Behavioral Economics and Finance Managerial

high quality & original research with empirical evidence and realistic analysis

this book, with the focus on creating a scientific and practical view of the opportunities and challenges facing of the Iranian economy, is compiled and published the result of examining the empirical evidence and realistic analysis in most important field related to the Behavioral Economic and Financial Management on a large part of Iranian industries . so The main audience of this book are foreign organizations and categories of different levels of international firms and other entities that need the information about Iranian financial economics or interested to start trade with Iran and investing in it.

This series contain ten high quality & original research dedicated to MOSTAFA EMAMI(master of science in financial economic from Michigan Technological University).

in addition all the Essays have been selected under scientific supervision of Professor Amrollah Amini(Associate Professor of Economics Faculty Allameh Tabataba'i University) and in some cases are accompanied by his valuable opinions, which are the result of more than thirty years of teaching at Allameh University, so we believe this book can be used as a reference by respected professors in the master's degree program. Related disciplines should be used as the main source of teaching

Author of this Book:

Mostafa Emami:(M.S.C Finance, Michigan Technological University)

Researchers:

- K.Nazari
- A.Shakarbeigi
- H.Fardmanesh,
- H.Maleki
- H.Khanifar
- F.Eavani
- S.Teymorpor
- M.Darabi
- H.Soltani
- A.Khanifar
- Al Ansari
- H.bordbar
- Z.Alizadeh
- S.vafaei

- E.Rayegan
- M.Parveizi
- M.Veisi
- K.Veisi
- M.Doroodgar
- S.Teymorpor
- M.Saiedi
- M.Nikjoo
- A.ghasemi
- H.Hassanzadeh
- M.Malmira
- M.Esfahanib
- M.Malmira
- H.Tajnesaeic

Book details:

ASIN: B00K9BP65Y ISBN-10: 9798578061189

Publisher : Amazon and Kindle are trademarks of Amazon.com Inc. or its affiliates

Language: English

c

Contents

ESSAYS:

1) IT Diffusion in Developing and Developed Countries: A Conceptual Analytical Model

2) public accountability and government financial reporting African journal of business management

3) the survey of correlation between social capital and knowledge management Australian journal of basic and applied sciences

4) entrepreneurship, religion, and business ethics business and management research Australian journal of

5) knowledge management: from theory to practice business and management research Australian journal of

6) job appropriateness (theories, concepts and measure it. case study in Iranian oil refining and distribution company) interdisciplinary journal of contemporary research in business

7) the study of the relationship between social capital and organizational entrepreneurships (case study of governmental organizations)interdisciplinary journal of contemporary research in business

8) conceptual and theoretical foundations of business intelligence journal of applied sciences research

9) the investigation of the business ethics: reviews, appraises and critiques theoretical journal of applied sciences research

10) application of fuzzy topsis technique for strategic management journal of basic and applied scientific research

11) strategies of increasing non-oil exports of Iran-Qom state journal of basic and applied scientific research

12) a survey of the relationship between stress management and workforce productivity of one of Iran's industrial parks elixir online journals

13) accountability systems in the governmental centers of four countries elixir online journals

14) analysis of cost of governance and revenue assurance elixir online journals

15) investigating the relation between earnings management and long run stock

performance elixir online journals

16) social responsibility accounting elixir online journals

17) the effect of inflation on development of stock market elixir online journals

18) the investigation of the relation between corporate social responsibility activities and company financial performance elixir online journals

19) the investigation of the relation between financial development and economic development: reviews, appraises, and critiques theoretical and empirical elixir online journals

20) the special value assessment of bank's brand name on basis of cbbe model (case study: bank Saderat) elixir online journals

21) the investigation of the relation between entrepreneurship and globalization, government, market structure, and market resources (case study in the tourism industry of Iran) elixir online journals

22) a survey of the relationship between stress management and workforce productivity of one of Iran's industrial parks elixir online journals

23) brand strategy development elixir online journals

24) human resources, organizational culture and empowerment elixir online journals

25) investigating the job satisfaction and professional commitment between staffs elixir online journals

26) organizational commitment and the implications for employees and organizations elixir online journals

27) organizational justice: understanding, applying, and measuring elixir online journals

28) the inaccuracy of previous studies in evaluating of export performance determinants elixir online journals

29) the investigation of the relation between job involvement and organizational commitment Managements since letters

30) the investigation of the relation between organizational trust and knowledge management elixir online journals

31) the relationship between operational auditing the public response in iran elixir online journals

32) the study of the relation between organizational justice and knowledge management elixir online journals

33) the study of the relation between power and policy and policy making elixir online journals

34) antecedents and consequences of organizational citizenship behavior (ocb) interdisciplinary journal of contemporary research in business

35) antecedents and consequences of organizational commitment interdisciplinary journal of contemporary research in business corporate

36) social responsibility: approaches and perspectives interdisciplinary journal of contemporary research in business

37) fraud and admirative corruption interdisciplinary journal of contemporary research in business

38) government accounting: an assessment of theory, purposes and standards interdisciplinary journal of contemporary research in business

39) leadership a critical review of the concept interdisciplinary journal of contemporary research in business

40) relationship between customers ethnocentrism of service marketing in iran interdisciplinary journal of contemporary research in business

41) the role and position of policy making compiling networks in policy making system interdisciplinary journal of contemporary research in business

42) the study of the relation between emotional intelligence and burnout of staff (case study of staff at state universities in Qom) interdisciplinary journal of contemporary research in business

43) emotional intelligence: understanding, applying, and measuring journal of applied sciences research

44) social audit: from theory to practice journal of applied sciences research

45) social entrepreneurships: a critical review of the concept journal of applied sciences research

46) the investigation of the relation between job stress and job satisfaction (case study in faculty members of recognized public and private universities) journal of applied sciences research

47) the investigation of the relation between personnel's emotional intelligence and

professional commitment (case study in national company of purging and distribution of oil products in Iran (shiraz) journal of applied sciences research

48) the role of social entrepreneurship in community journal of applied sciences research

49) total quality management: understanding, applying, and measuring journal of applied sciences research

50) analysis of leadership styles in different cultures journal of basic and applied scientific research

51) chaos theory and its complexity and role in the analyzing of policy journal of basic and applied scientific research

52) relationship between individual characteristics and effectiveness of human resources staff journal of basic and applied scientific research

53) relationship between job satisfaction and employee satisfaction survey of accounting information systems (case study of government agencies in Ira) journal of basic and applied scientific research

54) relationship between organizational justice and professional commitment of staff (case study in public organization) journal of basic and applied scientific research

55) the relationship between operational auditing the public response in Iran journal of basic and applied scientific research

56) the role of information & communication technology (ICT) in constant journal of basic and applied scientific research

57) the study of the relation between marketing mix and attract customers journal of basic and applied scientific research

58) the study of the relationship between organizational trust and organization journal of basic and applied scientific research

59) the study of the relationship between organizational trust and organization creativity (case study in purge national company and distribution of petroleum products in Iran) journal of basic and applied scientific research

60) an investigation of relation between organizational justice and professional commitment of staff: a case study of public organization In Iran management science letters

61) an investigation leadership styles different cultures management science letters

Impacts corporate social responsibility activities on company financial performance

Hossein Khanifar

Teacher of Tehran University.

Kamran Nazari

Department of Business Management, Payam Noor University, Kermanshah, Iran

Mostafa Emami

Young Researchers Club, Branch, Islamic Azad University,

Hossein Ali Soltani

Abstract

In the modern commercial era, companies and their managers are subjected to well publicized pressure to play an increasingly active role in society – so called "Corporate social responsibility". It has been argued that an element in this development is simply enlightened self-interest in that social responsibility enhances corporate image and financial performance. To date the evidence to support this thesis derives from North America. Outside this continent evidence for any relationship is sparse. This study will initially attempt to define the concept of corporate social responsibility and to examine its guiding principles. Subsequently, the available empirical research into the link between corporate social responsibility and economic performance will be evaluated this study examines different impacts of positive and negative CSR activities on financial performance of hotel, restaurant and airline companies, theoretically based on positivity and negativity effects. Findings suggest mixed results across different industries and will contribute to companies' appropriate strategic decision-making for CSR activities by providing more precise information regarding the impacts of each directional CSR activity on financial performance.

Keywords: Corporate social responsibility; Financial performance; Commercial era

Introduction

It is no secret that many multinational enterprises (MNEs) have annual turnovers higher than that of the GDP of a significant number of less developed countries (LDCs) put together. At the same time, the grad-ual liberalization of trade at the global level, coupled with mounting external debt, lack of financial capital, and high unemployment in LDCs has resulted in many cases in the promulgation of enticing foreign investment legislation, rampant corruption, and lax control over the operations of MNEs, as far as the domestic law and enforcement by the host State is concerned. Since the addressees and bearers of human rights, labor, and environmental obligations under traditional treaty and customary international law have been States. Commentators have argued both for and against the view that corporate social responsibility is enlightened economic self-interest.

The controversy at the theoretical level will be considered here, while the empirical evidence for and against will be presented later. Similarly, in order to clarify what is a complex and at times convoluted debate, the discussion will be divided into the relationships suggested with:

• Concurrent and subsequent (to CSR) economic performance; and

• Past economic performance.

Those who have theorised that a negative relation exists between social responsibility and economic performance have argued that a high investment in social responsibility results in additional costs. According to McGuire *et al.* (1988, p. 855) the added costs may result from actions such as "making extensive charitable contributions, promoting community development plans, maintaining plants in economically depressed locations and establishing environmental protection procedures". These costs might put a firm at an economic disadvantage compared to other, less socially responsible, firms. In contrast, others have argued the case for a positive association. McGuire *et al.* (1988) cite the argument that a firm perceived as high in social responsibility may face relatively fewer labour problems or perhaps customers may be more favourably disposed to its products.

Alternatively, CSR activities might improve a firm's reputation and relationship with bankers, investors and government officials. Improved relationships with them may well be translated to economic benefits.

According to Spicer (1978a,b), Rosen *et al.* (1991), Graves and Waddock (1994) and Pava and Krausz (1996), a firm's CSR behavior seems to be a factor that influences banks and other institutional investors' investment decisions. Thus, a high CSR profile may improve a firm's access to sources of capital.

Corporate social responsibility

The pharmaceutical sector, an industry already facing stiff tests in the form of intensified competition and strategic consolidation, has increasingly become subject to a variety of other pressures. Significantly, in common with other large-scale businesses, pharmaceutical firms are being exhorted to respond positively to the challenge of corporate (social) responsibility (CSR). Clearly, for individual managers within pharmaceutical firms the issue of CSR in the form of closely connected questions relating to patient access to health treatment, patent protection and affordability presents major problems.

Part of the burden of addressing the demands of CSR is the need to engage effectively with a range of stakeholders. Individual managers in pharmaceutical companies have to confront the complicated task of choosing which stakeholder dialogue practices to adopt and why. This real-world management predicament runs parallel to an academic interest in CSR stakeholder dialogue theory and models. Accordingly, this paper contributes to primarily to the academic debate by reviewing past attempts to theorise CSR and stakeholder dialogue, identifying gaps and weaknesses, and proposing a diagram-type model as a refined prototype framework.

The amount of literature available on CSR is massive and its production continues to grow. In addition, there is considerable literature on related concepts, such as 'business ethics', 'corporate citizenships' and 'sustainable business', to mention a few. The readings suggested here focus on literature that explicitly discusses CSR. The Reader is therefore not a complete review of CSR-relevant literature, but rather an attempt to organize this complex and vast area of literature . CSR refers to the obligations of the firm to society or, more specifically, the firm's stakeholders—those affected by corporate policies and practices. Saltaire and other early examples of paternalistic capitalism reveal three important characteristics of CSR. First, it is not a new idea, the hype surrounding it today notwithstanding Second, firms engaging in CSR often have "normative case" for CSR. Third, while there is substantial agreement that CSR is concerned with the societal obligations of business, there is much less certainty about what these obligations might be or their scope. Salt's ideas for social betterment did not meet with universal approval and he opposed legislation to prohibit child labor. Even corporate champions of CSR today, such as Starbucks meet with opposition from NGOs (non governmental organizations) and others. As Sethi observed nearly 30 years ago, the operational meaning of corporate social responsibility is supremely vague and, he suggested, it can mean all things to all peopleThese three characteristics of CSR are particularly important as we consider its recent rise to prominence and the challenges it poses.

Bowen (1953) sets the scene in this field by suggesting that the concept of specifically corporate social responsibility emphasizes that:

• businesses exist at the pleasure of society and that their behaviour and methods of operation must fall within the guidelines set by society; and • businesses act as moral agents within society.

Wood (1991) expanded these ideas, encapsulating them into three driving principles of social responsibility, which are that:

(1) business is a social institution and thus obliged to use its power responsibly;(2) businesses are responsible for the outcomes relating to their areas of involvement with society; and (3) individual managers are moral agents who are obliged to exercise discretion in their decision making. In general, the social responsibilities of a firm seem to arise from the intersection (and compatibility) of the political and cultural systems with the economic system (Jones,1983). However, Friedman (1970) argued that the successful functioning of our society depends on the role specialisation of its institutions (or systems). According to him the corporation is an economic institution and thus should specialise in the economic sphere; socially responsible behaviour will be rectified by the market through profits. In Friedman's (1970) view business has only one social responsibility and that is to maximise the profits of its owners (to protect their property rights). Organisations are seen purely as legal entities incapable of value decisions. A manager who uses a firm's resources for non-profit social purposes is thought to be diverting economic efficiency and levying an "illegal tax" on the organisation. Opponents (Frederick *et al.*, 1992) of this view, challenge the very foundations of Friedman's thesis – the economic model. They claim that the economic model and role specialisation of institutions (or systems) are not working as suggested.

This comes as a result of the rise of oligopolies in certain sectors; the separation of ownership and management; government's involvement in the economy and conversely industry's involvement in the political process through lobbying. In addition, if corporations do not adopt "social responsibility", government with its potential for inefficiency and insensitive bureaucratic methods may be forced to step in. With respect to Friedman's argument that the legal conception of corporations' articles and memorandums of associations limits a firm's involvement solely to economic roles, it can be claimed that they are broad enough to allow departures from this narrow path. Social responsibility is also seen as a consequence of and an obligation following from the unprecedented increase of firms' social power (as tax payers, recruiters, etc.) (Davis, 1975). Failure to balance social power with social responsibility may ultimately result in the loss of this power and a subsequent decline of the firm (Davis, 1975).

Another school of thought sees social responsibility as a contractual obligation firms have towards society (Donaldson, 1983). It is society in the first place that has permitted firms to use both natural and human resources and has given them the right to perform their productive functions and to attain their power status (Donaldson, 1983).

As a result, society has an implicit social contract with the firm. Thus, in return for the right to exploit resources in the production process, society has a claim on the firm and the right to control it. The specifics of this contract may change as social conditions change but this contract in general always remains the basis of the legitimacy of the demand for or assertion of the need for CSR (Epstein, 1987). A growing number of scholars take the view that firms can no longer be seen purely as private institutions but as social institutions instead (Frederick *et al.*, 1992; Freeman, 1984; Lodge, 1977). The benefits flowing from firms need to be shared collectively. This thesis is similar to the stakeholders model (Freeman, 1984) and claims that a firm is responsible not only to its shareholders (owners) but to all stakeholders (consumers, employees, creditors, etc.) whose contribution is necessary for a firm's success. Thus, CSR means that a corporation should be held accountable for any of its actions that affect people, communities and the environment in which those people or communities live (Frederick *et al.*, 1992).

Carroll (1979) suggests that CSR is defined as the economic, legal, ethical and discretionary demands that society places on business. Similarly, Zanies conceptualized CSR as the degree of "fit" between society's expectations of business and the ethics of business. He argues that CSR is really nothing more than another layer of managerial responsibility resulting from the evolution of capitalism. An interesting twist to the argument is provided by Tuzzolino and Armandi (1981) who provide a motivational theory of organisational social response based on Maslow's hierarchy of needs. CSR is the fulfilment of a firm's "internal and external self-actualisation needs" which are located on the top of their organisational needs pyramid.

According to this view, firms adopt CSR after they have satisfied three earlier layers of needs (which include: "physiological" or survival needs fulfilled by corporate profits; "safety needs" such as dividend policy, conglomeration and competitive position; and "affiliative needs" such as participation in trade association, lobby groups, etc.). Epstein (1987) attempted to differentiate "business ethics" and CSR and to incorporate them into a strategic process. According to him "business ethics" refer to issues and dilemmas related to the morality of organisational actions or decisions. CSR focuses more on the consequences of organisational actions. He defined CSR as the "discernment of issues, expectations and claims on business organizations regarding the consequences of policies and behaviour on internal and external stakeholders" (Epstein 1987, p. 101). Angelidis and Ibrahim (1993) defined CSR as "corporate social actions whose purpose is to satisfy social needs". They developed an equilibrium theory based on social demand and supply, identifying a set of factors that affects them (social supply and demand).

Thus, opinions differ in terms of the basis or scope of CSR and even the very definition of the term. As a consequence different aspects of a firm's operations can be seen to come under its sway – depending on the stance one adopts. As has been shown, what can be conceived as "social responsibility" can range from simply maximisation of profits, to satisfaction of stakeholders' social needs, or fulfilment of social contractual obligations, fulfilment of a firm's needs, achievement of a social equilibrium, etc. – depending on the stance taken.

While academic debate abounds at the theoretical level, at the operational level insights are more sparse. Schwarts and Dahl observed that socially acceptable behaviour of North American firms at the time of writing – the 1970s included:

• Disclosure of information to shareholders;
• Disclosure of the board of directors;
• Monopolistic behaviour (predatory pricing, etc.);
• Equality of treatment for minorities;
• Profit sharing;
• Environmental protection;
• Ethics in advertising; and • Social impact of technology.

However, according to Vyarkarnam (1992), many of these have now been regulated by statute. Present day concerns have changed focus. He found that current CSR concerns, which are in substance the same for both North American and the UK firms, encompass such areas as:

• Environmental protection (e.g. reduction of emissions and waste and the recycling of materials);
• Philanthropy (donating to charities, etc.); • Involvement in social causes (involving anything from human rights to AIDS education);

• Urban investment (working with local government to regenerate small businesses and the inner city environment generally);and

• Employee schemes (higher standards of occupational health and safety, good standard of staff treatment, job-sharing, flexitime, etc.).

Empirical research into the effects of corporate responsibility has produced mixed results. Some studies have suggested a positive relation, whereas others have concluded that the effects are negative or inconsequential. For example, Belkaoui (1976) investigated the information content of pollution control disclosures. His results suggested a positive relationship between economic performance and social responsibility, at least in this area. Other studies produced results consistent with the notion that corporate social responsibility activities impact on the financial markets (Anderson and Frankle, 1980; Shane and Spicer, 1983; Spicer, 1978a,b). However, certain studies have replicated earlier research and found conflicting results. Frankle and Anderson (1978) rejected Belkaoui's (1976) interpretation and argued that nondisclosing firms had consistently performed better in the market. In a similar manner, Chen and Metcalf (1980) disagreed with Spicer's (1978a,b) conclusions, arguing that his results were driven by spurious correlations. In response Spicer (1980) stated that Chen and Metcalf (1980) misinterpreted the purpose of his study, emphasising that associations not causal relationships were being investigated.

Ingram (1978) concluded that the information content of social responsibility disclosures was conditional on the market segment with which a firm is identified. Alexander and Bulcholz (1978) and Abbott and Monsen (1979) found no significant relationship between a corporation's level of social responsibility activities and stock market performance.

In addition, Chugh (1978), Trotman and Bradley (1981) and Mahapatra (1984) concluded that corporate social responsibility activities may lead to increased systematic risk.

Cochran and Wood (1984) used corporate social responsibility rankings developed by Moskowitz (1972) to test the relationship between corporate social responsibility activities and firm's performance. After controlling for industry classification and corporate age, a weak positive association between corporate social responsibility activities and economic performance was found. Mills and Gardner (1984) concluded in their analysis of the relationship between social disclosure and economic performance, that companies are more likely to disclose social responsibility expenditures when their financial statements indicate favourable economic performance.

One drawback of the above empirical studies is that they failed to distinguish between past, concurrent and subsequent to CSR economic performance, and thus to make possible reliable inferences about direction of causation. In most of the previous studies, economic performance covered a (commonly five year) period "surrounding" the CSR performance and/or social disclosure periods. Routinely, the CSR performance and/or social disclosure periods were the midpoints of that period. However, in Mahapatra (1984) and Mills and Gardiner (1984) studies, economic performance periods were concurrent to the CSR performance period.

Only Shane and Spicer (1983) looked at economic performance subsequent to CSR disclosure period, finding a positive association. Practically, McGuire et al. (1988) were the first to break this tradition and to separate economic performance into past, concurrent and subsequent to CSR performance. They used Fortune magazine's ratings of corporate reputations to analyse the relationship between perceived corporate social responsibility and economic performance. Prior economic performance of the firms, as measured by both stock market returns and accounting based measures, were found to be more closely related to corporate social responsibility than was subsequent economic performance. McGuire et al. (1988) suggested that economic performance may be a variable influencing

Thus, the empirical research into the relationship between corporate social responsibility and economic performance is confusing and far from conclusive. According to Ullmann (1985) this may be attributed to the use of varying and questionable measures of CSR, differences in the research methodologies and the financial performance measures used. To overcome these limitations, this study will use a more comprehensive measurement of CSR performance (admittedly within the context of the UK social and business environment), a combination of economic performance measures and including the necessary intervening variables in the research design.

CSR and financial performance

A modern concept of CSR has evolved since the 1950s, formalized in the 1960s and proliferated in the 1970s (Carroll, 1999). Based on various studies from the CSR literature (Carroll, 1999; Engardio et al., 2007; Hart, 1995; Holme and Watts, 2000; McWilliams and Siegel, 2001; Nicolau, 2008; Tsoutsoura, 2004), CSR can be broadly defined as the activities making companies good citizens who contribute to society's welfare beyond their own self interests. Throughout the past several decades, numerous aspects of CSR have been the subject of investigation in academic and business literature, and according to the framework of Schwartz and Carroll (2003), economic, legal and ethical domains can be epitomized as the most common components of CSR. One aspect of CSR interesting to many financial economists is the economic domain: financial impact of CSR for profit-seeking corporations. Regarding the relationship between companies' CSR activities and their performances (especially, financial performance), the literature presents three assertions.

The first group of researchers, based on the viewpoint of Friedman (1970), has found a negative relationship between CSR activities and financial performance as measured by, for example, stock price changes (Vance, 1975), excess return (Wright and Ferris, 1997), or analysts' earnings-per-share forecasts (Cordeiro and Sarkis, 1997). Friedman argued that managements are selected by the stockholders as agents and their sole responsibility is acting on behalf of the principals' best interests. From Friedman's perspective, the one and only social responsibility of business is to use its resources and engage in activities designed to increase profits and wealth of owners. Any other activities disturbing the optimal allocation of scarce resources to alternative uses exert an adverse influence on firm performance.

The second group argued for positive impact from companies' CRS activities on financial performance (Arago´ n-Correa et al., 2008; Bird et al., 2007; Bragdon and Marlin, 1972; Klassen and McLaughlin, 1996; Nicolau, 2008; Orlitzky et al.,1997). This group's assertion, based on stakeholder theory (Freeman, 1984), suggests that firms expand the scope of consideration in their decision-making and activities beyond shareholders to several other constituencies with interests, such as customers, employees, suppliers and communities. The second group asserts that CSR activities, which encompass all legitimate stakeholders' implicit claims as stakeholder theory suggests, can improve firm value by (1) immediate cost saving, (2) enhancement of firm reputation, and (3) dissuasion of future action by regulatory bodies including governments which might impose significant costs on the firm (Bird et al., 2007). A third group has supported no particular relationship between CSR activities and financial performance (Abbott and Monsen, 1979; Alexander and Buchholz, 1978; Aupperle et al., 1985; Teoh et al., 1999), partially arguing for the existence of too many confounding factors for researchers to uncover a particular impact from CSR on firm performance.

Seemingly contradictory themes between Friedman's (1970) viewpoint and the stakeholder theory arise from the assumption that CSR, which considers the interests of a broad spectrum of stakeholders (suggested by stakeholder theory), is in fact detrimental to value maximization activities of the firm (asserted by Friedman's viewpoint). However, Jensen (2001) attempted to reconcile the potential conflict between these two viewpoints by proposing enlightened stakeholder theory, which asserts that a firmcannotmaximize its long-term value if it ignores the interests of diverse stakeholders. And, according to Post et al. (2002), a firm's capacity that generates sustainablewealth over time and its long-term value are determined by the relationship with both internal and external stakeholders. CSR, if it contributes to enhancing firm value, can be an appropriate corporate strategy as the stakeholder theory suggests, not an exploitation of shareholders' wealth to benefit other parties, as Friedman (1970) worried.

Conclusion

Modern corporate stakeholder theory (Cornell and Shapiro, 1987; Freeman, 1984; Jones, 1995; McGuire *et al.*, 1988) can also explain part of the CSR/economic performance relationship. According to stakeholder theory the value of a firm is related to the cost of both "explicit claims" and "implicit claims" on a firm's resources. Claimants include not only the legal owners of the firm but other constituencies such as lenders, employees, consumers, banks, government, etc. Stakeholders who have explicit claims on the corporation include – besides its owners – lenders, employees, government, etc. In addition, there are others with whom the firm has made implicit contracts, which could include the quality of service and CSR. According to McGuire *et al.* (1988), if the firm does not honour these implicit contracts, then it is argued that the parties to these contracts may attempt to transform them from implicit to explicit agreements. The latter may be more costly for the firms involved. According to Freeman (1984) and McGuire *et al.* (1988) the implications of the conversion of " implicit" to "explicit" contracts may have broader effects than the direct costs resulting from the forced change in its behaviour (e.g. cost of installment of gas emission control equipment). For example, socially irresponsible actions in one area (e.g. gas emissions) may spill-over and affect the corporate image in other areas as well (e.g. unregulated issues on labour relationships).

This could in turn result in other implicit stakeholders (e.g. trade unions) striving to make their claims explicit. Thus, firms with an image of high CSR may find that they face both fewer and lower-cost explicit claims than those with a less enlightened stance. Thus, from a theoretical perspective, arguments can and have been made both for and against a positive relationship between social responsibility and concurrent or subsequent (to CSR) economic performance. According to Parert and Eibert (1975), Ullmann (1985) and Roberts (1992), if corporate social responsibility is viewed as a significant cost, firms with relatively high past financial performance may be more willing to absorb these costs in the future. It is also expected that poor performers would seek more immediate results and consequently they may prefer short-term and highyield investments to the uncertain and in general longer-term CSR investments. A similar view is that policies and expenditures in discretionary areas such as social programmes may be especially sensitive to the existence of "slack" resources in the firm (McGuire *et al.*, 1988). Ullmann (1985) argued that corporations must reach an acceptable level of economic performance before devoting company resources to meet social demands. This is supported by the assertion that corporations with strong prior economic performance appear to be more likely to have high current levels of social disclosure. Ullmann (1985) also suggested that companies with less stable stock market patterns would be relatively less likely to commit resources to social activities.

References

Adams R., Carruthers, J. and Hamil, S. (1991), Changing Corporate Values, Kogan Page,London.

Alexander, G. and Bulcholz, R. (1978), "Corporate social responsibility and stock market performance", Academy of Management Journal, Vol. 21, pp. 479- 86.

Anderson, J. and Frankle, A. (1980), "Voluntary social reporting: an iso-beta portfolio analysis", Accounting Review, Vol. 55, pp. 468-79.

Angelidis, P. and Ibrahim, N. (1993), "Social demand and corporate supply: a corporate social responsibility model", Review of Business, Vol. 15, Fall, pp. 7-10.

Belkaoui, A. (1976), "The impact of the disclosure of the environmental effects of organization behaviour on the market", Financial Management, Vol. 5 No. 4,pp. 6-31.

Bowen, H.R. (1953), Social Responsibilities of the Businessman, Harper & Row, New York, NY.
Carroll, A.B. (1979), "A three-dimensional model of corporate performance", Academy of Management Review, Vol. 4 No. 4, pp. 497-505.

Chen, K. and Metcalf, R. (1980), "The relationship between pollution control record and financial indicators revisited", Accounting Review, Vol. 55, pp. 168-77.

Clarkson, M.B.E. (1995), "A stakeholder framework for analysing and evaluating social corporate performance", Academy of Management Review, Vol. 20 No. 1, pp. 92-117.

Cochran, P. and Wood, R. (1984), "Corporate social responsibility and financial erformance", Academy of Management Journal, Vol. 27 No. 1, pp. 42-56.

Cohen, J. and Cohen, P. (1983), Applied Multiple Regression for the Behavioral Sciences, Laurence Erlbaum, Hillsdale, NJ.

Copeland, T. and Weston, J. (1983), Financial Theory and Corporate Policy, AddisonWesley, Reading, MA.

Cornell, B. and Shapiro, A. (1987), "Corporate stakeholders and corporate finance", Financial Management, Vol. 16, pp. 5-14.

Davis, K. (1975), "Five propositions for social responsibility", Business Horizons, Vol. 18 No. 3, pp. 19-24.

Frankle, A. and Anderson, J. (1978), "The impact of the disclosure of environmental effects of organizational behaviour on the market: comment", Financial Management, Vol. 21, Summer, pp. 92-107.

Frederick, W.C. et al. (1992), Business and Society, McGraw-Hill International, New York, NY.

Freeman, R.E. (1984), Strategic Management : A Stakeholder Approach, Pitman, Boston, MA.
Graves, S.B. and Waddock, S.A. (1994), "Institutional owners and corporate social performance", Academy of Management Journal, Vol. 37 No. 4, pp. 1034- 46.

Spicer, B. (1980), "The relationship between pollution control record and financial indicators revisited: further comment", Accounting Review, Vol. 55, pp. 178-85.

Trotman, K. and Bradley, G. (1981), "Association between social responsibility disclosure and characteristics of companies", Accounting Organizations and Society, Vol. 6, pp. 355-62.

Tuzzolino, F. and Armandi, B. (1981), "A need – hierarchy framework for assessing corporate social responsibility", Academy of Management Review, Vol. 6 No. 1, pp. 21-8.

Ullmann, A. (1985), "Data in search of a theory: a criticalexamination of the relationships among social performance, social disclosure, and economic performance of US firms", Academy of Management Review, Vol. 10 No. 3, pp. 540-57.

Vyakarnam, S. (1992), "Social responsibility: what leading companies do", Long Range Planning, Vol. 25 No. 5, pp. 59-67.

Wartick, S. and Cochran, P. (1985), "The evolution of the corporate social performance model", Academy of Management Review, Vol. 10 No. 4, pp. 758-69.

Wood, D. (1991), "Corporate social performance revisited", Academy of Management Review, Vol. 16 No. 4, pp. 758-69.

Vol. 7(34), pp. 3272-3280, 14 September, 2013
DOI: 10.5897/AJBM12.127
ISSN 1993-8233 © 2013 Academic Journals
http://www.academicjournals.org/AJBM

African Journal of Business Management

Full Length Research Paper

The effect of marketing mix in attracting customers: Case study of Saderat Bank in Kermanshah Province

Bahman Saeidi Pour[1], Kamran Nazari[2] and Mostafa Emami[3]*

[1] Department of Educational, Payam Noor University, Iran. [2] Department of Business Management, Payam Noor University, Kermanshah, Iran. [3] Young Researchers Club, Kermanshah Branch, Islamic Azad University, Kermanshah, Iran.

Accepted 24 November, 2012

This study investigated the impact of marketing mix in attracting customers to Saderat Bank in Kermanshah Province. Questionnaire which included 30 questions was used to collect information in this research. The reliability of the questionnaire was calculated using Cronbach's alpha, and a value of 0.882 was obtained, greater than 0.7 which is the reliability of the questionnaire. The population used in this study is the customers of Saderat Bank in Kermanshah Province, with at least one account, interestfree loans and savings. 250 questionnaires were collected by stratified random sampling. The work has one main hypothesis and 5 sub- hypotheses. Pearson correlation test was used to test the hypotheses. It was established that factors in the marketing mix have a significant positive effect in absorbing customers. That means the bank has a significant positive effect.

Key words: Marketing, marketing mix factors, customers' orientation, customers' satisfaction.

INTRODUCTION

Progress and transformation in industries, institutions and companies has to do with their ability to deal with problems, activities, as well as competitors. Each institution should adopt policies with respect to long-term vision, mission, goals, opportunities, arrangements and using internal facilities of an external to develop comprehensive marketing (Industries, 1384), because in today's global business environment there is increasing complexity, rapid change and unexpected developments (Mason, 2007).

With the development of science in all fields, banks and financial markets have become competitive in recent years as seen in the development of their activities, creation of private banks and financial institutions and applying marketing techniques and strategies for attracting customers and increasing deposit. Using the marketing mix factors such as access to appropriate services and providing services to customers quickly and appropriately in a variety of services and advertising to attract customers, there is increase in financial institutions and banks. Marketing is one of the issues that is subject to change, due to market changes in consumption patterns and tastes of individuals. Population growth, urban expansion, changes in community structure, diversity of products, advance knowledge and generational changes are factors that will determine market variables (Lavak, 1382).

Each institution has the task of marketing managers by analyzing, planning, implementing and controlling effectively marketing programs in order to develop a superior competitive position in target markets. Marketing plan includes a process designed for predicting future events and determining strategies to achieve the objectives of an institute (Mnty and Trustee).

Institutions should try to obtain an appropriate share of the market by studying the market, applying marketing

*Corresponding author. E-mail: emamemostafa@yahoo.com.

mix variables, using appropriate methods of distribution and supplying of goods and services and be aware of the campaign and identification of opportunities. They should attract more resources to deal with scientific creativity and innovation to meet customers' needs; and match resources to increase market share and take care of customers. Strengthening financial markets in the country for its economic development and saving of resources for the health of the economy seem to be necessary. The savings rate in the banking and credit system and financial institutions can lead to increased investment and economic growth.

In Iran, the main hub of the financial markets, banks and financial institutions is the main source of capital for buying products and services, granting loans and as the funding source for all economic units in the country. In banks and institutions, appropriate activities and effective use of marketing are very effective for achieving their goals. A significant number of banks and institutions need to make more use of marketing variables in order to increase resources to customers. Apart from these categories in which the bank is not required in this research, institutions have found the effect of competition with some of the marketing mix strategies for increasing their deposits and investments.

Marketing

In the 1960s, the term was common in marketing. It says everything starts with consumer's needs and demands. Marketing and market management, an important branch of knowledge management, is the main task of understanding people's needs and desires and help them through the process; a process where resources are exchanged. Society needs are increasing today more than ever, especially with the growing shortage of human and other resources. Managers are faced with limited resources available to meet those demands which are unlimited; but knowledge management is here to help the economy scientifically as well a set of skills and knowledge for the optimal use of limited resources. Marketing also needs to recognize the efforts put up by the exchange of resources (Venus, 1386). Marketing is a social and managerial process by which needs and desires of individuals and groups are provided through the production, supply and exchange of useful goods (Holm, 2006).

Marketing management can be defined as follows: "The analysis, planning, implementation and monitoring of programs to create, provide and maintain a profitable transactions process with the buyers, in order to achieve organizational goals (Cutler, 2000). llMarketing management is the analysis, planning, implementation and controlling of programs to achieve organizational goals. It involves programs made to establish and maintain beneficial exchanges with buyers (Lavak, 1382).

Pour et al.   3273

"Marketing management opportunities, including analysis, planning, implementation, execution and monitoring of programs to establish and maintain a favorable exchange markets aim to achieve organizational goals. Thus marketing management or demand management, supply and demand caused by or in the form of motivation is essential (Alvdary, 1387).

According to the Marketing Association of America, _'marketing is the process of planning; the realization of an idea, pricing, advertisement and distribution of goods and services, where the exchange makes the individual and the organization in it a reality (Cutler, 2000; Belch and Belch, 2001). The art and science of marketing is to create or establish favorable conditions between supply and demand. The main task of marketing is to meet product and service needs of customers and focus on target market (Frank, 1994).

Marketing involves activities that provide a comprehensive definition. Marketing experts raise their own vision based on these activities. Some of the definitions of marketing involve a group of activities that take place in the market and others include the ways marketers have to comply with the definition. Table 1 shows some of these definitions.

The art of marketing entails carrying the correct amount and quality of product or service to meet the need of customers at the right place and time, and ensuring that customers benefit from its activities (Arto and Sample, 2005).

Today, advertisement is to be considered as part of marketing territory and all economic activities including manufacturing, distribution of a wide range of services, the management of sales and production and sales of goods and services.

In summary, the designing, manufacturing, packaging, distribution and sale of goods and services to consumers, which ultimately lead to customers' satisfaction play an important role (BolurianTehrani, 1376). In marketing services, field marketing is important. Service activities include features such as intangibility, indiscernible and being different and impossibility (Pickton and Broderick, 2001). The exchange of product marketing and marketing services with the different goods and services between the same characteristics such as inseparable, intangibility, lack of maintenance and service is different (Murrar, 1995). In recent years, branches and wide variety of services in the market over several service centers are more tangible (Table 2).

Marketing mix

This is a set of controllable elements of marketing tools and marketing strategies of a company in combining these elements. Cutler says that a set of marketing mix variables can be controlled by the marketing companies and institutions in their target market and its composition

Table 1. Definitions of marketing (Researcher).

Scholar	Year	Definition
Chisnall	1992	Marketing means finding a suitable position in the market
Mei	2011	Understanding what people want and seek in a market and supply and provision of goods and services to meet their needs and achieve goals.
Cohen	1998	The marketing activities such as buying and selling of goods, transport and storage.
Baker	1998	A series of activities called the flow of commercial goods and services from producer to final consumer.
Goharian	1374	Marketing structure and demand for products and services is estimated to predict the spread.
Ranjbariyan	1378	Satisfy human needs and to define the process was considered with the market. On the other hand, the buyer and seller in a market where it is located.
Hosseini	1379	A set of human and economic activities conducted in order to satisfy the needs and demands of the people through the exchange process .
Alvdary	1383	Process in which groups of people, goods and benefits from production and exchange with others to meet their wants and needs.
Events in Iran	1386	Targeted marketing enabling the company to plan and execute pricing, promotion and distribution of products, services and ideas.

Table 2. Community services sector (research).

Section	Example	Section		Example
Public sector	Hospitals, educational	Department Commerce	of	Hotels, insurance companies, banks and financial institutions and credit
Non-profit sector	Charitable institutions, mosques	Manufacturing sector		Computer operators

are required for the reaction (Cutler, 2000). Elements of the marketing mix are a set of marketing tools for achieving the goals of the institute of marketing (HaKansson and Waluszewski, 2005).

Marketers, in order to receive favorable responses from their target markets, use many tools. These tools comprise the marketing mix. In fact, it is a set of tools that institutions use to achieve their marketing goals. McCarthy classified these tools into four major groups, called the 4P's of marketing: product, price, place and promotion (Harrell and Frazier, 1999). Decisions about future marketing by marketers should also affect the final consumer and commercial channels. Thus, despite the decision of institutions concerning a number of variables of the marketing mix and because it requires a long time, little can change in the short term in their marketing mix. Robert's statement to the seller regarding the 4P's vs 4C's of customer is shown in Table 3.

Based on the 4C's, for institutions to meet the needs of consumers, their products should be economical; they should consider comfort, convenience and effective communication; they should take customers' interest into account and try to charge them less. Customers should be expected to benefit from their products. Price should commensurate with the capabilities of the buyer. Their product should be available to customers purchasing it. Finally, promotions should be made available to potential consumers of such products (Mohammadian, 1382). The concept of marketing mix is defined as the organization's performance using a set of controllable variables and uncontrollable factors of the environment (Newson et al., 2000).

Marketing mix of traditional management models overcomes dynamic market, where the beggar works, alongside other methods of Anderson and the theoretical parameters of a system developed by the University of Copenhagen in Europe. Methods such as vision of a new product, functional vision are faced with such geographical perspective. Just a few of these models were able to maintain their survival against the 4P's (Pourhassan, 1376). The concept of marketing mix, for the first time in 1950, was introduced by Neil Bvrdn and

Table 3. Component Model of 4Ps and 4Cs.

4C customer		The 4Ps	
Customer solution	Customer solution	Product	Product
Customer costs	Customer coast	Price	Price
Profits and customer comfort	Convenience	Location distribution	Place
Communications	Communication	Advance sales	Promotion

Table 4. Definitions of the four elements of marketing mix.

Product	Product is a physical object that is sold and has a palpable characteristic, a complex set of benefits that can be used to meet customer needs.
Price	Includes issues such as discounts, list prices, credit, repayment term and conditions .The price is included in the price, product or service offered for sale and will determine the level of benefits. Price is the only element that does not include costs charged to the customers to buy products they take.
Promotion	Includes issues such as advertising, personal selling, sales promotion, public relations and direct marketing. Distribution channels are the most important questions about how an organization can optimize a connection between inner and outer channels.
Place	Includes issues such as distribution channels, market coverage, product inventory, transportation and distribution sites.

became known as the 4P's (29). McCarthy, in the early 1960s, blends marketing with four variables known as the 4P's classification that included: product, price, place and promotion (30).

McCarthy has since created dramatic changes in the marketing mix, and the 4P's is still used a lot in literature as the main concept for coordinating many other aspects of marketing (31). Four elements of marketing mix are defined in Table 4:

The most important element in the marketing mix is product. What makes our product marketable? For pricesensitive element of the marketing mix, customer is liable for the amounts paid to deliver the product. The third element is the distribution of all the activities that aim to deliver the product to the customer. The fourth element of the marketing mix is promotion, which is used to communicate with customers. This association is to encourage customers to buy products. Figure 1 shows the elements of the marketing mix.

History and implementation of marketing mix

Borden (1965) claims to be the first to have used the term
—marketing mix‖ and that it was suggested to him by Culliton's (1948) description of a business executive as —mixer of ingredients‖. An executive is —a mixer of ingredients, who sometimes follows a recipe as he goes along, adapts a recipe to the available ingredients and experiments with or invents ingredients no one else has tried‖ (Mei, 2011).

The early marketing concept is similar to the notion of marketing mix, based on the idea of action parameters presented in the 1930s by Stackelberg (1939). Rasmussen (1955) then developed what became known as parameter theory.

He proposes that the four determinants of competition and sales are price, quality, service and advertising. Mickwitz (1959) applies this theory to the Product Life Cycle Concept.

Borden's original marketing mix had a set of 12 elements namely: product planning; pricing; branding; channels of distribution; personal selling; advertising; promotions; packaging; display; servicing; physical handling and fact finding and analysis. Frey (1961) suggests that marketing variables should be divided into two parts: the offering (product, packaging, brand, price and service) and the methods and tools (distribution channels, personal selling, advertising, sales promotion and publicity). On the other hand, Lazer and Kelly (1962) and Lazer et al. (1973) suggested three elements of marketing mix: the goods and services mix, the distribution mix and the communication mix. McCarthy (1964) refined Borden's (1965) idea further and defined marketing mix as a combination of all of the factors at a marketing manger's command to satisfy the target market. He regrouped Borden's 12 elements to four elements or 4Ps, namely product, price, promotion and place at a marketing manger's command to satisfy the target market (Mohammadian, 1382).

Especially in the 1980s onward, a number of researchers propose new _P' into the marketing mix. Judd (1987) proposes a fifth P (people). Booms and Bitner (1980) add 3 Ps (participants, physical evidence and process) to the original 4Ps to apply the marketing mix concept to service. Kotler (1986) adds political power and public opinion formation to the Ps concept. Baumgartner (1991) suggests the concept of 15 Ps. MaGrath (1986) suggests the addition of 3Ps (personnel, physical facilities and process management). Vignalis and Davis (1994) suggest the addition of S (service) to the marketing mix. Goldsmith (1999) suggests that there should be 8 Ps (product, price, place, promotion, participants, physical evidence, process and personalisation). Moller (2006) presents an up-to-date picture of the current standing in the debate around the mix as marketing paradigm and predominant marketing management tool by reviewing academic views from five marketing management sub-disciplines (consumer marketing, relationship marketing, services marketing, retail marketing and industrial marketing) and an emerging marketing (E-commerce) (Iranian Events, 1386).

Most researchers and writers that reviewed in these domains express serious doubts as to the role of the mix as marketing management tool in its original form; and therefore propose alternative approaches, which is adding new parameters to the original mix or replacing it with alternative frameworks altogether.

Use of the marketing mix concept

Like many other concepts, marketing mix concept seems relatively simple, once it has been expressed. Before they were ever tagged with the nomenclature of "concept," the ideas involved were widely understood among marketers as a result of the growing knowledge about marketing and marketing procedures that came during the preceding half century. But once the ideas were reduced to a formal statement with an accompanying visual presentation, the concept of the mix has proved to be a helpful device in teaching, in business problem solving, and, generally, as an aid to thinking about marketing. First of all, it is helpful in giving an answer to the question often raised: "what is marketing?" A chart which shows the elements of the mix and the forces that bear on the mix helps to bring understanding of what marketing is. It helps to explain why in our dynamic world the thinking of management in all its functional areas must be oriented to the market. In recent years, the authors have kept an abbreviated chart showing the elements and forces of the marketing mix in front of their classes at all times. In case discussion, it has proved to be a handy device by which queries were raised as to whether the student has recognized the implications of any recommendation he might have made in the areas of the several elements of the mix. Referring to the forces, we can ask if all the pertinent market forces have been given due consideration. Continual reference to the mix chart makes the authors to feel that the students' understanding of marketing is strengthened. The constant presence and use of the chart leaves a deeper understanding that marketing is the devising of programs that successfully meet the forces of the market. In problem solving the marketing mix chart is a constant reminder of the following (Mei, 2011):

1)   The fact that a problem seems to lie in one segment of the mix must be deliberated with constant thought regarding the effect of any change in that sector on other areas of marketing operations. The necessity of integration in marketing thinking is ever present.
2)   The need to study carefully the market forces as they might bear on problems in hand. In short, the mix chart provides an ever ready checklist as to which areas to think when considering marketing questions or dealing with marketing problems.

Marketing mix resource allocation and planning challenges

Marketing mix resource allocation and planning has assumed prominence as companies have attempted to optimize spending across all marketing activities. That is no surprise, considering that senior marketing executives are under increasing pressure to help their organizations achieve organic sales growth with tighter, top down- driven budgets and short time horizons to deliver tangible payback on their marketing campaigns. With less influence over the size of their budgets, senior marketers must instead attempt to maximize the impact of the dollars they distribute for programs across multiple products, markets, channels, and specific customers, using an increasingly complex mix of new and traditional media.

As a result, companies have looked toward analytical and modeling techniques in an attempt to better link marketing investments to meaningful and measurable market responses (and, ideally, to one or more financial metrics). Packaged goods and pharmaceutical marketers, in particular, were among the pioneers in exploring marketing mix analytics and data-driven econometric models. Marketing scholars also have contributed to a more sophisticated body of analytical and modeling literature that offers both theoretical and substantive insights for marketing mix resource allocation decisions and planning practices. In many respects, marketing practitioners and researchers were early advocates for bringing analytics to business practice (Hosseini, 1384).

Nevertheless, changing customer dynamics and advances in media technology presents novel challenges.

Nowhere is the challenge more evident than in the domain of new media that originated in and is energized by the digital environment. The rapid and ongoing emergence of new digital channels—from the static online banner ads of the 1990s to the social media and mobile platforms of the current environment—has changed the way people consume information and has left marketers scrambling to address the new digital landscape.

According to a recent report by Hamilton, —digital marketing still lags the shift in consumer behaviorǁ prompted by the Internet (Goharian, 1374). At the same time, the rise of digital communications channels has focused renewed attention on the efficiency and effectiveness of traditional media and the extent to which new media are a complement to or a substitute for television, print, and other established channels—all with an eye toward optimal allocation of marketing mix resources through marketing analytics.

—You have to be able to orchestrate a move toward emerging media,ǁ says Greg Welch, head of the CMO practice at Spencer Stuart. —How do you take a traditional media budget and figure out not just how much to allocate to [new] media, but also how to measure it and how to defend it in front of your peer group?ǁ (Iranian Events, 1386). Not surprisingly, many companies have adopted a measured approach to the inclusion of new media in their marketing communication programs until appropriate analytical and modeling techniques can provide better insight into their use. The description of marketing analytics contained in this book offers contemporary perspectives and practices that should provide direction for these marketing mix decisions.

Eighty-plus percent of U.S. consumers are online regularly, and 34% of their media time is spent online. Still, most marketers devote only approximately 5 to 10% of their advertising and promotion dollars to digital media (Murrar, 1995).

What are the likely reasons for the disconnection between consumer media usage and company media spending? Three are most commonly mentioned: (1) modest budgetary and organizational support for media experimentation, (2) limited business experience with and talent necessary to apply marketing analytics to new media, and (3) insufficient metrics and marketing analytics to measure the efficiency and effectiveness of new media alongside traditional media (Mei, 2011).

Hypotheses

The content of the main hypothesis of this study is as follows:

Marketing mix elements and the relationship between bank customers are significant. Five sub-hypotheses in this regard are as follows:

1. There is a significant relationship between income of customers and their deposit in the bank. 2- There is a significant relationship between providing quick and convenient services to the customers and their deposit in the bank.

3- There is a significant relationship among the variety of services and increase in the knowledge of customers and resources to attract customers to the bank. 4 -The use of advertising to attract customers to the bank is significant. 5 –Accelerating the transfer of facilities and resources to attract customers to bank is significant.

METHODS

Since in this study researchers sought to explore the relationship between combining elements of marketing and attracting customers to the bank in Kermanshah Province using survey method, the research is descriptive.

The population used in this study is the customers of the bank in Kermanshah Province (based on 14 cities), with at least one account, interest-free loans and savings. The formula is based on 230 samples in this study:

$$n \; \square \; \frac{Z^2P4}{\square} \Big/ 0_2 \qquad\qquad (1)$$

And 1-p = q, and p values are not available if it is equal to 5 / 0 set.

$$1\square\square\square0/95 \quad , \quad Z\square1/96 \quad q\square0/5 \quad p\square0/5$$

And the value of d (the amount of allowable error) with respect to similar research has been done based on empirical research. If the survey is collecting data to estimate the value of d p in the interval 4 to 7% is acceptable.

In this study, using statistical formulas, selected number of samples is 230.

Data for this study were collected using two methods: A library method and two field method.

A library method: This method involves collecting information from literature and history books, dissertations, articles, databases and Internet sources.

Two field method: This includes the use of questionnaire and distribution of statistical information on the relationship between marketing mix and attracting more customers. The questionnaire consists of three questions as well as the first, second and fifth hypotheses. Similarly the second hypothesis has questions 6, 7, 8, 9, 10, 11 and 12; third hypothesis, 13, 14, 15, 16 and 17 questions; fourth hypothesis, 18, 19, 24, 25 and 30; fifth hypothesis, questions 27 and 28, each in five levels (very low, low, medium, high and very high). They have been measured in the questionnaire design of university teachers in the field of management science and marketing, and financial consultants were used. The questionnaires were distributed among 30 customers. These individuals were selected according to the researcher to identify and complete a questionnaire about the appropriateness of the research questions, including questions on proper and demystification of the comments that people were using for the current exchange of ideas and thought with interviews and discussions on each of the questions. In this study, to describe and analyze the collected data, descriptive and inferential statistics were used.

FINDINGS

This study examined the hypotheses in section 6 and the results confirm or reject them.

The first hypothesis test

First hypothesis: the relationship between income of customers and their deposit in the bank is significant.

H_0. There is no significant relationship between income of customers and their deposit in the bank. H_1. There is significant relationship between income of customers and their deposit in the bank.

Since the Pearson correlation coefficient close to one is 878 / 0, H_0 is rejected and H_1 is accepted. There is significant relationship between income of customers and their deposit in the bank. The higher the income of customers, the more willing they would want to invest in the bank.

Testing the second hypothesis

Second hypothesis: There is a significant relationship between providing quick and convenient services to the customers and their deposit in the bank.

H_0. There is no significant relationship between providing quick and convenient services to the customers and their deposit in the bank.
H_1. There is a significant relationship between providing quick and convenient services to the customers and their deposit in the bank.

Since the H_0 is greater than 645/1, H_0 is rejected and is therefore against H_1, which is accepted.

Testing the third hypothesis

Third hypothesis: There is a significant relationship among the diversity of the customer service and increased awareness and resources to attract customers to the bank.

H_0. There is no significant relationship among the diversity of the customer service and increased awareness and resources to attract customers to the bank.
H_1. There is a significant relationship among the diversity of the customer service and increased awareness and resources to attract customers to the bank.

Considering the H_0 (674/17 = H_0) is larger than 645/1, the assumed H_0 is rejected and it is against the accepted H_1.

The fourth hypothesis test

The fourth hypothesis: The use of advertising to attract customers to the bank is significant.

H_0. The use of advertising to attract customers to the bank is not significant.
H_1. The use of advertising to attract customers to the
bank is significant

Considering the H_0 (844/26 = H_0) obtained is larger than 645/1, H_0 is rejected and it is against H_1, which is accepted.

Testing the fifth hypothesis

The fifth hypothesis: Accelerating the transfer of facilities and resources to attract customers to the bank is significant.

H_0. Accelerating the transfer of facilities and resources to attract customers to the bank is not significant. H_1. Accelerating the transfer of facilities and resources to attract customers to the bank is significant.

Considering that the H_0 (082/24 = H_0) is larger than 645/1, H_0 is rejected and H_1 is accepted.

Conclusion

Marketing involves a number of activities. To begin with, an organization may decide which of its target group of customers to be served. Once the target group is decided, the product is to be placed in the market by providing the appropriate product, price, place and promotion. These are to be combined or mixed in an appropriate proportion so as to achieve the marketing goal. Such mix of product, price, distribution and promotional efforts is known as _Marketing Mix' (Mei, 2011).

According to Kotler, —Marketing mix is the set of controllable variables that the firm can use to influence buyers' responsell. The controllable variables in this context refer to the 4P's [product, price, place (distribution) and promotion]. Each firm strives to build up such a composition of 4_P's, which can create highest level of consumer's satisfaction and at the same time meet its organizational objectives. Thus, this mix is assembled keeping in mind the needs of target customers, and it varies from one organization to another depending upon its available resources and marketing objectives (Iranian Events, 1386).

The major objective of this study is to investigate the effect of some of the marketing mix variables in attracting customers to the bank in Kermanshah Province, based on the primary hypothesis and the 5 secondary hypotheses proposed.

Based on the results of the first hypothesis, it is concluded that when there is more income, customers are more likely to deposit in the institution. Management and employees of the institution with high-income customers should implement plans and provide more benefits such as low-cost facilities in order to attract more resources.

According to the analysis and result of the second hypothesis, one can say that with the increasing competition between banks and financial institutions, management and employees should endeavor to shorten the time required to perform additional services to their customers. They should increase the number of staff in some branches which are more crowded and try to accelerate the delivery of services possible, as well as the payment of electricity and water bills. Payment facilities for customers and their physical presence should be reduced.

The third hypothesis shows there is a significant relationship among the diversity of the customer service and increased awareness and resources to attract customers to the bank. Banks also offer banking services to others banks as possible, which is now mostly done by the Institute of banking services. This leads to higher customers' deposit and particular variety of facilities and reduce the profits of the banks. This in turn would make bank customers to consider adopting appropriate policies of various facilities, and they are not forced to stop working with the institute.

Based on the result of the fourth hypothesis, the banks can diversify and expand their services through publicity and advertising, television messages and installation of banners on various sites to attract more customers. Some institutions are not aware that this is why higher deposit customers are with them.

The fifth hypothesis result indicates that accelerating the transfer of facilities and resources to attract customers to the bank is significant

SUGGESTIONS

From the assumptions and conclusions of this study based on the hypotheses, we conclude that there is a significant positive relationship to advance the goals of the bank. In connection with the study, the following suggestions are offered.

(1)   Proposals such as increasing profits, deposits and facilities from agency managers and policymakers offered to customers should be so cheap so that they can attract more resources to the institution.

(2)   Possible time of operation should be short and they should increase number of customer service staff

and Pour et al.   3279

expertise over the counter at any branch to be able to offer faster service to customers.

(3)   Institutions such as banks can provide complete management services for clients.

(4)   The institute should have broader campaign to engage in a variety of services and be more aware of its actual and potential customers. There should be advertising and television messages and banners installed at various sites to attract more customers because many customers will benefit from the variety of deposits and payments of services and facilities.

(5)   The bank should have major facilities to get the most important target customers. The type of facilities and their benefits should be made clear to customers, and in this way facilitating customers to deposit more.

(6)   Considering that one of the important goals in the bank is the transfer of account, the credit facilities should be given to 55% of respondents who have account in the bank to absorb more resources.

LIMITATION

Although all of our hypotheses are supported, this study has a few limitations that present opportunities for further research. First, our survey respondents were chosen from a convenience sample and the representativeness of our sample may be questioned. Second, this model was tested for validity and reliability only in the context of luxury restaurants in Iran. Ideally, national relationship quality indexing should be conducted in different sectors simultaneously, and the model should be tested periodically. Only then can the results be compared with other countries' relationship quality indices.

REFERENCES

Alvdary H (1383). "Marketing and market management," Tehran: Payam Noor University.

Alvdary H (1387). "Marketing and market management" (Fifth Edition). Tehran: Payam Noor University Press.

Arto A, Sample J (2005). Everybody's Selling Something: An Introductory Guide to Marketing Human Resource Development Programs. Anne M. Arto.

Baker MJ (1998). The Marketing Manual. (1 st ed), The Chartered Instituteb of Marketing Plant a Tree.

Belch George E, Belch Michael A (2001). Advertising And Promotion: An Integrated Marketing Communication Perspective, 5 Th Ed, New Delhi: Tata McGraw-Hill Publishing Company Limited.

BolurianTehrani M (1376). "Marketing Management" market, commercial printing and publishing.

Chisnall PM (1992). Marketing Research. (4 th Ed) McGraw Hill.

Cohen W (1998). Marketing Managemen. (2 nd ed), Macmillan publishing co.

Cutler RP (2000). "Principles of Marketing" translation Parsayyan A. (1383), published Birthdays.

Events Iranian GH (1386). "The most important factor in the marketing mix factors used to replace carpet with carpet in Tehran." Tehran: MS Thesis, University of Science and Research Branch.

Frank E (1994). Marketing HRD: An Overview. J. Eur. Ind. Train. 18(8):4-9.

Goharian MI (1374). "Management of non-oil exports", Tehran, Institute of Business Research.

HaKansson H, Waluszewski A (2005). Developing New Understanding of Market: Reinterpreting the 4ps. Journal of Business & Industrial Marketing.

Harrell GD, Frazier GL (1999). Marketing connecting with customer. (1 st ed). USA: Prentice Hall Inc.

Holm O (2006). Integerated Marketing Communication: From Tactics to Strategy Corporate Communication. An International Journal, Vol.11, No 1.

Hosseini MH (1384). "International Marketing", Tehran: Payam Noor University.

Industries A (1384). "principles of marketing and market management," the question of publication, second edition.

Ivy J (2008). A new higher education marketing mix: the 7ps for MBA marketing. Int. J. Educ. Manage. 22(4).

Lavak C (1382). "Marketing of Services", translated Tajzadeh
    Artaxerxes, the publishing, printing.

Mason RB (2007). A Marketing Mix Model for a Complex and Turbulent.

Mei LS (2011). Marketing mix (7P) and performance assessment ofwestern fast food industry in Taiwan: An application by associating DEMATEL and ANP, Afr. J. Bus. Manage. 5(26):10634-10644,

Mnty H, Trustee AK, Mastication "Marketing Plan", Published by term. Mohammadian M (1382). "Advertising Management", Sayhnma Publishing, Printing.
Murrar J (1995). Success in Advertising and promotion. (1 st ed), Don Milner.
Newson D, Vanslyke TJ, Kruckerburg D (2000). Public relation (7th ed). USA: wada worth.
Pickton D, Broderick A (2001). Integrated Marketing Communication. (1 st ed). Barcelona: Financial Times / Prentice Hall. Pourhassan E (1376). "International Marketing Management", Open University Press.
Ranjbariyan B (1378). "Marketing Management" market, the publication of the Institute of Business Research.
Venus referee, the rosta of Ahmad, Abdul Hamid Ebrahimi (1386).
    "Marketing management" of the publisher.

Sharifi, H; Zhang, Z (1999). A Methodology for Achieving Agility in Manufacturing Organizations, International Journal of Production Economics, 20(4): 7-22.

Sharifi, H and Zhang, Z (2000). Agile Manufacturing in Practice: Application of a Methodology, International Journal of Operations & Production Management, 21(5/6): 772-794.

Sharp, J; Irani, Z; Desai, S (1999). Working Towards Agile Manufacturing in The UK Industry, International Journal of Production Economics, 62(5): 155-169.

Sherehiy, B; Karwowski, W and Layer, J (2007). A review of enterprise agility: Concepts, frameworks, and attributes, International Journal of Industrial Ergonomics 37(5): 445–460.

Thompson, J (1967). Organization in Action, McGraw-Hill, New York, NY.

Tsourveloudis, N.C., Valavanis, K.P (2002). On the measurement of enterprise agility. Journal of Intelligent and Robotic Systems, 33 (3): 329–342.

Vernadat, F (1999). Research Agenda for Agile Manufacturing, LGIPM, ENIM/University, International Journal of Agile Management Systems, 1(1): 37-40.

Vokurka, R; Fliedner, G (1998). Journey toward Agility, Industrial Management & Data Systems, 98(4): 165–171.

Youssuf, Y; Sarhadi, M; Gunasekaran, A (1999). Agile Manufacturing: The Drives, Concepts and Attributes; International Journal of Production economics, 62(1-2): 33-43.

Impacts corporate social responsibility activities on company financial performance

Hossein Khanifar

Teacher of Tehran University.

Kamran Nazari

Department of Business Management, Payam Noor University, Kermanshah, Iran

Mostafa Emami

Young Researchers Club, Branch, Islamic Azad University,

Hossein Ali Soltani

Abstract

In the modern commercial era, companies and their managers are subjected to well publicized pressure to play an increasingly active role in society – so called "Corporate social responsibility". It has been argued that an element in this development is simply enlightened self-interest in that social responsibility enhances corporate image and financial performance. To date the evidence to support this thesis derives from North America. Outside this continent evidence for any relationship is sparse. This study will initially attempt to define the concept of corporate social responsibility and to examine its guiding principles. Subsequently, the available empirical research into the link between corporate social responsibility and economic performance will be evaluated this study examines different impacts of positive and negative CSR activities on financial performance of hotel, restaurant and airline companies, theoretically based on positivity and negativity effects. Findings suggest mixed results across different industries and will contribute to companies' appropriate strategic decision-making for CSR activities by providing more precise information regarding the impacts of each directional CSR activity on financial performance.

Keywords: Corporate social responsibility; Financial performance; Commercial era

Introduction

It is no secret that many multinational enterprises (MNEs) have annual turnovers higher than that of the GDP of a significant number of less developed countries (LDCs) put together. At the same time, the grad-ual liberalization of trade at the global level, coupled with mounting external debt, lack of financial capital, and high unemployment in LDCs has resulted in many cases in the promulgation of enticing foreign investment legislation, rampant corruption, and lax control over the operations of MNEs, as far as the domestic law and enforcement by the host State is concerned. Since the addressees and bearers of human rights, labor, and environmental obligations under traditional treaty and customary international law have been States. Commentators have argued both for and against the view that corporate social responsibility is enlightened economic self-interest.

The controversy at the theoretical level will be considered here, while the empirical evidence for and against will be presented later. Similarly, in order to clarify what is a complex and at times convoluted debate, the discussion will be divided into the relationships suggested with:

• Concurrent and subsequent (to CSR) economic performance; and

• Past economic performance.

583

Those who have theorised that a negative relation exists between social responsibility and economic performance have argued that a high investment in social responsibility results in additional costs. According to McGuire *et al.* (1988, p. 855) the added costs may result from actions such as "making extensive charitable contributions, promoting community development plans, maintaining plants in economically depressed locations and establishing environmental protection procedures". These costs might put a firm at an economic disadvantage compared to other, less socially responsible, firms. In contrast, others have argued the case for a positive association. McGuire *et al.* (1988) cite the argument that a firm perceived as high in social responsibility may face relatively fewer labour problems or perhaps customers may be more favourably disposed to its products.

Alternatively, CSR activities might improve a firm's reputation and relationship with bankers, investors and government officials. Improved relationships with them may well be translated to economic benefits.

According to Spicer (1978a,b), Rosen *et al.* (1991), Graves and Waddock (1994) and Pava and Krausz (1996), a firm's CSR behavior seems to be a factor that influences banks and other institutional investors' investment decisions. Thus, a high CSR profile may improve a firm's access to sources of capital.

Corporate social responsibility

The pharmaceutical sector, an industry already facing stiff tests in the form of intensified competition and strategic consolidation, has increasingly become subject to a variety of other pressures. Significantly, in common with other large-scale businesses, pharmaceutical firms are being exhorted to respond positively to the challenge of corporate (social) responsibility (CSR). Clearly, for individual managers within pharmaceutical firms the issue of CSR in the form of closely connected questions relating to patient access to health treatment, patent protection and affordability presents major problems.

Part of the burden of addressing the demands of CSR is the need to engage effectively with a range of stakeholders. Individual managers in pharmaceutical companies have to confront the complicated task of choosing which stakeholder dialogue practices to adopt and why. This real-world management predicament runs parallel to an academic interest in CSR stakeholder dialogue theory and models. Accordingly, this paper contributes to primarily to the academic debate by reviewing past attempts to theorise CSR and stakeholder dialogue, identifying gaps and weaknesses, and proposing a diagram-type model as a refined prototype framework.

The amount of literature available on CSR is massive and its production continues to grow. In addition, there is considerable literature on related concepts, such as 'business ethics', 'corporate citizenships' and 'sustainable business', to mention a few. The readings suggested here focus on literature that explicitly discusses CSR. The Reader is therefore not a complete review of CSR-relevant literature, but rather an attempt to organize this complex and vast area of literature . CSR refers to the obligations of the firm to society or, more specifically, the firm's stakeholders—those affected by corporate policies and practices. Saltaire and other early examples of paternalistic capitalism reveal three important characteristics of CSR. First, it is not a new idea, the hype surrounding it today notwithstanding Second, firms engaging in CSR often have "normative case" for CSR. Third, while there is substantial agreement that CSR is concerned with the societal obligations of business, there is much less certainty about what these obligations might be or their scope. Salt's ideas for social betterment did not meet with universal approval and he opposed legislation to prohibit child labor. Even corporate champions of CSR today, such as Starbucks meet with opposition from NGOs (non governmental organizations) and others. As Sethi observed nearly 30 years ago, the operational meaning of corporate social responsibility is supremely vague and, he suggested, it can mean all things to all peopleThese three characteristics of CSR are particularly important as we consider its recent rise to prominence and the challenges it poses.

Bowen (1953) sets the scene in this field by suggesting that the concept of specifically corporate social responsibility emphasizes that:

• businesses exist at the pleasure of society and that their behaviour and methods of operation must fall within the guidelines set by society; and • businesses act as moral agents within society.

Wood (1991) expanded these ideas, encapsulating them into three driving principles of social responsibility, which are that:

(1) business is a social institution and thus obliged to use its power responsibly;(2) businesses are responsible for the outcomes relating to their areas of involvement with society; and (3) individual managers are moral agents who are obliged to exercise discretion in their decision making. In general, the social responsibilities of a firm seem to arise from the intersection (and compatibility) of the political and cultural systems with the economic system (Jones,1983). However, Friedman (1970) argued that the successful functioning of our society depends on the role specialisation of its institutions (or systems). According to him the corporation is an economic institution and thus should specialise in the economic sphere; socially responsible behaviour will be rectified by the market through profits. In Friedman's (1970) view business has only one social responsibility and that is to maximise the profits of its owners (to protect their property rights). Organisations are seen purely as legal entities incapable of value decisions. A manager who uses a firm's resources for non-profit social purposes is thought to be diverting economic efficiency and levying an "illegal tax" on the organisation. Opponents (Frederick *et al.*, 1992) of this view, challenge the very foundations of Friedman's thesis – the economic model. They claim that the economic model and role specialisation of institutions (or systems) are not working as suggested.

This comes as a result of the rise of oligopolies in certain sectors; the separation of ownership and management; government's involvement in the economy and conversely industry's involvement in the political process through lobbying. In addition, if corporations do not adopt "social responsibility", government with its potential for inefficiency and insensitive bureaucratic methods may be forced to step in. With respect to Friedman's argument that the legal conception of corporations' articles and memorandums of associations limits a firm's involvement solely to economic roles, it can be claimed that they are broad enough to allow departures from this narrow path. Social responsibility is also seen as a consequence of and an obligation following from the unprecedented increase of firms' social power (as tax payers, recruiters, etc.) (Davis, 1975). Failure to balance social power with social responsibility may ultimately result in the loss of this power and a subsequent decline of the firm (Davis, 1975).

Another school of thought sees social responsibility as a contractual obligation firms have towards society (Donaldson, 1983). It is society in the first place that has permitted firms to use both natural and human resources and has given them the right to perform their productive functions and to attain their power status (Donaldson, 1983).

As a result, society has an implicit social contract with the firm. Thus, in return for the right to exploit resources in the production process, society has a claim on the firm and the right to control it. The specifics of this contract may change as social conditions change but this contract in general always remains the basis of the legitimacy of the demand for or assertion of the need for CSR (Epstein, 1987). A growing number of scholars take the view that firms can no longer be seen purely as private institutions but as social institutions instead (Frederick *et al.*, 1992; Freeman, 1984; Lodge, 1977). The benefits flowing from firms need to be shared collectively. This thesis is similar to the stakeholders model (Freeman, 1984) and claims that a firm is responsible not only to its shareholders (owners) but to all stakeholders (consumers, employees, creditors, etc.) whose contribution is

585

necessary for a firm's success. Thus, CSR means that a corporation should be held accountable for any of its actions that affect people, communities and the environment in which those people or communities live (Frederick *et al.*, 1992).

Carroll (1979) suggests that CSR is defined as the economic, legal, ethical and discretionary demands that society places on business. Similarly, Zanies conceptualized CSR as the degree of "fit" between society's expectations of business and the ethics of business. He argues that CSR is really nothing more than another layer of managerial responsibility resulting from the evolution of capitalism. An interesting twist to the argument is provided by Tuzzolino and Armandi (1981) who provide a motivational theory of organisational social response based on Maslow's hierarchy of needs. CSR is the fulfilment of a firm's "internal and external self-actualisation needs" which are located on the top of their organisational needs pyramid.

According to this view, firms adopt CSR after they have satisfied three earlier layers of needs (which include: "physiological" or survival needs fulfilled by corporate profits; "safety needs" such as dividend policy, conglomeration and competitive position; and "affiliative needs" such as participation in trade association, lobby groups, etc.). Epstein (1987) attempted to differentiate "business ethics" and CSR and to incorporate them into a strategic process. According to him "business ethics" refer to issues and dilemmas related to the morality of organisational actions or decisions. CSR focuses more on the consequences of organisational actions. He defined CSR as the "discernment of issues, expectations and claims on business organizations regarding the consequences of policies and behaviour on internal and external stakeholders" (Epstein 1987, p. 101). Angelidis and Ibrahim (1993) defined CSR as "corporate social actions whose purpose is to satisfy social needs". They developed an equilibrium theory based on social demand and supply, identifying a set of factors that affects them (social supply and demand).

Thus, opinions differ in terms of the basis or scope of CSR and even the very definition of the term. As a consequence different aspects of a firm's operations can be seen to come under its sway – depending on the stance one adopts. As has been shown, what can be conceived as "social responsibility" can range from simply maximisation of profits, to satisfaction of stakeholders' social needs, or fulfilment of social contractual obligations, fulfilment of a firm's needs, achievement of a social equilibrium, etc. – depending on the stance taken.

While academic debate abounds at the theoretical level, at the operational level insights are more sparse. Schwarts and Dahl observed that socially acceptable behaviour of North American firms at the time of writing – the 1970s included:

• Disclosure of information to shareholders;
• Disclosure of the board of directors;
• Monopolistic behaviour (predatory pricing, etc.);
• Equality of treatment for minorities;
• Profit sharing;
• Environmental protection;
• Ethics in advertising; and • Social impact of technology.

However, according to Vyarkarnam (1992), many of these have now been regulated by statute. Present day concerns have changed focus. He found that current CSR concerns, which are in substance the same for both North American and the UK firms, encompass such areas as:

• Environmental protection (e.g. reduction of emissions and waste and the recycling of materials);
• Philanthropy (donating to charities, etc.); • Involvement in social causes (involving anything from human rights to AIDS education);
• Urban investment (working with local government to regenerate small businesses and the inner city environment generally);and

586

• Employee schemes (higher standards of occupational health and safety, good standard of staff treatment, job-sharing, flexitime, etc.).

Empirical research into the effects of corporate responsibility has produced mixed results. Some studies have suggested a positive relation, whereas others have concluded that the effects are negative or inconsequential. For example, Belkaoui (1976) investigated the information content of pollution control disclosures. His results suggested a positive relationship between economic performance and social responsibility, at least in this area. Other studies produced results consistent with the notion that corporate social responsibility activities impact on the financial markets (Anderson and Frankle, 1980; Shane and Spicer, 1983; Spicer, 1978a,b). However, certain studies have replicated earlier research and found conflicting results. Frankle and Anderson (1978) rejected Belkaoui's (1976) interpretation and argued that nondisclosing firms had consistently performed better in the market. In a similar manner, Chen and Metcalf (1980) disagreed with Spicer's (1978a,b) conclusions, arguing that his results were driven by spurious correlations. In response Spicer (1980) stated that Chen and Metcalf (1980) misinterpreted the purpose of his study, emphasising that associations not causal relationships were being investigated.

Ingram (1978) concluded that the information content of social responsibility disclosures was conditional on the market segment with which a firm is identified. Alexander and Bulcholz (1978) and Abbott and Monsen (1979) found no significant relationship between a corporation's level of social responsibility activities and stock market performance.

In addition, Chugh (1978), Trotman and Bradley (1981) and Mahapatra (1984) concluded that corporate social responsibility activities may lead to increased systematic risk.

Cochran and Wood (1984) used corporate social responsibility rankings developed by Moskowitz (1972) to test the relationship between corporate social responsibility activities and firm's performance. After controlling for industry classification and corporate age, a weak positive association between corporate social responsibility activities and economic performance was found.

Mills and Gardner (1984) concluded in their analysis of the relationship between social disclosure and economic performance, that companies are more likely to disclose social responsibility expenditures when their financial statements indicate favourable economic performance.

One drawback of the above empirical studies is that they failed to distinguish between past, concurrent and subsequent to CSR economic performance, and thus to make possible reliable inferences about direction of causation. In most of the previous studies, economic performance covered a (commonly five year) period "surrounding" the CSR performance and/or social disclosure periods. Routinely, the CSR performance and/or social disclosure periods were the midpoints of that period. However, in Mahapatra (1984) and Mills and Gardner (1984) studies, economic performance periods were concurrent to the CSR performance period.

Only Shane and Spicer (1983) looked at economic performance subsequent to CSR disclosure period, finding a positive association. Practically, McGuire et al. (1988) were the first to break this tradition and to separate economic performance into past, concurrent and subsequent to CSR performance. They used Fortune magazine's ratings of corporate reputations to analyse the relationship between perceived corporate social responsibility and economic performance. Prior economic performance of the firms, as measured by both stock market returns and accounting based measures, were found to be more closely related to corporate social responsibility than was subsequent economic performance. McGuire et al. (1988) suggested that economic performance may be a variable influencing

Thus, the empirical research into the relationship between corporate social responsibility and economic performance is confusing and far from conclusive. According to Ullmann (1985) this may be attributed to the use of varying and questionable measures of CSR, differences in the research methodologies and the financial performance measures used. To overcome these limitations, this

587

study will use a more comprehensive measurement of CSR performance (admittedly within the context of the UK social and business environment), a combination of economic performance measures and including the necessary intervening variables in the research design.

CSR and financial performance

A modern concept of CSR has evolved since the 1950s, formalized in the 1960s and proliferated in the 1970s (Carroll, 1999). Based on various studies from the CSR literature (Carroll, 1999; Engardio et al., 2007; Hart, 1995; Holme and Watts, 2000; McWilliams and Siegel, 2001; Nicolau, 2008; Tsoutsoura, 2004), CSR can be broadly defined as the activities making companies good citizens who contribute to society's welfare beyond their own self interests. Throughout the past several decades, numerous aspects of CSR have been the subject of investigation in academic and business literature, and according to the framework of Schwartz and Carroll (2003), economic, legal and ethical domains can be epitomized as the most common components of CSR. One aspect of CSR interesting to many financial economists is the economic domain: financial impact of CSR for profit-seeking corporations. Regarding the relationship between companies' CSR activities and their performances (especially, financial performance), the literature presents three assertions.

The first group of researchers, based on the viewpoint of Friedman (1970), has found a negative relationship between CSR activities and financial performance as measured by, for example, stock price changes (Vance, 1975), excess return (Wright and Ferris, 1997), or analysts' earnings-per-share forecasts (Cordeiro and Sarkis, 1997). Friedman argued that managements are selected by the stockholders as agents and their sole responsibility is acting on behalf of the principals' best interests. From Friedman's perspective, the one and only social responsibility of business is to use its resources and engage in activities designed to increase profits and wealth of owners. Any other activities disturbing the optimal allocation of scarce resources to alternative uses exert an adverse influence on firm performance.

The second group argued for positive impact from companies' CRS activities on financial performance (Arago´n-Correa et al., 2008; Bird et al., 2007; Bragdon and Marlin, 1972; Klassen and McLaughlin, 1996; Nicolau, 2008; Orlitzky et al.,1997). This group's assertion, based on stakeholder theory (Freeman, 1984), suggests that firms expand the scope of consideration in their decision-making and activities beyond shareholders to several other constituencies with interests, such as customers, employees, suppliers and communities. The second group asserts that CSR activities, which encompass all legitimate stakeholders' implicit claims as stakeholder theory suggests, can improve firm value by (1) immediate cost saving, (2) enhancement of firm reputation, and (3) dissuasion of future action by regulatory bodies including governments which might impose significant costs on the firm (Bird et al., 2007). A third group has supported no particular relationship between CSR activities and financial performance (Abbott and Monsen, 1979; Alexander and Buchholz, 1978; Aupperle et al., 1985; Teoh et al., 1999), partially arguing for the existence of too many confounding factors for researchers to uncover a particular impact from CSR on firm performance.

Seemingly contradictory themes between Friedman's (1970) viewpoint and the stakeholder theory arise from the assumption that CSR, which considers the interests of a broad spectrum of stakeholders (suggested by stakeholder theory), is in fact detrimental to value maximization activities of the firm (asserted by Friedman's viewpoint). However, Jensen (2001) attempted to reconcile the potential conflict between these two viewpoints by proposing enlightened stakeholder theory, which asserts that a firmcannotmaximize its long-term value if it ignores the interests of diverse stakeholders. And, according to Post et al. (2002), a firm's capacity that generates sustainablewealth over time and its long-term value are determined by the relationship with both internal and external stakeholders. CSR, if it contributes to enhancing firm value, can be an appropriate corporate strategy as the stakeholder

588

theory suggests, not an exploitation of shareholders' wealth to benefit other parties, as Friedman (1970) worried.

Conclusion

Modern corporate stakeholder theory (Cornell and Shapiro, 1987; Freeman, 1984; Jones, 1995; McGuire *et al.*, 1988) can also explain part of the CSR/economic performance relationship. According to stakeholder theory the value of a firm is related to the cost of both "explicit claims" and "implicit claims" on a firm's resources. Claimants include not only the legal owners of the firm but other constituencies such as lenders, employees, consumers, banks, government, etc. Stakeholders who have explicit claims on the corporation include – besides its owners – lenders, employees, government, etc. In addition, there are others with whom the firm has made implicit contracts, which could include the quality of service and CSR. According to McGuire *et al.* (1988), if the firm does not honour these implicit contracts, then it is argued that the parties to these contracts may attempt to transform them from implicit to explicit agreements. The latter may be more costly for the firms involved. According to Freeman (1984) and McGuire *et al.* (1988) the implications of the conversion of " implicit" to "explicit" contracts may have broader effects than the direct costs resulting from the forced change in its behaviour (e.g. cost of installment of gas emission control equipment). For example, socially irresponsible actions in one area (e.g. gas emissions) may spill-over and affect the corporate image in other areas as well (e.g. unregulated issues on labour relationships).

This could in turn result in other implicit stakeholders (e.g. trade unions) striving to make their claims explicit. Thus, firms with an image of high CSR may find that they face both fewer and lower-cost explicit claims than those with a less enlightened stance. Thus, from a theoretical perspective, arguments can and have been made both for and against a positive relationship between social responsibility and concurrent or subsequent (to CSR) economic performance. According to Parert and Eibert (1975), Ullmann (1985) and Roberts (1992), if corporate social responsibility is viewed as a significant cost, firms with relatively high past financial performance may be more willing to absorb these costs in the future. It is also expected that poor performers would seek more immediate results and consequently they may prefer short-term and highyield investments to the uncertain and in general longer-term CSR investments. A similar view is that policies and expenditures in discretionary areas such as social programmes may be especially sensitive to the existence of "slack" resources in the firm (McGuire *et al.*, 1988). Ullmann (1985) argued that corporations must reach an acceptable level of economic performance before devoting company resources to meet social demands. This is supported by the assertion that corporations with strong prior economic performance appear to be more likely to have high current levels of social disclosure. Ullmann (1985) also suggested that companies with less stable stock market patterns would be relatively less likely to commit resources to social activities.

References

Adams R., Carruthers, J. and Hamil, S. (1991), Changing Corporate Values, Kogan Page,London.

Alexander, G. and Bulcholz, R. (1978), "Corporate social responsibility and stock market performance", Academy of Management Journal, Vol. 21, pp. 479- 86.

Anderson, J. and Frankle, A. (1980), "Voluntary social reporting: an iso-beta portfolio analysis", Accounting Review, Vol. 55, pp. 468-79.

Angelidis, P. and Ibrahim, N. (1993), "Social demand and corporate supply: a corporate social responsibility model", Review of Business, Vol. 15, Fall, pp. 7-10.

Belkaoui, A. (1976), "The impact of the disclosure of the environmental effects of organization behaviour on the market", Financial Management, Vol. 5 No. 4,pp. 6-31.

Bowen, H.R. (1953), Social Responsibilities of the Businessman, Harper & Row, New York, NY.
Carroll, A.B. (1979), "A three-dimensional model of corporate performance", Academy of Management Review, Vol. 4 No. 4, pp. 497-505.

Chen, K. and Metcalf, R. (1980), "The relationship between pollution control record and financial indicators revisited", Accounting Review, Vol. 55, pp. 168-77.

Clarkson, M.B.E. (1995), "A stakeholder framework for analysing and evaluating social corporate performance", Academy of Management Review, Vol. 20 No. 1, pp. 92-117.

Cochran, P. and Wood, R. (1984), "Corporate social responsibility and financial erformance", Academy of Management Journal, Vol. 27 No. 1, pp. 42-56.

Cohen, J. and Cohen, P. (1983), Applied Multiple Regression for the Behavioral Sciences, Laurence Erlbaum, Hillsdale, NJ.

Copeland, T. and Weston, J. (1983), Financial Theory and Corporate Policy, AddisonWesley, Reading, MA.

Cornell, B. and Shapiro, A. (1987), "Corporate stakeholders and corporate finance", Financial Management, Vol. 16, pp. 5-14.

Davis, K. (1975), "Five propositions for social responsibility", Business Horizons, Vol. 18 No. 3, pp. 19-24.

Frankle, A. and Anderson, J. (1978), "The impact of the disclosure of environmental effects of organizational behaviour on the market: comment", Financial Management, Vol. 21, Summer, pp. 92-107.

Frederick, W.C. et al. (1992), Business and Society, McGraw-Hill International, New York, NY.

Freeman, R.E. (1984), Strategic Management : A Stakeholder Approach, Pitman, Boston, MA.
Graves, S.B. and Waddock, S.A. (1994), "Institutional owners and corporate social performance", Academy of Management Journal, Vol. 37 No. 4, pp. 1034- 46.

Spicer, B. (1980), "The relationship between pollution control record and financial indicators revisited: further comment", Accounting Review, Vol. 55, pp. 178-85.

Trotman, K. and Bradley, G. (1981), "Association between social responsibility disclosure and characteristics of companies", Accounting Organizations and Society, Vol. 6, pp. 355-62.

Tuzzolino, F. and Armandi, B. (1981), "A need – hierarchy framework for assessing corporate social responsibility", Academy of Management Review, Vol. 6 No. 1, pp. 21-8.

Ullmann, A. (1985), "Data in search of a theory: a criticalexamination of the relationships among social performance, social disclosure, and economic performance of US firms", Academy of Management Review, Vol. 10 No. 3, pp. 540-57.

Vyakarnam, S. (1992), "Social responsibility: what leading companies do", Long Range Planning, Vol. 25 No. 5, pp. 59-67.

Wartick, S. and Cochran, P. (1985), "The evolution of the corporate social performance model", Academy of Management Review, Vol. 10 No. 4, pp. 758-69.

Wood, D. (1991), "Corporate social performance revisited", Academy of Management Review, Vol. 16 No. 4, pp. 758-69.

JOB APPROPRIATENESS (THEORIES, CONCEPTS AND MEASURE IT) (A CASE STUDY IN IRANIAN OIL REFINING AND DISTRIBUTION COMPANY)

MOSTAFA EMAMI

Young Researchers Club, South Tehran Branch, Islamic Azad University, Tehran, Iran.

KAMRAN NAZARI

Department of Business Management, Payam Noor University, Kermanshah, Iran

HAMID MALEKI

Teacher of Payam-noor University.

Abstract:

Job Appropriateness (fit between personal characteristics and job requirements), one of the fundamental issues of human resource management has been proven that this is a Job Appropriateness for the organizational efficiency of human resources is essential. Given the importance of Job Appropriateness , Job Appropriateness in this study were reviewed and evaluated solutions and suggestions for improvement are presented. The main aim of this study and assess the appropriateness of the company's professional staff is the National Iranian Oil Refining and Distribution. In order to assess the appropriateness of international job bank job [1] (O * NET) was used, with regard to this subject in the population studied, 37 were identified as existing staff who work in these jobs, according to the job description The job description business standards in the database of job internationally are available to compare and match was the 27th title of the job with the international code and the score of knowledge, skills and abilities required to determine and were identified and 27 were given the average job titles of each of the questionnaire included 21 questions were developed to be designed. Reliability of job suitability assessment 0 / 87 respectively and Cronbach questionnaires because of 0 / 7 are the reliability of the questionnaire were necessary. The population size is about 150. Based on stratified random sampling of 80 sample was selected and the 78 questionnaires were collected and analyzed. Data obtained from tests to determine the normal Kolmogorov - Smirnov normality test was used and the results confirmed the data, to determine suitability for the job of comparing the scores obtained from standardized questionnaires with scores in the bank job International (O * NET) is available to use are the findings of this study indicate the fact that only about 40 percent of the employees of these companies in terms of Job Appropriateness , and these findings indicate that the issue is that the population studied, the proportion not have a good job.

Key words: Job knowledge, job skills, job ability.

Introduction

Human life in society are incorporated into the work, other living organisms owe their gifts of nature and their own instincts without thought and effort, especially with direct donations from living nature,

532

but humans only in the short period since the status of mere and the dam has lived esurience content of the dawn of human history, using his intelligence and knowledge of complex brain as tool and material and the nature of their service has had to rely on what is not directly available , but always try and rush the search is to use what is available does not have access to what it feels the need to achieve, and thus his work every day more complex and the normal phase and The distance is more instinctive and cultural aspects of man-made artifacts, and every day more and more of the natural environment around him and made of fabric that he has made for himself is caught, the social life requires cooperation and the mutual needs, leading to division of labor and the development of expertise and skills and the development of quantitative and qualitative results of the added work and social relations and institutions and organized in his more or less extensive and specialized agencies and departments has expanded. (prayer: 8:1384).

Important element of course work and building societies and organizations. For they are not associated with alienation, we must consider the technical and physiological psychology is favorable. Economic and social situation in which the work must be done so that the worker feels he is fair and proportionate to the skill and effort and also pay the appropriate fee is paid to other Working Groups (Boom, 1380: 24).

In doing so, where are the jobs, it features a job working with properties measured and could be considered. It should do the job well and to have the job analysis, job design and people with the next step in the job and the job was done (Sadeghi, 1375:23).

The proper design of jobs and job satisfaction, effectiveness, and not wanting to leave the service and get rid of the service is important. Here, since the characteristics of jobs and how to organize how the structure depends on the first issue that must be examined in the context of the special importance of a varied and extensive career in the making. Division of labor as Scientists believe that all the main classical management and productivity has been the traditional paradigm with advantages and disadvantages are. Among the benefits of increased skills and reduced work time, but the division of labor intensive tasks due to repeated minor decrease in long-term productivity and reduced job satisfaction is a. Therefore, an important role in enhancing the spirit of service, job satisfaction and productivity of the workforce there. However, a detailed explanation of the tasks and missions, redesigning jobs, participation in decision making regarding health and fitness programs work with organizations working in human resources, efficiency increases (figural [2] on: 23:2001).

Proportion employed in jobs with the organization as an effective strategy in the maintenance of human resources is considered .The match begins from the moment the first person to work and pick up his sleeve jobs. Second, the employee organization for finding, selecting, hiring and appointment will be ready. May be hired at the start, according to the needs and requirements Volunteers work to a limited extent, but gradually the proportion of individuals in the course of his career continues and leaves behind his life, this proportion is expected to be more .. If the job is designed in such a way that is commensurate with the individual characteristics, is the motivation and productivity in the workforce increases. (Skinner [3,] 2005: 342).

Proportion of employment (the proportion of employed jobs)

In the past two decades, organizations have to significantly change the characteristics of organizations with decentralization, globalization and leadership on the team have become. In these organizations,

533

organized labor is a major capital and organizational capabilities and skills in the use of human resources in order to maximize their efficiency and productivity, in order to utilize and use of the proportion of knowledge, ability and skills of human resources is very important. Proportion of individual types of jobs fit with their surroundings - [4] is employed, the proportion of costs between the individual and his job could be on the lookout for the organization. The main character fit the job - working in the different definitions that are clear and in research in this area fit the definitions of employment and occupation is presented (Antal [5:] 336:2008).

[6] David proportion of jobs - working as such defines "compatibility between individual and organization that is doing business" in other words, knowledge, skills and abilities of the individual's knowledge, skills and abilities of the individual jobs in the organization It needs to be (David: 6:2007).

Match between job requirements and working theory is that such a variety of job skills, [7, 8] task identity, task autonomy [9, 10] job knowledge, job skills, [11, 12,] and dozens of other variables, there are potential occupational ability and has the capability of the personal characteristics such as age, sex, education, marriage and celibacy, experience, knowledge, skills and abilities appropriate to the individual, and therefore not compatible with the employee and his job affects the individual behaviors and attitudes. (Chang and Klyndr [13:] 33:2001)

Hvsaka similar values of jobs and personal values consistent with the values of the important aspects of fitness jobs - that is employed, provided by Hvska within the framework of the Stretching - Select - weakening (ASA) is adapted to fit the individual and I have a job, according to this theory, people are attracted to jobs in organizations that jobs are a means of achieving individual goals. (Hvsaka [14:] 560:2008).

Four groups of [15] Chaynvy fitness routine job - working with the above examples are as follows (Chaynvy: 23:2008):

1   - Fitness Supplement [16:] When a person has characteristics that are similar to the job profile, what I value in life are very similar to the values that exist in my career.

2   - The proportion of the additional [17:] When a person can be enough to revitalize the jobs lost in the characteristics or properties will provide additional knowledge, skills and abilities I offer things that other people do the job the operator.
3   - fit the demands - abilities [18:] When a person's ability to meet job requirements, skills, abilities and the abilities and skills that I needed a job.

4   - fitness needs - providing [19:] When a person needs can be met by the job, a job that I expect a job to fulfill my needs, can meet.

As very different definitions of fitness has been observed that the results can be influential.

In studies on the proportion of jobs - jobs that are sometimes very different results and consequences of the breach has been made for each other are also major sources of incompatibility and lack of coordination based on the results of these studies have been diagnosed:

534

- How to think and understand and define the proportion of jobs - working.

- Define a job operation.

- The realm of concept and methods used to assess Job Appropriateness .

- Individual differences that can lead to different perceptions.

The proportion of jobs in the job - working to distinguish the two methods are considered:

The first method:

In the first method people are asked to do the job profile (values, mission, etc.) The second

method:

In the second method, people are asked to note that the profile of staff members.

Some researchers believe that people are not separate and distinct from the operator's job in the job to be considered (and Dymz Ktystal [20:] (1999

Levin, Nottingham, Payj, Lewis [21] (2006) to study the effect of fitness work on job satisfaction of employees in 2006, 12 factories, plants, petrochemical West America conducted a statistical population included 14,500 people, with a sample of 822 questionnaires were collected, including technicians, engineers and managers, the results show, only fifty-eight percent of subjects in terms of employment were appropriate, and higher job satisfaction scores of other individuals who have acquired, also professionals (chemical engineering, petrochemical, oil) that the job than other occupations in the study population had a higher proportion of job satisfaction scores were higher than the other businesses. Http://Www.onetcenter.org)).

Smart [22] In a study that investigated the relationship between job satisfaction and job suitability, the subjects were 792 men and 1077 women in the first year of college and six years after graduating from the University to undertake the job, the question were those who had high job relevance of the knowledge, skills and their ability to be consistent with their job, while studying at the university who wish to build their current jobs and were in the field of expertise directly to the job that was. Thus the acquisition of desired skills and were grown men and women who had shown a high proportion of employment income from their benefits, and opportunities satisfied with the promotion of their jobs, who were fit to the higher It had very little coordination between the knowledge, skills, abilities, and there was a job; lineage to present a dream job in no time and no specialized university that did not get it to work (Smart 2003).

Other research includes a survey of 253 university graduates in jobs at various time periods longer than 7 years, and another survey of 345 bank employees who were working during 4 months, that both Investigation of the relationship between Job Appropriateness and job satisfaction are supported (Beer [23:] 2004).

Job satisfaction is highest when the best fit between their abilities and job demands exist (Frykv [24:] 2006 Brank [25:] 2005).

535

Another study about the appropriateness of the individual - [26] of the nearly 15,000 teachers and 356 school managers were asked the researchers to conclude an agreement on goals achieved (proportion of) the fundamental skills of students or to increase the physical facilities Job satisfaction is positively associated with leaving the job to be a negative relationship (Van Kvvr [27:] 2003).

David fit between the person and the relationship between job attitudes and outcomes examined. The results showed that the proportion of jobs - working to concepts such as freedom, job satisfaction and organizational commitment is related. The results showed that the proportion of persons with a job (of consistency versus other forms of adaptation) and the method used to measure the proportion of jobs - working (internal, external, perceived) between the proportion of jobs - working and attitudinal outcomes makes the adjustment. In general, poor internal communication and behavior are among the criteria (David: 17:2007).

Recently, "an emphasis on individual fitness - a job as a way to reach the needs of recruitment agencies," changing nature of work "is. Understanding of organizational fitness, job skills and job performance are essential for understanding and essential part of any employment decisions, and improved form (Rezaei Nejad: 1382).

Entries are listed according to relevance and importance of job evaluation study will try to fit the job to pay the National Iranian Oil Refining and Distribution.

The research hypothesis

In the present study is the following hypothesis:
Staff participate in professional fitness level Iranian Oil Refining and Distribution has been in good health.

The aim of the research

The main objective of this study are the following:

Evaluate the appropriateness of existing jobs and provide guidelines and suggestions to improve the National Iranian Oil Refining and Distribution.

Materials and Methods

Since in this study, researchers sought to assess the suitability of the job and provide guidelines to improve the staff at National Iranian Oil Refining and Distribution products is based on the research arm of the survey method of research and descriptive research is.

Total population of 150 members of the headquarters staff of National Iranian Oil Refining and Distribution form. The study is based on the following formula 74.

 $n== 74$

Data for this study were collected from the two following methods.

Library method: This method of data collection related to the research literature and history books, dissertations, articles, databases and Internet sources were used.

Field Methods: In this method, questionnaire design and distribution of the sample information about Job Appropriateness was obtained. In order to assess the appropriateness of the job (knowledge, skills and abilities with the knowledge, skills and abilities needed to perform the job) of the various databases that are used by different countries to create jobs for introducing one of the best and most complete Bank Information Occupational Information Network (O * NET [28]) which is supported by the Washington State Department of Labor in the database all the necessary information about defined jobs, meet the conditions of physical, environmental, skills and knowledge and required capabilities, are available.

In these conditions, taking any job site, divided into three components, which includes knowledge, skills and abilities required for the profession is employed and the conditions specified above and is defined in terms of three (Http://Www.onetcenter . org). With regard to information about available jobs in the job database, 27 questionnaires (depending on the job in 37 organizations and businesses with the implementation of existing jobs in the job database and identified as 27 career matches at the site available jobs in the organization) with respect to three variables of knowledge, skills and ability to work with cooperation and guidance of faculty members, academic advisers and industrial design were developed. Any questions concerning the appropriateness of the job an average of 21 questions, which consists of the current state of knowledge and skills and employment potential of those deals .The first questionnaire was distributed among 30 of the Staff. These individuals were selected according to the researcher to identify and then completed questionnaires about the appropriateness of the research questions, including questions of proper and demystification of these comments was that the flow of ideas and intellectual exchange and discussion of the interview performed on individual questions, the questionnaire was distributed to the necessary reforms. The presence and distribution of questionnaires to provide an explanation on how to complete a questionnaire regarding different questionnaires in terms of content and appearance of the questionnaire was common. To ensure the validity of the questionnaire [29] (it means the validity of the How much research tool for gathering information about what is to be measured) is used in the study of the formal validity of the use of faculty members and consultants and experts to assess the reliability of (it means How reliable is the measurement tool in the same situation would obtain the same results) Cronbach's alpha test was used. (This test was designed to examine and discuss the coordination questionnaires) alpha coefficient obtained for the questionnaire employed to measure the proportion of jobs with 872 /. Obtained and the reliability of more than 70 /. They are, therefore, the reliability of the questionnaire are required.

Results

To test this hypothesis in this study must first be determined whether or not the normal distribution of data collected. Normal or abnormal test data using Kolmogorov - Smirnoff is measured by the test results Kolmogorov - Smirnoff Table 1 are:

Table 1: Test of a two-sample Kolmogorov - Smirnov

Test Statistics

Z	

537

864.	Most Extreme Absolute
000.	Differences Positive
864 .-	Negative
3.979	Kolmogorov-Smirnov Z
000.	Asymp.Sig. (2-talied)

a. Grouping Variable: GROUP

The table above for the z-test at 95 percent of the 979 / 3 is. The statistical tables in table z-value of 95%, 64 / 1. From there, ready to test the value of z is larger than the zvalue, 95% confidence level can be argued that the data collected from a sample has a normal statistical distribution.

Studied in 37 professional staff in these positions were identified and defined according to the job description with the standard of service in the American job database (o * net) are available (Http://Www.onetcenter . org) and finally 27 were compared and matched with the job title and grade of the International Code of knowledge, skills and abilities required was determined that the information is contained in Table 2.

Table 2: Titles, job codes, and frequency

Row	Job titles on the Iranian Oil Refining and Distribution Company	O * NET job codes in the database	The number of people who fit the job	Job of the disproportionate number of people who are	Many people in each job
			Frequency	Frequency	Frequency
1	Hire an expert	43 to 4061.00	2	4	6
2	Social worker	43 to 4061.00	A	2	3
3	Property Accountant	13 to 2011.00	2	3	5
4	Training and Development	13 to 1073.00	A	A	2
5	Integrated Accounting	43 to 3011.00	A	3	4
6	Pension Management	11-3.41.00	A	0	A
7	Human Resource Management	11-304 .. 00	A	0	A
8	Auditor	13 to 2011.01	A	3	4
9	The development of clay	13 to 2061.00	A	0	A
10	Planning Expert	15 to 1081.00	A	2	3
11	Environmental Expert	19 to 4091.00	A	A	2

12	Administrative staff	43 to 3011.00	2	5	7
13	Expert Press	27 to 3031.00	A	A	2
14	International Affairs	19 to 3094.00	A	2	3
15	Social worker	21-1093 .. 00	A	A	2
16	Head of Commercial Services	11 to 3031.02	A	0	A
17	Expert land	23 to 2011.00	A	2	3
18	Budget and finance expert	13-2031.100	A	2	3
19	Rights experts	23 to 1022.00	A	2	3
20	Evaluation methods and fields	13 to 1111.00	A	0	3
21	Industrial Health	29 to 9012.00	A	A	2
22	Service Personnel and Labor Relations	13 to 1072.00	A	3	4
23	Fire safety expert and	33 to 2021.01	A	A	2
24	Expert Home	27 to 3031.00	A	A	2
25	Integrated management planning	11 to 9021.55	2	4	6
26	Buying Expert	13 to 1023.00	A	A	2
27	Mortgage and Retirement specialists	13 to 1072.00	A	A	2

An overall look at the frequency (number and percent) of employees who fit the job or not suit is as follows:

Table 3: Prevalence (number and percent) of employees on the appropriateness or inappropriateness of job

Index	Of employees	
	Total	Percent
Employees who are suited to the job	31	39.7 / 0
Employees who do not fit the job	47	59.3 / 0
Workers studied	78	100 / 0

As can be seen in Table 3, 39.7 / 0% of teller samples were matched to suit the job, the highest proportion of occupational pension managers and human resources management, planning, advertising experts, legal experts and experts in occupational employment and the lowest proportion, administrative staff, and experts in integrated planning and management accountants have the property.

Conclusion

People do not just mixed it with his experience and knowledge as a cultural value that has been manifested, and thus the thought, work and social relationships has emerged linked unbroken. This requires that all matters relating to the scope of work is rigorous, because it must do one of the characteristics of the life of mankind. Man is a social ecology, and even today, despite the variety of collections variety of technical progress and momentum in the evolution of the social construction of communities, the work deals with the life and work in common and necessary condition of human life in society (Shafee, 1378: 17).

Since the work done in the form of jobs and is expected to feature in a job working with properties measured and could be considered. It should do the job well and to have the job analysis, job design and people with the next step in the job and the job was done. Jobs and proper design of job satisfaction efficacy and lack of freedom of leaving the service and the service is important. Since the characteristics of jobs depend on how organized and how the organization structure, the first issue that must be examined in this context is important professional jobs in a wide variety to it. division of labor as a major management scholars who believed in the classical and the traditional paradigm of productivity has been the advantages and disadvantages. Among the benefits of increased skills and reduced work time, but the division of labor intensive tasks due to repeated minor decrease in long-term productivity and reduced job satisfaction is a. Therefore, an important role in enhancing the spirit of service, job satisfaction and productivity of the workforce there. However, a detailed explanation of the tasks and missions, redesigning jobs, participation in decision making, compliance with health and fitness programs employed in jobs with an eye to how the efficiency of human resources to increase the proportion employed in jobs Organization as an effective strategy in maintaining human resources are used. The proportion of the first moment a person begins to work and pick up his sleeve jobs, secondly, the organization seeking to employee selection, recruitment and appointment will be ready. May be hired at the beginning, the organization needs volunteers to work, but gradually in proportion to the limited extent that the person continues his career in the organization and the organization makes the period of his life behind the. Variables and other factors into the culture and needs of individuals and organizations will be used if the job is designed to be motivational in nature and individual characteristics is appropriate in this case the productivity of human resources increased (Kazemi HAGHIGHI , 1379: 5).

540

The main objective of this study and assess the appropriateness of materials listed in the job and provide suggestions to improve it in the National Iranian Oil Refining and Distribution. Important result of this study was obtained from the research community about 40 percent of the Job Appropriateness for this Iranian Oil Refining and Distribution Company as one of the largest companies in the process of developing an effective and fundamental There is an economic good and is not based on the research objectives and results achieved during the research and observations, suggestions and recommendations for increasing fitness for this job, which in turn increase productivity, satisfaction occupational and organizational commitment of employees to be considered are:

1.   Given that the people working in this organization with the job of education that are now the operator should not have been appropriate and in accordance with international standards in the hiring process, which in terms of attracting jobs and recruitment for vacant posts, or the existing requirements are created by human resource professionals should be carefully explained to the selection criteria of democracy and international standards should be based on merit.

2.   Emphasis on human development through education and promotion as a process for improving the capabilities and abilities, increase knowledge and change attitudes and staff attitudes toward jobs in recent years have been enormous changes (parts inspection, purchasing and advertising).

3.   To determine the relative value of jobs and wages adjusted for other jobs inside and outside the company by the directors of human resources and personnel (in jobs such as accountant, senior accountant, purchasing agent and the development of clay).

4.   Sharing and integration of business activities and duties with respect to the same job, especially in legal and accounting sectors.

5.   Prepare a catalog, brochure, billboard about the latest changes in employment issues in the organization and its installation in high traffic locations such as the woman card, self-service and .. The information to employees.

6.   Increase their skills for the promotion and implementation of training programs promotion to higher posts, sending employees to training for jobs outside the organization and similar organizations.

7.   Offering a reward and promote employees who work abroad and voluntary organizations in the areas of job training programs that they are motivated to maintain and strengthen their competitiveness and create a healthy and productive employees in the other.

Suggestions for future research:

1   - In the present study was to evaluate the proportion of employees in a small part of the National Iranian Oil Refining and Distribution (headquarters), as is recommended in all branches and agencies related to the company and the results should be The research study will be compared to a more solid basis for assessing the appropriateness of the selection and recruitment agencies in the future should be.

541

2   according to the study of the job only three components: knowledge, skills and ability to find employment and other aspects of employment such as work style, personality and psychological characteristics have been studied, the researchers suggested that be paid to research on this topic.

References

1 - Prayer, Habib A. ... (1384), *"Human resource management approach to application"* Mashhad, the direction of light emission, the fifth printing.

2 - Rezaei Nejad, F. (1382) *"Analysis of manufacturing jobs in Kurdistan,"* MS Thesis, University, School of Management.

3 - boom, Y. (1380) *"The standard of work and jobs,"* Tehran, published by the Center for Public Management

4 - Sanjar Khrvdy, AR (1383) *"Re-design jobs in human resources management",* Journal of Command and Staff College, No. 22, p. 31-46

5 - Shafi Abadi, Abdullah (1378), *"Career counseling and vocational guidance and career choice theory",* Tehran, Ministry of Culture and Islamic Guidance.

6 - Sadeghi, M. (1375), *"Job analysis in Spad Khorasan»* Mashhad, Spad.

7 - Kazemi real-Din (1378) *"The psychology and management,"* Tehran, under the cursor.

8. Acorn *S,* Ratner PA, Crawford M (2008). *"Decentralization as determinant of autonomy, job satisfaction, and organizational commitment among nurse manager".* Nurse Res, Vol33, No3, pp.80-88 ..

9. Antall, Gloria, F. (2008). *"Assessing Job Candidates for Fit".* Merlin Press.

10.Beer, Duane P, (2004) *"Psychology and work today an introduction to industrial an organizational psychology".* Macmillan co.

11.Bennett, H. (2002) *"Employee commitment: the key to absence management in local government? Leadership & Organization Development Journal ",* Vol .23, No. 8, pp.430-441.

12. Brunk, R (2005) *"The nature of work".* London: Macmillan.

13.Chinoy, E, (2008). *"Automobile workers and the American Dream"* New York: Beacon press.

14.   David, T (2007) *"A quantitative review of the relationship between personorganization fit and outcome".* Journal *of* Industrial Teacher *Education.* Vol44, No2.

15.   Durkin, M. *and* Bennett, H. (1999) *"Employee commitment in retail banking: identifying* and exploring *hidden dangers",* International Journal of Bank Marketing, Vol.17, No.2, pp.80-88.

16.   . Frico, Paule (2006) *"E. industrial and organizational psychology "*. John wiley & sns, inc.

542

17.   Hosaka, Takaashi & et al. *(2008). "Assessing Person-Organization Fit to Reduce Turnover (Presented to 24th Annual IMPAAC Conference on Personnel Assessment)"*

18.   Mc Kenna, S. (2005). *"Organizational commitment in the small entrepreneurial business in Singapore",* Cross Cultural Management,, Vol.12, No.2, pp.16-37.

19.Paul AK, Anantharaman RN. (2006). *"Influence of HRM practice on organizational commitment: A study among software professional in India"* Hum Resource Manage R Vol16, No4, pp.46-87.

20. Van couver, Tony (2003) *"Professions in the class system of present day societies".* Currnt sociology.

The twenty first. Http://Www.onetcenter.org

European Journal of Scientific Research
ISSN 1450-216X Vol.58 No.4 (2011), pp.532-541
© EuroJournals Publishing, Inc. 2011 http://www.eurojournals.com/ejsr.htm

Job Appropriateness Survey and its Relationship with Staff Organizational Commitment (The Case Study in National Iranian Oil Refining and Distribution Company)

Hamidreza Hassanzadeh
Faculty Member of Tehran University
E-mail: Drhassanzadeh@gmail.com

Mostafa Emami
D   D*Faculty Member of Tarbiat Modares University*

Mahdi Beiruti
Student of Payam-Noor University

Reza Abachian Ghasemi
Student of MBA at Tehran University

Vahid Fahimi
Student of MBA at Tehran University

Abstract

Job Consistency (job-employed fit) is a basic issue in human resource management. The assumption has been approved that existence of this appropriateness of organizational necessity is for human resource productivity.

There fore ,the main purpose of this article is studying job consistency and its relationship with organizational commitment of national Iranian oil refining and distributing company head qarters Staff .Information collection tools for measurement of organizational commitment was Allen and Meyer questionnaire including 15 questions and for measuring Occupational proportion the Knowledge questionnaires ,Job skill and ability of international job databank (occuptional Information Network)were used .Each of the questionnaires on the average includes 21 questions. Stability of organizational Commitment questionnaire was 0.89 and stability of job fit measurement was 0.87 , because kronbakh Alfa in both is over 0,70 ,thus both questionnaires had enough stability.

Statistical community was 150 people. According to the accidental Sampling method 80 People as a statistical Sample were chosen and finally78 questionnaires were collected.

For identifying normality of information Two– Sample kolmogorov Smirnov Test was used and the data normality rate accepted .the research assumptions using independent T-Test were tested and their meaningful positive effects were proved , so that some staffs that were consistence in occupational necessities had more organizational commitment .The other result of this paper reveals the fact that only 40% of staffs in this company were completely appropriate in occupational necessities and this company is weak in this

Keywords: Organizational commitment , job appropriateness, occupational knowledge ,occupational skill ,occupational ability.

Introduction

Work is a major and, of course, constructive element of communities and organizations .In order for work does not get along with self –denying it must be technically, physiologically, and psychologically favorable .

The social and economic situations that in which work fulfils must be a way that worker feels that his labor is fair and appropriates to his /her skill and effort , and also his labor is fair and appropriates to his / her skill and effort, and also his/her wage is proportional to other work groups (shafi ، abadi 14:1999).

Since work fulfillment takes a job form ,it is necessary to measure and observe job specifications in relation with employee ’s characteristics .First , job and its fulfillment stages must be well known and its analysis considered ,next step it must be designed and appropriate individual for each job appointed to the necessary position (sadeghi 23:1996).

Since work fulfillment stages must be well known and its analysis considered , next step it must be designed and appropriate individual for each job appointed to the necessary position (sadeghi23:1996).

Job and its accurate designing play a crucial role in job consent .effectiveness ,and not willing to quit job. Since job characteristics depend on organizational procedure and designing quality of organization structure, the first factor that must be studied is the importance of specializing a job versus making it vast various.

Division of labor that all classic management scientists believed it as a principle and has been propounded as a traditional productivity.

Paradigm has advantage and disadvantage ,Its advantages include skill increment and reduction time of work fulfillment .But strict division of labor for the reason of less important jobs frequencies in long – term causes reduction in job consent and productivity .Hence , job designing plays a vital role in increasing moral , job consent and finally human productivity .Any was ,organization can by accurate clarifying duties and missions , new designing of jobs, participation in decision making , sanitation programs and observing job – employed fit in organization improve the human resources efficiency .

The occupational appropriateness is considering as an effective strategy in maintaining human resources in organization ; first this proportion starts from an instant that a person chooses a job and prepares himself to do it.

Second , organization will de prepared to find employees , select , hire, and appoint to the job.

May be at the hiring commencement ,with due attention to organization and applicants needs , the considering consistency sets up in a limited amount , but gradually that the individual continues his work and organization moves forward , it is expected that the proportion increases If job designing fits with individual characteristics , it will motivate and increase human productivity (kazemi – Haghighi,5:2000).

With due attention to above mentioned the main part of this research is whether occupational consistency causes improvement in organizational commitment or doesn't have any relations with it.

Occupational Appropriateness (Job-Employed Fit)

In two recent decades , organizations have changed meaningfully , and converted into organizations with decentralized features , global , and having team leadership . In such organizations human resource is considering as a main capital of them and they try to take advantage of his skill and abilities to maximize their efficiencies and productivities ,using job fit concept for better use of human know ledge m ability , and skill is very important.

A division of individual fitness with his peripheral invironment is job proportion (job – employed fit) , the inconsistency between employee and his job costs a lot for an organization . the main nature of job fitness clears in its various definitions, and in previous researches on job fitness clears in its various definitions , and in previous researches on this subject a variety of its definitions has been given (Ental 336,2008).

The occupational fitness theory , that identity , job autonomy , work knowledge , job skill , ability to be consistance with personal featwres , like age , gender , education level , being single or married , job experience , employee knowledge , skill , and abilities . And consequencely the adaptation of employee and his job affects his behavior and attitude.

David defines job fitness as follows :the adaptability of employee and organization, in the job which he performs , in other word his knowledge , skill , and abilities should the same as the knowledge , skills ,and abilities that his job in organization needs (David 6:2007).

Husaka assumes the similarity of job and personal values , that is , occupational proportion.

In his framework , I .e .,stretch – selection – weakening (ASA) framework the target adaptability of job – employed fit important dimension has been hypothesized . Based on this theory people attract to jobs in organizations which they take for granted to achieve individual goals (Husaka 560 :2008):

1. Supplementary fit: when an employee specifications are similar to job characteristics, i.e., things which are values in his life , they are very similar to those of his job .

2. Complementary fit : when an individual sufficiently fills the lost specifications of job , or offers additional characteristics , i.e., his knowledge , skill , and abilities offer things which other people in presiding over that job can't offer .

3. Demands – abilities fit= when employed abilities meet the job needs , in this case, his abilities and skills are those that job needs.

4. Needs – Supplies fit : when job meets individual needs , his job meets the needs which he is expected it to meet .

As can be observed , a lot various definitions of consistency have been suggested that affect its results.

Research shows that individuals fail or un succeed more for the reason of job inconsistency than lack of skills or unwilling to do the job well. Following steps to identify occupational consistency.

- Identifying successful people specifications in that job .
- Identifying failure and unsuccessful people specifications in that job .
- Identifying specifications that caused people succeed in that job if one could take it.

In studies about occupational appropriateness different results have been obtained that sometimes they are contradictory .

The main sources of results in consistency and disagreement based on accomplished studied are identified as follows (chinoy 25;2008):

- Quality of imagination , perception , definition of job consistency job operational definition.
- Concept domain and the method used for evaluating job proportion
- Individual differences that lead to different understandings

JOB concept in occupational appropriateness is considered in two organization distinctive methods (Husaka , 560;2008) .

First Method

In this method , the individuals will be asked to notice the job specifications .

Second method:

In this procedure , the people will be asked to consider the emplored members specifications .

Acron classifies job consistency measurement procedures into three categories (Acron , 42;2008).

1. Subjective fit :In this method the employee will be asked directly and by person that how much his specification are adapting with organizational specifications , here none of the individual or organizational characteristics would be concentrated on directly , and should be assumed that respond ants have a background knowledge of organization and diagnostically address the consistency rate of their characteristics and organizational specifications.

2. Perceived fit :In this type of proportion , the people will be asked to describe them selves , and also express their perceptions of organizational specification then the appropriateness degree by assessing consistency between the individual's self – descriptive and his similar desription of organization will be measured.

3. Objective fit (external) . I n this procedure , the individual will be asked to explain his specifications, then the other organization members would be asked to explain organization specifications, after that the organization members ideas will be combined and an assessment criterion will be provided that indicates the organizational specifications , and the proportion of consistency rate between his description of himself and the agreed criterion about organization specifications will be measured.

Difference in measurement scales of occupational proportion belonging to an special concept domain is used for evaluating occupational proportion.

Values are most common sources of occupational consistency . many studies evaluate the adaptation of occupational consistency . many studies evaluate the adaptation of valuing (my values appropriate will present staff values of this organization).In some researches the personation proportion has been measured (Dose your personality fit with organization mode ?) , some researches have studied the Objectives consistency (assessment of proportion degrees between one's goals and organization goals) , few studies in clued KSA consistency (my skills and abilities reflect the abilities and skills that organization is looking for) , some studies don't use an especial criterion for research accomplishment (Is the organization the one that the employee was looking for ?)

The criterion that uses for assessing proportion can affect the outcomes and the consequences.

In general, as mentioned above the type of proportion definition , consistence criterion , measurement method , and Organization definition , etc. ,affect the job fitness relationship with its outcomes .

Vancouver et al . show that job fitness leads to attitude and behavioral Consequences . Their findings indicate that job fitness depends on job consent and organizational commitment ; it also has a less effect on behavioral results such as occupational accomplishment , OCB (organizational controlling behaviors) and staff transferring . The above said researchers by studies fulfilment concluded that perceived and objective measurement method show the dependency of behavioral outcomes further , and the relation between values adaptation and behavioral outcomes is a bit stronger than other forms of job fitness (van couver 19 , 2003) .

Confirmative findings encouraged the dependency of objection fit measurement to behavioral outcomes of using appropriateness in selection systems, but subjective and perceived fits measurements were used less in individuals selecting systems ,because both of them were selfreporting and require the know leg and familiarity with respondent to organizational value system. But objective fit scales only needs that respondent expresses his specifications and than will be compared with organizational specifications and doesni't need the familiarity of respondent to organizational specifications , and this procedure can be used in individuals selection system.

In Acron et al . research , different resuits of van couver et al . studies were obtained , So that job – employed subjective fit leads to workplace various outcomes such as organizational attractiveness , job selection , organizational commitment , no job transferring , etc . Findings show that better matching of proportion and person to organization causes higher job consent , organizational commitment , and less transferring and movement , and consequently causes the organizational system survival and preserved (Acron 42 ,2008).

Another research includes a background finding of 253 university graduated people in different full-time jobs in more that 7 years m and the ther background finding of 345 banklers that while for four months were working in the job , they were studied , showed that both studies support the relation between job – employed fit and job consent (Beer , 2004) .

Fric and Brunk in their research concluded that there is the most job consent when there is the best fit between individuals abilities and job requirements (Frico , 2006;Brunk ,2005).

David studied the relation between job – employed fit and attitude outcomes . Results showed that job – employed fit depends on concepts like freedom, job consent ,and organizational commitment .In addition , they showed that the job – employed fit dimensions (adaptability of value Vs . other forms of consistencies), and the used method in measuring job proportion (subjective, objective, perceived)regulate the relation between job – employed fif and the attitude consequences .

Organizational Commitment

In early 1980 s, staff organizational commitment was one of the most important problems that drew many researchers attention and a lot of researches accomplished on that subject . Till1985 that Walton published his famous article titled " management by commitment" , that in this work he reminds that necessity to move from management by control to management by commitment and by doing this he gave a right path to the studies in this area (Mc kenna , 16 , 2005) Organizational commitment is a structure that its different definitions have been offered , for example , marrow (1999) suggests over 25 meanings related to organizational commitment . porter et al .(1974) defines the commitment as follows :" the rate that an individual belongs himself to an organization and determines his identity with it " .They used motivation , identifying organization values and staff willing rate to membership in organization , for its measurement . Buchanan (1974) also , defines commitment as follows : organization proponents, rate of emotional belonging in proportion to organizational goals and values , their role in relation with these goals and values , and to the organization for the sake of its existence that is somewhat for the benefit that organizational has for them of course , it is worth noting that in this definition it is a different between a belonging that is based on exchanging (involvement for receiving external reward) and moral and valuable belonging (involvement for homogeneous and perfect agreement of individual and organization values . kelman (1958) diffretiates between commitment by compliance (I.e.,a commitment in which staff accepts behavioral patterns and special ideas for definite rewards), commitment by identification (when accepted behaviors and opinions are for the sake of joining to a third party that is valuable for that person) , and subjective commitment (in that the individual acts the Special behaviors and ideas that their contents are in agreement with his system value).So , the staff commitment can be studied on different views , Oreill and chatman (1986) based on kelman opinions identified that the mentally belonging (i.e., individual mentally dependent on organization)as main an key issue in staff commitment . they defined mentally belonging as:it reflects a degree in which individuals accept and internalize organizational views and specifications . oreilly and chatman (1986)based the saff mentally belonging on three following items which were similar to kelman (1958) suggestions (Durkin and Bennett, 127 ;1999)

1. Acceptance or staff physically presence in organization for definite external rewards .
2. Identifying , or staff presence in organization based on willing to solidarity .
3. Internalizing , Or staff active participation in organization rely on organizational and individual values consistency .

This multifactor approach to staff commitment , has been supported by other researcher . For example, Jaros et al . (1993)using factoral analysis method proved this multifactor approach to commitment , and concluded that organization commitment monofactor models whether conceptually Or empirically are not supported . Each of mentioned dimensions of commitment (internalized , identified , compliance) also in a way relates to organization changing process . In fact, staff commitment in changing process management play a key role . on one hand staff,s higher commitment enforces (enhances) the accomplished changes and on the other hand guarantees the change schedukes (Bennett 433,2002).

One of the most important studies regarding commitment is the multifactoral one which belongs to Meyer and Allen (1997) .

In their points of view , there are there kinds of commitments :

1. Affective commitment , means the staff emotional belonging to organization , unity sensation with organization , and an active presence in organization .

Staffs which have affective commitment usually tend to remain in organization and this is one of their wishes.

2. Continuance commitment , is in relation with benefits and charges which relate to remaining or quitting the organization . staffs which have continuance commitment , usually remain in organization in have continuance commitment , usually remain in organization in case that quitting it has no enormous charges for them .

3. Normative commitment , which shows the staff obligation or duty to stay in organization . therefore , staff will remain in organization until their remaining in organization is a right and appropriate task in their views (Mc Kenna , 17 ;2003).

Thus, the organizational commitment can be defined as follows:

1. Strong tendency to remain in a typical organization .

2. Willing to do enormous efforts for organization .

3. Decisive belief in supporting organization ,s goals and values .

Hence ,Organizational commitment can be known as an attitude toward staff loyalty to organization and a continuance process , which thanks to individuals participations in organizational decisions , individuals attention to organization and organization 's success and welfare will be determined (Moghimi 392 ,2004) .

Research assumptions

Regarding above mentioned the main assumption of this paper is as follow : occupational appropriateness with organizational commitment at the national Iranian oil refining and distribution company head quarters staff level has a positive an meaningful relationship .

With due attention to the main assumption of this article , three sub – hypotheses will be given :

1. The proportion between staff occupational knowledge and requirement knowledge for job accomplishment with organizational commitment. At the national Iranian oil refinery and distributing company headquarters staff level has a positive and meaning relationship .

2. The consistency between staff occupational skill and required skill for the job fulfillment along with organizational commitment at the national Iranian oil refining and distribution company headquarters staff level has a positive and meaningful relationship .

3. The fitness between staff job ability and ability needs for job accomplishment along with organizational commitment at the national Iranian oil refining and distributing company head quarters stafflevel has a positive and meaningful relationship.

Research method

Since in this research , the authors want to study and measure job – employed fit and its relation with organizational commitment in national Iranian oil refining and distributing company headquarters staff , the research is based on descriptive and measuring type.

Statistical community was 150 people of national Iranian oil company headquarters Staff . the research sample by following equation will be 74 people.

$$n = \frac{(150)(1.96)^2(0.5)(0.5)}{(0.5)^2(150-1)+(1.96)^2(0.5)(0.5)} = 74$$

The needed data for this research was gathered in two following ways . library method :In this method for gathering the data related to subject matter and research background books ,theses , articles , databases, and internet sources were used .

Field method :In this procedure by designing questionnaires and distributing them among statistical sample , the necessary data regarding occupational appropriateness and its relationship with organizational commitment obtained . For job – employed fit measurement by data related to available jobs in American job database (occupational Information Network),27questionnaires by considering three knowledge variables . job skills and abilities guided and cooperated by university professors and industrial advisers were compiled and designed (http: //www. Onetcenter . org) .

Allen and meyer organizational commitment questionnaire was used for measuring the organizational commitment parameters.

Organizational commitment has 15 questions that deal with organizational commitment . Each questionnaire related to job fit on the average consists of 21 questions , that deals with available situation of individuals job knowledge, skill, and ability . first both measurement tools were distributed among30 people of headquarters staff. These people were selected on their research data , and after completing the questionnaire , we used their ideas about the questions consistency with research context , proper writing and removing the ambiguities in the questions . this the ought exchange flow and Co – thinking along with interviewing in person and discussing all questions One by one were accomplished . In this paper the descriptive and inferential statistics were used for describing and analyzing gathered data . by these tests first normality of information was identified by two – sample kolmogorov smirnov test .In the case of data distribution normality , the independent T- Test was used . Based on this test a meaningful difference between staff organizational commitment regarding job consistency or in consistency was identified . But if data distribution were abnormal , to determine a meaningful difference of organizational

Commitment refer to job consistency or in consistency man wittney – Test should be used.

Research Findings

In this research to check its assumption , first must be specified whether or not the data distribution is normal . Data normality or its abnormality is measured by kolmogorov – smirnov statistic test , the kolmogorov Smirnov test results were accordant to following table:

Table 1:   Two – Sample kolmogorov – smirnov test.

Test Statistics

		z
Most Extreme	Absolute	.864
Differences	Positive	.000
Negative		-.864
Kolmogorov – Smirnov Z		3.979
Asymp .Sig.(2-talied)		.000

A .Grouping Variable : GROUP

According to above table the prepared Z amount of the test at a certainty level of 95% equals 3.979 Based on statistics tables the Z amount of table at Certainty level of 95% is 1.64 . since the Z amount of test is higher than the Z of the table , Can be argued that at the certainty level of 95% the data gathered from statistics sample has normal distribution .

Therefore , to test the meaningfulness of the rate difference of the organizational commitment of the staffs that regarding job are appropriate with the staffs that are inappropriate , independent test was used . this test identifies the rate difference of staff organizational difference of staff – organizational commitment in terms of job consistency or inconsistency .

In a general look the average score of organizational commitment of staffs that referring occupation were suitable or inconsistence is as follows :

Table 2: The average score of staff organizational commitment in terms of job consistency or in consistency .

organizational commitment average score	Staff aboundant		index
	percent	numbers	
5.2	39.7/0	31	Occupational proper staffs
3.9	59.3/0	47	Occupational improper staffs.

T-Test results show (Table 2) that a group with job consistency obtained organizational commitment score of 5.2, which in comparison with the Same Subject score of a group that was in job in consistency ,namely(3.9) was high .The score difference shows that occupational consistency with organizational Commitment in national Iranian oil refining and distributing Company headquarter staff has a positive and meaningful relationship .And the more increment in this proportion the more increase in rate of staff organizational commitment would be .Also Table 2 shows that in this refinery and distributer company 39.7 % of staff refer to job are appropriate .

Conclusions and Suggestions

Job – employed fit is a basic issue in human resource management, the assumption has been approved that existence of this proportion is an organizational necessity for human resource productivity .And job_employed fit in an organization is considered as an effective strategy in preserving human resources. This consistency starts from the moment that the individual gets prepare for the job and its selection. Second organization gets prepare to find employees, select, hire and appointment. May at the commencement of employing, regarding organization and applicants needs, the considering proportion set up in a limited amount, but gradually along with the individual continuing his work in an organization and organization itself get life experience , it is expected that the consistency in creases .If job design is in a way that fits that individual specifications , it will motivate and increase human productivity (kazemi –Haghighi , 5 ;2000).

For this paper the independent T-Test was used to study occupational consistancy and it relation with organizational commitment in national Iranian oil refining and distributing company headquarters staff .the test shows that the meaning and difference of staff organizational commitment average scores refer to occupation are whether or not cot consistence .Its results at certainty level of 95% are meaningful since organizational commitment average scores of those that are in consistence , then it can be argued that job employed fit has a positive and direct relationship with staff organizational commitment .that is , the more job – employed fit , the more staff organizational commitment . that is ,the more job –employed fit , the more staff organizational commitment could be or vice versa , that less job – employed fit , the less staff organizational commitment , and this conclusion totally matches with the research results (David , 2007; Acron ,2006;Frico ,2006 ;Brunk ,2005 ;Beer , 2004 , van couver , 2003). The other important outcome of this research is that in statistical community about 40% were job – employed fit which for the national Iranian oil refinement and distribution company , as one of the biggest an most in come bearer companies of the country ,is very weak and unacceptable . Based on this and refer to research goal and accomplished results and also researchers observation during the research , the following suggestions and recommendations for in creasing occupational proportion that in turn causes more productivity ,job consent , and staff organizational commitment will be offered :

1. Regarding this issue the education certificates of employees who work in researched organization don ,t match the jobs that they do and aren't accordant with international standards .In employment process , attracting and finding employees for job position vacancies or job positions that become available of existence necessities infinite precision must be taken by hwman resource specialists , so that people' s selection criteria be on merit laddering and international standards .

2. To lay emphasis onhuman development through education as a process of improvement and promotion of abilities , knowledge and consciousness in cerement and changing the staff attitudes toward the jobs that in recent years greatly have been changed (investigative, perchase and advertisement sections).

3. Job relative value determination for detemining and regulating payment wage with other internal and external jobs by personnel and human resources managers (in jobs like accountant , senior accountant , civil senders , and perchase official).

4. Division of labor and merging certain jobs refer to similar job duties and activities especially in law and accounting sections .

5. Preparing catalog , brochure , brochure , billboard refer to last changes in occupational issues and problems domain in organization and installing them in much traffic place such as :hour recorder card machine , messhall , etc. for in forming staffs.

6. People 's skill increment for promoting to higher positions through implementing job training schedules , sending staffs to occupational training courses out of organization or in similar organizations .

7. Giving reward job position to staff that are out of the organization and voluntarily participate in education schedules that relate to their job domain to preserve and enhance people motivation and create a sound and constructive competition sensation in other staffs.

References

[1]   Shafi,a Abadi , Abdallah (1999). "*Professional and occuputinal counseling and guiding* , and job option opinions" Islamic culture and guidance ministry" " Tehran"

[2]   Sadeghi , Mansooreh (1996) *" job analysis in mashad sepad company"* , khorasan .

[3]   Kazemi Haghighi , Nasereddin (1999) , *" psychology for laborand management"* , sayeh nama press , Tehran.

[4]   Moghimi , Mohammad.(2004). " *Researching and approaching Organization and management* " Third edition, termeh press, Tehran .

[5]   Acorn S, Ratner PA, Crawford M(2008).*"Decentralization as determinant of autonomy, job satisfaction, and organizational commitment among nurse manager"*. Nurse Res, Vol33,No3,pp.80-88..

[6]   Antall, Gloria,F.(2008). *"Assessing Job Candidates for Fit"* .Merlin Press.

[7]   7.Beer,Duane P,(2004) *"Psychology and work today an introduction to industrial an organizational psychology "*. Macmillan co.

[8]   Bennett, H.(2002) *"Employee commitment: the key to absence management in local government? Leadership & Organization Development Journal"* ,Vol .23,No. 8, pp.430-441.

[9]   Brunk,R(2005) " *The nature of work*". London:Macmillan.

[10]   Chinoy, E , (2008). *"Automobile workers and the American Dream* " New York: Beacon press.

[11]   David, T(2007) *" A quantitative review of the relationship between person–organization fit and outcome"*. Journal of Industrial Teacher Education. Vol44,No2.

[12]   Durkin, M. and Bennett, H.(1999) *"Employee commitment in retail banking: identifying and exploring hidden dangers"*,International Journal of Bank Marketing, Vol.17,No.2,pp.80-88.

[13]   Frico, Paule(2006) *"E. industrial and organizational psychology"*. John wiley &sns,inc.

[14]   Hosaka, Takaashi & et al.(2008). *" Assessing Person-Organization Fit to Reduce Turnover (Presented to 24th Annual IMPAAC Conference on Personnel Assessment)"*

[15]   Mc Kenna, S.(2005). *"Organizational commitment in the small entrepreneurial business in Singapore"*,Cross Cultural Management ,, Vol.12,No.2, pp.16-37.

[16]   Paul AK, Anantharaman RN. (2006). *"Influence of HRM practice on organizational commitment: A study among software professional in India"* Hum Resource Manage R Vol16,No4,pp.46-87.

[17]   Van couver,Tony(2003) *"Professions in the class system of present day societies"*. Currnt sociology.

[18]   *http://www.onetcenter.org*

© 2012,

Scienceline Publication Asian Journal of Social and Economic Sciences **AJSES**

www.science-line.com Asian J. Soc. Econ. Sci. 1(1): 23-33, 2012

The Relationship between Job Involvement, Job Satisfaction and Organizational Commitment among lower-level Employees

Mostafa Emami

Young Researchers Club, Kermanshah Branch, Islamic Azad University, Kermanshah, Iran

*Corresponding author's Email: Emamemostafa12@yahoo.com

ABSTRACT: This study investigated the relationship between job satisfaction, job involvement, and organizational commitment among lower-level employees. Job satisfaction and job involvement were used as independent variables in the study while organizational commitment was used as the dependent variable. Data was gathered from a random sample of 100 lower-level employees of the company concerned. A questionnaire consisting of four-parts was used for data collection. To gather biographical and occupational data, a self-designed 40-item questionnaire was used. To measure job involvement, Kanungo's (1982) 10-item 5-point rating scale was used. To measure job satisfaction, Halpern's (1966) 10-item 7-point rating scale was used. To measure organizational commitment, Mowday, et al. (1982) 15-item 5-point scale was used. Data analysis was done by means of various statistical techniques, including the Pearson Product Moment Correlation Technique and Multiple Regression Analysis. The results indicated that though both job satisfaction and job involvement are strongly associated with organizational commitment, job satisfaction accounts for a higher proportion of variance in organizational commitment than job involvement. Intrinsic job satisfaction, extrinsic job satisfaction, and overall job satisfaction were found to be significantly and highly inter-correlated, an indication that they are all equally associated with organizational commitment. The paper therefore recommends that managers must do all in their power to promote job satisfaction and job involvement in their companies, but especially job satisfaction.

Key words: Job satisfaction, Job involvement, and Organizational commitment

INTRODUCTION

Organizational commitment can be defined as an employee's psychological attachment to the organization (Organizational commitment Wikipedia, 2008). It can be measured by the following factors: identification with the goals and values of the organisation, the desire to belong to the organisation and the willingness to display effort on behalf of the organisation. Maxwell and Steele (2003) carried out a study to identify the determinants of organizational commitment and its effects in the organisation. The results suggested that organizational commitment is determined by job characteristics such as the job scope and work experiences such as rewards and employee importance. The findings further suggested that organizational commitment was positively related to employee performance.

Organizational commitment has been one of the most widely researched areas in the field of management in relation to different job-related variables but in South Africa very few studies have explored this concept. Various researchers identify multiple factors affecting organizational commitment among employees but the present study focuses on investigating the impact of job involvement and job satisfaction on organizational commitment. Organizational commitment is considered to be one of the most important and crucial outcomes of human resource strategies. Furthermore employee commitment is seen as the key factor in achieving competitive performance (Sahnawaz and Juyal, 2006). A significant relationship has been identified between job satisfaction and organizational commitment (Narimawati, 2007). Samad (2007) also tried to determine the level of influence job satisfaction facets will have on organizational commitment. Job satisfaction, on the other hand, can be defined as a pleasurable feeling that results from the perception that one's job fulfils or allows for the fulfilment of one's important job values (Wagner and Hollenbeck, 1998). It is more of an attitude that an employee possesses, which reflects how content an individual is with his or her job. Job satisfaction is of great importance because it seems to affect overt organisational behaviour.

Kanungo (1982) views job involvement as a cognitive or belief state of psychological identification with one's job. In other words, this approach suggests that an individual's psychological identification with a particular job depends on the saliency of his or her needs and the perceptions he or she has about the need satisfying potentialities of the job (Kanungo, 1982). Brown (1996) argues that job involvement will be highest when the work environment: makes one believe that one's work is meaningful; offers control over how work is accomplished; maintains a clear set of behavioural norms;

 To cite this paper: Emami M. 2012. The Relationship Between Job involvement, Job satisfaction and Organizational commitment among lower-level employees. *Asian J. Soc. Econ. Sci.* 1 (1): 23-33.

makes feedback concerning completed work available; and provides supportive relations with supervisors and co-workers. Many theorists have hypothesized that highly involved employees will put forth substantial effort towards the achievement of organisational objectives and are less likely to turnover.

Argyris (1957) and McGregor (1960) saw job involvement as a means of aiding productivity and of creating work situations in which there would be better integration of individual and organisational goals. Marcson (1960) presented an argument and findings suggesting that one of the best ways to increase productivity in organisations was to provide employees with jobs that are more demanding and challenging. Recent studies of job involvement show that such involvement enhances the individual's satisfaction, while at the same time increasing productivity for the organization (Hall and Lawler, 2000).

Statement of the problem

Assuming that management have been using the independent variables mentioned below, the fundamental questions that need to be addressed then are: does job satisfaction and job involvement have a negative or a positive impact on organizational commitment? The economic woes which afflicted South Africa recently have made it impossible for many organisations to take significant strides in their drive towards achieving organisational excellence. Many organisations are struggling to survive the hostile economic environment. Many employees are unhappy with their current situation and would prefer leaving should they get an alternative job elsewhere. The labour turnover is being instigated by the decline in the quality of life due to poor remuneration levels and poor organisational policies on benefits (Financial Gazette, 2009).

According to Robert (1997) labor turnover is positively related to job dissatisfaction and is costly to an organisation. Such costs include that of recruitment, training of new employees, high scrap and waste rates as well as high accident costs for new employees. Job dissatisfaction manifests itself in the form of labour turnover in many organisations; hence, it is likely to have negative implications for organizational commitment, a factor identified as critical to organizational success". According to Werner (2007) only satisfied employees seem more likely to display positive behaviour that contributes to the overall functioning of the organisation. In this regard, management in organisations must be more concerned with the extent to which their employees experience job satisfaction and are involved in their jobs. Organ, Podsakoff and McKenzie (2005) state that the ability of an organisation to innovate and successfully implement business strategy and to achieve competitive advantage depends on how much employees are involved in their jobs and are satisfied in doing their jobs.

Purpose of the study

The main objective of this study was to investigate the relationship between job involvement and job satisfaction on organizational commitment among lower-level employees.

This study seeks to answer the following questions: o Is there an association between job involvement and organizational commitment?

o   Is there an association between job satisfaction and organizational commitment?

o   What is the relative strength of the association of each of the two independent variables (job involvement and job satisfaction), on the one hand, and organizational commitment, on the other hand? o What is the combined strength of the association of the two variables as factors that explain the variance in organizational commitment?

Significance of the study

Establishing a link between job involvement and job satisfaction, on the one hand, and organizational commitment, on the other, could be to the benefit of organisations as management could put in place human resources practices that increase the levels of job involvement and job satisfaction among employees and hence impact positively on their commitment to the organisation. The results of this study will show whether job satisfaction and job involvement have an impact on organizational commitment. If so, future managers would know that to improve organizational commitment, they must improve job satisfaction and job involvement. Research has shown that job involvement and job satisfaction may result in positive outcomes in organisations such as low absentee levels and higher productivity rates among employees (Robbins, 2005). This study aims to determine the relationship between job involvement and job satisfaction, on the one hand, and organizational commitment on the other. Organizational commitment has been identified as critical for organisational success. Koys (2001) contends that organizational commitment is very vital to the survival of many organisations. It maximizes the efficiency and productivity of both the employees and the organisation, which ultimately contribute to the effective functioning of an organisation.

METHODOLOGY

Selection of   the   sample and   sampling procedure

According to Sekaran (2003), the population of a study is the entire group of people, events, or things of interest that the researcher wishes to investigate. It is the aggregate of all units that have a chance of being included in the sample to be studied. The population involved in this study was made of male and female lower-level employees of motor car manufacturing companies. The population for the research included about 1000 employees from MBSA, East London. From the total population 10% of the lower-level employees were used as a sample. Their job titles included: assemblers, material handlers, inspectors, machineoperators, coordinators and drivers.

Gray (2004) defines a sample as a set of objects, occurrences or individuals selected from a parent population for a research study. The sample selected was a fairly large portion of the non-managerial employees of MBSA and was thus fairly well representative of the population. In this sense, the characteristics of the sample represent those of the entire population. The method used to collect the sample in this study was the stratified probability sampling method. A sample of 100 lower-level employees of Mercedes Benz South Africa, East London was selected. Random sampling was used because it ensures representativeness and generalisability of results.

Random sampling is a probability sampling method, whereby each element in the population has some known chance or probability of being selected as a subject (Uma, 2003). In this study employees were divided according to their work stations, for example work station 1, 2, 3, 4, etc. Each work station represented a stratum. To ensure that samples adequately represented the relevant strata (work stations), respondents were randomly selected from within strata, that is, from each work station using a table of random numbers. The sampling procedure for the research began with a preliminary compilation of a sampling frame. A sampling frame is "a complete list in which each unit of analysis is mentioned only once". The sampling frame was required for clarity about the population of interest. As stated before, a table of random numbers was used to ensure that the sample was representative of the sample frame. The research site (i.e. Mercedes Benz South Africa East London) was visited for data collection.

Research instruments

A four-part questionnaire was used to collect the data. Nachmias and Nachmias (1996) define a questionnaire as a list of questions that is presumably formulated, constructed and sequenced to produce the most constructive data in the most effective manner.

The questionnaire consisted of the following four parts:

The biographical and occupational data questionnaire

The first part tapped data related to biographical and occupational variables, i.e., age, gender, marital status, educational qualifications, position held in the organisation, and tenure. This data was tapped with a view to obtaining a clear understanding of the sample used in the study.

Kanungo's (1982) job involvement scale (JIS)

The second part of the questionnaire consisted of Kanungo's (1982) 10-item job involvement scale. This scale measures job involvement on a five-point Likert scale with responses ranging from "Strongly disagree" (1) to "Strongly agree"(5). Kanungo (1982) found this scale to have a Cronbach Alpha coefficient of 0.81, which indicates a reasonably high level of internal consistency, and therefore a reasonably high level of reliability and construct validity.

Halpern's (1966) job satisfaction scale (JSQ)

The third part of the instrument consisted of Halpern's (1966) job satisfaction questionnaire. It is a seven-point Likert scale ranging from "Very dissatisfied" (1) to "Very satisfied" (7). The scale measures satisfaction both of Herzberg's (1959) motivator and hygiene aspects of the job (Halpern 1966). Fields (2002) reports that this job satisfaction scale has an alpha co-efficient ranging from 0.81 to 0.90

Mowday et al.'s Organizational commitment Questionnaire

The fourth part of the questionnaire was adopted from Mowday et al. (1979). It is a 15- item questionnaire that measures organizational commitment , using a fivepoint Likert scale ranging from "Strongly disagree" (1) to "Strongly agree" (5). This instrument has been tested with several groups such as public employees and university employees. Such tests have yielded reliability coefficients ranging from 0.82 to 0.93 with a median value of 0.90 (Reyes & Pounder, 1993).

Administration on the questionnaire

In this study, questionnaires were "selfadministered." This means that the respondents filled the questionnaire on the spot. The researcher handed over each questionnaire by hand to the respondents. The respondents took about 30 minutes to fill in the questionnaire. The covering letter was drawn carefully to convey the research objectives and to persuade respondents to give frank responses. The covering letter also explained the nature of the study, as well as assuring respondents of the confidentiality of all information provided. Respondents were also provided with detailed instructions as to how the questionnaires were to be completed and returned. This was also reinforced on the days of completion of the questionnaires by the researcher orally, so that the respondents could for clarity where it was needed. The rationale behind providing clear instructions and assuring confidentiality of information was that this significantly reduces the likelihood of obtaining biased responses (Sekaran, 2003). Respondents' names were not asked for. This was done to give them an assurance that their responses would be kept confidential. This approach involves the researcher having direct contact with the respondents. The researcher utilized this method because it is less expensive, ensures anonymity of the respondents and has a high return rate as the researcher can make follow-ups for unreturned questionnaires. The co-operation of the Human Resources Department of Mercedes Benz South Africa made the administration process much easier and quicker. This was facilitated by the HR Manager who arranged one to one meetings between the researcher and the prospective respondents for purposes of questionnaire administration.

Methods of Analysis

In analyzing the data collected, graphs were used to describe the data. Also descriptive statistics, Pearson Correlation and Multiple Regression Analysis were employed to analyze the collected data.

Descriptive statistics

Descriptive statistics describe the phenomena of interest (Sekaran, 2003). They include the analysis of data using frequencies, dispersions of dependent and independent variables and measures of central tendency and variability and to obtain a feel for the data (Sekaran, 2003). The mean and standard deviation was primarily be used to describe the data obtained from the JSQ, JIS and the OCQ.

Inferential statistics

Inferential statistics allow the researcher to present the data obtained in research in statistical format to facilitate the identification of important patterns and to make data analysis more meaningful. According to Sekaran (2003), inferential statistics is employed when generalisations from a sample to the population are made. The statistical methods used in this research include the Pearson Product Moment Correlation and Multiple Regression Analysis.

The Pearson Product Moment Correlation

For the purposes of determining whether a statistically significant relationship exists between job involvement and job satisfaction on the one hand, and organizational commitment on the other, the Pearson Product Moment Correlation Coefficient was used. It provides an index of the strength, magnitude and direction of the relationship between two variables at a time (Sekaran, 2003). The Product Moment Correlation Coefficient was, therefore, suitable for the purpose of this study.

Multiple Regression Analysis

Multiple Regression Analysis: is a multivariate statistical technique that is used for studying the relationship between a single dependent variable and several independent variables. It provides a method to predict the changes in the dependent variable in response to changes in more than one independent variable. Hence, it allows the researcher to determine the relative importance of each predictor as well as to ascertain the collective contribution of the independent variables (Sekaran, 2003).

Ethical considerations

The researcher observed and abided by the three major areas of ethical concern, ethics of data collection and analysis, treatment of human subjects, and the ethics of responsibility to society (Reese and Fremouw, 1984). To successfully conduct the study, several ethical issues were addressed during the process of collecting data. In this regard, permission to carry out the study in the designated organisation was sought from respective senior managers. The researcher also obtained informed consent from the participants through the covering letter; all responses were treated as confidential; and the respondents as anonymous. The researcher informed the respondents orally of their right to acceptance or withdrawal from participation in the research at any point in time during the research. Finally the researcher, to the best of his ability, ensured that no harm befell any of the respondents, their employer, their families or anyone else that may have had anything to do with the study.

RESULTS
Descriptive statistics

The descriptive statistics in the form of arithmetic means and standard deviations were computed for Halpern's (1966) Job Satisfaction questionnaire,
Kanungo's Job Involvement questionnaire (1982) and Mowday et al. (1979) Organizational commitment Questionnaire. These are presented in Table 1 together with the number of cases (sample size) that responded to each questionnaire.

Table 1. Mean, standard deviation and total number of cases in relation to organizational commitment, job satisfaction, and job involvement

Item	Mean	Std. Deviation	N
Organizational commitment	51.29	11.217	100
Job satisfaction	38.43	13.383	100

Job involvement	33.92	7.519	100

The level of organizational commitment, job satisfaction, and job involvement among the sample of 100 lower level employees at Mercedes Benz South Africa, east London is depicted in Table 1. The results indicate that organizational commitment has a mean of 51.29 and a standard deviation of 11.217. The results also indicate that the mean for job satisfaction is 38.43 and the standard deviation is 13.383. The results also indicate that job involvement has a mean of 33.92 and a standard deviation of 7.519.

Hypothesis testing

This study sought to investigate the relationship between job involvement and job satisfaction, on the one hand, and organizational commitment, on the other. It also sought to determine the relative strength of the association of each of the two independent variables (job involvement and job satisfaction), on the one hand, with organizational commitment, as a dependent variable, on the other. To measure job involvement, Kanungo's (1982) 10-item five-point Likerttype rating scale was used. To measure job satisfaction, Halpern's (1966) 10-item seven-point Likert-type rating scale was used. To measure organizational commitment, Mowday et al. (1979) 15-item five-point Likert-type rating scale was used. Data analysis was done by means of the Pearson Product Moment Correlation Technique, and Multiple Regression Analysis.

Table 2. Pearson inter-correlations of job satisfaction, job involvement and organizational commitment.

Item	Organizational commitment	Job satisfaction	Job involvement
Organizational commitment	---	-0.62**	-0.53**
Job satisfaction	-0.62**	---	-0.44**
Job involvement	-0.53**	-0.44**	---

*n = 100   ** Significant to 0.01

Hypothesis 1

The first null hypothesis of the study (H_0) was stated as, "there is no significant positive correlation between job satisfaction and organizational commitment" and the corresponding alternative hypothesis (H_1) was that, "there is a significant positive correlation between job satisfaction and organizational commitment". This hypothesis was tested by means of the Pearson Product Moment Correlation technique. The correlation coefficient between overall job satisfaction and overall organizational commitment was found to be $r = 0.62$; $p < 0.001$. This shows that the two variables are significantly and highly positively correlated. This leads to a rejection of the null hypothesis and acceptance of the alternative hypothesis.

Table 3. Correlation for overall job satisfaction, extrinsic job satisfaction and intrinsic job satisfaction

item	Extrinsic	Intrinsic	Overall Satisfaction
Extrinsic (Pearson Correlation)	---	-0.83**	-0.57**

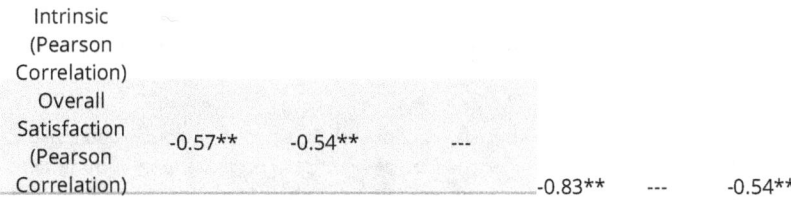

Intrinsic (Pearson Correlation)					
Overall Satisfaction (Pearson Correlation)	-0.57**	-0.54**	---	-0.83**	---	-0.54**

*n = 100; ** Correlation is significant at 0.01

The two main components of overall job satisfaction, that is, intrinsic and extrinsic job satisfaction were found to be highly inter-correlated. The correlation coefficient between the two was $r = 0.83$; $p < 0.001$. This suggests that both are highly correlated with overall organizational commitment. The results also indicated that there is a highly significant relationship between overall job satisfaction and extrinsic job satisfaction ($r = .57$, $p < 0.01$). There is also a highly significant positive relationship between overall job satisfaction and intrinsic job satisfaction ($r = .54$, $p < 0.01$).

Table 4 below indicates the relationship between total organizational commitment and its dimensions. The three main components of organizational commitment , according to Mowday et al., 1979, that are, loyalty to the employing organisation (Loyalty), acceptance of the organisation's values and goals (Value) and willingness to expend a great deal of effort on behalf of the organisation (Effort). These are all highly inter-correlated with overall organizational commitment (see Table 4). The correlation between

Loyalty and overall organizational commitment is $r = 0.91$; $p < 0.001$. Between Value and overall organizational commitment, the correlation is $r = 0.99$; $p < 0.001$. For Effort and overall organizational commitment, the correlation is $r = 0.98$; $p < 0.001$.

These high correlations suggest that all three components of organizational commitment are as significantly positively correlated with overall job satisfaction as overall organizational commitment. These high correlations also suggest that the subcategories of job satisfaction (intrinsic and extrinsic job satisfaction) are highly correlated with the subcategories of organizational commitment (Loyalty, Value and Effort).

Table 4. Inter-correlations for the subscales of organizational commitment

	Loyalty	Value	Effort	Overall organizational commitment
Loyalty (Pearson Correlation)	---	0.84**	0.82**	0.91**
Value (Pearson Correlation)	0.84**	---	0.99**	0.99**
Effort (Pearson Correlation)	0.82**	0.99**	---	0.98**
Total organizational commitment	0.91**	0.99**	0.98**	---

*n = 100; **. Correlation is significant at 0.01 **Hypothesis 2**

The second null hypothesis of the study (H_0) was stated as, "there is no significant positive correlation between job involvement and organizational commitment" and the corresponding alternative hypothesis (H_1) was that, "there is a significant positive correlation between job involvement and organizational commitment". This hypothesis was tested by means of the Pearson Product Moment Correlation technique. The correlation coefficient between job involvement and organizational commitment was found to be $r = 0.53$; $p < 0.001$. This shows that there is a significant positive association between job involvement and organizational commitment. This leads to a rejection of the null hypothesis and acceptance of the alternative hypothesis. The fact that all the subcategories of overall organizational commitment (Loyalty, Value and Effort) are highly inter-correlated (see Table 2) suggests that job involvement is highly correlated with each of these.

Hypothesis 3

The third null hypothesis of the study (H_0) was stated as, "there is no additive effect between job satisfaction and job involvement whereby the two put together account for a higher proportion of variance in organizational commitment than each of them separately" and the corresponding alternative hypothesis (H_1) was that, "there is an additive effect between job satisfaction and job involvement whereby the two put together account for a higher proportion of variance in organizational commitment than each of them separately". This hypothesis was tested by means of Multiple Regression Analysis (see Table 5).

Table 5. Multiple regression between job satisfaction and job involvement, on the one hand, and organizational commitment, on the other

Multiple R	0.70		
R-Squared	0.47		
Adjusted R-Squared	0.46		
Standard Error	0.44		
F	44.00		
Sign F	0.000*		
Variable	Beta	T	Sig T
Job satisfaction	0.48	5.90	0.000
Job involvement	0.32	3.95	0.000

Table 5 presents the results of the regression analysis, regressing organizational commitment (dependent variable) against the independent variables, that is, job involvement and job satisfaction. The results indicate that the multiple correlation value is 0.70, with the R-squared value being 0.47. This indicates that approximately 47% of the variance in organizational commitment can be attributed to the independent variables (job satisfaction and job involvement) entered into the regression. The F-statistics of 0.44 is significant at the 0.001 level indicating that this is a highly significant relationship.

Table 5 shows a Beta weight of $\beta = 0.48$; $p < 0.001$ for the relationship between job satisfaction and organizational commitment. This means that job satisfaction accounts for 0.48 or 48% of the variance in organizational commitment and that this is a highly significant proportion of variance. The same table (Table 3) also shows a Beta weight of $\beta = 0.32$; $p < 0.001$ for the relationship between job involvement and organizational commitment. This means that job involvement accounts for 0.32 or 32% of the variance in organizational commitment, and that this is a highly significant proportion of variance. While job satisfaction accounts for a higher amount of variance in organizational commitment, than job involvement, therefore, both account for a highly significant proportion of variance.

Table 5, however, shows that R-squared is $R^2 = 0.47$. This means that the two independent variables, that is, job satisfaction and job involvement, together account for 0.47 or 47% of the variance in organizational commitment. This result is in support of H_0 of hypothesis 3 in that, though 0.47 is higher than the Beta weight for job involvement ($\beta = 0.32$), it is lower than that for job satisfaction ($\beta = 0.48$). The two independent variables therefore do not have an additive effect that results in them accounting for a greater among of variance in organizational commitment than the two of them independently. The results therefore lead to the acceptance of the null hypothesis that there is no additive effect between job satisfaction and job involvement whereby the two put together account for a higher proportion of variance in organizational commitment than each of them separately. The lack of an additive effect of job satisfaction, and job involvement is probably due to the high correlation between the two variables ($r = 0.44$; $p < 0.001$).

DISCUSSION AND CONCLUSION

The first null hypothesis of the study (H_0) was stated as: "there is no significant positive correlation between job satisfaction and organizational commitment," and the corresponding alternative hypothesis (H_1) was that: "there is a significant positive correlation between job satisfaction and organizational commitment." This hypothesis was tested by means of the Pearson Product Moment Correlation technique.

The correlation coefficient between job satisfaction and organizational commitment was found to be significantly and highly positively correlated. This leads to a rejection of the null hypothesis and acceptance of the alternative hypothesis. The two main components of overall job satisfaction, that is, intrinsic and extrinsic job satisfaction were found to be highly inter-correlated. The three main components of organizational commitment, according to Mowday et al. (1979), that is, Loyalty, Value and Effort, are all highly correlated with overall organizational commitment (see Table 2). These high correlations suggest that all three components of organizational commitment are as significantly positively correlated with job satisfaction as overall organizational commitment.

The significant positive correlation between job satisfaction and organizational commitment that was found in the present study suggests that job satisfaction is an important factor whose presence must be ensured in an organisation. Such a significant positive correlation was also one of the findings in the study carried out by Yang and Chang (2008) involving a sample of nursing staff. The study carried out by Guleryuz et al. (2008) also found a significant positive relationship between job satisfaction and organizational commitment ($r = 0.667$, $p < 0.01$). Mosadeghrah *et al.* (2008), in their study, found moderate levels of job satisfaction and organizational commitment among the sample of hospital employees. Among other results of that study, it was found that the employees' job satisfaction and organizational commitment were highly inter-related. These findings are both in support of the findings of the present study, despite the different working environments.

A study was conducted in Turkey by Gunlu, Aksarayle and Percin (2010) regarding the relationship between job satisfaction and organizational commitment among hotel managers. The study investigated whether there was a significant relationship between the characteristics of the sample, job satisfaction and organizational commitment. The results obtained from this study indicated, *inter alia*, that extrinsic, intrinsic and general job satisfaction have a significant effect on normative and affective commitment. The findings further suggested that the dimensions of job satisfaction had no significant impact on continuance commitment among the hotel managers.

Chang et al. (2010) conducted a cross-sectional questionnaire survey to study the mediating role of psychological empowerment on the relationship between job satisfaction and organizational commitment for school health nurses. The findings of the research were that psychological empowerment did not fully mediate the relationship between job satisfaction and organizational commitment due to the strong direct effect of job satisfaction on organizational commitment. The influence of empowerment on organizational commitment was mediated through job satisfaction. The researchers suggested that improving the job satisfaction levels of school health nurses would help school leaders achieve greater organizational commitment.

While many studies generally support a positive association between job satisfaction and organizational commitment , the causal ordering between these two variables is both controversial and contradictory (Martin and Bennett, 1996). According to Mowday et al. (1982), "although day-to-day events in the workplace may affect an employee's level of job satisfaction, such transitory events should not cause an employee to re-evaluate seriously his or her attachment to the overall organisation."

The second null hypothesis of the study (H_0) was stated as: "there is no significant positive correlation between job involvement and organizational commitment," and the corresponding alternative hypothesis (H_1) was that: "there is a significant positive correlation between job involvement and organizational commitment." This hypothesis was tested by means of the Pearson Product Moment Correlation technique. The correlation coefficient between job involvement and organizational commitment was found to be significant and positively correlated. This leads to a rejection of the null hypothesis and acceptance of the alternative hypothesis. The findings of the present study suggest that job involvement is an important factor whose presence in an organisation must be ensured. The following studies are in support of the significant positive correlation between job involvement and organizational commitment that was found in the present study:

Moynihan and Pandey (2007) investigated the relationship between job involvement and organizational commitment using a sample of public sector health and human services managers. The study showed that there is a moderate positive correlation between job involvement and organizational commitment. This concurs with the results of the current study.

The organizational commitment meta-analysis conducted by Mathieu and Zajac (1990) also revealed that among the foci of commitment, the job involvement and organizational commitment relationship is frequently investigated. The two variables are also considered to influence some forms of workrelated behaviour independently. O'Reilly and Chatman (1986) reported that job involvement is an outcome of psychological commitment to an organisation.

Uygur and Kilic (2009) studied the level of organizational commitment and job involvement of the personnel at Central Organisational, Ministry of Health in Turkey. Questionnaires were distributed to a total of 210 subjects. Of this number, 180 (86%) returned the questionnaire and of these, 168 were found to be useable. A significant positive correlation was found between organizational commitment and job involvement ($r = 0. 44$, $p < 0.001$). There have been many other studies into organizational commitment and job involvement especially related to the heath-care workers and nurses (Brewer and Lok, 1995; Brooks and Swails, 2000; Ors et al., 2003; Ozsoy et al., 2004; Sjoberg and Sverke, 2000; Blau and Boal, 1989). In a study conducted by Sjoberg and Sverke in a Swedish Emergency Hospital (2000), it was found that organizational commitment and job involvement are significantly positively correlated. Blau and Boal (1989) found that nurses with a higher level of job involvement and organizational commitment had significantly less unexcused absences than nurses with lower levels of job involvement and organizational commitment.

One value of this study is that it was conducted in a developing country, unlike most similar studies that have traditionally been conducted in the highly industrialised countries of the Western world. The present study showed that there is a significant positive correlation between job involvement and organizational commitment. This concurred with different previous studies conducted as mentioned earlier on. One significant difference between the present study and previous studies is that, the present study was conducted in a different geographical area.

The third null hypothesis of the study (H_0) was stated as: "there is no additive effect between job satisfaction and job involvement whereby the two put together account for a higher proportion of variance in organizational commitment than each of them separately" and the corresponding alternative hypothesis (H_1) was that: "there is an additive effect between job satisfaction and job involvement whereby the two put together account for a higher proportion of variance in organizational commitment than each of them separately". This hypothesis was tested by means of Multiple Regression Analysis. Job satisfaction accounts for a higher proportion of variance in organizational commitment than job involvement, both accounts for a highly significant proportion of variance. The two independent variables therefore do not have an additive effect that results in them accounting for a higher proportion of variance in organizational commitment than the two of them independently. The null hypothesis was therefore accepted.

Ha-Young and Hyun (2009) conducted a study with the prime aim to analyze an empirical test to classify workers' character in private and public organisations. He sought to answer the question, "what are important organisational determinants of job involvement and job satisfaction?" The study findings suggested that job satisfaction has greater power to influence organizational commitment than job involvement. The results also suggested that, the higher the degree of job involvement, the greater the organizational commitment and effectiveness. They further argued that an increase in the work related attitudes and wage satisfaction results in an increase in organizational commitment. Moynihan and Pandey (2007) made a comparison of job satisfaction, job involvement and organizational commitment using a sample of public sector health and human services managers. The results showed that managers had the greatest influence over job satisfaction and the least influence over job involvement.

The results also showed that job satisfaction accounts for a higher proportion of variance in organizational commitment than job involvement. In the study, it was also shown that there are moderate positive correlations between job satisfaction, job involvement and organizational commitment. The findings of this study concur with the results of the present study as far as the independent correlations are concerned. This study, however, did not investigate the issue of an addictive effect of job satisfaction and job involvement on organizational commitment.

The present study showed that job satisfaction has a greater power to influence organizational commitment that job involvement, therefore the results tell us that companies must pay more attention to promoting job satisfaction in order to ensure higher levels of organizational commitment. The aim of this research was primarily to determine the relationship between job involvement and job satisfaction, on the one hand, and organizational commitment on the other among lower-level employees in the motor-car manufacturing industry. The results indicate that there is a statistically significant relationship between the two independent variables, that is, job satisfaction and job involvement on the one hand, and the dependent variable, that is, organizational commitment , on the other. However, the results also indicated that there is no additive effect between job satisfaction and job involvement whereby the two put together account for a higher proportion of variance in organizational commitment than each of them separately.

This study mainly investigated the relationship between job satisfaction, job involvement and organizational commitment among lower-level employees at Mercedes Benz South Africa, East London, as a representative of the motor-car manufacturing industry. The results obtained from this study showed that there is a significant positive association between job involvement, job satisfaction, and organizational commitment. The two main components of overall job satisfaction, that is, intrinsic and extrinsic job satisfaction were found to be significantly and highly inter-correlated with overall job satisfaction. This suggested that both components of overall job satisfaction are also highly correlated with overall organizational commitment. The results indicated that there is no additive effect between job involvement and job satisfaction whereby the two put together account for a higher proportion of variance in organizational commitment than each of them separately. The results further showed that though both job involvement and job satisfaction are strongly associated with organizational commitment, job satisfaction accounts for a higher proportion of variance in organizational commitment than job involvement.

The fact that job satisfaction was found to account for a higher proportion of variance in organizational commitment than job involvement means that companies must pay more attention to promoting job satisfaction in order to ensure a higher level of organizational commitment. The main practical implication of this study relate to employee retention or prevention of a high rate of labour turnover. Organizational commitment is likely to be strongly associated with employee retention. To ensure organizational commitment, companies must promote both job involvement and job satisfaction. This is likely to lead to employee retention. The fact that intrinsic job satisfaction, extrinsic job satisfaction and overall job satisfaction were found to be highly inter-correlated means that they are all equally important as probable determinants of organizational commitment . Companies must, therefore, constantly upgrade both intrinsic and extrinsic job satisfaction. The future research studies should incorporate an investigation of the outcomes of organizational commitment, such as retention. The present study assumed that organizational commitment is associated with employees' retention. This needs to be confirmed in actual empirical research.

REFERENCES

Argyris, C. (1957). Personality and Organization, New York: Harper Collins.

Avolio, B. J. and Bass, B. M. (1991). The full range of leadership development. Binghamton, NY: Bass, Avolio & Associates.

Baron, R. A., Bryne, D., Nyler, R., and Branscombe, D. (2006). Social Psychology. London: Allyn & Beacon.

Blau, G., and Boal, K. B. (1989). Using job involvement and organizational commitment interactively to predict turnover. *Journal of Management*, 15 (1): 115-127.

Brewer, A. M., and Lok, P. (1995). Managerial Strategy and Nursing Commitment in Australian Hospitals. *Journal Advanced Nursing.* 21: 769-799.

Brooks, I., and Swailes, S. (2002). Analysis of the relationship between nurse influences over flexible working and commitment to nursing. *Journal of Advanced Nursing*, 38 (2):117-126.

Brown, S. P. (1996). A meta-analysis and review of organizational research on job involvement. Psychology Bulletin, 120, 235-255.

Chang, L., Shih, C., and Lin S. (2010). The mediating role of psychological empowerment on job satisfaction and organizational commitment for school health nurses: A cross-sectional questionnaire survey. *International Journal of Nursing Studies*, 47 (4): 247-276.

Gray, D. E. (2004). Doing research in the real world. London: Sage Publications limited.

Gunlu, E., Aksarayli, M. and Percin, N. S. (2010). Job satisfaction and organizational commitment of hotel managers in Turkey. *International Journal of Contemporary Hospitality Management,* 22 (5): 693717.

Ha-Young, H. (2009). Analysis the factors impact on the Job Involvement and Organizational commitment . Department of Public Administration Korea University

Hall, D. T. and Lawler, E. E. (2000). Job characteristics and job pressures and the organizational integration of professionals. Administrative Science Quarterly, 15, 271-281.

Hisrchfeld, R. R. and Field, H. S. (2000). Work centrality and work alienation: Distinct aspects. Of a general commitment to work. *Journal of Organisational Behavior, 21(7), pp.789-800.*

Hufnagel, E. M. and Conca, C. (1994). User Response Data: The Potential for Errors and Bias Information Systems Research, 5, 48-73.

Kanungo, R. N. (1982). Measurement of Job and Work Involvement. *Journal of Applied Psychology, 67(3): 341-349.*

Martin, C. L., and Bennett, N. (1996). The role of justice judgments in explaining the relationship between job satisfaction and organizational commitment. Group & Organization Management, 21(1) 84-105.

Maslow, A. (1954). Motivation and Personality; New York: Harper.

Mathieu, J. E. and Zajac, D. M. (1990). A review and Meta analysis of the antecedents correlates and consequences of organizational commitment.
Psychological Bulletin 108, 171-199.

Maxwell, G. and Steele, G. (2003). Organizational commitment : a study of managers in hotels, International: *Journal of Contemporary Hospitality Management, 15(7), pp. 362–369.*

McGregor, D. (1960). The Human Side of Enterprise. New York: McGraw-Hill Book Co., Inc.

Mowday, R., Porter, L., and Steers, R. (1982). Employee organisational linkages- The psychology of commitment, absenteeism and turnover. London:
Academic Press.

Mowday, R. T., Steers, R. M. and Porter, L. W. (1979). The measurement of organizational commitment.
Journal of Vocational Behaviour, 14 (2): 224-247.

Moynihan, D. P and Pandey, S. K. (2007). Finding workable levers over work motivation: Comparing job satisfaction, job involvement and organizational commitment. *Administration &*
Society, 39 (7): 803-832.

Nachmias, C. F., and Nachmias, D. (1997). Research Methods in Social Sciences. London: ST Martins Press Inc.

Organ, D. W, Podsakoff, M. P. and McKenzie, S. B. (2005). Organizational Citizenship Behavior, Its Nature, Antecedents and Consequences. London: Sage Publications.

O'Reilly, C. A and Chatman, J. (1986). Organizational commitment and psychological attachment: the effects of compliance, identification and internalization on pro-social behaviour. *Journal of Applied Psychology, 71 (3): 492-499.*

Reese H. W, and Fremour W. J. (1984). Normal and normative ethics in behavioral sciences, American Psychologist, 39(8): 863-876.

Robbins, S. P. (2005). Essentials of Organisational Behaviour. New Jersey: Pearson.

Robert, L. (1997). Human Resources Management. London: West Publishing Company.

Sekaran, U. (2003). Research methods for business: A skill-building approach. (3rd ed.). New York: John Wiley & Sons, Inc.

Uygur, A., and Kilic, G. (2009). A study into Organizational commitment and Job Involvement: An Application towards the Personnel in the Central Organization for Ministry of Health in Turkey. Ozean journal of applied sciences
2(1).2009.

Werner, A. (2007). Organizational Behavior: A Contemporary South African Perspective.

Pretoria: Van Schaik Publishers.

Knowledge Management: FROM THEORY TO PRACTICE

Kamran Nazari

Department of Business Management, Payam Noor University, Kermanshah, Iran
Kamrann0156@yahoo.cm

Mostafa Emami

Young Researchers Club, Kermanshah Branch, Islamic Azad University, Kermanshah, Iran.
Emamemostafa@yahoo.com

ABSTRACT

Knowledge management is a process that helps organizations to find important information, select, organize and publish them; and it's a proficiency that will be necessary for actions like solving problems, dynamic learning, decision making. Knowledge management can improve a wide range of organization performance properties by enabling company to more intelligent performance, but it's not enough alone; because knowledge management to be useful needs undertaking staff to organization and their job, that accept the knowledge management process with spirit and heart and perform it (Wiig, 1999:14).Knowledge management is the leveraging of collective wisdom to increase responsiveness and innovation. It is important that you discern from this definition three critical points. This definition implies that three criteria must be met before information can be considered knowledge. » Knowledge is connected. It exists in a collection (collective wisdom) of multiple experiences and perspectives Knowledge management is a catalyst. It is an action – leveraging. Knowledge is always relevant to environmental conditions, and stimulates action in response to these conditions. Information that does not precipitate action of some kind is not knowledge. In the words of Peter Drucker, "Knowledge for the most part exists only in application." » Knowledge is applicable in un-encountered environments. Information becomes knowledge when it is used to address novel situations for which no direct precedent exists. Information that is merely "plugged in" to a previously encountered model is not knowledge and lacks innovation.

Keywords: *Knowledge, Knowledge Management Innovation, Collective Wisdom.*

INTRODUCTION

Technologists never evangelize without a disclaimer: "Technology is just an enabler." True enough – and the disclaimer discloses part of the problem: enabling what? One flaw in knowledge management is that it often neglects to ask what knowledge to manage and toward what end. Knowledge management activities are all over the map: building databases, measuring intellectual capital, establishing corporate libraries, building intranets, sharing best practices, installing groupware, leading training programs, leading cultural change, fostering collaboration, creating virtual organizations – all of these are knowledge management, and every functional and staff leader can lay claim to it. But no one claims the big question: why? (Tom Stewart in The Case Against Knowledge Management, Business 2.0, February 2002).

Under increasing competitive pressure, many companies are examining how they can better manage their intellectual capital. As the pace of global competition quickens, executives realize that their edge lies in more efficiently transferring knowledge across the organization. The emerging field of knowledge management addresses the broad processes of locating, organizing, transferring and more efficiently using information and expertise within an organization. New market forces and infrastructure changes have prompted an interest in knowledge management. Market forces include new corporate models that emphasize corporate growth and efficiency, the need for cycle time reduction, knowledge lost from downsizing and the need to share information across the organization, which often means across the globe. Recent infrastructure changes have significant positive impact on an organization.s ability and desire to manage knowledge.

The barriers to sharing information have been dramatically lowered by intranet technologies. Now companies comprehend the extent to which knowledge can be shared across the organization; however, they also realize how many of their existing knowledge assets are accessible only to a small part of the organization. To lower these barriers to sharing knowledge, leading executives recognize the need to institute new knowledge-centric practices. Information technology plays an important role in enabling these processes across distributed enterprises. What executives want to avoid, however, is the cost and disruption of a wholesale change to the organization's information systems. The promise of technologies aimed at knowledge management is that they will help organizations use the knowledge they have more efficiently without changing the tools they currently use to create it and process it. This is the promise, but unfortunately what many software vendors tout as knowledge management systems are only existing information retrieval engines, groupware systems or document management systems with a new marketing tagline. What executives really need are new technologies designed to implement the revolutionary changes in the way knowledge workers create, communicate and manage knowledge. To help answer that question, this white paper examines the practical aspects of knowledge management and evaluates how various new and existing technologies can be used to create a .knowledge management system. that meets the needs of the organization.

The recent summit on knowledge management (KM) at the pre-eminent ASIST conference opened on a rather upbeat note. The preface noted that KM has evolved into a mature reality from what was merely a blip on the ''good idea'' radar only a few years ago. Growing pervasiveness of KM in worldwide industries, organizations, and institutions marks a watershed event for what was called a fad just a few years ago. KM has become embedded in the policy, strategy, and implementation processes of worldwide corporations, governments, and institutions. Doubling in size from 2001, the global KM market has been projected to reach US$8.8 billion during this year. Likewise, the market for KM business application capabilities such as CRM (Malhotra, 2004a) is expected to grow to $148 billion by the next year. KM is also expected to help save $31 billion in annual reinvention costs at Fortune 500 companies. The broader application context of KM, which includes learning, education, and training industries, offers similarly sanguine forecasts. Annual public K-12 education is estimated at $373 billion dollars in US alone, with higher education accounting for $247 billion dollars. In addition, the annual corporate and government training expenditures in the US alone are projected at over $70 billion dollars.

One can see the impact of knowledge management everywhere but in the KM technology-performance statistics (Malhotra, 2003). This seems like a contradiction of sorts given the pervasive role of information and communication technologies in most KM applications. Some industry estimates have pegged the failure rate of technology implementations for business process reengineering efforts at 70 percent. Recent industry data suggest a similar failure rate of KM related technology implementations and related applications (Darrell et al., 2002). Significant failure rates persist despite tremendous improvements in sophistication of technologies and major gains in related price-performance ratios. At the time of writing, technology executives are facing a renewed credibility crisis resulting from cost overruns and performance problems for major implementations (Anthes and Hoffman, 2003). In a recent survey by Hackett Group, 45 percent CIOs attribute these problems to technology implementations being too slow and too expensive. Interestingly, just a few months ago, some research studies had found negative correlation between tech investments and business performance (Alinean, 2002; Hoffman, 2002). Financial performance analysis of 7,500 companies relative to their IT spending and individual surveys of more than 200 companies had revealed that:

companies with best-performing IT investments are often most frugal IT spenders; top 25 performers invested 0.8 percent of their revenues on IT in contrast to overall average of 3.7 percent; and highest IT spenders typically under-performed by up to 50 percent compared with best-in-class peers.

Based upon multi-year macroeconomic analysis of hundreds of corporations, Strassmann (1997) had emphasized that it is not computers but what people do with them that matters.

He had further emphasized the role of users' motivation and commitment in IT performance[1]. Relatively recent research on implementation of enterprise level KMS (Malhotra, 1998a; Malhotra and Galletta, 1999; Malhotra and Galletta, 2003; Malhotra and

Galletta, n.d. a; Malhotra and Galletta, n.d. b) has found empirical support for such socio-psychological factors in determining IT and KMS performance. An earlier study by Forrester Research had similarly determined that the top-performing companies in terms of revenue, return on assets, and cash-flow growth spend less on IT on average than other companies. Surprisingly, some of these high performance ''benchmark'' companies have the lowest tech investments and are recognized laggards in adoption of leading-edge technologies. Research on best performing US companies over the last 30 years (Collins, 2001) has discovered similar ''findings''. The above findings may seem contrarian given persistent and long-term depiction of technology as enabler of business productivity (cf. Brynjolfsson, 1993; Brynjolfsson and Hitt, 1996; Brynjolfsson and Hitt, 1998; Kraemer, 2001). Despite increasing sophistication of KM technologies, we are observing increasing failures of KM technology implementations (Malhotra, 2004b). The following sections discuss how such failures result from the knowledge gaps between technology inputs, knowledge processes, and business performance. Drawing upon theory, prior research, and industry case studies, we also explain why some companies that spend less on technology and are not leaders in adoption of most hyped RTE technologies succeed where others fail. The specific focus of our analyses is on the application of KM technologies in organizational business processes for enabling real time enterprise business models. The RTE enterprise is considered the epitome of the agile adaptive and responsive enterprise capable of anticipating surprise; hence our attempt to reconcile its sense making and information processing capabilities is all the more interesting. However, our theoretical generalizations and their practical implications are relevant to IT and KM systems in most enterprises traversing through changing business environments.

KNOWLEDGE MANAGEMENT

In the early 1990, knowledge management seriously entered topics of organization, although discussion and negotiation about knowledge had started from a long time ago; in 1965 Marshall claims that a major part of capital includes knowledge. Also, he believe that knowledge is the most powerful engine of generation, so the organizations should increasingly focus on its management. Kohn (1970) insists that knowledge is per se the capital of a group. In 1972, Hubremass points to this matter that knowledge should not beconsidered as a abstract existence, but it's a product based on volition and sometimes non conscious activities of human. (Radding,1998:41) . Complexity and breadth of the concept of knowledge management has led that the same attitudes about knowledge management don't be formed. Therefore, different experts have seen that from different angles and paid to define it. Despite this fact, some of the most common definitions of knowledge management is expressed here:

Knowledge management refers to a series of regular and systematic activities of organization that is performed to obtain the larger value trough the available knowledge. The available knowledge includes all experiences and learning of organization persons and all documents and reports inside an organization(Marwick, 2001;2). Knowledge management includes behaviors of human, attitudes and capabilities of human, philosophies of business, patterns, operations, procedures and complex technologies(Wiig, 2002:1). In another definition, knowledge management is considered as a commercial process with two basic aspects(Future Development consults, 2007) :

- Considering of the element of knowledge in commercial processes: so that the element of knowledge displays prominently itself in all of strategies, lines and employing these principles.
- Creation of intellectual capitals of organization: that includes both explicit capitals(registered) and implicit capitals(individual knowledge) and it takes positive results of that.
- In practice, knowledge management is proposed to identify and characterize intellectual capitals and creating new knowledge to prefer competitive in the global scene outside the organization and to facilitate data availability, share appropriate processes, and obtain information and communication technology inside the organization) Barclay& Murray, 2000).
- Knowledge management is knowledge creating and sharing, transferring and retention process so that it can effectively apply it in the organization(Hoffman, Holster, Sheriff, 2005: 178)
- Knowledge management means improving knowledge word processes. Improving knowledge word requires reduction of top-down interferences. Staff should have freedom and necessary independence in their work until they can utilize their knowledge in problem solving and decision making.
- Perost and Rebb and Romhard(2000) designed a model called " The model of cornerstones of knowledge management building" for knowledge management. The designers of this model see knowledge as a dynamic cycle that it is in constant rotation. The steps of this model includes eight subsets consisting of two outer and inner cycles. a) Outer cycle:
  1. Determination of knowledge aims: the aims of knowledge management should rise the main aims of organization and should be characterize in two strategic and operational levels.
  2. Knowledge evaluation: the method to achieve specific aims and use of its results as feedback, to aim determination or modification, relates to this section.
  b) Inner cycle:
  1. Identification of knowledge: outer knowledge is analyzing and explaining of environmental knowledge. Lack of transparency, leads to effectiveness of decisions and cause errors to be repeated.
  2. Knowledge acquisition: many companies import a significant part of their knowledge from external resources. Communication with customers, suppliers, competitors and partners in cooperative and collaborative work is a considerable potential for providing knowledge.
  3. Knowledge development: How to create a new specialty? Knowledge development is a cornerstone that it is the processor of process of knowledge acquisition. Its main focus is on developing new skills, new products, and better ideas and more efficient processes.
  4. Knowledge sharing and distribution: How knowledge can be put in place right? Fundamental requirement for data conversion and individual experiences is something that organization will be able to use it. In this stage. the necessary preconditions are:
  -Everyone should know how much and with what level of knowledge about a problem and be able to do it. -How to facilitate knowledge sharing?

It's not necessary that everyone know everything. Therefore, the principle of dividing the people capability in the range of distribution and sharing of knowledge should be defined as significant. Here, the most important step is analysis of how knowledge transfer from individual to group and organization.

5. Applying the knowledge: How can we ensure that knowledge is used? Concept of knowledge management is to ensure that current knowledge in an organization be used to benefit the entire organization effectively and productively.
6. Preservation of knowledge: How can we ensure that we do not lose knowledge? Obtained abilities will not be forever available. Preservation and selection of information, documents and experiences require management. Organization have often complained of the fact that reorganization has caused them to lose a part of their memory, hence the selection process, the processes of storing and updating the knowledge that will be valuable in future should be organized with complete accuracy. If this is not done, valuable expertise will be unintentionallyabandoned , (Probst,Raub&Romhardt, 2000: 30).

Fig1. The model of cornerstones of knowledge management

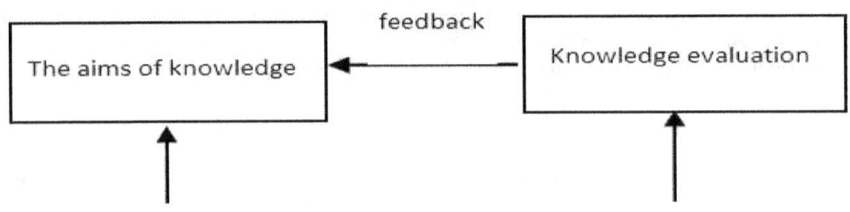

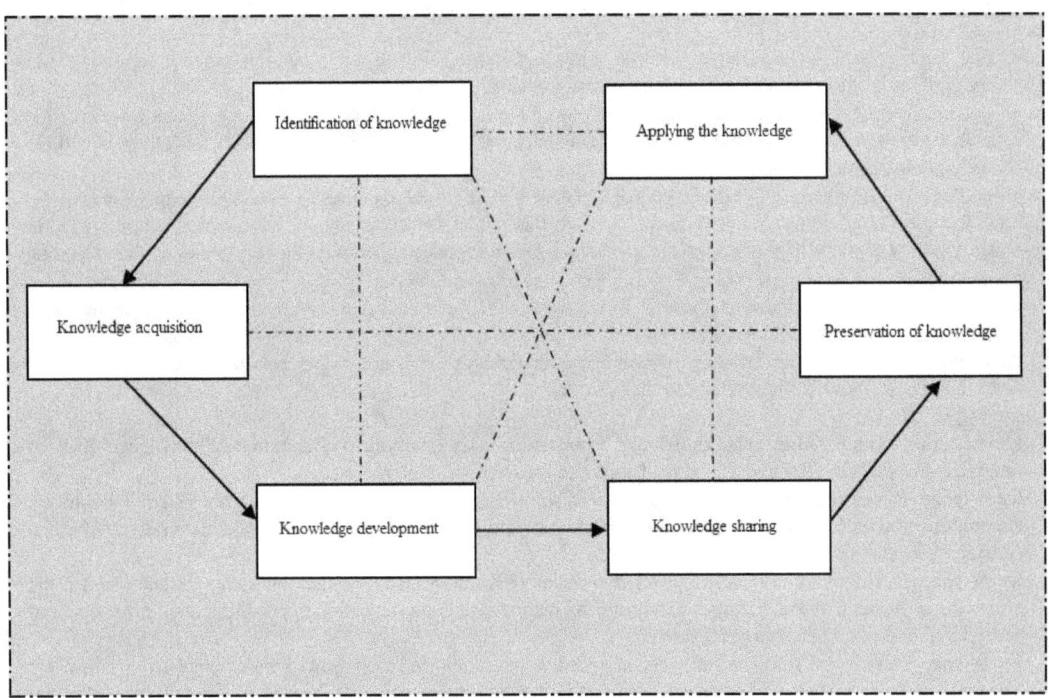

Source:)Probst, Raub&Romhardt, 2000)

Technologies for Enabling Knowledge Management

Vendors of information-oriented products are rushing to introduce new knowledge management products and re-label their existing products as knowledge management products in an effort to quickly gain mindshare and marketshare in a potentially enormous market. But computer applications have addressed aspects of knowledge management for years. No single technology fills all the criteria required of a knowledge management system, because knowledge management is not solely about technology. It is a multi-disciplinary field that draws on aspects of information science, interpersonal communications, organizational learning, cognitive science, motivation, training, publishing and business process analysis. The following sections look at the roles specific technologies play in an enterprise-wide knowledge management environment.

Intranet

Intranets have sprung up across corporations at a rate that challenges any previous introduction of new technology. They are ideal environments for sharing information that is both dynamic and richly linked. However, most large organizations quickly reach a point where so much information exists on the intranet that it begins to suffer the same problems that exist on the World Wide Web; no one knows where everything is, so no one can quickly find what he or she is looking for. Although some evangelists profess that all of an organization.s knowledge should be transferred to the intranet, many others take a modified view of what it is best suited to do. The intranet can be broken down into two distinct areas: the technology infrastructure (IP networks, universal web browser, thin client and the HTML format), and the web server as a content repository. These recent changes.the web browser and the web server being the most visible.have enabled greater access to information for broader groups of knowledge workers and increased the speed of integration for application developers. Allowing users to access all corporate knowledge through a web browser is not equivalent to forcing all knowledge assets onto the web server. Applications, specialized repositories and various other knowledge silos will always exist because they have capabilities that are distinct from those of a generalized knowledge management system. Web sites are best used for hosting and managing content that is constantly changing and linked in a complex manner. But to the organization as a whole, each intranet site is just another type of knowledge silo, the content of which must be integrated in the organization.s knowledge management system along with the other silos that exist across the enterprise.

DOCUMENT MANAGEMENT SYSTEMS

Document management systems are repositories of important corporate documents and are therefore important stores of explicit knowledge. They are also valuable tools for creating and processing complex documents, such as new drug applications in pharmaceutical companies. Document management systems excel at controlling the process of document creation, processing and review. Some companies are approaching enterprise knowledge management based on document management. However, many have found that the bulk of knowledge workers resist using highly structured document management processes for all of their document creation and management tasks. Most users do not participate directly in complex document creation and therefore do not realize enough value from those systems to make an investment in learning how to use them. Therefore, document management systems are important knowledge silos that must be integrated into the corporate knowledge infrastructure, but are not used by most organizations as the basis for a complete knowledge management system.

INFORMATION RETRIEVAL ENGINES

Information retrieval technology, whether it be in the form of corporate text repositories or intranet search facilities, exists in many organizations as a knowledge silo containing legacy information. Information retrieval vendors continue to be concerned with satisfying the needs of information seekers and have added features such as relevancy ranking, natural language querying, summarization and others that have increased the speed and precision of finding information.

ROUPWARE AND WORKFLOW SYSTEMS

Organizations use groupware systems when users in workgroups or departments need to communicate and collaborate. Groupware allows formal and ad hoc conversations in cases when the participants can not communicate in real time. This makes groupware an important technology for enhancing the exchange of tacit information. However, like other applications, groupware databases become knowledge silos that must be integrated into the enterprise knowledge architecture. Knowledge transfer processes often occur on an ad hoc basis when the need for specific knowledge arises somewhere in the organization, but organizations also have a large number of formalized processes that regulate the flow of information.

Workflow systems enable users to codify knowledge transfer processes when they require a more rigid method of dissemination. For example, proposal generation processes often require the proposal writer to collect prior knowledge assets, create new information and gain approval on the entire proposal. This process necessitates structured and ordered information preparation and review, which is what a workflow system facilitates.

PUSH TECHNOLOGIES AND AGENTS

Technologies that automate the transfer of information to end users have received considerable attention recently. Although e-mail served this purpose for over a decade, new web-based technologies have added better presentation, real-time updates and the ability to push applications as well as content. Content push is a dynamic form of electronic publishing and is therefore an important feature of a knowledge management system.

Agents are a specialized form of push technology. Agents are controlled by the end user, who can specify the type of knowledge he or she wants to receive. Agent capabilities are extremely valuable in knowledge-intensive environments, where knowledge workers do not have the time to continually monitor discreet information resources. Knowledge management systems should provide the means for users to easily capture the particular kinds of knowledge assets they need to monitor without requiring them to learn a complex search syntax.

HELP-DESK APPLICATIONS

Many organizations use help-desk technology to respond to both internal and external requests for information. However, the knowledge accumulated in help-desk systems can have much broader applications than answering specific questions. For example, service request logs are valuable tools to assist in product design and improving services. To tap this potentially valuable information, companies will want to integrate their help-desk applications into the knowledge management system.

BRAINSTORMING APPLICATIONS

Brainstorming tools help inspire creative thinking and convert tacit into explicit knowledge. These end user applications help categorize, organize and identify knowledge resources and are therefore useful knowledge creation tools. While it should not try to replicate their functionality, an organization.s knowledge management system must provide an easy way for users or these applications to identify, capture and share the results of these activities with others across the enterprise.

DATA WAREHOUSES AND DATA MINING TOOLS

Organizations are creating data warehouses and arming their business managers with data mining tools to optimize existing relationships and discover new ones between customers, suppliers and internal processes. Used primarily by business managers, leading organizations are now broadening their use since everyone in a knowledge-based organization needs to make decisions based on increasingly complex sets of data. Knowledge management systems must provide meaningful access to data warehouses by supporting standard protocols such as Open Database Connectivity (ODBC) and Structured Query Language (SQL). Knowledge management systems also need to provide a way to describe and provide access to common reports so that users not intimately familiar with data mining tools and techniques can find and access current reports on subject areas they are investigating.

THE KNOWLEDGE WAREHOUSE

First RDBMSs, then document management/groupware systems and now web servers. All of these systems have aimed to replace the organization.s knowledge silos with a single application. However, stand-alone applications are too feature rich to make this practical or even desirable. The goal of a knowledge warehouse.the core component of the knowledge management system.is to preserve the creation and processing functionality inherent in knowledge silos, while offering all users access to the knowledge contained in the silos. In addition, a knowledge warehouse allows users to submit valuable knowledge even when they are not frequent contributors and therefore do not work through an established knowledge silo.This eliminates the need for all end users in the organization to install and maintain complex client software for all of the application silos.

KNOWLEDGE CONTRIBUTION & COLLECTION

End users should be able to easily add content to a knowledge warehouse through their web browsers. The knowledge warehouse must support all of the various desktop document formats as well as graphics, video clips, sound clips and others.

Some knowledge assets benefit from a more structured approach than that provided by a simple document. For example, if all an organization.s knowledge workers were asked to contribute skill profiles as word processor documents, they will probably produce thousands of variations in format. However, if they fill out a web-based form instead, they will submit this information in a consistently organized way. Administrators should be able to easily create such forms to allow users to enter such structured knowledge. This not only allows the user to perform fielded searches on the class of knowledge assets, but also enforces a uniform presentation of the resulting information.

To enable or increase the accuracy and speed of information retrieval, knowledge assets need to be associated with categories from the corporate taxonomy or knowledge map. This categorization can be accomplished by the end user on submission or by a content manager. The knowledge warehouse must incorporate categorization into the submission process, yet be flexible enough to adapt to each organization.s processes,

KNOWLEDGERETRIEVAL

The other half of a knowledge management system concerns itself with access to the organization.s knowledge assets regardless of whether they were contributed to the knowledge warehouse by end users, or to a knowledge silo linked to the knowledge warehouse by the administrator. This section discusses some of the knowledge retrieval features that make it easier for end users to find the specific knowledge assets they require.

Search Knowledge workers now demand searching tools that are sophisticated yet easy to use. Some of the more useful advanced searching features for a knowledge warehouse include: Natural language searching; Boolean searching; Automatic root expansion; Proximity searching; Numeric searching; Term weighted searching;Thesaurus integrationSearch by object type (e.g., PowerPoint files, internal documents, etc.). Search by metadata fields (e.g., knowledge map (taxonomy) categories, author, date, location, etc.) Concept searching (e.g., find .more like this.)

KNOWLEDGEMANAGEMENTROLES

Knowledge management has brought with it new corporate roles and titles. The most visible of these is the Chief Knowledge Officer, or CKO. As Tom Davenport, professor and director of the Information Management Program at the University of Texas at Austin, describes it, .CKOs have two critical responsibilities: creating a knowledge management infrastructure and building a knowledge culture. Most organizations that have successfully implemented knowledge management have created a corporate level knowledge management team led by a high level executive (often the CKO, CIO or a line-of-business head). These teams usually consist of a small group (under a dozen) of employees dedicated to coordinating and evangelizing knowledge management principles. In many cases they are responsible for designing, piloting and implementing a knowledge management system.

This small knowledge management group cannot effect enterprise-wide changes by itself. Content managers or knowledge editors are needed to manage the capture and classification of knowledge to guard against information pollution. They are typically spread throughout an organization and spend some part of their job framing and structuring knowledge. Tom Davenport has remarked that: In the rosy future I envision, categorization and organization of knowledge will be a core competence for every firm.

This will require strategic thinking about what knowledge is important; development of a knowledge vocabulary (and a thesaurus to accommodate near misses); prolific creation of indices, search tools and navigation aids; and constant refinement and pruning of knowledge categories. Knowledge editors will have to combine sources and add context to transform information into knowledge.

CONCLUSIONS

The current period of human life is associated withamazing developments and changes. Organizations as a subset of human life, should be ready to deal with these major developments (Druker, 2002). Knowledge management is a process which helps organizations to find important information, select, organize and publish them and it is a proficiency which is necessary for activities such as problem solving, dynamic learning and decision making. Knowledge management can improve a range of organizational performance features with enabling the company to function more intelligently (Wiig, 1999:14‹). technology have observed that real knowledge is created and applied in the processes ofsocialization, externalization, combination, and internalization (Nonaka and Takeuchi, 1995) and outside the realm of KM technologies. Practitioners' inability to harness relevant knowledge despite KM technologies and offices of the CKOs caused the backlash and KM was temporarily branded as a fad. Scholarly research on latest information systems and technologies, or lack thereof, has further contributed to the confusion between data management, information management, and knowledge management. The outcomes-driven paradigm of KM has its primary focus on business performance. Key emphasis is on strategic execution for driving selection and adaptation of processes and activities, and carefully selected technologies. For instance, if collaborative community activities do not contribute to the key customer value propositions or business value propositions of the enterprise, such activities are replaced with others that are more directly relevant to business performance (Malhotra, 2002a). If these activities are indeed relevant to business performance, then appropriate business models, processes, and culture are grown (Brooks, 1987) as a precursor to acceleration of their performance with the aid of KM technologies. Accordingly, emphasis on business performance outcomes as the key driver ensures that relevant processes and activities, as well as, related technologies are adopted, modified, rejected, replaced, or enhanced in service of business performance.

REFERENCES

1. Ackoff, R. (1979), "The future of operations research is past", Journal of the Operations Research Society, Vol. 30, p. 93.
2. Argyris, C. (1990), Integrating the Individual and the Organization, Transaction, New Brunswick, NJ. Argyris, C. (1994), "Good communication that blocks learning", Harvard Business Review, Vol. 72 No. 4, pp. 77-85.
3. Alavi, M. and Leidner, D. (2001), "Review: knowledge management and knowledge management systems: conceptual foundations and research issues", MIS Quarterly, Vol. 25 No. 1, pp. 107-36.
4. Alinean (2002), "Alinean identifies why certain companies achieve higher ROI from IT investments", available at: www.alinean.com
5. Arthur, B. (1996), "Increasing returns and the new world of business", Harvard Business Review, Vol. 74 No. 4, pp. 100-9.
6. Barth, S. (2000), "KM horror stories", Knowledge Management, Vol. 3 No. 10, pp. 36-40.
7. Brynjolfsson, E. (1993), "The productivity paradox of information technology", Communications of the ACM, Vol. 36 No. 12, pp. 66-77.
8. Charles, S.K. (2002), "Knowledge management lessons from the document trenches", Online, Vol. 26 No. 1, pp. 22-9.
9. Churchman, C.W. (1971), The Design of Inquiring Systems, Basic Books, New York, NY.
10. Collins, J. (2001), Good to Great: Why Some Companies Make the Leap and Others Don't,
11. Harper-Business, New York, NY.
12. Conway, S. (2002), "Knowledge searching and services", in Holsapple, C.W. (Ed.), Handbook on
13. Darrell, R., Reichheld, F.F. and Schefter, P. (2002), "Avoid the four perils of CRM", Harvard Business Review, February, pp. 101-9.
14. Dragoon, A. (1995), "Knowledge management: Rx for success", CIO Magazine, Vol. 8 No. 18, pp. 48-56.
15. Drucker, P.F. (1994), "The theory of business", Harvard Business Review, September-October, pp. 95-104.
16. eMarketer (2001), "Knowledge management: executive brief", available at: www.info-edge.com/ samples/EM-2001free.pdf
17. Emery, F.E. and Trist, E.L. (1965), "The causal texture of organizational environments", Human Relations, Vol. 18, pp. 21-32.
18. Gartner, Inc. (2002), "The real time enterprise", available at: http://rte.gartner.com/
19. Greenemeier, L. (2003a), "HP looks to utility computing for growth", Information Week, May 12, available at: www.informationweek.com/story/showArticle.jhtml?articleID ¼ 9800052
20. Grover, V. and Davenport, T.H. (2001), "General perspectives on knowledge management: fostering a research agenda", Journal of Management Information Systems, Vol. 18 No. 1, pp. 5-21.
21. Hammer, M. (1990), "Reengineering work: don't automate", Harvard Business Review, July, pp. 10412.
22. Hansen, M.T. and Nohria, N. (1999), "What's your strategy for managing knowledge?", Harvard Business Review, March-April, pp. 106-16.
23. Hapgood, F. (2003), "Plug and pay", CIO Magazine, April 15, available at: www.cio.com/ archive/ 041503/plug.html
24. Hildebrand, C. (1999), "Intellectual capitalism: does KM ¼ IT?", CIO Magazine, September 15, available at: www.cio.com/archive/enterprise/091599_ic_content.html
25. Hoffman, T. (2003), "Survey points to continuing friction between business, IT", Computerworld, May 12,p. 10.
26. Holsapple, C.W. (2002), "Knowledge and its attributes", in Holsapple, C.W. (Ed.), Handbook on Knowledge Management 1: Knowledge Matters, Springer-Verlag, Heidelberg, pp. 165-88.
27. Jackson, C. (2001), "Process to product: creating tools in knowledge management", in Malhotra, Y.(Ed.), Knowledge Management for Business Model Innovation, Idea Group Publishing, Hershey, PA,pp. 402-13.
28. Khosla, V. and Pal, M. (2002), "Real time enterprises: a continuous migration approach", March, available at: www.asera.com/technology/pdf/RTE-WHITEPAPER-PDF-VERSION.pdf

29. Malhotra, Y. (1997), ''Knowledge management in inquiring organizations'', Proceedings of 3rd Americas Conference on Information Systems (Philosophy of Information Systems Mini-track), Indianapolis, IN, August 15-17, pp. 293-5, available at: www.kmnetwork.com/km.htm
30. Malhotra, Y. (1998a), ''Role of social influence, self-determination, and quality of use in information technology acceptance and utilization: a theoretical framework and empirical field study'', PhD thesis, Katz Graduate School of Business, University of Pittsburgh, Pittsburgh, PA.
31. Nonaka, I. and Takeuchi, H. (1995), The Knowledge-Creating Company, Oxford University Press, New York, NY.
32. Porter, M.E. and Millar, V.E. (1985), ''How information technology gives you competitive advantage'', Harvard Business Review, Vol. 63 No. 4, pp. 149-60.
33. Rayport, J.F. and Sviokla, J.J. (1995), ''Exploiting the virtual value chain'', Harvard Business Review, Vol. 73 No. 6, pp. 75-99.
34. Sawhney, M. (2003), ''Reality check'', CIO Magazine, March 1, available at: www.cio.com/
35. archive/030103/netgains.html
36. Schrage, M. (2002), ''Wal-Mart trumps Moore's law'', Technology Review, Vol. 105 No. 2, p. 21.
37. Schultze, U. and Leidner, D. (2002), ''Studying knowledge management in information systems resarch: discourses and theoretical assumptions'', MIS Quarterly, Vol. 26 No. 3, pp. 213-42.
38. Siegele, L. (2002), ''The real-time economy: how about now?'', CFO (The Economist), February 1, available at: www.cfo.com/printarticle/0,5317,6651%7C,00.html
39. Sliwa, C. (2003), ''Event-driven architecture poised for wide adoption'', Computerworld, May 12, p. 8.
40. Stewart, T.A. (2000), ''How Cisco and Alcoa make real time work'', Fortune, May 29.
41. Strassmann, P. (1997), The Squandered Computer: Evaluating the Business Alignment of Information Technologies, Information Economics Press, New Canaan, CT.
42. Tsui, E. (2002), ''Tracking the role and evolution of commercial knowledge management software'', in Holsapple, C.W. (Ed.), Handbook on Knowledge Management 1: Knowledge Directions, SpringerVerlag, Heidelberg, pp. 5-27.

African Journal of Business Management Vol. 6(29), pp. 8475-8482, 25 July, 2012
Available online at http://www.academicjournals.org/AJBM
DOI: 10.5897/AJBM12.072
ISSN 1993-8233 ©2012 Academic Journals

Review

Public accountability and government financial reporting

Mostafa Emami[1]* , Kamran Nazari[2] ,Farzad Eivani[3]

[1]Young Researchers Club, Kermanshah Branch, Islamic Azad University, Kermanshah, Iran.
[2]Department of Business Management, Payam Noor University, Kermanshah, Iran. [3]
Department of Accounting, School of Social Science, Razi University, Kermanshah, Iran.

Accepted 5 June, 2012

New Public Management" requires the introduction of competition within the Government to increase financial transparency and improve government performance. The major role of financial reporting is the effective transfer of financial data to people who are outside the organization in a way that is valid and timely one of the most important goals of which is to provide necessary data to evaluate the function of an economic agencies and its ability to make profits. The necessary condition to achieve this is to provide financial data in such a way that the evaluation of the previous functions becomes possible and effective in measuring the ability to make profits and in predicting future activities of economic agencies. The major role of financial reporting is the effective transfer of financial data to people who are outside the organization in a way that is valid and timely; one of the most important goals of which is to provide necessary data to evaluate the function of an economic agencies and its ability to make profits. Government accounting and financial reporting aims to protect and manage public money and discharge accountability. These purposes, and the nature of public goods and tax financing, give rise to differences with commercial accounting. In order to achieve ambitious socioeconomic goals, developing countries require public sector institutional capacity for setting and implementing public policy, which in turn necessitates government accounting reform. The social value of government accounting reform therefore lies in its contribution to development goals, including poverty reduction. Public accountability of government is demonstrated in part by accounting standards that require fair presentation and full disclosure. In the United States, many of these standards are developed by the Governmental Accounting Standards Board (GASB). The paper revealed that the effective implementation of development policies and programmes is anchored on purity of action, honesty of purpose, probity and integrity, which are important hallmarks of accountability and transparency. Financial reporting is the best index of accountability. The accountability and control apparatus in the public service has some minimum technical components that should elicit tolerable standards of accountability and transparency. There are reasonable regulations, adequate albeit outdated accounting procedures, stringent sanctions and financial auditing. The major problem however, is with the human component indices of commitment, honesty, integrity and transparency. The apparatus for managerial and programme accountability are either weak or non-existent. Consequently, the quality of the financial statements should be improved, the system should create room to inculcate both managerial and programme accountability apparatus. The human component-individual accountability should be seriously considered.

Key words: Public accountability, government, accounting reform, government financial.

INTRODUCTION

Today, business operations and financial position reporting have a direct or indirect influence on the individual's decisions and it is important for them. In fact, financial reports provide a picture of how the company is run and can also be a way to monitor the business unit and its activities from the perspective of management and the board. External financial reporting should be able to present such a view to individuals. That there is a serious problem of lacking accountability and transparency in the public service is not only well known but fairly documented. General and specific observations within the service and comments from international bodies like World Bank (WB), transparency international (TI), all seem to suggest that the problem is not only real but also enduring.

Accountability; the concept of its importance and the concept of accountability are a pervasive one which impacts on all aspects of government operations. The notions underlying it are those accounting for, reporting on, explaining and justifying activities, and accepting responsibility for the outcomes.

Accountability involves an obligation to answer for one's decisions and actions when authority to act on behalf of one party (the principal) is transferred to another (the agent). According to the Management Advisory Board (MAB) of the Commonwealth Government (Neilson, 1993), the responsibility for accountability in the public sector exists ". . .where there is a direct authority relationship within which one party accounts to a person or body for the performance of tasks or functions conferred [. . .] by that person or body.

Accountability requires openness, transparency and the provision of information, and the acceptance of responsibility for one's actions. The concept underlies all accounting as well as the operations of democratic governments (Hines, 1989).

It has been argued that sustainability reporting represents one of, if not the most important advance in organizational reporting in the last few decades.

However, while this form of reporting has been taken up by the private sector, in comparison, progress within the public sector appears patchy and in many respects, is seen as an emerging field (Dickinson et al., 2005; Ball, 2004). Slowly this is changing with recent shifts in momentum within the public sector and there is evidence of increasing interest and engagement in the practice of sustainability reporting by public agencies (Ellis, 1997). The responsibilities arising from accountability in the public sector are very broad-ranging ones which encompass the entire structure of government. There is a continuous chain of accountability from governments and the public service to citizens (Funnell and Cooper, 1998: 27 to 29). Governments are responsible to their citizens for the good governance of the nation; ministers and cabinet to parliament for policy formulation and general implementation; and ministers and their departmental staff for detailed policy implementation and the provision of specified public services as authorised by parliament to eligible citizens. It should be noted that the word "democratic" comes from the classical Greek work of "demos", meaning the people (Funnell and Cooper, 1998: 9).

---

*Corresponding author. E-mail: mostafa.emami@modares.ac.ir. Tel +989127001816

Democratic governments are elected by citizens to act in the best interests of the nation on their behalf and citizens have a right to know what their governments are doing on their behalf.

They are answerable to their citizens. There is an implicit requirement for public trust in the operations of government and this is embodied in the responsibility for accountability (Funnell and Cooper, 1998: 1). The provision of appropriate information by government to parliament and the people is critical to the accountability obligation, and hence to democracy.

The necessity for maintaining the accountability of governments in democratic societies is attested to in various Royal Commission reports, government committee reports and High Court judgments. For example, the Report of the Royal Commission into Commercial Activities of (the Western Australian) Government and Other Matters stated in 1992 that: If Government is to be truly government for the people, if the public is to be able to participate in government and to experience its benefits, the public must be properly informed about government and its affairs (Miller, 1996).

The organisation for economic co-operation and development (OECD) believes strongly that sound governance is necessary for economic stability and social cohesion. The study would like to take a moment to discuss the word "governance" because it is sometimes casually used and often misused to represent several ideas. By governance, the study means the way power is embodied in public institutions and is exercised, as well as arrangements that keep policy making sound over time.

The concept of governance incorporates how decisions are made, the balance of powers and institutions, and in ways politicians and managers are held accountable. It refers not to public policies *per se*, but to the settings within which public policy is decided and executed. When it is effective, governance serves to provide (Talebnia et al, 2011):

1. An environment in which people are treated fairly and equitably;
2. An atmosphere of transparency which limits monopolistic behavior and stimulates efficiency and innovation;
3. Stability and predictability for social investments;
4. A way of bringing coherence to diverse policy objectives, including both short and long term interests; and
5. Separated responsibilities and accountabilities to prevent the misuse of power by individuals or groups.

Governmental accounting recognises that financial benefits may not reflect economic benefits and that it is measurement of the latter that is sought: Future economic benefits have sometimes been used in accounting texts to signify access to future cash inflow. However, the term is used ... with broader meaning –
namely the capacity to provide goods and services in accordance with the entity's objectives, whether those objectives are the generation of net cash inflows or the provision of goods and services of a particular volume and quality to beneficiaries (Miller, 1995).

Financial benefits (in terms of expected cash flow) are subsumed within economic benefits, pecuniary and nonpecuniary. Non-pecuniary service potential is generated by a wide range of community assets. Despite tangibility not being an essential characteristic of an asset (AARF, 1995, para. 33), their valuation and inclusion in government financial reports rests on the conclusion that, for accounting purposes, they cannot be readily distinguished from other physical assets (Rowles, 1998: 44), and they meet the asset definition test of SAC (Bolo and Hosseini, 2007).

The new accounting rule dramatically increases the amount of quality information included in government financial reports particularly in regard to retiree healthcare and other retiree benefits. State and local governments must take a series of steps that include quantifying the unfunded liabilities association with retiree health benefits. Results of these assessments must be reported in governmental audits and updated regularly.

Government financial statements will then list an actuarially determined amount known as an annual required contribution. In regard to healthcare this contribution includes (1) the 'normal costs – the amount that needs to be set aside in order to fund future retiree health benefits earned in the current year and (2) unfunded liability costs- the amount needed to pay off existing unfunded retiree health liabilities over a period (Salehi and Abedini, 2009) of no longer than 30 years.

The spectre of two sets of accounts offering competing numbers, such as the net worth of government, with which to assess the economic performance of government, is unlikely to assist decision making by potential users of either set of accounts unless they can reconcile the differences. If both accounts seek to provide information about the economic performance of either the economy as a whole or government as an institutional unit within that economy (Gittins, 1995: 34), they should rely upon similar theory and measurement. In addition, savings in information collection and processing would be an obvious advantage if the two accounting systems were compatible.

Government regulatory bodies have also been identified in the literature as being constituents in the public sector accounting standard setting process. In Australia, despite the existence of the Public Sector Accounting Standards Board (PSASB), government regulatory bodies - Departments of Local Government (or their equivalent) in each Australian jurisdiction, have the responsibility for the determination of accounting requirements for local governments. Prior research has documented that these bodies have lobbied on public sector accounting standards (Ryan, 1999). Public sector accounting standard s etters in numerous jurisdictions internationally has adopted the user needs perspective as their framework for general purpose financial reporting (Van Peursem and Pratt, 1992). This perspective suggests that resource providers, recipients of goods and services and parties performing a review or oversight function are the primary users of financial reports.

Despite this emphasis, the response rate of these groups to exposure drafts has been found to be low, even where the proposed standard adopts a user perspective (Weetman et al., 1996; Gaffney, 1986; Butterworth et al., 1989; Hay, 1994; Dixon et al., 1994).

The fact that the accounting standard was issued with requirements largely unchanged from the original exposure draft suggests a number of possibilities: either the ED gained general constituent approval; respondents who did not agree with the proposals chose not to lobby; or the positions of opponents to the requirements failed to influence the standard-setters to alter the outcome.

By documenting the level of evident constituent participation in the 'due process', the key issues, the positions held by respondents and any strategies employed by them in an attempt to influence the standard-setters, this case study will add to other public sector case studies and enable conclusions to be drawn about the operation of the public sector 'due process (Puro, 1984).

A considerable body of literature has developed, particularly examining the nature of governmental accounting and financial reporting. Research in this category typically explains the practical application of accounting standards in the governmental settings, discusses currently unresolved governmental accounting issues, and or questions current practices in governmental accounting and financial reporting (Gittins, 1995).

Some of the major issues identified include: a perceived gap in the information content of government financial report and information need of users and lack of external accountability (Tamlin, 1997), the need to integrate budgeting, accounting and financial reporting and that a strong and enduring relationship exists between government accounting and budgeting (Tutticci et al., 1994), and the need to reform budgeting processes in view of large budget variances (Watts and Zimmerman, 1978).

The government financial reporting function seems to have been subjected to the greatest amount of criticism in recent years with regard to its information content and its apparent inability to meet the assumed need of a variety of user-groups.

In addition, individuals and institutions outside the government have become virtually interested in the   financial activities and status of governments. Example of such users includes creditors, citizen groups (that is, taxpayers, service recipients or voters), business enterprises and others, yet the Government Financial Reports remain the singular picture of the resources entrusted, how the resources are employed during a fiscal year, and in what form the resources are now held. However, there are overwhelming calls on government to shift emphasis from traditional stewardship financial reporting to the presentation of more informative Government Financial Statements (Solomons, 1978).

Sutton (1984) observes that various persons who have written on the subject of financial reporting in the Federal Government have termed it 'antiquated, fragmented, incomplete, unreliable and lacking timeliness...' Gary further submits that to a person schooled in government accounting, the Federal Government Financial reporting is disgraceful. All of these epithets may have merit, especially in respect of the statutory background of government accounting, the adequacy of the information content and the extent to which it satisfies public accountability criteria.

Morey (1926) acknowledged that many errors of principle will be committed if there are no material modification to the public accounts, in adopting private sector accounting procedures. In addition, if relevant information contained in Government Financial

Statements could provide financial information, the timing of publication can impair its reliability, completeness, and usefulness and so adversely affect users of Published Government Financial Statements (Tandy and Wilburn, 1996).

VALUING FUTURE ECONOMIC BENEFITS

In valuing future economic benefits, national accounting seeks an approximation of the cost of using, or using up, some existing asset or good in one particular process of production is measured by the amount of the benefits that could have been secured by using the asset or good in alternative ways. The best practical approximation to opportunity cost accounting is current cost accounting, whereby assets and goods used in production are valued at their actual or estimated current market prices at the time the production takes place" (Salehi and Azary, 2008).

The link between opportunity cost and welfare also is established: the prices used to value different goods and services should reflect not only their relative costs of production but also the relative benefits or utilities to be derived from using them in production or consumption. This establishes the link between changes in aggregate production and consumption and changes in welfare
(Greenall et al., 1988).

National accounting seeks to measure the current exchange value in money terms; that is, the values at which assets and other goods, services, labour or the provision of capital are in fact, exchanged or else, could be exchanged for cash (UN, 1993, para.3.72). If no actual exchange values are at hand, values should be taken from markets in which the same or similar items are traded currently in sufficient numbers and in similar circumstances against cash.

Based on market prices, such measurement treats the financial value of an asset as equivalent to its economic value. The absence of readily observable market prices creates a problem. A market, such as the stock exchange, is acknowledged in SNA93 as an ideal source of price observations which can be used for valuing balance sheet items. A market's utility in valuation decisions is derived from trading a homogeneous product in considerable volume, with the price obtained listed at regular intervals (Deegan et al., 1990), such markets are rare. Where there is no appropriate market from which the value of a particular non-monetary flow or stock item can be taken, by analogy its valuation could be derived from prices that are established in less closely related markets.

Some goods and services may need to be valued by the amount that it would currently cost to produce them (UN, 1993, para. 13.73). These pricing methods - observing market values, accumulating and revaluing transactions, and calculating the present value of future returns - relate to the assessment of current opportunity cost.

According to Hone (1997: 40), there are two ways of interpreting the future flows of economic benefits. Firstly, the benefits represent an increase in the utility of wellbeing of society that comes from the stewardship of the community asset.

Secondly, the benefits represent a gain achieved by the steward-managers from achieving their entity's objectives and obligations to the community. Accordingly, in valuing economic benefits, both commercial and social values are appropriate because economic benefits can flow from the use of community assets, from the option to use them in the future, or from the knowledge that they exist. Implicit market prices exist for the provision of social, cultural and environmental services and, by extension, for the assets which generate them.

Measuring these distortion-free prices is an exercise which separates financial analysis from economic analysis which, with its focus on community welfare, is an extension of financial analysis (Perkins, 1994: 3, ch.16). Carnegie and Wolnizer (1997: 45 and 47) dispute whether non-financial benefits can be quantified in commercial terms.

Although, social valuations may assist government's allocations of scarce resources among competing potential recipients, verifiable financial valuations are necessary for inclusion of assets in statements of financial position As a recent report discussing ways of valuing Australia's native forests observed, the identification of financial with economic values occurs because of "the easy but methodologically sloppy habit of referring to the financial activities of the Australian society as the 'economy'" (Mian and Smith, 1990). If government accounts and national accounts have a similar economic focus, similar definitions, and are based on the use of accrual accounting with similar valuation practices, reconciliation should be possible. Superficially, asset definitions used in Australian national and government accounting appear to be similar. While the key to determining what is an asset, the definition of "economic benefit", is similar, recognition criteria vary, leading to differences in the grounds for asset inclusion (MacArthur, 1988).

FROM ACCOUNTABILITY TO ACCOUNTING

Accountability has an economic focus, requiring information which can be used to assess "the economy, efficiency and effectiveness of entity operations" (Parker, 1993: 162; PSACE, 1995: 13). This represents a "hijacking" (Rentschler and Potter, 1996: 110) by accountants of traditional notions of accountability, in which the emphasis is on effectiveness.

Effectiveness is determined by reporting entities' objectives, objectives which span cultural, heritage, scientific and educative values. Such accountability lies outside the market (Carnegie and Wolnizer, 1995: 84) and is difficult to quantify in financial terms. Financial notions of accountability also may trivialise the notion inherent in the Westminster model of government, a notion based on ethical and equity considerations (McCrae and Aiken, 1994: 66).

Others, such as Micallef and Peirson (1997), adopt the strong economic focus inherent in the Australian conceptual framework, a focus which is reflected in the standards governing governmental accounting. This economic focus leads Hone (1997: 40) to declare that resource allocations must be based on increases in the utility or well-being of the community, and on gains achieved by public sector asset managers by meeting their entity's objectives and obligations to the community.

The global rise of government accounting is fundamentally due to the greater demand for accountability in a democracy and market economy. Democratic governance and market transactions require and foster the norm of reciprocity the expectation of exchange of benefits of comparable value upon which accountability is based. Accounting information can be used to monitor and enforce the terms of economic, social and political contracts. When a government engages in market transactions whether buying or selling services, lending or borrowing money it is subject to economic accountability. When it levies taxes to finance public services, it incurs political accountability (Dolley and Priest 1994).

While all governments engage in some degree of planning and control, only democratic governments are mandated to open their books directly to auditors and indirectly to the public through financial reports. Fiscal transparency is therefore an attribute of limited government, for to give out information is to cede authority. Government officials rationally do not volunteer more information than is required or in their interest. It is therefore not surprising that, while some accounting is done on a voluntary basis, financial disclosure is often made only in response to demand.

The regulatory structure for government financial disclosure mirrors the pattern of accountability in government and the political system. In an administrative hierarchy, the superior holds subordinates accountable and requires feedback information on their performance. A legislature monitors the conduct of the executive branch, for example, in executing the approved budget.

Furthermore, a government has the incentive to disclose information in order to induce others to provide resources to it. These include potential buyers of   government securities; vendors of goods and services on credit; and grantors of financial aid. In these voluntary exchanges, information is used to predict a government's ability to carry out the   terms of contracts, after the transactions are made; accounting information is used to monitor contractual performance (O'Keefe and Soloman, 1985).

Governments are less inclined to disclose financial information to those without leverage over it, at least in the short-term, such as individual taxpayers. It is here that mandatory standards seek to increase the information access of those who are least able to demand it, or to enforce their right to know. The exercise of accountability requires institutions in both senses of the term: namely, organizations; and rules of the game (World Bank, 2002: 4).

In government accounting, these refer to standardsetting bodies and the standards they promulgate. These institutions of government accounting in individual countries are extensively documented in the CIGAR literature and will not be covered in this article. It is, how ever, important to describe the general purposes of government accounting, in order to contrast it with commercial accounting. The Commission on Audit shall have the power, authority, and duty to examine, audit, and settle all accounts pertaining to the revenue and receipts of, and expenditures or uses of funds and property, owned or held in trust by, or pertaining to, the Government, or any of its subdivisions, agencies, or instrumentalities, including government-owned or controlled corporations with original charters, and on a post-audit basis: (a) constitutional bodies, commissions and offices that have been granted fiscal autonomy under this constitution; (b) autonomous state colleges and universities; (c) other government owned or controlled corporations and their subsidiaries; and (d) such nongovernmental entities receiving subsidy or equity, directly or indirectly, from or through the Government, which are required by law or the granting institution to submit to such audit as a condition of subsidy or equity.

However, where the internal control system of the audited agencies is inadequate, the Commission may adopt such measures, including temporary or special pre-audit, as

are necessary and appropriate to correct the deficiencies. It shall keep the general accounts of the Government and, for such period as may be provided by law, preserve the vouchers and other supporting papers pertaining thereto. The Commission shall have exclusive authority, subject to the limitations in this Article, to define the scope of its audit and examination, establish the techniques and methods required therefor, and promulgate accounting and auditing rules and regulations, including those for the prevention and disallowance of irregular, unnecessary, excessive, extravagant, or unconscionable expenditures or uses of government funds and properties (Section 3). No law shall be passed exempting any entity of the Government or its subsidiaries in any guise whatever, or any investment of public funds, from the jurisdiction of the Commission on Audit (Scanlan, 1999) (Section 4). The Commission shall submit to the President and the Congress, within the time fixed by law, an annual report covering the financial condition and operation of the Government, its subdivisions, agencies, and instrumentalities, including government-owned or controlled corporations, and nongovernmental entities subject to its audit, and recommend measures necessary to improve their effectiveness and efficiency. It shall submit such other reports as may be required by law.

ORGANIZATIONAL ROLES AND RESPONSIBILITIES

The following organizations play central roles in budgeting, accounting and auditing arrangements. The COA audits the general accounts of the Government, promulgates accounting rules and regulations, and submits the annual financial report of the Government, its subdivisions, and agencies (including government owned or controlled corporations).

The Department of Finance (DOF): The DOF is responsible for (i) formulating, institutionalizing, and administering fiscal policies in coordination with other concerned subdivisions, agencies, and instrumentalities of the government; (ii) managing the financial resources of government; (iii) supervising the revenue operations of all LGUs; (iv) reviewing, approving and managing all public sector debt; and (v) rationalizing, privatizing and ensuring the public accountability of corporations and assets owned, controlled or acquired by the Government (187). The DOF oversees three operating bureaus: the

Bureau of the Treasury (BTr), the Bureau of Internal Revenue (BIR), and the Bureau of Customs. The Bureau of the Treasury (BTr): The BTr plays a pivotal role in the cash operations of the national government. It is responsible for (i) receiving and keeping national funds; (ii) managing and controlling disbursements of national funds; and (iii) maintaining accounts of financial transactions of all national government offices, agencies, and instruments.

Department of Budget and Management (DBM): The DBM is responsible for the design, reparation and approval of the accounting systems of government agencies. It is also responsible for coordinating and implementing the annual budget process. Furthermore, the Department manages the process of cash disbursement as well as monitoring compliance with appropriations.

Development   and   Budget   Coordinating   Council
(DBCC): The DBCC comprises representatives from DBM, DOF, Bureau of Treasury, NEDA, and BSP. All agency budgetary requirements must pass through the Council. Its objectives are to (i) set budget parameters based on

available resources; (ii) conduct budget hearings; and (iii) submit the resulting consolidated budget to the House of Representatives (particularly the Committee on Appropriations).

CONCLUSION

Financial reports are an important source of information for stakeholders, who use them for investing, contracting, and regulating decisions. Low quality reporting can lead to suboptimal decisions and potential misallocation of resources and as such, financial reporting quality is important (Ellis, 1997).

Traditional public administration is internationally widespread and has been durable, because the ideal of rules ensuring equal service delivery to every citizen has strong popular and political appeal. Moreover it is durable because traditional public administration can continue to operate where bureaucrats do not have highly specialised skills and where they may not be trusted to exercise discretion. The kinds of changes we are talking about are crucially dependent on relatively specialised skills (for example, the transition to and use of accrual accounting) (Chua and Sinclair, 1994).

These new approaches will not work at either the political or the bureaucratic level in the absence of a supportive culture. It may not be possible for a government to leap frog to such reforms. Rather system changes should occur gradually as public officials internalise values and attitudes to the point where there is a supportive culture for rule compliant behaviour oriented to the public interest. It is only in such an atmosphere of relatively high trust and low enforcement costs, that the full advantages of high managerial discretion will be realised.

The work of the Organisation for Economic Cooperation and Development (OECD) is to promote stable and sound governance arrangements. The budget is a nation's, a province's or a city's most important policy document. Consequently, to promote sound governance arrangements, the Member countries of the organisation for economic co-operation and development (OECD) are committed to producing well-crafted budgeting and reporting systems that are tailored to the business of government.

Budgets are constructed in a way that encourages politicians and public servants to act coherently in the larger public interest. This is achieved:

1.   Vertically, by connecting policy intent to administrative action,
2.   Horizontally, by ensuring that one action of government is consistent with another, and
3.   Temporally, by recognising that sound governance includes care for the interests of future generations.

Conditions of separated decision-making, transparency and accountability help these processes to be selfcleansing over time and thus provide the insurance of a successful society in the long-run. The accounting system should measure the cash and other financial consequences of past transactions and events, including, but not limited to, budget execution. The accounting system should be capable of keeping track of the levels and changes in assets, liabilities, revenues and expenditures or expenses, relative to budgeted amounts. These principles do not prescribe accounting choices. Rather, they provide a foundation for deliberating and setting government accounting standards.

Generally, accounting standards take on a greater social role as accountability requirements in countries that require higher standards of ethical behaviour. Government accounting standards in effect become government accountability standards. (Recently the U.S. General Accounting Office was renamed Government Accountability Office). Government must answer for the resources or authority it receives from others in the society and economy.

In conclusion, fundamental to the development of accrual accounting in developing countries is the ability to identify and measure the government's assets and liabilities. Corruption tends to result in the understatement of government's assets or the overstatement of government's liabilities.

Unless financial integrity is assured, the credibility of government's financial information suffers. Thus both financial integrity assurance and accurate accrual accounting are accountants' professional contribution to developing countries. The most significant factors to push the change forward have been as follows: a favourable political approach, civil servants wholeheartedly working to successfully implement the reforms and the continuous point of reference of business accounting. Even though there is still a clear need to improve the financial statements that are now prepared, especially in the case of local administrations, the Spanish model seems rather advanced in comparison to others in its environment.

From the mid-1990s, the priorities and criteria to qualify under-development of managerial culture in public administration have changed the focus of the process and reduced the speed of reforms. The interest is now moving towards National Accounts, and therefore, microeconomic aspects are rather overlooked.

Nonetheless, this move towards aggregated information is also taking place in other European countries, so the international stimuli for micro-economic accounting harmonisation are reduced. However, this process implies a high support for full accrual accounting and budgeting, in the lines of the magnitudes used by National Accounts. This will undoubtedly lead to a significant push to adopt Generally Accepted Accounting Principles (GAAP) in public sector accounting and budgeting.

Last but not least, in Spain we use the accounting and budgeting model derived from the change of political regime in the late 1970s. The budgetary accounting is based in the modified cash basis of accounting, whereas the financial accounting is based on the modified accrual basis. Even though in the short-term the interest is moving towards National Accounts, the need to provide an effective financial management and rendering of accounts by public administrations will imply a further development and improvement of the initiated reforms.

Elaborate financial regulation and rigid accounting system are deliberately designed to guide the actions and conduct of public officers in the conduct of and accounting for scheduled activities. In scope and content the financial regulations appear to be quite adequate. There are sufficient provisions to guide every responsible officer and to safeguard official resources. The cash basis of accounting which the Finance (Control and Management) Act, 1958 imposes would also appear to be realistic going by the traditional activities of government; financial account However, there is the added need for managerial and programme accountability which the prevailing system has not adequately catered for; value for money is not a feature of the present system. The problems related to wrong approvals, wrong payments, wasteful expenditure, fake acquisitions and ghost disbursements are directly traceable to weak internal control system. The individual accountability, an important element of the system is at its lowest ebb of accountability and transparency (Butterworth et al., 1989).Taking all these together, one is tempted to infer that though the accountability and control apparatus in the public service may not be the best, it has some minimum technical components that should elicit tolerable standards of accountability and transparency.   The findings and conclusions of the paper necessitated the following recommendations on legislative requirement, and report content and presentation (Coleman, 1996):

(1) Legislative Requirement:

(a) The right of users to request special financial reports must be legally mandated, and be made accessible; (b) The timing of reports publication should be made 3months as against the statutory 7-months;

(c)   Establishment of Governmental Accounting Standard Board, to determine the detailed procedures, principles, and standards that should operate within the public sector, as public Accounting Standard Board is to the private sector accounting; and :

(d)   The present statue makes the accrual basis of accounting illegal, in view of the importance now attached to it; the modified accrual basis of accounting should be adopted in reporting government financial transactions. (e) Value for money audit should be mandated by law as well as a shift from stewardship reporting to emphasis on external accountability and programme planning budgeting systems.

(f) The office of the Auditor-General whose constitutional duty it is to examine and authenticate the books of accounts is deliberately designed to be party of government but yet outside it. Efforts have to be made to enhance the autonomy and staffing situation and facilities too.

(2) Content and presentation:

(a)   Provision of information showing the relationship between services rendered and operating outlays, to enable groups external to the government obtain accounting information to assist them in evaluating the performance of functionaries in charge of government operations.

(b)   Improvement in the quality and style of presentation of the statements with focus to make it understandable, complete, reliable and consistent. This could be achieved through:

(i)   Expansion of the contents of the notes to financial statements; notes to include: basis of presentation and explanation of funds and fund accounts, basis of accounting- for measuring and reporting constituents of the financial statements;

(ii)   Disclosure of the reconciliation between actual expenditures on the budget basis and the modified accrual basis, and disclosure on adverse situationsdeficits in fund balances or retained earnings of individual funds, excess expenditures over appropriations, material violations of finance related legal and contractual provisions.

REFERENCES

AARF(1996)a, Australian Accounting Research Foundation, AAS 27 Financial Reporting by Local Governments, Australian Accounting Research Foundation, Melbourne.
Bolo G, Hosseini SA (2007). Profits' management and its measurement Official Account. J. 12:72-78.
Butterworth P, Tam A, Frick J (1989). 'The Local Authority Annual Report in the UK: An Exploratory Study of Accounting Communication and Democracy', Financ. Account. Manage. 5(2):7378.
Carnegie G, Wolnizer B (1995). 'Observing the PSASB: ED 50 and the Recognition of Infrastructure Assets'. Austr. Account. Rev. 7(2):3039.
Carnegie G, West B (1997). 'Observing the PSASB: ED 50 and the Recognition of Infrastructure Assets', Aust. Accoun. Rev. 7(2):30-39.

Chua WF, Sinclair A (1994). 'Interests and the Profession-State Dynamic: Explaining The Emergence of the Australian Public Sector Accounting Standards Board', Bus. Financ. Account. 21(5):669-705.
Coleman M (1996). 'Valuation of Public Sector Assets – Where are we at?' August, Valuer Land Econ. 34:236-243.
Deegan CM , Benson PG, Schroeder RG (1990). 'Audit Firm Lobbying on Proposed Disclosure Requirements', Aust. J. Manage. 15(2):261280.
Dolley C, Priest A (1994). 'Voluntary Financial Disclosure Prior to the Introduction of AAS27', Account. Res. J. 7(2):42-52, 28. Ellis M (1997). 'Public Sector Accounting Standards board Land Under Roads Working Party', (February), Valuer Land Econ. pp. 435-436.
Gaffney MA (1986). 'Consolidated versus Fund-Type Financial Statements: The Perspectives of Constituents', J. Account. Public Policy 5(3):167-190.
Greenall D, Chin KS, Gill R (1988). 'Financial Reporting by Local Governments, Melbourne. Aust. Account. Res. Found. p. 12.
Hines RD (1989). 'Financial Accounting Knowledge, Conceptual Framework Projects and the Social Construction of the Accounting Profession', Account. Audit. Account. J. 2(2): 72-91.
MacArthur JB (1988). 'An Analysis of the Content of Corporate Submissions on Proposed Accounting Standards in the UK', Account. Bus. Res. 18(1):213-226.
Mian SL, Smith CW (1990). 'Incentives Associated with Changes in Consolidated Reporting Requirements', J. Account. Econ. 13:249266.
Miller MC (1995). 'The Credibility of Australian Financial Reporting: Are Co-regulation Arrangements Working', Aust. Account. Rev. 5(2):3-16.
Miller MC (1996). 'Accounting Regulation and the Roles Assumed by the Government and the Accounting Profession: The Case of Australia', presented at The 19th Annual Congress of the European Accounting Association NHH, Bergen, Norway 2-4 May. Neilson J (1993). 'AAS 27: Expensive and Unnecessary', Charter (March) pp. 53-55.
O'Keefe TB, Soloman SY (1985). 'Do Managers Believe in the Efficient Market Hypothesis?Additional Evidence', (Spring). Account. Bus. Res. pp. 67-79.
Puro M (1984). 'Audit Firm Lobbying Before the Financial Accounting Standards Board: An Empirical Study', (Autumn). J. Account. Res. 22(2):624-646.
Rowles T (1998). 'AAS 27: A Survey of Local Government Views', Aust. Account. 68(4):46-49, 29.
Ryan C (1999). 'Australian Public Sector Financial Reporting: A Case of Cooperative Policy Formulation', Account. Audit. Account. J. 12(5):561-582.
Salehi M, Azary Z (2008). Fraud Detection and Audit Expectation Gap: Empirical Evidence from Iranian Bankers, Int. J. Bus. Manage. 3(10):65-77.
Salehi M, Abedini B (2009). Financial Distress Prediction in Emerging Market: Empirical Evidence of Iran, Interdisciplinary J. Contemp. Res. Bus. 1(1):6-26.
Scanlan L (1999). Queensland Audit Office: an Insight, Business Links Seminar, Queensland University of Technology, April 21.
Solomons D (1978). 'Poiliticization of Accounting', November. J. Account. pp. 65-72.
Sutton TG (1984). 'Lobbying of Accounting Standard Setting Bodies in the UK and the USA: A Downsian Analysis', Account. Org. Soc. 9(1):81-95.
Talebnia G, Salehi M, Kangarluei S (2011). "A study of the impact of collapse on financial reporting quality of listed companies: Some Iranian evidence", (May), Afr. J. Bus. Manage. 5:3858-3865. Tamlin AR (1997). "The Valuation of Land Under Roads". Valuer Land Econ. 34:230-235.
Tandy P, Wilburn N (1996). 'The Academic Community's Participation in Standard Setting: Submission of Comment Letters on SFAS Nos. 1117', (September). Account. Horizons 10(3):92-111.
Tutticci I, Boocock G, Smith A, Whittaker J (1994). 'Respondent Lobbying in the Australian Accounting Standard Setting Process: ED 49 A Case Study', Account. Audit. Account. J. 7(4):86-104.
Watts RL, Zimmerman JL (1978). 'Towards a Positive Theory of the Determination of Accounting Standards', Account. Rev. 53(1):112-134.

J. Basic. Appl. Sci. Res., 2(10)10111-10117, 2012

ISSN 2090-4304
Journal of Basic and Applied Scientific Research *www.textroad.com*

Social Responsibility Accounting: From Theory to Practice

Mostafa Emami[1], Mehdi Parvizi[2], Ayat TamriNeia[1], Shahram Nemati[2], Maryam Abgineh[3], Sajad Gholami [4]

[1] Young Researchers Club, South Tehran Branch, Islamic Azad University, Tehran, Iran
[2] Eslamabad -e-Gharb Branch, Islamic Azad University, Eslamabad -e-Gharb, Iran
[3] Harsein Branch, Islamic Azad University, Harsein, Iran
[4] Eyvan-e-Gharb Branch, Islamic Azad University, Eyvan -e-Gharb, Iran

ABSTRACT

Social responsibility of organizations has been the most important elements of philosophy, So that it is important to abide by organizations within the social identity theory, Satisfaction of stakeholders outside the organization to legitimate organizations will strengthen.Many of the behaviors and actions of managers and employees, was influenced by moral valuesrooted in ethics. Due to lack of work ethic in management, organizations, societies such as Iran, which was one rich in moral values? The advanced countries have a considerable distance, can create problems for organizations. In addition to increasing the social expectations of organizations, societies, such issues as the environment, women, children, minorities, disabled people, equal employment and staffing reductions, are more sensitive. Organizations ignoring these rights and ethics in dealing with external stakeholders can cause problems for the organization and the organization and action of legitimacy put it, profits, and thus affects the success of the organization.
Poor work ethic, the attitude of jobs, organized and effective managers, can affect the performance of individual, group and organizational influence.
KEY WORDS: accountability, social Accounting, public responsibility, social responsibility.

INTRODUCTION

Due to the complex relationship between the companies in the community and also with the government and those conditions were created in the community that corporations should be accountable not only stakeholders but also to individual people. Companies from the 60s to have realized the importance of social resources so that their importance in social reportingshowed a decade later. In 70s starts and is considered the peak period, accounting and social reporting. Many articles were written in this decade that the social information of interest to managers.

So that, in the first decade of social accounting and social reporting went to many companies many problems also exist in the direction of social reporting and the development of this report is limited in this paper is to point out some problems.(Zhang & Hill, 1998).

Accounting concept of social responsibility in the early 60s by writers such as Anderson, furniture, and Lin was Abs. Anderson should be named as the father of social responsibility accounting. America in the early 70's this concept of America Accounting Association to review the obstacles and problems related to social responsibility was measured in Accounting.

Social responsibility in accounting standards due to pressure from pro-environment and human rights organizations in industrialized countries, the International Federation of Accounts (IFAC) has focused its attention focused on this topic And a series of statements issued in connection with these standards.

J. Basic. Appl. Sci. Res., 2(10)10111-10117, 2012

Reports provided by the financial accounting system, certain aspects of the business unit's performance can be evaluated and business unit profitability and financial strength of the success or failure as the most attention focused on groups that benefit most include(OECD , 2005):

- Actual and potential investors;
- Managers of business units;
- Actual and potential creditors;
- Government agencies;
- Employee business unit; - Customers; - Vendors.

But in America the concept of social responsibility accounting, with a delay in the early seventies, America Accounting Association (AA A) forming a committee to review the obstacles and difficulties related to measuring and reporting process began in the accounting responsibilities and despite the passage of more than

Corresponding Author: Mehdi Parvizi, Eslamabad -e-Gharb Branch, Islamic Azad University, Eslamabad -e-Gharb, Iran.

four decades, this concept is still in early stages of the latest accounting issues to take over and run the application and not much progress has so far been published in most papers, the More descriptive and based on concepts described, less attention to implementation and provide appropriate solutions to practical problems it had.

Of foreign works, the group of business activities and results of operations that go beyond the stated interest groups, and works like the social costs, social benefits and social returns are included.

Social accounting

Social accounting is part of the knowledge of accounting and reporting that aims to measure the social effects (social costs and benefits) arising from the business unit's activities.(McNamara, 1999).

Since each business unit is part of a community that works and is constantly interacting with other community members And incomplete contracts by citing social and community members that have been enacted to protect the interests of all, it is necessary Business unit is aware of their obligations and responsibilities and know their limits to protect shareholders' interests But other obligations and responsibilities towards other social groups such as creditors, employees, customers and vendors and groups in the community and its surrounding environment feels.

The social accounting can be issued by an organization with information that allows stakeholders to the organization's performance in dealing with social issues (positive and negative) to assess, define (Richmond&Etal 2003).

Social accounting process to collect, measure and report transactions and interactive effects of these transactions between business and society surrounding him Social Accounting and Reporting by measuring the effects of cross-business unit and its surrounding community, to assess the fulfillment of social obligations makes possible.

Social responsibilities, duties and obligations of the organization should help in the maintenance of a society in which the activity will do. ""Understanding Frnch" and "HineStarved" book "management culture" regarding social responsibility write: "social responsibility & duty is the responsibility of private institutions, meaning that adversely impact the social life in which work, do not. This task generally consists of tasks such as: not infected, not discriminated against Drastkhdam, evasion, unethical activities and to inform consumers of product quality. Task is also based on positive participation in community life(Hopkins, 2001).

"Robinson" says the same about "social responsibility is one of the duties and an obligation toward the organization has benefited the community so that the primary goal of maximizing profits if the noble cause." "Keith Davis" believes that "the sense of social responsibility commitment by the managers of business organizations, the private sector as it may decide that the profits for the Institute, improve the welfare of society as a whole."

The other definitions of social responsibility are(Higgins& Vince 1993):

1   - "Social responsibility of management commitment is in addition to maintaining and expanding the organization's interests, individual and general welfare of the community is done."

2   - "Commercial enterprises are working in a society that society has created many opportunities for them to pay profits. Instead, the agencies must be committed to meet the needs and demands of society. Call this commitment to social responsibility. "

3   - "social responsibility, commitment, decision-makers for that general measures in addition to their own interests, also provides improved welfare. In this definition, there are several elements: firstly, social responsibility, an obligation that the institutions should be accountable to its economy. Secondly, the institutions responsible for polluting the environment, discrimination in employment, ignored the needs of their employees (O'Dwyer, 2005).

Products harmful to health and the like that can do damage, avoid. Finally, organizations should allocate financial resources, in improving social welfare majority wider community. Such measures include: helping the country's culture and cultural institutions and improve the quality of life. ". Simply put, organizations should be linked as part of a larger system in which there are, actIt is between management ethics, social responsibility and social commitment with social responsibility, there are differences. In this regard, "Anderson" in his book writes: "The terms of management ethics and social responsibility in relation to compliance with the norms and values and morals of the community and aims to provide managers are hand ... With the difference that social responsibility and ethics in relation to the major issues associated with the behavior of individual managers and employees. ""Stephen Robbins" also wrote about it: "If the concept of social responsibility with the concepts of social commitment and social responsibility, we compare, we realize that social responsibility is in the moderate evolution of social participation. (Social commitment to social responsibility)."One organization, the social commitment of his works to their economic and legal responsibilities to act and no more. In other words, he asked that the law is at least responsible acts. If the organization does not encourage social goal, only to achieve its economic goals are and nothing else. With its social responsibility, an ethical governance framework, adding that it is based on the activities of organizations that have improved the community, doing things that worsen the

10112

condition of society can be avoided. Finally, the social accountability of the organization's capacity to act and move toward the demands and expectations of society(Poesche, 2002).

Assumptions of social responsibility accounting system

Four basic assumption of social responsibility accounting system include:(William , Frederick & Mildred, 2001).

1 - Each business unit has obligations towards its surrounding communities that do not adhere to them.

2 - goods that were previously free, others are not so available for free.

3 - of the inalienable rights of the community that the social obligations, and also the conduct of its business units to increase their awareness and knowledge is required to be based on principles of accounting reporting. Accounting of costs and social benefits to the business units of social return on investment can be calculated.

Framework and the concepts, provides practical viewpoints. As mentioned, one of the goals of social accounting, determination and measurement of net social benefits and social costs and ultimately is a business unit. Accounting profit because only part of this partnership shows based solely on market transactions, measured, and numerous other transactions that simultaneously with the informal economic transactions between business units and the data is ignored. Residents and staff was the first branch to the new bank branch, loss of property values and business units and the area will further the economic downturn. In contrast, if the Bank to expand its branches to act in such neighborhoods and areas, gradually causing the boom in regional and community banks will ultimately increase profitability. For these reasons, non-commercial transactions such as accounting, must recognize the economic transactions and to report. It is essential to the basic concepts such as social dealings; social benefits, Social Structure, Social Capital and Social Net assets are defined.

1 - socialtransactions: Social transactions, dealings and transactions between business units and its surrounding community is the result of economic, business and community decisions and actions around him. These types of transactions that are not reflected in market economies. Identification and reporting of social transactions, as the net effect of net profit in the fiscal period, the appropriate criteria for examining the social impact of business units

.2 - Social benefits: Net social benefits of participation and social effects of business transactions with the financial community during social costs and benefits is achieved. The calculation of social benefits, social benefits should be consistent with true social costs.

3 - Social Structure: Social elements, the informal social groups that have signed a social contract with business units and business unit are responsible for the consequences of its social obligations. The system of social accounting, social rights to this business unit, the account ((social capital)), is the identification and reporting.4 - Social Capital: Social capital, the interests, rights and claims of the social pillars of the business unit. Registration and reporting of such rights and interests may not match the conventional accounting system, but also social capital measurement and reporting as a basis to decide when it will be beneficial to users. Thus, the business unit management in everyday economic decisions, with regard to financial considerations, rights and social interests identified, including the effects and how to establish a new factory on the production environment, employment, public facilities and ... And claims and benefits and expenses that each social group to pursue such measures will take into consideration.5 - Net Social assets: Net social assets, the difference in our community resources and community resources in analysis of business activity in his lifetime.

Different views and opinions in relation to the accounting concept of social responsibility and there is also the appellation. In terms of concept, it is part of a group of financial accounting and knows it is possible to consider expanding the scope of financial accounting and accounting responsibilities to include these groups, only a simple extension of the traditional accounting role. While most groups believe that the accounting system, social responsibilities, principles, and concepts has its own rules, so that it can be a completely separate issue, such as management accounting, cost accounting, governmental accounting and others who knew Its purpose is to deal with social issues:

1 - evaluate the social impact of business activities;

2 - Measuring the social costs and obligations of the entity;

3 - Measuring the social interests of the entity;

4 - Provide internal and external information systems in the community

Trade can help. But the naming of some aspects of the social accounting and social accounting entity called the group, but the term was coined, is the social responsibility accounting. Social costs and social responsibilities resolution of accounting problems, many of the costs can be divided into both categories. Accounting aspects of the concept of social responsibility, we must say that the experts and scholars have provided different definitions of the most important and most common is as follows: know, but other obligations and responsibilities towards other social groups such as creditors, employees, customers and vendors and groups in society and the environment around you. For example, the accounting system, social responsibilities,

reporting the results of business operations costs will be limited to the traditional method of dealing with income, but it is necessary to expand the scope and the costs and benefits in the commercial unit

Benefits and problems of social responsibility accounting system:

The main advantages of the social responsibilities of the accounting system can be pointed to the following:

providing conditions for entering environmental issues in national accounts, which will lead to two results:

First, to provide important information for planning economic and social development at national level;

Second, to provide improved methods and components for the calculation of GDP

Social costs and economic costs of each business unit have grown from the commitments to social and economic entity, which may be due to legal obligations or the entity to be voluntary.

Producers are faced with the problem of social reports, the separation of these two types of costs. Immixture because some of these commitments together, creates problems in drawing the line between them.

While the other may be considered as an economic cost to increase sales volume and ability to compete with other producers while these costs can be looked at as well as economic costs to increase productivityand ultimately increase profitability have been made.

The theoretical basis of accounting for such costs from each other, there are two criteria that include:

1- The aim of an activity or cost criteria;

2- The legal criteria. The first criterion, the cost of that entity to improve its standing with the public can do to contribute to the costs and environmental cleanliness, staff and community education, provision of travel and tourism is the holiday period, will be a social cost, what will be on what they do on the legal requirements. costs to increase profit entity that is done, the economic costs are considered. But the second criteria, legal requirements, criteria for distinguishing the social costs of economic costs will be. Therefore, based on legal expenses that the entity will do, as the economic costs are considered. If the law requires an entity to be used by transportation and environmental health staff and also provide safety equipment, such costs will be social costs, but and costs. But the cost of that legal entity of the request and does not require, as a kind of social costs are considered.

Ducker's first and most important social responsibility and the duty of every institution knows and says it works well if the firm fails to perform its main task, no can do no other. According to him, bankrupt businesses, employers are not good, neither good neighbor, not a member of the party and cannot even provide enough capital to expand its work. Therefore, more work should not be considered. According to Drucker, the "constraint" social responsibility of enterprises, high volume and level of responsibility in performing their mission is successful. This seems very similar to the "Friedman" The main responsibility of its social responsibility to the firm knows economy.

According to Druker, the most important form of social responsibility, legitimacy and authority is restored. Responsibility without authority is meaningless, so the responsibility is always with authority. Therefore, anyone who makes a claim of responsibility, authority is really a lawsuit. Indeed, whoever has the authority, is responsible. He says humor and authoritarian regimes that are at full strength, its own against anyone and anything, do not charge! Thus, Drucker when the firm is asked to accept responsibility for solving one of the troubles and problems of society, think carefully and see whether the authority embodied in this responsibility, it is legitimate or not. If this authority is legitimate and justified, accept responsibility, the responsibility is in fact frowned upon. Due to these constraints and limitations, firms do indeed have Responsibilities? According to Drucker, the social responsibilities of firms can be outlined as follows: Responsible products and services: firm and its managers responsible for the consequences and effects of its products and the consequences should, be held responsible. Processes responsible for: firm and its managers are responsible for the production processes. Social costs of production and production processes should not be necessary if conditions, such a situation occurs, the rate must be at least as much as possible. For example, if the target firm, chipboard manufacturer is considered to be supplying the raw material from forests, this should not be associated with the destruction of forest resources. Exploitation of forests must be a way that did not damage it. On the other hand, care must be taken in the production process so that its losses "especially glues and chemicals" does not pollute the environment. Aerosols and dust control, and in cases such as the inevitable noise pollution, damage to reach the lowest possible. The problem is considered transparency in financial statements. Financial statements to be prepared so that all stakeholders such as universities and the whole community to be used. In the Europe Union to the international standards and is interested in approaching

But something was not adopted as international standards in Europe standard board have made this work Krdndv something like Germany and France and Italy.

What social report should be prepared to gain the satisfaction of shareholders?

But I think from my perspective to environmental issues, financial issues, particularly if used in conjunction

with institutions that are particularly sensitive issues that they demonstrated. (Financial problems in the financial crisis that already exists) (Zhang & Hill, 1998).

10114

Generally there are three approaches in corporate social responsibility concept that can be explained as follows: First of classical economic theory, theories of origin is. According to this concept and the company has only one goal to maximize profits and consequently maximize the shareholders wealth. This concept has so far been accepted and supported the effort to achieve the goal of ethical and legal framework exist. The second theory is presented in the 1970s and based on social goals related to bringing maximum benefit to be considered. According to this theory, corporate managers must make decisions that are between the rights of shareholders, employees, customers and the general public to create balance. The result should be a coalition and solidarity between the various interests and concerns, and this coalition is the only way the company from the Max to ensure long-term profits. This decision is necessary organization in order to maximize profits rather than trying to earn the profit level that is appropriate and will provide a good level of social goals. Theresults of their activities are considered. And organizational decisions based on those ways in which society creates more responsibility must be taken. On this basis, to achieve social and economic welfare based on the theory and May lead to decisions based mentality is not helpful to the community. The government's role as a determinant of power is remarkable. Lobbying the government may be done in three(OECD , 2005):Determine the social and illegal activities.) adopt rules and laws in order to limit the activities of the community itself had been useful, but without enforcement it is disadvantageous to the health community.) dealing with a series of activities that have social costs and negative effects on the community. As for the taxes to pay for damages to the community.The main purpose of such taxes to encourage companies to reduce the effects of such activities and control them.Azbhs about the nature of government regulation to solve social problems is characterized in that the definition of corporate social responsibility is very difficult.

Profits and social responsibility in companies: You can also profit companies, they operate in? Yes, sometimes the idea that companies are required to take interest and benefit of the way is fundamentally incorrect. Currently, large companies frequently claim that the financial goals are to think of social services. Management Association and the United Nations, encourage companies to follow such a line. No wonder that this interesting idea has already attracted numerous people, because they benefit both companies' social responsibilities of the cases where private interests and public interests are equals, the idea of corporate social responsibility seems to be irrelevant. Companies to increase profits, the resort to do anything, will ultimately lead to increased social welfare, but on condition that the interests and welfare are in direct contrast, almost no recourse to social responsibility will result, because managers are reluctant interest in public affairs act against the interests of shareholders. Companies should private interests or public interests are the way in, they choose, but sometimes the situation is more difficult than a simple choice. When the interests and conflicts of interests are focusing on social responsibility, more effective measures to enhance social welfare will delay. Since companies are expected to provide a solution to deal with problems, real solutions are not ignored. Proper performance and profitability: For a better understanding of the concepts of private and public interests, the circumstances of which we have no contradiction with the interests and welfare. Consider the market for healthy foods. Fast market to attract customers who offering suggestions are important to your health choices such as salads and other benefits are many.Other companies with a focus on low fat foods, whole grains and other foods to the public interest, their income.Progress in various fields of social welfare because investors are successful. Similarly, auto manufacturers to meet the needs of consumers and producers less fuel and benefit the environment, as well as numerous companies have benefited by increasing welfare and reducing energy consumption and costs, have found the frequency of the profit.But the motives and strategies, these are not social welfare. Healthy food and fuel for vehicles with less time for their manufacturers, with no benefit, not common. Many of the company until the energy value was not increased to this size did not matter to preserve energy. Until such companies are to benefit the community take steps towards their interests. Less effect on changing the ways that social activists have emphasized. The goal is to increase profits, not the organization's commitment towards social responsibilities, but in such cases has been proven that the methods of social activities for the benefit of society. Unfortunately, the use of the opportunities presented by companies to social welfare and the interest is persona (Mcnamara, 1999).

Conclusions

J. Basic. Appl. Sci. Res., 2(10)10111-10117, 2012

Since the relationship between the social, political, environmental, economic, trade has been increasing, organizations are faced with new dynamism. The challenge facing organizations is that they need time to increase profitability and respond to new social expectations and the simultaneous administration of these two seemingly contradictory outcomes that require Develop practical strategies and has positive effects on society and on the organization's reach. Implementation of social responsibility in organizations, including the mechanisms and strategies are effective in this regard. In fact, many organizations in addition to their traditional tasks are required to perform other activities, the purpose of these activities, responding to the expectations of society and its organizations are referred to as social responsibility. In this period, effective management, the

10115

management of ideas within their organizations and to release the built environment and wider society thinks, Why not separate from society organizations can make their Society cannot continue without the organization.

Corporate income and also long-term risk of future profit company, will oppose. Resorting to social responsibility, none of the above does not solve the problems of pressure from shareholders on a sustainable growth in profitability, will fix the problem and causing managers with incentives to replace incompetent managers are focusing on the long-term goals The company will compensate the damages. Choices(Richmond&Etal 2003). Otherwise, it would solve these problems long ago. The best example in this regard, it is industrial pollution. Manufacturers to reduce pollution, high cost of factory pay dividends. Poverty, another example is given.(Hess ,2001).

Companies could pay higher wages to workers, lower costs for products, reduce poverty, in this case the losses were incurred. In such circumstances, regardless of whether managers should pay attention to their social role of corporate interests? Can assume that should happen, but in practice expect managers to focus solely on social responsibility. Duty and responsibility of managers to increase profits in the company's shareholders. Even if the directors of the company regardless of who is to benefit society, they will certainly lose their jobs, because shareholders, hiring managers that keep profits at the highest level possible. In such circumstances, the move towards the social responsibilities of management is in conflict because of the expected management task is in line with shareholder interests, directors should otherwise have to think of another job. Many companies in social responsibility not only speak and do virtually nothing and it is due to tactical called Green washing. (Which supporters claim are environmentally friendly).Managers of the company profits in order to lose Mamas No, actually impose tax on the shareholders and decide how to spend its own arbitrary will, and instead of the elected government officials are even on a small scale. Private companies are a different story. If the manager to raise social welfare is willing to accept lower profits, the shareholders should not impose such. The successful managers of public companies, private investors wishing to spend part of their charitable purposes, like many companies that has been active in charity work, but managers should not private companies using shareholder capital, realize their philanthropic goals. In fact, the majority shareholder, significant amounts of their incomes from investment spending to help charities, or other methods to help improve social welfare are. Of course this does not mean that companies are free regardless of social consequences following their huge profits.(Cherry, 1978).

However, resorting to corporate social responsibility through effective balance between corporate profits Vnf not public. Theregulations: The best way to bring balance profit public benefit corporation and is The best way is to bind the organization. The government has the power to enforce rules and would no longer need to rely on people.But government regulation is not perfect and sometimes due to decreased cost and inefficiency welfare. Industrial groups to influence policy in ways that are mostly useless, used or intended use of the expensive resort to profitability. Public corruption, the situation is worse, plus, all the causes of government failure in developing countries due to weak and often corrupt governments worsened. Despite all the problems, governments, trade unions towards social responsibility, more effective role in support of their common interests. Observers and supporters: Civil society as observers and supporters, and provide an important role in imposing the kind of behavior is integrated into the social welfare is reduced. Types of nonprofit organizations and movements for a broad range of interests of different views of social, political, environmental, ethnic, social and cultural offer. For example, «Rainforest Action Network», an organization that often works in the field of environmental protection and natural resource consumption. The website mentioned that the campaign to increase public sensitivity towards the environment and consumers is that environmental degradation and stigma spot for U.S. companies to know and this nightmare is to accept responsibility liability policies are adopted to preserve the environment. This approach tries to convince managers that we are in the interests of the community, is quite different because in this case does not adversely affect the financial balance sheets. Generally, such a hypothesis is specified and cannot record it as a way to impose restrictions on the behavior of the main labor union presidents, especially in most developing countries that lack sufficient resources to the influence of civil society and people to the release shares are not sufficient. Its branches were: Another alternative is the creation of autonomous systems, but it is on the same forms of social responsibility strategy. This means that investment firms are unlikely to benefit shareholders in the public interest. The system of regulations that the government will be and variable environmental conditions, reaction is more efficient. Emphasis on transparency, commitment and consistent with what people expect from the concerns of governmental laws and approaches to this system. Morph types responsible government to ensure autonomy, according to the standards. If the industry in order to be successful, government must intervene and to enforce its regulations. Financialestimates: Finally, other aspects such as social responsibility of business managers are charged. Only safe and effective for long-term decisions, impose penalties, such as regular supervision, taxes, criminal penalties and public embarrassment, for social behavior is unacceptable.Social responsibility theory of trade, which is only accepted by managers Bazkavty know when work is done correctly, it should focus on the profit.Conclusion:Research has shown that managers tend to be limited to corporate social reporting in accordance with the shareholder wealth maximization should be used. Research has also shown that managers believe that social pressures are causing companies to respond ((O'Dwyer, 2005).

10116

Consistent with the rules seem to be companies that led to the development and delivery of appropriate social reports

REFERENCES

Cherry, Alan Abraham(1978)."Testing the Effects of Social Accountig Information on Desisio Making And Attitudes A Laboratory Expriment." A dissertation submitted in partial fulfillment of the requirement for the degree of Doctor of philosophy (management). University of California-Los Angeles

Hess, David(2001). "Reguulation Corporate Social Performance- A New Look At Social Accounting. Auditing and Reporting." Business Ethics Quarterly, Vol. 11, No. 2, pp. 307-330.

O'Dwyer, Brendan (2005). "Stakeholder democracy- challenges and contributions from social accounting." Business Et‿ihics: A European Review, Vol. 14, No. 1, pp.28-41.

Richmond, Betty Jane Etal (2003). " Social Accounting for Nonprofits-Two Models." Nonprofit Management & Leadership, Vol. 13, No. 4, pp.308-324.

Hopkins willie E,(2001)» Diversity And Organizationapplreformance» ,Routledge,Ny,120-128

Higgins, J M. &Vincze J.W. (1993) ," Strategic Management Concepts", Fort Worth,Tx: Dyden. McNamara,carter, (1999), «Complete Guide To Ethics Management»,

Poesche,(2002)»Agile Manufacturing Straegy& Business Ethics»,Journal Of Business Ethics 38,No.4

OECD Productinty Database, (2005), www.axiss.com.au/assets/document/ Buckly M. R. ,Ds.Beu,D. D. Frink (2001)»Ethical Issues in Human Resources Systems»,Human Resource Management Review,No.11,11-29.

William C. Frederick and Mildred S. Myers, (2001)."The Hidden Politics of Social Auditing".Business andSociety Review.

Zhang, J., I. Fraser and W.Y. Hill, (1998) A Comparative Study of Social Audit Models and Reports. GlasgowCaledonian University, UK.

J. Basic. Appl. Sci. Res., 2(10)10111-10117, 2012

10117

J. Basic. Appl. Sci. Res., 2(10)10111-10117, 2012

ISSN 2090-4304
Journal of Basic and Applied Scientific Research *www.textroad.com*

Social Responsibility Accounting: From Theory to Practice

Sajad Gholami[1], Mehdi Parvizi[2], Ayat TamriNeia[1], Shahram Nemati[2], Maryam Abgineh[3], Mostafa Emami[4]

1 Eyvan-e-Gharb Branch, Islamic Azad University, Eyvan -e-Gharb, Iran
2 Eslamabad -e-Gharb Branch, Islamic Azad University, Eslamabad -e-Gharb, Iran
3 Harsein Branch, Islamic Azad University, Harsein, Iran
4

Young Researchers Club, Kermanshah Branch, Islamic Azad University, Kermanshah, Iran

ABSTRACT

Social responsibility of organizations has been the most important elements of philosophy, So that it is important to abide by organizations within the social identity theory, Satisfaction of stakeholders outside the organization to legitimate organizations will strengthen.Many of the behaviors and actions of managers and employees, was influenced by moral valuesrooted in ethics. Due to lack of work ethic in management, organizations, societies such as Iran, which was one rich in moral values? The advanced countries have a considerable distance, can create problems for organizations. In addition to increasing the social expectations of organizations, societies, such issues as the environment, women, children, minorities, disabled people, equal employment and staffing reductions, are more sensitive. Organizations ignoring these rights and ethics in dealing with external stakeholders can cause problems for the organization and the organization and action of legitimacy put it, profits, and thus affects the success of the organization.
 Poor work ethic, the attitude of jobs, organized and effective managers, can affect the performance of individual, group and organizational influence.
KEY WORDS: accountability, social Accounting, public responsibility, social responsibility.

INTRODUCTION

Due to the complex relationship between the companies in the community and also with the government and those conditions were created in the community that corporations should be accountable not only stakeholders but also to individual people. Companies from the 60s to have realized the importance of social resources so that their importance in social reportingshowed a decade later.   In 70s starts and is considered the peak period, accounting and social reporting. Many articles were written in this decade that the social information of interest to managers.

So that, in the first decade of social accounting and social reporting went to many companies many problems also exist in the direction of social reporting and the development of this report is limited in this paper is to point out some problems.(Zhang & Hill, 1998).

Accounting concept of social responsibility in the early 60s by writers such as Anderson, furniture, and Lin was Abs. Anderson should be named as the father of social responsibility accounting. America in the early 70's this concept of America Accounting Association to review the obstacles and problems related to social responsibility was measured in Accounting.

Social responsibility in accounting standards due to pressure from pro-environment and human rights organizations in industrialized countries, the International Federation of Accounts (IFAC) has focused its attention focused on this topic And a series of statements issued in connection with these standards.

Reports provided by the financial accounting system, certain aspects of the business unit's performance can be evaluated and business unit profitability and financial strength of the success or failure as the most attention focused on groups that benefit most include(OECD , 2005):

-Actual and potential investors;
- Managers of business units;
- Actual and potential creditors;
- Government agencies;
- Employee business unit; - Customers; - Vendors.

But in America the concept of social responsibility accounting, with a delay in the early seventies, America Accounting Association (AA A) forming a committee to review the obstacles and difficulties related to measuring and reporting process began in the accounting responsibilities and despite the passage of more than

---

Corresponding Author: Mehdi Parvizi, Eslamabad -e-Gharb Branch, Islamic Azad University, Eslamabad -e-Gharb, Iran.

four decades, this concept is still in early stages of the latest accounting issues to take over and run the application and not much progress has so far been published in most papers, the More descriptive and based on concepts described, less attention to implementation and provide appropriate solutions to practical problems it had.

Of foreign works, the group of business activities and results of operations that go beyond the stated interest groups, and works like the social costs, social benefits and social returns are included.

Social accounting

Social accounting is part of the knowledge of accounting and reporting that aims to measure the social effects (social costs and benefits) arising from the business unit's activities.(McNamara, 1999).

Since each business unit is part of a community that works and is constantly interacting with other community members And incomplete contracts by citing social and community members that have been enacted to protect the interests of all, it is necessary Business unit is aware of their obligations and responsibilities and know their limits to protect shareholders' interests But other obligations and responsibilities towards other social groups such as creditors, employees, customers and vendors and groups in the community and its surrounding environment feels.

The social accounting can be issued by an organization with information that allows stakeholders to the organization's performance in dealing with social issues (positive and negative) to assess, define (Richmond&Etal 2003).

Social accounting process to collect, measure and report transactions and interactive effects of these transactions between business and society surrounding him Social Accounting and Reporting by measuring the effects of cross-business unit and its surrounding community, to assess the fulfillment of social obligations makes possible.

Social responsibilities, duties and obligations of the organization should help in the maintenance of a society in which the activity will do. ""Understanding Frnch" and "HineStarved" book "management culture" regarding social responsibility write: "social responsibility & duty is the responsibility of private institutions, meaning that adversely impact the social life in which work, do not. This task generally consists of tasks such as: not infected, not discriminated against Drastkhdam, evasion, unethical activities and to inform consumers of product quality. Task is also based on positive participation in community life(Hopkins, 2001).

"Robinson" says the same about "social responsibility is one of the duties and an obligation toward the organization has benefited the community so that the primary goal of maximizing profits if the noble cause." "Keith Davis" believes that "the sense of social responsibility commitment by the managers of business organizations, the private sector as it may decide that the profits for the Institute, improve the welfare of society as a whole."

The other definitions of social responsibility are(Higgins& Vince 1993):

1   - "Social responsibility of management commitment is in addition to maintaining and expanding the organization's interests, individual and general welfare of the community is done."

2   - "Commercial enterprises are working in a society that society has created many opportunities for them to pay profits. Instead, the agencies must be committed to meet the needs and demands of society. Call this commitment to social responsibility. "

3   - "social responsibility, commitment, decision-makers for that general measures in addition to their own interests, also provides improved welfare. In this definition, there are several elements: firstly, social responsibility, an obligation that the institutions should be accountable to its economy. Secondly, the institutions responsible for polluting the environment, discrimination in employment, ignored the needs of their employees (O'Dwyer, 2005).

Products harmful to health and the like that can do damage, avoid. Finally, organizations should allocate financial resources, in improving social welfare majority wider community. Such measures include: helping the country's culture and cultural institutions and improve the quality of life. ". Simply put, organizations should be linked as part of a larger system in which there are, actIt is between management ethics, social responsibility and social commitment with social responsibility, there are differences. In this regard, "Anderson" in his book writes: "The terms of management ethics and social responsibility in relation to compliance with the norms and values and morals of the community and aims to provide managers are hand ... With the difference that social responsibility and ethics in relation to the major issues associated with the behavior of individual managers and employees. ""Stephen Robbins" also wrote about it: "If the concept of social responsibility with the concepts of social commitment and social responsibility, we compare, we realize that social responsibility is in the moderate evolution of social participation. (Social commitment to social responsibility)."One organization, the social commitment of his works to their economic and legal responsibilities to act and no more. In other words, he asked that the law is at least responsible acts. If the organization does not encourage social goal, only to achieve its economic goals are and nothing else. With its social responsibility, an ethical governance framework, adding that it is based on the activities of organizations that have improved the community, doing things that worsen the

10112

condition of society can be avoided. Finally, the social accountability of the organization's capacity to act and move toward the demands and expectations of society(Poesche, 2002).

Assumptions of social responsibility accounting system

Four basic assumption of social responsibility accounting system include:(William , Frederick & Mildred, 2001).

1   - Each business unit has obligations towards its surrounding communities that do not adhere to them.

2   - goods that were previously free, others are not so available for free.

3   - of the inalienable rights of the community that the social obligations, and also the conduct of its business units to increase their awareness and knowledge is required to be based on principles of accounting reporting. Accounting of costs and social benefits to the business units of social return on investment can be calculated.

Framework and the concepts, provides practical viewpoints. As mentioned, one of the goals of social accounting, determination and measurement of net social benefits and social costs and ultimately is a business unit. Accounting profit because only part of this partnership shows based solely on market transactions, measured, and numerous other transactions that simultaneously with the informal economic transactions between business units and the data is ignored. Residents and staff was the first branch to the new bank branch, loss of property values and business units and the area will further the economic downturn. In contrast, if the Bank to expand its branches to act in such neighborhoods and areas, gradually causing the boom in regional and community banks will ultimately increase profitability. For these reasons, non-commercial transactions such as accounting, must recognize the economic transactions and to report. It is essential to the basic concepts such as social dealings; social benefits, Social Structure, Social Capital and Social Net assets are defined.

1 - socialtransactions: Social transactions, dealings and transactions between business units and its surrounding community is the result of economic, business and community decisions and actions around him. These types of transactions that are not reflected in market economies. Identification and reporting of social transactions, as the net effect of net profit in the fiscal period, the appropriate criteria for examining the social impact of business units

.2 - Social benefits: Net social benefits of participation and social effects of business transactions with the financial community during social costs and benefits is achieved. The calculation of social benefits, social benefits should be consistent with true social costs.

3 - Social Structure: Social elements, the informal social groups that have signed a social contract with business units and business unit are responsible for the consequences of its social obligations. The system of social accounting, social rights to this business unit, the account ((social capital)), is the identification and reporting.4 - Social Capital: Social capital, the interests, rights and claims of the social pillars of the business unit. Registration and reporting of such rights and interests may not match the conventional accounting system, but also social capital measurement and reporting as a basis to decide when it will be beneficial to users. Thus, the business unit management in everyday economic decisions, with regard to financial considerations, rights and social interests identified, including the effects and how to establish a new factory on the production environment, employment, public facilities and ... And claims and benefits and expenses that each social group to pursue such measures will take into consideration.5 - Net Social assets: Net social assets, the difference in our community resources and community resources in analysis of business activity in his lifetime.

Different views and opinions in relation to the accounting concept of social responsibility and there is also the appellation. In terms of concept, it is part of a group of financial accounting and knows it is possible to consider expanding the scope of financial accounting and accounting responsibilities to include these groups, only a simple extension of the traditional accounting role. While most groups believe that the accounting system, social responsibilities, principles, and concepts has its own rules, so that it can be a completely separate issue, such as management accounting, cost accounting, governmental accounting and others who knew Its purpose is to deal with social issues:

1 - evaluate the social impact of business activities;

2 - Measuring the social costs and obligations of the entity;

3 - Measuring the social interests of the entity;

4 - Provide internal and external information systems in the community

Trade can help. But the naming of some aspects of the social accounting and social accounting entity called the group, but the term was coined, is the social responsibility accounting. Social costs and social responsibilities resolution of accounting problems, many of the costs can be divided into both categories. Accounting aspects of the concept of social responsibility, we must say that the experts and scholars have provided different definitions of the most important and most common is as follows: know, but other obligations and responsibilities towards other social groups such as creditors, employees, customers and vendors and groups in society and the environment around you. For example, the accounting system, social responsibilities,

10113

reporting the results of business operations costs will be limited to the traditional method of dealing with income, but it is necessary to expand the scope and the costs and benefits in the commercial unit

Benefits and problems of social responsibility accounting system:

The main advantages of the social responsibilities of the accounting system can be pointed to the following:

providing conditions for entering environmental issues in national accounts, which will lead to two results:

First, to provide important information for planning economic and social development at national level;

Second, to provide improved methods and components for the calculation of GDP

Social costs and economic costs of each business unit have grown from the commitments to social and economic entity, which may be due to legal obligations or the entity to be voluntary.

Producers are faced with the problem of social reports, the separation of these two types of costs. Immixture because some of these commitments together, creates problems in drawing the line between them.

While the other may be considered as an economic cost to increase sales volume and ability to compete with other producers while these costs can be looked at as well as economic costs to increase productivityand ultimately increase profitability have been made.

The theoretical basis of accounting for such costs from each other, there are two criteria that include:

1- The aim of an activity or cost criteria;

2- The legal criteria. The first criterion, the cost of that entity to improve its standing with the public can do to contribute to the costs and environmental cleanliness, staff and community education, provision of travel and tourism is the holiday period, will be a social cost, what will be on what they do on the legal requirements. costs to increase profit entity that is done, the economic costs are considered. But the second criteria, legal requirements, criteria for distinguishing the social costs of economic costs will be. Therefore, based on legal expenses that the entity will do, as the economic costs are considered. If the law requires an entity to be used by transportation and environmental health staff and also provide safety equipment, such costs will be social costs, but and costs. But the cost of that legal entity of the request and does not require, as a kind of social costs are considered.

Ducker's first and most important social responsibility and the duty of every institution knows and says it works well if the firm fails to perform its main task, no can do no other. According to him, bankrupt businesses, employers are not good, neither good neighbor, not a member of the party and cannot even provide enough capital to expand its work. Therefore, more work should not be considered. According to Drucker, the "constraint" social responsibility of enterprises, high volume and level of responsibility in performing their mission is successful. This seems very similar to the "Friedman" The main responsibility of its social responsibility to the firm knows economy.

According to Druker, the most important form of social responsibility, legitimacy and authority is restored. Responsibility without authority is meaningless, so the responsibility is always with authority. Therefore, anyone who makes a claim of responsibility, authority is really a lawsuit. Indeed, whoever has the authority, is responsible. He says humor and authoritarian regimes that are at full strength, its own against anyone and anything, do not charge! Thus, Drucker when the firm is asked to accept responsibility for solving one of the troubles and problems of society, think carefully and see whether the authority embodied in this responsibility, it is legitimate or not. If this authority is legitimate and justified, accept responsibility, the responsibility is in fact frowned upon. Due to these constraints and limitations, firms do indeed have Responsibilities? According to Drucker, the social responsibilities of firms can be outlined as follows: Responsible products and services: firm and its managers responsible for the consequences and effects of its products and the consequences should, be held responsible. Processes responsible for: firm and its managers are responsible for the production processes. Social costs of production and production processes should not be necessary if conditions, such a situation occurs, the rate must be at least as much as possible. For example, if the target firm, chipboard manufacturer is considered to be supplying the raw material from forests, this should not be associated with the destruction of forest resources. Exploitation of forests must be a way that did not damage it. On the other hand, care must be taken in the production process so that its losses "especially glues and chemicals" does not pollute the environment. Aerosols and dust control, and in cases such as the inevitable noise pollution, damage to reach the lowest possible. The problem is considered transparency in financial statements. Financial statements to be prepared so that all stakeholders such as universities and the whole community to be used. In the Europe Union to the international standards and is interested in approaching

But something was not adopted as international standards in Europe standard board have made this work Krdndv something like Germany and France and Italy.

What social report should be prepared to gain the satisfaction of shareholders?

But I think from my perspective to environmental issues, financial issues, particularly if used in conjunction

with institutions that are particularly sensitive issues that they demonstrated. (Financial problems in the financial crisis that already exists) (Zhang & Hill, 1998).

10114

Generally there are three approaches in corporate social responsibility concept that can be explained as follows: First of classical economic theory, theories of origin is. According to this concept and the company has only one goal to maximize profits and consequently maximize the shareholders wealth. This concept has so far been accepted and supported the effort to achieve the goal of ethical and legal framework exist. The second theory is presented in the 1970s and based on social goals related to bringing maximum benefit to be considered. According to this theory, corporate managers must make decisions that are between the rights of shareholders, employees, customers and the general public to create balance. The result should be a coalition and solidarity between the various interests and concerns, and this coalition is the only way the company from the Max to ensure long-term profits. This decision is necessary organization in order to maximize profits rather than trying to earn the profit level that is appropriate and will provide a good level of social goals. Theresults of their activities are considered. And organizational decisions based on those ways in which society creates more responsibility must be taken. On this basis, to achieve social and economic welfare based on the theory and May lead to decisions based mentality is not helpful to the community. The government's role as a determinant of power is remarkable. Lobbying the government may be done in three(OECD , 2005):Determine the social and illegal activities.) adopt rules and laws in order to limit the activities of the community itself had been useful, but without enforcement it is disadvantageous to the health community.) dealing with a series of activities that have social costs and negative effects on the community. As for the taxes to pay for damages to the community.The main purpose of such taxes to encourage companies to reduce the effects of such activities and control them.Azbhs about the nature of government regulation to solve social problems is characterized in that the definition of corporate social responsibility is very difficult.

Profits and social responsibility in companies: You can also profit companies, they operate in? Yes, sometimes the idea that companies are required to take interest and benefit of the way is fundamentally incorrect. Currently, large companies frequently claim that the financial goals are to think of social services. Management Association and the United Nations, encourage companies to follow such a line. No wonder that this interesting idea has already attracted numerous people, because they benefit both companies' social responsibilities of the cases where private interests and public interests are equals, the idea of corporate social responsibility seems to be irrelevant. Companies to increase profits, the resort to do anything, will ultimately lead to increased social welfare, but on condition that the interests and welfare are in direct contrast, almost no recourse to social responsibility will result, because managers are reluctant interest in public affairs act against the interests of shareholders. Companies should private interests or public interests are the way in, they choose, but sometimes the situation is more difficult than a simple choice. When the interests and conflicts of interests are focusing on social responsibility, more effective measures to enhance social welfare will delay. Since companies are expected to provide a solution to deal with problems, real solutions are not ignored. Proper performance and profitability: For a better understanding of the concepts of private and public interests, the circumstances of which we have no contradiction with the interests and welfare. Consider the market for healthy foods. Fast market to attract customers who offering suggestions are important to your health choices such as salads and other benefits are many.Other companies with a focus on low fat foods, whole grains and other foods to the public interest, their income.Progress in various fields of social welfare because investors are successful. Similarly, auto manufacturers to meet the needs of consumers and producers less fuel and benefit the environment, as well as numerous companies have benefited by increasing welfare and reducing energy consumption and costs, have found the frequency of the profit.But the motives and strategies, these are not social welfare. Healthy food and fuel for vehicles with less time for their manufacturers, with no benefit, not common. Many of the company until the energy value was not increased to this size did not matter to preserve energy. Until such companies are to benefit the community take steps towards their interests. Less effect on changing the ways that social activists have emphasized. The goal is to increase profits, not the organization's commitment towards social responsibilities, but in such cases has been proven that the methods of social activities for the benefit of society. Unfortunately, the use of the opportunities presented by companies to social welfare and the interest is persona (Mcnamara, 1999).

Conclusions

Since the relationship between the social, political, environmental, economic, trade has been increasing, organizations are faced with new dynamism. The challenge facing organizations is that they need time to increase profitability and respond to new social expectations and the simultaneous administration of these two seemingly contradictory outcomes that require Develop practical strategies and has positive effects on society and on the organization's reach. Implementation of social responsibility in organizations, including the mechanisms and strategies are effective in this regard. In fact, many organizations in addition to their traditional tasks are required to perform other activities, the purpose of these activities, responding to the expectations of society and its organizations are referred to as social responsibility. In this period, effective management, the

10115

management of ideas within their organizations and to release the built environment and wider society thinks, Why not separate from society organizations can make their Society cannot continue without the organization.

Corporate income and also long-term risk of future profit company, will oppose. Resorting to social responsibility, none of the above does not solve the problems of pressure from shareholders on a sustainable growth in profitability, will fix the problem and causing managers with incentives to replace incompetent managers are focusing on the long-term goals The company will compensate the damages. Choices(Richmond&Etal 2003). Otherwise, it would solve these problems long ago. The best example in this regard, it is industrial pollution. Manufacturers to reduce pollution, high cost of factory pay dividends. Poverty, another example is given.(Hess ,2001).

Companies could pay higher wages to workers, lower costs for products, reduce poverty, in this case the losses were incurred. In such circumstances, regardless of whether managers should pay attention to their social role of corporate interests? Can assume that should happen, but in practice expect managers to focus solely on social responsibility. Duty and responsibility of managers to increase profits in the company's shareholders. Even if the directors of the company regardless of who is to benefit society, they will certainly lose their jobs, because shareholders, hiring managers that keep profits at the highest level possible. In such circumstances, the move towards the social responsibilities of management is in conflict because of the expected management task is in line with shareholder interests, directors should otherwise have to think of another job. Many companies in social responsibility not only speak and do virtually nothing and it is due to tactical called Green washing. (Which supporters claim are environmentally friendly).Managers of the company profits in order to lose Mamas No, actually impose tax on the shareholders and decide how to spend its own arbitrary will, and instead of the elected government officials are even on a small scale. Private companies are a different story. If the manager to raise social welfare is willing to accept lower profits, the shareholders should not impose such. The successful managers of public companies, private investors wishing to spend part of their charitable purposes, like many companies that has been active in charity work, but managers should not private companies using shareholder capital, realize their philanthropic goals. In fact, the majority shareholder, significant amounts of their incomes from investment spending to help charities, or other methods to help improve social welfare are. Of course this does not mean that companies are free regardless of social consequences following their huge profits.(Cherry, 1978).

However, resorting to corporate social responsibility through effective balance between corporate profits Vnf not public. Theregulations: The best way to bring balance profit public benefit corporation and is The best way is to bind the organization. The government has the power to enforce rules and would no longer need to rely on people.But government regulation is not perfect and sometimes due to decreased cost and inefficiency welfare. Industrial groups to influence policy in ways that are mostly useless, used or intended use of the expensive resort to profitability. Public corruption, the situation is worse, plus, all the causes of government failure in developing countries due to weak and often corrupt governments worsened. Despite all the problems, governments, trade unions towards social responsibility, more effective role in support of their common interests. Observers and supporters: Civil society as observers and supporters, and provide an important role in imposing the kind of behavior is integrated into the social welfare is reduced. Types of nonprofit organizations and movements for a broad range of interests of different views of social, political, environmental, ethnic, social and cultural offer. For example, «Rainforest Action Network», an organization that often works in the field of environmental protection and natural resource consumption. The website mentioned that the campaign to increase public sensitivity towards the environment and consumers is that environmental degradation and stigma spot for U.S. companies to know and this nightmare is to accept responsibility liability policies are adopted to preserve the environment. This approach tries to convince managers that we are in the interests of the community, is quite different because in this case does not adversely affect the financial balance sheets. Generally, such a hypothesis is specified and cannot record it as a way to impose restrictions on the behavior of the main labor union presidents, especially in most developing countries that lack sufficient resources to the influence of civil society and people to the release shares are not sufficient. Its branches were: Another alternative is the creation of autonomous systems, but it is on the same forms of social responsibility strategy. This means that investment firms are unlikely to benefit shareholders in the public interest. The system of regulations that the government will be and variable environmental conditions, reaction is more efficient. Emphasis on transparency, commitment and consistent with what people expect from the concerns of governmental laws and approaches to this system. Morph types responsible government to ensure autonomy, according to the standards. If the industry in order to be successful, government must intervene and to enforce its regulations. Financialestimates: Finally, other aspects such as social responsibility of business managers are charged. Only safe and effective for long-term decisions, impose penalties, such as regular supervision, taxes, criminal penalties and public embarrassment, for social behavior is unacceptable.Social responsibility theory of trade, which is only accepted by managers Bazkavty know when work is done correctly, it should focus on the profit.Conclusion:Research has shown that managers tend to be limited to corporate social reporting in accordance with the shareholder wealth maximization should be used. Research has also shown that managers believe that social pressures are causing companies to respond ((O'Dwyer, 2005).

10116

Consistent with the rules seem to be companies that led to the development and delivery of appropriate social reports

REFERENCES

Cherry, Alan Abraham(1978)."Testing the Effects of Social Accountig Information on Desisio Making And Attitudes A Laboratory Expriment." A dissertation submitted in partial fulfillment of the requirement for the degree of Doctor of philosophy (management). University of California-Los Angeles

Hess, David(2001). "Reguulation Corporate Social Performance- A New Look At Social Accounting. Auditing and Reporting." Business Ethics Quarterly, Vol. 11, No. 2, pp. 307-330.

O'Dwyer, Brendan (2005). "Stakeholder democracy- challenges and contributions from social accounting." Business Et⌐ihics: A European Review, Vol. 14, No. 1, pp.28-41.

Richmond, Betty Jane Etal (2003). " Social Accounting for Nonprofits-Two Models." Nonprofit Management & Leadership, Vol. 13, No. 4, pp.308-324.

Hopkins willie E,(2001)» Diversity And Organizationapplreformance» ,Routledge,Ny,120-128

Higgins, J M. &Vincze J.W. (1993) ," Strategic Management Concepts", Fort Worth,Tx: Dyden. McNamara,carter, (1999), «Complete Guide To Ethics Management»,

Poesche,(2002)»Agile Manufacturing Straegy& Business Ethics»,Journal Of Business Ethics 38,No.4

OECD Productinty Database, (2005), www.axiss.com.au/assets/document/ Buckly M. R. ,Ds.Beu,D. D. Frink (2001)»Ethical Issues in Human Resources Systems»,Human Resource Management Review,No.11,11-29.

William C. Frederick and Mildred S. Myers, (2001)."The Hidden Politics of Social Auditing".Business andSociety Review.

Zhang, J., I. Fraser and W.Y. Hill, (1998) A Comparative Study of Social Audit Models and Reports. GlasgowCaledonian University, UK.

10117

European Journal of Scientific Research
ISSN 1450-216X Vol.58 No.4 (2011), pp.532-541
© EuroJournals Publishing, Inc. 2011 http://www.eurojournals.com/ejsr.htm

Job Appropriateness Survey and its Relationship with Staff Organizational Commitment (The Case Study in National Iranian Oil Refining and Distribution Company)

Hamidreza Hassanzadeh
Faculty Member of Tehran University
E-mail: Drhassanzadeh@gmail.com

Mostafa Emami
D   D*Faculty Member of Tarbiat Modares University*

Mahdi Beiruti
Student of Payam-Noor University

Reza Abachian Ghasemi
Student of MBA at Tehran University

Vahid Fahimi
Student of MBA at Tehran University

Abstract

Job Consistency (job-employed fit) is a basic issue in human resource management. The assumption has been approved that existence of this appropriateness of organizational necessity is for human resource productivity.

There fore ,the main purpose of this article is studying job consistency and its relationship with organizational commitment of national Iranian oil refining and distributing company head qarters Staff .Information collection tools for measurement of organizational commitment was Allen and Meyer questionnaire including 15 questions and for measuring Occupational proportion the Knowledge questionnaires ,Job skill and ability of international job databank (occuptional Information Network)were used .Each of the questionnaires on the average includes 21 questions. Stability of organizational Commitment questionnaire was 0.89 and stability of job fit measurement was 0.87 , because kronbakh Alfa in both is over 0,70 ,thus both questionnaires had enough stability.

Statistical community was 150 people. According to the accidental Sampling method 80 People as a statistical Sample were chosen and finally78 questionnaires were collected.

For identifying normality of information Two– Sample kolmogorov Smirnov Test was used and the data normality rate accepted .the research assumptions using independent T-Test were tested and their meaningful positive effects were proved , so that some staffs that were consistence in occupational necessities had more organizational commitment .The other result of this paper reveals the fact that only 40% of staffs in this company were completely appropriate in occupational necessities and this company is weak in this

Keywords: Organizational commitment , job appropriateness, occupational knowledge ,occupational skill ,occupational ability.

Introduction

Work is a major and, of course, constructive element of communities and organizations .In order for work does not get along with self –denying it must be technically, physiologically, and psychologically favorable .

The social and economic situations that in which work fulfils must be a way that worker feels that his labor is fair and appropriates to his /her skill and effort , and also his labor is fair and appropriates to his / her skill and effort, and also his/her wage is proportional to other work groups (shafi · abadi 14:1999).

Since work fulfillment takes a job form ,it is necessary to measure and observe job specifications in relation with employee ʼs characteristics .First , job and its fulfillment stages must be well known and its analysis considered ,next step it must be designed and appropriate individual for each job appointed to the necessary position (sadeghi 23:1996).

Since work fulfillment stages must be well known and its analysis considered , next step it must be designed and appropriate individual for each job appointed to the necessary position (sadeghi23:1996).

Job and its accurate designing play a crucial role in job consent .effectiveness ,and not willing to quit job. Since job characteristics depend on organizational procedure and designing quality of organization structure, the first factor that must be studied is the importance of specializing a job versus making it vast various.

Division of labor that all classic management scientists believed it as a principle and has been propounded as a traditional productivity.

Paradigm has advantage and disadvantage ,Its advantages include skill increment and reduction time of work fulfillment .But strict division of labor for the reason of less important jobs frequencies in long – term causes reduction in job consent and productivity .Hence , job designing plays a vital role in increasing moral , job consent and finally human productivity .Any was ,organization can by accurate clarifying duties and missions , new designing of jobs, participation in decision making , sanitation programs and observing job – employed fit in organization improve the human resources efficiency .

The occupational appropriateness is considering as an effective strategy in maintaining human resources in organization ; first this proportion starts from an instant that a person chooses a job and prepares himself to do it.

Second , organization will de prepared to find employees , select , hire, and appoint to the job.

May be at the hiring commencement ,with due attention to organization and applicants needs , the considering consistency sets up in a limited amount , but gradually that the individual continues his work and organization moves forward , it is expected that the proportion increases If job designing fits with individual characteristics , it will motivate and increase human productivity (kazemi – Haghighi,5:2000).

With due attention to above mentioned the main part of this research is whether occupational consistency causes improvement in organizational commitment or doesn't have any relations with it.

Occupational Appropriateness (Job-Employed Fit)

In two recent decades , organizations have changed meaningfully , and converted into organizations with decentralized features , global , and having team leadership . In such organizations human resource is considering as a main capital of them and they try to take advantage of his skill and abilities to maximize their efficiencies and productivities ,using job fit concept for better use of human know ledge m ability , and skill is very important.

A division of individual fitness with his peripheral invironment is job proportion (job – employed fit) , the inconsistency between employee and his job costs a lot for an organization . the main nature of job fitness clears in its various definitions, and in previous researches on job fitness clears in its various definitions , and in previous researches on this subject a variety of its definitions has been given (Ental 336,2008).

The occupational fitness theory , that identity , job autonomy , work knowledge , job skill , ability to be consistance with personal featwres , like age , gender , education level , being single or married , job experience , employee knowledge , skill , and abilities . And consequencely the adaptation of employee and his job affects his behavior and attitude.

David defines job fitness as follows :the adaptability of employee and organization, in the job which he performs , in other word his knowledge , skill , and abilities should the same as the knowledge , skills ,and abilities that his job in organization needs (David 6:2007).

Husaka assumes the similarity of job and personal values , that is , occupational proportion.

In his framework , I .e .,stretch – selection – weakening (ASA) framework the target adaptability of job – employed fit important dimension has been hypothesized . Based on this theory people attract to jobs in organizations which they take for granted to achieve individual goals (Husaka 560 :2008):

1. Supplementary fit: when an employee specifications are similar to job characteristics, i.e., things which are values in his life , they are very similar to those of his job .

2. Complementary fit : when an individual sufficiently fills the lost specifications of job , or offers additional characteristics , i.e., his knowledge , skill , and abilities offer things which other people in presiding over that job can·t offer .

3. Demands – abilities fit= when employed abilities meet the job needs , in this case, his abilities and skills are those that job needs.

4. Needs – Supplies fit : when job meets individual needs , his job meets the needs which he is expected it to meet .

As can be observed , a lot various definitions of consistency have been suggested that affect its results.

Research shows that individuals fail or un succeed more for the reason of job inconsistency than lack of skills or unwilling to do the job well. Following steps to identify occupational consistency.

- Identifying successful people specifications in that job .

- Identifying failure and unsuccessful people specifications in that job .

- Identifying specifications that caused people succeed in that job if one could take it.

In studies about occupational appropriateness different results have been obtained that sometimes they are contradictory .

The main sources of results in consistency and disagreement based on accomplished studied are identified as follows (chinoy 25;2008):

- Quality of imagination , perception , definition of job consistency job operational definition.

- Concept domain and the method used for evaluating job proportion

- Individual differences that lead to different understandings

JOB concept in occupational appropriateness is considered in two organization distinctive methods (Husaka , 560;2008) .

First Method

In this method , the individuals will be asked to notice the job specifications .

Second method:

In this procedure , the people will be asked to consider the emplored members specifications .

Acron classifies job consistency measurement procedures into three categories (Acron , 42;2008).

1. Subjective fit :In this method the employee will be asked directly and by person that how much his specification are adapting with organizational specifications , here none of the individual or organizational characteristics would be concentrated on directly , and should be assumed that respond ants have a background knowledge of organization and diagnostically address the consistency rate of their characteristics and organizational specifications.

2. Perceived fit :In this type of proportion , the people will be asked to describe them selves , and also express their perceptions of organizational specification then the appropriateness degree by assessing consistency between the individual's self – descriptive and his similar desription of organization will be measured.

3. Objective fit (external) . I n this procedure , the individual will be asked to explain his specifications, then the other organization members would be asked to explain organization specifications, after that the organization members ideas will be combined and an assessment criterion will be provided that indicates the organizational specifications , and the proportion of consistency rate between his description of himself and the agreed criterion about organization specifications will be measured.

Difference in measurement scales of occupational proportion belonging to an special concept domain is used for evaluating occupational proportion.

Values are most common sources of occupational consistency . many studies evaluate the adaptation of occupational consistency . many studies evaluate the adaptation of valuing (my values appropriate will present staff values of this organization).In some researches the personation proportion has been measured (Dose your personality fit with organization mode ?) , some researches have studied the Objectives consistency (assessment of proportion degrees between one's goals and organization goals) , few studies in clued KSA consistency (my skills and abilities reflect the abilities and skills that organization is looking for) , some studies don't use an especial criterion for research accomplishment (Is the organization the one that the employee was looking for ?)

The criterion that uses for assessing proportion can affect the outcomes and the consequences.

In general, as mentioned above the type of proportion definition , consistence criterion , measurement method , and Organization definition , etc. ,affect the job fitness relationship with its outcomes .

Vancouver et al . show that job fitness leads to attitude and behavioral Consequences . Their findings indicate that job fitness depends on job consent and organizational commitment ; it also has a less effect on behavioral results such as occupational accomplishment , OCB (organizational controlling behaviors) and staff transferring . The above said researchers by studies fulfilment concluded that perceived and objective measurement method show the dependency of behavioral outcomes further , and the relation between values adaptation and behavioral outcomes is a bit stronger than other forms of job fitness (van couver 19 , 2003) .

Confirmative findings encouraged the dependency of objection fit measurement to behavioral outcomes of using appropriateness in selection systems, but subjective and perceived fits measurements were used less in individuals selecting systems ,because both of them were selfreporting and require the know leg and familiarity with respondent to organizational value system. But objective fit scales only needs that respondent expresses his specifications and than will be compared with organizational specifications and doesni't need the familiarity of respondent to organizational specifications , and this procedure can be used in individuals selection system.

In Acron et al . research , different resuits of van couver et al . studies were obtained , So that job – employed subjective fit leads to workplace various outcomes such as organizational attractiveness , job selection , organizational commitment , no job transferring , etc . Findings show that better matching of proportion and person to organization causes higher job consent , organizational commitment , and less transferring and movement , and consequently causes the organizational system survival and preserved (Acron 42 ,2008).

Another research includes a background finding of 253 university graduated people in different full-time jobs in more that 7 years m and the ther background finding of 345 banklers that while for four months were working in the job , they were studied , showed that both studies support the relation between job – employed fit and job consent (Beer , 2004) .

Fric and Brunk in their research concluded that there is the most job consent when there is the best fit between individuals abilities and job requirements (Frico , 2006;Brunk ,2005).

David studied the relation between job – employed fit and attitude outcomes . Results showed that job – employed fit depends on concepts like freedom, job consent ,and organizational commitment .In addition , they showed that the job – employed fit dimensions (adaptability of value Vs . other forms of consistencies), and the used method in measuring job proportion (subjective, objective, perceived)regulate the relation between job – employed fif and the attitude consequences .

Organizational Commitment

In early 1980 s, staff organizational commitment was one of the most important problems that drew many researchers attention and a lot of researches accomplished on that subject . Till1985 that Walton published his famous article titled " management by commitment" , that in this work he reminds that necessity to move from management by control to management by commitment and by doing this he gave a right path to the studies in this area (Mc kenna , 16 , 2005) Organizational commitment is a structure that its different definitions have been offered , for example , marrow (1999) suggests over 25 meanings related to organizational commitment . porter et al .(1974) defines the commitment as follows :" the rate that an individual belongs himself to an organization and determines his identity with it " .They used motivation , identifying organization values and staff willing rate to membership in organization , for its measurement . Buchanan (1974) also , defines commitment as follows : organization proponents, rate of emotional belonging in proportion to organizational goals and values , their role in relation with these goals and values , and to the organization for the sake of its existence that is somewhat for the benefit that organizational has for them of course , it is worth noting that in this definition it is a different between a belonging that is based on exchanging (involvement for receiving external reward) and moral and valuable belonging (involvement for homogeneous and perfect agreement of individual and organization values . kelman (1958) diffretiates between commitment by compliance (I.e.,a commitment in which staff accepts behavioral patterns and special ideas for definite rewards), commitment by identification (when accepted behaviors and opinions are for the sake of joining to a third party that is valuable for that person) , and subjective commitment (in that the individual acts the Special behaviors and ideas that their contents are in agreement with his system value).So , the staff commitment can be studied on different views , Oreill and chatman (1986) based on kelman opinions identified that the mentally belonging (i.e., individual mentally dependent on organization)as main an key issue in staff commitment . they defined mentally belonging as:it reflects a degree in which individuals accept and internalize organizational views and specifications . oreilly and chatman (1986)based the saff mentally belonging on three following items which were similar to kelman (1958) suggestions (Durkin and Bennett, 127 ;1999)

1. Acceptance or staff physically presence in organization for definite external rewards .
2. Identifying , or staff presence in organization based on willing to solidarity .
3. Internalizing , Or staff active participation in organization rely on organizational and individual values consistency .

This multifactor approach to staff commitment , has been supported by other researcher . For example, Jaros et al . (1993)using factoral analysis method proved this multifactor approach to commitment , and concluded that organization commitment monofactor models whether conceptually Or empirically are not supported . Each of mentioned dimensions of commitment (internalized , identified , compliance) also in a way relates to organization changing process . In fact, staff commitment in changing process management play a key role . on one hand staff,s higher commitment enforces (enhances) the accomplished changes and on the other hand guarantees the change schedukes (Bennett 433,2002).

One of the most important studies regarding commitment is the multifactoral one which belongs to Meyer and Allen (1997) .

In their points of view , there are there kinds of commitments :

1. Affective commitment , means the staff emotional belonging to organization , unity sensation with organization , and an active presence in organization .

Staffs which have affective commitment usually tend to remain in organization and this is one of their wishes.

2. Continuance commitment , is in relation with benefits and charges which relate to remaining or quitting the organization . staffs which have continuance commitment , usually remain in organization in have continuance commitment , usually remain in organization in case that quitting it has no enormous charges for them .

3. Normative commitment , which shows the staff obligation or duty to stay in organization . therefore , staff will remain in organization until their remaining in organization is a right and appropriate task in their views (Mc Kenna , 17 ;2003).

Thus, the organizational commitment can be defined as follows:

1. Strong tendency to remain in a typical organization .

2. Willing to do enormous efforts for organization .

3. Decisive belief in supporting organization ,s goals and values .

Hence ,Organizational commitment can be known as an attitude toward staff loyalty to organization and a continuance process , which thanks to individuals participations in organizational decisions , individuals attention to organization and organization 's success and welfare will be determined (Moghimi 392 ,2004) .

Research assumptions

Regarding above mentioned the main assumption of this paper is as follow : occupational appropriateness with organizational commitment at the national Iranian oil refining and distribution company head quarters staff level has a positive an meaningful relationship .

With due attention to the main assumption of this article , three sub – hypotheses will be given :

1. The proportion between staff occupational knowledge and requirement knowledge for job accomplishment with organizational commitment. At the national Iranian oil refinery and distributing company headquarters staff level has a positive and meaning relationship .

2. The consistency between staff occupational skill and required skill for the job fulfillment along with organizational commitment at the national Iranian oil refining and distribution company headquarters staff level has a positive and meaningful relationship .

3. The fitness between staff job ability and ability needs for job accomplishment along with organizational commitment at the national Iranian oil refining and distributing company head quarters stafflevel has a positive and meaningful relationship.

Research method

Since in this research , the authors want to study and measure job – employed fit and its relation with organizational commitment in national Iranian oil refining and distributing company headquarters staff , the research is based on descriptive and measuring type.

Statistical community was 150 people of national Iranian oil company headquarters Staff . the research sample by following equation will be 74 people.

$$n = \frac{(150)(1.96)^2(0.5)(0.5)}{(0.5)^2 (150-1) + (1.96)^2 (0.5)(0.5)} = 74$$

The needed data for this research was gathered in two following ways . library method :In this method for gathering the data related to subject matter and research background books ,theses , articles , databases, and internet sources were used .

Field method :In this procedure by designing questionnaires and distributing them among statistical sample , the necessary data regarding occupational appropriateness and its relationship with organizational commitment obtained . For job – employed fit measurement by data related to available jobs in American job database (occupational Information Network),27questionnaires by considering three knowledge variables . job skills and abilities guided and cooperated by university professors and industrial advisers were compiled and designed (http: //www. Onetcenter . org) .

Allen and meyer organizational commitment questionnaire was used for measuring the organizational commitment parameters.

Organizational commitment has 15 questions that deal with organizational commitment . Each questionnaire related to job fit on the average consists of 21 questions , that deals with available situation of individuals job knowledge, skill, and ability . first both measurement tools were distributed among30 people of headquarters staff. These people were selected on their research data , and after completing the questionnaire , we used their ideas about the questions consistency with research context , proper writing and removing the ambiguities in the questions . this the ought exchange flow and Co – thinking along with interviewing in person and discussing all questions One by one were accomplished . In this paper the descriptive and inferential statistics were used for describing and analyzing gathered data . by these tests first normality of information was identified by two – sample kolmogorov smirnov test .In the case of data distribution normality , the independent T- Test was used . Based on this test a meaningful difference between staff organizational commitment regarding job consistency or in consistency was identified . But if data distribution were abnormal , to determine a meaningful difference of organizational .

Commitment refer to job consistency or in consistency man wittney – Test should be used.

Research Findings

In this research to check its assumption , first must be specified whether or not the data distribution is normal . Data normality or its abnormality is measured by kolmogorov – smirnov statistic test , the kolmogorov Smirnov test results were accordant to following table:

Table 1:   Two – Sample kolmogorov – smirnov test.

Test Statistics

		z
Most Extreme	Absolute	.864
Differences	Positive	.000
Negative		-.864
Kolmogorov – Smirnov Z		3.979
Asymp .Sig.(2-talied)		.000

A .Grouping Variable : GROUP

According to above table the prepared Z amount of the test at a certainty level of 95% equals 3.979 Based on statistics tables the Z amount of table at Certainty level of 95% is 1.64 . since the Z amount of test is higher than the Z of the table , Can be argued that at the certainty level of 95% the data gathered from statistics sample has normal distribution .

Therefore , to test the meaningfulness of the rate difference of the organizational commitment of the staffs that regarding job are appropriate with the staffs that are inappropriate , independent test was used . this test identifies the rate difference of staff organizational difference of staff – organizational commitment in terms of job consistency or inconsistency .

In a general look the average score of organizational commitment of staffs that referring occupation were suitable or inconsistence is as follows :

Table 2: The average score of staff organizational commitment in terms of job consistency or in consistency .

organizational commitment average score	Staff aboundant		index
	percent	numbers	
5.2	39.7/0	31	Occupational proper staffs
3.9	59.3/0	47	Occupational improper staffs.

T-Test results show (Table 2) that a group with job consistency obtained organizational commitment score of 5.2, which in comparison with the Same Subject score of a group that was in job in consistency ,namely(3.9) was high .The score difference shows that occupational consistency with organizational Commitment in national Iranian oil refining and distributing Company headquarter staff has a positive and meaningful relationship .And the more increment in this proportion the more increase in rate of staff organizational commitment would be .Also Table 2 shows that in this refinery and distributer company 39.7 % of staff refer to job are appropriate .

Conclusions and Suggestions

Job – employed fit is a basic issue in human resource management, the assumption has been approved that existence of this proportion is an organizational necessity for human resource productivity .And job_employed fit in an organization is considered as an effective strategy in preserving human resources. This consistency starts from the moment that the individual gets prepare for the job and its selection. Second organization gets prepare to find employees, select, hire and appointment. May at the commencement of employing, regarding organization and applicants needs, the considering proportion set up in a limited amount, but gradually along with the individual continuing his work in an organization and organization itself get life experience , it is expected that the consistency in creases .If job design is in a way that fits that individual specifications , it will motivate and increase human productivity (kazemi –Haghighi , 5 ;2000).

For this paper the independent T-Test was used to study occupational consistancy and it relation with organizational commitment in national Iranian oil refining and distributing company headquarters staff .the test shows that the meaning and difference of staff organizational commitment average scores refer to occupation are whether or not cot consistence .Its results at certainty level of 95% are meaningful since organizational commitment average scores of those that are in consistence , then it can be argued that job employed fit has a positive and direct relationship with staff organizational commitment .that is , the more job – employed fit , the more staff organizational commitment . that is ,the more job –employed fit , the more staff organizational commitment could be or vice versa , that less job – employed fit , the less staff organizational commitment , and this conclusion totally matches with the research results (David , 2007; Acron ,2006;Frico ,2006 ;Brunk ,2005 ;Beer , 2004 , van couver , 2003). The other important outcome of this research is that in statistical community about 40% were job – employed fit which for the national Iranian oil refinement and distribution company , as one of the biggest an most in come bearer companies of the country ,is very weak and unacceptable . Based on this and refer to research goal and accomplished results and also researchers observation during the research , the following suggestions and recommendations for in creasing occupational proportion that in turn causes more productivity ,job consent , and staff organizational commitment will be offered :

1. Regarding this issue the education certificates of employees who work in researched organization don ,t match the jobs that they do and aren·t accordant with international standards .In employment process , attracting and finding employees for job position vacancies or job positions that become available of existence necessities infinite precision must be taken by hwman resource specialists , so that people· s selection criteria be on merit laddering and international standards .

2. To lay emphasis onhuman development through education as a process of improvement and promotion of abilities , knowledge and consciousness in cerement and changing the staff attitudes toward the jobs that in recent years greatly have been changed (investigative, purchase and advertisement sections).

3. Job relative value determination for detemining and regulating payment wage with other internal and external jobs by personnel and human resources managers (in jobs like accountant , senior accountant , civil senders , and perchase official).

4. Division of labor and merging certain jobs refer to similar job duties and activities especially in law and accounting sections .

5. Preparing catalog , brochure , brochure , billboard refer to last changes in occupational issues and problems domain in organization and installing them in much traffic place such as :hour recorder card machine , messhall , etc. for in forming staffs.

6. People ·s skill increment for promoting to higher positions through implementing job training schedules , sending staffs to occupational training courses out of organization or in similar organizations .

7. Giving reward job position to staff that are out of the organization and voluntarily participate in education schedules that relate to their job domain to preserve and enhance people motivation and create a sound and constructive competition sensation in other staffs.

References

[1] Shafi,a Abadi , Abdallah (1999). "*Professional and occuputinal counseling and guiding* , and job option opinions" Islamic culture and guidance ministry" " Tehran"

[2] Sadeghi , Mansooreh (1996) "*job analysis in mashad sepad company*" , khorasan .

[3] Kazemi Haghighi , Nasereddin (1999) , "*psychology for laborand management*" , sayeh nama press , Tehran.

[4]   Moghimi , Mohammad.(2004). " *Researching and approaching Organization and management* " Third edition, termeh press, Tehran .

[5]   Acorn S, Ratner PA, Crawford M(2008).*"Decentralization as determinant of autonomy, job satisfaction, and organizational commitment among nurse manager"*. Nurse Res, Vol33,No3,pp.80-88..

[6]   Antall, Gloria,F.(2008). *"Assessing Job Candidates for Fit"* .Merlin Press.

[7]   7.Beer,Duane P,(2004) *"Psychology and work today an introduction to industrial an organizational psychology "*. Macmillan co.

[8]   Bennett, H.(2002) *"Employee commitment: the key to absence management in local government? Leadership & Organization Development Journal"* ,Vol .23,No. 8, pp.430-441.

[9]   Brunk,R(2005) " *The nature of work*". London:Macmillan.

[10]   Chinoy, E , (2008). *"Automobile workers and the American Dream* " New York: Beacon press.

[11]   David, T(2007) *" A quantitative review of the relationship between person–organization fit and outcome".* Journal of Industrial Teacher Education. Vol44,No2.

[12]   Durkin, M. and Bennett, H.(1999) *"Employee commitment in retail banking: identifying and exploring hidden dangers"*,International Journal of Bank Marketing, Vol.17,No.2,pp.80-88.

[13]   Frico, Paule(2006) *"E. industrial and organizational psychology"*. John wiley &sns,inc.

[14]   Hosaka, Takaashi & et al.(2008). " *Assessing Person-Organization Fit to Reduce Turnover (Presented to 24th Annual IMPAAC Conference on Personnel Assessment)"*

[15]   Mc Kenna, S.(2005). *"Organizational commitment in the small entrepreneurial business in Singapore"*,Cross Cultural Management ,, Vol.12,No.2, pp.16-37.

[16]   Paul AK, Anantharaman RN. (2006). *"Influence of HRM practice on organizational commitment: A study among software professional in India"* Hum Resource Manage R Vol16,No4,pp.46-87.

[17]   Van couver,Tony(2003) *"Professions in the class system of present day societies"*. Currnt sociology.

[18]   *http://www.onetcenter.org*

J. Basic. Appl. Sci. Res., 2(3)2991-2998, 2012

ISSN 2090-4304
Journal of Basic and Applied Scientific Research *www.textroad.com*

Strategies Of Increasing Non-Oil Exports of Iran-Qom State Case Study : Sohan

Hossein Khanifar[1]; Hamed bordbar[2]; Mostafa Emami[2]; Kamran Nazari[3]; Azadeh Feyzi[2];

Azadeh Pezhman[2]

[1]
Teacher of Tehran University

[2]
M.Sc FIN.ECO, Department of Accounting,Tarbiat Modares University,Iran

[3]
Department of Business Management, Payam Noor University, Iran

---

ABSTRACT

Introduction: Productions and outputs known as souvenirs of a city Can be good opportunities for growing businesses and economic in that area. Sohan as a cookie is one of the main souvenirs of Qom. If producers want to use the opportunity of exporting Sohan, they should apply proper strategies for their targets and have strategic plans. This study is to know the present position of exporting Sohan by means of internal and external analysis.
Methodology: Interviews, books and documents are used in this survey; for studying information, SWOT analysis model is used and for strategy compiling, Quantitative Strategic Planning Matrix (QSPM) is used.
Findings: Data shows that exporting Sohan has more weaknesses and opportunities in external and internal factors and it is in a situation that can use opportunities to decrease weaknesses by help of the strategies.
Conclusion: Based on evaluation of scores conservative strategies in quantitative strategic planning matrix, focusing strategy on products and market penetration in the region and the solvent was selected as the best strategy.
KEYWORDS: *Non-Oil Exports, Swot, QSPM.*

INTRODUCTION

Development is one of the important challenges of every society. Export development and increase directly affects the foreign exchange income of the country and there will be potentialities for indispensable investments for growing businesses and economic through supplying these foreign exchange sources. On the other hand, export development creates opportunities to take the advantage of global markets for growing local products. Therefore production merchants will be able to escape from local market limits and in addition to foreign exchange incomes they will benefit from financial benefits resulted from production scale through increasing production scale for the purpose of increasing exports. (Salehiyan Omran, 1382, p17).

Considering different weather conditions and agricultural products, one of the advantages of the country in production and export of non-oil products is food and beverages industry. Programming for development and enrichment of these industries, with the purpose of increasing exchanging agricultural products export, will increase the benefits of agricultural products and prevent wastage of them. It would not be surprising if we say that these days, as a group of exchanging agricultural products, different kinds of candies and sweets are one of the most favored products throughout the world and the demand is increasing from day to day. Our country is not an exception and lots of candies and sweets are being used in ceremonies and special occasions.

This study considers examination and proposal of Sohan expert strategies which is one of the most important local sweets in Iran and most of the producers of this sweet are in Qom state. This study includes analysis opportunities, threats, strength and weakness and proper strategies for increasing Sohan expert.

The process of internal and external environment evaluation is called internal and external analysis which is a realistic and reliable scale for evaluating organization, because contains detecting strength, weakness, opportunity and threat. Mostly, information found in this process result in detecting strategic issues (Rowly, DJ. ,Lugan, HD. ,Dolence, MG. ,1997 :44).

The main idea of organization internal and external analysis (SWOT Analysis) is progress based on strengths, minimizing weaknesses, providing opportunities, taking advantage of opportunities and removing threats(Garner, R., 2005:74).

Strategic management process can be considered as a systematic goal for main organic decisions (Breene, R.S, 2007:84).

Not only defining a good strategy can guarantee organization success, but also those strategies should be fulfilled successfully (Weilun , Z.William, 2007:10).

1. An overview of research precedence

Comprehensive experimental studies has been done on non-oil expert and proposing strategies. Some of them include:
Haghighi (1374); p22, in his thesis entitled "Research into Possibility of exchanging agricultural products export in Khorasan state and its foreign marketing challenges" found that one of the obstacles in industry export is foreign exchange

*Corresponding Author: Mostafa Emami, Tarbiat Modares University, Iran Tehran, P.O BO:1767778151

TEL:18162370018-989127001816   EMAIL: Mostafa.Emami@Modares.ac.ir

problems. Khorasan state exporters believe that foreign exchange problems prevent having a safe condition for exporting products.

Lotfabadi(1374); p45, in his thesis entitled: "Research into Non-oil Export and Estimation of Date Export Supply Function" found that increase in internal prices has negative effects on export supplies. Lack of attention to date export at the time of foreign exchange income increase from oil sales, which results from the absence of a centralized organization for date export in the country, is another important finding of this study.

Dodangi and Amoozade (1376); p25, in their research entitled "examining effective factors in developing Mazandaran state export and detecting main difficulties" pointed that in 1374 the amount of non-oil export comparing 1370-1373 has been reduced, they considered the main problems of Mazandaran state in developing export activities and has proposed some political points regarding potentials of this state.

Akbar Zarezade Mehrizi (1379) has analyzed the functionality of Iran non-oil export programs. Not considering country advantages in export, not observing quality standards and loosing market, not having firm foreign exchange policies, not having precise information about the market of exported goods, optimistic goal defining and lack of coordination among different parts are the main causes of failure in achieving pre-defined goals in non-oil export in his idea.

Mohammadreza Zargarzade (1380); p42, has used Analytical Hierarchy Process (AHP) method for designing marketing strategies for agricultural products exporters. Long term interests of export merchants is affected by proper selection of exportable goods and target markets regarding variety of factors. Choosing goods and target markets should take place considering these factors.

Jafari Samimi and Peikani (1381); p61, in their study entitled " The Role of Exportation Reliability in Iran Non-oil Export Development" mentioned internal and external effective factors and non-oil export development obstacles, optimize production weakness, export organization weakness and … as non-oil export problems through a forecasting study pattern.

Mostafa Ghazizade (1382); p98, in his P.H.D thesis considers examination and detection of effective factors in Iranan export companies success in middle east markets and proposes strategies for increasing non-oil export. In his research, Ghazizade, has studied the effect of four variables including target market environment, national and internal environment of the company and mixed marketing elements.

Darvishkhani (1383); p35, in his thesis considers the effects of marketing management on local and global Sohan selling. He introduces marketing management as a local and global Sohan selling facilitator. He has studied the role of packing, mixed marketing elements and hygienic and nutritious standards and proved their positive effects on increasing local and global selling from producer's perspective.

Madhooshi and Tari (1386); p195, in their study entitled "non-oil export development strategies in Mazandaran state" consider proportional advantages of mazandaran state using revealed comparative advantage. After studying target markets for the exportable productions of the state, they introduced strategies for developing plants, citrus fruits and kiwi export of the city analyzing environmental and internal factors with SWOT method.

Narseri and his colleagues (1386); p46, in their study entitled : " detailed observation of Iran tea supply chain" has evaluated global and local condition of tea trading and studied strengths, weaknesses, opportunities and threats of tea industry using Gornport Dimond Model as framework of competitiveness study. Also, Tea supply chain of Kenya as an advanced country in tea production and trading is evaluated.

2. Research style

This study is descriptive regarding the aim, efficiency, data process and resulting and includes studying Sohan export of Qom state.

The main purpose of organization SWOT analysis is progress based on strengths, minimizing weaknesses, providing opportunities and taking advantage of them and removing threats (Garner ,R. ,2005:74).

In this study, information is taken from Qom state commerce organization documents. It also includes interviews on Sohan export with experts which are presented through SWOT table.

1.2. Comprehensive strategy defining matrix

SWOT matrix is an effective device through which managers compare data and represent 4kinds of strategies:

1.1.2 SWOT analysis stages

1- Holding the SWOT analysis meeting
2- Brief explanation of meeting goals and performance stages
3-Detecting internal (strengths and weaknesses) and external (opportunities and threats) factors through brainstorming.
4-Proioritizing internal and external factors
5-SWOT matrix formation and inserting selected factors regarding priorities
6-Comparing internal and external factors and defining aggressive strategy(SO), conservative strategy (WO) , competitive strategy (ST), defense strategy (WT).
7-Defining necessary measurements for fulfilling defined strategies
8-Measurments fulfillment and studying their results
9-Updating SWOT matrix in proper intervals (David, 1385; p54)

1.2.2fulfilling Quantitative Strategic Programming Matrix stages

Generally strategic management process includes three separate stages:
1) Strategy defining
2) Strategy fulfillment
3) Strategy evaluation

Quantitative Strategic Programming Matrix technique is an efficient device for strategy defining stage. This device assists us in selecting best strategy and provides a plain framework for giving priority to available strategies.

After recognizing external factors (opportunities and threats) through asking expert ideas we have allocated 2992 weight factor between zero (unimportant) to one (very important) to every factor. Then, according to the amount of conformity with opportunities and threats, a score between 1 to 4 is allocated to every factor. At next stage, weighted score (each factors importance score multiple accumulated score) and total score is computed. Then the environmental condition evaluation matrix is computed through this total score. Internal condition evaluation matrix is computed in the same way. Then by setting external and internal strategic factors, which are the basements for defining strategies, SWOT matrix is extracted and based on final matrix of defined priorities proper strategies are introduced. also, for the purpose of examining results of the matrix, Quantitative Strategic Programming Matrix is used. In this method:
1-first, the data related to factors (S, W, O, T) and weight score are moved from internal and external factors analysis table on the right column of QSPM matrix.
2-all of the strategies from SWOT strategic programming matrix is written on the upper horizontal column.
3-attractiveness score: based on the importance of each factor in defining each strategy is between 1 to 4. 1=unattractive, 2= relatively attractive, 3=acceptably attractive, 4= very attractive.
4- Importance factor TAS equals weight score multiple AS
5-the TAS for every strategy is summed up and the best programs are selected according to the priorities.
Its worthy to mention that, the results has been confirmed by this matrix. (David,1379; p54)

4- Statistics of Qom state customs function on export in the first 6 months of 1389

In the first 6 months of the year 1389, 14400ton of goods such as shoes, sandals, books, hand-woven carpet, Sohan, sweets, glass products and… 47. 448 million dollars is exported to countries like Iraq, Afghanistan, Imarat and china which, regarding the value, had 31 percent growth (documents represented in Islamic Republic of Iran customs website).

1-4- Qom state Sohan production and export condition

Right now more than 500 units that produce and sell Sohan are a member of Qom state Sohan merchant union. These units are some small ones with less than 10 workers. Most of these units produce Sohna traditionally.

Based on statistics represented by Qom state commerce organization Sohan export in the first nine months of 1389 is 477ton and 477 thousand dollars.

Considering small amount of export it can be deduced that Soahn has been exported under sweet category or has not been exported in an organized way. Probably Sohan is mostly exported to other countries through tourists and pilgrims. Experts has announced in the interviews that sohan has been exported to Middle East countries, Iraq and…), Lebanon, Syria, Afghanistan, Germany, Poland, Australia, America and Canada (documents of commerce organization of Qom state 1389) .

5-Soahn industry rivals 1-5 local rivals

Main local rivals for Qom state Sohan industry are Isfahan sweets (Gaz), Yazd sweets (Baghlava and Ghotab and…) and Tabriz and Oroumiye sweets. Because of the quality and beautiful packing, these product are the most favored in the country.

2-5- foreign rivals

In the last few years, Turkey had been one of the main sweet producer and exporters. Also Some other countries, like Syria, had been sweet producers.

6-possibility of exporting Sohan to global halal food market

Halal food market is developing throughout the world and can be a safe and stable market for these products. Considering this issue that up to the year 2025, 30 percent of the world population will be Muslims, many producers plan investing in this market. Because halal food shows high quality of healthy food, these products are not only for Muslim consumers and all people around the world use them. (FArmiran news, 1389).

7- Findings analysis and representation 1-7- External factors evaluation Matrix

This Matrix helps strategists to evaluate environmental, economical, social, political, cultural, legal, technological and marketing condition in a defined interval. This Matrix is useful for governmental and private organizations (Arabi, 1385; David,1379)(Forbes, P. , 1996:45).

2-7-Internal factors evaluation Matrix:

This Matrix helps evaluating inter-organization factors and considers organizational units strength and weakness. Mostly this Matrix is formed based on managers and staffs ideas (Arabi, 1385; David,1379).

8-comparision and contrasting stage 1-8- SWOT Matrix

SWOT Matrix includes a two dimensional table of coordinates and every one of the four areas represents a set of strategies (David, 1385 and Ali Ahmadi and colleagues, 1382). These strategies are (Richard, 2005:69):
1. Aggressive strategies (SO):
Strategies for taking advantage of environmental opportunities using organization
strengths 2. Conservative strategies (WO):
Strategies for using potential advantages in environmental opportunities for compensating organization weaknesses.
2993 3.competitive strategies (ST)
Strategies for using organization strengths in order to prevent threats
4.defense strategies (WT)
Strategies for minimizing damages resulting from threats and weaknesses.

Table 1. Sohan Export external factors evaluation Matrix (EFE)

External strategic factors	Code	Weight	Score	Weighted score	Explanation
Opportunity					
1.presenting products in international sweet and chocolate festival	01	0.02	3	0.06	Opportunity for presenting products and acquaintance with rivals products
2.exploiting geographical condition of neighbor countries	02	0.06	4	0.24	Placing Iran in geographical area of middle east

3. studying possibilities of Sohan export to "halal" global market	O3	0.06	4	0.24	Supporting Sohan producers for granting "halal" label and appropriate function in halal food market
4. governmental facilities	O4	0.06	4	0.24	Governmental consideration to nonoil export and providing enough credits for market researches, proprgandas and sale expansion in target markets
5.eliminating legal obstacles for Sohan export and production	O5	0.09	4	0.36	Legal obstacles prevent exportations
6.expration date, calories and vitamin insertion on the Sohan canister	O6	0.045	4	0.18	Lack of attention to observing quality standards (ISO 22000) in production and supply
7.scientific promotion of production units	O7	0.015	3	0.045	Purposeful teaching is the first and most important development tool
8. on-line selling possibility	O8	0.025	4	0.1	On-line selling and marketing improvement are the main reasons of GAZ export
9. supporting establishment of export institutes	O9	0.08	4	0.32	Small units mostly are not able to participate in global markets
10.ranking products based on their quality	O10	0.015	3	0.045	Results in competitive condition for Sohan production
11. utilizing artificial saccharin in Sohan production	O11	0.025	3	0.075	Leads to calories reduction
12. modern packing and design based on export	O12	0.045	4	0.18	Proper packing leads to demand increase and attracts customers attention
Threats					
1.progressing function of neighbor countries like Turkey and Syria	T1	0.06	1	0.06	Rivals marketing and extensive propagandas and market share growth
2. lack of management and technical knowledge of some managers and producers	T2	0.03	2	0.06	Not knowing new technical issues about production and new management tips
3.not necessary middlemen existence which leads to price increase	T3	0.02	2	0.004	Sohan price increase and Sohan demand reduction against favored foreign production in global market
4.lack of Sohan export union	T4	0.06	1	0.06	A fundamental factor in supporting exporters
5.political prohibitions	T6	0.09	1	0.09	Obstacles on Iranian goods export
6.governmental effects	T7	0.045	1	0.045	Governmental credits elimination and energy cost increase and governments emphasis on not increasing the price of goods
7. inflation	T8	0.04	2	0.08	Increasing the price of raw materials because of inflation
8.inefficient banking system for providing credits	T9	0.055	1	0.055	Lack of financial plan for protecting producers and exporters
9.lack of investment insurance for export	T10	0.06	1	0.06	Not having a proper plan for reducing performance risk and financial investment
Total		1		2.635	

Source: (Arabi, 1385; David, 1379 & 1385; Ali Ahmadi and colleagues, 1382)

Table2. . Sohan Export internal factors evaluation Matrix

Strength	

Internal strategic factors	code	weight	Score	weighted score	Explanation
1.utilizing natural ingredients	S1	0.055	4	0.22	Ingredients include: flour, sugar, wheat sprout, oil, cardamom, pistachio, almond, saffron, rosewater, egg, cocoa powder
2. full of vitamins E &B	S2	0.033	3	0.099	Because of having wheat sprout, pistachio and almond
3. easy access to ingredients	S3	0.053	4	0.212	All of the ingredients are made in the country
4.non competitive Sohan price in export market	S4	0.08	4	0.32	Sohan is the monopoly of Iran
5.various production styles	S5	0.025	3	0.075	Butter Sohan(with butter oil), mixed Sohan(butter and plants oil) and Sohan with plants oil in different shapes like circle, rectangle, diamond and....
6.Qom state fame and precedence in producing Sohan	S6	0.06	4	0.24	Most Sohan producers are in Qom
7.long lasting of Sohan	S7	0.031	3	0.093	If it is kept in cold place, Sohan will last for a whole year
8.educated and young work force in Qom	S8	0.03	3	0.09	Young and educated population of the state
9. foreign pilgrims	S9	0.031	3	0.093	Neighbor countries Muslims take Sohan to their country as a souvenir(indirect marketing)
10. low production prices	S10	0.051	4	0.204	Because of existing facilities in the state and easy access to ingredients
11. ability for production in large scale	S11	0.03	3	0.09	Having lots of factories in Qom state
weakness 1.large amount of sugar and fat in it	W1	0.054	1	0.054	Although this product is very restorative, it has a large amount of calories
2.not proper packing	W2	0.054	1	0.054	Not enough developments in packing industry comparing to the amount of production
3.lack of stability in providing ingredients regarding price and quality	W3	0.035	2	0.07	Changing prices of ingredients
4.Lack of a comprehensive strategy for having better performance local and foreign markets	W4	0.08	1	0.08	Unfortunately thete is no long term program for having better performance in local and foreign markets
5.lack of whole mechanized Sohan cooking process	W5	0.035	2	0.07	Some of the producer still use traditional Sohan production style
6.not having a good program for introducing brands	W6	0.031	1	0.031	There is no suitable branding process in this industry because of lack of programs in this field
7.lack of comprehensive distribution network	W7	0.071	1	0.071	Customs problems
8.not inserting expiration date, amount of calories and vitamins on the Soahn canister	W8	0.051	1	0.051	Leads to customer uncertainty about Sohan health
9.weak marketing and propaganda	W9	0.08	1	0.08	Lack of scientific programs on marketing and totally commerce
10. lack of observation on Sohan quality and production	W10	0.03	2	0.06	Observation increase on SOhan production regarding quality and hygienic issues leads to customer satisfaction and sales increase
		1		2.357	

2994

Source: (Arabi, 1385; David, 1379 & 1385; Ali Ahmadi and colleagues, 1382)

Table3. Qom Soahn SWOT matrix

External factors	opportunities	Threats
	1.presenting products in international sweet and chocolate festival 2.exploiting geographical condition of neighbor countries 3. studying possibilities of Sohan export to "halal" global market 4. governmental facilities 5.eliminating legal obstacles for Sohan export and production 6.expration date, calories and vitamin insertion on the Sohan canister 7.scientific promotion of production units 8. on-line selling possibility 9. supporting establishment of export institutes 10.ranking products based on their quality 11. utilizing GHANDE MASNOOI in Sihan production 12. modern packing and design based on export	1.progressing function of neighbor countries like Turky and Syria 2. lack of management and technical knowledge of some managers and producers 3.not necessary middlemen existence which leads to price increase 4.lack of Sohan export union 5.political prohibitions 6.governmental effects 7. inflation 8.inefficient banking system for providing credits 9.lack of investment insurance for export
Internal factors		
Strengths: 1.utilizing natural ingredients 2. full of vitamins E &B 3. easy access to ingredients 4.non competitive Sohan price in export market 5.various production styles 6.Qom state fame and precedence in producing Sohan 7.long lasting of Sohan 8.educated and young work force in Qom 9. foreign pilgrims 10. low production prices 11. ability for production in large scale	aggressive strategies (SO): 1.recognizing potevtial target markets 2.export development and insertion into area and global markets 3.introducing Sohan to international markets 4. gaining governments satisfaction through utilizing job making power of Soah production and export 5.producing high quality Sohan in accordance with customers taste	Conservative strategies (WO): 1.focuse on products and insertion into halal markets 2.control increase on distribution system 3.control increase on product quality and packing 4.sale increase through research and marketing activities 5.modeling after advanced countries in sweet and chocolate industry
Weaknesses: 1.large amount of sugar and fat in it 2.not proper packing 3.lack of stability in providing ingredients regarding price and quality 4.Lack of a comprehensive strategy for having better performance local and foreign markets 5.lack of whole mechanized Sohan cooking process 6.not having a good program for introducing brands 7.lack of comprehensive distribution network 8.not inserting expiration date, amount of calories and vitamins on the Soahn canister 9.weak marketing and propeganda 10. lack of observation on Sohan quality and production	Competitive strategies (ST) 1.financial and performance risk management 2.propeganda increase for introducing Sohan and attracting customers 3.establishment of Sohan unions and export organizations	defense strategies (WT) 1.constant products improvement 2.long term programming based on export policies 3.expanding contrasts with credible ingredient suupliers 4.improving production instruments and mechanizing the whole production process

Source: (Arabi, 1385; David, 1379 & 1385; Ali Ahmadi and colleagues, 1382)

2-8-internal and external factors matrix

Considering internal and external factors matrix, conservative strategies are used for Sohan export:

1. focus on products and insertion into halal markets
2. control increase on distribution system
3. control increase on product quality and packing
4. sale increase through research and marketing activities
5.modeling after advanced countries in sweet and chocolate industry

Table3. Sohan export internal and external matrix

"aggressive" strategy Strength	Opportunity "conservative strategy" IFE=2.357 Weakness EFE=2.635
"competitive strategy"	"defense strategy" Threat

Source: (Arabi, 1385; Ali Ahmadi and colleagues, 1382)

9-decision making stage

Regarding the results derived from Sohan export internal and external factors matrix, we have inserted defined strategies for SO into quality strategy matrix to select the best strategy for the organization.

Table 4. quality strategic programming matrix for Sohan export external factors

External factors strategy	Factor importance (weight)	1. focus on products and insertion into halal markets		2. control increase on distribution system		3. control increase on product quality and packing		4. sale increase through research and marketing activities		5. modeling after advanced countries in sweet and chocolate industry	
		Attractiveness Factor	Score	Attractiveness factor	Score	Attractiveness factor	Score	Attractiveness factor	Score	Attractiveness factor	Score
										Strength (S)	
S1	0/055	4	0/22	1	0/055	2	0/11	2	0/11	1	0/055
S2	0/033	4	0/132	1	0/033	1	0/033	2	0/066	1	0/033
S3	0/053	4	0/212	1	0/053	1	0/053	4	0/212	1	0/053
S4	0/08	4	0/32	1	0/08	3	0/24	4	0/32	2	0/16
S5	0/025	4	0/1	1	0/025	2	0/05	3	0/075	2	0/05
S6	0/06	3	0/18	1	0/06	1	0/06	3	0/18	1	0/06
S7	0/031	4	0/124	3	0/093	2	0/062	4	0/124	1	0/031
S8	0/03	2	0/06	2	0/06	4	0/12	4	0/12	3	0/09
S9	0/031	4	0/124	2	0/062	3	0/093	4	0/124	2	0/062
S10	0/051	4	0/204	1	0/051	2	0/102	1	0/051	2	0/102
S11	0/03	4	0/12	1	0/03	1	0/03	3	0/09	3	0/09
										Weakness(W)	
W1	0/054	3	0/162	1	0/054	4	0/216	2	0/108	2	0/108
W2	0/054	4	0/216	1	0/054	4	0/216	3	0/162	4	0/216
W3	0/035	4	0/14	1	0/035	4	0/14	2	0/07	1	0/035
W4	0/08	4	0/32	3	0/24	3	0/24	4	0/32	3	0/24
W5	0/035	3	0/105	1	0/035	2	0/07	2	0/07	4	0/14
W6	0/031	2	0/062	1	0/031	4	0/124	4	0/124	3	0/093
W7	0/071	4	0/284	4	0/284	1	0/071	3	0/213	4	0/284
W8	0/051	4	0/204	1	0/051	4	0/204	4	0/204	4	0/204
W9	0/08	4	0/32	2	0/16	3	0/24	4	0/24	4	0/32
W10	0/03	2	0/06	1	0/03	4	0/12	3	0/09	4	0/12
		1 2/546		3/669		1/576		2/594		3/073	

Table 5. quality strategic programming matrix for Sohan export internal factors

internal factors strategy	Factor importance (weight)	1. focus on products and insertion into halal markets		2. control increase on distribution system		3. control increase on product quality and packing 299 6		4. sale increase through research and marketing activities		5. modeling after advanced countries in sweet and chocolate industry	
		Attractiveness Factor	Score	Attractiveness factor	Score	Attract veness factor	Score	Attractiveness factor	Score	Attractiveness factor	Score
										Strength (S)	
O1	0/02	3	0/06	1	0/02	3	0/06	4	0/08	4	0/08
O2	0/06	4	0/24	4	0/24	4	0/24	4	0/24	1	0/06
O3	0/06	4	0/24	4	0/24	4	0/24	4	0/24	1	0/06
O4	0/06	4	0/24	4	0/24	3	0/18	2	0/12	2	0/12
O5	0/09	4	0/36	4	0/36	2	0/18	2	0/18	1	0/09
O6	0/045	4	0/18	2	0/09	4	0/18	2	0/09	2	0/09
O7	0/015	3	0/045	2	0/03	4	0/06	4	0/06	4	0/06
O8	0/025	4	0/1	1	0/025	3	0/075	4	0/1	4	0/1

O9	0/08	4	0/32	4	0/32	3	0/24	2	0/16	2	0/16
O10	0/015	2	0/03	1	0/015	4	0/06	2	0/03	3	0/045
O11	0/025	3	0/075	1	0/025	4	0/1	2	0/05	3	0/075
O12	0/045	4	0/18	1	0/045	4	0/18	3	0/135	4	0/18
										Weakness(W)	
T1	0/06	3	0/18	2	0/12	3	0/18	3	0/18	3	0/18
T2	0/03	3	0/09	3	0/09	4	0/12	4	0/12	3	0/09
T3	0/02	2	0/04	4	0/08	2	0/04	3	0/06	3	0/06
T4	0/06	3	0/18	3	0/18	3	0/18	3	0/18	3	0/18
T5	0/09	4	0/36	3	0/27	1	0/09	3	0/27	3	0/27
T6	0/045	4	0/18	4	0/18	3	0/135	3	0/135	2	0/09
T7	0/04	3	0/12	3	0/12	2	0/08	2	0/08	3	0/12
T8	0/055	4	0/22	4	0/22	2	0/11	3	0/165	3	0/165
T9	0/06	4	0/24	4	0/24	1	0/06	1	0/06	1	0/06
	1		3/68		3/15		2/79		2/735		2/335

10- Conclusion

Considering tables 4 &5, this table can be represented as the conclusion.

Table6: strategies attractiveness regarding Sohan export internal and external factors

strategy	Strategy 1: focus on products and insertion into halal markets	Strategy 2: control increase on distribution system	Strategy control 3: on increase quality luct and packing	Strategy 4: sale increase through research and marketing activities	Strategy 5: modeling after advanced countries in sweet and chocolate industry
Internal factors attractiveness score	3.68	3.15	2.79	2.735	2.335
External factors attractiveness score	3.669	1.576	2.594	3.073	2.546
Average score	3.6745	2.363	2.692	2.904	2.4405

According to the average score of conservative strategies in quality strategic programming matrix, focus on products and insertion into halal markets has been selected as the best strategy.

Sohan is one of the traditional sweets and is favored by a lot of people. Soahn production, which one can say is only produced in Qom, faces many challenges that may be extinct. These challenges include not suitable packing, lack of programming and scientific strategies in marketing, not defining necessary standards and.... In this research we tried to study proper strategies for increase Sohan export and find solutions through researching about production and export condition and asking experts ideas.

11-suggested solutions

1)purposeful teaching is the main device for development. Teaching issues like country laws, export, packing and modern management tips to producer units managers can help development of this industry.

2)mostly small units are not able to take part in global markets and export. Taking part in these markets will be possible through establishing export organizations and cooperation of these units.

3)regarding production unit weaknesses in recognizing markets, collecting global information for Sohan producers to get familiar with these markets is effective. Iran commerce agents and ministry in other countries can present useful information about other countries marketing condition. Also, tourist and pilgrims attendance in Qom is another opportunity for recognizing these markets.

4) attractive packing for consumers is the main opportunity for profitability and competitive progress. But this opportunity has practically changed into a threat for our Sohan producers.

5) the first priority in Sohan export is protecting producers to grant "halal" sign and effective performance in halal markets. As mentioned before, progressing halal food market which belongs to Muslims should be the main target market for producers regarding common cultural backgrounds.

6) one of the strategies for gaining customer satisfaction and sales increase is quality promotion and producing different kinds of Sohan. Of course, differentiating should take place according to scientific knowledge of market and production process.

7) governmental credits for paying the costs of researches, propagandas and sales increase in target markets can assist these producers marketing in local and global markets.

REFERENCES

1. Amin Naseri, Mohammad; MOradi, MOrteza and MAlihi, eyed ehsan (1386); **"MEMERIYE KALANE Iran tea supply chain"**, scientific commerce magazine(1387), pp119-143.
2. Arabi, Seyed Mohammad(1385), "strategic programming, Tehran", cultural research office: p54
3. Haghighi, Mohsen (1374); **"considering export possibility of agricultural changing products of Khorasan state and its foreign marketing problems"**, thesis, Tehran university;p22.
4. Jafari Samimi, ahmad and Katrin Peykani (1381); **"the role of export credit on non-oil export development "**, commerce research magazine, commerce research and study institute, magazine no24,p p61-75.
5. Darvish Khani, Mahdi (1383); **"studying the effect of marketing management on Sohan export local and global sales increase"**, thesis, economy and official university of Isfahan, p35.
6. David, Fred.R (1379); **"strategic management"**, Parsaiian, Ali; Arabi, Seyed Mohammad, Tehran, cultural research office. P74.
7. Dodangi, Mahmood and MohamaAli Amoozade Khalili (1376); **"considering effective factors in MAzandaran state export development and its challenges"** , collection of articles of first conference on knowing the commerce talents of Mazandarn state, commerce research and study institute; pp25-36.
8. Zargarazad, Mohammad reza (1380); **"using AHP in strategic marketing in agricultural export merchants"**, thesis, Tehran university, p42.
9. .Islamic Republic of Iran customs website: www.irica.gov.ir, Dey 1389 10. Islamic Republic of Iran customs website: www.qomcustoms.ir, Dey1389.
11. Farmiran news website: www.farrmiran.ir; Dey1389.
12. Salehian Omran, Abolfazl. 1382. " **studying the relation between carpet roduction and export companies with utilizing simulative export government rules"**. University thesis with the guidance of Dr.Nahavandian. Tarbiyate Modares University;p17.
13. Ali Ahmadi, Alireza; Fathollah,Mahdi; TAjodin,Iraj (1382); **"comprehensive study of strategic management**: views, paradigms, processes, models, techniques and tools.p45
14. .Ghazi Zade, Mostafa (1382); **"study and determination of effective factors in export company success in Iran in Middle east and representation of strategies for non-oil export increase"**, thesis, Tehran university. P98.
15. Lotfabadi, Ali Shams (1374); **"considering non-oil export and estimation of date export function"**, thesis, Shahid BEheshti University; p45.
16. Madhoosh, Mehrdad and Ghafartari; **"non-oil export development strategies"**, commerce research magazine, commerce research and study institute, no44, pp195-223.
17. Breene , R.S., Nunes, Paul F., Shill , Walter E. (October 2007)"**The Chief Strategy Officer"**. *Harvard Business Review*;p 84.
18. Garner ,R. (2005),"**SWOT Tactics: Basics for strategic planning.FBI Low Enforcement Bulletin**"; 74(11);pp17-
9.
19. Forbes, P. (1996) ,"**Handbook of strategic planning ; Air Dole Group**";p45
20. Meredith , E., Forest , R. , Fred , R. (Spring 2009), " **The Quantitative Strategic Planning Matrix (QSPM) Applied To A Retail Computer Store"**, *The Coastal Business Journal* Spring 2009: Volume 8, Number 1;p23
21. .Richard ,W. (2005), **"The evolution of Business Strategy"**, Journal of Business Strategy;p69.
22. Rowley ,D. , Lugan , H., Dolence ,MG.(1997)," **Strategic change in colleges and universities** ". San Francisco: Jossey-Bass Publishers ;p44.
23. Weilun , Z.William, (2007), " **Analysing Company Strategy: The Case of EMC Corporation"**, Journal of University of Nottingham; P10.

2998

Journal of Applied Sciences Research, 8(6): 2949-2958, 2012 ISSN 1819-544X
This is a refereed journal and all articles are professionally screened and reviewed

ORIGINAL ARTICLES

The investigation of the business ethics: reviews, appraises and critiques theoretical

¹Ahmad Khanifar Al Ansari, ¹Hossein Khanifar, ²Kamran Nazari, ³Mostafa Emami

¹Associate Professor of Faculty of Management of Tehran University, Qom College, Iran ²Department of Business Management, Payam Noor University, Kermanshah, Iran ³Young Researchers Club, South Tehran Branch, Islamic Azad University, Tehran, Iran.

ABSTRACT

As an academic discipline, business ethics emerged in the 1970s. Since no academic business ethics journals or conferences existed, researchers published in general management journals, and attended general conferences. Over time, specialized peer-reviewed journals appeared, and more researchers entered the field. Corporate scandals in the earlier 2000s increased the field's popularity. As of 2009, sixteen academic journals devoted to various business ethics issues existed, with Journal of Business Ethics and Business Ethics Quarterly considered the leaders. Business ethics (also corporate ethics) is a form of applied ethics or professional ethics that examines ethical principles and moral or ethical problems that arise in a business environment. It applies to all aspects of business conduct and is relevant to the conduct of individuals and entire organizations. Business ethics has both normative and descriptive dimensions. As a corporate practice and a career specialization, the field is primarily normative. Academics attempting to understand business behavior employ descriptive methods. The range and quantity of business ethical issues reflects the interaction of profit-maximizing behavior with non-economic concerns. Interest in business ethics accelerated dramatically during the 1980s and 1990s, both within major corporations and within academia. For example, today most major corporations promote their commitment to non-economic values under headings such as ethics codes and social responsibility charters. Adam Smith said, "People of the same trade seldom meet together, even for merriment and diversion, but the conversation ends in a conspiracy against the public, or in some contrivance to raise prices." Governments use laws and regulations to point business behavior in what they perceive to be beneficial directions. Ethics implicitly regulates areas and details of behavior that lie beyond governmental control. The emergence of large corporations with limited relationships and sensitivity to the communities in which they operate accelerated the development of formal ethics regimes.

Key words: ethics, Business ethics, Behaving Ethically

Introduction

A business (also known as enterprise or firm) is an organization engaged in the trade of goods, services, or both to consumers. Businesses are predominant in capitalist economies, where most of them are privately owned and administered to earn profit to increase the wealth of their owners. Businesses may also be not-for-profit or state-owned. A business owned by multiple individuals may be referred to as a company, although that term also has a more precise meaning.

The etymology of "business" relates to the state of being busy either as an individual or society as a whole, doing commercially viable and profitable work. The term "business" has at least three usages, depending on the scope — the singular usage to mean a particular organization; the generalized usage to refer to a particular market sector, "the music business" and compound forms such as agribusiness; and the broadest meaning, which encompasses all activity by the community of suppliers of goods and services. However, the exact definition of business, like much else in the philosophy of business, is a matter of debate and complexity of

J. Appl. Sci. Res., 8(6): 2949-2958, 2012

meanings. Look in the newspaper on virtually any day of the week and you will find at least one business scandal in which a corporation appears to have violated the rules or standards of behavior generally accepted by society. Company finances have been manipulated in order to show a better balance sheet than actually exists, toxic waste has been allowed to flow into a river, bribes have been paid to secure a business deal, child labor has been used to assemble a product, discriminatory practices have prevented the employment or promotion of members of a particular group. When businesses behave unethically, they act in ways that have a harmful effect on others and in ways that are morally unacceptable to the larger community. This is very serious because corporate power and impact are increasing as corporations become larger (indeed, global) and as profit-making concerns take over functions that were once publicly controlled, such as the railroads, water utilities, and healthcare.

Corresponding Author: Ahmad Khanifar Al Ansari, Associate Professor of Faculty of Management of Tehran University, Qom College, Iran

Increasingly, it is the private sector that determines the quality of the air we breathe, the water we drink, our standard of living, and even where we live and how easily we can move around.

The philosophy of ethics: ethical theory Ethical theory is generally based upon moral philosophy and may be classified on many different dimensions, however, there are several basic 'types' of moral philosophy which are used in business ethics, such as egoism, utilitarianism, deontology, rights and relativism. Most of the different approaches may be considered as revolving around a focus on either the outcome of a situation (a consequentialist view) or upon the process or means to that outcome (nonconsequentialist).

Two examples of consequentialist or teleological philosophies are egoism and utilitarianism, while nonconsequentialist philosophies include deontological approaches such as that of Immanuel Kant. While some of Kant's writings are rather esoteric, his theory is often associated with the moral rights and duties of an individual; each person has both the right to expect to be treated according to universal moral laws and the corresponding duty to behave according to that law. The particular moral law according to which people should behave is known as the 'categorical imperative' and Kantproposed several versions of this law which, he claimed, were equivalent although their similarity is sometimes rather difficult to apprehend. In its first form, the categorical imperative states that one should 'act as if the maxim of thy action were to become by thy will a universal law of nature' (Kant, translated 1964). As Velasquez (1988) points out, the categorical imperative may be understood in a far less cumbersome and more readily accessible way by reference to the 'Golden Rule': 'Do unto others as you would have them do unto you'. As well as such general theories of ethics, many theories of ethics in particular situations or in relation to particular problems have been proposed. The field of applied ethics is, however, too specialist and voluminous to consider in any depth here. Furthermore, the ever-widening theory–practice gap has resulted in what Bowie (1991) calls a 'crisis of legitimacy' in business ethics. Kaler (1999) went even further in his call to dispense entirely with ethical theory. Even if one accepts the importance and achievements of ethical philosophy, the types of universal laws which are proposed as a guide to human behaviour are often difficult to apply in a practical way during the everyday life of organizational actors or, indeed, during the academic research process. Of course, depending upon one's view of the 'project' of business ethics, or what it aims to achieve, it could be argued that ethical theory need not concern itself with application to issues or problems, but could simply be about identifying what are good or bad reasons for particular courses of action. Such a view, however, fails to address the pragmatic concern for the management of organizational ethics (as well as the ecological validity of research into business ethics) because it ignores the actual acting out of ethical incidents within organizations. In any case, many authors (e.g. Bowie, 2000) have concurred with earlier suggestions (e.g. Brady and Logsdon, 1988; Randall, 1989) that much of the business ethics literature has a misplaced emphasis upon underlying philosophical theory and that researchers should focus instead upon the more psychological aspects of business ethics, such as behavioural intentions and the beliefs that shape those intentioshow generally weak, if statistically significant, links to both ethical decision-making and subsequent behaviour. The theory does, at least, provide a teleological account of how an individual may develop morally and a rudimentary understanding of moral reasoning processes. The weaknesses of this approach, however, necessitate the drawing together of other strands in the diverse literature on organizational ethics if we are to move towards more integrated and practically useful theoretical frameworks.

Business ethics reflects the philosophy of business, one of whose aims is to determine the fundamental purposes of a company. If a company's purpose is to maximize shareholder returns, then sacrificing profits to other concerns is a violation of its fiduciary responsibility. Corporate entities are legally considered as persons in USA and in most nations. The 'corporate persons' are legally entitled to the rights and liabilities due to citizens as persons.

Economist Milton Friedman writes that corporate executives' "responsibility... generally will be to make as much money as possible while conforming to their basic rules of the society, both those embodied in law and those embodied in ethical custom".Friedman also said, "the only entities who can have responsibilities are individuals ... A business cannot have responsibilities. So the question is, do corporate executives, provided they stay within the law, have responsibilities in their business activities other than to make as much money for their stockholders as possible? And my answer to that is, no, they do not." A multi-country 2011 survey found support for this view among the "informed public" ranging from 30-80%. Duska views Friedman's argument as consequentialist rather than pragmatic, implying that unrestrained corporate freedom would benefit the most in long term. Similarly author business consultant Peter Drucker observed, "There is neither a separate ethics of business nor is one needed", implying that standards of personal ethics cover all business situations. However, Peter Drucker in another instance observed that the ultimate responsibility of

2951

J. Appl. Sci. Res., 8(6): 2949-2958, 2012

company directors is not to harm—*primum non nocere*. Another view of business is that it must exhibit corporate social responsibility (CSR): an umbrella term indicating that an ethical business must act as a responsible citizen of the communities in which it operates even at the cost of profits or other goals. In the US and most other nations corporate entities are legally treated as persons in some respects. For example, they can hold title to property, sue and be sued and are subject to taxation, although their free speech rights are limited. This can be interpreted to imply that they have independent ethical responsibilities. Duska argues that stakeholders have the right to expect a business to be ethical; if business has no ethical obligations, other institutions could make the same claim which would be counterproductive to the corporation. Ethical issues include the rights and duties between a company and its employees, suppliers, customers and neighbors, its fiduciary responsibility to its shareholders. Issues concerning relations between different companies include hostile take- overs and industrial espionage. Related issues include corporate governance; corporate social entrepreneurship; political contributions; legal issues such as the ethical debate over introducing a crime of corporate manslaughter; and the marketing of corporations' ethics policies.

Business Ethics:

 The business ethics can also be understood generally in terms of corporate social responsibility (CSR) (Singer, 1993). CSR is can be catagorally defined as the level of economic legal, morality or ethical adapted to values of society expectation (Andrews, 1987; Carrroll, 1979, Sathi 1975). The term corporate social responsibility is understood as a subject of manager level but it is also consider in the business ethics literature (Frietman,1962). The researcher, on the other side business ethics is divided into main Approaches (i) conceptual & (ii) empirical (Preble & Reichel, 1988), The main objective of conceptual approach to maximum clarity in the meaning of business ethics, moral conduct and social responsibility and also used with the recommended guideline to help the corporate leader to reach on ethical business decision (Braybrooke, 1983; Cavanagh et al, 1981; Hoffman & Moore, 1984). According to the second approach- empirical approach ((Preble & Reichel, 1988), is used to places emphasis on examining the prevailing ethics, perceptions and attitude / behavior of general public, business peoples and universities students who regarded as the future business leader oftenly. The behavior or the attitude towards ethics of the business is referred to have "the subjective assessment by given individuals with respect to sets of premises that make a various business phosiphies (Preble & Reichel, 1988 p 942).
 The behavior towards business ethics shaping the core component of empirical study of business ethics. They also lighted the importance that some particular groups of individuals attaching to each of the philosophies underline the concept of business ethics.
 The literature in classical text in which formed the managerial foundation had researched to recognize the themes as they evolved in literature recognizing the perceptional changing in the concept over time. More over recently literature available also reviewed the concepts and can available to use to understanding the recently changing brought in the concept.
 Peter Drucker explicitly addressed the "social responsibility of business (The practices of management, book 1954, p. ix) Drucker also focusing on the CSR in which he considered the public responsibility as one of the eight key areas would be used for setting the business objectives. He, furtherly, the objective narrated in this areas must be in compliance of social condition and political arena which are concede organizational management (1954, p82).Drucker fatherly identified that the manager has assumed responsibilities in the references to the public good, as he subordinated by his actions to an ethical standard of conduct. In the mean time he also pronounced in a clear way that the organization has to give first priority to the society in which it is doing business and he also realized that it is also important to pay attention on every business policy and actions effecting on the society. "it has to consider whether to action is likely to promote the public good, to advance to basic beliefs of our society , to contribute to its stability, strength and harmony" (1954, p388), Durcker also said that it is an ultimate responsibility of the management for, itself, enterprises, heritage, society, and the way of life (1954, p392).
 The other researchers like Batrnard (1938) and Simon (1945) paid attention more to the moral ethical damnations of the individual behavior in organization. Philip Selznicx has done his basic work on values, he also worked to exploring to ethical/moral consideration and corporate social responsibility, (leadership in administration: A sociological perspective, 1957, p. ix) further said that a sound leadership of an organization would have to required the proper ordering of human affairs, incorporating the social order establishment, the determination of public interest, and defense of critical values". He also strongly follower of this thought but peter Durker (1954) that the organizations had becoming publicly in natures that is why needed to handling of the problems off effecting the welfare of entire society. He also understood that the organizations which shifted from a narrow emphasis on profit making to a large social responsibility" had required to build special values into the corporation (1957, p.26-27) in general theory of marketing ethics, Hunt and Vittel proposed that "cultural norms/values affect the perceived ethical situation, alternatives, consequences probabilities of consequences, desirability of consequences and importance of the stakeholders" (1986 p. 10) but they were not specify in what way or extent the norms/values affect the ethical decision making. In 1992 Hunt & Vitell revised their general theory in which they again not specified how values affected in the ethical decision making besides the empirical test also did not examined the extent of influence of cultural values on the ethical making decision (Vitell & Hunt, 1990; Mayo & Marks, 1990; Singhapakdi & Vitell 1990; & Singhapakdi & Vitell 1991).
 Kenneth R. Andrews in the concepts of corporate strategy concepted the ethical behavior as an outcome of values. He also identified emerging importance of the values, ethical/moral considerations and CSR (Corporate social responsibility). He further explained that

2952

J. Appl. Sci. Res., 8(6): 2949-2958, 2012

the forms doing business only for the profit earning these forms had to obey the ethical behavior to earn the profit. He also advised that a company should follow good worked which are connected its plans of action with present and futuristic economics functions. He also suggested that a corporation should have economic and non-economic objectives which are harmony with the views as of Durker (1954) and Ansoff (1965), Andrew stated that the firms with having further action planning will have a strategy for support of its community institutions as explicit as its economic strategy and as its decision about the kind of organization it intends to be and the kid of people it intends to attract to its membership. R. Edward Freeman in his book, strategic management: a stakeholder approach, also acknowledge the developing the importance of ethics which are evidenced in building of ethics codes in business and increasing so, of ethics courses in business schools.

Presently the business are effects the most powerful institutions in the world, the expense of social responsibility has enlarged to include areas formally considered the domain of governments: quality of education and support of acts, funding and facilities for basic research, urban planning and development, would hanger and poverty, hard core unemployment. The more powerful business becomes in the world, the more responsibility for well being of the world it will be expected to bear" (Soloman, 1997; p. 204-206).

We obviously understand that CSR concept envisaged the social concerns in the business (Branda Joyer & Dinah Payne, 2002). It is question about our understanding level for values and ethics at present and how our leaders do supportive and ranking the ethical behavior in a corporation shown by individuals.

".... Cultures set up the network of people and positions with whom we feel comfortable and, given enormous power of peer pressure in ethics, one should not be surprised that the culture of the corporation – rather than individual values- is the primary determinant of business ethics, different business provide different cultural, and different cultural define different values, different ethics, different lives". (Solomon 1997, p. 140)Common Ethical Problems Within Corporations Given the increasing social impact of business, business ethics has emerged as a discrete subject over the last 20 years. Business ethics is concerned with exploring the moral principles by which we can evaluate business organizations in relation to their impact on people and the environment. Trevino and Nelson (2004) categorize four types of ethical problems that are commonly found in business organizations.

First are the *human resource problems*: These relate to the equitable and just treatment of current and potential employees. Unethical behavior here involves treating people unfairly because of their gender, sexuality, skin color, religion, ethnic background, and so on.

Second are ethical problems arising from *conflicts of interest*, when particular individuals or organizations are given special treatment because of some personal relationship with the individual or group making a decision. A company might get a lucrative contract, for example, because a bribe was paid to the management team of the contracting organization, not because of the quality of its proposal. Third are ethical problems that involve *customer confidence*. Corporations sometimes behave in ways that show a lack of respect for customers or a lack of concern with public safety. Examples here include advertisements that lie (or at least conceal the truth) about particular goods or services, and the sale of products, such as drugs, where a company conceals or obfuscates negative data about safety and/or efficacy.

Finally, there are ethical problems surrounding the *use of corporate resources* by employees who make private phone calls at work, submit false expense claims, take company stationery home, etc. The financial scandals that have rocked the corporate world in recent years (Enron, WorldCom, Parmalat, Lehman Brothers, for example) have involved a number of these different ethical issues. In these cases, senior managers have engaged in improper bookkeeping, making companies look more financially profitable than they actually are. As a consequence the stockholder value of the company increases, and anyone with stock profits directly. Among those profiting will be those making the decisions to manipulate the accounts and so there is a conflict of interest. However, the fallout from the downfall of these companies affects stockholders, employees, and society at large negatively, with innocent people losing their retirement reserves and/or savings, and employees losing their jobs.

Another category can be added to this list—ethical problems surrounding the *use of the world's environmental resources*. Many organizations have externalized the costs associated with their negative impact on the environment, whether in relation to their own operations to produce goods and services, or in terms of the use and later the disposal of the goods that they have sold. Externalizing means that organizations do not themselves pay for the environmental costs that they create. For example, carbon dioxide emissions, a byproduct of energy use for all kinds of organizations, are now recognized as contributing to global warming; computer equipment contains toxic waste that pollutes the land where it is dumped; and packaging of all kinds, including plastic bags that are handed out by supermarkets, are creating mounting problems as local authorities run out of landfill sites. Increasingly, ethical business is seen to require that a business takes into account and offsets its "environmental footprint" so that it engages in sustainable activity. Sustainability broadly means that a business meets the needs of the present without compromising the ability of future generations to meet their needs.

Accounting for Ethical and Unethical Behavior:

While it may be very easy to identify and blame an individual or small group of individuals, to see these individuals as the perpetrators of an unethical act—the "bad apple"—and hold them responsible for the harm caused, is an oversimplification. Most accounts of unethical behavior that are restricted to the level of the individual are inadequate. Despite popular belief, decisions harmful to others or the environment that are made within organizations are not typically the result of an isolated, immoral individual seeking to gain

2953

J. Appl. Sci. Res., 8(6): 2949-2958, 2012

personally. Although an individual's level of moral maturity or the locus of control (for example, the degree to which they perceive they control their behaviors and actions) are factors, we also need to explore the decision-making context—the group dynamics and the organizational practices and procedures—to understand why an unethical decision was made.

Group dynamics influence the decision-making process. A particularly important group-level influence is *groupthink*, a phenomenon identified by Irving Janis (1982) in his research on US foreign policy groups. The research demonstrates the presence of strong pressures towards conformity in these groups: individual members suspend their own critical judgment and right to question, with the result that they make bad and/or immoral decisions. Janis defines groupthink as "the psychological drive for consensus at any cost that suppresses dissent and appraisal of alternatives in cohesive decision-making groups." The degree to which decisions are ethical is also influenced by organizational culture or climate.

Organizational ethical climates can differ; some are more egoistic, others are more benevolent, still others are highly principled, and these contexts can shape a manager's ethical decision-making. Smith and Johnson (1996) identify three general approaches that organizations take to corporate responsibility:

• **Social obligation**: The corporation does only what is legally required.
• **Social responsiveness**: The corporation responds to pressure from different stakeholder groups.
• **Social responsibility**: The corporation has an agenda of proactively trying to improve society.

In a company in which the dominant approach to business ethics is social obligation, it is likely to be difficult to justify a decision based on ethical criteria; morally irresponsible behavior may be condoned as long as it does not break the law. Legal loopholes, for example, may be exploited in such a company if these can benefit the company in the short term, even if they might have a negative influence on others in society.

Ethical Dilemmas:

Sometimes it is clear that a business has behaved unethically—for example, where a drug is sold illegally, the company accounts have been falsely presented, or where client funds have been embezzled. Of more interest, and much more common, are situations that pose an ethical dilemma—situations that present a conflict between right and wrong or between values and obligations—so that a choice is necessary. For example, a corporation may want to build a new factory on a previously undeveloped and popular tourist site in a location where there is large-scale unemployment among the local population. Here we have a conflict between the benefits of wealth and job creation in a location in which these are crucial and the cost of spoiling some naturally beautiful countryside. Philosophers have attempted to develop prescriptive theories providing universal laws that enable us to differentiate between right and wrong, and good and bad, in these situations

Prescriptive Ethical Theories:

Essentially there are two schools of thought. The consequentialists argue that behavior is ethical if it maximizes the common good (happiness) and minimizes harm. The opposing nonconsequentialists argue that behavior is ethical if it is motivated by a sense of duty or a set of moral principles about human conduct — regardless of the consequences of the action.

Casuistry was so thoroughly discredited that the only mention of it to be found in most textbooks on the history of philosophy is in connection with its ultimate adversaries-Spinoza and Pascal. Indeed, only 10 or 15 years ago, few if any philosophers would have thought it possible for anything like "business ethics" to emerge. "Particularist ethics," a set of ethics that postulates that this or that group is different in its ethical responsibilities from everyone else, would have been considered doomed forever by the failure of casuistry. Ethics, almost anyone in the West would have considered axiomatic, would surely always be ethics of the individual and independent of rank and station.But there is another, non-Western ethics that is situational. It is the most successful and most durable ethics of them all: the Confucian ethics of interdependence.Confucian ethics elegantly sidesteps the trap into which the Casuists fell; it is a universal ethics, in which the same rules and imperatives of behavior hold for every individual. There is no "social responsibility" overriding individual conscience, no costbenefit calculation, no greater good or higher measure than the individual and his behavior, and altogether no casuistry. In the Confucian ethics, the rules are the same for all. But there are different general rules, according to the five basic relationships of interdependence, which for the Confucian embrace the totality of individual interactions in civil society: superior and subordinate (or master and servant); father and child; husband and wife; oldest brother and sibling; friend and friend. Right behavior-what in the English translation of Confucian ethics is usually called "sincerity" is that individual behavior which is truly appropriate to the specific relationship of mutual dependence because it optimizes benefits for both parties. Other behavior is "insincere" and therefore wrong behavior and unethical. It creates dissonance instead of harmony, exploitation instead of benefits, manipulation instead of trust. An example of the Confucian approach to the ethical problems discussed under the heading of "business ethics" would be "sexual harrassment." To the Confucian it is clearly unethical behavior because it injects power into a relationship that is based on function.

This makes it exploitation. That this "insincere,"-that is, grosslyunethical-behavior on the part of a superior takes place within a business or any other kind of organization, is basically irrelevant.

2954

J. Appl. Sci. Res., 8(6): 2949-2958, 2012

The master/servant or superior/subordinate relationship is one between individuals. Hence, the Confucian would make no distinction between a general manager forcing his secretary into sexual intercourse and Mr. Samuel Pepys, England's famous 17th century di- * No word has caused more misunderstanding in East/West relations than "sincerity." To a Westerner, "sincerity" means "words that are true to conviction and feelings"; to an Easterner, "sincerity" means "actions that are appropriate to a specific relationship and make it harmonious and of optimum mutual benefit." For the Westerner, "sincerity" has to do with intentions, that is, with morality; to the Easterner, "sincerity" has to do with behavior, that is, with ethics. Arist, forcing his wife's maids to submit to his amorous advances. It would not even make much difference to the Confucian that today's secretary can, as a rule, quit without suffering more than inconvenience if she does not want to submit, whereas the poor wretches in Mrs. Pepys' employ ended up as prostitutes, either because they did not submit and were fired and out on the street, or because they did submit and were fired when they got pregnant. Nor would the Confucian see much difference between a corporation ice-president engaging in "sexual harrassment" and a college professor seducing coeds with implied promises to raise their grades. And finally, it would be immaterial to the Confucian that the particular "insincerity" involves sexual relations. The superior would be equally guilty of grossly unethical behavior and violation of fundamental rules of conduct if, as a good many of the proponents of "business ethics" ardently advocate, he were to set himself up as a mental therapist for his subordinates and help them to "adjust."

No matter how benevolent his intentions, this is equally incompatible with the integrity of the superior/subordinate relationship. It equally abuses rank based on function and imposes power. It is therefore exploitation whether done because of lust for power or manipulation or done out of benevolence-either way it is unethical and destructive. Both sexual relations and the healer/patient relationship must be free of rank to be effective, harmonious, and ethically correct. They are constructive only as "friend to friend" or as "husband to wife" relations, in which differences in function confer no rank whatever.

This example makes it clear, I would say, that virtually all the concerns of "business ethics," indeed almost everything "business ethics" considers a problem, have to do with relationship of interdependence, whether that between the organization and the employee, the manufacturer and the customer, the hospital and the patient, the university and the student, and so on. Looking at the ethics of interdependence immediately resolves the conundrum which confounds the present discussion of "business ethics": What difference does it make whether a certain act or behavior takes place in a "business," in a "non-profit organization," or outside any organization at all? The answer is clear: None at all. Indeed the questions that are so hotly debated in today's discussion of "business ethics," such as whether changing a hospital from "nonprofit" to "proprietary and for profit" will affect either its behavior or the ethics pertaining to it, the most cursory exposure to the ethics of interdependence reveals as sophistry and as nonquestions. The ethics of interdependence thus does address itself to the question which "business ethics" tries to tackle. But today's discussion, explicity or implicity, denies the basic insight from which the ethics of interdependence starts and to which it owes its strength and durability:It denies interdependence.

The ethics of interdependence, as Confucian philosophers first codified it shortly after their Master's death in 479 B.C., considers illegitimate and unethical the injection of power into human relationships. It asserts that interdependence demands equality of obligations. Children owe obedience and respect to their parents. Parents, in turn, owe affection, sustenance and, yes, respect, to their children. For every paragon of filial piety in Confucian hagiology, such as the dutiful daughter, there is a paragon of parental sacrifice, such as the loving father who sacrificed his brilliant career at the court to the care of his five children and their demands on his time and attention. For every minister who risks his job, if not his life, by fearlessly correcting an Emperor guilty of violating harmony, there is an Emperor laying down his life rather than throw a loyal minister to the political wolves. In the ethics of interdependence there are only "obligations," and all obligations are mutual obligations. Harmony and trust-that is, interdependence-require that each side be obligated to provide what the other side needs to achieve its goals and to fulfill itself. But in today's American-and European-discussion of "business ethics," ethics means that one side has obligations and the other side has rights, if not "entitlements." This is not compatible with the ethics of interdependence and indeed with any ethics at all. It is the politics of power, and indeed the politics of naked exploitation and repression. And within the context of interdependence the "exploiters" and the "oppressors" are not the "bosses," but the ones who assert their "rights" rather than accept mutual obligation, and with it, equality. To "redress the balance" in a relationship of interdependence- or at least so the ethics of interdependence would insist-demands not pitting power against power or right against right, but matching obligation to obligation. To illustrate: Today's "ethics of organization" debate pays great attention to the duty to be a "whistle-blower" and to the protection of the "whistle-blower" against retaliation or suppression by his boss or by his organization. This sounds high-minded. Surely, the subordinate has a right, if not indeed a duty, to bring to public attention and remedial action his superior's misdeeds, let alone violation of the law on the part of a superior or of his employing organization. But in the context of the ethics of interdependence, "whistle-blowing" is ethically quite ambiguous. To be sure, there are misdeeds of the superior or of the employing organization which so grossly violate propriety and laws that the subordinate (or the friend, or the child, or even the wife) cannot remain silent. This is, after all, what the word "felony" implies; one becomes a partner to a felony and criminally liable by not reporting, and thus "compounding" it. But otherwise? It is not primarily that to encourage "whistle-blowing" corrodes the bond of trust that ties the superior to the subordinate. Encouraging the "whistle-blower" must make the subordinate lose his trust in the superior's willingness and ability to "protect his people." They simply are no longer "his people" and become potential enemies or political pawns. And in the end, encouraging and indeed even permitting "whistle-blowers" always makes the weaker one-that is, the subordinate-powerless against the unscrupulous superior, simply because the superior no longer can recognize or meet his obligation to the subordinate.

2955

J. Appl. Sci. Res., 8(6): 2949-2958, 2012

"Whistle-blowing," after all, is simply another word for "informing." And perhaps it is not quite irrelevant that the only societies in Western history that encouraged informers were bloody and infamous tyranniesTiberius and Nero in Rome, the Inquisition in the Spain of Philip II, the French Terror, and Stalin. It may also be no accident that Mao, when he tried to establish dictatorship in China, organized "whistle-blowing" on a massive scale. For under "whistle-blowing," under the regime of the "informer," no mutual trust, no interdependencies, and no ethics are possible. And Mao only followed history's first "totalitarians," the "Legalists" of the Third Century B.C., who suppressed Confucius and burned his books because he had taught ethics and had rejected the absolutism of political power.

The limits of mutual obligation are indeed a central and difficult issue in the ethics of interdependencies. But to start out, as the advocates of "whistle-blowing" do, with the assumption that there are only rights on one side, makes any ethics impossible. And if the fundamental problem of ethics is the behavior in relations of interdependence, then obligations have to be mutual and have to be equal for both sides. Indeed, in a relationship of interdependence it is the mutuality of obligation that creates true equality, regardless of differences in rank, wealth, or power. Today's discussion of "business ethics" stridently denies this. It tends to assert that in relations of interdependence one side has all the duties and the other one all the rights. But this is the assertion of the Legalist, the assertion of the totalitarians who shortly end up by denying all ethics. It must also mean that ethics becomes the tool of the powerful. If a set of ethics is one-sided, then the rules are written by those that have the position, the power, the wealth. If interdependence is not equality of obligations, it becomes domination. Looking at "business ethics" as an ethics of interdependence reveals an additional and equally serious problem-indeed a more serious problem.

Can an ethics of interdependence be anything more than ethics for individuals? The Confucians said "no"--a main reason why Mao outlawed them. For the Confucian-but also for the philosopher of the Western traditiononly/aw can handle the rights and objections of collectives. Ethics is always a matter of the person.

But is this adequate for a "society of organizations" such as ours? This may be the central question for the philosopher of modern society, in which access to livelihood, career and achievement exist primarily in and through organizations-and especially for the highly-educated person for whom opportunities outside of organization are very scarce indeed. In such a society, both the society and the individual increasingly depend on the performance, as well as the "sincerity," of organizations.

But in today's discussion of "business ethics" it is not even seen that there is a problem.

Business ethics," this discussion should have made clear, is to ethics what soft porn is to the Platonic Eros; soft porn too talks of something it calls "love." And insofar as "business ethics" comes even close to ethics, it comes close to casuistry and will, predictably, end up as a fig leaf for the shameless and as special pleading for the powerful and the wealthy.

Clearly, one major element of the peculiar stew that goes by the name of "business ethics" is plain oldfashioned hostility to business and to economic activity altogether-one of the oldest of American traditions and perhaps the only still-potent ingredient in the Puritan heritage. Otherwise, we would not even talk of "business ethics." There is no warrant in any ethics to consider one major sphere of activity as having its own ethical problems, let alone its own "ethics." "Business" or "economic activity" may have special political or legal dimensions as in "business and government," to cite the title of a once-popular college course, or as in the antitrust laws. And "business ethics" may be good politics or good electioneering.

But that is all. For ethics deals with the right actions of individuals. And then it surely makes no difference whether the setting is a community hospital, with the actors a nursing supervisor and the "consumer" a patient, or whether the setting is National Universal General

Corporation, the actors a quality control manager, and the consumer the buyer of a bicycle.

But one explanation for the popularity of "business ethics" is surely also the human frailty of which Pascal accused the Casuists of his day: the lust for power and prominence of a clerisy sworn to humility. "'Business ethics" is fashionable, and provides speeches at conferences, lecture fees, consulting assignments, and lots of publicity. And surely "business ethics," with its tales of wrongdoing in high places, caters also to the age-old enjoyment of "society" gossip and to the prurience which-it was, I believe, Rabelais who said it-makes it fornication when a peasant has a toss in the hay and romance when the prince does it.

Altogether, "business ethics" might well be called "ethical chic" rather than ethics-and indeed might be considered more a media event than philosophy or morals.

But this discussion of the major approaches to ethics and of their concerns surely also shows that ethics has as much to say to the individual in our society of organizations as they ever had to say to the individual in earlier societies. They are just as important and just asneeded nowadays. And they surely require hard and serious work.

A society of organizations is a society of interdependence. The specific relationship which the Confucian philosopher postulated as universal and basic may not be adequate, or even appropriate, to modern society and to the ethical problems within the modern organization and between the modern organization and its clients, customers, and constituents. But the fundamental concepts surely are. Indeed, if there ever is a viable "ethics of organization," it will almost certainly have to adopt the key concepts which have made Confucian ethics both durable and effective:

-clear definition of the fundamental relationships;

-universal and general rules of conduct-that is, rules that are binding on any one person or organization, according to its rules, function, and relationships; --focus on right behavior rather than on avoiding wrongdoing, and on behavior rather than on motives or intentions; and finally, -an effective organization ethic, indeed an organization ethic that deserves to be seriously considered as

J. Appl. Sci. Res., 8(6): 2949-2958, 2012

"ethics," will have to define right behavior as the behavior which optimizes each party's benefits and thus makes the relationship harmonious, constructive, and mutually beneficial. But a society of organizations is also a society in which a great many people are unimportant and indeed anonymous by themselves, yet are highly visible, and matter as "leaders" in society. And thus it is a society that must stress the Ethics of Prudence and selfdevelopment.It must expect its managers, executives, and professionals to demand of themselves that they shun behavior they would not respect in others, and instead practice behavior appropriate to the sort of person they would want to see "in the mirror in the morning."

Consequentialist Accounts of Ethical Behavior:

Philosophers who adopt the consequentialist approach (sometimes also referred to as utilitarianism) consider that behavior can be judged ethical if it has been enacted in order to maximize human happiness and minimize harm. Jeremy Bentham (1748–1832) and John Stuart Mill (1806–73) are two of the best-known early proponents of this view. Importantly it is the common good, not personal happiness, that is the arbiter of right and wrong. Indeed, we are required to sacrifice our personal happiness if doing so enhances the total sum of happiness. For someone faced with a decision choice, the ethical action is the one that achieves the greatest good for the greatest number of people after weighing the impact on those involved. Common criticisms of this approach are that it is impossible to measure happiness adequately and that it essentially condones injustice if this is to the benefit of the majority.

Nonconsequentialist Accounts of Ethical Behavior:

Philosophers who adopt a nonconsequentialist approach (also referred to as deontological theory) argue that behavior can be judged as ethical if it is based on a sense of duty and carried out in accordance with defined principles. Immanuel Kant (1724–1804), for example, articulated the principle of *respect for persons*, which states that people should never be treated as a means to an end, but always as an end in themselves; leading to the easy to remember maxim – do as you would be done by. The idea here is that we can establish moral judgments that are true because they can be based on the unique human ability to reason. One common criticism of this approach is that it is impossible to agree on the basic ethical principles of duty or their relative weighting in order to direct choices when multiple ethical principles are called into question at the same time, or when decisions cut across cultures with different ethical principles.

Why Behaving Ethically Is Important for Business:

Choosing to be ethical can involve short-term disadvantages for a corporation. Yet in the long term it is clear that behaving ethically is the key to sustainable development. When you're faced with an ethical dilemma in which the immoral choice looks appealing, ask yourself three questions:

1.   **What will happen when (not if) the action is discovered?** Increasingly, the behavior of corporations is under scrutiny from their various stakeholders—customers, suppliers, stockholders, employees, competitors, regulators, environmental groups, and the general public. People are less willing to keep quiet when they feel an injustice has been done, and the internet and other media give them the means to make their concerns very public, reaching a global audience. Corporations that behave unethically are unlikely to get away with it, and the impact when they are discovered can be catastrophic. This leads to the second question.

2.   **Is the decision really in the long-term interests of the corporation?** Many financial services companies in the United Kingdom generated short-term profits in the 1990s by miss selling personal pensions to people who would have been better off staying in their company's pension plan. However, in the long term these companies have suffered by having to repay this money and pay penalties. Most significantly, the practice has eroded public confidence. The same is true of many banks and mortgage brokers in the first part of the 21st century when they sold mortgages to individuals who could not afford to repay their debts. The eventual result was that large numbers defaulted, causing a meltdown in the global financial system beginning in 2008.

3.   **Will organizations that behave unethically attract the employees they need?** Corporations that harm society or the environment are actually harming their own employees, including those who are making the decisions. For example, corporations that pour toxins into the air are polluting the air their employees' families breathe. Ultimately, a business relies on its human resources. If a company cannot attract high-quality people because it has a poor public image based on previous unethical behavior, it will certainly flounder.

Behaving ethically is clearly key to the long-term sustainability of any business. Focusing on the triple bottom line—the social and environmental as well as the economic impact of a company—provides the basis for sound stakeholder relationships that can sustain a business into the future.

Conclusions:

Business ethics is part of the philosophy of business, the branch of philosophy that deals with the philosophical, political, and ethical underpinnings of business and economics. Business ethics operates on the premise, for example, that the ethical operation of a private business is possible—those who dispute that premise, such as libertarian socialists, (who contend that "business ethics" is an oxymoron) do so by definition outside of the domain of business ethics proper.

The philosophy of business also deals with questions such as what, if any, are the social responsibilities of a business; business management theory; theories of individualism vs. collectivism; free will among participants in the marketplace; the role of self interest; invisible hand theories; the requirements of social justice; and natural rights, especially property rights, in relation to the business enterprise.

Business ethics is also related to **political economy,** which is economic analysis from political and historical perspectives. Political economy deals with the distributive consequences of economic actions. It asks who gains and who loses from economic activity, and is the resultant distribution fair or just, which are central ethical issues.

Although theoretical bases for the study of business ethics have been offered in the form of both moral philosophies and the psychology of moral development, these approaches are only of limited value when it comes to attempting to apply ethical theory to real-life situations (e.g.Bowie, 2000; Cornelius and Gagnon, 1999). In this connection, Maclagan (1995) has suggested that business ethics researchers need to recognize the complexity and disorder of real-life management practice and adopt methods of investigation and theoretical and conceptual frameworks that allow for this, rather than attempting to borrow from the abstract concepts of philosophical ethics theory. The limited description of the ethical decision-making process offered by Kohlberg's stages of CMD, coupled with the theoretical criticisms and limitations of this approach (e.g. Marnburg, 2001) also make this a less than satisfactory theoretical framework for understanding ethical decision-making at work.

Codes of ethics are probably the most visible sign of a company's ethical philosophy. In order for a code of ethics to be meaningful, it must clearly state its basic principles and expectations; it must realistically focus on the potential ethical dilemmas which may be faced by employees; it must be communicated to all employees; and it must be enforced. Further, a meaningful code of ethics cannot rely on blind obedience. It must be accepted and internalized by the employees who are required to implement it. This means that managers must attend not only to the content of the code but also to the process of determining that content. To be most effective, a code should be developed and disseminated in an open, participative environment involving as many employees as possible. Since individuals are likely to face ethical issues most of their lives, there is little doubt that potential employees have significant ethical decision histories when they apply. Thus the first line of defense against unethical behavior in the organization is the employment process. There are several methods available to organizations for ethical screening. These techniques vary widely in terms of costs and benefits. Further, these techniques may vary widely in terms of their legality and may themselves have ethical implications. Paper and pencil honesty tests are one technique which may be used for ethical screening in organizations. These tests seem to be reasonably valid with low costs and short time periods involved in administration (Sackett and Harris, 1984).Employees need to have an experiential awareness of the types of ethical dilemmas they may face, and they need to know what actions to take in these dilemmas. Providing ethics training for employees is one key to increasing this awareness. Ethics training normally begins with orientation sessions and open discussions of the firm's code of ethics. Employees should be encouraged to participate at a high level in these sessions as well as in other training that follows. This is often followed by the use of fictitious ethical scenarios which simulate situations that employees may face on the job. Providing sales persons with scenarios involving improper gifts or kickback offers gives employees a chance to make ethical decisions in realistic situations and to discuss these decisions openly with peers, supervisors, etc. Organizations such as McDonnell Douglas and General Dynamics have used scenario training to transform their codes of ethics from simple documents to tools for training, education and communication about ethical standards (Otten, 1986).

References

Andrew, K.R., 1987. *"The concept of corporate strategy"* (Richard D Irwin, Inc., New York, N.Y).

Ansoff, H.I., 1965. *"Corporate strategy: an analytic approach to business policy for growth and Expansion"* (MaGraw Hill New York, N.Y).

Carroll, A.B., 1978. "Linking business ethics to behavior in organization." Advance Management Journal, 43: 411.

Drucker, P.F., 1954. *"The practice of Management"* (Harper & Raw publishers, New York. N.Y).

Freeman, R.E. and D.E. Gilbert Jr., 1988. *"Corporate strategy and the search for ethics"* (Prentice Hall, Englewood Cliffs, NJ)

Friedman, Milton, 1962. *"Capitalism and freedom"* The university of Chicago Press, Chicago, IL.

Hunt, S.D. and S. Vitell, 1986. "A General theory on Marketing Ethics"

Kotter, J.P. and A. Heskett, 1992. *"Corporate Culture and Performance",* Free Press, New York, NY.

Liu, A.M.M., 1999. "Culture in the Hong Kong real estate profession: a trait approach", Habitat International, 23(3): 417-25.

Mason, D.E., 1992. "Values of ethical choices: Rate yourself", Non profit world, 10(3): 23-25.

Nahapiet, J., S. Goshal, 1998. Business Ethics Preble, J.F., & Reichel, A. (1998), "Attitude toward business ethics of future managers in the USA and Isreal". *Journal of Business Ethics*, 9, 941-949

J. Appl. Sci. Res., 8(6): 2949-2958, 2012

Raiborn, Cecily A. and D. Payne, 1990. "Corporate codes of conduct; A collective conscience and continuum", *Journal of business Ethics,* 9: 897-889.

Rokeach, M., 1972. "Beliefs, Attitudes and Values: A Theory of Organization and Change", Josey Bass, San Francisco, CA.

Rosenthal, R. and R.L. Rosnow, 1991. Essentials of Behavioral Research: Methods and Data Anlaysis, 2nd ed., McGraw- Hill, Boston, MA.

Schein, E.H., 1985. Organizational Culture and Leadership, Jossey-Bass, San Francisco, CA. Simon, H.A.,

1945. Administrative behavior (Free Press, New York, NY.) Stodder, Gayle Sato, 1998. "Goodwill hunting",

Entrepreneurs (July), 118-121.

Vitell, S.J. and S.D. Hunt, 1990. "the general theory of marketing ethics: A partial test of the model, research in the marketing, 10: 237-265.

Management Science Letters 3 (2013) 511–518

Contents lists available at GrowingScience

Management Science Letters

homepage: www.GrowingScience.com/msl

The investigation of the relation between job involvement and organizational commitment

Mohammad Javad Esfahani[a*], Mostafa Emami[b] and Hamid Reza Tajnesaei[c]

[a]Department of Industrial Engineering, Young Researchers Club, Naragh Branch, Islamic Azad University, Naragh, Iran [b]Young Researchers Club, Kermanshah Branch, Islamic Azad University, Kermanshah, Iran [c]Department of Management, Sanandaj Branch, Islamic Azad University, Sanandaj, Iran

C H R O N I C L E

A B S T R A C T

Article history:
Received September 18, 2012
Received in revised format
21 December 2012
Accepted 21 December 2012
Available online
December 22 2012

Keywords:
Job involvement
Organizational commitment
Iran automaker industry

This paper investigates the relationship between job involvement and organizational commitment among lower-level employees in Iranian automaker industry. In this study, job involvement is an independent variable, organizational commitment is dependent variable, and the analysis is performed using 100 randomly selected data through a questionnaire, which consists of four-parts. The study gathers biographical and occupational data using a self designed 40-item questionnaire. The survey measures job involvement using Kanungo's 10 item 5-point rating scale and organizational commitment is measured based on Mowday's 15 item 5-point scale. The study uses different statistical techniques including Pearson Product Moment Correlation Technique and Multiple Regression Analysis. The results indicate that job involvement is strongly associated with organizational commitment. The paper therefore suggests that managers must put in all their efforts to promote job involvement in their companies.

1. Introduction

During the past few years, there have been enormous evidences recommending that organizational commitment could possibly lead to organizational success and efficiency (Mowday et al., 1982; Robbins, 2005). Organizational commitment plays an important role for management of organizations and learns more on what variables are useful for organizational commitment. Knowledge enables managers to build necessary conditions, which are conducive to the development of such antecedents of organizational commitment in their organizations. Organizational commitment can be described as employees' psychological attachments to the organization (Organisational Commitment Wikipedia, 2008) and it is possible to compute it through different factors including organizational objectives, the desire to belong to the organization and the willingness to display effort on behalf of the organization.

*Corresponding author. Tel: +9891876 54910
E-mail addresses: mohammadjavadesfahani@gmail.com (M. J. Esfahani)

© 2013 Growing Science Ltd. All rights reserved. doi:
10.5267/j.msl.2012.12.023

Maxwell and Steele (2003) carried out an investigation to identify the determinants of organizational commitment and its factors within the firm. They reported that organizational commitment can be determined by job characteristics such as the job scope and work experiences such as rewards and employee importance. They also suggested that organizational commitment was positively associated with employee performance.

Organizational commitment is one of the most widely researched areas in the field of management in association with various job-related variables in the world but there are few related studies in Iran. Different studies have identified factors influence organizational commitment among employees but the present study concentrates more on the effect of job involvement on organizational commitment. Organizational commitment is one of the most important and crucial outcome of human resource strategies and employee commitment is the key factor in reaching competitive performance (Sahnawaz & Juyal, 2006). A meaningful relationship is identified between job satisfaction and organizational commitment (Narimawati, 2007). Samad (2007) attempted to detect the effect of job satisfaction on organizational commitment.

According to Kananga (1982) job involvement as a cognitive or belief state of psychological identification with one's job. In other words, this method recommended that an individual's psychological identification with a particular job depends on the saliency of his/ her needs and the perceptions he/she had about the need satisfying potentialities of the job (Kanungo, 1982). Brown (1996) criticized that job involvement would be in the highest level when the work environment makes one believe that one's work is helpful; offers control over how work is taken place; keeps a clear set of behavioral norms; creates feedback concerning completed work available; and provides supportive relationships with supervisors and co-workers. Many other works have investigated that highly involved employees perform substantial efforts towards the achievement of organizational objectives and would less likely to turnover.

Argyris (1957) and McGregor (1960) considered job involvement as a method for aiding productivity and for creating better integration of individual and organizational goals. Marcson (1960) presented an argument and his findings recommended that one of the best ways to increase productivity in organizations was to incorporate employees with jobs, which were more demanding and challenging. Recent studies of job involvement have demonstrated that such involvement enhances the individual's satisfaction, while at the same time, and increases productivity for the organization (Hall & Lawler, 2000).

This purpose of this study is to investigate the relationship between job involvements on one hand and organizational commitment on the other hand. The independent variable is job involvement whereas organizational commitment is the dependent variable. Recent research findings recommend that a positive and significant relationship exists between job involvement and job satisfaction on the one hand and organizational commitment on the other (Sahnawaz & Juyal, 2006). These authors further contend that, although both independent variables are strongly associated with organizational commitment, the effect of job satisfaction on organizational commitment is relatively stronger than job involvement is. The focus of this study is to investigate this further.

The primary aim of this study was to investigate the relationship between job involvements on organizational commitment and lower-level employees at Iran. This company was used as a representative of the automaker industry in the province.
This study seeks to answer the following question:

o Is there an association between job involvement and organizational commitment?

Establishing a link between job involvement, on the one hand, and organizational commitment, on the other, could benefit organizations, significantly. Managers are, therefore, able to use human resources practices, which increase the levels of job involvement among employees and hence influence positively on their commitment to the organization. The results of this study will demonstrate whether job satisfaction and job involvement have any effect on organizational commitment. If so, future managers would realize how to improve organizational commitment and job involvement.

According to Robbibs (2005), job involvement may result in positive outcomes in organizations such as low absentee levels and higher productivity rates among employees. This study aims to determine the relationship between job involvement and organizational commitment on the other hand. Organizational commitment plays important role for organizational success. Koys (2001) emphasized the significance of organizational commitment for the survival of many organizations. It maximizes the efficiency and the productivity of both the employees and the organization, which ultimately contribute to the effective functioning of organizations.

2. Methodology

According to Sekaran (2003), the population of a study is the entire group of people, events, or things of interest that the researchers intend to investigate and it must include the sample to be studied. The population involved in this study was made of people with lower-level employees of auto-maker firms as represented by Iran Khodro. The population for the research included about 1000 employees from the total population 10% of the lower-level employees were used as a sample. Their job titles included: assemblers, material handlers, inspectors, machine-operators, coordinators and drivers.

Gray (2004) defined a sample as a set of objects, occurrences or individuals selected from a parent population for the purpose of research study. The selected sample was a fairly large portion of the non-managerial employees and was thus fairly well representative of the population. The technique implemented to collect the sample in this study was the stratified probability sampling technique. A sample of 100 lower-level employees of Iran Khodro has been selected based on random sampling technique. Random sampling is a probability sampling technique, whereby each element in the population contains some known chance or probability of being selected as a subject (Uma, 2003).

In this study employees were divided according to their work stations, for instance work station 1, 2, 3, 4, etc. where each work station represented a stratum. To ensure that samples adequately represented the relevant strata (work stations), respondents were randomly selected from within strata, that is, from each work station using a table of random numbers. The sampling procedure for the research began with a preliminary compilation of a sampling frame. A sampling frame is "a complete list in which each unit of analysis is mentioned only once". As stated before, a table of random numbers was applied to ensure that the sample was representative of the sample frame. The research site was visited for data collection.

3. Research instruments

A four-part questionnaire was designed to gather the necessary data. Nachmias and Nachmias (1996) introduced a questionnaire as a list of questions presumably formulated, constructed and sequenced to produce the most constructive data in the most effective manner. The questionnaire consisted of the following four parts:

The first part tapped data associated with biographical and occupational variables including age, gender, marital status, educational qualifications, position held in the organization, and tenure. This data was tapped with a view to obtaining a clear understanding of the sample used in the study.

3.1. Kanungo's (1982) job involvement scale (JIS)

The second part of the questionnaire consisted of Kanungo's (1982) 10-item job involvement scale. This scale measures job involvement on a five-point Likert scale with responses ranging from "Strongly disagree" (1) to "Strongly agree"(5). Kanungo (1982) found this scale to have a Cronbach Alpha coefficient of 0.81, which indicates a reasonably high level of internal consistency, and therefore a reasonably high level of reliability and construct validity.

3.2. Mowday et al.'s Organizational Commitment Questionnaire

The third part of the questionnaire was adopted from Mowday et al. (1979). It is a 15-item questionnaire, which measures organizational commitment, using a five-point Likert scale ranging from "Strongly disagree" (1) to "Strongly agree" (5). This instrument has been examined with several groups such as public employees and university employees. Such tests have yielded reliability coefficients ranging from 0.82 to 0.93 with a median value of 0.90 (Reyes & Pounder, 1993).

3.3. Methods of Analysis

In analyzing the data collected, graphs were implemented to describe the data. In addition, descriptive statistics, Pearson Correlation and Multiple Regression Analysis were employed to analyze the collected data.

3.4. Descriptive statistics

Descriptive statistics describe the phenomena of interest (Sekaran, 2003). They include the analysis of data using frequencies, dispersions of dependent and independent variables and measures of central tendency and variability and to obtain a feel for the data (Sekaran, 2003). The mean and standard deviation was primarily be used to describe the data obtained from the JIQ and the OCQ.

4. Results

4.1 Descriptive statistics

The descriptive statistics in terms of means and standard deviations were measured for Kanungo's Job Involvement questionnaire (1982) and Mowday et al.'s (1979) Organizational Commitment Questionnaire. Table 1 shows the number of cases (sample size) that responded to each questionnaire. Table 1 shows the level of organizational commitment and job involvement for the sample of 100 lower level employees of the company.

Table 1
Mean, standard deviation and total number of cases in relation to organizational commitment and job involvement

	Mean	Std. Deviation	N
Organizational commitment	51.29	11.217	100
Job involvement	33.92	7.519	100

The results indicate that organizational commitment has a mean of 51.29 and a standard deviation of 11.217. The results also indicate that job involvement has a mean of 33.92 and a standard deviation of 7.519.

4.2 Hypothesis testing

This study sought to investigate the relationship between job involvement and organizational commitment. It also sought to determine the relative strength of the association of each of the two independent variable (job involvement), on the one hand, with organizational commitment, as a dependent variable, on the other. To measure job involvement, Kanungo's (1982) 10-item five-point Likert-type rating scale was used. To measure organizational commitment, Mowday et al. (1979) 15item five-point Likert-type rating scale was implemented. Data analysis was performed by means of the Pearson Product Moment Correlation Technique, and Multiple Regression Analysis.

Table 2
Pearson inter-correlations of job involvement and organizational commitment

	Organizational commitment	Job involvement
Organizational commitment	---	.53**
Job involvement	.53**	---

*n = 100   ** Significant to 0.01

4.3 Research Hypothesis

The research hypothesis of the study (H_0) was stated as, "there is no significant positive correlation between job involvement and organizational commitment" and the corresponding alternative hypothesis (H_1) was that, "there is a significant positive correlation between job involvement and organizational commitment". This hypothesis was tested by means of the Pearson Product Moment Correlation technique. The correlation coefficient between job involvement and organizational commitment was found to be $r = 0.53$; $p < 0.001$. This shows that there was a significant positive association between job involvement and organizational commitment. This leads to a rejection of the null hypothesis and acceptance of the alternative hypothesis. The fact that all the subcategories of overall organizational commitment (Loyalty, Value and Effort) are highly inter-correlated (see Table 2) suggests that job involvement is highly correlated with each of these.

5. Discussion and Conclusion

The research hypothesis of the study (H_0) was stated as: "there is no significant positive correlation between job involvement and organizational commitment," and the corresponding alternative hypothesis (H_1) was that: "there is a significant positive correlation between job involvement and organizational commitment". This hypothesis was tested by means of the Pearson Product Moment Correlation technique. The correlation coefficient between job involvement and organizational commitment was found to be significant and positively correlated. This leads to a rejection of the null hypothesis and acceptance of the alternative hypothesis.

The findings of the present study have suggested that job involvement was an important factor whose presence in an organization must be ensured. The following studies are in support of the significant positive correlation between job involvement and organizational commitment found in the present study: Moynihan and Pandey (2007) investigated the relationship between job involvement and organizational commitment using a sample of public sector health and human services managers. The study showed that there was a moderately positive correlation between job involvement and organizational commitment. This concurs with the results of the current study.

The organizational commitment meta-analysis conducted by Mathieu and Zajac (1990) also disclosed that among the factors of commitment, the job involvement and organizational commitment relationship were frequently investigated. The two variables were considered to study the impact of some forms of work-related behavior independently. O'Reilly and Chatman (1986) reported that job involvement is an outcome of psychological commitment to an organization. Uygur and Kilic (2009) studied the level of organizational commitment and job involvement of the personnel at Central Organizational, Ministry of Health in Turkey. Questionnaires were distributed to a total of 210 subjects. Of this number, 180 (86%) returned the questionnaire and of these, 168 were found to be useable. A significant positive correlation was found between organizational commitment and job involvement ($r = 0.44$, $p < 0.001$).

There have been many other studies into organizational commitment and job involvement especially associated with the healthcare workers and nurses (Brewer & Lok, 1995; Brooks & Swails, 2000; Ors et al., 2003; Sjoberg & Sverke, 2000; Blau & Boal, 1989). In a study conducted by Sjoberg and Sverke in a Swedish Emergency Hospital (2000), it was reported that organizational commitment and job involvement were significantly positively correlated. Blau and Boal (1989) found that nurses with a higher level of job involvement and organizational commitment had significantly less unexcused absences than nurses with lower levels of job involvement and organizational commitment did.

One of the significance of the present study is that it was conducted in a developing country, unlike most similar studies that have traditionally been conducted in the highly industrialized countries of the Western world. The present study showed that there was a significant and positive correlation between job involvement and organizational commitment. This concurred with various previous studies conducted as mentioned earlier on. One significant difference between the present study and previous studies is that, the present study was conducted in a various geographical area.

The present study demonstrated that job involvement has a great power to impact organizational commitment therefore the results tell us that companies must pay more attention to promote job involvement in order to ensure higher levels of organizational commitment. The aim of this research was primarily to determine the relationship between job involvement and organizational commitment on the other among lower-level employees in the automaker industry. The results indicate that there was a statistically significant relationship between the independent variable, that is, job involvement and the dependent variable, that is, organizational commitment, on the other.

References

Argyris, C. (1957). *Personality and Organization*. New York: Harper Collins.

Blau, G., & Boal, K. B. (1989). Using job involvement and organisational commitment interactively to predict turnover. *Journal of Management*, 15 (1), 115-127.

Brewer, A. M., & Lok, P. (1995). Managerial Strategy and Nursing Commitment in Australian Hospitals. *Journal Advanced Nursing*, 21, 769-799.

Brooks, I., & Swailes, S. (2002). Analysis of the relationship between nurse influences over flexible working and commitment to nursing. *Journal of Advanced Nursing*, 38 (2), 117-126.

Brown, S. P. (1996). A meta-analysis and review of organizational research on job involvement. *Psychology Bulletin*, 120, 235-255.

Gray, D. E. (2004). *Doing research in the real world*. London: Sage Publications limited.

Gunlu, E., Aksarayli, M. & Percin, N. S. (2010). Job satisfaction and organisational commitment of hotel managers in Turkey. *International Journal of Contemporary Hospitality Management*, 22 (5), 693-717.

Ha-Young, H. (2009). Analysis the factors impact on the Job Involvement and Organisational commitment. Department of Public Administration Korea University

Hall, D. T. & Lawler, E. E. (2000). Job characteristics and job pressures and the organizational integration of professionals. *Administrative Science Quarterly*, 15, 271-281.

Hisrchfeld, R. R. & Field, H. S. (2000). Work centrality and work alienation: Distinct aspects. Of a general commitment to work. *Journal of Organisational Behavior*, 21(7), pp.789-800.

Hufnagel, E. M. & Conca, C. (1994). User Response Data: The Potential for Errors and Bias . *Information Systems Research*, 5, 48-73.

Kanungo, R. N. (1982). Measurement of Job and Work Involvement. *Journal of Applied Psychology*, 67(3), 341-349.

Koys, L. (2001). The effects of employee satisfaction, organisational citizenship behaviour, & turnover on organisational effectiveness: A unit level, longitudinal study, *Personnel Psychology*, 54(1), 101-114

Marcson, S. (1960). *The scientist in American industry*. New York: Harper.

Martin, C. L., & Bennett, N. (1996). The role of justice judgments in explaining the relationship between job satisfaction and organisational commitment. *Group & Organisation Management*, 21(1) 84-105.

Maslow, A. (1954). *Motivation and Personality*; New York: Harper.

Mathieu, J. E. & Zajac, D. M. (1990). A review and Meta analysis of the antecedents correlates and consequences of organisational commitment. *Psychological Bulletin*, 108, 171-199.

Maxwell, G. & Steele, G. (2003). Organisational commitment: a study of managers in hotels. *International Journal of Contemporary Hospitality Management*, 15(7), 362–369.

McGregor, D. (1960). *The Human Side of Enterprise*. New York: McGraw-Hill Book Co., Inc.

Mowday, R., Porter, L., & Steers, R. (1982). *Employee organisational linkages- The psychology of commitment, absenteeism and turnover*. London: Academic Press.

Moynihan, D. P and Pandey, S. K. (2007). Finding workable levers over work motivation: Comparing job satisfaction, job involvement and organizational commitment. *Administration & Society*, 39 (7), 803-832.

Nachmias, C. F., & Nachmias, D. (1997). Research Methods in Social Sciences. London: ST Martin's Press Inc.

Organ, D. W, Podsakoff, M. P & McKenzie, S. B. (2005). *Organizational citizenship behaviour, its nature, antecedents and consequences*. London: Sage Publications.

O'Reilly, C. A & Chatman, J. (1986). Organizational commitment and psychological attachment: the effects of compliance, identification and internalization on pro-social behaviour. *Journal of Applied Psychology*, 71 (3), 492-499.

Örs, M., Acuner, A. M., Sarp, N., & Önder, Ö. R. (2003). Antalya Tıp Fakültesi Hastanesi'nde, Antalya Sosyal Sigortalar Kurumu Hastanesi'nde ve Antalya Devlet Hastanesi'nde çalısan hekimler ile hemsirelerin örgütlerine baglılıklarına iliskin görüslerinin degerlendirilmesi. *Ankara Üniversitesi Tıp Fakültesi Mecmuası*, 56(4), 217-224.

Reese H. W, & Fremour W. J. (1984). Normal and normative ethics in behavioral sciences, American Psychologist, 39(8), 863-876.

Robbins, S. P. (2005). *Essentials of Organizational Behaviour*. New Jersey: Pearson.

Robert, L. (1997). *Human Resources Management*. London: West Publishing Company.

Samad, S. (2007). *Assessing the effects of job satisfaction and psychological contract on organisational commitment among employees in Malaysian SMEs*. The 4th SMEs IN A Global Economy Conference 2007.

Sahnawaz, M. G., & Juyal, R. C. (2006). Human resources management practices and organisational commitment in different organisations. *Journal of the Indian Academy of Applied Psychology*, 32, 171-178.

Sekaran, U. (2003). *Research methods for business: A skill-building approach*. 3rd ed., New York: John Wiley & Sons, Inc.

Sjoberg, A., & Sverke, M. (2000). The interactive effect of job involvement and organisational commitment on job turnover revisited: A note on the mediating role of turnover intention. *Scandinavian Journal of Psychology*, 41, 247-252.

Uygur, A., & Kilic, G. (2009). A study into Organizational Commitment and Job Involvement: An Application towards the personnel in the central organisation for ministry of health in Turkey. *Ozean journal of applied sciences*, 2(1).2009.

Wagner, J. A. III, & Hollenbeck, J. R. (1998). *Organizational behavior: Securing competitive advantage*, 3rd. ed. Upper Saddle River, NJ: Prentice Hall.

Werner, A. (2007). *Organizational Behaviors: A Contemporary South African Perspective*. Pretoria: Van Schaik Publishers.

www.thefinancialgazate.co.zw accessed May 2010. www.wikipedia.com accessed May 2010.

Journal of Applied Sciences Research, 8(2): 983-991, 2012 ISSN 1819-544X
This is a refereed journal and all articles are professionally screened and reviewed

ORIGINAL ARTICLES

The Investigation Of The Relation Between Personnel's Emotional Intelligence And Professional Commitment (case study in National company of purging and Distribution of Oil Products in Iran (Shiraz))

[1]Kamran Nazari, [2]Mostafa Emami, [3]Ali Reza Shakarbeigi

[1]Department of Business Management, Payam Noor University, Kermanshah, Iran
[2]Young Researchers Club, Kermanshah Branch, Islamic Azad University, Kermanshah, Iran. [3]Department of Law, Payam Noor University, Kermanshah, Iran

ABSTRACT

The main goal in this paper is to investigate the relation of emotional intelligence and career commitment of the personnel. The statistical society in this survey includes 300 employees of Iran (Shiraz) National Oil Products Infiltration and Distribution. Considering the sample volume by using Cockrun formula, 148 targets were selected which answered both questionaries, emotional intelligence standard by Mayer and Salvey and career commitment by and Mayer et al. in order to analyze the data, the software SPSS and also the average tests of some statistical society, Colmograph-Smironeph, Spearman adhesion coefficient and Freadman test were implemented. The results obtained from analyzing the information showed that in the studied society, there is some constant positive significant relation between self-controlling, sympathy, social skills and career commitment, and regarding the previous studies theories and backgrounds, these results were expected. But, unlike what we expected the analysis illustrated that self-controlling and social skills have negative significant relation with normative career commitment. The results, also, showed that in the considered statistical society, the emotional intelligence and career commitment were in a bad situation. Between the career commitment, the emotional career components and normative career commitment were in a bad situation and the constant career commitment, conversely, had a good situation.

Key words: emotional intelligence, career commitment, constant career commitment, normative career   commitment, emotional career commitment.

Introduction

In past decade, the issue presented in management literature has attracted the management researchers and scientists. The emotional intelligence is the issue in here. This issue that studies the personnel's feelings and emotions in working with others tries to explain the personnel's emotions place in their efficiency. A set of reports published from the investigation related to emotional intelligence issue, provided some promising results on personnel's emotional intelligence and their success. Some of these investigations show that the personnel with high emotional intelligent, has better functionality, organizational and career commitment, and are more satisfied of their own jobs than the others. These people have some characteristics such as self-controlling, selftraining, self-managing and controlling their emotions in workplace (Doostar, 1385).

The emotional intelligence includs the ability to pursuit and be incentive, to control the strokes, to control the emotion and to sympathy (Megarvey, 1997).

The emotional intelligent is known as the important resource of incitement, information, personal power, innovation, creativity and influence, that plays a vital role in improving the organization. Because, the emotional intelligent results in person's loyalty and organizational dependency, better compatibility with organization changes, technical improvements, human relations and making more logical decisions (Antonacopoulou & Gabriel, 2001).

J. Appl. Sci. Res., 8(2): 983-991, 2012

According to the subjects mentioned above and regarding the emotional intelligence importance, the main goal in this research is that is there any relation between emotional intelligent components and personnel's carrer commitment in Iran National (Shiraz) Oil Products Infiltration and Distribution Company, or not.

The emotional intelligence:

Corresponding Author: Kamran Nazari, Department of Business Management, Payam Noor University, Kermanshah, Iran
E-mail: Kamrann0156@yahoo.cm

The emotional intelligence is not a new concept, and Aristotle seems to be the first one who considered the importance of emotions in human relations. It is easy to get angry, everyone could get angry, but it is not easy to get angry on right person, at the correct time, for some sensible reason and in a correct way (Calman, 1382).

Here, the emotional intelligence means the academic studies and researches conducted on emotional intelligence and emotions, in twenty century. Based on the criterion presented with Thomas Cohen in his remarkable book, "scientific revolutions structure" about the paradigm, there could be seen some signs of maturation in emotional intelligence paradigm. The emotional intelligence has entered to psychology literature as a concept, which is rooted in Thorndike and Gardner works and is resulted from connecting intellectual and emotional minds, and the correlation between emotion and reason. The emotional intelligence is a new component in studies that many researchers are intended to use it in various fields. The emotional intelligence theory is some modern view about predicting the success factors in life, including work activities and efficient opposition against stressful factors as the mental disorders resource, because many characteristic significances such as sympathy, self-propensity, optimism, self-simulating, stress controlling, self-awareness and emotions managing, result in success in different fields of life. Emotional intelligence illustrates the social and personality emotional dimensions, which are often considered and appeared in daily activities (Saboori Moghadam, 1372).

Intelligence is one of the human's critical mechanisms that include the ability to be compatible with environment. Some part of intelligence is appeared in social and personal relations. Regarding to Thorndike, social intelligence includes ability to understand internal situations, incentives and self and others behavior and optimal functions according to the information. Gardner in his octoploid theory, considers the personal (inter and intera personal) intelligence and explains the person's ability to be aware of emotions, to distinguish between them and to use the data to give efficient answer against the environment, as one of the intelligent aspects (Plaamer & Donaldson, 2001). Obviously, since very early in the intelligence studies, cognitive aspects such as memory and problem solving have been emphasized. While, non-cognitive dimensions including emotional and functional abilities are not only acceptable but also necessary. Gradually, the insights on intelligence quotient have been replaced by studying other effective abilities in human functionality. For example, Thorndike (1920) explained the intelligent behavior including visual intelligence (fabricating skills and implementing the instruments), abstract intelligence (the ability to use the words, numbers and scientific principals) and social intelligence (recognizing the people and the ability to perform creative behaviors in human relations). Wechster, D (1943) offers that the intelligence non-cognitive aspects like emotional- sentimental, social and personal abilities to prospect self- abilities to be obtain success and compatibility in life, are important (Chiva & Alegre, 2008).

Basically, the emotional phenomenon, provide a particular resource for people about the environment and searching for them, and these data form the concepts, behaviors and feelings. It is supposed that people use various amounts of understanding, intellect and implementing these emotional data. The emotional intelligence theory provides a new insight about predicting the effective factors of success and also initial prevention from mental disorders, which is a supplementary to cognitive science and nervous science and the emotional intelligence abilities are so important for emotional self-controlling and subtle contraptions (King & Gardner, 2006).

Giving the general intelligence alone is not sufficient to reach success and the research show that in best situations the general intelligence is just 25% percent of success and the rest is depend on fortune, emotional and social intelligence (Golman, 1380).

Genetically, the emotional intelligence is not stable and is not formed just in childhood period, unlike the general intelligence which is slightly changed after adolescence. The emotional intelligence is more often learned and during the life it is formed based on the experiment. The research on determining the emotional intelligence level during the life show that the human is getting better and also is obtaining more skills to manage self-emotions (Golman, 1383).

The emotional intelligence frame, it's formal definition and the offers on how to measure it, were appeared in 1990, in two articles by Salovey, P & Mayer, J, for the first time. The initial definition was based on some two-part procedure, in which the first part includes total general data processing and the second part consists of personalizing the emotions, compatibly in order to improve the life progress. The emotional intelligence as some ability includes the capacity of understanding the instruments, recognizing, implementing and managing self and others emotions (Khaef Elahi & Doostar, 1382).

985

J. Appl. Sci. Res., 8(2): 983-991, 2012

Golman explains the emotional intelligence as the ability to keep the incentives and to resist against the problems, to control the anger and to postpone the success, to adjust the mental conditions and to prevent distress from disturbing the thoughts, to have sympathy with others and to be hopeful. According to Goldman, the emotional intelligence includes recognizing and controlling self-emotions, having sympathy with others and keeping satisfactory relations. In other words, the person with high emotional intelligence combines three emotional components (cognitive, physiological and behavioral components), successfully (Golman, 1380).

Since the critical components of emotional intelligence include the ability to understand the others emotions and to adjust self and others consistency, it is expected that the people with high emotional intelligence show better social skills and compatibility. Therefore, the social skills include the social life expeditors that help people to have efficient and reciprocal relations; moreover, the social skills are bilateral and the people with good social skills receive good behaviors and are liked with the others (Palmer & Donaldson, 2001).

Bar-on & Parker consider the emotional intelligence as a form of intelligence that is resulted from thoughts and emotions and they mean to reach the total structure of emotional, personal and social abilities that affect on ability to insist against requests and environmental stress (Chiva & Alegre, 2008).

In some research between 19 organizations in Arab states, it was illustrated that there is some negative significant relation between emotional intelligence and opposition. In this research, when the emotional intelligence was evaluated as the selected sample with supervisors, the adhesion coefficient was -0.52 and when emotional intelligence was evaluated by the personnel, the adhesion coefficient was -0.22, and it shows that the personnel and supervisors have different insights on the amount of emotional intelligence (Suliman & Shaikh, 2007; 208-220).

In some research conducted on big manufacturing organizations in England, the relation between emotional intelligence and leadership efficiency was investigated. In order to investigate the leadership efficiency, the supervisors' ideas were implemented. The selective sample included 38 supervisors and 1258 personnel. The Pierson adhesion coefficient between emotional intelligence and leadership efficiency was 39%, and it shows that there is some positive relation with 99% confidence between emotional intelligence and leadership efficiency. The emotional intelligence components in this research were: self- sentiment understanding, sentiments implementing, others feelings understanding and sentiments managing, and no significant relation was obtained between two first components with leadership efficiency and two other components (Stein & Sitarenio, 2009).

Koman & Wolff in some research between 81 teams in military organizations investigated the relation between emotional intelligence of group leaders and the amount of organizational intelligence in group level. In this research, also, the effect of group emotional intelligence on the group functionality was investigated. In fact, in this survey the group emotional intelligence is considered as interfering variable. The results of this research showed that the group emotional intelligence has completely positive relation with the leader emotional intelligence and also there is some positive relation between group emotional intelligence and functionality (Koman & Wolff, 2008).

In some study, Grant investigated the short-time and long-time training on the amount of emotional intelligence. The results in his study showed that the long-time training plan (in this study, 13 weeks) could improve the emotional intelligence, significantly (Grant, 2007).

Some research was conducted on 92 managers from general communications and 129 managers from Australia banks on the relation between emotional intelligence and financial function. The results illustrated that there is some significant positive relation between emotional intelligence and financial function of the banks (Heffernan & Droulers. M, 2008).

In some research on 8 ceramic companies in Spain, the results showed that the organizational learning capacity is as a regulator variable that could affect the relation between emotional intelligence and work satisfactory. The results illustrated that there is some positive relation between emotional intelligence and organization learning capacity. Also, the results of this research showed that there is no significant relation between emotional intelligence and work satisfactory, unless the organization learning capacity, affect the relation between these two variables, as a regulator factor (Chiva & Alegre, 2008).

In some research conducted on 156 professional personnel in New Zealand, it was illustrated that there is some positive relation between understanding the others feelings and social support (King & Gardner, 2006).

The adults showed better emotional intelligence skills than the others. Mayer, in his research, showed that the emotional intelligence improves with aging and experience from childhood to adulthood (Golman, 1383).

The research illustrate that people with lower emotional intelligence, facing with life stressful situations will have less conformity, and as a result they would get into trouble with depression, disappointment, and other negative consequences. Conversely, people with higher emotional intelligence, choose their life style in such a way that they face with less negative consequences and they also skilful in creating high quality relations. Totally, the emotional intelligence is related to the life events and helps the people to understand and predict the different daily aspects (Chiva & Alegre, 2008).

Siarochi et al pointed that the emotional intelligence regulates the relation between stress and psychological conformity. By psychological conformity, we mean the characteristics related to depression and disappointment and suicide tenets. In other research, they found that the people with skills in regulating the feelings are provided with higher social support, and this social support prevents them against depression and suicide tenets. Some people believe that today emotional intelligence plays a significant role in being succeeded in life and work. The studies show that bravery, sympathy, happiness and emotional self-awareness, as various factors of emotional intelligence, have the most effect on new success for employees, and also implementing the emotional intelligence test in

J. Appl. Sci. Res., 8(2): 983-991, 2012

selecting new employees shows that most newly employed persons would reach to significantly higher scores in bravery, sympathy, happiness and emotional self-awareness (Khaef Elahi and Doostdar, 1382). Investigating about 200 global organizations and companies indicates that one-third of differences is related to cognitive ability and technical skills and two-third of them is related to emotional potencies (Golman, 1998).

In some research conducted on 105 personnel from health care sector in U.S., it was concluded that sentimental intelligence has a critical role in investigating the relation between organizational commitment and ability to have sentimental conformity. This research showed that the personnel with high sentimental conformity ability, with a higher sentimental intelligence, will have more commitment. It means that, if it is proved that in some organization the emotional intelligence scores are in a high level, so it could be concluded that the personnel with higher sentimental intelligence will have more organizational commitment (Humphreys, Brunsen & Davis, 2005).

In some other research conducted on 200 officers in Niger police office, it was found that work experience, self-efficiency, emotional intelligence and incentive could affect on the amount of commitment (in order to analyze data in this research, we used the regression model and the Fischer statistics 5.856 was obtained: Aremu, 2005).

In some investigation on students graduated in gob course from 3 Malaysia, Poon found that for personnel with average to high sentimental intelligence, the work commitment will affect the work direction improvement. The results, also, showed some positive relation between work satisfactory and the amount of salary (Poon, 2004.

Career commitment:

The term carrer commitment is derived from psychology and has been improved from the current term organizational commitment (Hall *et al*, 2005). It has the study directions same as the organizational commitment (Herr, 2005). The definitions related to career commitment differ from the amount of work the person has to do in his work place to the important role of the work in life (Somech & Bogler, 2002).

The career commitment is considered as one of the most important determinant factors for the persons' work behaviors and it is the favorite issue for many managers and people in educational places (Kannan & Pillai, 2008).

The "career commitment theory" also presents that more the person invests on some issues, more hard is the commitment. Therefore, more encouraged the person to enter the work and more activities performed to provide such encouragement, 1988). The professional people, consider themselves as someone with full-time career which they should all their best for that and they feel limitless commitment on their career, because it is valuable for them (Favela & Fuzessery, 1974).

The career commitment is described as the insight of the person on his/ her career (Fjortof & W.I. Lee, 1994). The career commitment pointes to the dependency people have on their career. In fact, the career commitment includes believing the aims and the career values and having tendency to try considerably to reach the career and to get involved in it (Elias, 2006).

The career commitment is defined as the level of designating the functional standards to be performed (Jones, 2000). Wallas et al define the career commitment same as Allen and Mayer's for organizational commitment. They consider three normative, sentimental and continuum dimensions to the career commitment and define the career commitment as feeling personality with some career, needing to continue serving in some career and having a high sense of duty against it (Osinsky & Mueller, 2004).

In some study on accountants' career commitment, Arnya, Bullak and Arming, define the career commitment by replacing the word career for the term organizational in Porter's definition for organizational commitment.

1.   Believing the aims and their values and accepting them;
2.   Having tendency to do the best in performing the career; 3. Having tendency to continue and keep involvement in career.

So, the people with high commitment in their career do their best to perform their career and this would result in career success and fail internalizing as their own success or fail (Giffords, 2003).

Considering the career as some desired professional value is derived from initial activities conducted on career characteristics. Career commitment has mostly favored by Gouldner, who determined the difference between career commitment and organizational commitment for professional people in Borkeratic organizations (Tayler, 1988). And additionally, this interest toward the career commitment was formed after the researchers found that the career commitment in people has various positive effects (Hall *et al*, 2005).

Llee et al, address four reasons for the career commitment importance:

1.   Most of the time, in the life, is spent for the career.
2.   Because career commitment affects maintenance, keeping and remembering, therefore, it has considerable meanings to manage the human source.
3.   Because the career skills are resulted from experience, so, functionality could be related to the career commitment.
4.   Further studies on career commitment may show that how people combine different internal and external commitments (Elias, 2007).

J. Appl. Sci. Res., 8(2): 983-991, 2012

Career commitment is related to considerable aspects including functional improvement, replacement decrease and satisfactory increase in organizational and professional levels (Elias, 2006). The research show that personnel's high level commitment results in more incentive and satisfaction and therefore decreases the possibility to leave the organization (Huang, 2006).

The career commitment, probably, affects the functionality of personnel such as their observable theories, their opinions on work output and their involvement in professional groups. The career commitment is related to positive behaviors which are useful for the organization and consequently the people with higher career commitment would less get involved in inadvisable activities for organization (Greenfield, 2008).

A dutiful person is interested in keeping the involvement or presents a considerable endeavor, not because of getting advantage but for the reason that he/ she believes it is better to behave in such a way because it's true and because he/ she is expected to do so (Raju & Shrivastava, 1994).

Goals of research

This research by considering the importance of emotional intelligence and professional commitment of the workers pursues the following goals:

1.   Survey the relation between emotional intelligence and professional commitments of the workers of Iran's national refinery and oil products Distribution Company (in Shiraz).

2.   Presenting necessary solutions to improve emotional intelligence and increase professional commitment of the workers based on the findings of the research.

Method

As in this paper researcher tries to determine and survey emotional intelligence and its relation with professional commitment of the workers of Iran's national refinery and oil products distribution company (in Shiraz), so the paper follows the method of descriptive researches of quantifiable branch. Statistical population is 300 workers of Iran's national refinery and oil products distribution company (in Shiraz) and the research sample is 148 workers based on the following formula;

$$n = \frac{(300)(1/96)^2(0/5)(0/5)}{(0.5)^2(300-1) + (1/96)^2(0/5)(0/5)} = 148$$

Main information of this paper has been collected through two ways;

Library method: in this method books, theses, essays, information bases and internet sources were used to collect information about the history and literature of the matter.

Free method: In this method sage counseling and interview were used to design and analyze questionnaire. The main tool of this paper is the questionnaire which is one of the common tools of research and a direct way of getting research's data. Two kinds of questionnaire have been used to scale the variables. One of the questionnaires was Maier's and et al which was used for scaling the workers professional commitments and the other was emotional intelligence questionnaire of Maier and Slave which was used for scaling the components of emotional intelligence and descriptive and illative statistics have been used. Colmogrof-Smirnof tests of average of a statistical population, correlation factor of Spearman and Freedman test have been used.

Findings

In this research in order to test the research hypothesis, it must be determined whether the distribution of the collected data is normal or not. Being normal or not will be evaluated based on statistic test of Clomongr ofSnirnof, the results of this test are in following table;

Distribution of observations follow the normal distribution	H0:ρ=0
Distribution of observations don't follow the normal distribution	H1: ρ≠0

Table 1: Colemogrof-Smirnof

variable	Sample amount	اماره ازمون	Sig amount	Test result
Emotional intelligence	148	0.993	0.278	Normal distribution
Professional commitment	148	0.991	0.280	Normal distribution

As we can see in table 1 the amount of اماره ازمون in level of 0.05 is less than the critical amount, so the zero hypothesis that means the data are normal is accepted and the corresponding hypothesis which means data are not distributed normally is rejected. Therefore as the data are normal in order to test these hypotheses Spearmen correlation test is used.

Based on the research's goals a main and fifteen particular hypotheses have been mentioned and tested which their results come as follow:

988

J. Appl. Sci. Res., 8(2): 983-991, 2012

main hypothesis

there is a positive and meaningful relation between emotional intelligence and professional commitments of the workers of Iran's national refinery and oil products distribution company (in Shiraz).

Particular hypotheses

Based on the main hypothesis fifteen particular hypotheses as follow came to the researcher's mind:

1. There is a positive and meaningful relation between self-control and emotional professional commitments of the workers of Iran's national refinery and oil products distribution company (in Shiraz).

2. There is a positive and meaningful relation between self-consciousness and emotional professional commitments of the workers of Iran's national refinery and oil products distribution company (in Shiraz).

3. There is a positive and meaningful relation between self- stimulation and emotional professional commitments of the workers of Iran's national refinery and oil products distribution company (in Shiraz).

4. There is a positive and meaningful relation between sympathy and emotional professional commitments of the workers of Iran's national refinery and oil products distribution company (in Shiraz).

5. There is a positive and meaningful relation between social skills and emotional professional commitments of the workers of Iran's national refinery and oil products Distribution Company (in Shiraz).

6. There is a positive and meaningful relation between self- control and continuous professional commitments of the workers of Iran's national refinery and oil products Distribution Company (in Shiraz).

7. There is a positive and meaningful relation between self-consciousness and continuous professional commitments of the workers of Iran's national refinery and oil products Distribution Company (in Shiraz).

8. There is a positive and meaningful relation between self-stimulation and continuous professional commitments of the workers of Iran's national refinery and oil products Distribution Company (in Shiraz).

9. There is a positive and meaningful relation between sympathy and continuous professional commitments of the workers of Iran's national refinery and oil products Distribution Company (in Shiraz).

10. There is a positive and meaningful relation between social skills and continuous professional commitments of the workers of Iran's national refinery and oil products Distribution Company (in Shiraz).

11. There is a positive and meaningful relation between self-control and regulated professional commitments of the workers of Iran's national refinery and oil products Distribution Company (in Shiraz).

12. There is a positive and meaningful relation between self-consciousness and regulated professional commitments of the workers of Iran's national refinery and oil products Distribution Company (in Shiraz).

13. There is a positive and meaningful relation between self- stimulation and regulated professional commitments of the workers of Iran's national refinery and oil products Distribution Company (in Shiraz).

14. There is a positive and meaningful relation between sympathy and regulated professional commitments of the workers of Iran's national refinery and oil products Distribution Company (in Shiraz).

15. There is a positive and meaningful relation between social skills and regulated professional commitments of the workers of Iran's national refinery and oil products Distribution Company (in Shiraz).

Conceptual model of the research

In this paper Meir and Solve's model has been used for emotional intelligence, and for professional commitment Meir's and et al model has been used which we can see in figure number 1.

Fig. 1: Conceptual model of the research

Dimensions of emotional intelligence	professional commitment
Self-regulation	Emotional professional commitment
self-consciousness	
	continuous professional commitment
self- stimulation	
	regulated professional commitment
sympathy	

989

J. Appl. Sci. Res., 8(2): 983-991, 2012

social skill

In order to survey the condition of emotional intelligence dimensions, the average test of statistical population has been used and its results are shown in the table 2.

Table 2: condition of emotional intelligence professional commitment's variables

variable	Variable's condition	average
emotional intelligence	undesirable	2.8659
professional commitment	undesirable	2.7569
self-control	undesirable	2.7799
self-consciousness	undesirable	2.8595
self- stimulation	mean	3.0714
sympathy	undesirable	2.8056
social skill	undesirable	2.5594
Emotional professional commitment	undesirable	2.0933
continuous professional commitment	undesirable	1.4683
regulated professional commitment	desirable	4.0488

In order to test the hypotheses Spearman correlation factor has been used. In table 3 we can see correlation and meaningfulness factors between emotional intelligence's and professional commitments' variables.

Table 3: Correlation and meaningfulness factors between emotional intelligence's and professional commitment's variables.

variables	Emotional commitment	professional	continuous professional commitment		regulated commitment	professional
	correlation factor	meaningfulness factors	correlation factor	meaningfulness factors	correlation factor	meaningfulness factors
self-control	0.433	0.000	0.301	0.009	-0.451	0.000
Selfconsciousness	0.190	0.105	0.190	0.105	0.057	0.635
self- stimulation	0.123	0.284	-0.074	0.518	-0.029	0.804
sympathy	0.384	0.003	0.298	0.011	-0.202	0.093
social skill	0.281	0.019	0.244	0.043	-0.303	0.013

The amount of correlation factor of emotional intelligence and professional commitment was 0.344 and because their meaningfulness factor was less than 0.05 and was 0.012 we come to this conclusion that there is a positive and meaningful relation between emotional intelligence and professional commitment, therefore the main hypothesis is accepted.

By considering table 3 we come to the following conclusions about particular hypotheses:

1. There is no relation between self- consciousness and emotional professional commitment, continuous professional commitment and regulated professional commitment. As the meaningfulness factor is more than0.05, therefore hypotheses 2,7 and 12 are rejected.

2.   As the meaningfulness factor is less than 0.05 and correlation is positive, there is a positive relation between self-control and emotional professional commitment. Therefore hypothesis 1 is accepted.

3.   As the meaningfulness factor is more than 0.05, there is no relation between self-control and regulated professional commitment. Therefore the hypothesis 11 is accepted.

4.   As the meaningfulness factor is less than 0.05 and correlation factor is negative, there is a negative relation between self-control and continuous professional commitment. Therefore hypothesis 6 is accepted

5.   As the meaningfulness factor is more than 0.05, there is no relation between self- stimulation and regulated professional commitment and continuous professional commitment. Therefore hypotheses 3,8 and13 are rejected.

6.   As the meaningfulness factor between sympathy and emotional professional commitment and continuous professional commitment is less than 0.05 and their correlation factors are positive. Therefore hypotheses 4 and 9 are accepted. However as the meaningfulness factor between sympathy and regulated professional commitment is more than 0.05, hypothesis 14 is rejected.

7.   As the meaningfulness factor between social skill and emotional professional commitment and continuous professional commitment is less than 0.05. Therefore hypotheses 5, 10 and 15 are accepted. However as the correlation factor between social skill and emotional professional commitment is positive, there is a positive relation between social skill and emotional professional commitment, but their correlation factors are negative, so there is a negative relation between social skill and regulated professional commitment.

Freedman test has been used to rank emotional intelligence's and professional commitment's variables. These variables are shown based on their importance in table 4.

Table 4: ranking of the intelligence's and professional commitment's variable.

Rank	emotional intelligence's variable	Average of score
1	stimulation	5.77
2	Self-consciousness	4088
3	self-control	4.42
4	sympathy	4.63
5	social skill	3.57
Rank	professional commitment's variable	Average of score
1	regulated professional commitment	2.88
2	emotional professional commitment	1.91
3	continuous professional commitment	1.20

Conclusion:

In nowadays world economic power and comfort of a country are functions of expert, commitment and capable human force. As a result of growing and developing organizations, one of the problems that they are faced is the reduction of professional commitments of their workers which has resulted in absence and delay of their workers, clash and contrast in work environments, growing lack of realism and reduction of energy for doing profitable activities. Different approaches have been offered to increase professional commitment in different sources; one of these approaches has prescribed the use of emotional intelligence's variables. Emotional intelligence is a matter which tries to explain and interpret the place of emotions and feelings in man's capabilities. Workers who have emotional intelligence are effective workers and eagerly accept organization goals and with high level of satisfaction try to gain the goals and they have the highest level of commitment and their approaches to control are a kind of self-control based on self-consciousness.

Emotional intelligence studies the role of individual emotions and feelings in their personal and social life, their works with others and it is an effort to explain and emplace individual emotions and feelings in their effectiveness. A set of researches and reports published by survey relevant to the matter of emotional or thrilling intelligence, have presented a hopeful conclusion about the relation between individual's emotional intelligences and their successes. Some of these researches claim that those workers who have a better function, work commitment and high level of job satisfaction, they have some features like; self- control, self- regulation, self- management and also are able to control their emotions , feelings and thrills in job environment (Xaefellahi and Dostar, 2006).

In this paper by considering the importance of emotional intelligence, the relation between emotional intelligence and professional commitments of workers of Iran's national refinery and oil products Distribution Company (in Shiraz) has been surveyed. Its findings show that in this statistical population there is a positive and meaningful relation between self-control, sympathy, social skill and emotional and continuous professional commitment. Based on relevant precedent theories and literature of the matter these findings were expected, however something that was unexpected was that; there was a negative meaningful relation between self-control, social skill and regulated professional commitment. These findings also showed that in the statistical population emotional intelligence and professional commitment had undesirable conditions. All components of emotional intelligence except for self-

991

J. Appl. Sci. Res., 8(2): 983-991, 2012

control which had a mean condition had undesirable conditions. But continuous professional commitment had a desirable condition. Based on the paper's goal and findings and the researcher's observations during the research, some advices and offers come as follow that will result in increasing the emotional intelligences of the workers and as its consequence increasing their professional commitment:

1. To increase sympathy workers must be sensitive to their own emotional signs and improve their effective eavesdrops.

2. By holding some training sessions we must inform the managers of the importance of nonmaterial requirements of the workers and also train them so that by relying on their cognition, knowledge and acquired skills will be capable to feel sympathy with the workers.

3. Social skills must be increased so that organizational structures will be more flexible and a premise will be prepared for increasing the horizontal relations and team work.

4. Managers and workers must try to use win-win strategy in their negotiations so that a desirable atmosphere will be made for negotiations in the organizations.

5. The organization must consider the workers emotional capabilities in choosing them and giving them promotions because based on this paper's findings worker's high level of emotional intelligence results in increasing their professional commitment and affecting the better function of the organization.

6. By considering this fact that the relation between emotional intelligence and job success and worker's professional commitment has been proved, the researcher's offer for human sources' managers and the organization industrial psychologists is to design some tests and mechanisms to evaluate applicants emotional intelligences before their entrance t o the organization.

References

Antonacopoulou, E.P., Y. Gabriel, 2001. Emotion, learning and organizational change: Towards an intergration of psycchanalytic and other perspectives" Journal of Organizational Change Management, 14(5): 435-451.

Aremu, A.O., 2005. "A confluence of credentialing,career experience,self-efficacy, Emotional intelligence & motivation on the career commitment of young police in Ibadan ,Nigeria" ,policing:international Journal of police strategies and management, 28(4): 609-618.

Carman, A., 2001. "staf burnout and patient satisfaction" Journal of occupational health psychology,7: 235-241.

Cherniss, C., 1992. "long term consequences of burn out : An exploratory study "journal of organizational behavior, 13: 2-11.

Chiva, R & J. Alegre, 2008." Emotional intelligence and job satisfaction: the role of organizational learning capability" ,personnel review, 37(6): 680-701.

Elias, R.Z., 2006. Theimpact of professional commitment and anticipatory socialization on accounting students ethical orientation; Journal of Business Ethics, pp: 83-90.

Freudenberger, H.J., 1974. "staff burn out"Jornal of social issues, 30: 15o-165.

Fullerton, G., 2003. When does commitment lead to loyalty?; Journal of Ghage Management, 14(4): 333-334.

Giffords, E.D., 2003. An examination of organizational and professional commitment among public; not profit and proprietary social service employees; Administration in Social Work, 27(3): 5-23.

Golman, Denial, 2001. "Emotional Intelligence" , Parsa, Nasrin, Tehran, Roshed Publication.

Golman, Denial, 2004. "Emotional Intelligence in Work" Ebrahimi, Bahman; Joyandeh, Mohsen,Tehran, Bahin Danesh Publication.

Grant, A.M., 2007. "Enhancing coaching skills and emotional intelligence through training" 39(5): 257-266.

Hall, M., D. Smith and K. Smith, 2005. Accountants commitment to their profession: multiple dimensions of professional commitment and opportunities for future research ; Behavioral Research in Accounting, 17: 89-109.

Heffernan, T., G. Oneill, T. Travaglion & M. Droulers, 2008. "relationshipe marketing" ,international Journal ofbank marketing, 26(3): 183-199.

Humphreys, J., B. Brunsen. & D. Davis, 2005. "Emotional structure and commitment:implications for health care management" ,Journal of health organization and management, 19(2): 120-129.

Jones, J., 2000. The impact of hospital mergers on organizational culture, organizational commitment, professional commitment , job satisfaction and intent to turnover on registeral nurses on medical, surgical hospital units; State University of New York.

Kanan, R. and S.M. pillai, 2008. An examination on the professional commitment of engineering college teacher; International Business Management, 2(6): 218-224.

Kerr, R., J. Garvin, N. Heaton. & E. Boyle, 2006. "emotional intelligence and leadership effectiveness" ,leadership & organizational development Journal, 27(4): 265-279.

King, M. & D. Gardner, 2006. "emotional intelligence and occupational stress among professional staff in NewZealand" ,international Journal of organizational analysis, 14(3): 186-203.

Koman, E.S. & S.B. Wolff, 2008."emotional intelligence competencies in the team and team leader ,Journal of management development, 27(1): 55-75.

J. Appl. Sci. Res., 8(2): 983-991, 2012

Maslach, C., & S.E. Jackson, 1993. "Manual of the Maslach Burn out Inventory"(2nded).Palo Alto: Consulting psychologist press Inc.

Mcgarvey, R., 1997. Final score:get more from employees by upping your EQ; Enterpreneur., 25(7): 78-81.

Osinsky, P. and C. Wmueller, 2004. Professional commitment of Russian provincial sp Paul .

Palmer, B, & C. Donaldson, 2001. "Emotional intelligence and life statisfaction"Retrieved from: http:///www.genos.com.au/pdg/EI-satisfaction.pdf.

Parry, J., 2006. The effect of workplace exposure on professionsl commitment : a longitudinal study of nursing professionals; Central Queensland University.ecialist; Journal of Work and Occupations, 31(2): 193-224.

Poon, J.M., 2004."Career commitment & career success : moderating rol of emotion perception",career development international., 9(4): 374-390.

Rraju, P.M and R.C. Shriavastava, 1994. Factors contributing to commitment to the teaching profession; International Journal of Educational Management, 8(5): 713.

Saborimoghadam, Hasan, 1993. "The Relation Between Control Focus and Individual's Work under Stress", M.A thesis of Clinical Psychology, Tahran Psychiatric Institute.

Stein, S.J., P. Papadogiannis, J.A. Yip. & G. Sitarenios, 2009. " Emotional Intelligence of leaders: aprofile top executives" , ,leadership & organizational development Journal., 30(1): 87-101.

Suliman, A.M. & F.N. Al-Shaikh, 2007. "Emotional intrlligence at work links to confilict and innovative", employee relations, 29(2): 208-220.

Ting, C. and S. Chun Hua, 2000. Understanding the professional Career commitment of medical laboratory professionals; The Journal of Health Sience, 2(4): 369-380.

Xaefallahi, Ahmadali; Dostar, Mohammad, 2003. "Emotional Intelligence's Dimensions", Chronicle Management and Development, 18: 52-62.

FRAUD AND ADMINRATIVE CORRUPTION

Kamran Nazari

Department of Business Management, Payam Noor University, Kermanshah, Iran Mostafa Emami

Assistant Professor, Faculty of Economic and Managements Tarbiat Modares University, Tehran, Iran

Ali Reza Shakarbeigi

Department of Law, Payam Noor University, Kermanshah, Iran

Abstract

The Royal Government of Bhutan has been pursuing a very prudent, well thought out and balanced socio- economic development policy. Under the dynamic leadership of His Majesty the King, the country has achieved unprecedented economic growth in just over the last two decades. Blending socio economic growth with the real happiness of the people, His Majesty the King declared a vision and theme of Gross National Happiness, which not only provided a unique measurement yardstick but also gained wide recognition and acceptance. While developmental initiative brings about improvement in the living conditions of the people, Government has been very wary of many evils which are synonymous to the developmental activities. Fraud and corruption go hand in hand with the development process. Perhaps, it is only a question of degree and methodologies adopted in perpetrating corruption and fraud in different countries which may be in variance. His Majesty the King has always been very concerned on this issue and its likely effect in our small social set up. His Majesty has always aspired for a small, effective and clean government. Number of Royal kashas had been issued to step up due vigil over the public spending hoping for a clean and corruption free administrative set up.

To mark the Silver Jubilee Celebration of His majesty's enthronement, there is perhaps no other better alternatives than to express our solidarity on His Majesty's dynamism and reaffirm our commitment in establishing a corruption free society. The Royal Institute of Management has organized this seminar on Corruption and fraud and a much wider representation has been expected to deliberate on this issue. The Royal Audit Authority and the Division of Revenue and Customs have been advised to present a paper on the Extent and Magnitude of Corruption while papers on other themes will be covered by other agencies.

Key words: FRAUD, CORRUPTION, ROYAL AUDIT AUTHORITY, GOVERNMENTS

Introduction

Comparative academic studies have been focused on unethical behaviour, maladministration and mismanagement in public sector organizations. Governments all over the world and international organizations have designed strategies to fight corruption.

Corruption is a multi-faced phenomenon, linking multiple issues together such as abuse of entrusted power for private gains, low integrity, taking bribes, maladministration, fraud, and nepotism. The big question is how to prevent the increase of administrative corruption in a single country? But, how to get a grip on the control of corruption in a single-case comparison, and how to identify properly the most important implications of corruption? There are studies which

469

concentrate on explaining the effects of corruption (e.g. Mauro 1995; 1998; Rose-Ackerman 1999), elaborating upon the implications, forms, and types of corruption (e.g. Caiden 2001; Levin & Satarov 2000; Stohs & Brannick 1999), and analysing anti-corruption mechanisms and effective ways of minimizing harms and preventing corruption (e.g. Maor 2004; OECD 2000; Clark & Jos 2000; Johnston 1999; United Nations 2004; OECD 2003a). The proper diagnosis of the causes and logic behind corruption plays an important role in combating it (Quah 1999; Maor 2004; Schwartz 2003). Huberts, Lasthuizen and Peeters (2006: 290) make clear the fact that researchers will never be able to reveal all corruption to the public. They compare corruption to an iceberg, in which only the tip can be seen and only known facts can be taken into consideration.

Conventional histories of nineteenth and early twentieth century America portray its corrupt elements as similar, and at times equal, to those found in many of today's modern transition economies and developing regions. Nineteenth-century American urban governments vastly overpaid for basic services, such as street cleaning and construction, in exchange for kickbacks garnered by elected officials. Governments gave away public services for nominal official fees and healthy bribes.[2] As late as the 1950s, reports Robert A. Caro (2002, pp. 403- 13), cash-filled envelopes floated in the hallowed halls of the U.S. Senate. Harry Truman made it into the Senate as an agent of the notoriously corrupt Pendergast machine (McCullough 1992).

Some of the greatest U.S. universities were funded by individuals infamous for their roles in extracting public resources through allegedly corrupt political influence— Leland Stanford and George D. Widener, whose surname adorns Harvard's largest library, come to mind. The presidential legacies of Ulysses Grant and Warren Harding were forever marred by the Crédit Mobilier and Teapot Dome scandals, respectively. The list could go on and on.

If the United States was once more corrupt than it is today, then America's history should offer lessons about how to reduce corruption. After all, the dominant political movement of the early twentieth century—Progressivism—was dedicated to the elimination of corruption. From 1901 to 1917, under Presidents T. Roosevelt, Taft, and Wilson, a national legislative an administrative agenda was justified in part by a perceived need to reduce corruption.

Municipalities and states throughout the twentieth century regularly elected reform slates that promised to exercise a strong hand to root out corruption. Crusading journalists and ambitious prosecutors have frequently taken aim at corruption. While scholars can debate the impact of these various forces, there is no doubt that U.S. history offers many examples of reform movements that claimed as a primary goal to reduce corruption, similar to the stated goals of reformers in developing countries today. In this volume we take stock of corruption and reform in American history. Because conceptual clarity is a pre-condition for measuring the level of and temporal change in corruption, the first three chapters—this introduction, the essay by John Wallis, and that by Rebecca Menes—each squarely confront what is meant by corruption.

Because corruption is generally illegal, or at least embarrassing, it tends to be hidden, and understandably, as the modern cross-national empirical literature has found, difficult to measure. Time-series measurement is yet more difficult. Despite these problems there is great value in searching U.S. history for evidence on corruption and its time trend. Several of the chapters address the measurement of corruption over time. The Menes essay uses information on the number of corrupt mayors and municipal administrations. That by Stanley Engerman and Kenneth Sokoloff uses evidence on cost overruns for major governmental projects. This introductory essay uses data on the reporting of corruption by hundreds of newspapers for the 160 year period from 1815 to 1975. The contributions by Howard Bodenhorn and Wallis, Price Fishback and Shawn Kantor add evidence on the time path but focus on shorter time periods.

470

After the discussion of the meaning and measurement of corruption, two of the essays in this volume address the consequences of corruption or of weak legal regimes more generally.

Naomi Lamoreaux and Jean-Laurent Rosenthal discuss the rise of corporations during the late nineteenth century and how their emergence was accompanied by decreased protection of minority shareholder rights. David Cutler and Grant Miller examine the diffusion of plentiful water in America's cities during an era of legendary municipal corruption. Clearly corruption does not alone determine the extent of public good formation.

According to Lamoreaux and Rosenthal, the number of corporations in the late nineteenth century exploded, despite inadequate protection of minority shareholders, because returns to scale in production increased. Cutler and Miller argue, in a somewhat similar manner, that despite the corruption of municipal governments the increasing availability of municipal credit during the Gilded Age made large-scale water projects feasible. Of course, the increase in municipal credit availability must have had something to do with improvements in accountability, suggesting that some forms of corruption had been curtailed. Both essays suggest that despite substantial corruption in government and fraud in private dealings economic growth was curtailed far less in America than in today's developing economies.

The volume then turns to the causes and consequences of reform. Reform and regulation were often rationalized as tools to protect consumers and workers, but as three of the essays—by Fishback, Bodenhorn, and Marc Law and Gary Libecap—note the actual situation was often more complex. Fishback suggests the importance of a Stiglerian view of workplace safety regulation. Workplace safety regulations in the manufacturing and mining industries, he finds, were supported by unions and opposed by certain manufacturers. Because workplace safety laws in manufacturing disproportionately raised costs for small firms, the laws were championed by large firms. Because they were perceived as protecting workers, the laws were supported by unions.

Bodenhorn's essay emphasizes that reform can be the result of self-interested, competing politicians. He analyzes one of the first episodes of anti-corruption reform in U.S. history the fight against corruption in the chartering of New York State banks during the late 1830s.

Bodenhorn argues that reform emerged from the Whigs' desire to deprive their opponents Van Buren's Democratic Regency—of the rents of patronage. Deregulation was the weapon of choice against corruption since reducing chartering requirements limited the ability of government to manage their monopoly in a corrupt manner.

Though definition of fraud and corruption is not part of our paper, for proper understanding of the subject matter in the context of our presentation, fraud and corruption have been defined as follows;

Fraud : Fraud is usually characterized as an act of willful deceit, trickery, concealment or breach of confidence that are used to gain some unfair or dishonest advantage.

Corruption : Corruption is a much broader and multi - layered phenomenon. It is an unethical, illegal, dishonest act aimed at obtaining an unfair gain by one or more persons.

Definitions of corruption often found are:

Any form of unethical use of public authority for personal or private advantage ; the perversion of integrity by bribery or favor.

Action by a government functionary that is different from the standard, in order to favor someone in exchange for a reward. **Forms of corruption:**

It is intended to give an international dimension and perspective to this paper. As such, nature and forms of corruption presented in this paper depict a global scenario of corruption. It may not be necessary that some or all types of corruption discussed here may be prevalent in this country.

Many of us have wrong notions about our understanding as to what constitute corruption and fraud. Gift and presentations are generally not included under this category. Certainly, if gift and presentations of significant amounts are given with the intention of influencing present or future decisions in favour of the donors, it would be unethical to accept such calculated gestures. Similarly, acts of favouring close friends and relatives for employment related issues and contract works etc. in preference to others or carried out in a manner generally not permitted or not extended to others, would also constitute fraud and corruption. Many would still argue that such acts are gratuitous in nature and as such are not unethical. Perhaps, the question we should be asking is whether the recipients/ beneficiaries would or would not have got it in the normal course.

In the professional circle, it has been generally understood that manifestations of corruption include, amongst others, the following:

  Bribery and extortion: commission, unreasonable gifts, Kickbacks etc.

  Fraud, embezzlement and theft: Forgery, manipulation of records, shortage of cash, pilferage of store etc.

   Misappropriation of resources :Irregular diversion of fund/properties/stores

  Undue favors in exchange for gains : Award of contracts to favored ones, Undue payments i.e. advances, escalation and not provided in the agreement etc

   Abuse of authority : Exercising discretionary powers for personal gains, Misuse of office equipment, Misuse of funds and human resources,

  Nepotism : Favoring near and dears

    Under/over assessments of taxes and duties with personal motives

  Tax evasion and smuggling

 Over/under invoicing with a view to financial benefit

    Unfair recruitment /promotion/placements/training

  Non compliance of rules and regulations with a view to gain

  Inaction by the rules enforcing authorities/regulatory bodies for violation Corruption is often kept in check by the media and the role of the press is directly confronted in the chapter by Matthew Gentzkow, Glaeser, and Goldin. In 1870, the press was partisan, histrionic, and prone to omit facts that went against acknowledged political biases. But by 1920, most newspapers eschewed party affiliations, used more moderate and civil language, and made at least a pretense of reporting the facts of the day without spin. The chapter argues that the rise of the independent press and the remarkable transformation in U.S. newspapers between 1870 and 1920 was fundamentally the result of the increasing financial returns to selling newspapers rather than placating politicians for patronage and other reasons. While the essay does not document the impact that the press may have had on corruption, it does discuss circumstantial evidence suggesting that the rise of the independent press was an important factor in movements to reform American political corruption.

Detection of Fraud and Corruption:

Most audits are conducted on a test basis using audit sampling and other techniques. To carry out 100% checking of all transactions would be an expensive proposition and meaningless as it would still not be possible to derive complete assurance and satisfaction on the existence and detection of fraud and corruption. Most corruption cases that are serious in nature often take place out side the records e.g. Bribery, commission, kickbacks, etc. It is also difficult to detect systematic frauds. Authorities normally succeed in detecting some of the fraud and corruption cases through in-depth investigations that would require;

472

Detailed scrutiny of accounts, records and operations

Unrestricted access to information

Unrestricted scope of examination

Investigations and interviews and obtaining written statements

Analysis and comparisons

Individuals wealth assessment and inquiring as to the sources

Gathering information from out side sources

Since both the Royal Audit Authority and the Division of Revenue and Custom primarily depend on the accounting records for their audit exercise, the cases of corruption noted do not give indication of extent and magnitude of corruption. Thus it would not be appropriate to draw conclusion from the observed cases. It is, however, evident that corruption in some form or other do exist in our society. During the nineteenth century, the definition of corruption morphed into one specifically related to the bribery of public officials by private agents. Bribery was generally an illicit payment in exchange for some government controlled resource, such as a service or a public property or an exemption from government regulation. These forms of bribery, detailed in the chapter by Menes, form the lion's share of what is known about nineteenth century municipal corruption. City governments were corrupt in the purchase of inputs, such as street cleaning or construction services, and bribes were routinely given in exchange for overpayment for these inputs. City governments were corrupt in the distribution of publicly-owned property—land or access to a port— that was sold, not to the highest bidder for the good of the citizens, but to the most generous briber for the benefit of the few. Finally city governments were corrupt in the administration of rules, such as prohibitions on gambling and prostitution, and officials accepted bribes for leniency in the administration of such regulations.

In this volume we will use the word "corruption" to refer to what Wallis terms "venal corruption." We view corruption to have three central elements: (1) payments to public officials beyond their salaries; (2) an action associated with these payments that violates either explicit laws or implicit social norms; and (3) losses to the public either from that action or from a system that renders it necessary for actions to arise only from such payment. Two examples from the volume illustrate how these elements describe corruption.

Areas prone to Fraud and Corruption:

It is generally understood that certain areas are more prone to corruption than others.

The following areas are considered to be more prone to fraud and corruption:

Procurements

Construction works

Stores / equipment

Revenue receipts and cash collections / handling

Filing of tax returns i.e., incidence of under declaration of income, inflated expenditure etc.

Assessment of taxes and duties

Commission on Sales : Usually documentation is not adequate

The Determinants of Corruption

The economic approach to corruption (as in Rose-Ackerman 1975) starts with the costs and benefits facing potentially corrupt public officials. Since economics predicts that we should expect to see corruption when the benefits are high and costs are low, it is worth analyzing what factors should impact the benefits and costs of corrupt behavior by a government official. The benefits from being

473

corrupt are determined by the ability of a government official to increase someone's private wealth; the costs come from the expected penalties from being caught.

What determines the ability of a government official to increase someone's private wealth? The most obvious means is to pay the person out of the public purse. In extreme circumstances, the person can just be the official himself; embezzlement is one example of corrupt behavior. More usually, paying someone out of the public purse occurs in exchange for services of some form, either labor or subcontracting. If fees are close to the costs of contracting firms or the opportunity costs of workers, then the opportunities for corruption are limited. If fees are significantly above free market prices, then there is opportunity for corruption in the assignment of work. High public sector wages and discretion over hiring has traditionally created some of the best opportunities for corrupt earnings.

This simple analysis helps us to understand some of the most popular reforms attempted to arrest corruption. Civil service reform which would take patronage out of the hands of politicians and replace discretion with test-based rules would naturally serve limit the opportunity for corruption, especially when combined with a rigid pay scale for civil servants Rules concerning procurement fees have also tended to be a popular tool against corruption.

Competitive bids for public projects linked to the requirement that the government accept the low cost bid is one of the simplest means of limiting corruption in administration of government projects. The approach relies on the existence of a competitive supply of contractors.

The second means that public officials have to create private wealth is to transfer government property to private individuals for their own profit. The transfer of government land to traction companies was a popular form of corruption in the nineteenth century. Information about future government actions is a more subtle form of in-kind transfer. The returns to corruption in these cases depend on the size of the assets at the government's disposal and the discretion that individuals have in the distribution of these assets.

The third primary means that governments have to create private wealth is the manipulation of legal rulings or the enforcement of rules, such as regulations. Rules banning gambling and prostitution, for example, create the opportunity to extract bribes from potential providers. These bribes can be extracted by any and all members in the chain of enforcement.

As the amount of regulation increases, the opportunity to extract bribes also rises and leads reformers to fight against regulation and government monopoly (as in Bodenhorn's essay).

Conversely, the connection between the intrusiveness of regulation and the ability to extract bribes creates an incentive for politicians to push for further regulation. Even in a libertarian's dream world where government is restricted to enforcing disputes over property rights, there would still be considerable scope for corruption in the arbitration of these disputes. Every dispute over ownership creates the possibility for a corrupt ruling. After all, a corrupt judge can extract bribes even if when he rules in favor of the rightful owner. As the legal system has the ability to redistribute all of the wealth in society, the opportunities for corruption within the system are enormous. As corruption within the courts destroys the clear definition of property rights, this corruption has the potential to turn the libertarian dream into a Hobbesian nightmare. In practice, this ability may be limited by the ability of private litigants to rely on private arbitration and avoid a corrupt legal system.

Together these factors suggest that the benefits from corrupt practices for bribe-taking politicians or bribe-giving businessmen will rise with the size and discretion of the government and the amount of social and economic regulation. Benefits from corruption will also rise when the size of assets or damages involved in property rights disputes increases (Glaeser and Shleifer 2003). The late nineteenth century was a period of increasingly larger governments, more valuable public assets, more aggressive regulation, and bigger stakes litigation. The potential benefits from corruption rose along almost every conceivable dimension. The prediction is an absolute increase in the total amount of

474

corruption (measured in either bribes given or in social losses). But the increase in corruption might not translate into an increase relative to the size of government or the size of the economy.

The limits on corruption have customarily come from three sources: legal penalties, career or social costs, and internal psychic pain. Thus, the overall costs of corruption come from the size of the potential penalties and the probability that these costs are imposed which are in turn a function of information flows, social opprobrium, and the legal system.

The most obvious parameter influencing the cost of illegal corruption is thestated legal penalty for corrupt practices (the cost of corruption that violates social norms, but not laws, will not be connected to legal penalties). While this is certainly obvious, it is also important to remember that these penalties have changed significantly over time. For example, while Plunkitt's honest graft the use of insider information by politicians to enrich themselves was surely corruption, at least by our definition, it was fully legal during Plunkitt's time. Even the gifts of railway stock given to congressmen and others during the Crédit Mobilier scandal were perfectly legal at the time. In the 1790s, the number of laws regarding corruption was so modest that legal penalties against corruption were often negligible. Since that time, there has been a steady increase in the range of behaviors by public officials that are punishable by law and a steady increase in the attempt to craft laws, such as the RICO statute, that render illegal as yet unspecified forms of corrupt behavior.

Magnitude of Fraud and Corruption:

As already mentioned it is not possible to quantify the magnitude of corruption. Cases of fraud and corruption often reported, including those providing indication there of, includes:

I.   Bribery and Extortion
    Extending/availing undue favours
    Presentation of Gifts of large amounts

II. Fraud, Embezzlement and Irregular payments
    Forgery of documents
    Misuse of funds and properties
    Pilferage of stores
    Inclusion of dummy workers in Muster Rolls
    Double claims
    Intentional Irregular claims and payments
    Concealment of information

III. Procurement and construction works related corruption
    Direct procurements/ award of works from/ to some preferred suppliers/contractors
    Preferring a bidder without valid justification(s)
    Accepting a non responsive bid
    Non enforcing contractual terms
    Accepting defective, inferior and unspecified items
    Paying at higher rates than the agreed rates
    Incorporating terms and conditions prejudicial to the interest of procuring agencies
    Payment of unjustified escalation, freight, insurance claims etc.
    Extending undue favour to suppliers/ contractors i.e. unauthorized advances, non recovery of security money, non recovery of advances in time etc.
    Non processing and passing of bills in time without any reasons
    Indication of undue harassment to contractors for insignificant issues
    Disparities in enforcing contract terms

Payments made for works not executed/ materials not received

Procurements at exorbitant rates from private/ unauthorized sources

Payments made without any valid documents

Additional payments by showing excess measurements

Deliberately under estimating quantities of works and paying at higher rates for quantities beyond deviation limit

Non/short accountal of items procured

Procurement of excessive materials/supplies

Not inquiring into rates to be charged by the sub vendors and   paying at higher rates to the main vendors

Unjustified payment of compensation/recommending such payments

IV Misappropriation of public resources

Unauthorized diversion of funds

Payment/withdrawal of unauthorized /excessive advances

Retention of excessive cash in hand

Non/short accountal of revenue

Non/short deposit/remittances of revenue

Abnormal delays in accountal/deposit of revenue

Unauthorized issue of stores for private purposes

Non raising of bills for supplies/hiring charges to favour individuals

Non deduction of house rent from employees occupying Government accommodation

V   Abuse of Public Office and Nepotism

Use of facilities for personal purposes

Requiring public office to pay expenses of private nature

Awarding supply orders / contracts to relatives

Paying for self and relatives in preference to others

Granting discounts/write off to favoured ones

Using daily wages workers etc. for domestic purposes/personal works

Sanctioning loans without proper scrutiny and appraisal

VI Over/Under invoicing

Over invoicing sales to inflate sales to depict better results

Over invoicing to share the difference   Under invoicing

to share the difference **Division of the Surplus**

The division of the surplus from administrative corruption can be thought of as a cooperative game among the Payers and the Collector. The issue we face is that of dividing the potential gains from cooperation between the tax collector and a large number of taxpayers. We would like to have a rule that reflects the maximum tax liabilities of each payer and the fact that the tax collector is an essential party in the corruption process. It should be pointed out that this cannot be solved as a simple bargaining problem between a single taxpayer and the tax collector.

This is because there exists an aggregate revenue target, and therefore the current surplus available to be shared between the Collector and a Payer depends on the taxes that have already been collected elsewhere.

In this paper we use a simple solution to this problem – namely, the *Shapley value*. This solution concept defines the payoff to each person in a multiperson game as a function of their marginal

476

contributions to the total surplus (see Moulin, 1988, for an excellent overview). We could have defined a noncooperative game, as in Gul (1989). However, this would have greatly complicated the analysis without offering a more convincing approach. The outcome predicted by the Nash equilibrium of an extensive form game is very sensitive to the way we define the extensive form. Furthermore, the extensive form is never observed in practice, and therefore its choice is necessarily arbitrary. The Shapley value has the attractive feature of ignoring the details of the strategic game and defining the payoffs only in terms of observable actions. Therefore, it is much more amenable to being confronted with the data.

The Shapley value is the unique division of the total surplus that satisfies the following conditions:

• Individuals are treated symmetrically. That is, their identities are irrelevant; it is only the way they are able to affect payoffs that matters.

• The value is additive. That is, if two different situations or games are combined, the payoff to an individual is equal to the sum of his/her payoffs from each game.

It can also be shown that the Shapley value allocation to each individual is an amount equal to the expected marginal contribution of that individual in a randomly chosen coalition.

This potential marginal contribution can be interpreted in terms of each coalition member's relative power in the group. The power of the Collector in this particular surplus division game derives from his or her ability to effect a reduction in tax liabilities. The power of the Payers derives from their ability to pay their full tax liabilities and deprive the Collector ofsupplementary income in the form of bribes. **Recommendations**:

Existence of a proper system of check and balance reduces the risks of wrong doings and chances of indulging in fraud and corruption. Strong internal controls, proper rules and regulations, motivated employees, a rational taxation structure etc. tend to act as deterrent against perpetuating fraud and corruption. We are offering some suggestions and recommendations in controlling fraud and corruption for deliberations with the hope that more realistic recommendations will emerge from it.

Establishment of Adequate Regulatory Framework

Formulation of appropriate rules and regulations clearly stipulating punitive measures

Professional development programmers for accountants, auditors, taxofficials and administrators

Establishment of anti corruption Agency

Further strengthening legal System   Widening Tax Base

Power of Back Duty Investigations

Index linked Salaries of civil servants and others

Protection of salaries at least in monetary terms

Periodic transfers of employees

Rotation of duties

Appropriate representations on the Boards/ Committees avoiding conflicting decisions

Appropriate reward and incentive schemes- not necessarily directly linked to individual act of performance

Establishment of appropriate bodies to review reports on fraud and corruption

Rules and regulations to be developed with positive frame of mind. They should be perceived to be facilitating and not be seen as too prohibitive and restrictive.

A progressive and liberalized economic policy

Promoting self regulations of enterprises and greater accountability

Dissemination of information and creating awareness

477

Commissioning independent inquiries on large procurements and construction contracts by appropriate authorities

Establishment of independent quality control units to inspect quality of works, materials and equipment

Strengthening BCCI to look into grievances of business communities and offer business counseling / advise

A definitive and clear policy guidelines on privatization including post privatization commitments of corporations and role of government

Formulation of Unfair Trade Practices Act

Strengthening internal controls in the organizations

Introducing internal audits

Rules / laws with wider implication to be discussed and scrutinized at different levels before approval for their general acceptance and removing inconsistencies

Publicity and greater transparency

Adequate enforcement and monitoring by law enforcing bodies

Establishment of Consumer Protection and Advisory board

Announcements of adequate reward schemes to informers

Formulation of Essential commodities Act

Establishment of Bhutan Standards for manufactured and imported items

Development of Safety regulations

Strengthening Tax Administration and Audit System and other Regulatory Bodies

Conclusions:

Corruption undermines the entire administrative system and functioning of the public offices. It adversely effects the integrity and morale of the employees of the public offices including those who are responsible to enforce laws, rules and regulations. It encourages those responsible to deliberately keep loopholes in the rules. Corruption may be prevalent at any level and any where thus effecting day to day activities and causing harassment and inconveniences to the general public. Detection of fraud and corruption alone is not sufficient. We must take preventive measures to control it. A proper study of causes of corruption and environment favouring it would help initiate effective remedial measures.

Individual cases of corruption can be rooted out by the application of organizational sanctions Systemic corruption cannot be handled so easily. There is no guarantee that if the most serious offenders are dismissed, or if everyone who is guilty is replaced, corruption will not persist. The old patterns will continue with new players. Moreover, in the wider society, systemic corruption impedes rather than aids change.

(a)   Systemic corruption perpetuates closed politics and restricts access, preventing the reflection of social change in political institutions.

(b)   Systemic corruption suppresses opposition contributing to increasing resentment.

Thus corruption, far from being an alternative to violence, is often accompanied by more violence.

(c)   Systemic corruption perpetuates and widens class, economic, and social divisions, contributing to societal strain and preventing cohesion.

478

(d)   Systemic corruption prevents policy change, particularly where this works against immediate market considerations. Individual or sectional interests are not the best guide to the public interest.

(e)   Systemic corruption blocks administrative reform, and makes deleterious administrative practices profitable, e.g., induced delays.

(f)   Systemic corruption diverts public resources and contributes to a situation of private affluence and public squalor, especially serious where affluence is confined to the few.

(g)   Systemic corruption contributes to societal anomie in shoring up or transmuting traditional values into inappropriate areas.

(h)   The effects of systemic corruption are not limited to a specific case: there is an accumulator effect upon public perceptions and expectations which subverts trust and cooperation far beyond the impact upon the individuals immediately concerned.

(i)   Systemic corruption is not confined to poor, developing, or modernizing countries, but found in all organizational societies."

Existence of adequate regulatory and legal framework as well as a clean and efficient civil service with high morale reduces the risk of rampant corruption in the society. A sound fiscal and monetary policy with due encouragement and incentives for investment will certainly act as deterrent against corruption. Corruption weakens the economy, efficiency and effectiveness of the government systems. Rampant corruption should not be allowed to occur at any cost.

References

CARTIER-BRESSON, J., "A Few Suggestions for a Comparative Analysis of Corruption in Western Europe", Revue Internationale de Politiques Comparées v. 4, n° 2, 2003.

CLARK, WILLIAM A. & JOS, PHILIP H. (2000). "Comparative Anti-Corruption Policy: The American, Soviet and Russian Cases", International Journal of Public Administration 23:1, 101– 148.

DOBEL, PATRICK J. (1999). Public Integrity. Baltimore and London: The Johns Hopkins University Press.

GALTUNG, FREDRIK (2006). Measuring the Immeasurable: Boundaries and Functions of (Macro) Corruption Indices. In Sampford, Charles & Shacklock, Arthur & Connors, Carmel & Galtung, Fredrik (eds). Measuring Corruption. Great Britain: Ashgate Publishing Limited: 101– 130.

HARISALO, RISTO & STENVALL, JARI (2001). Luottamus kansalaisyhteiskunnan peruskivenä: Kansalaisten luottamus ministeriöihin. [Trust as Cornerstone of Civic Society: Citizens trust to ministries]. Helsinki: Edita.

HOLMES, LESLIE (1993). The End of Communist Power. Anti-Corruption Campaign and Legitimation Crisis. New York: Oxford University Press.

HUBERTS, LEO & LASTHUIZEN, KARIN & PEETERS, CAREL (2006). Measuring Corruption: Exploring the Iceberg. In Sampford, Charles & Shacklock, Arthur & Connors, Carmel & Galtung, Fredrik (eds). Measuring Corruption. Great Britain: Ashgate Publishing Limited: 265– 293.

VAN HULTEN, MICHEL (2007). Ten years of Corruption (Perceptions) Indices. Methods – Results – What Next? An analysis.

JOHNSTON, MICHAEL (1999). A Brief History of anticorruption Mechanisms. In Schedler, Andreas & Diamond, Larry & Plattner, Marc F. (eds). The Self-Restraining State: Power and Accountability in New Democracies. Boulder:Lynne Rienner Publishers: 217–226.

KAUFMANN, DANIEL (2004). Corruption, Governance and Security: Challenges for the Rich

Countries and the World. In The Global Competitiveness Report 2004/2005. The World Bank: 83–102.

KONTTINEN, E. (1991). Perinteisesti moderniin: Professioiden yhteiskunnallinen synty Suomessa. [Traditionally to Modern: The Birth of Professions in Finland.] Tampere, Finland: Vastapaino.
KOSKINEN, PEKKA (2001). Johdatus rikosoikeuteen. [Introduction to Criminal Law.] Helsinki: University of Helsinki.

LANGSETH, PETTER (2006). Measuring Corruption. In Sampford, Charles & Shacklock, Arthur & Connors, Carmel & Galtung, Fredrik (eds). Measuring Corruption. Great Britain: Ashgate Publishing Limited: 7–44.

LEVIN, MARK & SATAROV, GEORGY (2000). Corruption and Institutions in Russia, European Journal of Political Economy, vol. 16, no. 1: 113-132.

MAOR, MOSHE (2004). Feeling the Heat? Anticorruption Mechanisms in Comparative Perspective, Governance, vol. 17, no. 1: 1–28.

MAURO, P., "The Effects of Corruption on Growth, Investment and Government Expenditure", in Elliot, K. (ed.), Corruption and the Global Economy, pp. 83-108, 1997.

WEI, S-J., "How Taxing Ades, A. and R. Di Tella , "Rent, Competition and Corruption", Oxford University, mimeo,2005. is Corruption on International Investors?", NBER Working Paper, no. 6030, 2001.

WORLD BANK, Using Surveys for Public Sector Reform, Premnotes No. 23, Washington, 2005.

481

Government Accounting: An Assessment of Theory, Purposes and Standards

Mostafa Emami
M.Sc Eco.Fin , Department of Accounting, Tarbiat Modares University ,Iran,Tehran **Mehdi Parveizi**
Thecher of Islamic Azad University, Giylan gharb, Iran
Kamran Nazari
Department of Business Management, Payam Noor University, Kermanshah, Iran **Ehsan Rayegan**
Department of Accounting,Scool of Social Since , Razi University, Kermanshah, Iran

Abstract

Developments in governmental activities in recent years have raised concerns over whether the cash basis of accounting is sufficient for governmental accounting and reporting. Accrual accounting, previously thought to be only suitable in the private sector, has been seen to be an alternative for better reporting of government activities. Although there is a continuing debate over the use of cash versus accrual accounting, accrual accounting has been adopted in he governments of several countries including Australia, New Zealand and the United Kingdom. Government accounting and financial reporting aims to protect and manage public money and discharge accountability In order to achieve ambitious socioeconomic goals, developing countries require public sector institutional capacity for setting and implementing public policy, which in turn necessitates government accounting reform. The social value of government accounting reform therefore lies in its contribution to development goals, including poverty reduction. This rationale has led international and multilateral lenders and donors to endorse International Public Sector Accounting Standards (IPSAS) for adoption by developing countries. An emphasis on assuring financial integrity and a shift to accruals can make IPSAS more useful in government accounting reform in developing countries. All of these are heavily influenced by private sector practices, which favour the accrual basis and consolidated reporting. This article argues for a gradual symmetric approach to accruals and a combination of government-wide and fund reporting. The author also proposes some broad accounting principles to promote political and economic accountability .

Key words: Government Accounting, government, accounting reform, International Public Sector Accounting Standards (IPSAS.

Introduction
Miller (1995) p10 argues that a "healthy" accounting standard setting process needs representation from the entire spectrum of stakeholders to retain its integrity. He concludes that "a transparent due process allows outsiders to see the interactions and compromises among the key participants in the development of acceptable accounting rules". Prior Australian research has raised questions about the veracity of various aspects of the operation of the 'due process' for public sector standard setting. Ryan et.

521

Institute of Interdisciplinary Business Research

al. (1999) concluded that there were fundamental problems with the 'due process' as it operated in AAS29, which was released in 1993. There was a lack of input from account preparers and a close working relationship existed between the Treasuries and the standard setters. Carnegie and West (1997) conducted an analysis of the responses to ED 50 in relation to the recognition of infrastructure assets only. They contended that, for this particular issue, the standard setters placed more weight on a sample of 26 responses which were deemed to be "of particular interest" by the staff of the Australian Accounting Research Foundation (AARF) (p32). This led to their raising the concern that the PSASB may not have been responsive to its constituents. The Philippines realized fiscal surpluses between 1994 and 1997, prior to the Asian financial crisis.176 However, indicators have deteriorated significantly in the past 3 years. The Arroyo administration faces a worsening fiscal position. Unless the Government curbs expenses and improves revenue collection, the 2001 budget deficit could reach P200 billion ($4.2 billion).177 The weak fiscal position is creating tensions with multilateral development banks.178 Moreover, it restricts the Government's ability to address infrastructure issues and poverty reduction.

Furthermore, the Philippines experiences significant ongoing problems with corruption. With annual capital expenditure exceeding $3.5 billion, the procurement of goods and services, and implementation of infrastructure projects, by the Government present significant opportunities for graft.179 Government accounting and auditing arrangements were formulated in 1947. They have many strengths including the use of doubleentry bookkeeping, a mixed cash-accrual accounting base, a cadre of well-trained accountants, and potential access to a large external pool of trained accountants. Public management arrangements are characterized by institutional and regulatory rigidities. Efforts to modernize the public sector have gathered pace in recent years. Among other things, the Government intends to (i) develop a MediumTerm Expenditure Framework (MTEF); (ii) introduce output and outcome performance measures and targets; (iii) overhaul procurement practices; (iv) introduce 3-year baseline budgeting; (v) modernize auditing practices; (vi) introduce computerized financial management information systems; and (vii) prepare for the introduction of full accrual accounting.180he Constitution of the Philippines 1987 mandates the keeping of government accounts, the promulgation of accounting rules, the audit of financial reports, and the submission of reports covering the Government's financial operations and position.181 In particular, Article IX defines three constitutional commissions as being separate and independent bodies.

From Accountability to Accounting

The global rise of government accounting is fundamentally due to the greater demand for accountability in a democracy and market economy. Democratic governance and market transactions require and foster the norm of reciprocity the expectation of exchange of benefits of comparable value upon which accountability is based. Accounting information can be used to monitor and enforce the terms of economic, social and political contracts. When a government engages in market transactions whether buying or selling services, lending or borrowing money it is subject to economic accountability. When it levies taxes to finance public services, it incurs political accountability. The development of government accounting is related to the

522

Institute of Interdisciplinary Business Research

constitutional form of government that provides for separation of powers, and checks and balances among the legislative, executive, and judicial branches of government (Chan and Rubin, 1987). While all governments engage in some degree of planning and control, only democratic governments are mandated to open their books directly to auditors and indirectly to the public through financial reports. Fiscal transparency is therefore an attribute of limited government, for to give out information is to cede authority. Government officials rationally do not volunteer more information than is required or in their interest. It is therefore not surprising that, while some accounting is done on a voluntary basis, financial disclosure is often made only in response to demand. The regulatory structure for government financial disclosure mirrors the pattern of accountability in government and the political system. In an administrative hierarchy, the superior holds subordinates accountable and requires feedback information on their performance. A legislature monitors the conduct of the executive branch, for example, in executing the approved budget. Furthermore, a government has the incentive to disclose information in order to induce others to provide resources to it. These include potential buyers of government securities; vendors of goods and services on credit; and grantors of financial aid. In these voluntary exchanges, information is used to predict a government's ability to carry out the terms of contracts, .\fter the transactions are made, accounting information is used to monitor contractual performance. Governments are less inclined to disclose financial information to those without leverage over it, at least in the short-term, such as individual taxpayers. It is here that mandatory standards seek to increase the information access of those who are least able to demand it, or to enforce their right to know. The exercise of accountability requires institutions in both senses of the term: namely, organizations; and rules of the game (World Bank, 2002, p. 4). In government accounting, these refer to standard-setting bodies and the standards they promulgate. These institutions of government accounting in individual countries are extensively documented in the CIGAR literature and will not be covered in this article. It is, how ever, important to describe the general purposes of government accounting, in order to contrast it with

commercial accounting. The Commission on Audit shall have the power, authority, and duty to examine, audit, and settle all accounts pertaining to the revenue and receipts of, and expenditures or uses of funds and property, owned or held in trust by, or pertaining to, the Government, or

any of its subdivisions, agencies, or instrumentalities, including government- owned or controlled corporations with original charters, and on a post-audit basis: (a) constitutional bodies, commissions and offices that have been granted fiscal autonomy under this Constitution; (b) autonomous state colleges and universities; (c) other government owned or controlled corporations and their subsidiaries; and (d) such nongovernmental entities receiving subsidy or equity, directly or indirectly, from or through the Government, which are required by law or the granting institution to submit to such audit as a condition of subsidy or equity. However, where the internal control system of the audited agencies is inadequate, the Commission may adopt such measures, including temporary or special pre-audit, as are necessary and appropriate to correct the deficiencies. It shall keep the general accounts of the Government and, for such period as may be provided by law, preserve the vouchers and other supporting papers pertaining thereto. (2) The Commission shall have exclusive authority, subject to

the limitations in this Article, to define the scope of its audit and examination, establish the techniques and methods required therefor, and promulgate accounting and auditing rules and regulations, including those for the prevention and disallowance of irregular, unnecessary, excessive, extravagant, or unconscionable expenditures or uses of government funds and properties Section 3. No law shall be passed exempting any entity of the Government or its subsidiaries in any guise whatever, or any investment of public funds, from the jurisdiction of the Commission on Audit.

Section 4. The Commission shall submit to the President and the Congress, within the time fixed by law, an annual report covering the financial condition and operation of the Government, its subdivisions, agencies, and instrumentalities, including governmentowned or controlled corporations, and nongovernmental entities subject to its audit, and recommend measures necessary to improve their effectiveness and efficiency. It shall submit such other reports as may be required by law.

Organizational Roles and Responsibilities

The following organizations play central roles in budgeting, accounting and auditing arrangements. The COA audits the general accounts of the Government, promulgates accounting rules and regulations, and submits the annual financial report of the Government, its subdivisions, and agencies (including government owned or controlled corporations).

The Department of Finance (DOF) The DOF is responsible for (i) formulating, institutionalizing, and administering fiscal policies in coordination with other concerned subdivisions, agencies, and instrumentalities of the government; (ii) managing the financial resources of government; (iii) supervising the revenue operations of all LGUs; (iv) reviewing, approving and managing all public sector debt; and (v) rationalizing, privatizing and ensuring the public accountability of corporations and assets owned, controlled or acquired by the Government.187 The DOF oversees three operating bureaus: the Bureau of the Treasury (BTr), the Bureau of Internal Revenue (BIR), and the Bureau of Customs.

The Bureau of the Treasury (BTr) The BTr plays a pivotal role in the cash operations of the national government. It is responsible for (i) receiving and keeping national funds; (ii) managing and controlling disbursements of national funds; and (iii) maintaining accounts of financial transactions of all national government offices, agencies, and instruments.

Department of Budget and Management (DBM) The DBM is responsible for the design, reparation and approval of the accounting systems of government agencies. It is also responsible for coordinating and implementing the annual budget process. Furthermore, the Department manages the process of cash disbursement as well as monitoring compliance with appropriations.

Development and Budget Coordinating Council (DBCC) The DBCC comprises representatives from DBM, DOF, Bureau of Treasury, NEDA, and BSP. All agency budgetary requirements must pass through the Council. Its objectives are to (i) set budget parameters based on available resources; (ii) conduct budget hearings; and (iii) submit the resulting consolidated budget to the House of Representatives (particularly the Committee on Appropriations).

Accounting Information Systems

The national government accounting system is largely paper based. Financial reports from national agencies, including those with computerized systems, are manually processed and consolidated by COA. Existing computerized systems are of varying types.191 This variation is to be expected in such a diversified environment comprising a wide range of organizations with differing roles and objectives.

524

Government versus Commercial Accounting

Business accounting has often been used as a benchmark for evaluating government accounting. Two hundred years ago, Thomas Jefferson (quoted by Arthur Andersen, 1986) wished to see *the finance of the Union as clear and intelligible as a merchant's books, so that every member of Congress, and every man of any mind in the Union, should be able to comprehend them to investigate abuses, and consequently to control them'. Is it possible that government and business accounting are fundamentally alike in unimportant respects as public and private management are (Allison, 1980)? What are the important respects that set government accounting apart from its business counterpart?

In order to serve the three identified purposes, financial accounting and management accounting cannot be so neatly compartmentalized in the public sector, where management accounting refers to budgeting and control, rather than accounting solely in the service of managers. The budget is an expression of public policy and political preferences. It is an instrument of fiscal policy on revenue and spending to achieve macroeconomic objectives. It provides benchmarks for performance measured partly by the accounting system. Given their close relationship, it is often difficult to tell where budgeting ends and accounting begins. They reinforce each other in demonstrating and discharging fiscal accountability to the government's stakeholders, who are more numerous and diverse than the owners of a firm. Indeed, governments do not have owners.

The absence of ownership in government makes it problematic to apply the accounting equation (assets = liabilities + owners' equity) and its corollary (profit = revenuesexpenses) to the public sector. An exception may be local governments. These are municipal corporations chartered by the state to perform certain public services, which in many cases are private goods (for example water) or only quasipublic goods (for example elementary education). These entities have clear origins, and own identifiable assets and liabilities. Unfortunately, the assets and liabilities of the national government of a sovereign state are difficult to identify and harder still to measure in financial terms. With regard to assets, except in rare instances (such as the United States' purchase of Louisiana from France, or Alaska from Russia), few nations acquire new territories through buy-and-sell transactions. Most occupy their ancestral lands and some acquired their territories through military conquests or colonization. Historical costs, even if data are available, are not meaningful, yet market prices, even ifjustifiable. are hard to come by. The same problems arise in the case of natural resources and heritage assets. On the liability side, it is not easy to draw the line between a national government's contractual or legal obligations and its political

commitments and social responsibilities for the general welfare. In contrast to corporations' limited liabilities, governments in a democracy are prone to expand their responsibilities, resulting in larger budgets and frequent deficits (Buchanan and Wagner, 1977).

Accounting principles allow a business, whether private or state-owned, to recognize revenues only to the extent of goods or services provided. Governments uniquely provide public goods and finance them through taxation. Public goods are consumed collectively, and non-payers cannot be excluded— hence requiring tax financing. These characteristics sever the link between service delivery and revenue recognition, making it impossible to match revenues and expenses (Sunder, 1997). This accounting problem is also exacerbated by the involuntary nature of many transactions between government and people. The government's operating statement tracks resource flows, and only incidentally measures the government's service efforts and accomplishments. These unique characteristics of government are the primary source of the differences between government and commercial accounting. These differences, argues Sunder (1997, p. 198), 'do not constitute prima facie evidence that the former are defective and should be altered to conform to the latter'. More specifically, Nobes (1988, p. 198) challenged the assertion that 'Anglo-Saxon commercial accounting involving accrualsbased annual financial statements is necessary for accountability, control and

525

decision-making relating to government'. From the research perspective, theories underlying government accounting standards are mostly normative, in contrast to the development of positive theory in (business) financial accounting. The latter (Watts, 1977; Watts and Zimmerman, 1978, 1990) draws its inspiration from the contract-cost theory of the firm originating from Coase (1937). A similar incipient conceptual revolution started tentatively with Zimmerman's (1977) paper linking government financial reporting to political incentives. It is time to resume the search for a positive theory of government accounting standards. One way would be to build on the work of Chester Barnard and Herbert Simon.

At about the same time Goase wrote his famous paper explaining the existence of the firm in terms of transaction costs, Barnard (1938) identified the functions of the executive as securing the co-operation of the stakeholders of an organization. Barnard's work is currently enjoying a revival, primarily through the efforts of Oliver Williamson (1990). Much earlier, Simon (1945) applied Barnard's insight to government in his hook Administrative Behavior. In Simon's view, an organization is in equilibrium if Barnard's executive succeeds in securing the contributions of stakeholders by offering them adequate inducements to stay in the organizational coalition. A business can be viewed in the same way (Gohen and Gyert, 1965). In both types of organization, the challenge for managers is to negotiate satisfactory terms of contracts to keep the coalition intact. In such a theory, owners are important as contributors of equity capital, but they are not the only group managers try to please. In other words, the owner-centred theory of the firm and the single-principal agency theory are a special case of the Barnard- Simon organization theory.

This theory can be used to identify potential users of government's financial information by postulating that they use the information to predict their inducements from government (Ghan, 1981). Recently, Sunder (1997) applied contract-cost theory to explain and justify the differences betw-een accounting for government and nonprofit organizations and business accounting. Much more research is needed before the multiple-stakeholder perspective can have an impact on standards. In the meantime, government accounting has shifted closer to the business (financial) accounting model.

Internal Auditing

The Internal Auditing Act 1962 (RA 3456) introduced internal auditing requirements to the national government. A 1965 amendment (RA 4177) extended the Act's coverage to government-owned and controlled corporations (GOCCs) and local government units (LGUs). In 1992, President Aquino directed that government internal-control systems be strengthened (AO 278) – the Association of Government Internal Audi- tors (AGIA), among others, was instructed to ensure that internal audit practices, methods, and procedures be improved through continuing education and be conducted in accordance with internal auditing standards.

192 The AGIA represents internal auditors in government and promotes their professional development. It had 1,177 members at January 1999.

Public Financial Management Reform Program

The objectives of the Government's public financial management reforms are to (i) allocate and manage expenditures via a Medium Term Expenditure Framework (MTEF); (ii) strengthen feedback mechanisms for budget formulation through enhanced budget and performance monitoring; (iii) improve the performance management environment by simplifying budgeting rules; (iv) introduce incentives for better performance management; and (v) increase management flexibility to ensure performance results.197 The reforms are based on a benchmarking study of the Philippine expenditure management system vis-à-vis its neighboring countries (Australia, Korea, Malaysia, New Zealand,

526

Singapore, and Thailand) in terms of the three important expenditure outcomes: maintaining fiscal discipline, facilitating strategic prioritization at the oversight level, and enhancing the implementation efficiency of line agencies.198 The reform program comprises several activities as follows: 199 • Sectoral budget ceilings. Six-year sectoral budget ceilings were introduced for the Fiscal 2000 budget. These sectoral budgets were developed with the multi-sector Planning Committees of the National Economic and Development Authority (NEDA). These Committees include representatives from Congress, local government, academia, the private sector and nongovernment organizations. The process involved various government implementing agencies in a participative and proactive manner. Three-year budget baselines. The 6-year sectoral ceilings served as the basis for allocating resources to implementing agencies using a budget baseline approach. • Strengthening evaluation mechanisms. First, locally funded projects will be subjected to the same approval process that applies to those funded from foreign sources. Second, the performance measurement will be mainstreamed. A set of performance indicators will have to accompany all new policies or projects that are submitted to NEDA or DBM. The ultimate objective is to foster an evaluation culture.

•   Improving government accounting and internal control. Adopting private sector accounting and reporting practices, such as full accrual accounting will enhance the usefulness of accounting information. It will also enable organizational outputs to be meaningfully costed.

•   Separating accounting and auditing functions. COA, the Philippines' supreme audit institution, undertakes accounting, internal control and auditing functions in government. These groupings are incongruous.

•   Improving procurement procedures. The DBM has launched the Electronic Procurement System to improve the efficiency and transparency of the government procurement process.200

Issue Synopsis: Government Budgeting and Accounting
Chapter VIII – Issues and Recommendations – identifies and describes constraints and proposes corrective actions. With minor departures, these include the following selected issues that have already been identified by the UNDP-sponsored studies:

•   The Commission on Audit is responsible for promulgating accounting and auditing rules. These responsibilities are defined in Article IX of the Constitution 1987. The coexistence of these responsibilities is inconsistent with the concept of auditor independence.

•   The absence of computerized accounting information systems, combined with complex accounting regulations (i) relegates the role of most government CPAs to that of highly qualified bookkeepers.
Little time is left for value-added activities, such as financial analysis; and (ii) means that financial reports are rarely prepared in time to be useful for decision-making purposes.

•   There is no consistent set of accounting standards for budgeting and reporting. Major reporting differences result.

•   Auditors spend the majority of their time on compliance auditing (checking transactions). Minimal time is spent on financial attest auditing as more effort is applied to value-for-money audits.

•   Comparatively attractive starting salaries attract high-quality personnel into government accounting. A flat earnings structure means that higher-level salaries are far from competitive. This creates retention problems and provides a supportive environment for graft and corruption.

Summary and Proposals
Over the past 25 years, there have been some notable institutional and conceptual innovations in government accounting, contributing to its greater visibility and influence. Its emphasis has shifted from bureaucratic control to accountability reporting to the public. In some countries, government

527

accounting standards are no longer set by government officials, but by relatively independent boards. While acknowledging the importance of cash the lifeblood in government as in business contemporary accounting standards aim at tracking the long-term consequences of decisions and actions. Government officials are held accountable for their stewardship of both

financial and capital assets. Finally, it is not enough to keep the books accurately; the books have to be open to the public. When the public does not have the time or ability to inspect the accounts, governments have to make the task easier by preparing comprehensible as well as comprehensive financial statements.

Many challenges remain, especially at the global and international level. A major issue is the proper balance between international norms and domestic practices arising from national political ideology, economic system and culture. As a mechanism of governance, government accounting is subject to political forces that distribute power, and economic forces that determine the supply of and demand for resources. Therefore, unless accounting standards boards ally themselves with the institutions that can withhold something of value to a government a grant, a loan, an unqualified audit opinion, a favourable bond rating their pronouncements would remain

ineffectual. Unfortunately, at the international level, there are relatively few levers available to

a body such as the IFAC Public Sector Committee to enforce its standards. However, accountants could make the case that fiscal accountability is an international norm applicable to all governments regardless of their political and economic system. Once this transcendent value of fiscal accountability is embraced, it is a technical matter to work out the means of implementation. These include not only yearend financial statements the current focus of IPSASs—but also budgets, internal controls and external audits. 1 urge the IFAC Public

Sector Committee to rectify its neglect of the budget and to include 'actual versus budget' comparisons in financial statements. Furthermore, putting aside differences of opinions on accounting choices, the entire body of detailed standards should be framed by a set of broader principles aimed at promoting government fiscal accountability, such as:

•The objectives of government accounting are to safeguard the public treasury and pr()pert\, to accurately measure and communicate the government's fmancial condition so as to demonstrate financial accountability, and to facilitate decisionmaking. •Agovernment should prepare and publish its budgets, maintain complete financial records, provide full financial disclosure, and subject itself to independent audits.

•The form and content of financial reports should be guided by the rights and need to know of intended users.

•The accounting system should measure the cash and other financial consequences of past transactions and events, including, but not limited to, budget execution.

•The accounting system should be capable of keeping track of the levels and changes in assets, liabilities, revenues and expenditures or expenses, relative to budgeted amounts. These principles do not prescribe accounting choices. Rather, they provide a foundation for deliberating and setting government accounting standards.

Generally, accounting standards take on a greater social role as accountability requirements in countries that require higher standards of ethical behaviour. Government accounting standards in effect become government accountability standards. (Recently the U.S. General Accounting Office was renamed Government Accountability Office.). Government must answer for the resources or authority it receives from others in the society and economy. Government provides both public goods and private goods, in return for the authority to govern, as well as economic and financial resources, Government accountability requirements are expressed as the terms in the political contracts, social contracts, and economic contracts that government enters into with its stakeholders (see Exhibit 2).

528

The asset-liability perspective of accrual accounting described in Exhibit 1 is compatible with this contract theory of government: the government's assets come from the stakeholders' voluntary and involuntary contributions, and its liabilities originate from providing incentives to the stakeholders. In conclusion, fundamental to the development of accrual accounting in developing countries is the ability to identify and measure the government's assets and liabilities. Corruption tends to result in the understatement of government's assets or the overstatement of government's liabilities. Unless financial integrity is assured, the credibility of government's financial information suffers. Thus both financial integrity assurance and accurate accrual accounting are accountants' professional contribution to developing countries.

References

Allen, R. and Tommasi, D. (2001), Managing Public Expenditure: A Reference Book for Transition Countries, OECD, Paris.

Bourmistrov, A. and Mellemvik, F. (2000) «Russian Local Government Accounting: New Norms and New Problems», in Caperchione E. and Mussari, R. eds., Comparative Issues in Local Government Accounting, Kluwer Academic Publishers, Boston, pp. 159- 174.

Bourmistrov, A. and Mellemvik, F. (2001), «Accounting and Democratic Governance: A Comparative Study of One Norwegian and One Russian County», in Bac, A. ed. International Comparative Issues in Government Accounting, Kluwer Academic Publishers, Dordrecht, The Netherlands, pp. 91-122.

Chan, J.L., Jones, R.H. and Lüder, K.G. (1996), «Modeling Government Innovations: An Assessment and Future Research Directions», Research in Governmental and Nonprofit Accounting, Vol. 9, pp. 1-19.

Chan, J.L. (2000), «A Sino-American Comparison of Budget and Accounting Coverage», in Caperchione, E. and Mussari, R., eds., Comparative Issues in Local Government Accounting, Kluwer Academic Publishers, Boston, pp. 11-34.

Chan, J.L., Cong, S.H. and Zhao, J.Y. (2001), «The Effects of Reform on China's Public budgeting and Accounting System», in Bac, A., ed. International Comparative Issues in Government Accounting, Kluwer Academic Publishers, Dordrecht, The Netherlands, pp. 297-314.

Chu, K-Y, and Hemming, R. (1991), «Public Expenditure Handbook: A Guide to Public Policy Issues in Developing Countries», International Monetary Fund, Washington, D.C. Coombs, Hugh M. and Mohamad Tayib, (2000), «Financial Reporting Practice: A Comparative Study of Local Authority Financial Reports Between the UK and 12 Malaysia», in Caperchione, E. and Mussari, M. eds., Comparative Issues in Local Government Accounting, Kluwer Academic Publishers, Boston,, pp. 53-68.

Deutsch, K.W. (1966), The Nerves of Government: Models of Political Communication and Control, The Free Press, New York.

Godfrey, A.D., Devlin, P.J. and Merrouche, C., (1996), «Governmental Accounting in Kenya, Tanzania and Uganda» in Chan, J.L., ed., Research in Governmental and Nonprofit Accounting, Vol. 9, JAI Press, Greenwich, Connecticut, pp. 193-208.

Godfrey, A.D., Merrouche, C. and Devlin, P.J. (1999), «A Comparative Analysis of the Evolution of Local Governmental Accounting in Algeria and Morocco,» in Copley, P.A. and Sanders, G.D., eds. Research in Governmental and Nonprofit Accounting, Vol. 10, JAI Press, Greenwich, Connecticut, pp. 201-234.

Grindle, Merilee S. (2000), «Ready or Not: The Developing World and Globalization,» in Nye, J.S. and Donahue, J.D., eds. Governance in a Globalizing World, Brookings Institution Press, ashington, D.C., pp. 178-207.

Hopwood, A. and Miller, P., eds. (1994), Accounting as a Social and Organizational Practice, Cambridge University Press, Cambridge.

International Federation of Accountants (IFAC) (1996), «Responding to an Increasing Demand for Accountability in the Public Sector,» IFAC Quarterly, October.

IFAC (2003), Handbook on International Public Sector Accounting Standards. IFAC, New York.

IFAC, International Public Sector Accounting Standards Board (2005), Exposure Draft 24, Financial Reporting Under the Cash Basis of Accounting – Disclosure Requirements for Recipients of External Assistance, IF AC, New York.

IFAC, International Public Sector Accounting Standards Board (2005), «Background and Update,» unpublished paper, March.

IFAC, Public Sector Committee (2000), Study 11, Government Financial Reporting: Accounting Issues and Practices. IFAC, New York, May.

Jaruga, A. (1988), «Governmental Accounting, Auditing and Financial Reporting in East European Countries,» in Chan, J.L. and Jones, R.H. eds., Governmental Accounting and Auditing: International Comparisons, Routledge, London, pp. 105-121. Keefer, P. and Khemani, S. (2004), «Democracy, Public Expenditure and the Poor,» World Bank Research Observer. World Bank, Washington, D.C.

Nowak, W.A. and Bakalarska, B. (2001), «Polish Public Sector Accounting in Transition: The Landscape after 1999 Step in the State Redefining,» in Bac, A. ed., International Comparative Issues in Government Accounting, Kluwer Academic Publishers, Dordrecht, The Netherlands, pp. 265-278.

Ouda, Hassan A.G. (2001), «Central Governmental Accounting of Egypt and the Netherlands: Similarities and Differences,» in Bac, A. ed., International Comparative Issues in Government Accounting, Kluwer Academic Publishers, Dordrecht, The Netherlands, pp. 71-90.

Rose-Ackerman, S. (1999), Corruption and Government: Causes, Consequences and Reform, Cambridge University Press, Cambridge.

Reuters (2003), «World Bank urges crackdown on government corruption», December 10.

Sachs, J.D. (2005), The End of Poverty: Economic Possibilities for Our Time, Penguin Books, New York.

Schiavo-Campo, S. and Tommasi, D. (1999), Managing Government Expenditure, Asian Development Bank, Manila.

Simon, H.A. (1954), Centralization vs. Decentralization in Organizing the Controller's Department, Controllership Foundation, New York.

Sutcliffe, P. (2003), «The Standards Programme of IFAC's Public Sector Committee,» Public Money and Management, January, pp. 11-12.

World Bank (1998), Public Expenditure Management Handbook, World Bank, Washington, D.C.

530

J. Basic. Appl. Sci. Res., 2(9)8606-8611, 2012

ISSN 2090-4304
Journal of Basic and Applied Scientific Research *www.textroad.com*

The Relationship between Operational Auditing the Public Response in Iran

Mostafa Emami [1], Farzad Eavani[2], Kamran Nazari[3], Mahdi Nikjoo [4]

[1]Young Researchers Club, South Tehran Branch, Islamic Azad University, Tehran, Iran
[2]Department of Accounting, School of Social Science , Razi University, Kermanshah, Iran
[3]Department of Business Management, Payam Noor University, Kermanshah, Iran
[4]Department of Accounting ,Gilan-E-Gharb Branch, Islamic Azad University, Gilan-E-Gharb, Iran

ABSTRACT

This study investigated the relationship between operational auditing The Government Accountability Supreme Audit Court of Auditors is the view. The study population included 1072 persons, The official technical expert Computing the whole country Court of Auditors to the Auditor General In 1389 are working in this field. 330 people in this study using simple random sampling As the sample is selected. Using survey data gathered with data and raw data into meaningful And values for each variable using data from the questions it has been calculated Using SPSS software Considering both descriptive statistics and the statistics And inferential statistics Has been processed and analyzed. For data analysis of two test T-TEST Correlation test was used. Results confirm the existence of the relationship between operational audit on government accountability Supreme Audit Court of Auditors is the view.
KEY WORDS: operational auditing, accountability, Supreme Audit Court of Iran, transparency

INTRODUCTION

In advanced and developing countries, Public accountability as a fundamental responsibility of, The data has been accepted. Auditing and financial experts believe the government is
Governmental accounting and financial reporting system Playing an important role as the main tool of public accountability is responsible. a special place to work on the concept of accountability The theoretical basis of accounting and financial reporting to the And the concept of accountability as the foundation Governmental accounting and financial reporting system and the center of gravity Attention and emphasis has been. Thus, accountability,
The government requires that the acts that will perform Explain to the citizens
And the results of the risk assessment program approved Independent regulatory agencies, and ultimately people will judge. Full preservation of the public interest through traditional auditing methods (Financial Accounting), along with the ideas and attitudes, more comprehensive approach towards, a more completeMore accurate formed more And with "the performance and management audit" or "Audit management activities" began its move.
Decades until the late eighties the performance audit Management and compliance audit was limited toIn the framework of laws, regulations and has been operating instructions.
In recent years the focus and scope of audits In public and private sector have been changed And the Financial Alone is not the management information needs Therefore, managers in private and public sectors Looking for more information to evaluate and judge about the quality of operations and operational improvements are Techniques in such areas to be audited to evaluate the performance of operations has increased dramatically So that the operational audit Participation in the accountability process is because they provide an independent assessment about the performance of government agencies, Project, activity or special duties

to provide information to increase the accountability process and facilitate the decision is made by hand Responsibility for monitoring or corrective actions are taken. (Babajani, 2005)

Statement of Problem

Theoretical framework based on responsibility and accountability, Create a proper system of accounting Accountable or responsible for information flow between And the answer is right, whether or owners. This framework is based on two-way communication. Based on this relationship has a right to know whether, As respondent has the right The disclosure of information privacy in their use is legal. Most of the theoretical framework based on accounting decisions, Interpretations have been developed to benefit users, While the theoretical framework based on responsibility and accountability Mutual interests of both parties and ensures(-KarbasiYazdi, Hossein (2005)

*Corresponding Author: Mahdi Nikjoo, Department of Accounting ,Gilan-E-Gharb Branch, Islamic Azad University,

In today's complex societies that people's expectations of government increasingly diversified and increased No doubt having a large organization and complex public

Or interpretation is inevitable bureaucracy. Theoretically, Organizations need effective, efficient and economical to operate. Through operational audits to determine Operational failure and offers practical suggestions and making positive changes to help organizations in this direction. If the operation is successful audit its cost would be justified And auditing environment rather than a cost center Effectively become a profit center is. Success in implementing the operational audit Management is also rapidly Operational audit be carried out more than and proposals in the areas of efficacy, (Babajani, J. & Poor Yansb, A. (2003)

Will provide efficiency and economy, And the results will be significant savings. Now that economic development programs, Social and Cultural A new trend has And a new outlook changes have appeared, The directors have paid special attention to the operational audit And enabling The more the internal audit Units under its management With new knowledge and methods of auditing Make a full operational audit And its share in economic prosperity than before, Cultural and social play.(- Dae-Zadeh, N. (2006)

Generally, the need for accountability, More information about programs And government services are demanded. Officials, legislators and citizens Data are demanding and require Confirm whether the public funds as appropriate And compliance with laws and regulations have been taken? They also want to know Do government agencies, projects and services have achieved their objectives? And the organizations, programs and services are managed efficiently or economically?(Williams and Gall, Gher. 1987) In this study to discuss About the operational audit The Government Accountability And also to answer For the questions below. 1 - Whether the operational audit And accountability of government, there is significant? 2 - Do Operational Audit Transparency leads to accountability to the community? 3 - Operational Audit Enhance the quality of government accountability to the community? 4 - Operational AuditQualitative characteristics of information (being understood, being comparable) It provides a benefit to government accountability?

Importance and necessity of research

Due to growing companies and organizationsIn public and private sectorAnd the distance created between managementAnd corporate business units,Audit needs to be feltThe routine audit (financial audit)Major emphasis on identifying the optimal (fair) being

The financial condition and results of operationsAnd no assessment of actual performance are not managers.Develop relationships with organizations and become more complex And technological progress of the rectifier andNeed for optimal use of resources

The more rare the growth accounting And requires the use of operational auditing for successful management of organizations In order to reduce the dissatisfaction expressed

The audit focused on the traditional role To follow the rules and regulations And the increasing expectations of citizens Responsibility of the Government Accountability About the acts that will perform Appropriate stimulus to induce the public sector To perform operational audits for Engage in acts that would increase government accountability.

Research hypotheses

With regard to questions Expressed in the following hypothesis Is formulated The main hypothesis is that a number of research hypotheses And hypotheses, two, three and four Secondary research hypotheses are: Hypothesis 1: There is a significant relation between audit government operations and accountability. Hypothesis 2: Audit of operational transparency of government accountability to the community. Hypothesis 3: Operational Audit of the quality of government accountability to the community.

Hypothesis 4: Auditing the operational characteristics of qualitative information (Being understood, being comparable)To be beneficial in order to meet the government provides.(Williams and Gall, Gher. 1987)

Variables

In the present studySince the effects of the operational auditOn government accountability, we Variables have been developed so as follows:Independent variables:The main hypothesis ofOperational auditAs the independent variable is consideredDependent variable:The main hypothesisAccountability of governmentAs the dependent variable is considered.

MATERIALS AND METHODS

Study Application of Descriptive, Survey was conducted and solidarity. Applied research is Because its results to facilitate operations Or solve problems Normally that should be solved in the long run Is used. The research

8607

J. Basic. Appl. Sci. Res., 2(9)8606-8611, 2012

is descriptive It includes a set of methods Their aim is to describe the conditions or phenomena studied The current status of the subject is studied. Survey is Based on the generalized information Of small Of society as a sample group Is the total population. R is the correlation Because this type of research is to identify cases That all changes in the dependent variable Expression of the independent variable does not And other variables in the expression changes are effective.

Methods of data collection

In this study, Library of methods and questionnaires Is used to collect information. Methods of data collection

Theoretical research in the field, Literature, research background and access to data Research efforts in the past The type of secondary data Library method has been used. For this jack using vector addition, Of a digital library, Search in the spreadsheets, Review of scientific articles And seminars are also used.

For data collection, A questionnaire using Likert scale range(The effect of low, medium, high, very high)Has been extracted Given that this scale Measurement, the qualitative responses, So, to convert themThe quantitative response,For each of the options allocated numbers 5,4,3,2,1And coefficient of some importanceThe coefficients are multiplied by the frequencyTo resultsUsed for statistical work.Measure of reliabilityCronbach's alpha statistic was usedThe obtained valueMore than 70% isThe reliability of measuring instruments is considered acceptableAlso provide for the validity of AndahThe ((validity-related content))And judging teachersAs subject specialistsIs used.

Population sample and sampling

In this study,The study population included 1072 persons,The official technical expert

Computing the whole country CourtThe auditor is the Auditor GeneralIn 1389 Are working in this field.In the present studySample usingSimple random sampling method is selected.Considering that the numberStatistical research has shownAnd community members were allTo study possible and not possible,Mathematical method is the most accurate methodIs used.Given the range of questionsOf five options - is a LikertIf the level of statistical confidenceIn this study, 95%And the rate of 6% to be considered carefully

Sample size was calculated as follows:

$$n = \frac{N \cdot Z_{\alpha/2}^{2} \cdot \sigma^{2}}{\sigma^{2} \cdot (N-1) + Z_{\alpha/2}^{2} \cdot \sigma^{2}} = \frac{1072 \cdot (1.96)^{2} \cdot (0.667)^{2}}{(0.06)^{2} \cdot (1072-1) + (1.96)^{2} \cdot (0.667)^{2}} = 330$$

Methods of data analysis

Statistical Information Collected using a questionnaire Data and raw data into meaningful And values for each variable using data Questions it has been calculated Using SPSS software And according to both statistics The descriptive statistics and inferential statistics processing Is taken and analyzed. To describe the data Two-dimensional frequency tables and charts have been used.

Descriptive statistics of Information theory and Illation in the field of statistics for data analysis Two techniques of T-TEST Friedman test and correlation

In order to confirm or refute this hypothesis has been used.

TEST RESULTS

The first hypothesis

H0: There is a significant relation between audit government operations and accountability

.H1 Operational audit and accountability, there is no significant relation between government   The first hypothesis test statistic calculated

d.f	T-statistics calculated	The standard error of the mean	The average	Number of Visits
329	13.68	.07	3.72	330

After comparing the test statistic (13.68)The critical value (1.64)It is clear thatThe test statistic is in the H1 area,The 95% confidence levelThe approval does not imply that the observations can be said HoSince Ho isStater is conflicting research hypothesisIt can be said at 5% errorResearch hypotheses were confirmed.The hypothesis"There is a significant relation between audit government operations and accountability."Is acceptable.The operational audit on the impact of government accountability.

Hypothesis 2

H0: Operational audits of government accountability to the community is clear.

8608

H1:Operational audits of government accountability to the community is not clear.

The second hypothesis test statistic calculated

d.f	T-statistics calculated	The standard error of the mean	The average	Number of Visits
329	11.89	.08	3.63	330

After comparing the test statistic (11.89)The critical value (1.64)It is clear thatThe test statistic is in the H1 area,The 95% confidence levelHo does not imply that the observations can be confirmed.Since Ho isStater is conflicting research hypothesisIt can be said at 5% errorResearch hypotheses were confirmed.The hypothesis"Operational audit led to the transparency of government accountability to the community."Is acceptable.

Hypothesis 3

First step: definition of the statistical assumptions

H0: Operational audit of the quality of government accountability to the community.

H1: Operational audit of the quality of government accountability to the community does not. Table III hypothesis test statistic calculated

d.f	T-statistics calculated	The standard error of the mean	The average	Number of Visits
329	14.02	.08	3.73	330

Step IV: Decision

After comparing the test statistic (02/14) The critical value (64/1)Is characterized

The test statistic is in the H1 area; The 95% confidence level The approval does not imply that the observations can be said Ho. Since Ho is Stater is conflicting research hypothesis

The 5% error in Research hypothesis can be confirmed. The hypothesis "Operational audit of the quality of government accountability to the community. "Is accepted

Hypothesis 4:

H0: Audit of operational characteristics of data quality (To be understandable and comparable) Into useful In order to meet the government provides.

H1: Audit of operational characteristics of data quality (To be understandable and comparable) Into useful In order to meet the government does not provide. Hypothesis test statistic calculated in Table IV

d.f	T-statistics calculated	The standard error of the mean	The average	Number of Visits
329	11.86	.12	3.65	330

After comparing the test statistic (86/11)The critical value (64/1)It is clear thatThe test statistic is in the H1 area;The 95% confidence levelObservations imply that not enough can be said Ho confirmation.Since Ho isStater is conflicting research hypothesisIt can be said at 5% errorResearch hypotheses were confirmed.The hypothesis"Audit quality attributes of operational information(To be understandable and comparable)Into usefulIn order to meet the government provides. "Is acceptable.

In the end, making notes Statistical data analysis and And we test the hypotheses. As observed did All hypotheses were confirmed, Employing the operational audit Increased transparency, quality and features of qualitative information And thus promote greater accountability And government acts that will perform better Be.

The results

During the studyFour hypotheses were tested.Testing the hypothesisThe study included 1072 people,The total computing power of the Court's formal technicalThe auditor is the Auditor GeneralIn 1389 are working in this field.The results of this test is as follows:

Hypothesis 1: There is a significant relation between audit government operations and accountability. After comparing the test statistic (13.86)The critical value (1.64)It is clear that The test statistic is in the H1 area, The 95% confidence level The approval does not imply that the observations can be said Ho. Since Ho is Stater is conflicting research hypothesis

The 5% error inResearch hypothesis can be confirmed. The hypothesis"There is a significant relation between audit government operations and accountability." Is acceptable.

The operational audit on the impact of government accountability.

Hypothesis 2: Operational Audit Transparency of government accountability To be community. After comparing the test statistic (11.89) The critical value (1.64)It is clear that

8609

J. Basic. Appl. Sci. Res., 2(9)8606-8611, 2012

The test statistic is in the H1 area, The 95% confidence levelHo does not imply that the observations can be confirmed. Since Ho is Stater is conflicting research hypothesis

It can be said at 5% error Research hypotheses were confirmed. The hypothesis "Operational audit led to the transparency of government accountability to the community."

Is acceptable.

Hypothesis 3:

Operational AuditEnhance quality, accountabilityThe state is society.After comparing the test statistic (14.02)The critical value (1.64)Is characterizedThe test statistic is in the H1 area;The 95% confidence level can be said Ho does not imply that the observations upon approval.Since Ho isStater is conflicting research hypothesis It can be said at 5% error Research hypotheses were confirmed. The hypothesis "Enhance the operational audit

Quality of government accountability to the community. "Is accepted.

Hypothesis 4: Operational Audit

Qualitative characteristics of information(Being understood, being comparable)To be beneficial in order to meet the government provides. After comparing the test statistic (14.02) The critical value (1.64)It is clear thatThe test statistic is in the H1 area, The 95% confidence level The approval does not imply that the observations can be said Ho.

Since Ho is Stater is conflicting research hypothesis The 5% error in Research hypothesis can be confirmed. The hypothesis "Operational Auditing Enhance the quality of government accountability The community is. "Is acceptable.

Suggestions

Although demand For operational audit Iran is growing day by day, But the service was And sometimes without the quality of services offered, The demand for this type of service has overshadowed Operational auditing is causing inefficiency. Therefore recommended:

1. Legislative and legal authorities with the adoption of binding rules and regulations, Public sector required to meet Unconditional Able to perform operational audits.
2. Public administration and public companies, Reform of the corporate budgeting the traditional method of operating budget Action to audit quality may be achieved.
3. Public sector Accounting systems and E and its operational and monitoring and auditing system Audit to be equipped to quickly Operational audits to reduce costs.
4. LegislatureBinding legislation Regulatory devices And audit Required to provide audited And the Court of AuditAnd Auditing OrganizationTowards operational auditing standards

Immediate   action   to.

5. The monitoring and auditingTo create trainingAnd professional seminarsThe operational audit action.
6. As regardsStill a large part of the activitiesIn our country are performed by government Moreover, inefficiency and management activities by the government,One of the actions that seem appropriate in present circumstancesOperational audit is conducted.With this type of audit,In addition to encouraging people to use the effective charge,Economic and efficient use of limited resources can beThey will also create a sense of accountabilityAnd thereby the citizens want the right answerThat one of their natural rightsIn democratic societies is to be respected.

REFERENCES

1-A. - Babajani, J. (1998), accounting and financial reporting system of accountability of the government of Iran. PhD thesis, University of AllamehTbabayy.

. 2 - Babajani, J. (2003), accounting, governmental auditing. Payam Noor University Press.

. 3 - Babakhani, J. (2008), governmental accounting and financial controls. TabatabaiUniversity Press, third edition.

4. - Babajani, J. & Poor Yansb, A. (2003), a conceptual framework based on CARE's accountability. Proceedings of the auditor, No. 40.

. 5 - Babajani, J. (2004), public sector accountability and internal controls. CPA Journal, No. 146 and 147.

6.   - Hussein in Iraq, Hassan (2009), Public Audit (theoretical and practical). Faculty of Economics, Publication No. 19.

7.   - Large, Hussein (1996), based on accountability in public sector accounting. Proceedings of the auditor, No. 4.

. 8 - KarbasiYazdi, Hossein (2005) Accounting Theory. Publications Higher Education Center of Imam Khomeini Relief Committee (RA), 374 to 420.

. 9 - A large, Hussein (2007), audit of performance management in Ireland and its relation to the control system. Proceedings of the auditor, No. 4.

10.   - Momeni, Qayum Mohammad and Ali. 2003.statistical data analysis using SPSS, publishing a new book, ¬ -110 to 115.

11.   - Dae-Zadeh, N. (2006), Guide to Preparing research proposals (proposals). Publication language culture.

12.   - Babajani, J. (2009), the benefits of performance auditing in the DrpaskhgvyyKshvrvnqsh. Conference Proceedings Vskhnrany performance audit.

13.-Abroadus ,Jospd . 1998, Comtoic.Performance Accounting.AICPA.

14.-Brown, Williams and Gall, Gher.1987 , Auditing Performance in Government.

Nikjoo *et al.*, 2012

J. Basic. Appl. Sci. Res., 2(9)8606-8611, 2012

ISSN 2090-4304
Journal of Basic and Applied Scientific Research *www.textroad.com*

The Relationship between Operational Auditing the Public Response in Iran

Mostafa Emami [1], Farzad Eavani[2], Kamran Nazari[3], Mahdi Nikjoo [4]

[1]Young Researchers Club, South Tehran Branch, Islamic Azad University, Tehran, Iran
[2]Department of Accounting, School of Social Science , Razi University, Kermanshah, Iran
[3]Department of Business Management, Payam Noor University, Kermanshah, Iran
[4]Department of Accounting ,Gilan-E-Gharb Branch, Islamic Azad University, Gilan-E-Gharb, Iran

ABSTRACT

This study investigated the relationship between operational auditing The Government Accountability Supreme
Audit Court of Auditors is the view. The study population included 1072 persons, The official technical expert Computing the
whole country Court of Auditors to the Auditor General In 1389 are working in this field. 330 people in this study using simple
random sampling As the sample is selected. Using survey data gathered with data and raw data into meaningful And values for
each variable using data from the questions it has been calculated Using SPSS software Considering both descriptive statistics and
the statistics And inferential statistics Has been processed and analyzed. For data analysis of two test T-TEST Correlation test was
used. Results confirm the existence of the relationship between operational audit on government accountability Supreme Audit
Court of Auditors is the view.
KEY WORDS: operational auditing, accountability, Supreme Audit Court of Iran, transparency

INTRODUCTION

In advanced and developing countries, Public accountability as a fundamental responsibility of, The data has been accepted.
Auditing and financial experts believe the government is
Governmental accounting and financial reporting system Playing an important role as the main tool of public accountability is
responsible. a special place to work on the concept of accountability The theoretical basis of accounting and financial reporting to
the And the concept of accountability as the foundation Governmental accounting and financial reporting system and the center of
gravity Attention and emphasis has been. Thus, accountability,
 The   government   requires   that   the   acts   that   will   perform   Explain   to   the   citizens
And the results of the risk assessment program approved Independent regulatory agencies, and ultimately people will judge. Full
preservation of the public interest through traditional auditing methods (Financial Accounting), along with the ideas and attitudes,
more comprehensive approach towards, a more completeMore accurate formed more And with "the performance and management
audit" or "Audit management activities" began its move.
Decades until the late eighties the performance audit Management and compliance audit was limited toIn the framework of laws,
regulations and has been operating instructions.
In recent years the focus and scope of audits In public and private sector have been changed And the Financial Alone is not the
management information needs Therefore, managers in private and public sectors Looking for more information to evaluate and
judge about the quality of operations and operational improvements are Techniques in such areas to be audited to evaluate the
performance of operations has increased dramatically So that the operational audit Participation in the accountability process is
because they provide an independent assessment about the performance of government agencies, Project, activity or special duties

to provide information to increase the accountability process and facilitate the decision is made by hand Responsibility for monitoring or corrective actions are taken. (Babajani, 2005)

Statement of Problem

Theoretical framework based on responsibility and accountability, Create a proper system of accounting Accountable or responsible for information flow between And the answer is right, whether or owners. This framework is based on two-way communication. Based on this relationship has a right to know whether, As respondent has the right The disclosure of information privacy in their use is legal. Most of the theoretical framework based on accounting decisions, Interpretations have been developed to benefit users, While the theoretical framework based on responsibility and accountability Mutual interests of both parties and ensures(-KarbasiYazdi, Hossein (2005)

*Corresponding Author: Mahdi Nikjoo, Department of Accounting ,Gilan-E-Gharb Branch, Islamic Azad University,

In today's complex societies that people's expectations of government increasingly diversified and increased No doubt having a large organization and complex public

Or interpretation is inevitable bureaucracy. Theoretically, Organizations need effective, efficient and economical to operate. Through operational audits to determine Operational failure and offers practical suggestions and making positive changes to help organizations in this direction. If the operation is successful audit its cost would be justified And auditing environment rather than a cost center Effectively become a profit center is. Success in implementing the operational audit Management is also rapidly Operational audit be carried out more than and proposals in the areas of efficacy, (Babajani, J. & Poor Yansb, A. (2003)

Will provide efficiency and economy, And the results will be significant savings. Now that economic development programs, Social and Cultural A new trend has And a new outlook changes have appeared, The directors have paid special attention to the operational audit And enabling The more the internal audit Units under its management With new knowledge and methods of auditing Make a full operational audit And its share in economic prosperity than before, Cultural and social play.(- Dae-Zadeh, N. (2006)

Generally, the need for accountability, More information about programs And government services are demanded. Officials, legislators and citizens Data are demanding and require Confirm whether the public funds as appropriate And compliance with laws and regulations have been taken? They also want to know Do government agencies, projects and services have achieved their objectives? And the organizations, programs and services are managed efficiently or economically?(Williams and Gall, Gher. 1987) In this study to discuss About the operational audit The Government Accountability And also to answer For the questions below. 1 - Whether the operational audit And accountability of government, there is significant? 2 - Do Operational Audit Transparency leads to accountability to the community? 3 - Operational Audit Enhance the quality of government accountability to the community? 4 - Operational AuditQualitative characteristics of information (being understood, being comparable) It provides a benefit to government accountability?

Importance and necessity of research

Due to growing companies and organizationsIn public and private sectorAnd the distance created between managementAnd corporate business units,Audit needs to be feltThe routine audit (financial audit)Major emphasis on identifying the optimal (fair) being

The financial condition and results of operationsAnd no assessment of actual performance are not managers.Develop relationships with organizations and become more complex And technological progress of the rectifier andNeed for optimal use of resources

The more rare the growth accounting And requires the use of operational auditing for successful management of organizations In order to reduce the dissatisfaction expressed

The audit focused on the traditional role To follow the rules and regulations And the increasing expectations of citizens Responsibility of the Government Accountability About the acts that will perform Appropriate stimulus to induce the public sector To perform operational audits for Engage in acts that would increase government accountability.

Research hypotheses

With regard to questions Expressed in the following hypothesis Is formulated The main hypothesis is that a number of research hypotheses And hypotheses, two, three and four Secondary research hypotheses are: Hypothesis 1: There is a significant relation between audit government operations and accountability. Hypothesis 2: Audit of operational transparency of government accountability to the community. Hypothesis 3: Operational Audit of the quality of government accountability to the community. Hypothesis 4: Auditing the operational characteristics of qualitative information (Being understood, being comparable)To be beneficial in order to meet the government provides.(Williams and Gall, Gher. 1987)

Variables

In the present studySince the effects of the operational auditOn government accountability, we Variables have been developed so as follows:Independent variables:The main hypothesis ofOperational auditAs the independent variable is consideredDependent variable:The main hypothesisAccountability of governmentAs the dependent variable is considered.

MATERIALS AND METHODS

Study Application of Descriptive, Survey was conducted and solidarity. Applied research is Because its results to facilitate operations Or solve problems Normally that should be solved in the long run Is used. The research

8607

J. Basic. Appl. Sci. Res., 2(9)8606-8611, 2012

is descriptive It includes a set of methods Their aim is to describe the conditions or phenomena studied The current status of the subject is studied. Survey is Based on the generalized information Of small Of society as a sample group Is the total population. R is the correlation Because this type of research is to identify cases That all changes in the dependent variable Expression of the independent variable does not And other variables in the expression changes are effective.

Methods of data collection

In this study, Library of methods and questionnaires Is used to collect information. Methods of data collection

Theoretical research in the field, Literature, research background and access to data Research efforts in the past The type of secondary data Library method has been used. For this jack using vector addition, Of a digital library, Search in the spreadsheets, Review of scientific articles And seminars are also used.

For data collection, A questionnaire using Likert scale range(The effect of low, medium, high, very high)Has been extracted Given that this scale Measurement, the qualitative responses, So, to convert themThe quantitative response,For each of the options allocated numbers 5,4,3,2,1And coefficient of some importanceThe coefficients are multiplied by the frequencyTo resultsUsed for statistical work.Measure of reliabilityCronbach's alpha statistic was usedThe obtained valueMore than 70% isThe reliability of measuring instruments is considered acceptableAlso provide for the validity of AndahThe ((validity-related content))And judging teachersAs subject specialistsIs used.

Population sample and sampling

In this study,The study population included 1072 persons,The official technical expert Computing the whole country CourtThe auditor is the Auditor GeneralIn 1389 Are working in this field.In the present studySample usingSimple random sampling method is selected.Considering that the numberStatistical research has shownAnd community members were allTo study possible and not possible,Mathematical method is the most accurate methodIs used.Given the range of questionsOf five options - is a LikertIf the level of statistical confidenceIn this study, 95%And the rate of 6% to be considered carefully

Sample size was calculated as follows:

$$n = \frac{N \square Z_{\alpha 2} \square \square_2^2}{\square_2^2 \square N \square 1 \square \square Z_{\alpha 2}^2 \square \square_2^2} = \frac{1072 \square \square 1.96 \square^2 \square (0.667)^2}{(0.06)^2 \square (1072 \square 1) \square \square 1.96 \square_2^2 \square (0.667)_2^2} \square 330$$

Methods of data analysis

Statistical Information Collected using a questionnaire Data and raw data into meaningful And values for each variable using data Questions it has been calculated Using SPSS software And according to both statistics The descriptive statistics and inferential statistics processing Is taken and analyzed. To describe the data Two-dimensional frequency tables and charts have been used.

Descriptive statistics of Information theory and Illation in the field of statistics for data analysis Two techniques of T-TEST Friedman test and correlation
In order to confirm or refute this hypothesis has been used.

TEST RESULTS

The first hypothesis

H0: There is a significant relation between audit government operations and accountability
.H1 Operational audit and accountability, there is no significant relation between government   The first hypothesis
test statistic calculated

d.f	T-statistics calculated	The standard error of the mean	The average	Number of Visits
329	13.68	.07	3.72	330

After comparing the test statistic (13.68)The critical value (1.64)It is clear thatThe test statistic is in the H1 area,The 95% confidence levelThe approval does not imply that the observations can be said HoSince Ho isStater is conflicting research hypothesisIt can be said at 5% errorResearch hypotheses were confirmed.The hypothesis"There is a significant relation between audit government operations and accountability."Is acceptable.The operational audit on the impact of government accountability.

Hypothesis 2

H0: Operational audits of government accountability to the community is clear.

8608

H1:Operational audits of government accountability to the community is not clear.

The second hypothesis test statistic calculated

d.f	T-statistics calculated	The standard error of the mean	The average	Number of Visits
329	11.89	.08	3.63	330

After comparing the test statistic (11.89)The critical value (1.64)It is clear thatThe test statistic is in the H1 area,The 95% confidence levelHo does not imply that the observations can be confirmed.Since Ho isStater is conflicting research hypothesisIt can be said at 5% errorResearch hypotheses were confirmed.The hypothesis"Operational audit led to the transparency of government accountability to the community."Is acceptable.

Hypothesis 3
First step: definition of the statistical assumptions
H0: Operational audit of the quality of government accountability to the community.
H1: Operational audit of the quality of government accountability to the community does not. Table III hypothesis
test statistic calculated

d.f	T-statistics calculated	The standard error of the mean	The average	Number of Visits
329	14.02	.08	3.73	330

Step IV: Decision

After comparing the test statistic (02/14) The critical value (64/1)Is characterized
The test statistic is in the H1 area; The 95% confidence level The approval does not imply that the observations can be said Ho.
Since Ho is Stater is conflicting research hypothesis

The 5% error in Research hypothesis can be confirmed. The hypothesis "Operational audit of the quality of government accountability to the community. "Is accepted

Hypothesis 4:

H0: Audit of operational characteristics of data quality (To be understandable and comparable) Into useful In order to meet the government provides.

H1: Audit of operational characteristics of data quality (To be understandable and comparable) Into useful In order to meet the government does not provide. Hypothesis test statistic calculated in Table IV

d.f	T-statistics calculated	The standard error of the mean	The average	Number of Visits
329	11.86	.12	3.65	330

After comparing the test statistic (86/11)The critical value (64/1)It is clear thatThe test statistic is in the H1 area;The 95% confidence levelObservations imply that not enough can be said Ho confirmation.Since Ho isStater is conflicting research hypothesisIt can be said at 5% errorResearch hypotheses were confirmed.The hypothesis"Audit quality attributes of operational information(To be understandable and comparable)Into usefulIn order to meet the government provides. "Is acceptable.

In the end, making notes Statistical data analysis and And we test the hypotheses. As observed did All hypotheses were confirmed, Employing the operational audit Increased transparency, quality and features of qualitative information And thus promote greater accountability And government acts that will perform better Be.

The results

During the studyFour hypotheses were tested.Testing the hypothesisThe study included 1072 people,The total computing power of the Court's formal technicalThe auditor is the Auditor GeneralIn 1389 are working in this field.The results of this test is as follows:

Hypothesis 1: There is a significant relation between audit government operations and accountability. After comparing the test statistic (13.86)The critical value (1.64)It is clear that The test statistic is in the H1 area, The 95% confidence level The approval does not imply that the observations can be said Ho. Since Ho is Stater is conflicting research hypothesis

The 5% error inResearch hypothesis can be confirmed. The hypothesis"There is a significant relation between audit government operations and accountability." Is acceptable.

The operational audit on the impact of government accountability.

Hypothesis 2: Operational Audit Transparency of government accountability To be community. After comparing the test statistic (11.89) The critical value (1.64)It is clear that

8609

J. Basic. Appl. Sci. Res., 2(9)8606-8611, 2012

The test statistic is in the H1 area, The 95% confidence levelHo does not imply that the observations can be confirmed. Since Ho is Stater is conflicting research hypothesis

It can be said at 5% error Research hypotheses were confirmed. The hypothesis "Operational audit led to the transparency of government accountability to the community."

Is acceptable.

Hypothesis 3:

 Operational AuditEnhance quality, accountabilityThe state is society.After comparing the test statistic (14.02)The critical value (1.64)Is characterizedThe test statistic is in the H1 area;The 95% confidence level can be said Ho does not imply that the observations upon approval.Since Ho isStater is conflicting research hypothesis It can be said at 5% error Research hypotheses were confirmed. The hypothesis "Enhance the operational audit

Quality of government accountability to the community. "Is accepted.

Hypothesis 4: Operational Audit

Qualitative characteristics of information(Being understood, being comparable)To be beneficial in order to meet the government provides. After comparing the test statistic (14.02) The critical value (1.64)It is clear thatThe test statistic is in the H1 area, The 95% confidence level The approval does not imply that the observations can be said Ho.

Since Ho is Stater is conflicting research hypothesis The 5% error in Research hypothesis can be confirmed. The hypothesis "Operational Auditing Enhance the quality of government accountability The community is. "Is acceptable.

Suggestions

Although demand For operational audit Iran is growing day by day, But the service was And sometimes without the quality of services offered, The demand for this type of service has overshadowed Operational auditing is causing inefficiency. Therefore recommended:

1. Legislative and legal authorities with the adoption of binding rules and regulations, Public sector required to meet Unconditional Able to perform operational audits.

2. Public administration and public companies, Reform of the corporate budgeting the traditional method of operating budget Action to audit quality may be achieved.

3. Public sector Accounting systems and E and its operational and monitoring and auditing system Audit to be equipped to quickly Operational audits to reduce costs.

4. LegislatureBinding legislation Regulatory devices And audit Required to provide audited And the Court of AuditAnd Auditing OrganizationTowards operational auditing standards

Immediate   action   to.

5. The monitoring and auditingTo create trainingAnd professional seminarsThe operational audit action.

6. As regardsStill a large part of the activitiesIn our country are performed by government Moreover, inefficiency and management activities by the government,One of the actions that seem appropriate in present circumstancesOperational audit is conducted.With this type of audit,In addition to encouraging people to use the effective charge,Economic and efficient use of limited resources can beThey will also create a sense of accountabilityAnd thereby the citizens want the right answerThat one of their natural rightsIn democratic societies is to be respected.

REFERENCES

1-A. - Babajani, J. (1998), accounting and financial reporting system of accountability of the government of Iran. PhD thesis, University of AllamehTbabayy.

. 2 - Babajani, J. (2003), accounting, governmental auditing. Payam Noor University Press.

. 3 - Babakhani, J. (2008), governmental accounting and financial controls. TabatabaiUniversity Press, third edition.

4. - Babajani, J. & Poor Yansb, A. (2003), a conceptual framework based on CARE's accountability. Proceedings of the auditor, No. 40.

. 5 - Babajani, J. (2004), public sector accountability and internal controls. CPA Journal, No. 146 and 147.

6.   - Hussein in Iraq, Hassan (2009), Public Audit (theoretical and practical). Faculty of Economics, Publication No. 19.

7.   - Large, Hussein (1996), based on accountability in public sector accounting. Proceedings of the auditor, No. 4.

. 8 - KarbasiYazdi, Hossein (2005) Accounting Theory. Publications Higher Education Center of Imam Khomeini Relief Committee (RA), 374 to 420.

. 9 - A large, Hussein (2007), audit of performance management in Ireland and its relation to the control system. Proceedings of the auditor, No. 4.

10.   - Momeni, Qayum Mohammad and Ali. 2003.statistical data analysis using SPSS, publishing a new book, ¬ -110 to 115.

11.   - Dae-Zadeh, N. (2006), Guide to Preparing research proposals (proposals). Publication language culture.

12.   - Babajani, J. (2009), the benefits of performance auditing in the DrpaskhgvyyKshvrvnqsh. Conference Proceedings Vskhnrany performance audit.

13.-Abroadus ,Jospd . 1998, Comtoic.Performance Accounting.AICPA.

14.-Brown, Williams and Gall, Gher.1987 , Auditing Performance in Government.

J. *Basic. Appl. Sci. Res.*, 2(3)2881-2888, 2012

© 2012, TextRoad Publication

www.textroad.com

ISSN 2090-4304
Journal of Basic and Applied
Scientific Research

The Role of Information & Communication Technology (ICT) in Constant Development (with a look at twenty years vision of Iran)

; Mostafa Emami[1] Kamran Nazari [2]; Hassan Moradi[3]; Sozan

vafaei[4] 1

Department of Accounting,   Tarbiat Modares University
,Tehran , Iran 2
Department of Business Management, Payam Noor University, Kermans   hah, Iran
3
Master of Scince , Public Management, Organizational change, University of Tehran
4 Master of Scince, Accounting , Islamic Azad University,
Malayer, Iran

ABSTRACT

The world in 21st Century is a world full of Competition development of markets, appearance and Circulation of superior technology and extension of Commerce. Condition for Success on this area is Profit of opportunities and Pacify of in front of challenges and these necessitate that the process of Social–Economic development with Strategic approach to definition of international new Condition and recognition Changes in Composition and relations procedure of economic, political, global and regional issues and also with an attitude towards the most important subjects and problems of national economy, rout of performance of technological–structural Changes and responsibility to necessities of Constant growing and development, Smooth the economy of Country away. Since the good of development is empower so con stat development is a development which focus on continuance development of peoples request and satisfaction with increasing of quality of human's life. Deny and threaten the ability of next generations for satisfaction of their own needs. Entering to third millennium and facing up to critical phenomena for becoming global and development of information and communication technology and using of these two phenomena have been Caused moving communities towards informational societies and this information technology has become the main motivation of world economy and constant development without reliance on application of ICI almost will be impossible. Mainly industry of information and Communication technology has created more revolution in human's life at new term than mechanics in industrial revolution period and this industry has wonderfully affected both private and social life. In this essay is attempted mean while defining development and Constant development is considered to information and communication technology for achieving constant development with a look at twenty years vision of Iran.
KEY WORDS: Information and Communication technology, Development, Constant development, Global economy, Wisdom, Electronic State.

1- INTRODUCTION

J. Basic. Appl. Sci. Res., 2(3)2881-2888, 2012

The word has seen the main changes in technology and economy–social development sciences in our country in recent half century. The world changes and constant development in based of knowledge and management development can extend extremely competition in the world changes. Thus, it is clear, the necessary of attention to social substructures and compiling the systems of society and development in various dimensions [3].

Therefore, the study and considering of the world changes and 21 century's challenges in science and technology areas can establish the administrative conditions of re–engineering of the scientific and technological substructures in country, the extension of new information and communication with another, access to information and the all aspects of human's life and specially in economic activities of each country [10].

It is clear, choosing strategic approach for determination of priorities and basic orientations for the future of country with international– regional changes is not only based on programs and middle–term and short–term policies. But it must be based on long–term planning, given views and the analysis of the m with far horizon according to obvious and clear aims and orientations. Long–term planning based on economic, social, cultural and biological principles of future, ideal society can create the conditions for the making of changes and reforms and re–regulation of national economy and the frames for the designing and accomplishment of middle–term and short–term programs. This subject only proves by using of new instruments and technology and information and communication technology has the main role in this direction [13].

Communication technology is a kind of technologies that the all of internal and external activities operate by using of informational elements and factors, therefore, the all of forming technologies can have its own analogous informational form [22].

*Corresponding Author: Mostafa Emami, Department of Accounting, Tarbiat Modares University,Tehran, Iran P.O

BO:1767778151ˉ . Tel:989127001816-18162370018Email: Mostafa.Emami@Modares.ac.ir

Information and communication technology like its name is limit of technology which is based on new communication improvements. These two terms use each other because of new strong affiliation of these two technologies and their remarkable influences on international economic area [25].

By attention to this role, Information in Informational technology becomes more important and becomes clear the concentration point of Informational technologies from other elements of Informational technology and Informational–technical knowledge. We live in age of Informational technology and knowledge and early we will enter to the fourth wave i.e. the virtual world. In this world, the all of economic, social, cultural and political affairs will be differ from today world's conditions [22].

The management of planning in the age of knowledge and virtual area has its own special complexity and differ totally from the traditional planning methods, based on people and limited information. This traditional planning in world's countries is changing by entering to third millennium and using of new instruments and methods has situated in the instruction of the world's planners [16].

In new age, the major managers of country must use of the skills, expertise and general knowledge of the society in basic planning, effectively and by using of informational technology instruments benefit from the useful experiences of the advanced countries and Iranian experts out of country. Unfortunately, there are not necessary conditions and mechanism for using of the wide information mass and global experiences in our country and isn't used from this global free capital. If this methods use experimentally in the development of country's planning and for special cases can create important influences in the future and environment full of hope and happiness [20].

New conditions of the world and knowledge age and complexity of major planning because of rapid changes in a lot of main parameters of planning need to the new methods for managing of major and development planning of country because traditional methods of planning are not usable. Tomorrow world will be virtual world that unfortunately. Not only our country but also some of extended countries are unable to understand that [15].

2- The concept of development

Let's review the concept of development before considering the concept of constant development. Maybe, you had heard this phrase that "Society is changing because people would like to change". Strict consideration of this term shows that at the first, the change is the desire of people and is not any changes without their desire. Second, people who would like changes want changes with development from their government not any changes. Hence, we must clarify what the concept of development is. The world of development and its root refers to a process which can observe its natural flow. In this century, there is a thought that human is able for creating regular and continuance changes in a desirable way in his own life [14].

The root of this thought must be finding in industrial culture of the west because they believe, improvement is practical. Primarily, the thought of improvement has been stated for access to development. The vast usage of this thought can be seen in most of independent societies which try to make better biological conditions for their people in the past three decade. Briefly, the aim of development is empower [24].

3- The concept of constant development

Constant development has many definitions, focus on continuance providing of needs and satisfaction of people with increasing the quality of human's life. Constant development in general concept emphasizes on main issues such as, the control of health, proper technology, providing pure water, independence for providing health food and shelter for all people and also focuses on important of human's creativities, innovations and inventions [5].

Also, it has been stated development means growing economic– social changes and the aim of constant development doesn't prevent for development or delays its process. But it means dynamic and purposive development according future vision. Indeed, the constant development is development doesn't limit the ability of future generations for fulfilling their needs [16].

Global commission of environment and development defined the constant development in report of "Our common future" in the year 1989. According to it, constant development fulfills current needs without threaten and renouncing the ability of next generations for supplying their needs. Therefore, constant development is a path or aspect of development and according to commission; it causes to protect human improvement in all of the world and far future not only in some places and for some years [24].

Constant development states we must use our forces and even native technologies, information and cultural structures and proper parts of classical finding and joint them with postmodern instructions and finding [22].

Concerning to given definitions, constant development must fulfill the current needs of present generation and provide the conditions for supplying human's future needs. When a society provides initial needs of people can access to constant development. Also it must specify the fields for future correct planning and use of essential instruments and mechanism for implementing this planning [3].

Experiences of current two decade of 20 century show the basic evolution in the concept of development and its status clarifies in the pattern of constant development. There are some components for access to constant development and briefly have been shown in below figure.

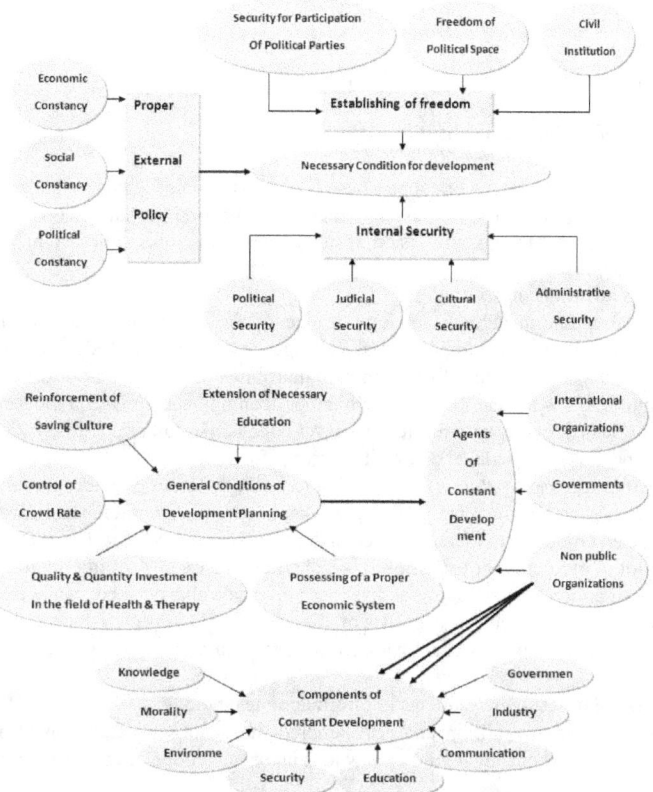

Figure 1: The process of access to the components of constant development [2]

As you see in figure 1, constant development consists of between economic, social, political and environmental dimensions in regional and international levels. Hence, because of existence of these factors, the orientations of national development must be regional and global with attention to general, external and future conditions [7].

Today, the planning of processes is not based on this subject, how balance changes to imbalance but it is based on this matter, how the simultaneous processes of balance and imbalance handle. In these conditions, there are three kinds of looks to future.

First: passive look, second: active look and third: futurist look. It's necessary for active and futurist looks, notice to the management of vision which means, the understanding status quo and its factors, analysis of national and international environment and finally recognition of ideal vision. When there is an ideal vision, personal and social actions conduce to make future and it can reduce undesirable outcomes of crisis [18].

Iran is placed on sensitive and strategic area in the world and possesses a lot of personal and natural resources for recognition of its own future vision. Thus, it has most of various alternatives and choices and naturally each of them follow different challenges. Iran will meet two basic challenges in next year. Country must make job and earnings and generative activities for young population and applicant of job by the constant and continuance growth. On the other hand, it is necessary the reducing of made distance between Iran and most of forward and industrial countries (and even most of neighbor countries) as soon as possible because of rising of regional and international situation of Iran [11].

Using of opportunities and confrontation with current likely threats in following challenges is necessary for taking strategies which can advance society and economy of Iran in the smooth path in direction of achievement to ideal goals of country in the horizon of vision according to below basic axles. These axles are challenges which country will meet them in future and they will transform to the basic threats in all aspects of economic, social, cultural and political if they don't have correct and proper management. These axles consists of

- Constant and continuance growth
- Development based of wisdom
- Active communication with global economy
- Competition in economy

- Personal security and social justice
- National security
- Rising of life's quality
- Environment and constant development
- Cultural development
- Development of public management
- Security and judicial development
- Regional equation and balance of country based on preparation of region's standards [5].

By attention to these basic axles, for making structures and various social and economic functions of country and expanding of society can expect long – term vision of Iran names with global approach in horizon of "national constant development" in the year 2015.

4- The importance of information technology

Information and communication technology is one of the important factors of improvement in 21 century. Information and communication technology will make changes in life, work and educational methods. ICT is a product of using of computer and transmission in information area and joints the entire world to information area after industrial revolution in 19 century. ICT is a means for development of economy and the world moves rapidly toward information - oriented or wisdom - oriented society with this technology. Globalism becomes possible with this technology and countries try to achieve the proper position in global competition area [15].

Considering of changes and nature of information technology shows, we need to culture for the best usage of ICT and making given and systematic structures for doing works and enjoyment of its future advantages until we can reinforce this technology. Usually, productivity increases in each domain by entrance of ICT to that domain but, ICT must enter to the domains with a lot of problems for extension this technology in Iran. Most important domains consists of; banking, economic systems, distribution of productions and services after sale channels, education and transportation [8].
Usage of this technology in some countries consists of;

India used IT industry by exports of software from eleven years ago and now, makes occupations for more than 3.2 million people.
South Korea allocates %4 of future investments to information technology.

Italy made more than one million and two hundred thousand occupations in IT industry in 2000 and finally researches and statistics show that almost %80 of new jobs in expansive societies depend to ICT and IT industries directly or indirectly [19].

Evidence shows the usage of IT is extending between expanding countries. Making change is one of IT characteristics and causes to make revolution in life, work and educational methods. The effects of ICT in educational and economic aspects consist of;
1-4) Economic aspects
1-1-4) changing of nature of market by e- commerce
2-1-4) exposure of new methods in marketing and propaganda
3-1-4) participation of international markets
4-1-5) access to global commerce
5-1-5) moving toward exports of production by more advanced technology 6-1-4)
development of occupational skills and making new jobs [20]. 2-4) Educational
Aspects
1-2-4) access to virtual schools and universities
2-2-4) rising of education by using of E-mail
3-2-4) access to a lot of resources
4-2-4) access to new educational methods
Classrooms with teacher-oriented education have been changed to creative and innovative environment by the entrance of ICT to educational environment [19].

5- The role of information and communication technology in development of wisdom

Wisdom means "the use of information by receiver of information makes the store of information and skills" [9]. Also, wisdom is collection of experiences, values, existent information and systemic expertise attitudes and a framework for evaluating and using of new existent information in person's mind. Wisdom is necessary in organization both evidences, resources and methods of work, organizational processes, activities and values [12].

Generally, wisdom is basic engine for development and making capital in today world and has more important role in national development than traditional factors such as; work and capital. We can achieve proper situation in international area and increase power of competition for entering to new markets, only by internalization of knowledge, technology and wisdom in country. Growth is not only effect of wisdom-oriented development and other effects consist of; basic cultural changes in economy (work market, financial organs …) and cultural and institutions, increasing of life quality (education, health, public welfare …), decreasing of social damages, expansion cultural and scientific productions [9].

Basic components of wisdom are;
- Organic and economic motivational system
- Human capital
- Information and communication technology □   Innovation and making wisdom flow [12].

As be told, Information and communication technology is a main factor and a component of wisdomoriented development and it is a combination of skills, knowledge, information, hardware and management in information and communication fields and finally conduces to preparation of goods and supplying of services. Information and communication technology means for production, distribution and consumption and useful and continuance usage of ICT in economic and social networks moves economy and reinforce communication and transaction of information and that is a powerful factor for making competition. Therewith, Information technology commerce is a factor for development of private part and transmission services which are dynamic parts of economy. This technology causes to obtain opportunities and new situations especially in the field of ecommerce and electronic services such as; e-government. This technology has the main role for making movement in small and medium companies and makes conditions for operation of these companies in the word of e-commerce and situations for their competitions in international levels by increasing economic abilities, expansion of activities and finally transforms them to larger companies [9].

6- Information and communication technology and its role in development planning

Maybe, most important place for applying of Information and communication technology is development and development planning both organization level and country level. Following the concept of Information and communication technology, it's necessary, considering of development planning according to ICT domain. Hence, we consider publication of changes layers which make by using of computerized systems for becoming clear this subject. Made changes from using of computers and computerized systems is stated in various five layers. Kinds of made changes is different in these five layers. First layer is direct applications of computerized system. This layer makes direct changes in instruments. The effect limit of these changes is local domain which uses from these systems. In other words, changes make in places where use from this system. Second layer is methods of management. This layer makes changes in ways of guidance and implementation. Third layer is engineering of systems. This layer changes structure and mechanisms. Changes in these two layers don't influence only on local domain of using of these systems, therefore, effect limit of system is whole of domain of organization. In other words, making decision and guidance about these changes connect to whole of organization.

Fourth layer is layer of principles. This layer makes change in strategies, missions, policies, structures and environmental and social major rules and makes evolution in equations of organization, too. Fifth layer is layer of concepts. This layer changes scientific theories. In other words, the effect of usage of computerized systems emerges in to changing of scientific theories in this layer. The effect limit of these changes in fourth and fifth layers is local, organizational domains and farther up, major domain of major systems and government and even farther up the government [6].

The functional limit of Information and communication technology is determined well according to especial attitude of Information and communication technology to recent two layers. When we speak about Information and communication technology, our intention isn't only using of one unit or even an organization of computerized systems but it points to attitudes of society, government and major system. When development planning become propounded, it's necessary, using of ICT for whole of development planning. Therefore, ICT leads us for making new basic attitude in development planning. In other words, when we speak about using of IT in first and second layers, it means using of instruments and at the most, changing of guidance and implementation ways and it leads us for buying and providing instruments and at the most making of technical substructures. When we speak about using of IT in second and third layers, it means making change in ways of guidance and implementation, structures and mechanism, Therefore, it leads us for reforming of structure. In fourth and fifth layers, we don't speak about buying and providing of instruments and making of technical substructures and even structures but would like to reform social and environmental fields and structures and rules according to scientific theories. This subject changes our attitude about development planning relative to current attitudes. Of course, this change has two aspects. First, ICT is main issue in development planning. This aspect makes challenges for development planners of country in recent years and that is initial objective in procedure of fourth development program of country. It means, fourth development program was based on ICT in initial stages but it Is forgotten at next stages. Second, for compiling of development program based on ICT, it's necessary, collection of scientific and theoretical foundations for doing this subject. In other words, it is necessary, formation of scientific theories in various fields based on information and technology. But it needs to definition of scientific system which their scientific theories have been formed based on Information and communication technology.

A scientific system is coherent collection of views, ideas and education and there is not any crack, conflict and ambiguities within. It means, we know that ICT makes conditions for new definition of various fields such as; operational, scientific and technological and linking and generalizing them to scientific theories and subjects therefore, subjects should be continued by various scientific dimensions and views and shouldn't be analyzed separately.

According to ICT, subjects are multidimensional and each dimension reflects an especial attitude in scientific and theoretical fields but whole of them have recognizable coherence and cohesion. Hence, mental and practical systems should be settled in architecture of extending system [20].

7- Information and communication technology and objectives of twenty vision of Iran

According to existence flow, growth rate of communication in economy of Iran is remarkable and it has high growth rate in last two decades. Statistics showed growth rate of population was %1.5, growth rate of existence telephones was %20.3 in last five years and growth rate of influence index of telephone was %14.6 in recent ten years therefore, according to current flow it has been forecasted, influence index of telephone becomes %46 in the year 2015 and will be %96.9 in the year 2015, by existence growth rate, the number of telephone will be 76.4 million line and population will be almost 78.2 million persons in the year 2015.

In this direction, with look at general objectives and major development strategies in IT unit and administrative policies for access to objectives of twenty vision of Iran, it is necessary; these objectives become division to three sections which consist of; qualitative major objectives, sectional major strategy and quantitative objectives [2].

1-7) Qualitative major objectives

1-1-7) possessing of informational society (citizen-oriented)

2-1-7) possessing of electronics government (making service and responsibility)

3-1-7) possessing of e-commerce

4-1-7) possessing of electronics health

5-1-7) possessing of electronics education

6-1-7) possessing of human resources and information technology

7-1-7) possessing of security, information and communication

8-1-7) possessing of structures of information & communication technology

2-7) Sectional major strategy

1-2-7) increasing and empowering of quality of access to information technology

2-2-7) extensive education and training of human resources

3-2-7) being up date of rules

4-2-7) using of information technology

5-2-7) promoting of monolith automation

6-2-7) attracting of participation of financial and international resources

7-2-7) attracting of customers satisfaction

3-7) Quantitative objectives

- Quantitative objectives have been brought in table 1.
- Policies and administrative strategies have been selected in vision of realizing of given objectives.
- Supporting of people and families for becoming equipped to information technology structures by cooperation of other institutions (regional council and mayoralty), national organization of youth
- Development of public centers which access to information technology
- Focus on making policies and national supervision and non focus on administrative management and implementation
- Rising of existent rules and compiling of new rules for adaptation to information technology needs
- Expansion of general knowledge about IT for whole society, especially managers and personnel of public organization
- Encouragement and supporting of users for using of IT
- Supporting of nonpublic institutions (NGO) for development of usage of IT
- Extension automation of general and especial systems in public organization
- Empowering of hardware in public organization, educational institution and medical centers
- Increasing of capacity and quality of IT educational center
- Making monolith planning system and providing of human resources for IT
- Making code system and IT standards
- Compiling of rules and IT juridical system of country   [2].

Table1: Quantitative goals of information technology in twenty vision of Iran

Goal	Unit	From	To
Increasing of number of public organizations with monolith, mechanism, general systems	Percent	50	90
Increasing of number of public organizations with monolith, mechanism, private systems	Percent	1	80
Using of communicational services in electronic environment by public organizations	Percent	-	50
Increasing of active companies in electronics trades	Percent	-	20
Access to web by companies	Percent	-	40
Increasing of electronic cards per 100 person	Card	6.6	45
Using of electronic cards	Percent	-	70
Connecting of medical centers to internet	Number	-	800
Access to computer systems by medical centers	Percent	-	50
Access to internet by medical centers	Percent	-	90
Increasing of computer per 100 student	Unit	/16	2
Increasing of computer per 100 scholar	Unit	20	25
The number of rapid computers per 100 student	Unit	/03	1
The number of rapid computers per 100 scholar	Unit	20	25
Increasing of teaching lessons by electronics education	Percent	-	20
Increasing of ratio of technological expertise to whole of population	Percent	-	/13
Increasing of secure servers per one million person	Number	-	10
Increasing of internet capacity of country	Mega byte	800	5000
Increasing of up-to-date personal computers' number per 100 person of country population	Unit	3	7.4
Increasing of user's influence index of data	Percent	7	30
Increasing of villages connected to informational network	1000	-	10
Increasing of number of communication services offices & civil information technology	Office	800	2500
Increasing of rapid ports' number	1000Pprt	1000	5000
Number of network of digital – radio sender	Number	-	2
Number of network of digital – television sender	Number	-	1

Conclusion

The experiences of last two decades of 20 centuries showed the basic evolution in concept of development which has been emerged in constant development model. In these two decades and the beginning of 20 century, alliance flows in regional and global levels became important despite the increasing of competitions, expansion of markets, spreading of major technologies and making new managerial structures for recognition of challenges and using of opportunities in international level. The alliance of economics, social, political and environmental dimensions both regional and global levels is expanding according to constant development model. The orientation of national development must be holistic, internal, external (regional and global) and futurist because of existence of these facts. We need to management, thought, research and evolution for movement toward economic development; therefore, Iran must increase its own abilities of economic capitals higher than other society levels and at least at the same level, if it wants to an active country in global society and plays role in global family in the future. This fact is possible only by using of new instruments and technologies which today extending and expansive societies use them. One of these technologies is ICT. When society moves toward knowledge-oriented, all of people use clear information and process for implementing of his planning and achieve higher productivity. Earned economic value from this mechanism is a basic factor for economic growth and improvement in this society. ICT as a main factor decreases distances in time and place dimensions in various programs as this fact causes to make new productions and services in these areas which it wasn't possible before [11].

In planning of twenty vision (2005-2015) which has been distinguished strategies and procedures to economics, social, political and cultural development, Traditional instruments and forces change to thought, knowledge and new technologies such as; ICT, internet, nanotechnology and …. The results of this vision which emphasize on ICT consist of;

- Access to constant and continuance growth

- Changing of all aspects in agriculture, industry, economics services and natural resources to a various and dynamic economy
- Dependence on knowledge and wisdom of human capital and new technologies
- Making proper environment for growth of innovation activities and entrepreneurship technical capacities

The importance of using of new informational and communicational technologies has been distinguished in these given goals. Therefore, Iran needs to basic evolution in technology and knowledge fields for access to these goals [17].

REFERENCES

1. Amini,GH.,2006,"Lookation to Draft Development National Dacument of section ICT",Tehran , Secretariat of top Council in Informiniticatio of Congress.pp. 21-39

2. Aron, Raimon , 1990," The final years of century", Translate by Assadolah, Mobasharifm, Tehran , Pblication of Safir.

3. Azadi,GH., Eftekhari ,R.,2000,"Economic and Constant Development",Tehran, Publication of Commercial.

4. Badie, Pol,1980," Growth polici economic", Translate to Azadmanesh, Kavah, Tehran ,Publication of Ghumes

5. Bahramzade , Hosinali,2004, " Constant Development" ,Tadbir Magazine.No.134, PP 35-42

6. Batini,carlo,Viscusi,Gianluigi,Cherabini,Daniela,2009,"Go7Qual":A quality driven methodology for EGovernment project planning ",journal Government Information Quarterly ,pp 106-117

7. Busha Charles H.and Stephen P.HarterT1980T "Research methodsin Librarianship, techniques and interpretation" ,Newyork :Academic press, p 180

8. Ghasemi , Akbar, 2006,IT season publication, 1 year, No.2, pp.16-32

9. Gottschalk,Peter,2009,"Maturity levels for intro perability in digital government" ,Jornal government information Quarterly ,pp 75-81

10. Hejazi , Abdoreza,2005," Research for resource IT in U.A", http//www. systems eroup.net

11. Jaefari, A.,2006," Vision public Season", Management and Planing Organization of Esfahan ,One year, No.2, pp.75-94

12. Kim,Senogsceol,Kim jeong,Hyun,Lee,Heejin,2009,"An institutional analysis of an e-government system for anti-Corruption: the case of open",Journal Government information Quarterly ,pp 42-50

13. Majidi, Ardowan2002," Future of top system traning and Upbringing" Termeh Publication.

14. Majidi, Ardowan,2001," Technology Science is challenge in traning Viewpoint", Latter Specific of technology traning Congress in public traning, Behaviorism and Upbringing scinces college of Tehran university, pp. 25-39

15. Mohamadi , Fateme, 2003," IT knowing",Technology traning Growth,No.6, pp.35-

16. Muldan,B., Bilhard,s.,2003," consulnt development and live envirovment", Translate by Hadadadel, Nshat, Moharamzade , Naser, Ney Publication.

17. Nickravesh, Mohamadreza,2004, Development Traning Mounth publication ,18th term,pp.20-30

18. Pillai,C.V.Rajan,1985,"Research methodology in social sciences", Herald of library science V24 .N12,January-april,pp.15-18

19. Rezaie, Hamid,2006, season publication of IT development,3 year, No.6, pp. 80-94

20. Sarafizade , Asghar,2005" IT in organizarion", Amir Publication.

21. Selltiz, Jahoda, deutsch,Cook, 1998,"research method in Entrepreneurial Management" proceedings of republican scientific Conference<Vilnius,pp17-29

22. Shahidi ,Mehdi,2000," Eectronic Trade is tool for decrace rake of digital",Saie nama Publication.

23. Steven son, H.H .and Jaarillo,J.C.1990,"A paradigm of Entrepreneurial Management. Strategic Management Journal, pp 17-27

24. Unesco Consultants, 2002, Traning planning,Translate by Mashaiekhi, Faride. GHumes Publication.

25. Wilson, J.1999.'How information Technology Entrepreneurship has changed the world', Harward Business review ,pp 75-85

2888

Advances in Environmental Biology, 6(7): 2069-2081, 2012
ISSN 1995-0756

ORIGINAL ARTICLE

The Special Value Assessment of Bank's Brand Name on Basis of CBBE Model (Case Study: Bank Saderat)

¹Motahar Ebrahimi Gara Tekan, ²Mohsen Emami Far, ³Majid Hajipoormashaiee, ⁴Ali Taheri Heshi

1,4Department of management ,science and research branch, Islamic Azad university, Kerman, Iran ²,³Firouz Kooh branch, Islamic Azad university, Firouz kooh, Iran

Motahar Ebrahimi Gara Tekan, Mohsen Emami Far, Majid Hajipoormashaiee, Ali Taheri Heshi; The Special Value Assessment of Bank's Brand Name on Basis of CBBE Model (Case Study: Bank Saderat)

ABSTRACT

This paper is in junction with special value assessment of bank's brand name on basis of CBBE model. The research questions are: 1) what factors effect on special valuebr and of bank Sade radon basis of CBBE model? 2) Which factors of CBBE model has more effect on special value brand of bank Saderat? And assumptions of researchare formed based on indictors of CBBE model. In this statistical universe study consists of the entire depositors who have opened account since 2006 in branches of bank Saderat in Amol Township. Through make use of Korjesi& Morgan table, the quantity of research sample obtained as 384 individuals. The research approach is of type descriptive –measurement in which questionnaire tool was used for collecting data which have judgmental admissibility and since the coefficient of Alpha-Conbakh obtained as 0.949 showed that it has required reliability and distributed among individuals based on simple random sampling. After collecting data from two terms distribution test were used for responding to assumptions and results shows that four indicators of: tendency to pay higher prices, familiarity with brand, organizational relationships and permanency of brand image have effect in determination of special value brand of bank Saderat. The five indicators of customers 'appreciated quality, appreciated quality based on cost, brand uniqueness, awareness form brand name and popularity of brand have not effect in determination of special value brand of bank Saderat. Based on freedman test the priority of indicators are brand image permanency, familiarity with brand, tendency to pay higher price and organizational relationships respectively and at the end of this research for enhancement of effective factors some recommendation have presented.

Key words: Customers' Appreciated Quality , Appreciated Value based on Cost, Tendency to Pay Higher Price, Familiarity with brand, Brand Uniqueness, Awareness from Brand Name, Brand Popularity, Organizational relationships and Brand Image Permanency.

Introduction

Nowadays, brand name is no longer a useful tool on hands of managers. Brand is a strategic necessity which makes contributions to organization toward creation of more value for customers as well as permanent competitive advantages [1]. Brand could be creator of issues such as assessment rate of customers' loyalty, tensile reactions against price change, assessment of market outlooks and etc….in the organization. The researcher in this search is after studying on this valuable concept of "Marketing" (which will be discussed in detail).

Adv. Environ. Biol., 6(7): 2069-2081, 2012

Undoubtedly, the bank industry is known as one of expensive bases of economy' stone of each country. Dynamic, effectiveness and capability of banking system not only benefits business spaces but also makes high effects on external environment (mega economic and commerce environment).

To achieving economic goals of governments without assistance of banking system is actually impossible. It is for the same reason that compiling part of policies of financial, monetary, economic and commerce is performed with respect to conditions and status of banks with using two ways discussions. Therefore, the scientific –research study of these giant institutions is not only responding to questions of manager of banking system, even it could be assisting governmental authorities specifically to explain economic & commerce conditions of country and compiling effective and applicable regulations.

2- Statement of Issue:

Corresponding Author

Motahar Ebrahimi, Department of Management, Science and Research Branch, Islamic Azad university, Ardebil, Iran Email: m0820@yahoo.com.

Brand is a concept more than a product or service. Nowadays, many computers, automobiles, shoes, bank accounts don't have much differences with each other, but these are brands which make essential distinctions in many industries and markets. These differences go up to a point that the many market leaders look to their brand as a competitive advantage. According to definition of interbrand (one of the most superior valid consulting company in the field of brand), brand is " an aggregate from tangible & non-tangible elements have placed aside to each other in a brand name such that to create & mange prestige and superiority for company and develops more value for customers [2].

A strong brand makes a positive effect on perception ofconsumer'sattitude to identify of the company. A positive perception forms along a good experience. awareness for name and mark and participation with that, effect on conceptual quality of customers and directly leads to loyalty [1]. Executive managers & researcher of knowledge management have high interest to make quantitative making of brand' value rate. This value in marketing definitions is express as brand equity. The definition of Mr. Aaker as one of famous theorist in this field have presented in the year 2000 is referred: the special value brand is defined as assets (or liabilities) of name & mark which is connected to it which would either cause its value creation or its destruction.

What would approved in all special value definitions by various researchers is that the special value brand, is an added value which is created due to existence of brand [3]. In addition to environmental & legal issue in frontof banks, electronic banking by propagation of receipt and electronic payment caused the dependency reduction of daily transaction to cash & check and ultimately reduction of costs related to print & maintaining money and rapid increase of performance and elevating the consumers' satisfactions. In a report announced this year by Forester institution; stated that between year 2002 to 2006, on average every year 50% have added to volume of commercial trades via electronic base with its amount reaches from 2,293 million dollars in 2002 to 12,8737 million dollars in 2006.

All aforesaid factors, are assisted by expansion of electronic banking system and more use of modern banking system. If these conditions are studied in the customers' viewpoint, the first mooted point, is image, identity and place of brand on the mind of society and specially potential and de facto customers. This is perception of customers relative to status of substructures and electronic capabilities of banks which encourage them toward bank services in the future. The commercial banks currently must prepare proper mental image for their adoption as electronic banking via customers. Therefore, the study of current status of special value of brand name & mark as a value making indicator in the mind of customer could guides banks. The special value brand not only is set forth for discussion as an indicator in explaining current financial value of organization, but also could be expressed as one of ground making & effectiveness indicator in the future activities of organization. Not to forget that the significance of special value brand is not limited to discussed issues and could be set forth for discussion as a guide for future planning and decision making of managers of organization. Issues such as assessment rate of customers' loyalty, tensile interactions against price change, assessment of market outlook, are extracted for study of special value brand.

From effective factors on value of brand name & mark based on Aaker in 1991 are four dimensions of : Awareness, Appreciated Quality, Associations and Loyalty to Brand Name and Mark which was approved by Mr. Yoo et al. Another model is CBBE which has been used in this study for assessing brand name & mark of bankSaderat. The main issue in this study is assessment of value brand of bank Saderat with respect to customers' viewpoint (customers who have acted to open account since 2005).After assessment of special value brand.at the end the effective indicators on special value brand of bank of Saderat will be graded.

3- A review on Research Literature:

Brand Equity:

2071

Adv. Environ. Biol., 6(7): 2069-2081, 2012

As mentioned in the past, the issue of measuring power of brand specially in service industry is one of important duties of management. Managers always confronted by these type of questions as how much values our brand creates for customers? Alongside of rivals and in this market which brand name is more reliable from customers viewpoint? What effect the brand names put on consumers' behavior in this market? Is it important for customers that to what name this product have supplied to market? Is it only this interest which a powerful brand to be created in market will lead to its creation? This is question which in past two decade have attracted major branding studies to itself. The answer to this question hasgiven as a concept under title special value brand. Actually, what is it that causes the brand of companies and our products become powerful? What sort of tool could be used to create such situation? The special value brand and its constituent dimensions is the answer to all these questions. It's a paradigm that will come to existence toward creation of value for customers and make use of all hidden potentials in the marketing unit of the organization [4].

Executive managers and researchers of knowledge management have high interest to quantitative making the value rate of the brand. In the marketing definition this value isexpressed as special value brand. For defining this marketing slang, numerous cases have performed which the definition of Mr. Aaker as one of famous theorists in this field have presented in the year 2000 and referred to: the special value brand is defined as assets (or liabilities) of brand which is connected to it and would causes either its value creation or its destruction.

The concept & nature of special value brand have been studied from various aspects with different purposes. Special value brand could be subject of study in the view of producer, retailer and customer. While the producers consider special value brand for its strategic values, invertorsconsider the financial value of brand as important. Supporters of financial aspect of special value brand define it as price of brand as independent and separate and wish to mention it into the profit/loss statement. Others who consider special value brand in terms of financial viewpoint, present different definition: The special value brand is flows of cash which generate more with products having brand than product without having brand[5].

What is approved by researchers in the entire definitions of special value brand is that the special value brand is added value which will create because of existence of brand [3]. This process of value creation have depicted in the diagram No. 1. This conceptual model was presented by Mr. Aker in 1991 and approved by Yu, et. al. in this process is observed that the efforts of the organization toward creation of brand is achieved via various dimensions of special value brand. These dimensions, ultimately create special value brand and supply the means of value creating for company and consumers.

Two well know scholars from Stanford University have conducted separate research in the ground of brand and branding and have published many books and articles which forms the source and references of most projects. Almost all published scientific research papers in valid international magazine have used their conceptual models.

Diagram 1: Outcomes of Special Value Brand [6].

[7] Considers the dimensions of special value brand as awareness from brand, relationships of brand, loyalty to brand, appreciated quality and other brand assets. While [1] has two main approaches (direct & indirect) to measuring special value and emphasizes on two parts from special value brand from customer viewpoint: Awareness form Brand, and Image of brand. The direct approach of Clair emphasizes on marketing actions such as distribution channel, effective marketing communications, and indirect approach have attention to respond of customer to various elements of company's marketing [5].A powerful brand strengthen the positive perception of consumers relative to the entire products related to brand. Positive perception results from product engagement and experience.

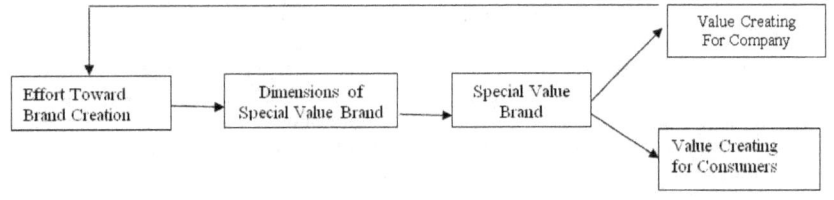

The customers' awareness and continual connection with brand leads to appreciated quality, complete appreciation from product and ultimately customers' loyalty. The viewpoint from following theory of special value brand creation results based on customer-oriented. The advantage of this type viewpoint is that, in this form marketers could achieve in methods in which to increase the way of engagement and customer's loyalty. Based on the outcome results from prior research, successful marketing compaing particularly branding have influenced on mind of customers. In many this sort of researches is observed that awareness from brand name prior and after enforcing campaign have made a great differences. Loyalty and tendency to pay higher prices have increased in customers and consequently the special value band also would increase as well [8].

Past research have shown that brand as market connecting tool has higher efficiency since brand is actually is in connection with main and final customers and this value creation could develops a connecting sense. Theoretical and academic researches aside with

Adv. Environ. Biol., 6(7): 2069-2081, 2012

findings from heart of business shows that confidence indicator is the most important factor which could form this mutual dependency. To create connection and strengthening that exactly develops confidence on both sides of consumers and producers [4].

 A perception have developed toward expansion in the world of marketing management: Creation of intangible assets to develop loyalty and more than ever connection with customer. Quality, experienceof personal, corporate culture, knowledge and special value brand is among such assets. Like many other intangible assets, the special vale brand could transform to a powerful tool in competitive market. These value creating ultimately transform to tool for obtaining higher profit, higher sales, bigger market share, more attractive advertisement [1], faster penetration in market, cheaperproduction line [7].

 To the opinion of many worlds' marketing thinkers the most valuable intangible assets of an organization is special value brand. According to recent performed studies, there is a direct relationship between special value brand and financial performance of organization. Indicators such as profitability and volume of sales are in direct connection with special value brand of company. As customers express opinion about success or failure of company, they also think about special value brand [9]. Performed studies on brand issue shows that indicators such as awareness from brand, loyalty to brand and appreciated quality (as effective factor on special value brand) are in direct connection with operational and financial indicators such as rate of profitability, performance of brand in market and customers' appreciated quality.

 Value creation for customers supplies the means of financial benefits for organization. Actually the financial indicators of company benefits towards increase of its special value brand from two ways cycle.This trend have shown in the Diagram No. 2 [9].

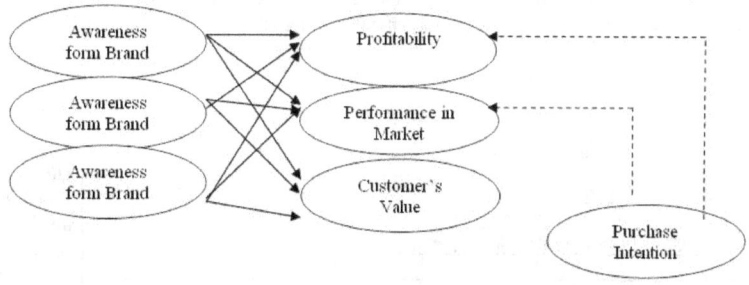

The special dimensions of brand consists of appreciated quality, customers' loyalty and awareness from brand make direct and positive influence on profitability of brand and volume of sales. Here we

Diagram 2: The effect of Special Dimensions of Brand on Performance of Organization [9].

point to two constituent parts of customer's special value : The perceived customer value and purchase intention. The essential issue is that that value creation for customer shows its value via brand in the entire value chains. The marketing managers must always consider this point that the right of retailingof product also effect in value creation process and special value brand.

The Constituent Dimensions of Special Value Brand:

 Up to this points, in regard to special value brand as well as relation among them and performance of organization were discussed. However, as pointed out earlier, the essential issue of marketing managers is the assessment of special value brand. In other words, wish to know the place of their brand name & mark in comparison with other rivals. In this section will review various theories which have been presented and at the end present the model which used in this research. In dimension of customer-oriented, the special value brand is assessed from customers' viewpoint or producers. With respect to indicators, they assess the rate of created value via brand. If the issue to be looked at in financial dimension, part of intangible assets of organization which are related to brand considered as added value. With a composite look at this issue both, customer-oriented dimension as well as financial dimension could be assessed.

 The dimensions which have presented by various authorities in particular to special value brand could fit them into three groups (dimensions): Customer-Based Perspective, financial Perspective and combined Perspective [3].

1- Customer-oriented Dimension of Special Value Brand:

 The customer-oriented dimension of special value brand is consist of two multi-dimensions concept of brand strength and brand value. The power of brand is defined based on observations, perceptions and behavior of customers who allows the brand to be likeable for them and form superior competitive advantage. The value brand is financial spending which give management the brand's expansion power inside strategies of organization. The value of brand are include benefits which organization will have in the future. Through these the special value brand would prepare means of value creation [10].

Adv. Environ. Biol., 6(7): 2069-2081, 2012

If we define special value brand in two dimensions of brand value, and brand meaning, the brandmeaning consists of brand's saliency, brand's assets and personality of brand. and brand's value means financial spending of brand management. To the belief of Mr. Keller the special value brand is the same differential force which brand makes itself distinct and superior from other rivals [8] . The customer-oriented special value brand usually effects on two indicators: Perceptions of customers (awareness from brand, assets of brand and appreciated quality) and behavior of customer (loyalty to brand and willingness to pay higher prices). The special value brand is an increase rate that appreciated desirability and eagerness of customer for consumption of goods and services are developed following creation of relation with partner's brand [11]. In this study the same paradigm will be used for looking at special value brand which will discuss about it in more detail.

2- Financial Dimension of Special Value Brand:

The financial dimension of special value brand could be defined as balance financial revenue of a product which once supplied with brand and brand management and once supplied without any brand. certainly a product which is supplied with a special brand will be blended with increase or decrease of value for customer and financial results for organization. This is the same thing which is defined as dimension of special value brand [12]. the value that appears through brand for products would show its effect in financial balance sheet of company. Financial dimension make use of financial techniques based on market value so that to estimate the special value brand. these are same approaches which the issuers of the list superior brand makes use of them every year [13]. Every year the inter-brand company through computation of profit of products based on brand and comparing financial performance of brands sets a place for itself. In this approach, the company's assets is separated to tangible and intangible in carrying on special value brand will be deducted from intangible assets.

Researchers	Concepts (Indicators)	Measurement
Customer-Oriented Dimension		
Aaker (1991-1996)	Awareness from brand	Behavioral and Perceptional Concepts
	Loyalty to brand	
	Appreciated Quality	
	Brand's Assets	
Srivastava&Schoaker, 1991	Power of Brand	Power of brand + suitability of brand = Value of brand
Keller (1993-2001)	Knowledge of Brand	Knowledge of Brand = Awareness from brand + Brand's image
Black Stone (1995)	Meaning of brand	Model of brand's relations: The subjective & objective goals
Kamakora&Russel (1993)	Value of brand	Value of brand= tangible values + intangible values
Suite et, al (1993)	Total desirability	Price measurement equality
Ransis&Maclushlez(1995)	Power of brand	Internal power of brand
Laser e. al (1995)	Performance	Measurement of perceptual dimension of brand
	Social Image	
	Commitment	
	Confidence	
Agharival&Raou (1996)	Total Quality	Brand' outlook perception/brand preference/ brand selection
	Selection intention	
Yoo&Dento (2001)	Brand's loyalty	Validation of Aker' s concepts
	Appreciated quality	
	Awareness from brand	
CoobWalgren et. al (1995)	Awareness from brand	Relation among brand preference and

Table 1: Performed Studies in Particular to Special Value Brand [8].

The value of intangible assets show itself in a place which the company would not purchase any new financial assets, but the value of shares would increase in investment market. This price increase is not resulted only by receiving higher profits in end of fiscal year, but these are intangible assets of organization which have supplied means of this value creation in longer term. This viewpoint is formed based on discounted cash flow (DCF). The future analysis in the context of future cash flow increase of company could present positive analysis.

3- Composite Dimension of Special Value Brand:

It will be looked at incomposite dimension of special value brand in a way which both prior dimension (Customer-oriented &Financial) to be included. This outlook approach applied for elimination of deficiencies in prior two viewpoints. The effect of special value brand on organization is two dimensional and would not show its effect only in the context of relation with customer or financial [14].

Adv. Environ. Biol., 6(7): 2069-2081, 2012

Moutemie&Shahrokhei in their project in 1998 under title " Special Value Brand : A Global Perspective" designed a research system in which relation between dimension of customer-oriented and financial completely were explained. The outcome resulted through testing this system on various organization showed that based on that there exist a convergent and positive relation among special value brand in two dimensions of customer-oriented and financial. Actually the two perspectives marketing and financial are intertwined with each other. In table No. 1 a summary of various perspectives in particular to special value brand and constituent factors in each of them is presented.

	Appreciated quality	goods' consumption
	Brand's assets	
Financial Dimension		
Simon & Sullivan (1993)	Cash flow related to products with brand	Special value brand= tangible assets – (unrelated factors with brand + industry uncompetitive structure)
Composite Dimension		
Farquhar (1989)	Added value to a product with respect to its brand	Assessment of company with respect to customers' perspective
Dyson el. al (1996)	Loyalty to brand	Model of consumer's value : ratio of consumption x weight of consumption
	Perception to the brand	
MotameiShahrokhie	Global Special value of Global	Power of brand (Global ability, consumer and competitive) x brand revenue

AppreciatedQuality:

The appreciated quality is one of cases that have always caught attention of researchers [15,14]. A definition presented by researchers are: judgment of customers relative to advantage, preference, credibility and superiority of a brand in compare with other competitors' brand, the appreciated quality is main parts to effect special value brand because they could effect the tendency to pay higher price, purchase intention and selection of brand. The appreciated quality not only effect other dimensions of brand but also effects onclassification of products in customers' perspectives [15,1].

Perceived Value for the Cost:

PVC, is one of the main dimensions &structural framework of customer-oriented special value brand. The appreciated value on the basis of cost is consists of all brand desirability dimension which customer takes (like quality) and gives (like prices or costs after purchase) in relation and comparison to other available brand.

PVC is a balance between " Things I take" (functionality benefits and sentiment) with " What I give" (Like time, money and effort) [16].

Theories of ultimate assets chain and expected value also could express good relation between expected value on the basis of cost with other dimensions of special value brand on basis of brand. in theory the final asset chain of appreciated quality on basis of cost is on the highest contact level relative to other dimensions. The benefits of receivable could be functionality, empirical, symbolic or even qualitative. The first dimension of this receivable include things customer gets from product consumption. Also in here we see a trace of appreciated quality, this is one of main dimensions of receivable value [17].

According to many presented theories, there s not much differentiation exist between appreciated quality and appreciated value [7, 18]. According to studies of Mr. Aker in 1996, appreciated quality gives 80% meaning of appreciated value. But due to difference in meaning and as well as section cost exist in definition, could separate these two from each other. The appreciated quality has more property of prestige in particular to brand, but the appreciatedvalue describe more in particular to functional desirability. This is the same verifier line that separate these two concepts[7].

To be Exclusive (uniqueness):

To be exclusive consist of a degree in which separatesa customer of a brand from competitor's brand. if a brand could not be separated from competitors, then higher prices or more profitcan not be imagined. As a result, to be exclusive is set forth for discussion as one of main dimensions of special value brand [7]. This judgment could be resulted from direct product consumption or promotional programs. In any way this differencebe formed the producer could offer higher price to the consumer [17]. According to choisetheory of "to be exclusive" is one of main dimensions of customer-oriented special value brand. with oppositeness with other brands, the qualities of substituting competitors could make influence on opinion of consumer. The more customer's information in particular to a brand to bo more that other rivals , the more accurate selection could be assumed [19]. The information of customer's mind could express separation between brand and their rate of exclusiveness. Customers' Knowledge directs and peruses them to logical selection in comparison to illogical decision. Recent studies distinctively states that tendency to pay higher prices in these conditions has higher probability [20].

Adv. Environ. Biol., 6(7): 2069-2081, 2012

Tendency to Pay Higher Prices:

Tendency to pay higher prices consist of the tendency rate of consumer to pay higher prices for obtaining considered brand in same conditions (In terms of volume and equal amount) in oppositeness with other rivals. This is one of important dimensions influencing on special value brand [1]. Although the tendency to pay higher prices is defined as one of main dimensions constituents of special value brand, but in terms of structure has many differences with the dimensions. This differenceis resulting from tendency to pay higher prices following correct management of other dimension of special value brand. if the brand gives the quality, value and considered differences of customer, consequently the tendency to pay higher prices will be concluded [17]. Numerous theories have explained the relation between tendency to pay higher price and other dimensions of special value brand. According to Memory theory, when information is stored, a associative network connects numerous dimensions of special value brand [21]. Other dimensions make brand congruence effect on tendency to pay higher price. This suitability means that which one of brand's dimensions special value brand effect on other dimensions. For example, higher quality, more value and product exclusiveness effects customer to pay higher price [17].

The pricing theories also show strong relation between tendency to pay higher price and dimensions of special value brand. for example in 1990 Monore presented a model in which tendency to pay higher price is impressed from quality and appreciated value of product and services. Other performed studies also shows that there are high correlation between tendency to pay higher priceand other dimensions of special value brand [22]. The selection theory, also relate the exclusiveness to tendency to pay higher price. Any time a customer consider a brand to be exclusive from other rivals, he/she is willing to pay higher price for having this exclusiveness. Difference among various brands is distinguished with paying of various prices. The more strong point in mind of consumer of brand relative to rivals, he/she will have higher tendency to accept paying higher price [20]. Tendency to pay higher price could be somehow interpreted the same as brand loyalty. The more loyalty of customer to a brand, in same condition show higher tendency in comparison to rivals.

Attention to this point is necessary that the loyalty doesn't appear itself only by spending higher money to obtain the brand. Instances such as enduring more inappropriate conditions or mere expenditure also could placed in the range of this concept definition. In many definitions presented by marketing researchers tendency to pay higher price include loyalty as well.

Awareness from Brand:

The main goal of brand management, expansion and protection of brand awareness, because, it is the awareness of brand that contributes in its entire decision making stages as well as value creation process of the company. Awareness of brand is consist of ability of a consumer toward recognition or remembering a brand in the arena of similar products [7].

[46]states that for obtaining special value brand based on customers, customer must be aware and familiar relative to what is offered [23]. When by hearing the name of product, what brand hits the consumers' mind for the first time is an important issue which in this index will be subject of an assessment. Main part of marketing managers' effort is spent to develop an image in the mind of addressers.If addressers have no awareness from brand then expectation to develop an image in their mind is useless. The awareness from brand could encourage customers who have not yet tried the brand to consume it for the first time and this process could come out of promotional business activities. To develop and protect for awareness is very importantsince only brands which are recalled by customer have ability to compete with others in the customer's mind and at the end also have chance to purchase for these brands is much higher than others. To select customer in this form not only becomes simpler but also develop assurance more than ever for him. However, the brand which to be recalled by customer could be identity, categorized and ultimately be purchased [9].

Familiarity with Brand:

Familiarity with brand consist of scope of information which a consumer be able to present in particular to a brand; information about short history, identity, products, type of service…all are aggregated in this concept. The more familiarity of customer with brand, probably intelligent selection also will be increased [21]. The more information particular to a brand, the familiarity with brand will be increase, in the selection conditions of brand among rivals the rate of familiarity with brand will have direct and positive effect with section of consumer. Thus when the customer not having familiarity with brand will be confused in choise process and for selecting best choice will use from quality analogy and considered cases [24]. In a study which performed at automobile auction market in Holland proved that there exist high relation between familiarity with brand and comparison & selection process of brand. the more familiarity with a brand the selection test of aforesaid brand among existing choices will be higher.

The main part of familiarity with brand is from marketing activities and public relation of organization, this familiarity is not involved direct advertisement. The public relation programs also have high effect on customer's selection. Public relation form a big volume from customer's knowledge in particular to a brand; also word of mouth advertisement have high influence on familiarity of

Adv. Environ. Biol., 6(7): 2069-2081, 2012

addressers over brands. An image which exist in the mind of customer very highly depends on what friends and families have expressed about that brand [25].

Brand Popularity:

Brand popularity consist of scope of interest which consumer express relative to brand in comparison with other rivals. It is a degree of interest which is expressed in particular to products in a category. According to the studies performed have proven that the more popularity of a brand over time, more profit will go to shareholders, in other words, there is direct relation between brand popularity and profit making for organization. these popularity is not personal judgment only, but is general assessment of brand popularity at the level of society.

Nowadays many brands which created many supporters develop competitive advantage. Supporters who not satisfy only by purchasing the products. They consider themselves as a family members of brand consumers. They register in consumer's associations, sleep in long line of presenting new product and under any condition consider themselves as supporter of the company. Even in some instances male enmity with opposite brand. the supporter of Adidas during 2006 world cuphave conducted damaging outdoor advertisement to its arrival Puma company. Brandesteem is one of the factor which have defined to effect on special value brand. The degree of credibility that consumers announce relative to brand effect on their purchasing decision and mouth to mouth advertisement. announced that the prestige of brand is from brand popularity as well as customer's perception from quality and services of the company. Interesting issue is that the popularity of brand is not from identity, personality and feature. Cultural issues of society and market and other conditions of rivals also have great effect on the degree of popularity on a brand. The brand , with respect to perspective of customer and what they have made in their mind must behave in a way that with respect to cultural structure of society to create the goal of popularity. The popularity is more than creation of product and type of services, it comes out of integratedcommunications of marketing [26].

Organizational relationships:

Anything that could relates the customer to the brand including: The mental image of user, characteristics, make use of situations, organizational assets, brand personality, logo, company's marks, special standards of company, exclusive technologies of company and anything else that could connects the customer's mind to the brand. Many managers effort are spent so that somehow to connect exclusive company's assets to the brand. This is done in a way that some programs are designed toward expansion and development of brand activities scope and mind of addressers would be full of connected sings to the brand [15].

Potential ability of developing an exclusive asset for a brand is a wining card on the hand of marketing manager. Specially in cases that the goods form the customer perspective is in need of up to date knowledge, this issue makes itself more exposed. Many active companies in field of high technology make more effort toward creating exclusive assets [15]. Brand assets not only contribute in the field of product sales to the customer, but also supply possible sales of technical licenses for he organization. Nowadays many companies with the help of technical knowledge on hand and as well as promotional and advertisement activities make available part of their asset to other brands such that via this approach attract trust of their customers and possible more sales as well. This is in addition to profits resulting from sales of approved licenses.

Adv. Environ. Biol., 6(7): 2069-2081, 2012

As shown in the diagram No. 3. one of the dimension of new brand build is creation of its exclusive assets. For build of a brand must plan, enforce and manage anvisiblity difference, exclusive assets and wide communications with customer.

Image processing of consumer is associated with perceptions related to individual who make use of considered product or services. This characteristics could form via personal experience of customer in relation with consumers of brand or an image which have depicted through marketing communications. If image processing of brand with its image is admired by customer, then his desire based on increase stability of personality and his confidence would direct him toward positive assessment of the brand.Usage imagery processing lead to creation of brand identity [23].

Diagram 4: Conceptual Model of Research.

4- Goal of Research:

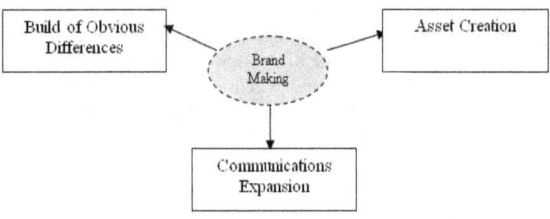

Diagram 3: Build of Brand Duties.

The goal of performing this research, assessment and prioritizing of effecting indicators on special value brand in bank Saderat from customers' perspective.

Permanency of Brand Image:

Various researcher have used variety of terms for description of brand image [7] employs the term as personality of brand [1] points to image of brand and Berri employs the brand meaning. Although they have similar approach and usually being used with similar meaning in contexts [27].

For acquiring customer-oriented special value brand, the customer must know the factors related to

brand in comparison with what other brands present in this category as strong, arbitrary and exclusive; this is the brand image which is in mind of customer [28]. Major part of Keller (1998) model, describes various types of factors relate with brand as characteristics product- related and non-productunrelated attributes [23]. For measurement of brand images could either use the list which have already prepared or act to re-extract the factors related to brand, then measure the power these factors [15].

5- Research Questions:

Question 1- what factors effect on special value brand of bank Saderat based on model of CBBE? Question 2- Which factors of CBBE model has more effect on special value brand?

7- Research Assumptions:

1- " Appreciated quality of customers" has effect on special value brand of bank Saderat. 2- " Appreciated value based on cost has effect on special value brand of bank Saderat. 3- " Uniquenessof

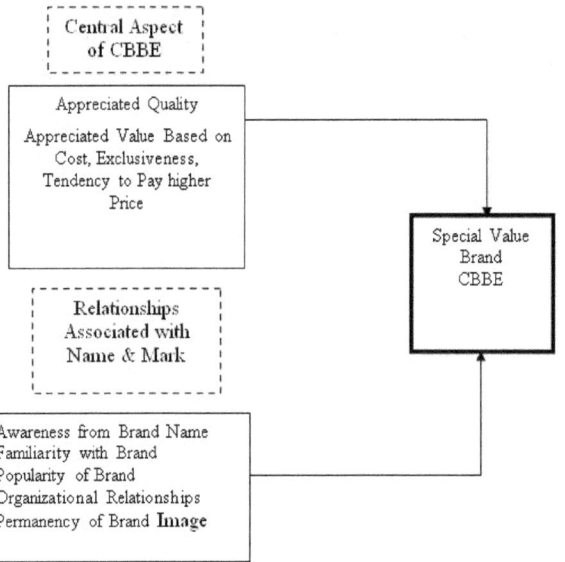

2078

Adv. Environ. Biol., 6(7): 2069-2081, 2012

Brand" has effect on special value brand of bank Saderat.

4-   " Tendency to pay higher price has effect on special value brand of bank Saderat.
5-   " Awareness from name of brand" has effect on special value brand of bank Saderat.
6-   " Familiarity with brand" has effect on special value brand of bank Saderat.
7-   " Brand Popularity" has effect on special value brand of bank Saderat.
8-   " Organizational relationships" has effect on special value brand of bank Saderat.
9-   " Permanency of Brand Image" has effect on special value brand of bank Saderat.

7- Implementation Approach of Research:

Research Approach:

In terms of applicable research goal and in respect to nature of subject , the research approach is of type descriptive- measurement.

Statistical Universe:

The statistical universe consists of entire depositors of banksaderat branches in Amol township who have acted to open an account with aforesaid bank since 2006.

Statistical Sample & Sampling Approach:

For determination of sample volume " Kerjesi& Morgan" have presented a good decision making model with table of volume [29] for universes with volume more than 10,000and up, sample volume of 384 would be acceptable. Same quantity questionnaire were randomly distributed and analyzed. For selection of statistical sample, the simple random sampling approach have used.

Information Collection Approach:

The tool used in this research is questionnaire. Since the questions of this study have prepared and compiled based on theory. For the purpose of admissibility assessment of designed questionnaire, the approach of judgmental validity assessment was used. For this purpose consultation performed from experts associated with research subject. Also, in addition to considering the questionnaire to be standard type, and for the purpose of determining reliability, the prepared questionnaire distributed randomly between 30 persons for statistical universe and after collection of questionnaires, the coefficient of Alpha Cronbakh have estimated using SPSS software to be $\square = 0.949$. with the quantity of this number which is above 0.7 indicates the desired reliability and validity of the questionnaire.

Approach Analysis of Research Information:

In this study, both, descriptive statistics and inferential statistics were used for analysis of information. In inferential statistics, binomial distribution test for responding to research questions and Freidman test for classification of effective factors have been used.

8- Conclusion:

    8-1 Conclusion from Descriptive Statistics:

In current research, for the purpose of demographical features, three question have designed in the questionnaire which consists of age, gender and education level. Based on the extracted information from questionnaire 384 individuals from sample members; 147 were male, 237 female , 63 between 20-30 years old, 142 between 31-40 years old, 137 between 41-50, 42 above 50 years old. 23 having education below high school diploma, 203 having diploma, 28 having associate degree, 118 having B.S degree, 12 having M.S degree or above. In respect to median of studied variables, observed that median respond were more in females that males. Also observed that in the variable,"Appreciated Quality" has the highest median related to individuals with high school diploma (3.23) and lowest medium related to individuals with education below high school diploma (2.87).observed that in the variable "Appreciated Value" based on cost; highest median related to individuals with B.S education (3.42) and lowest median related to individual below diploma (2.74). in variable value of being exclusive , the highest median related to individual with diploma (3.97) and lowest median

2079

Adv. Environ. Biol., 6(7): 2069-2081, 2012

related to individual under diploma (2.52). in variable " tendency to pay higher price", the highest median related to individual with B.S education (3.87) and lowest median related to individuals with education below diploma (3.22). variable in "Awareness from brand" highest median related to individuals with B.S education (3.49) and lowest median goes to individuals with below diploma education (2.67). in variable- "familiarity with brand" highest median related to individuals with associate degree (3.49) andlowest median goes to individuals with diploma education (2.97). in variable- "Organizational relationships" highest median related to individuals with M.S education and higher (3.45) and lowest median goes to individuals with M.S education (2.84). in variable – "Permanency of brand image, the highest median related to individuals with M.S education (3.49)and lowest median related to individuals with below diploma education (3.06).

8-2 Conclusion from Inferential Statistics (Test Assumption):

Before test assumption for entire research assumption two assumptions H_0 , H_1 compiled as following:
H_0 : Indicator "…………………………….." has no effect on special value brand of bank Saderat.
H_1 : Indicator "…………………………….." has
effect on special value brand of bank Saderat.
 In this section, outcome results from test of research assumption is shown in table No.2.   In concluding from such tests, when the obtained meaningful level to be less than 0.05, then the assumption (H_1) is accepted and when the obtained meaningful level to be bigger than 0.05, then assumption (H_0) is accepted.

8-3 Result of Friedman Test:

H_0 : There is no meaningful difference between research variables
H_1 : There is meaningful difference between research variables
Since the meaningful level is than 0.05, therefore H_1 assumptions is approved. Asunp Sig $= 0.007 < 0.05$
 For ranking of effecting factors on special value brand (answer to question No.2), the freedman test have been used .the output result of SPSS software is observed in table below:

Table 2: The results of research assumptions testwith the help of binomial distribution test.

Standard	Classification	Quantity	Percent (Observed ratio)	Test Ratio	Meaningful Level	Result
Appreciated Quality	3 3	201 183 384	0/6 0/4 1/0	0/60	0/097	Approval of zero Assumption
Perceived Value for the Cost	3 3	247 137 384	0/6 0/4 1/0	0/60	0/422	Approval of zero Assumption
Tobe Exclusive (uniqueness)	3 3	283 101 384	0/7 0/3 1/0	0/60	0/431	Approval of zero Assumption
Tendency to PayHigher Prices	3 3	87 297 384	0/2 0/8 1/0	0/60	0/017	Approval of alternative Assumption
Awareness from Brand	3 3	216 168 384	0/6 0/4 1/0	0/60	0/422	Approval of zero Assumption
Familiarity with Brand	3 3	119 265 384	0/3 0/7 1/0	0/60	0/031	Approval of alternative Assumption
Brand Popularity	3 3	231 153 384	0/6 0/4 1/0	0/60	0/497	Approval of zero Assumption
Organizational relationships	3 3	136 248 384	0/3 0/7 1/0	0/60	0/021	Approval of alternative Assumption

2080

Adv. Environ. Biol., 6(7): 2069-2081, 2012

Permanency of Brand Image	3 3	134 250 384	0/3 0/7 1/0	0/60	0/021	Approval of alternative Assumption

Table 3: Result of Friedman Test.

Parameter	Mean of Rank
Tendency to Pay Higher Prices	5.02
Familiarity with Brand	5.68
Organizational relationships	4.85
Permanency of Brand Image	6.03

In respect to rate of desirability an importance the results are as follow:

1- The Permanency of brand image indicator is in the first level

2- The familiarity with brand is in second level

3- The tendency to pay higher price is in third level 4- The organizational relationships is in fourth level.

9- Research Recommendation:

In this section is presented in two operational domains (notable to financial institutions and banks) and some researches (notable to researcher who wish to study the issue of branding and special value brand).

9-1 Recommendations for Managers and Organizations:

There are some applicable and operational recommendation available to managers in regard to dimensions which effects on special value.

1) the satisfied and loyal customers are willing to pay higher price for obtaining their considered brand. whatever brand which is important in the mind of customer, he/she is wiling to pay higher costing in the Cost-value equation since the brand itself is value creation for him.

If bank Saderat enhancesperformance of services equal to other banks, the customer keep using the services of the bank Saderat. In future the new electronic services of bank must always be updated. This variable has high relation with other indicators, therefore with creation of differentiation and desired service could attract customer to the bank in equal conditions.

2) Focus on visual elements of branding (Like; advertisement slogan, equalizing the facets of branch, creation of common visual identification for bank..) aside with powerful public relation activities could be introduced the bank beyond a giant economic organization and this affair is effective for familiarity of brand.

For example public perception is not appropriate relative to uses of bank's resources in accounts of loan without interest, banks could enhance this perception with presence in charity programs and participation with non-profit organization. Unfortunately, many banks with not having branding strategy toward creation of self visual image commit big mistakes. Lack of organizational color is one of common problem. An appropriate organizational color as a connecting loop could connect entire organizational communications activities which unfortunately many organization do not consider this issue accurately.

3) The bank Saderat must participate in social affairs and be honest to customers in all fields and consider itself liable relative to society. Also the personnel of bank Saderat must have a good relation with customers. For this affair must make effort with required planning for getting feedback from bank's customers so the relationships indicator in the organization would be strengthen. Creation of an image beyond an economic organization which were reviewed in past pages is one of approaches that could assist bank in creation of arms in keeping customers.

Adv. Environ. Biol., 6(7): 2069-2081, 2012

4)   To establish creation of permanent image strategy from brand is the first step in the context of penetration to the mind of addressers.

Implementation of this strategy must be performed with care, patience and desirable form. The entire relation activities of organization with customer must be performed in such a way that to make appear in the mind of customer as an appropriate image of organization. The thing here to be emphasized again is that the brand image not only must be function of branding strategy of organization, but also must always develop and equal image in the mind of customers. Specially in the modern bank services which banks are need of creating distinct and new image from themselves; this issue must be followed seriously.

9-2 Recommendations for future research:

❖   It is recommended which that special value brand of bank to be subject of study based on other models (Aker &etc).

❖   It is recommended that research to be performed in wider geographical range relative to this study. ❖ Study in particular to brand of a bank via questioning customers of other banks also could have interesting results.

❖   The relation between special value brand and performance of bank's personnel to be assessed.

References

1. Keller, K.L., 1993. Conceptualizing, measuring, ang managing consumer-based brand equity, Marketing Management, 57(1).
2. Rita Clifton and eshermaughan, 2000. The future of the brands: twenty- five visions, new York university press and interbrand.
3. Srivastava, R.K.S., A.D. Choker, 1991. Brand equity :aprespective on its meaning and measurement, Cambridge, MA: Marketing
    Science Institute.
4. Delgado Elena, Ballester and Jose Luis Munuera, Alema'n, 2005. Does brand trust matter to brand equity ?, journal of product & Brand Management, 14/3: 187-196.
5. Fahimi, A., 2006. Review of factors affecting for selection and customer loyalty in banking: the depositors of Bank Mellat, Tehran University School of Management. (in Persian).
6. Yoo, B., N. Donthu and S. Lee, 2000. An examination of selected marketing mix elements and brand equity, journal of the Academic of Marketing Science, 28.
7. Aaker, D.A., 1991. Managing brand equity, the free press, New YORK, NY.
8. Kim Hong-Bomm, Kim Woo Goon, 2005. The Relationship between brand equity and firms ' performance in luxury hotels and chain resataurants , tourism Management, 26: 549-560.
9. Baladuf Artur, Cravens Karen, Binder Gudrun, 2003. Performance consequences of brand equity management: evidence from organizations in the value chain, journal of product & brandmanagement, 12(4): 220-236.
10. Blackstone, M., 1995. The qualitatiyedimesion of brand equity journal of advertisifresearch, 35(4).
11. Coob-Walgren, C.J., C.A. Ruble, N. Donthu, 1995. Brand Equity, Brand preferenceand
                          Purchase intent, journal of advertising, 24(3).
12. Simon, C.J., M.W. Sullivan, 1993. The measurement and determinants of brand equity: A financial approach, Marketing Science, 12(1).
13. Ourusoff, A., 1993. Who said brands are dead?, Brandweek, 34(32).
14. Dyson, P., A. Farr, N.S. Hollis, 1996. Understanding, Measuring and using brand equity, journal of advertising research, 36(6).
15. Aaker D.A. and Joachimsthaler, 2001. Erich, Brand leadership, the Free press, New York, NY.
16. Kirmani, A., V.A. Zeithmal, 1993. Advertising, perceived qualityand brand image, in Aaker DA, Biel A, editors Brand equity and advertising, hillsdale (NJ): Lawrence Erlbaum Associates.
17. Netmeyer Richard, G., KrishanBalaji, Pullig Chris, Wang Guangping, Mehmet Yagci, Dean Dwane, Rick Joe, Wirth Ferdinand, 2004. Developin and alidating measures of facets of customer-based brand equity, journal of Business Research, 57.
18. Holboork, M.B., C.F. Corfiman, 1994. Quality and value in the consumptionexperience: phaedurs rides againg, Marketing Science, 12(5).
19. Dhar, R., S.J. Sheramn, 1996. The effect of common and uinique features in consumer choise, journal of Consume Research, 23.
20. Kalra, A., R.C. Goodstein, 1998. The Impact of advertising positioning strategies on consumer price sensitivity, journal of Marketing Research, 35.
21. Alba, W.J., W. Hutchinson, J.H. Lynch, 1990. Memory and decision making. in: kassarjian H.H., Robertson T.S., editors. Hand book of Consumer Theory & Research Englewood Cliffs (NJ): Prentic Hall.

Adv. Environ. Biol., 6(7): 2069-2081, 2012

22. Sethuraman, Re, C. Cole, 1997. Why do consumers pay more for national brands than for store brand ?, Cambridge: Marketing Science
    Institute.

23. Khoshparvar, Z., 2006. Determine the factors influencing to personal Behavior in order to strategic implementation services Branding to create competitive differentiation: a case study of Bank Mellat, Tehran University School of Management. (in Persian).

24. Park, C.W. and P.V. Lessig, 2001. Familiarity and its impact on consumer decision biases and heuristics. jounal of consumer Research, 8: 223230.

25. Holden Stephen, J.S., Vanhuele Marc, 1999. Know the Name, Forget The Exposure: Brand Familiarity versus Memory of Exposure Context, psychology & Marketing, 16(6): 479496.

Adv. Environ. Biol., 6(7): 2069-2081, 2012

26. Scally, R., 1999. Upscale mix lifts image above the fray journal of Advertising Research, 38(8).

27. O'cass, Aron Grace, Debra, 2003. An explanatory prespective of service brand associations, journal of services marketing, 17(5).

28. Keller, K., 2003. Strategic Brand Management: Building Measuring and Managing Brand Equity, 2 ed., Prentice-Hall, Englewood Cliffs, Nj.

29. Skaran, U., 2001. Research methods in management, translation Mahmoud Shirazi and Mohammad Saberi, Tehran, published by the State Management Training Center, First
Printing. (in Persian).

J. Basic. Appl. Sci. Res., 2(9)9211-9215, 2012

© 2012, TextRoad Publication

ISSN 2090-4304

Journal of Basic and Applied

Scientific Research

www.textroad.com

The Study of Supervision System

Nasrin Heidarizadeh[1], Mostafa Emami[2], Hassan Moradi[3]

1 Department of Science Education, Payam Noor University,
Iran 2 Young Researchers Club, South Tehran Branch, Islamic Azad University, Tehran, Iran.
3

Department of management, Payam Noor University, Iran

ABSTRACT

This research is an attempt to study the supervision system of elementary school teachers in Kermanshah Province in order to develop a conceptual framework applying a descriptive-method. To do these first 176 factors were derived through studying the literature of models and theories in Iran which resulted in 93 factors after surgery. The main findings are: 1. in studying the current situation of the teachers' supervision system, the factors of class management and the school regulations had better results than other factors. In the factor of evaluation from the students learning the performance was average but in sustainable development of educational quality, teacher professional development and commitment, motivating students, determining educational and curricular objectives, teacher performance evaluation less work has been carried out. And in analysis of the factors, the factors classification has changed from seven to 13 factors. 2. Developing a suggested framework in order to study the teacher supervision including five categories of philosophy and objectives, theoretical principals, supervision functions in 13 branches, operation stages, and evaluation system. 3. The findings from validity of questionnaires from scholars indicate a 91.78% suitability ranking by the scholars which shows a high validity of the model in the eyes of the scholars.

KEYWORDS: Supervisor, mentor, teacher, elementary level, supervision model, Kermanshah Province

INTRODUCTION

The education and training system is one of the small parts of society system which is responsible for training peoples. It has critical mission to follow. The function and the role of the system are more critical than the function of other society system such as economic and social system. Therefore the result and the outcome must be evaluate and modified continuously. As a matter of fact based on the quality systematic approach, the output of the system is the result of input and the process of the education and training system. In the circle of the education and training system, teachers have a key role and in order to reach the class goals, they must have essential knowledge and skills.

Supervision system is going to define such vision for the system. Its definition has been changed as long as the other environmental changes as now there some limited conception in its definitions (Vaylz & Bandi, 2004); Administrative, education planning, teaching, human relationship, management and Leadership. Eye, Netzer and Krey defined concentrate supervision as; supervision is a stage of administrative management of school which considers education expectation appropriate with education and training system. So school staffs and facilities must integrate till school can reach to their education goal (Vaylz & Bandi, 1986). Glic man has also defined administrative supervision as; teachers are stand in the front position while supervision is at the behind to make teachers able in their work and support and provide them skills and knowledge they would need. Also from the view of Haris and Bezent administrative supervision is; supervision about school staffs along with adults and facilities to keep and change schools function to be effective in main lessons goals achievement (Vaylz and Bandi, 2004). Cogan define concentrate supervision on education planning as; supervision consist of activities such as plan writing, review of education planning, syllabus and lessons preparedness, facilities and tool use, family reporting and considering the whole evaluation system.

Marks, Stoops and King Stoops defined concentrate supervision on teaching as: supervision is an action and experience to education and teaching improvement (Vaylz and Bandi, 1986). Komoski has also defined supervision on teaching as; supervision is a process of leadership with a final goal to promote education (Vaylz and Bandi, 2004).

The fourth definition will go to human relationship. Comeil Vaylz define supervision as; supervisors are those who foster performance and works. They help in creating and transferring massage till people can hear each other. Beside they help people solve their problems and courage people to do new things. They would listen to people critics and objects about the system and policy and suggest the administrative to listen to the

*Corresponding Author: Nasrin Heidarizadeh, Department of Science Education, Payam Noor University, Iran. Email:Malakihamid12@yahoo.com

9211
Heidarizadeh *et al.*, 2012

staff words to solve their problems. In the fifth definition supervision is limited to management. As Alfonso, Firth and Nevi defined it as;

Supervision is in all complicated organization to conserve and improve the system. The relation between supervision and communicative organization is clear and straight forward. The organization results would be used in organization efficiency and effectiveness. This kind of supervision especially could be applicable in production system for those who do educational supervision. School is considered as a production system. The sixth definition is on the leadership concept on Mosher and Purper view as define: the supervision duty is the knowhow of teaching to teachers how to teach and professional leadership in general reeducation.

Ben Harris has also defined supervision and teaching guide as; what school staffs do with adults and things to keep school performance or to change it, in the way to effect on the process of promotion and students learning system. Supervision and education guide is often regarding to education and would not involve in students. It is the main function of school. It's a skill, guide and supervision to keep and improve learning and teaching process. Comeil Vaylz stated that education leadership is a kind of assistance and help to education promotion and is kind of action that would help teachers to take step. Khadivi, 1993 presented a conceptual model of supportive supervision in education and training system of the country and recognized the following factors:

Factors are annual evaluation, monitoring, professional development, goals determination, lessen and syllabus designing and professional commitment. The model has been accepted with 0.088 agreements.

Research method

The presented research with goal of description and investigation in supervision process, the research method is descriptive one. Moreover in presented research we use documentations, library study and data and information gathering in the area of research title, by studying books, articles, thesis, and electronic recourses in the case of supervision by doing some interviews with teachers, managers, and supervisions and questionnaires.

Statistical population and sampling techniques

The statistical population of the research would cover all Kermanshah elementary school teachers during 2006-2007 which accounted for about 7051 persons. The sampling was done by multi stage grape sampling from training and teaching area of province during 2006-2007. The numbers of sampling teachers are about
384 persons. For their selection we used 6 area(1- Kermanshah: region 2, 2- Eslam abad, 3- Ghasr shirin, 4- Kerend, 5- Kangavar, 6- Paveh) and we collected 6 girls and 6 boys school from each region.
Two researcher made questionnaires have been used to collect data. The first one with 3 questions was completed by elementary teachers and the second one was completed by university teachers specialized in supervision study for reaching to conceptual framework,Inferential statistics,Using a single factor analysis with Varimax and the tools reliability is over 0.95.

Research findings

Findings regarding to the first question:
Comparing the marks of the supervision factors with the average of 14.67 shows that class manager and school regulation has a better performance than other parameters. The evaluation situation of students learning is in the moderate position, while other factors as permanent quality education improvement, growth and teacher professional commitment, student encouragement, defining educational and teaching goals, and teacher evaluation were very low in position. The whole study results are alignment with Elyasi's result in 2000.

Table 1. Statistical elements of the questionnaire and comparing them with the average of 14.67

Supervision	mean	number of questions	Sig. (2-tailed)	df	t
Sustainable development of educational quality	13.36	30	0.000	267	-7.306
Professional growth and commitment	13.47	25	0.000	330	-6.069
Motivating students	14.22	15	0.08	351	-2.37
Class management, school administration and regulations	15.0043	9	0.049	365	1.94
Student learning evaluation	14.59	5	0.67	3	-0.424
Determining educational and curricular objectives	13.54	4	0 0.00	373	-4.606
Teacher evaluation	13.77	5	0 0.00	377	-4,562

9212

J. Basic. Appl. Sci. Res., 2(9)9211-9215, 2012

Findings regarding to the second question

The conceptual framework for quality improvement of supervision system quality has been prepared in 5 categories; the goals and philosophy, theories, conceptual framework, the implementation stages and the supervision model.

A. the aims and philosophy

In this section the main goal of presenting the supervision framework has been presented. The main goals are renewal and rethinking in supervision, introducing and centralization of education and training parameters, fostering and changing approach from traditional supervision to the modern one, concerning the practical aspect and implementation and access to integrative supervision model.

B. Theoretical Concept

Following the studies done regarding to supervision in theories, the researcher has recognized the conceptual models, approaches, theories and paradigms. The result set in 13 models: Synergic supervision model, the paradigm of knowledge work supervision, external supervision model, inter-school supervision, inschool supervision, model of self-evaluation, and model of clinical supervision,‹ supportive supervision, and peer supervision model, cooperative supervision

C. Supervision functions

Based on the studies the main seven factors have been extracted which consist of: permanent quality education improvement, growth and teacher professional commitment, student encouragement, class management and regulations, evaluation of students learning, defining educational and teaching goals, and teacher evaluation. In order to reach to conceptual framework, factor analyzing has been done for studying its reliability with 13 factors. So the conceptual framework with factor analyzing of Varimax has been changed as following:

The first main factor: participating in teachers council- designing and equipping essential teaching methods for problem solving, reviewing teaching methods, efficient use of technology and resources, providing teaching methods, interest making in teachers and opportunity making for teachers to visit best practice classes.

The second main factor: education feedback to teachers: providing appropriate context for getting assistance from others, getting feedback, regular visit of schools based on rules, helping teachers in teaching methods modification, post and after meeting schedule with teachers, presenting suggestions and offers about teacher behavior and teaching, recording of observations, and using check list in observation process.

The third main factor: adapting programs and methods with cultural situation, such as: encouraging teachers to innovative and inventive teaching skills- relating teacher reaching methods to local culture- time planning for permanent improvement- identifying and studying solutions for solving teaching problems- applying creativity in growth programs- introducing teachers who need knowledge synergy- teacher encouraging in using simple and comprehensive examples.

The forth main factor: teachers, students, parents and school commitment such as: commitment to students, teachers, school, parents and teaching quality

The fifth main factor: professional and growth commitment to teacher such as: providing learning opportunity and promoting teachers skills and abilities- increasing professional encouragement in teachers- providing job satisfaction context- providing professional commitment- providing appropriate atmosphere for teachers learning- showing teachers teaching best practice- providing facilities for teachers to do researches- introducing new internet sites for learning process- teacher learning- having sympathy with teachers to participate in professional growth opportunity

The sixth main factor: teacher participation in teaching quality promotion such as: assistance to new teachers in improving professional and teaching- providing opportunity for knowledge and experience sharing among teachers- encouraging teachers to do creative and innovative works- conducting teachers view and problems to the management levels.

The seventh main factor: providing studying and learning context: providing teachers, the last educational journals- introducing them the new educational results- persuading teachers in studying and learning to enhance their professional knowledge.

The eighth main factor: student's motivation and their need understanding: informing parents about the way of encouraging their child- adapting teaching material with students needs- providing suitable situation for students learning process- group teaching methods and increasing team work ability among students- recognizing geographical, economic and cultural situation of school- helping teachers to use the best incentive system for students- encouraging teachers to use creativity and innovative teaching methods- doing consulting activities with parents- helping teachers to know the wise and genus student for additional teaching and training materials- convincing teachers to understand the individual distinguish in time of teaching and assignment submission. The main ninth factor: administrative information such as: identifying rules and regulations in the class- reflecting class and school problems to the administration- knowing all guidelines and construction

The main tenth factor: class managing and school rules such as: class handling skills- educational, administrative, serving and health weakness identification and attempt to solve the problems- class and student's educational files investigation- supervising class schedule and development with its timetable- submitting information about class management style- teacher behaviors with annoyed students

The main eleventh factor: evaluating students learning such as: supervising the student's exam based on the time schedule- encouraging teacher in doing the final evaluation- helping teachers in studying students assignment and evaluating their works.

The main twelfth factor: educational goal and aims, such as; helping teachers in planning and providing teaching plan- helping teachers in performing the study materials, lessons modification and evaluation- informing teachers about the teaching necessities

The main thirtieth factor: supervision evaluation as: Teacher's performance evaluation after supervision process- studying learning level of students from quizzes – teacher's modification planning- using the evaluation results to promote, make official and to get other administrative decisions.

The result of factor analyzing of main factors is as follows:

1. Sustainable education quality improvement: the results based on principal components regarding to   graph indicate that four factors as permanent education quality improvement, education feedback, adaptability of plans and methods with cultural situation, commitment and responsibility to teachers, students and parents can be extracted. In the first main factor the weightiest factor goes to equipping and designing the essential means and teaching methods for teachers, with 0.721 weight and the lowest rate goes to provide opportunity for teachers to observe teaching style and to become familiar with the best practice with 0.486. in the second main factor, teaching feedback presentation, the weightiest factor goes to permanent visit from schools with factor of 0.765 and the lowest goes to commitment to education quality with factor of 0.613 and to prearrangement of attending in the class with 0.505 and in the third factor, plans and methods adaptation with culture, the highest score goes to establishing and relation making between local culture and teacher teaching methods with 0.659 and the lowest goes to schedule permanent development planning in school with 0.508 and in the fourth factor, commitment to teachers, students and parents, the highest score belongs to commitment to students with 0.786 and the lowest belongs to commitment to educational quality with 0.613.

2. The results of the second main factor, the professional growth and commitment: the result manifested that at least three main factors of supervision are; professional growth and commitment, teacher's contribution in quality improvement and providing study context. The most prominent factors in the first factor is providing opportunity for teachers to present their view and points with 0.768 and the lowest point fits for providing opportunity for teachers to participate in education training with 0.557 and in the second factor the highest score was job satisfaction with 0.807 and the lowest score was sympathy with teacher in professional opportunity with 0.547.

3. The result of the third factor, motivating students and recognizing their need: in this case only one factor can be extracted. Based on the table, helping teachers in using the best students encouragement and incentive system with 0.842 is the highest score and setting relationship with parents to provide encouraging methods with 0.391 is the lowest one.
4. The result of the main fourth factor, class management and school regulation: the two factors of class management, school administration and regulations can be considered. Findings indicates that information and methods submission in class management with 0.842 got the top score and studying class and education documents got the lowest score with 0.686. In the second factor reflecting the school and class problems to education and training ministry and having enough information about guidelines, and administrative got the highest and lowest score with 0.895 and 0.421 respectively Divek Daniel (1999) and Caroline Avrtsvn (1987) and Admin Achsvn and Gall (2004) is consistent.
5. The fifth score, students learning assessment: based on the analyzing, the highest score belongs to helping teachers in evaluating students with 0.897 and the lowest belongs to control and supervision of exams based on the timetable with 0.672.
6. The sixth factor analyzing result, education and lessons goal making: the highest score relates to help and assist teachers in lessons modification with 0.913 and the lowest relates to help teachers in lessons planning and designing with 0.619.
7. The seventh factor analyzing result, teacher evaluation: based on the table findings, planning for teachers improvement got the highest score with 0.87 and performance evaluation after supervision process and using evaluation results to promote,make official,and other administrative decision with
0.837 got the lowest score Antony Clarks and Steve Collins (1993 And Kojesky(2006)

Conclusions

Based on the findings and results, the following conclusion can be taken: The appropriate supervision which could work out for teachers of province must be based on the conceptual frame work extracted from this research. Providing workshops and training programs for supervisions to learn and promote their skills. The ministry of education and training must provide educational programs and plans for improving professional skills and teacher's commitment, encouraging students and providing evaluation system for teachers. Teacher's role in the cities and rural areas must be redefined.

REFERENCES

Beach, D.m.and Reinhartz, J.(2000). Supervisory Leadership: focus on instruction. Boston : Allyn and bacon.

Bouchamma,yamina.(2007). Evaluating Teaching personnel .Which Model Of Sopervision Do Canadian Teachers Prefer?,Springer ,Canada.

Bouchamma,yamina.(2007). Evaluating Teaching personnel .Which Model Of Sopervision Do Canadian Teachers Prefer?, Springer ,Canada.

Brady, M. P., Taylor, R. D., & Hamilton, R. (1989). Differential measures of teachers' questioning in mainstreamed classes: Individual and class wide patterns. Journal of Research and Development in Education, 22(4), 10-17.

Brophy, J., & Good, T. (1970). Teachers' communication of differential expectations for children's classroom performance: Some behavioral data. Journal of Educational Psychology, 61, 365-374.

Feiman-Nemser, S. (2001). From preparation to practice: Designing a continuum to strengthen and sustain teaching. Teachers College Record, 103, 1013-1055.

Geeta, Heble(2005) A Model Of Expert Instructional Supervision, Doctor Of Education , Wilmington College ,November 2005

Giebelhaus, C. R. (1994). The mechanical third ear device: A student teaching supervision alternative. Journal of Teacher Education, 45, 365-373.

Jossey-Bass. Swanson, J.L., & O'Saben, C.L. (1993). Differences in supervisory needs and expectations by trainee experience, cognitive style, and program membership. Journal of Counseling and Development, 71, 457-464.

Lindell, M. A. (2001). Audiocuing teacher clarity skills: The effects on preservice teachers during student teaching experiences (Doctoral dissertation, University of Wyoming, 2001). Dissertation Abstracts International, 62(05), 1801.

Madsen, C. H., Jr., Becker, W. C, & Thomas, D. R. (1968). Rules, praise, and ignoring: Elements of elementary classroom control. Journal of Applied Behavior Analysis, 1, 139-150.

Malott, R. W., & Suarez, E. T. (2004). Principles of behavior. Upper Saddle River, NJ: Pearson

Mehrunnisa, Ahmad Ali (2000)Supervision for teacher development , International of educational development 20 ,pergamon

Moran, D. J., & Malott, R. W (2004). Evidence-based educational methods. San Diego, CA: Elsevier Academic.

Neufeldt, S.A., Beutler, L.E., & Banchero, R.E. (1997). Research on supervisor variables in psychotherapy supervision. In C.E. Watkins, Jr. (Ed.), Handbook of psychotherapy supervision (pp. 508-524). New York: Wiley.

Ross, D. E., Singer-Dudek, J., & Greer, R. D. (2005). The Teacher Performance Rate and Accuracy Scale: Training as evaluation. Education and Training in Developmental Disabilities, 40, 411-123.

Stallings, J. (1984). Effective use of classroom time (Appalachia Educational Lab Occasional Paper 013). (ERIC Document Reproduction Service No. ED252515)

Stoltenberg, C., & Delworth, U. (1987). Supervising counsel ors and therapists. San Francisco, CA.

9215

J. Basic. Appl. Sci. Res., 2(8)7734-7740, 2012

ISSN 2090-4304
Journal of Basic and Applied Scientific Research *www.textroad.com*

The Study of the Relation between Marketing Mix and Attract Customers

Mohammad Reza Doroodgar[1], Kamran Nazari[2], Mostafa Emami[3]

[1] Master degree in IT Management, Shahid Beheshti University

Department of Business Management, Payam Noor University, Kermanshah, Iran
3 Young Researchers Club, South Tehran Branch, Islamic Azad University, Tehran, Iran

---

ABSTRACT

With competitive financial markets and the expansion of private banks and financial institutions and credit to the marketing and applying marketing techniques and strategies to attract customers and increase the deposit is more important. Using the marketing mix factors such as market access and good service and fast customer service and variety of services and appropriate advertising to attract customers, the increase in deposit institutions, especially financial and credit institutions shall. Given the importance of this issue, this study investigated the impact of marketing mix to attract customers in the bank is in Kermanshah Province. Collection of information is the researcher and the study questionnaire included 30 questions are the reliability of the questionnaire was calculated using Cronbach's alpha was 0.882 and the Cronbach values are greater than 0.7, the reliability of the questionnaire is. The population used in this study is the province of the customer's bank account with at least one interest-free loans, savings, and they are now. Stratified random sampling is that the 250 questionnaires were collected. The main hypothesis of this study and 5 with a particular hypothesis is the Pearson correlation test hypotheses were put to the test plant and a significant positive effect, it was established, meaning that factors in the marketing mix customers absorption process The bank has a significant positive effect.

KEYWORDS: Marketing, marketing mix factors, attract customers.

---

1 – INTRODUCTION

Progress and transformed the industry with institutions and companies to deal with problems and activities, along with competitors, and each institution should adopt policies with respect to long-term vision, mission, goals and opportunities and arrangements and the internal facilities of an external to develop comprehensive marketing [1], because today's global business environment with increasing complexity, rapid change and unexpected developments in the markets is [2].

With the development of science in all fields, especially banks and financial markets become competitive in recent years with the development of their activities with the creation of the private banks and financial institutions and credit to the marketing and applying marketing techniques and strategies in attract customers and increase the deposit was more important. Using the marketing mix factors such as access to appropriate services and provide services to customers quickly and appropriately in a variety of services and advertising to attract customers, the increase in deposit institutions and banks, especially the bank. Marketing is one of the issues that are subject to change, due to market changes in consumption patterns and tastes of individuals. Population growth, urban expansion and changes in community structure and diversity of products and advance knowledge, generation changes, etc. are factors that will determine market variables [3].

Each institution has the task of marketing managers with analyzing, planning, implementation and effective control of marketing programs for a superior competitive position in target markets to develop. Marketing plan includes a process designed to predict future events and determining strategies to achieve the objectives of the Institute [4].

Institutions should try to obtain an appropriate share of the market with a market study and application of marketing mix variables, and using appropriate methods of distribution and supply good service and well aware of the campaign and for the identification of opportunities and They attract more resources to deal with scientific creativity and innovation with customer needs and matching resources to increase market share and take care of customers. Strengthening financial markets in the country of its economic development and resource savings for the health of the economy seems to be necessary and the savings rate in the banking system and credit system and financial institutions can expect increased investment and economic growth there.

In Iran the main hub of the financial markets, banks and financial institutions and credit are the main source of capital in banks and financial institutions and credit to buy products and services, loans are granted, the funding source for all economic units in the country. The banks and institutes appropriate activities and effective use of marketing is very effective for achieving their goals. In recent years a significant number of banks and institutions need to make more use of the application of marketing variables that are trying to attract

---

*Corresponding Author: Mohammad Reza Doroodgar, Master degree in IT management Shahid Beheshti University

7734

more of the ways of marketing to increase resources and effort to customers. Apart from these categories in which the bank is not required in this research institute has found that the effect of competition with some of the marketing mix strategies for increasing deposits and investments in the institution.

2 - Marketing

In the 1960s, the term was common in marketing. It says everything starts with consumer needs and demands. Marketing and market management of the important branches of knowledge management is the main task of understanding human needs and desires and help them through the process, resources are exchanged. Because society needs today more than ever, especially with the demands of a growing shortage of human and other resource managers faced with limited resources available to meet those demands are unlimited, and that knowledge management is here to help science the economy and a set of skills and knowledge to the optimal use of limited resources, and marketing also need to recognize the efforts put up by the exchange of resources [5]. Marketing is a social and managerial process by which needs and desires of individuals and groups through the production, supply and exchange of useful goods and the value they provide to others [6].

Marketing Management can be defined as follows: "The analysis, planning, implementation and monitoring programs to create, provide and maintain a profitable process transactions with the buyers, in order to achieve organizational goals [7]. "Marketing management" as the analysis, planning, implementation and control programs are defined to achieve organizational goals are developed. Programs that establish and maintain beneficial exchanges with buyers is made [3].

"Marketing Management" opportunities, including analysis, planning, implementation, execution and monitoring programs to establish and maintain a favorable exchange markets aim to achieve organizational goals. Thus marketing management or demand management, supply and demand caused by or in the form of motivation is essential [8].

"Marketing Association of America [3]" marketing "the process of planning, the realization of an idea, pricing, advertising and distribution of goods and services or ideas considered so that the exchange is that the individual and the organization in its becoming a reality [7 and 9. The art and science of marketing is to create favorable conditions the to be established between supply and demand. The main task of the marketing of both product and service needs and focus on target market is [10].

Marketing involves activities that provide a comprehensive definition makes it difficult. Marketing experts are by definition as a way for these activities from their own angle of vision has been raised. Some of the term, see a group of activities that take place in the market and also some of the ways that marketers have to comply to the definition .Table 1 shows some of these definitions.

Table 1. Definitions of marketing (Researcher)

Scholar	Year	Definition
Chysnral	1992	Marketing means finding a suitable position in the market [11].
Mercer	1996	Understanding what people want and seek a market and supply and provision of goods and services and meet their needs and achieve goals [12].
Cohen	1998	The marketing activities such as buying and selling of goods, transport and storage of [13].
Baker	1998	A series of activities called the flow of commercial goods and services from producer to final consumer, it will lead [14].
Goharian	1374	Marketing structure and demand for products and services is estimated to predict the spread[15].
Ranjbariyan	1378	Satisfy human needs and to define the process was considered with the market. The other hand, the buyer and seller in a market where it is located [16].
Hosseini	1379	A set of human and economic activities conducted in order to satisfy the needs and demands of the people through the exchange process [17].
Alvdary	1383	Process in which groups of people, goods and benefits from production and exchange with others to meet their wants and needs 18.
Events in Iran	1386	Targeted marketing enabling the company to plan and execute pricing, promotion and distribution of products, services and ideas [19].

The art of marketing and product or service to meet the need, if the correct amount and quality of sound in the right place and right time to reach customers and to benefit from its activities should be] 20 [.

Today the range extends to the advertising and marketing so as to be considered as part of its territory and that all economic activities including manufacturing, distribution or marketing of a wide range of services includes the management of sales or production to the sale of goods and services to provide.

In summary, the design, manufacture, packaging, distribution and sale of goods and services to consumers and ultimately customer satisfaction through after sales activities play an important role [21]. In the field of services marketing, field marketing is important; service activities which include features such as being intangible, indiscernible being different and being held to be impossible [22]. The exchange of product marketing, marketing services, with the difference goods and services between the same characteristics inseparable, being intangible, lack of maintenance and service is different [23].

In recent years, branches and wide variety of services to the market so much over the last several service centers are more tangible, and that it can be listed as Table 2:

Table 2. Community services sector (research)

Section	Example	Section	Example
Public sector	Hospitals, educational	Department of Commerce	Hotels, insurance companies, banks and financial institutions and credit
Non-profit sector	Charitable institutions, mosques	Manufacturing sector	Computer operators

3 - marketing mix

Set of controllable elements of marketing tools and marketing strategies with the company in its marketing strategy in combining these elements form. By definition, "Cutler" a set of marketing mix variables can be controlled by the marketing companies and institutions in their target market and its composition are required for the reaction [7].Elements of the marketing mix is a set of marketing tools for achieving the goals of the Institute of Marketing in the market that uses [24].

Marketers in order to receive favorable responses from their target markets of many tools they use. These tools comprise the marketing mix. In fact, a set of tools that institutions of their marketing mix to achieve marketing goals of your target market use. McCarthy classified these tools into four major groups has, these four groups, which they called the 4P's of marketing: product, price, location, distribution, sales promotion] 25 [. Decisions about future marketing by marketers, should also affect the final consumer and commercial channels. Thus, despite the presence of institutions in a number of decision variables of the marketing mix because it requires a long time, little can change in the short term in their marketing mix to create. Robert Latr for the seller as to the 4P 4C customer is shown in Table 3:

Table 3. Component Model 4P and 4C

4C customer		The 4P	
Customer solution	**Customer solution**	**Product**	**Product**
Customer costs	Customer coast	Price	Price
Profits and customer comfort	Convenience	Location distribution	Place
Communications	Communication	Advance sales	Promotion

4C according to the customer, the customer needs to succeed with institutions more economical, more comfortable and more effective communication to meet the needs of the consumer satisfaction convenience, comfort, and their interests taken into account and try to charge less for their customers

Should the customer be expected product benefits. Price should be commensurate with the capabilities of the buyer. This product should be available to customers purchasing its not a problem. Finally, the promotions should be made to potential consumers of such products are available [26]. The concept of marketing mix, the organization's performance using a set of controllable variables and uncontrollable factors of the environment is defined [27].

Marketing mix of traditional management models and dynamic market such as the beggar working alongside other methods of Anderson and the theoretical parameters of a system that was developed by the University of Copenhagen in Europe to overcome. Methods such as new product vision, functional vision, and with such a geographical perspective he faced. just a few of these models were able to maintain their survival against 4P [28]. The concept of marketing mix for the first time in 1950 by Neil Bvrdn was introduced and became known as the 4P] 29 [. Jerome McCarthy in the early 1960s, blends marketing with four variables known as the 4P classification that included: product [4] the price of [5] the distribution [6] (place) and promotion of [7] which each of these marketing tools have the following collections are] 30 [.

McCarthy has since been created dramatic changes in the marketing mix and the 4P's still a lot of literature as the main concept is to coordinate the many other aspects of marketing are organizing a round] 31. Four elements of marketing mix is defined in Table 4:

Table 4. Definitions of the four elements of marketing mix (made)

Product [8]	Product is a physical object that is sold and has a characteristic palpable, a complex set of benefits that can be used to meet customer needs [32].

Price [9]	Includes issues such as discounts, list prices, credit, repayment term and conditions .The price is included in the price, product or service offered for sale and will determine the level of benefits. Price is the only element that does not include costs charged to the customers to buy products they take [32].
Promotion [10]	Includes issues such as advertising, personal selling, sales promotion, public relations and direct marketing. Distribution channels is the most important questions about how an organization can optimize a connection between inner and outer channels is [24].
Distribution of [11]	Includes issues such as distribution channels, market coverage, product inventory, transportation and distribution sites.

The most important element in the marketing mix is product. Is what makes our product to market. Pricesensitive element of the marketing mix, customer is liable for the amounts are paid to deliver the product. The

7736

third element is that the distribution of all the activities that aim to deliver the product to the customer. The fourth element of the marketing mix is promotion, which is used to communicate with customers. This association is to encourage customers to buy products. Figure 1 shows the elements of the marketing mix.

4 - hypotheses

The contents of the main hypothesis of this study is as follows:

Marketing mix elements and the relationship between bank customers are significant.

The main hypothesis of this study, five sub-hypotheses in this regard will be made as follows:

A significant relationship between income customers, and deposit in a bank there.

2 between providing services that offer quick and convenient services to their customers on deposit in the bank there is a significant relationship.

3 Among the variety of services and increase their knowledge of customers and resources to attract customers in the bank there is a significant relationship.

4 The use of advertising to attract customers in the bank there is a significant relationship.

5 and accelerating the transfer of facilities and resources to attract customers in the customer's bank, there is a significant relationship.

5 – METHODS

Since in this study, researchers sought to combine elements of relationship marketing and attracting customers in the bank in Kermanshah province is based on the research arm of the survey method of research is descriptive research.

The population used in this study is the province of bank customers (based on 14 city) with at least one account, interest-free loans, and savings are now. The formula is based on 230 samples in this study.

$$(1)\ n = \frac{Z^2 P4}{d^2}$$

And 1-p = q, and p values are not available if it is equal to 5 / 0 set.

$$1 - \alpha = 0/95 \qquad , \qquad Z = 1/96 \qquad q = 0/5 \qquad p = 0/5$$

And the value of d (the amount of allowable error) with respect to similar research has been done based on empirical research. If the survey is collecting data to estimate the value of d p in the interval 4% to 7% is acceptable.

In this study, using statistical formulas selected number of samples is 230.

Data for this study were collected from the two following methods.

A library method: This method of collecting information about the study of literature and history books, dissertations, articles, databases and Internet sources were used.

Two field methods: In this method, questionnaire design and distribution of statistical information about the relationship of the marketing mix and attract more customers to design questionnaire with three questions and hypotheses for the first hypothesis and the second and fifth Similarly for the second hypothesis, questions 6,7,8,9,10,11 and 12, the third hypothesis, 13,14,15,16 and 17 questions, for the fourth hypothesis, 18,19,24,25 and 30 as well as questions for the fifth hypothesis, Questions 27 and 28 each in five levels (very low, low, medium, high and very high) have been measured in the questionnaire design of university teachers in the field of management science and marketing and financial consultants were used. The questionnaires were distributed among 30 customers. These individuals were selected according to the researcher to identify and complete a questionnaire about the appropriateness of the research questions, including questions of proper and demystification of the comments that people were using the current exchange of ideas and thought with interviews and discussions on each of the questions was conducted. In this study, to describe and analyze the collected data, descriptive and inferential statistics were used.

6 - Findings

This study examined the hypothesis in section 6 and the results confirm or reject them.

6-1 - the first hypothesis test:

First hypothesis: the relationship between income customers, and there is a significant deposit in the bank. H_0. Income customers in the bank and deposit a significant relationship between No.

H_1. Income customers in the bank and deposit a significant relationship between There.

Since the Pearson correlation coefficient close to one of the 878 / 0 is the hypothesis H_0 is rejected and H_1 is acceptable to the customer and deposit the money in the bank there is a significant relationship. The higher the income customers are more willing to invest more in the bank are found.

7737

6-2 - test the second hypothesis:

Second hypothesis: The service offers quick and convenient services to their customers on deposit in the bank there is a significant relationship.

H_0. The service offers quick and convenient services to customers with a deposit by the customer, there is no significant relationship.

H_1. The service offers quick and convenient services to customers with a deposit by the customer, there is a significant relationship.

Since the H_0 t greater than t table, the 645 / 1 is H_0 is rejected and is therefore against the H_1 is accepted. Among the services offered fast and convenient services to their customers on deposit there is a significant relationship.

6-3 - test the third hypothesis:

Third hypothesis: the diversity of their customer service and increase awareness and resources to attract customers in the bank there is a significant relationship.

H_0. The diversity of their customer service and increase awareness and resources to attract customers, there is no significant relationship.

H_1. The diversity of their customer service and increase awareness and resources to attract customers, there is a significant relationship.

Considering the t H_0 (674/17 = H_0) of the t 645 / 1 = t is larger than the assumed H_0 is rejected and it is against H_1 is accepted. Among the variety of services and increase their knowledge of customers and resources to attract customers, there is a significant relationship.

6-4 - the fourth hypothesis test:

The fourth hypothesis: the use of advertising to attract customers in the bank there is a significant relationship.

H_0. Advertising to attract customers with a significant association between the use of operating there.

H_1. Advertising to attract customers with a significant association between the use of operating there. Considering the t H_0 (844/26 = H_0) obtained from the t table 645 / 1 = t is larger than H_0 is rejected and it is against H_1 is accepted. The operating result of advertising to attract customers with a significant relationship exists.

6-5 - test the fifth hypothesis:

The fifth hypothesis: the acceleration in the transfer of facilities and resources to attract customers in the customer's bank there is a significant relationship.

H_0. Accelerate the transfer of facilities and resources to attract customers with a customer, there is no significant relationship.

H_1. Accelerate the transfer of facilities and resources to attract customers with a customer, there is a significant relationship.

Considering that the t H_0 (082/24 = H_0) larger than the table t 645 / 1 = t is the result of the rejection of H_0 and H_1 is the front that indicates there was a significant correlation accelerate the transfer of facilities and resources to attract customers with a customer.

7 - Conclusion

The major objective of this study to investigate the effect some of the marketing mix to attract customers in the bank Kermanshah province is considering the hypothesis of a primary and 5 secondary hypothesis was proposed:

The results of the test the first hypothesis, significant relationship with the customers deposit money in the bank concluded that even when there is more income customers are more likely to deposit in the institution's management and employees of the institution in high-income customers and the implementation plans and providing more benefits such as increased customer deposits and low-cost facilities in order to raise the effective income customers to attract more resources.

According to the analysis and test the second hypothesis, results showed a significant relationship between early and offer appropriate services to customers with a deposit by the customer can say that with the increasing competition between banks and financial institutions and bank credit management and employees should endeavor Shortening the time required to perform additional services to our customers and do much to increase the number of staff in some branches are more crowded and the efforts to accelerate the delivery of services possible, in some service delivery and the payment of electricity and water bills ... Payment facilities for customers and the customer's physical presence is reduced.

Test the hypothesis that the diversity of their customer service and increasing the knowledge and resources to attract customers, there is a significant relationship. The bank also offers banking services to banks as possible, which is now mostly done by the Institute of banking services that will lead to higher customer deposit and pay particular variety of facilities and reduce the profits of the important that bank customers should also consider adopting appropriate policies to various facilities to the customers to pay for the needs of their customers are not forced to stop working with the Institute.

7738

The fourth hypothesis test result indicates a significant relationship between the advertising and attracting customers, the banks can diversify and expand their services in terms of publicity and advertising and television messages and Installation of banners on various sites that will attract more customers. Some customers because of the amount, status and pay ... Institutions are not aware that this is due to higher deposit customers are in the institution.

The fifth hypothesis test result indicates a strong significant correlation between the acceleration in the transfer of facilities and resources to attract customers with a customer.

8 - Suggestions

Analysis assumptions and conclusions from this study indicate that the hypothesis we conclude that there is a significant positive relationship to advance the goals of the bank in connection with the study offers the following suggestions.

1. Agency managers and policymakers with proposals such as increasing profits, deposits and facilities offered to customers in high-income customers have contributed so cheap that they can attract more resources to be added to the deposit institution.
2. Possible time to be in short time and with increasing number of customer service counter at any branch of service by the staff and expertise to be able to offer faster service to customers.
3. Institutions such as banks can provide complete management services for clients in institutions such as banks, which makes this the highest and most customers refer to the institution.
4. The Institute's broader campaign to engage in a variety of services and more aware of the actual and potential customers. Such as advertising and television advertising messages, banners installed at various sites to attract more customers because many customers will benefit from the variety of deposits and payments of services and facilities are not adequately informed by the institution.
5. Given the need for major facilities to receive the most important target customers in the deposit is recommended in the Institute's facilities as soon as possible and type of facilities and benefits for our customers clear and in this way facilities to the customers smoother hopefully more to do with the deposit and in collaboration with the Institute.
6. Considering that one of the important goals in the bank account by bank transfer is the use of the facilities in question concerning the account to 55% of respondents consider the facilities had received the account in the bank Along with banks and other financial institutions and credit facilities to customers in a variety of institutions can be absorbed more resources.

REFERENCES

[1]   industries, A. (1384), "principles of marketing and market management," the question of publication, second edition.

[2]   Mason, R. B, (2007) *a Marketing Mix Model for a Complex and Turbulent.*

[3]   Lavak Christopher (1382), "Marketing of Services", translated TajzadehArtaxerxes, the publishing, printing.

[4]   Mnty, H., trustee, A., K. mastication "Marketing Plan", published by term.

[5]   Venus referee, the rosta of Ahmad, Abdul Hamid Ebrahimi (1386). "Marketing management" of the publisher.

[6]   Holm, O. (2006) *Integerated Marketing Communication: From Tactics to Strategy Corporate Communication.* An International Journal, Vol.11, No 1.

[7]   andRmstranggry Philip Cutler (2000), "Principles of Marketing" translation Parsayyan A. (1383), published Birthdays.

[8]   Alvdary, Hassan. (1387). "Marketing and market management" (Fifth Edition). Tehran: Payam Noor University Press.

[9]   Belch, George E. & Belch, Michael A. (2001) *Advertising And Promotion: An Integrated Marketing Communication Perspective,* 5 Th Ed, New *Delhi:* Tata McGraw-Hill Publishing Company Limited.

[10] Frank, E. (1994) *Marketing HRD: An Overview.* Journal of European Industrial Training, Vol.18, No.8, 4-9.

[11] Chisnall. Peter M, (1992) *Marketing Research.* (4 th Ed) McGraw Hill.

[12] Mercer. David, (1996) *Marketing* (2 nd ed) USA: Black well.

[13] Cohen.William (1998) *Marketing Managemen.* (2 nd ed), Macmillan publishing *co.*

7739

[14] Baker. Michael J, (1998) *the Marketing Manual.* (1 st ed), The Chartered Instituteb of Marketing Plant a Tree.

[15] Goharian, Mohammed Ibrahim (1374) "Management of non-oil exports", Tehran, Institute of Business Research.

[16] Ranjbariyan B. (1378), "Marketing Management" market, the publication of the Institute of Business Research.

[17] Hosseini, MirzaHasan (1384) "International Marketing", Tehran: Payam Noor University.

18 Alvadr, H. (1383), "Marketing and market management," Tehran: Payam Noor University.

[19] Iranian Events, GH (1386) "The most important factor in the marketing mix factors used to replace carpet with carpet in Tehran." Tehran: MS Thesis, University of Science and Research Branch.

[20] Arto, A., & Sample, J. (2005, fall) *Everybody's Selling Something: An Introductory Guide to Marketing Human Resource Development Programs.* Anne M. Arto.

[21] BolurianTehrani M. (1376), "Marketing Management" market, commercial printing and publishing.

[22] Pickton. David & Broderick. Amanda (2001) *Integrated Marketing Communication.* (1 st ed). Barcelona: Financial Times / Prentice Hall.

[23] Murrar. John, (1995) *Success in Advertising and promotion.* (1 st ed), Don Milner.

[24] HaKansson, H., &Waluszewski, A. (2005) *Developing New Understanding of Market: Reinterpreting the 4ps.* Journal of Business & Industrial Marketing.

[25] Harrel.Gilbert D & Frazier. Gary L (1999) *Marketing connecting with customer.* (1 st ed). USA: Prentice Hall Inc.

[26] Mohammadian Mahmoud (1382), "Advertising Management", Sayhnma Publishing, Printing.

[27] Newson. Doug &Vanslyke Turk. Judy &Kruckerburg. Dean (2000) *Public relation.* (7 th ed). USA: wada worth.

[28] E. Pourhassan (1376) "International Marketing Management", Open University Press.

[29] S., Jamshid (1385), "Relationship marketing mix and consumer behavior", Journal of prudence, No. 176, pp. 64-59.

[30] Drgy, P. (1384) "Designing the marketing mix", Journal of prudence, No. 161, pp. 56-54.

[31] KhodadadHosseini, H., Rezvani, Mehran (1388) "marketing mix modeling phase (case study SntBaty personal vehicles", Journal of Business Research, No. 51, Summer 1388, 277-241.

[32] Ivy, J. (2008) *a new higher education marketing mix: the 7ps for MBA marketing.* International Journal of educational management, Vol.22, No.4.

J. Basic. Appl. Sci. Res., 2(3)2694-2700, 2012

© 2012, TextRoad Publication

ISSN 2090-4304
**Journal of Basic and Applied
Scientific Research**

www.textroad.com

The Study of the Relationship between Organizational Trust and Organization Creativity (Case Study in Purge National Company and Distribution of Petroleum products in Kermanshah – Iran)

Hossein khanifar[1],Kamran Nazari[2], Mostafa Emami[3], Hoseinali Soltani

[1] Teacher of Tehran University

[2] Department of Business Management, Payam Noor University, Iran

[3] Young Researchers Club, South Tehran Branch, Islamic Azad University, Tehran, Iran.

ABSTRACT

Purpose: The purpose of this study is the review of the relationship between organizational trust and organization creativity in the national company of refining and distribution of the oil production in Kermanshah – Iran. **Methods and materials**: this research is on the basis of the descriptive type, and the questionnaires are used in it. Aloonen, et al., (2008). Questionnaires are used for organizational trust and Randseep (1979) is used for organizational creativity, because Alpha in both of them is over 0.7 both of them had necessary lasting.

Capacity of statistical society consist of 300 employee of the national company on the basis of the class accidental sampling among them, some of them have selected as a statistical sample and finally, 156 questioner have collected. **Finding and results**: kolmogroph – smineroph test was used for the determining of the normality collected data, and to confirm the results of it. Hypothesis of the research were put in test container with spearman conjunction test. Results show meaning full and positive conjunction between trust and creativity. That is as trust of employees about their organization, in creases, they should show much creativity.

The result shows multiple linear regressions. That two various variance with organizational trust and vertical trust, have relationship with creativity dependant variance. Organizational trust with 78% coefficient had most share to determine of the various variance of creativity.

KEYWORDS: organizational trust, creativity- lateral trust, vertical trust, institutional trust.

INTRODUCTION

In 21 century, the secret of the survival of the human society should search in their creativity. In this time, societies will be able joint to the future that see creative think and don't fear from creativity. In the future word, growing people and their society is accordance with their creativity and in the information age, people have future who have creativity. Present thing about organization Doesn't solve this problem, and environmental condition had been complex and dynamic and non-trust that organization can not guarantee their long-life , without creativity . creativity is a reason for growing of organization, improving the productivity increasing in quality of production and services , success in matches development in employee motivation and their job satisfying, decreasing in cost, decreasing organization bureaucracy (Bowen, 2004)
Most of articles about creativity are began with general words that companies should creative if one company not be efficacy in the use of new ideas, destroy its resources and finally it defeats. In turn, each company create effective creative

process, it will attain social advantages that will be achieve through group action and employee motivation companies that one active in national and local economy and don't have comparison experience in the international level, can be successful with traditional ways. (McAdam & McClelland, 2002: 86) But world economy has many effects on the world, companies for their remaining don't option, except, finding same direction with management of new models as cross-trust culture.(Gibson, 2007;58) This idea, that trust is potential and main factor that lead to improving in organizational activity for acceptation of society successfully, effective group action –long- lasting aim for minimizing risks and operational costs. (Lamsa & Pucetaite, 2006: 130) More, trust provide, society discipline is effective in improving life quality. (Pucetaite & Lamsa, 2008: 325) In turn, costs of low trust is high, because of the lake of the willing to cooperation of employees, doing risk for unsuitable behaviors low quality of work, so low trust will be lost comparisons in the world market.

Organization trust:

Management on the basis of the trust is new expression of old ideas, that is certain in today relations and using of the ways can affect individual and organizational results. Management with trust is the technique that people use it in their relations. But not as behavioral technique that could teach it. Trust is the concept psychology, society, economy, history science. (Ratnasingham, 1998:313) It has been conceptualized over 40 years by researcher. For example, Deutsch (1958),

*Corresponding Author: Kamran Nazari, Department of Business Management, Payam Noor University, Iran. Email:kamranno57@yahoo.co

has described trust through expectations. Gabarro (1978), knows trust as open areas. Between 2 groups and has described as: trust predicts other behavior through what one expects individual action correctly and what one trust the other don't act wrongly (Smith & Birney, 2005: 473)

However, there isn't formal description in this field, instance, Barber (1983) define that the concept of the trust is similar. So, Lewis and Weigert, define confused concept in trust. (Ramo, 2004:762). Indeed trust is complex concept with different aspects. Although there are some problems in expressing of the trust concept, compressive analysis of this study shows some various ideas. (Smith & Birney, 2005: 473)

Some researchers believe that the trust is confidence of concurring events without the existence of some obligatory reasons oxford might describes as an idea or believe that person might rely on it. Other description that offers by Shaw (1997), is, the trust is a belief that we rely on it and sates-your expectations. These expectations are dependent of our determine of other duties for satisfying our need. (Yee & Yeung, 2002:138).

In the summary, the trust means beliefs that people have in the future behavior of other group. As one group has much believed, the other one acts his complaints. The trust in organizing of the new organization that was on the basis of the arbitrary has increased, improving and progressing of the trust might be over casting because, establishing of person relations friendly is a time – consuming job. More, lack of the trust contuses cooperation efforts (Lee, 2004: 625). In turn, organizations that have high level of the trust, can enjoy of cooperation efforts that lead to decreasing of operation cost in process. But organizations that have low trust, their strategic options are limited. there are wild plow in the trust , literature , (Ratnasingham, 1998,314) However , face to the trust is separate : first , he trust in cross – organization that , that , is as a phenomenon in organizations between employees and managers , that we focus on ham in this study , second trust between organizations , that is one phenomenon across – organizations and third , one , trust between organizations and their costumer . Third is expressed as a concept. (Dietz and Hartog, 2006: 557-558)

Butler and Cantrell (1984), know, integrity, competence, consistency, loyalty, Openness as key element. (Robbins, 2003: 337).Mayer, et al., (1995) believe that effective factors that that effect on trust levels consist of on ability – benevolence and competence. Other researchers have determined similar factors that are trust base. Cook and Wall (1980) described creativity, ability as a main factors and Liberman (1981) knows motive as a main factor.

Dietz and Hartog (2006) know competence and ability in a prediction as main factors that make trust.

Benevolence: Benevolence means friendly motives and amount of kind\ness of the other. Integrity refuses to the other ability that they can do their duty.

Competence: Competence consists of imitation (following) of some principle that accepted by the other group.

Ability of anticipation: Ability of anticipation is related to consistency in behavior so trust has multiple aspect concept. (Dietz and Hartog, 2006: 560)

Ellonen et al.,(2008) offer other classifying of the organizational trust ,they divide it in ,as interpersonal trust and impersonal. in this study both of them are reviewed. (Ellonen, 2008: 162). Impersonal trust can divide in2 aspect later trust that is related to trust between employees and vertical trust that refers to the trust between employees and their bosses. Trust is on the base of competence, benevolence or reliability. Trust between employees, and trust between teams in organization is one of the most important elements that prepare long – life of the organization(Bao, et al, 2004, 415) . Tan and Tan(2000) know trust to bosses as a willing of employee to vulnerability , toward boss behaviors that his action isn't in control . (Tan & Tan, 2000: 243) . In this study impersonal trust organization is named as institutional trust. Trust impersonal in the organization level hasn't studied widely, exception some cases such as mc McCauley and Kuhnret (1992) , Atkinson and Butcher(2003) , Costigan et al.(1998). For example in human resources, juctice , the justice is related to employees attitudes directly. Such as obligation to the organization. Institutional trust can determine as an element trust to strategy and vision of the organization, its business merit, process and construction (Ellonen et al. 2008, 161-162). Tan and Tan (2000) introduced trust to organization,

As determining of organizations that understands by employee. In fact, trust to organization is employee trust that means the organization behavior that are advantageous or don't have any harmful behavior. (Tan & Tan, 2000, 243) Institutional trust means that person believes that are necessary to prepare successful efforts and are determined as two various type. Situational normality and structural assurance. in first one all things have normal position and all of them are in the correct position . so situational normality means that success is attained because of the normality of situation on the other hand, assurance of constructs means that success is because of Con tracts and assurance .so, institutional trust indicates action and process of the organization that hasn't been personal for organization element such as technology and business integrity, strategy and human resource principle and relations. (McKnight et al. 1998, 478-479)

Organization creativity:

Study about creativity and its elements were begun by social science of one century but main motive of study was offered by Gilford in 1950.Gilford knew that creativity has some meaning with different thinning. Creativity in the point of view of psychology is determined new ideas by making evidence from know resource. Papilla knows creativity as ability in watching in a new ideas and face to face problems that haven't an ability of deterring of their existence.(Kueen, 1997; 137)

2695

Amabile (1976) described creativity as making combining of ideas of persons or groups in the new method " Bozerman", knows it as cognitive process from mentioned disable , we conclude that in creativity concept will be exist public but slow agreement (Sakie,2002).
Most important description is as below:
"Creativity is balance, repeat in production, difficult happiness.
Creativity is looking as possible as deeper, and is be leave from closed doors and is unifying with future."(Zherzh M-Parnis, 1963)
There is same factors in all of descriptions of creativity and is access to new combining of existing element , so creativity include existing mechanism one repletion and new process or change in a characteristic , such as shape , color , or size.(Van fanzhh, 1966).
rapid growing of economical agencies, rapid changes and environmental ambiguity and other problems lead to highest importance of the organizational creativity-creativity could be the reason of dynamic and moving of organizations and elements that, is an effective factor in economical action, because of acceleration of technical changes and world competence, ability of organization in vesting and offering of new product has vital effete on long- time action organization.(Momfared, 2000)
Malag a says that although various research's on creativity , aspects such as creativity of process, ability of person creativity and creative environment are important in the all of these researches- First creativity includes process as below:
1: making construct, cognition and description of the
problem. 2: preparing and attaining of data related to
problem 3: overviewing and giving idea.
Second, all person have normal level of inventive ability.Some factors affect this ability. These factors are: biology, personality, motive and training. However The factor such as biology doesn't have any effect .third , environment as a place that shapes creativity , Effects creativity action. He suggested 3 main principle include, ideas, be new and possibility of reviewing of creativity action.(Malaga, 2003;139)

Bear has mentioned learning method, creative thinking, motive and risk, supporting environment for creativity action. Researchers offer various processes in the field of creative solving. Values are the famous one that has expressed creative steps he mentioned 4 steps include (Valas, 1999:17):

Preparing:

in this step on actor or scientist should be familiar with his action from various aspects preparing , study , collecting of information and so on are the introduction for preparing of a creative person for getting creativity .

Hiddenness:

In this step, creative person doesn't do any action for getting of creation and doesn't think about any problem. This situation is hidden. That is person act in the mind and is a hidden.

Illumination:

In this step, subject is determined for person who attains new ideas without any think about it .

Proving:

Creative [person conclude any problem . Clegg et., al (2002) ,do wide study in American steel industry . to review that trust effected creativity or not ? they consider 2 aspects of the trust : 1: employee trust to considering idea organization 2: employee trust to share organization advantages. this research shows positive relation between trust and employee creation . Conceptualization of them is on the basis of general expectation that be heard and attaining of advantages is benefits act if employees don't trust to these expectations, they won't be creative. (Clegg et al. 2002).
 Murphy reviews the role of 3 levels of the trust on creation process. His finding indicated positive relation between small relation and medium trust. Trust doesn't have meaning full relation with creative but large trust had considerable effect on creation. (Murphy, 2002).

Research Hypothesis:

Main hypothesis of this study is there is a relation between organization trust and creativity the company of the oil productions of Iran – Kermanshah.
There is 3 sub - hypothesis in this situation .
1: there is relation between lateral trust and creativity between o:
Productions of Iran – Kermanshah Company.
2 : there is relation between vertical trust and creativity between o : productions of Iran – Kermanshah . Company.
3: there is relation between institutional trust and creativity between o : productions of Iran – Kermanshah . Company.

METHODS

 This research is on the basis of the research method , because of the determining of the organization trust aspects and its relation with employee creativity on employee in the oil production of Iran-Kermanshah company researcher is descriptive 300 person exist in statistical society on the basis of the below formula. There is 148 people in this research

$$(300)(1/96)^2(0/\ 5)(0/5)$$

$$n\square \underline{\hspace{5cm}}\square 148$$
$$(0.5)^2(300 \square 1) \square (1/96)^2(0/5)(0/5)$$

Necessary information for doing this research was collected from 2 method:

Library method: in this method, article , this and information agencies and internet resource, books are used for collecting information.

Field method: questionnaires are used and distribute, for test of creativity Randseap(1979) questionnaires are used , both of them first distribution between 30 employee. They were selected on the basis of the researchers cognition and their ideas were used after completing of the questionnaires. In this research , for describing and analysis of data descriptive statistical was used. The normality of data test using Coolmogreph - Smirnoph was used to description and analysis of data, description and understanding statistical was used. Used test in this research include, Coolmogreph and Smirnoph and Spearman unity coefficient.

Smirnoph- test:

To determine of type of used test for research hypothesis, first it should be determined normality or non- normality of data, so using conclusion of this test, we should use parametric and non- parametric test of these hypothesis.

Table (1): test Coolmogreph - Smirnoph

$H_0 : \square \square \, 0$		Normal distribution follows of observations distributions.		
$H_1 : \square \square \, 0$		Normal distribution doesn't follows of observations distributions.		
Variable	Number of sample	Test statistic	Percent of Sig	Test result
Creativity	156	0.993	0.278	Normal distribution
Organizational trust	156	0.639	0.809	Normal distribution
Lateral trust	156	0.991	0.280	Normal distribution
Vertical trust	156	0.833	0.491	Normal distribution
Organizational trust	156	0.966	0.308	Normal distribution

As you see in table (1), percent of test in 0.5 level is bellow of crisis percent so zero hypothesis that is, data normality is accepted and non-normality is rejected so Spearman unity coeffient is used for test of this hypothesis.

Hypothesis test:

Test of main hypothesis:
There is a meaningful relation between organizational trust and creativity in Kermanshah – Iran products company Statistic hypothesis of this hypothesis include:

$H_0 : \square \square \, 0$	There isn't meaning full relation between vertical trust and creativity in national company of refining oil production.
$H_1 : \square \square \, 0$	There is meaning full relation between vertical trust and creativity in national company of refining oil production.

The results of this test in 0.01 level for main hypothesis is as below:

	Trust	Creativity

Trust	Correlation coefficient Sig Number sample	1 0 156	0.881 0.000 156
Creativity	Correlation coefficient Sig Number sample	0.881 0.000 156	1 0 156

2697

Table 2 indicates that in 99 percent trust level, the percent is Sig=0.000 and blew of 0.01, as result , zero is rejected. That is, there is meaningful relation between organization trust and creativity. Spearman unity coefficient between 2 variance is 0.881 that shows positive relationship between them.

That of first sub hypothesis:

There is meaningful relation between lateral trust and creativity in national company of distribution of the oil product. Statistical hypothesis of this hypothesis is as bellow:

$H_0 : \mathcal{L}\square\ 0$	There isn't meaning full relation between lateral trust and creativity in national company of refining oil production
$H_1 : \mathcal{L}\square\ 0$	There isn't meaning full relation between vertical trust and creativity in national company of refining oil production

The results of this test of Spearman in 0.01 level is as be in 0.99% trust, the Sig= 0.000 and below 0.01, as a result, zero hypothesis is rejected and we accept following hypothesis:
There is certain relation between lateral trust and national company. Spearman correlation coefficient between 2 variance 52% that indicates positive relation.

Test of second sup-hypothesis:

There is a meaning full relation between vertical trust and creativity in the national company. Statistical hypothesis **include:**

$H_0 : \mathcal{L}\square\ 0$	There isn't meaning full relation between vertical trust and creativity in national company of refining oil production
$H_1 : \mathcal{L}\square\ 0$	There isn't meaning full relation between vertical trust and creativity in national company of refining oil production

The results of this test is as below:
In 99% level of this trust the percent of Sig= 0.000 is below 0.01. as a result, zero hypothesis is rejection , that is relation between vertical trust and creativity.
Spearman correlation between 2 variance is 0.659 that is indicates positive relation between them.

Test of third sub-hypothesis:

There is a meaning full relation between organizational trust and creativity in the national company. Statistical hypothesis is as below:

$H_0 : \mathcal{L}\square\ 0$	There isn't meaning full relation between organizational trust and creativity in national company of refining oil production

$H : \mathcal{L}\Box\ 0$ [1]	There isn't meaning full relation between organizational trust and creativity in national company of refining oil production

Result of the test of Spearman hypothesis in 0.01 level is as below:
In 99% trust level , percent of Sig=0.000 is below 0.01 and zero hypothesis is rejected and we accept that there is a meaningful relation between organizational trust and creativity Spearman correlation coefficient between two variance is 0.626 that indicates positive relation.

RESULTS

The trust is a mainly organization for successions of the organization – results indicate that low level of the trust caused increasing of stress and decreasing of efficiency , lack of creativity on the other hand , high level of the trust caused increasing of employee motivation , decreasing in absence , in creasing creativity of organization . making trust is begun with a culture based on same values . making trust needs assurance toward making relation between individuals based on openness of relation , and comprehension on the other hand creating is necessity of succession , and accordance of organization with environmental condition . so in this study , spearman unity test was used for reviewing of the relation between organizational trust and organizational creativity . The results of this test is meaning full in 0/99 level .
The results indicates positive and meaning full relation between organization trust and employees creativity that proves the result of Aloonen study . so
Suggestions and problems expresses for increasing of organizational trust as bellow:

1: increase of employees trust capacity through certain system can make trust capacity in the person.
2: improve of employee confidence, for this, the company can improve finding employee system.
3: making training periods to improve employee skills in their special field.

4: making same aim between employee so that can help each other
5: alternation to the same values in the organization
6: managers should prove, they try to their employee advantages they prefer group advantages on special individual advantages.
7: managers should show, they have enough ability in their special field.
8: managers should like their relations with employees and try to improve of these relations. They should ask employee need that employee can trust to them.

REFERENCES

Armestrung, Mickel,(2006) "management of human resource proactivity" translation of Sohrabi Abolfazl, Qum.

Bao, G.M., Yang, Z.R., Xie, Z.S. and Zhou, M.J.(2004), "The Dilemma of Trust and Commitment in the Construction of Innovative Team in Chinese Private Enterprises", International Engineering Management Conference.

Beir, j. (1995)," Managing Creatives" Vital Speeches of the Day,6,pp.501-506.

Bowen, Edward C.(2004), "Organizational Structure and The Creative Process. A. dissertation submitted in partial fulfillment of the requirement for the degree Doctor of Education . University of SanDiego

Clegg, C., Unsworth, K., Epitropaki O. and Parker, G.(2002), "Implicating trust in the innovation process", Journal of Occupational and Organizational Psychology, Vol. 75, December, PP. 409-422.

Connell, N.A.D and Mannion, R. (2006), "conceptualization of trust in the organisational literature", Journal of Health Organization and Management, Vol.20, No.5, PP.417-433.

Coyne, Richard (1997). "Creativity as Commonplace" Design study,18,pp.135-141

Dietz, G. (2004), "partnership and development of trust iv British workplaces", Human Resource Management Journal, Vol.14, No.1, PP.5-24.

Dietz, G. and Hartog, D.N.(2006), "Measuring trust inside organizations", Personnel Review, Vol.35, No.5, PP.557-588.

Ellonen, R., Blomqvist, K. and Puumalainen, K.(2008), "The role of Trust in organizational innovativeness", European Journal of Innovation Management, Vol.11, No.2, PP.160-181.

Gibson, Ran:(2007) " new think in changing age " translation of Ali Shirazi, organizational management industrial, Tehran.

Lamsa, A.M. and Pucetaite, R.(2006), "Development of organizational trust among employees from a contextual perspective", Business Ethics, Vol.15, No.2, PP.130-141.

Lee, H.J.(2004), "The role of competence-based trust and organizational identification in continuous improvement", Journal of Management Psychology, Vol.19, No.6, PP.623-639.

Lee, T-S., Tsai, H-J.(2005), "The effect of business operation mode on market orientation, learning orientation and innovativeness", Industrial Management & Data Systems, Vol. 105, No. 3, PP. 325-348.

Malaga, Ross(2000). " The Effect of Stimulus Modes and Associative Distance in Individual Creativity Support System" , Decision Support System , 29, pp135-141.

McAdam, R. and McClelland, J. (2002), "Individual and team-based idea generation within innovation management: organizational and research agendas", European Journal of Innovation Management, Vol. 5, No. 2, PP. 86-97.

McKnight, D.H., Cummings, L.I. and Chervany, N.I.(1998),"Initial trust formation in new organizational relationships", Academy of management Review, Vol.23, No.3, PP.473-490.

Moghimi, Sayed Mohammad: (2005), " the organization management and research performance" . Publication, Tehran.

Mumford, Michael D. (2000), "Managing Creative People", Human Resource Management Review, Vol.10, No3,pp.313-351.

Murphy, J.T. (2002), "Networks, Trust, and Innovation in Tanzania's Manufacturing Sector", World Development, Vol. 30, No. 4, PP. 591-619.

Pucetaite, R. and Lamsa, A-M. (2008), "Developing Organizational Trust Through Advancement of Employees' Work Ethic in a Post-Socialist Context", Journal of Business Ethics, No. 82, PP. 325-337.

Ramo, H. (2004),"Moments of Trust: temporal and spatial factors of trust in organizations", Journal of Management Psychology, Vol. 19, No.8, PP.760-775.

Ratnasingham, P. (1998), " The importance of trust in electronic commerce " , Electronic Networking Applications and Policy, Vol. 8, No. 4, PP. 313-321.

Robbins, S. P. (2005), "Organizational Behavior", 11th ed, Prentice Hall.

Smith, G.(2005), "How to achieve organizational trust within an accounting department", Managerial Auditing Journal, Vol.20, No.5, PP.520-523.

Smith, P.A. and Birney, L.L.(2005), "The organizational trust of elementary schools and dimensions of student bullying", International Journal of Educational Management, Vol.19, No.6, PP.469-485.

Suki Reza.(2001) "change and creativity in the organization training" , Vol 26.

Tan, H.H. and Lim, A.(2009), "Trust in coworkers and Trust in Organizations", The Journal of Psychology, Vol.143, No.1, PP.45-66.

Tan, H.H. and Tan, C.S.F.(2000), "Toward the Differentiation of Trust in Supervisor and Trust in Organization", Genetic, Social, and General Psychology Monographs, Vol. 126, No. 2, PP. 241-260.

Toorani, Heidar(2006) " Educational creativity , challenges and sloves" year 5, vol 15.

Tourence, Pall E.(1993) "Skills of creativity and methods of its test" translation of Hasanzadeh.

Walls, G(1999) "The Art of Thought" New York, Hncourt Brace.

Yee, W. and Yeung, R. (2002), "Trust building in investock farmers: an exploratory study", Nutrition & Food Science, Vol.32, No.4, PP.137-144.

The Study of the Relationship between Social Capital and Organizational Entrepreneurship (Case Study of Governmental Organizations in Kermanshah) Kamran Nazari

Department of Business Management, Payam Noor University, Kermanshah, Iran

Mostafa Emami

Department Of Economic&management, Faculty of Accounting ,Tarbiat Modares University,Iran, Tehran

Hoseinali Soltani

Department of public Management, Kermanshah Branch, Islamic Azad University, Kermanshah, Iran

Saber Sharifi

Department of Educational, Sciencesand Research Branch, Islamic Azad University, Ghaser Shiren, Iran

Shahram Gilaninia

Department of Business Management, Science and Research Branch, Islamic Azad University, Guilan, Iran

Seyyed Javad Mousavian

Department of Management, Astara Branch, Islamic Azad University, Astara, Iran

Abstract

Purpose: the main purpose of this project is scrutiny of the relationship between social capital and organizational entrepreneurship at Kermanshah governmental organization.**Materials and styles:** This research is based on research styles and it's type of descriptive and brunch of surveying. The implements for collection of social capital reporters questionnaire of Mallaie social capital (1380) that have constituted from 31 questions, read attentively social capital and its all aspects and for evaluation of organization of organizational entrepreneurship questionnaire of 22 question of Rabinsand Kotler(1996) entrepreneurship has been utilized. Perpetuity of social capital questionnaireis 0/88 and perpetuity of organizational entrepreneurship questionnaire is 0/79.becauseKoronbakh'salfa of both of questionnaires are over 0/7 thus, both of questionnaires had been embodied necessitous perpetuity. The considered statistic social content is, 978 persons of Kermanshah governmental organization employers.   Based on proportional classificatory of sampling style between them, 146 people have chosen as statistical samples. **Findings and result:** in order to specification of attained datum normality, Colomoro. Esmirnoph examination has been being utilized. And the conclusion of examination confirmed the normality of datum. The conclusions signifying direct and positive relationship between social capital and organizational entrepreneurship. It means that, in investigated society what so ever social capital is increased the tendency of organizational entrepreneurship will increase.

Key Words: Capital, Social Capital, Entrepreneurship, Organizational Entrepreneurship
Introduction:

Nowadays, social capital is innovative concept that It's more significant than Human and physical capital. Nowadays in sociology is economic and also in the management, the concept of social capital has enormously utilized. The concept of social capital implies joining and relations of members of one network as valuable source. That bring about the realization of purposes with creation of reciprocal confidence and Norms in the absence of social capital, other capitals will lose their efficacy. And also bring about harden pace ways of economic and cultural development. Social capital not only in the massive management bus also in organizational management, it will be able to create the new reorganization from social _ economical systems and helps managers to guide their system. Appropriately One the most important aspect of social capital concept.is this concept encompass different aspects. This reason is, social capital has plenty of power and capacity for accomplishment of enormous range of works. (Nahapiet and Ghoshal, p 248:1998) Motivation gives force and direction to behavior and people will mobilize to achieve its goals. (Faghirpour,Razaz Razaghi,Gilaninia&et al, 2011)

768

Institute of Interdisciplinary Business Research

In the current Age that environment changes is one of the most important challenges , encountering all organization appropriate profiting from peoples skills and abilities in order to compilation frames or structures and patterns of new thinking , real requirement cognizance of clientele and customers and successive improvement of services and productive out puts , social capital has excessively become significant.   Nowadays, one of the basis remedy in order to contrast with Threats of developed country is emphasis on human elements as the most important endless divine sources. Organization for being efficacious, need foresightful persons, that to know what kind of works must be done, that they easily communicate with those who are wakeful of changings and prepare themselves and their organization for encountering with prospective challenges. between the human who are named entrepreneur have particularly received attention , importance and necessity of entrepreneur presence in different section of industry , enterprise and services , weather in exclusive section , cooperative governmental organization weather profit _ making or nonprofit _ making have distinguished seriously in most of developed country and developing country different senders of researches and studies of entrepreneurship have been created and also with increasing of cognizance in comparison with entrepreneurs and entrepreneurship and its education to present generation and subsequent generation and even employees of big organization try to create entrepreneurship mood in the organization and with training of creative and entrepreneur managers and absorbent and utilization of them in in the organization , creation of providing situation of creative and entrepreneur organization the most important entrepreneurship achievement for developing of country is creation of , employment , welfare , wealth and cognition of appropriate opportunities , and even somebody believes that entrepreneurs are be able to bring about exploitation in organization as a mechanism. In this way , nowadays , developed countries have held their companies in a perfect and dynamic situation from a new vertex in addition to that it's investigation and training of special human that is playing role and cause of creation of situation for advancements.

Social capital:

The discussion of social capital of 1916 in an essay, has mentioned by Hony Fan from western Verginia for the first time. Never the less, its importance of social researches till 1960 has utilized by John Kob in urbanization programs that had been neglected. In 1970, this theory was interred to arena of economy; social asset is a concept between field that is utilizable in sociology, economic, Psychology and other social frameworks. (Bazergan, 1994)

Communication is the basic and the most important need for human beings (Rezvani,Gilaninia , Mousavian, 2011). The idea of social assed is summarized in word of communications that the social members will be able to contact and cooperate to gather, and by this way they'll achieve sth that they'll never get them singly or they'll catch them with too many problems.

The human race is linked with each other with collection of huge networks and they want to have common relationship with other members of network with developing of them, kind of wealthy was being formed that we have been considered it as wealthy. As money more standpoint are existence between the people we will have been had more abundant social asset (Rahmanpour, p79, 2003). About the importance necessity of social asset in organization we can say that in the past social asset wasn't a necessity appropriation for organization. but , currently , speeding changings of information and education , necessary requirements for creativity , progressive learning and development , changing toward planning of organizational structure and close relationship between customer's organizations and networks.

A) Structure dimension

Structure dimension consists of the rate of connection between peoples. The general pattern communication that is visible in the entire institute is representative of structure's dimension of social invest. This concept is valuable in three branches networks connection.

B) Communicational dimension:

Creating relationship by the networks is one of the main elements of the social investment. The main aspects of these dimensions are such as confidence, requirement, expectations, and identification.

769

C) A knowledge dimension:

It relates to the rate of that personnel in the social networks that they have similar visual in that field. According to Nahapit&Goshal in 1998 to sides understanding between employees with a union language by changing alike stories that they are the more important features in this part.

Organizational entrepreneurship

Institute of Interdisciplinary Business Research

This term in 1985 by GifordPienkat by mixing to terms Entrepreneur &IntracorPovate was invent and he tried to present some ways to create in inter institutional.

Many companies know knowledge as wealth (Gilaninia,Ganjinia & et al, 2011). Nowadays many of companies have found out the necessary of entrepreneurship. In fact this change in the strategy in answering to three needs that has been exposed on companies.

–Increasing new competitors

- Creation sense of unconfidenceness to the methods of traditional management
in the companies.

– Extrunce the best forces of compunise and their attempt to independent entrepreneurship (Ahmadpurdoryani 1961 – 2004)

Totally quickly development of knowledge and technology , changing of process of demographics and being affective of asseta of markets and managers with entrepreneurship's phenomena has caused tendency to entrepreneurship in strategy of companies extremely is emphasized. (Kuratko&Hodgetts, 1989).

Through processentrepreneurshipobservation knowledge with idea of entrepreneurship is turn to true. The process of entrepreneurship includes education and boost mood of entrepreneurship, tools of ideas. Forming teamof entrepreneurship .creation balance between members of tem, providing financial resources and gain agreement for training and advance of modern ideas. Process of organizational entrepreneurship , includes steps of followings. production of idea , executive idea un gained exploration

First step: forming an idea team

A creative person or entrepreneurship must be between some idea which may get in his mind in the same time. He selects the idea. The idea which is useful for market,company. Then a descriptive short text is about idea is competed that is called design of idea.(Hadizadeh and Rahimi, p89, 2005) Idea is given to the team for more investigation. The important note that must be created in the idea adaption of idea with present resources of organization for producing and new services .this problem is shown in the form.(Pardakhtchi and shafizadeh, p98, 2006)

Second step. Executive idea

If there is a need to investigation andwith need ofattachof opinions and recommendations, inventor team is entered with goal of gaining guarantee of idea. **Third step: gaining and exploitation**

If Guarantee or supportive is found, it turns into a formal projectofcompany. **The**

Goals of research:

In this research according to topic of social asset and it's relation with organizational entrepreneurship is followed the goal.

Main Goal:

Determine relation between social asset and organizational entrepreneurship is in stated organizations in Kermanshah. According to main goal of research, this goal is mentioned.

1-determine relation between social asset and production of idea in state organization in Kermanshah.

2-determine relation between social asset and executive in organization

3-determine relation between social asset and exploitation and gain of idea in the organization in Kermanshah

Hypothesis of research:

according to goals of exploitation, hypothesis , in the frame work of total or special hypothesis upon on relation between base indexes of social asset and processes of entrepreneurship is followed by this –

770

The main hypothesis of research:

Between social asset and organizational entrepreneurship in the state organizations in Kermanshah, there is significant relation.

The special hypothesis of research:

Between social asset and production of idea in the state organization, there is a significant relation. There is a significant relation between social asset and exploitation and gain of idea in the state organizations in Kermanshah. **Method of Research:**

Since that in this research it is verified to tangible and systematic description of social asset and it is deal to organizational entrepreneurship in the state organization in Kermanshah. It is analyzed this condition of

771

these two component on noticed society , so this survey is a cording of gathering data's in branch of descriptive measurement research. The members of statistic at community contain 978 workers of mentioned organization. Sampling method comparative classification method, volume sampling was used in the Morgan's form 1460.

The necessary information is gathered which followed their two methods.

LibraryMethod: it is used for gathering information which is relevant to subject literature and background of research of books and thesis's , data base and internet resources.

square method: in this mention , it has been used tools such as consul – interview with reports about design of questioner and analysis of them. In the present research , the main tool of research is questioner , which is one of the most current tools of research and is a direct method to gain data's of research for evaluation of variable it has been used two sorts of questionaries' , the questioner of social asset reporters (1380) which is contained 31 questions ,(kotler and Rabins, P160, 2001) that deals to social asset, the other one is 22 questions Righer's entrepreneurship which deals to investigate to situation of werleers entrepreneurship .for describing gathered data analyzing . it is used descriptive statistical , the tests which are used in this research include Colmograph's test.

Colmograph _ Smironoph's test:

In order to determine the sort of test for using to phenomenas research , at first we should investigate being normal or unmoral of which relate to phenomenas , then by using of outcome of this test we use the methods of parametric statistic for test of hypothesizes

	$H_0 : p=0$	Distribution of observation follows of normal observation		
	$H_1 : P=0$	Distribution of observation don't follows of normal observation		
Outcome of test	Quantity Sig	Statistic of test	The number of sample	Variable
normal distribution	0/378	0/993	146	Social asset
normal distribution	0/ 809	0/639	146	Organizational entrepreneurship
normal distribution	0/280	0/991	146	Production of idea
normal distribution	0/491	0/833	146	Executive of idea
normal distribution	0/308	0/966	146	Exploitation and gain of idea

Table (1) Colmograph _Ismironoph's test

As you notice in the table (1) the quality of statistic test in the level of 0/5 less than crisis quantity .therefore Zero phenomenon being normal of data's . Acceptation and phenomena that dominate not being normal .therefore it is used test of index correlation of Spearman for being normal of data's. **Findings of research and outcome:**

The most important achievement of entrepreneurship for developing country is creation of employment .welfare, wealth and cognition suitable opportunities, and even some believe that entrepreneurship can be a mechanism which causes increasing exploitation in organizations. Today developed countries in the new aspect have held it's own companies in a quiet variable dynamic environment. In additional that exploration and training certain human that is playing role and causes of creation situation of success. "shompiter" believes that entrepreneurship is the main stimulus power in the economic development while japer owns it's progress because of some innovator and social worker after the world war. Sheita social working because of his believe and having self-confidence , innovating and he was able to research to the management stay (level) of one of the most successful industries in japer via working in Vietnam and also having have working in cement companies . so it's confessed that building and society improvement relay on social working endeavor and attempt of the people and managers , nowadays most of the companyin fact , such a change in the trends strategy , is in response of three necessities that has been imposed of companies :

1-Quick increasing in new opponents

2-Distrusting in the traditional management methods in companies

3-dismissing the best work forces from the companies and begin to put them to work into independent social working on the whole, progressing in the fast knowledge and technology.(Kuratko&Hodgetts, 1989).

changing in the precidares of demographic trends, the operative existence of the investment markets and the familiarity of the managers with the social working phenomenon have caused to placed highly emphasis in

772

the trends to social working in the companies strategies. According to social capital admires , it seems while these two concepts emphasizes associating and communicating of people in the companies , it's necessary to examine the level of social of company social working influencing from the level of social capital in the company the existence of social capital can also help in producing and operating and field operating of the ideas. Social capital increases the process of the company social working, because that shares in the firm abilities of valuating in the form of innovating by facilitating the associating and resources compound in the company.(Blanke and Fargment, P30, 2008)

According what mentioned above and the importance of social capital, the researcher determinedness in this project to study the relationship between the company social working through studying social capital in the governmental companies of Kermanshah city. According to the purpose of the research Y one important theory and three special theory were studied that their results are according to the below :

Project discoveries relating to main theory:

There is a meaningful relation between the social capital and company social working the Kermanshah city governmental companies

Using Spearman correlation coefficient between the social capital and company's social working in the Kermanshah city governmental companies it gained 0/373 , and the relating between these two variables is meaningful and the level of the correlation coefficient shows the move the amount of capital (investment) strong the more the trends towards company's social working would be increased findings based on this project , the studding results of Blanke and Fargment, (2008) emphasis on relating between the social capital and producing the ideas and Antonice and Porden in the field of relation and the social capital interacting using operating and field operation , this conclusion also coordinates with the findings resulted by Gerio (2005) , Kanson (2008) studings , based on the relation between the social capital and company social working.

Project findings related to the first side theory:

 the first project side theory specifies to the relation between producing the ideas and social capital , the first side theory verifies as this way that there is a meaningful relation between producing the ideas and social capital , this theory would be analyzed with the Sperman correlation examination , and it was resulted that producing the ideas has got a straight and meaningful relation with social capital in the 1% meaningful level and counting the correlation coefficient 0/375 so it could conclude that the move the company moves towards the progress and improving of the social capital the producing of idea will be facilitate and could be moved toward it's progress.

Project findings related to the second side theory:

The second adjunct theory of research dedicate to connection between perform of idea and social fund. Though, the second adjunct theory with this way cordificationed that there is meaning full connection between social fund and perform of idea.

To accept or reject idea , proved data's , the perform of the idea and social fund experimented and analyzed by " the Sperman's collection examination" and result showed that perform of idea in meaningful level by 1% and with count of collection factor by 0/348 has direct ad meaningful communication with social fund. So, we can take this result that for do the best of idea that one of the important stage of employ's structure , that must be improve by the social fund in the office.

The research of the third adjunct theory:

The third adjunct theory dedicate to connection between exploitation of idea and social fund. Though, the third adjunct theory with this way codification that there is meaningful connection between exploitation of idea and social fund. This theory experimented and analyzed by the Sperman's collection examinations, that the exploitation with 5% and with count of collection facto with 0/314 have direct and meaningful communication with social fund. We take result that by having well found social fund will have more exploitation from better ideas in the organization.

Any organization that has good social fund with importance upon exploitation would cause produce new ideas. According to the goals of research and proved researches by experts several suggestions have said:

1-Persude and establishment of the expertism and professional convention that take place with participation of experts that can increase the social fund in organizations

2-Educate clerks : one of the important condition that exist in organization for provide social fund is educational process pass the general education , specially pass communication particular class can take good role in provide the social fund.

3-Try to provide the phicelogical and securities of the personals from organize until according to respect to their social needs then could progress.

4-Use to process that not only don't attention to experiment but also focus to socialites :it's definition ability that exist in the person to connect to others and attract them to take place in the group works.

5-Guidance to clerks behaviors according obvious goals and way to get them with influencment of managers.

Management with oppointment the goals and way to get them can guide clerks to do good behavior and do best.

Having obvious goals let clerks know their path.

The duty that will perform in this path determinate several tasks that clerks must do.

6-provide information about the clerk's needs and requests, employ new clerk with having ability and talent that cause confidence and trust atmosphere.

7-persude clerk for offer new and artful ideas in atmosphere that full of confidence.

References

Ahmadpour ,Daryan , M and Moghimi y SaJyed M.(2005).Job creation based.

Antoncic, B &Prodan, I (2008). "Alliances, corporate technological entrepreneurship and firm performance: Testing a model on manufacturing firms", Technovation, Vol.28, PP: 257-265.

Baker , V(1382) . Management and social investment.

Bazergan , A.(1373). Educating for job creation in kantre economic part.

Blanker, P.   Dreisler,   P,   Fargement,   M   (2008). "Entrepreneurship   Educational
        University Context.AuarhusSchool of Business, Denmark

Casson, D.P &NisarT.M .(2007). " Entrepreneurship And Organizational desighn:investor specialization, management
        decision", Vol.45, PP: 883-896.

Coleman, J.S. (1988), "Social capital in the creation of human capital", American Journal of Sociology, Vol. 94, pp. 95-
        120.

Fukoyama , F.(2006) . End of principle (Social investment and Keeping ic). Translation by :GholamAbasTavasoli.

Faghirpour,M;Amoopour,M;Gilaninia,Sh;Alinejad Moghadam,M.(2011). The Relationship between Emotional
        Intelligence and Mental Health of Students,Journal Of Basic and Applied Scientific research.,1(12)3046-3052,
        www.textroad.com.

Fukuyama, F. (1995), Trust: The Social Virtues and the Creation of Prosperity, Hamish Hamilton, London.

Fukuyama, F. (1995), Trust: The Social Virtues and the Creation of Prosperity, Penguin Books, New York, NY.Glasser,
        P. (١٥,CIO ,"rotcaf egdelwonK ehT" ,(١٩٩٨ December, pp.1-9.

Gilaninia,Sh;Ganjinia,Hosein;Babaei,Z;Mousavian,S.J.(2011). Dimensions of Knowledge Management on Good Urban
        Governance (Case Study: Municipality of Rasht City, Iran), Journal of Management and Strategy, Vol. 2, No. 3;pp91-
        101.

Grave, Arent, Salaff. W. Janet. (2005). "Social net works and entrepreneurship", Baylor university. Vol.28, N.1.

Hadizade ,Moghadom , A. and RahimiFillAbadi , F.(2005). Organizational Job making.

Isobel Van derkuip& Ingrid Verheul, (2003)."Early Development of Entrepreneurial qualities: The role of Initial
        Education.

Jonan Publication: First Print.

Klemen , J.(1998). The bases of Social Ideology.

Kuratko, Donald &Hodgetts, Richard (2001), Entrepreneurship: A contemporary approach, Philadelphia: Harcourt college
        publishers

Moghimi , M.(2005) . Organization and research procedure management . Fourth Print. Tehran: Terma Publication.
Moghimi ,Saiyad Mohammad.(2005).Job Creation in State organizations. FaraAndish Publication: First Print.

Nahapiet, J. and Ghoshal, S. (1998), "Social capital, intellectual capital, and the organizational advantage", Academy of
        Management Review, Vol. 23 No. 2, pp. 242-66.

Pardaktchi , M.H and Shafizade , H.(2006). A review of organizational Job creation.

Patnom , R.(2001).Democracy and community costums(Italian experience and lessons for other countries)

Portes, A. (1998), "Social capital: its origins and applications in modern sociology", Annual Review of Sociology, Vol.
        24 No. 1, pp. 1-24.

Putnam, R. (2000), Bowling Alone: The Collapse and Revival of American Community, Simon & Schuster, New York,
        NY.

775

Rahmanpour , L (2010) . Management of social investment.

Razaz Razaghi.S.J; Gilaninia.Sh; Amoopour.M; Shakibaeic.Z,Mosavian.S.J. (2011).Critical Reading, Journal of Basic and Applied Scientific Research, J. Basic. Appl. Sci. Res., 1(9)1173-1176, www.textroad.com.

Rezvani,M;Gilaninia,Sh;Mousavian,S.J.(2011). Communicative Wisdom Model and its Impact on Employees Operation (A Case Study by Iran`s University Dins), Australian Journal of Basic and Applied Sciences, 5(6): pp1296-1308.

Riterz , J.(2000). Sociology idea in contemperory times". Translation by Mohsen Salasi . Tehran :Scientific Publication.

Tehran :HekayateGhalemeNavin Publication.

Translation :ManouchehrSabouri. Tehran :Nai Publication.

Winter, Lan. (2000), Towards a Theorised Understanding of Family Life and Social Capital, Working Paper No.21, April 2000 Australian Institute of FamilyStudies

Australian Journal of Basic and Applied Sciences, 5(12): 719-726, 2011
ISSN 1991-8178

The Survey of Correlation between Social Capital and Knowledge Management (The Case Study in National Refining and Distribution of Oil Company in Iran(shiraz))

[1]   [2]   [3]
Hossein Khanifar, Mostafa Emami, Kamran Nazari

[1] Teacher of Tehran University

[2] Department Of Accounting , Tarbiat Modares University ,Iran.

[3] Teacher of Payam-noor University.

Abstract: The aim of current study's aim is to investigate the relationship between social capital & the knowledge management in the Iranian National Company of Oil Refining and Distribution. Therefore, after a thorough literature review, the researcher has chosen the Filius knowledge management model, with the four dimensions of knowledge acquisition, knowledge documentation, knowledge transfer, knowledge creation and knowledge application and a model for social capital with five dimension that Mr.molaii used for her research. The standard scale for the KM is consisted of 33 statements and the social capital is consisted of 31 statements. The statistical sample of this study was the manager and employees of Iranian National Company of Oil Refining and Distribution, therefore based on a random sampling method, we have survey 60 respondents, among these respondents, 11 belonged to the general engineering unit and 8 belonged to refinement engineering unit, 8 belonged to technical inspection, 13 belonged to financial unit,15 belonged to supplies and store units and 5 belonged to clerical unit, Based on the proposed research model, we have examined the research hypothesis, which consisted of one main hypothesis and five sub hypothesis. At last, the research hypotheses were tested by Spearman Correlation Factor and four hypotheses were accepted and one of them weren't accepted and their significance factor was confirmed. Afterward, by the multi factor data analyze, it was noticed that the independent variables of research has multi dimension correlation with km as a dependent variable.

Key words: Capital , knowledge , social capital, knowledge management.

INTRODUCTION:

Social capital is a new concept that plays a greater vital role than physical and human capital in organizations. Nowadays in sociology and economics and quite recently in management and organization the social capital has been used widespreadly. The social capital concept considers the communications and relations of a net work members as a valuable resource that by creating norm ali ties and mutual confidence provides the members goals achievement. In the absence of social, then the other capitals lose their effectiveness and the continuation of development routines and cultural and economic evolution become difficult. Social capital either at macro-management lever or at management lever of an organization can create a new cognition of economic-social systems, and helps managers in better conducting of the system; many parameters have been mentioned for social capital and one of the aspects that in considering social capital must be dealt with is, this concept can contain many a spects, and the reason is, the social capital has a significant potential and capacity to fulfill a wide range of works (Nahapiet and Ghshal, 1998).

Modern management has found an endless resource of competitive benefits and advantages in knowledge for an organization , by considering wide and increasing spread of this organizational necessity and accurate management commitment of this vital aspect of organization, the concept and appreciation of its effect on factors and factors which affect is must be examined. Knowledge management is known as knowledge storing, collecting, creating process and facilitating its use, so that organization can use it effectively (Turban, *et al.,* 2000).

Also, social capital can facilitate the intellectual capital movement, since the intellectual capital from different aspects is based on combination of knowledge and experiences, the social capital existence facilitates the intellectual capital creation. Social capital has been theorized to play a role to develop axial merits, because they are necessary to create knowledge (kogut and zander, 1996).

Other knowledge management definitions have been suggested that the difference of definitions could be realized from the expressed dimensions, but in any in any case . the knowledge is a vital and necessary part of nowadays organizations and could be expressed as knowledge acquisition, recording, conveyance, creating and use (Filiusrenee and jan a. dejong erik-c. roelofs, 2000).

The social capital existence can help the knowledge recoding, compiling, and conveyance. Social capital promotes these knowledge management processes through sharing in organization capabilities to create value in

---

Corresponding Author: Mostafa Emami, Young Researchers Club, South Tehran Branch, Islamic Azad University, Tehran, Iran.
E-mail:MOSTAFA.EMAMI@MODARES.AC.IR

innovation model by facilitating exchange and combination of re sources in an organization (kanter,1988; kogut and zander, 1996).

Social capital:

In 1916, the social capital subject, for the first time was suggested by honey fun, university of west Virginia. Despite its significance in social research it was ignored until 1960 that jean Jacob used it in civil programming in 1970s Lury entered it into economic realm. Social capital is an inter- connection course, i.e., it is used in sociology, economy, psychology, and other social realms (renani, 2006). Social capital axial idea is summarized in relationships expression , society members by communicating with each other and making it sustainable they are capable to cooperate and through this they acquire something that in alone they cannot obtain, or by a lot of difficulty is obtainable. Human beings communicate with each other through an assembly of networks are willing to have a common relationship with other members of this network. By spreading that communication, they form a kind of property that consider it as a sort of capital. It is obvious that the more points of view among individuals the richer the social capital.

About social capital significance and necessity in organization, can be said that in the past social was not a necessary merit of organization. But at the moment, information technology's full accelerated changes, daily increased needs to information and education, necessary requirements to creativity, continuous learning and improvement, changing towards designing a flat and flexible organizational structure, and a close relation between organization and customers networks make the dealing with social capital an inevitable for organizations leaders (Rahmanpor, 2003). Social capital is an available resource from networks internal of work and business. These resources include: information, thoughts, instructions, job and business opportunities, financial capitals, influence power, emotional support, benevolence, confidence, and cooperation. The social expression denotes in the title of social capital, and these resources are not private properties per se. No single person is their sole owner. These resources are located in the center of relationship networks. The capital expression denotes that the social capital like human or economic capital has productive and generative nature, i. e. , enables human brings to achieve their goals, and creates additional value. It means without social capital nobody can succeed (Baker & wine, 2002).

Social capital is a collection of actual and potential benefits, that is created by membership in social networks of activists and organizations. In the other words, it is a definite assembly of normalities or informal values, that members of a group are sharing, whose cooperation is authorized and permitted (Fukuyama, 2005). Burdio suggests the social capital as the container of valuable social relations among people (Ritz, 1999). Social capital is considered as struchures, relations, and normalities which form the quantity and quality of social interactions in a society and like a glue sticks them to each other (world bank, 1999).

Social capital is the capital and resources, which individuals and groups can achieve through communicating with each other and regarding relationships (coleman, 1998). Social capital denotes the available resources in social structures internal including confidence, mutual interaction normal ties and goals that prepare individuals to fulfill collective aching, and it emerges as social relations by-product and civil engagement in informal organizations (Kawachi, 2001).

Social capital consists of social networks and its related normalities that influence the social utility; this denotes the horizontal relationships among people (Putnam, 1993). Bert defines the social capital as friends, colleagues, and more general relations that through them the opportunities to use the economic and human capital can be achieved (ports, 2005).

Ports considers the social capital as activist's capabilities for achieving benefits which can be concluded by membership in social networks or in other social structures (Narayan Cassidy, 2001).

Social capital consists of positive interpersanal and social relation ships and meanwhile based on confidence (winter, 2000).

Social capital is the individuals relations, social networks, mutual normalities, and the social confidence which is obtained through this (Putnam, 2000).

Knowledge Management:

Malhutra believes that, knowledge includes an organizational process which seeks a co-increment combination of data and information processing capacity by information technology, and creativity and innovation capacity by human being. (Buctiz William se, 1999) defines the knowledge management as a process that an organization through which produces value and wealth by utilizing the intellectual capabilities and relying on its own knowledge. (Pukek, *et al.,* 2000) following their own expremental research define the knowledge management as the using and offering process of individuals skills and specialties in an organization that is supported by information technology.

(Bahat, 2001) considers the knowledge management as the process of individuals knowledge creation, offering, distribution, and application in an organization. Although all of the above definitions have several differences in the knowledge management definition and explanation, it seems that these cases have an identical consideration of the knowledge management, i.e., a process to circulate knowledge among individuals and organization as a tool to achieve innovation in processing knowledge decision making services and products and organizational conformity with competitive market dynamic environment. One can separate several main activities from knowledge management.

(Bahat, 2001) mentions the five major processes as follows:

knowledge creation: knowledge confirmation: knowledge offering:
knowledge distribution;   knowledge use.

(Filius, *et al.,* 2000) separates the five major realms of knowledge management as follows:

Knowledge acquisition:

Knowledge recording:

Knowledge conveyance:

Knowledge creation:

Knowledge application (Alvani, 2007).

According to (simon, 1992) knowledge management is an intelligent designing of processes, tools, structures, etc. by the intention of increment, reconstruction, subscription or the use improvement of knowledge that appears in either elements of intellectual capital, i.e., structural, human, and social. According to (sint, 2004) the knowledge management definition puzzle solution is that which omits any articles that the knowledge management can not be inserted in. knowledge management includes knowledge creation, acquisition, storing, publication, subscription and use (Jafari moghadam, 2004). From the other point of view, knowledge management is the process of knowledge creation, confirmation, offering, distribution, and application (Ganp, 2005). Also the principles allocate to knowledge management are as follows (jafari moghadam, 2004):

Knowledge originates from thoughts and locates in individuals:

Knowledge sharing requires confidence:

Making the new knowledge behaviors are possible by technology: knowledge sharing must be couraged and a warded:

management support and allocating resources to knowledge management is necessary;   knowledge must be created;

starting the knowledge management programs, experimently first is better;   knowledge management enhances and supports the applied and major elements in a powerful organization (ray, 1994).

1.   The new knowledge discovery or creation processes, purifying the available knowledge, and creating the availability of the knowledge;

2.   share the knowledge among individuals and manage the knowledge circulation in all organizational borders level;

3.   Creation and the use of knowledge as a part of individuals daily routine and as a part of decision making to make knowledge applicable. Creating an effective knowledge management system is one of the key factors in improving job and business processes. Most of the knowledge management requirements are only available implicitly, and converting them to the clear models is a difficult tast and meanwhile it is vital. Specific organizational will form for knowledge management and distribution, and necessary processes create for promoting knowledge management. Too much money in these structures is spent to improve the members productivity. This is specially true about simulated work and business systems which exchange in formation through internet (knowledge management forms the interactive patterns among technologies, techniques, and individuals).

For example, information technology concerning data collecting, storing, and distributing works well, but it is unable to interpret it (Bhatt, 1998). Technical solutions achievement is possible, but for knowledge management, the organization must create the partnership, assistance, and sharing environment of knowledge. Human being behavior change is one of the management current problems, so in the knowledge management projects, the change of traditional processes and enhancing structures and technologies is recommended. (Classer, 1998).

One can say that the knowledge subject is a social phenomenon, computer, information technology, and alike s con not guarantee the knowledge management success. The knowledge management is endless, because the movement from data to information and from information to knowledge never ends. Organizational staff and managers (intrinsic environment), customers and other beneficiaries (extrinsic environment) belong to knowledge management realm (Abtahi and salavati, 2006). The researches about the social capita relation with knowledge management in a research by (Robert, D. may field, 2008) titled`` organizational culture and knowledge management in power producing industry``, he considers the electric power industry's big challenge as lack of knowledge and skill and knows the organizational culture as one of the most principal factors in the knowledge acquisition, conveyance, and application area. In the Iranian national company of oil refining and distribution(shiraz).

4   Determining the relationship between social capital and knowledge creation in the Iranian national company of oil refining and distribution(shiraz).

5   Determining the relation of social capital with knowledge application in the Iranian national of oil refining and distributing (shiraz).

Research hypotheses:

Concerning the research purposes and based on relation between social capital essential indexes and knowledge management process several hypotheses in combination with one most significant hypothesis and five specific hypotheses have compiled as follows:

The research main hypothesis:

There is a meaningful relation between social capital and knowledge management in the Iranian national company of oil refining and distribution(shiraz).

Specific hypotheses: there is a meaningful relationship between social capital and knowledge acquisition in the Iranian national company of oil refining and distribution (shiraz).

There is a meaningful relation between social capital and knowledge record in the Iranian national company of oil refining and distribution(shiraz).

There is a meaningful relation ship between social capital and knowledge transfer in the Iranian national company of oil refining and distributing (shiraz).

There is a meaningful relation between social capital and knowledge creation in the Iranian national company of oil refining and distribution (shiraz).

There is a meaningful relationship between social capital and knowledge application in the Iranian national company of oil refining and distributing (shiraz).

Research method:

Since, the researcher in this study deals with regular and irreplaceable description of social capital and knowledge management in the Iranian national company of oil refining and distribution (shiraz), and he analyses based on research findings, an organizational culture in which human resources management processes, education, utilizing, and pattern imitating are essential principles, can be concerned as a vital factor to prove the knowledge management aims.

In a re search by (we Hee, 2009) titled`` social communications and their roles in knowledge management application. He states, although the knowledge management has found an appropriate importance in organization, it doesn't guarantee that staff intend to spend time and money for applying it. He continues,`` we found that knowledge management stresses on social relationships``. The social capital theory is used specifically to create social communication and dimensions(strong relations, common norms, and confidence). In continuation, he says that in a research of a company that uses the knowledge management systems, he has figured out the significance of social relations and staff knowledge management stystems use.

Research objectives: this by concerning the social capital issue and its relation with knowledge management, follows the following purposes:

The main goal:

Determine the relationship between social capital and knowledge management in the Iranian national company of oil refining and distribution (shiraz). Concerning the research main purpose, the following minor aims are offered:

1.   Determining the relation between social capital and knowledge acquisition in Iranian national company of oil refining and distributing (shiraz).

2.   Determining the relationship between social capital and knowledge record in the Iranian national company of oil refining and distribution(shiraz).

3.   Determining the relation between social capital and knowledge transfer the existing condition of these tow parameters in the mentioned society; thus, this study is based on data collecting of the type of descriptive and measurement.

The number of statistical society members in this research include Iranian company of oil refining and distribution employees(shiraz),that contain 103people.This study sample based on following formula is 60people.

$$n = 3 + \frac{4c}{\left\{ \ln \left(\dfrac{1+r}{1-r} \times \dfrac{1-ro}{1+ro} \right) \right\}^2}$$

The required data to fulfill this study was collected in the two following method:

Library method: In this method to collect data, books, these, articles, databases, and internet resources that refer to subject literature and research background were used.

Field method:

In this procedure the factors like consoul ting and interviewing with experts of designing and analyzing questionnaire were used. In the present paper, the measurement major tool questionnaire, because it is one of the common tools for research and the direct method for research data collection.

Tow questionnaire types were used for measuring variables, one has been prepared to measure social capital and determine its type, and the other to measure knowledge management parameters.

Mullaii's social capital experts questionnaire (2001) consists of 31 questions that deals with social capital. The knowledge management questionnaire constitutes 33 questions which based on Filius model (2000) deals with knowledge management present situation. To describe and analyze gathered data, the descriptive and inferential statistic was used. The used tests in this paper include, the kolmogrov-smirnov Test and spearman correlation factor.

Kolmogrov-smirnov Test:

To determine the research hypotheses test type, first the hypo theses related data normality and abnormality should be verified, then the suitable parameteric and non- parameteric statistical methods to test hypotheses will be used by applying the test results.

Ho :p=o	→ observations distribution follows normal distribution.
H1:p≠o	→ observations distribution doesn't follows normal distribution.

Table 1: kolmogrov-smirnov test.

Normal distribution	→0.491	0.833	60	Social capital
Normal distribution	→0.308	0.966	60	Knowledge management

As it is shown in table 1 the statistical amount of the test in the level of 0.05 is less than critical amount , therefore , the zero hypothesis, i.e., the normality of data is acceptable and the opposite hypothesis which indicates the data abnormality is refused. thus, concerning the data normality, to test these hypotheses, the spearman correlation Factor is used.

Research Findings and Conclusion:

Nowadays organizations must be able to acquire their requirement knowledge to innovate and improve their products and processes and issue it among their employees and use it in all their daily activities. Only through this they are able to response to the competitive environment senses and the customers exteremly variable needs. Regarding the knowledge management significance and organizational learning importance, it is necessary to recognize the influential factors of facilitating this process. With due attention to social capital definitions, it seems that since both concepts emphasize on the individuals relations and interactions in organization, it is necessary to check the knowledge management impressible rate from social capital rate in organization. The social capital presence can also help the knowledge record, compile, and transfer. Social capital promotes the knowledge management processes by sharing in organization abilities to create value in the innovation model through facilitating resources and combination in an organization (schum peter, 1934; kanter, 1988; kogut and zander, 1993).concerning the above mentioned subject–matters , and the social capital significance in this paper the researcher tries to study its relation with knowledge management by studying social capital in the Iranian national company of oil refining and distribution (shiraz) regarding the research objectives the most significant hypothesis and five specific hypotheses were offered and tested then the results are as follows :

Research Findings Relates To Main Hypothesis:

There is a meaningful relation between social capitul and knowledge management in the Iranian company of oil refining and distribution. using spearman correlation factor between the social capital and knowledge management in the Iranian national company of oil refinery and distribution 0.373 was acquired, so the colleration of these two variables is meaningful , and this colleration factor rate indicates that the social capital in the Iranian national company of oil refining and distribution has an essential role in establishing knowledge management in this company, so the stronger the social capital the more successful the knowledge management establishment. This research findings support (Alderoun, 2002) studies results based on social capital relation with knowledge transfer, (kogut, 2004) in the area of social capital mutual relation and effect on knowledge creation and application. Also this conclusion agrees with the (Hunt studies, 1999; kohen, 1999; Hufman studies, 2005) based on relation between social capital and knowledge management.

Research Findings Relate To The First Minor Hypothesis:

The research first minor hypothesis allocates to the relationship between knowledge acquisition and social capital, it was compiled so that there is a meaningful relation between knowledge acquisition and social capital. This hypo thesis was analyzed by spearman correlation Test, the result was in such a way that the knowledge acquisition at a meaningful level of 1% and by considering correlation Factor of 0.375 has a direct and meaningful relation with social capital.

Knowledge acquisition deals with utilizing knowledge resources, and these resources are: individuals, databases, and documents. In relation with this hypothesis the social capital development and improvement through creating a stronger interactive relationship among individuals that it considers as one of the knowledge resources, provides improvement process and facilitates its fulfillment. Since the social networks and normalities belong to social capital dimensions and by a brief deep thought can realize that to inhance these networks and creating social normalities one can hope to have more interaction and co- aggrandizement among individuals towards facilitating the achievement of this knowledge management parameter through social capital improvement.

Thus, it can be concluded that the more movement of the company to work social capital development, the more facilitate the knowledge acquisition, and it can move to more improvement.

Research Findings Relate To Second Minor Hypothesis:

The research second minor hypothesis specifies to relation between knowledge record and social capital. Therefore, it was compiled so that there is a meaningful relationship between knowledge record and social capital. For confirming or rejecting the hypothesis, the knowledge record collected data and social capital were analyzed by spearman correlation Test, the result was such a way that the knowledge recording compatibility at a meaningful level of 1% and by considering the correlation Factor of 0.348 has a direct and meaningful relation with social capital.

Knowledge recording is a part of difficult knowledge management dimensions Among the other resources which in addition to individuals for the knowledge acquisition process was mentioned, is the use of databases and documents. The presence of rich data bases and referring to consultant and instructive instructive documents need an infrastructure under the title of knowledge recording. To create and inhance tendency in individuals for fulfillment this knowledge management dimension tow parameters must be considered, first the technological infrastructures existence, and the other the availability of a tendency and motivation to fulfill much more better the knowledge recording and documentation, but by referring to social capital dimensions may one be able to realize the essence of an atmosphere that confidence there, is felt, and a unity to achieve a goal that attracts all people's attention. Doubtless that paying attention to individuals moral ownership right in documentation their properties and knowledge and inhancing motivation and tendency to fulfill this dimension of knowledge management in a best way, acquires its share of social capital improvement. So it can be concluded that to fulfill the better knowledge recording, as one of the knowledge management parameters, the social capital must be inhanced and improved in the company.

Research Findings Relate To The Third Minor Hypothesis:

The research third minor hypothesis allocates to the relation between knowledge transfer and social capital. There fore, it was compiled so that there is a meaningful relation between knowledge transfer and social capital. This hypothesis was analyzed by speerman correlation Test, the obtained result was in such a way that compatibility at a meaningful level of 5% and by considering correlation Factor of 0.314, has a direct and meaningful relation with knowledge management.

The knowledge transfer dimension in knowledge management relates to that very knowledge acquisition process from several aspects. As earlier mentioned, individuals are the resources of knowledge acquisition and it should bear in mind that social capital development and inhancing by providing a position for improving interaction, solitary, common normalities and networks provide the main infrastructures for knowledge transfer. It can be concluded that the firm and stronger the social capital the better knowledge transfer in the company. An organization with a good social capital, boosts the individuals new ideas, because of its effect on information exchange and knowledge transfer implicitly and explicitly.

Research Findings Relate To The Fourth Minor Hypothesis:

The research fourth minor hypothesis allocates to the relation between knowledge creation and social capital. Therefore, it is compiled so that there is a meaningful relation between knowledge creation and social capital. This hypothesis is analyzed by spearman correlation Test, the result is so that the organizational mission at a meaningful level of 1% and by considering the correlation coefficient of 0.380, has a direct and meaningful relation with knowledge management.

Knowledge creation needs conditions to be emerged, knowledge creating is done either to improve the under ways of governing task and modifying the past errors or finding a higher of task accomplishment and or problem-solving and a spark to find new lines in scientific areas. But the achievement of anything that is based on knowledge creation requires a great at tempt in organization to accomplish that dimension of knowledge management. An atmosphere overwhelmed with confidence makes the problems and barriers pursuance possible, tolerance (interaction) and solitary to achieve a common goal that under a stronger social capital protection can hope a part of this dimension meets. Then it could be concluded that the higher the social capital the more successful the knowledge creation.

Research Findings Relate To The Fifth Minor Hypothesis:

The research fifth minor hypothesis specifies to the relation between the knowledge application and social capital. Thus it was compiled so that there is a meaningful relation between the knowledge application and social capital. To confirm or reject the hypothesis, the gathered data related to knowledge creation and social capital was analyzed by spearman correlation Test, the obtained result was in such a way that the knowledge application at a meaningful level of 1٪and by considering correlation coefficient of 0.229, There is no direct and meaningful relation with social capital. The knowledge application dimension in the knowledge management like the knowledge acquisition and recording is a part of the difficult knowledge management dimensions. The difficult knowledge management activities include those categories of activities in the knowledge management cycle, which are based on appropriate structure and technology in organization. Including the structural and technological factors are: information and telecommunication technology, formal methods and procedures of organization, awarding and encouraging system in organization, and management style. With due attention to the subject that a relation has been found between social capital and the knowledge application in this organization, the result can be obtained that this knowledge management dimension is affected by other parameters which among them notice to technological infrastructure is mentioned, so more work and studies that affect knowledge application are needed.

Concerning the research goals, produced results, and researchers observation during research the following suggestions are offered:
1 Provide the data relate to employees requests and requirements, employment and recruitment of staffs with needed abilities and information, causes more toleration and creates an atmosphere full of confidence. 2 Holding training courses and seminars proportion to staff information needs creates more dynamic to wards knowledge management establishing in the organization.

3   Facilitate more access to internet through free of charge subscription for staffs to use at home or after work hours in office to up-to-date the staff knowledge.

4   SWOT analyzing fulfillment (analyzing opportunity and strength, weakness and intimidation) by the research institutes and university assistance.

5   The knowledge will be stored in the organization's memory. This memory includes: documents, databases, and their creating possibility by using information technology; organization must record and documentarize individuals knowledge, create data base and/ or the information that the employees knowledge could be documentarized in their names, which causes a kind of sense creation of commitment in individuals.

6   Holding training classes under the experienced staff management supervision those who have quit the company and are retired. This itself creates a more dynamic atmosphere to learn duty- fulfillment methods. 7 To consider the moral ownership right which relate to the employees previous knowledge and findings, i.e., if a project based on employees researches has been improved to an acceptable stage its constant under those very people management or monitor ship and in the case of their absence, the organization should enjoy their assistance.

8   Creat data base (including web sites) to inform employees about their colleagues function and using their co-workers knowledge and abilities.

9   Publishing the journals that they offer the company accomplishments and finding at the colleagues disposal.

10   Using the electronic post systems- Email, chat- for establishing on- line communication inside organization.

REFERENCES

Abtahi, sayid Husein and salavati Adel, 2006. " knowledge management in organization". first edition, payvan- e- now press, Tehran.

Baker and wine, 2003. "management and social capital ".translated by sayid mehdi Alvani, mohammad Reza Rabiee mandjin, industrial management organization press.

Putnam and Robert, 2000. "democracy and civi traditions". Italian experience and lessons for developing counties » translated by Mohammad Taghi Delforooz, first edition, Interior ministry and political research office, Tehran.

Jafari Moghadam and saeed, 2004. "managers experiences documentation from knowledge management point of view". management training and research institution.

Rahman pour Loghman, 2010 "social capital management". development management journal, (19).

Riterz George, 2000. "contemporary sociology theory". translated by Mohsen salasi, Elmi press, Tehran.   United Nations organization, 2001. "New york, United Nations development program". Oxford university press, the world bank development indexes, world bank central computer, 2000.

Fukuyama, Francis, 2006. " End of discipline(social capital and preserve it ".translated by Gholam Abas Tavasoli, Hekayat-e-Oalam– e-nawin press, Tehran.

Coleman and James, 1999. "social theory foundations".translated by Manouchehr sabouri, Nashre ney, Tehran.

Gunp Bhat, 2005. "knowledge management in organizations, studying the mutual effect of technology, techniques and human being".translated by Mohammad Iranshahi, informing science 8th period, (1,2).

Alvani, sayid Mehdi and Ali Reza shirvani, 2006. "social capital (The theories and applications concepts) ". Mani, press, Esfahan.

Bhatt, G., 1998. "Managing Knowledge through people". Knowledge and Process Management: Journal of Business Transformational, 5(3): 95-7.

Coleman, J.S., 1988. "Social capital in the creation of human capital", American Journal of Sociology, 94: 95-120.

Filius renee & jan a.de jong & erik c.roelofs, 2000.knowledge management in the hrd office : A comparison of three cases" Journal of workplace lerning, vol12. nimber7.2000-PP286-295mcb univercity press issn, pp:1366-5626

Fukuyama, F., 1995. Trust: The Social Virtues and the Creation of Prosperity, Hamish Hamilton, London. Fukuyama, F., 1995. Trust: The Social Virtues and the Creation of Prosperity, Penguin Books, New York, NY.Glasser, P., (15 CIO ,The Knowledge factor"" (1998)December, pp:1-9.

Kanter, R.M., 1988. "When 1,000 flowers bloom: structural, collective, and social conditions for innovation in organizations", in Staw, B.M. and Cummings, L.L. (Eds), Research in Organizational Behavior, Vol. 10, JAI Press, Greenwich, CT, pp: 169-211.

Kogut, B. and U. Zander, 1993. "Knowledge of the firm and the evolutionary theory of the multinational corporation", Journal of International Business Studies, 24(4): 625-45.

Kogut, B. and U. Zander, 1996. "What do firms do? Coordination, identity, and learning", Organization Science, 7(5): 502-18.

Lewicki, R.J. and B.B. Bunker, 1996. "Developing and maintaining trust in work relationships", in Kramer, R.M. and Tyler, T.M. (Eds), Trust in Organizations: Frontiers of Theory and Research, Sage, Thousand Oaks, CA, pp: 114-39.

Nahapiet, J. and V. Ghoshal, 1998. "Social capital, intellectual capital, and the organizational advantage", Academy of Management Review, 23(20): 242-66.

Nahapiet, J. and S. Ghoshal, 1998. "Social capital, intellectual capital, and the organizational advantage", Academy of Management Review, 23(2): 242-66.

Portes, A., 1998. "Social capital: its origins and applications in modern sociology", Annual Review of Sociology, 24(1): 1-24.

Putnam, R., 2000. Bowling Alone: The Collapse and Revival of American Community, Simon & Schuster, New York, NY.

Ray, P., 1992. "Collaborative information systems and business process design using simulation",IEEE communications, 32: 22-50.

Schumpeter, J.A., 1934. The Theory of Economic Development, Harvard University Press, Cambridge, MA.

Simon, L. and G. Davies, 1996. "A contextual approach to management learning", Organization Studies, 17: 269-89.

Turban.E,Mclean, E., 2002. "Information technology for management" ,3rd ed, John wiley & Sons.Inc. Winter and Lan, 2000. Towards a Theorised Understanding of Family Life and Social Capital, Working Paper No.21, April 2000 Australian Institute of FamilyStudies.

ijcrb.webs.com

INTERDISCIPLINARY JOURNAL OF CONTEMPORARY RESEARCH IN BUSINESS

JANUARY 2012
VOL 3, NO 9

Government Accounting: An Assessment of Theory, Purposes and Standards

Ehsan Rayegan
Department of Accounting,Scool of Social Since , Razi University, Kermanshah, Iran
Mehdi Parveizi
Thecher of Islamic Azad University, Giylan gharb, Iran
Kamran Nazari
Department of Business Management, Payam Noor University, Kermanshah, Iran
Mostafa Emami
Teacher of Kermanshah University of Applied Science

Abstract

Developments in governmental activities in recent years have raised concerns over whether the cash basis of accounting is sufficient for governmental accounting and reporting. Accrual accounting, previously thought to be only suitable in the private sector, has been seen to be an alternative for better reporting of government activities. Although there is a continuing debate over the use of cash versus accrual accounting, accrual accounting has been adopted in he governments of several countries including Australia, New Zealand and the United Kingdom. Government accounting and financial reporting aims to protect and manage public money and discharge accountability In order to achieve ambitious socioeconomic goals, developing countries require public sector institutional capacity for setting and implementing public policy, which in turn necessitates government accounting reform. The social value of government accounting reform therefore lies in its contribution to development goals, including poverty reduction. This rationale has led international and multilateral lenders and donors to endorse International Public Sector Accounting Standards (IPSAS) for adoption by developing countries. An emphasis on assuring financial integrity and a shift to accruals can make IPSAS more useful in government accounting reform in developing countries. All of these are heavily influenced by private sector practices, which favour the accrual basis and consolidated reporting. This article argues for a gradual symmetric approach to accruals and a combination of government-wide and fund reporting. The author also proposes some broad accounting principles to promote political and economic accountability .

Key words: Government Accounting, government, accounting reform, International Public Sector Accounting Standards (IPSAS.

Introduction

Miller (1995) p10 argues that a "healthy" accounting standard setting process needs representation from the entire spectrum of stakeholders to retain its integrity. He concludes that "a transparent due process allows outsiders to see the interactions and compromises among the key participants in the development of acceptable accounting rules". Prior Australian research has raised questions about the veracity of various aspects of the operation of the 'due process' for public sector standard setting. Ryan et. al. (1999) concluded that there were fundamental problems with the 'due process' as it operated in AAS29, which was released in 1993. There was a lack of input from account preparers and a close working relationship existed between the Treasuries and the standard setters. Carnegie

521

and West (1997) conducted an analysis of the responses to ED 50 in relation to the recognition of infrastructure assets only. They contended that, for this particular issue, the standard setters placed more weight on a sample of 26 responses which were deemed to be "of particular interest" by the staff of the Australian Accounting Research Foundation (AARF) (p32). This led to their raising the concern that the PSASB may not have been responsive to its constituents. The Philippines realized fiscal surpluses between 1994 and 1997, prior to the Asian financial crisis.176 However, indicators have deteriorated significantly in the past 3 years. The Arroyo administration faces a worsening fiscal position. Unless the Government curbs expenses and improves revenue collection, the 2001 budget deficit could reach P200 billion ($4.2 billion).177 The weak fiscal position is creating tensions with multilateral development banks.178 Moreover, it restricts the Government's ability to address infrastructure issues and poverty reduction.

Furthermore, the Philippines experiences significant ongoing problems with corruption. With annual capital expenditure exceeding $3.5 billion, the procurement of goods and services, and implementation of infrastructure projects, by the Government present significant opportunities for graft.179 Government accounting and auditing arrangements were formulated in 1947. They have many strengths including the use of doubleentry bookkeeping, a mixed cash-accrual accounting base, a cadre of well-trained accountants, and potential access to a large external pool of trained accountants. Public management arrangements are characterized by institutional and regulatory rigidities. Efforts to modernize the public sector have gathered pace in recent years. Among other things, the Government intends to (i) develop a MediumTerm Expenditure Framework (MTEF); (ii) introduce output and outcome performance measures and targets;

(iii) overhaul procurement practices; (iv) introduce 3-year baseline budgeting; (v) modernize auditing practices; (vi) introduce computerized financial management information systems; and (vii) prepare for the introduction of full accrual accounting.180he Constitution of the Philippines 1987 mandates the keeping of government accounts, the promulgation of accounting rules, the audit of financial reports, and the submission of reports covering the Government's financial operations and position.181 In particular, Article IX defines three constitutional commissions as being separate and independent bodies.

From Accountability to Accounting

The global rise of government accounting is fundamentally due to the greater demand for accountability in a democracy and market economy. Democratic governance and market transactions require and foster the norm of reciprocity the expectation of exchange of benefits of comparable value upon which accountability is based. Accounting information can be used to monitor and enforce the terms of economic, social and political contracts. When a government engages in market transactions whether buying or selling services, lending or borrowing money it is subject to economic accountability. When it levies taxes to finance public services, it incurs political accountability. The development of government accounting is related to the constitutional form of government that provides for separation of powers, and checks and balances among the legislative, executive, and judicial branches of government (Chan and Rubin, 1987). While all governments engage in some degree of planning and control, only democratic governments are mandated to open their books directly to auditors and indirectly to the public through financial reports. Fiscal transparency is therefore an attribute of limited government, for to give out information is to cede authority. Government officials rationally do not volunteer more information than is required or in their interest. It is therefore not surprising that, while some accounting is done on a voluntary basis, financial disclosure is often made only in response to demand. The regulatory structure for government financial disclosure mirrors the pattern of accountability in government and the political system. In an administrative hierarchy, the superior holds subordinates accountable and requires feedback information on their performance. A legislature monitors the conduct of the executive branch, for example, in executing the approved budget. Furthermore, a government has the incentive to disclose information in order to induce others to provide resources to it. These include potential buyers of government securities; vendors of goods and services on credit; and grantors of financial aid. In these voluntary exchanges, information is used to predict a government's ability to carry out the terms of contracts, .\fter the transactions are made, accounting information is used to monitor contractual performance. Governments are less inclined to disclose financial information to those without leverage over it, at least in the short-term, such as individual taxpayers. It is here that mandatory standards seek to increase the information access of those who are least able to demand it, or to enforce their right to know. The exercise of accountability requires institutions in both senses of the term: namely, organizations; and rules of the game (World Bank, 2002, p. 4). In government accounting, these refer to standard-setting bodies and the standards they promulgate. These institutions of government accounting in individual countries are extensively documented in the CIGAR literature and will not be covered in this article. It is, how ever, important to describe the general purposes of government accounting, in order to contrast it with

commercial accounting. The Commission on Audit shall have the power, authority, and duty to examine, audit, and settle all accounts pertaining to the revenue and receipts of, and expenditures or uses of funds and property, owned or held in trust by, or pertaining to, the Government, or

any of its subdivisions, agencies, or instrumentalities, including government- owned or controlled corporations with original charters, and on a post-audit basis: (a) constitutional bodies, commissions and offices that have been granted fiscal autonomy under this Constitution; (b) autonomous state colleges and universities; (c) other government owned or controlled corporations and their subsidiaries; and (d) such nongovernmental entities receiving subsidy or equity, directly or indirectly, from or through the Government, which are required by law or the granting institution to submit to such audit as a condition of subsidy or equity. However, where the internal control system of the audited agencies is inadequate, the Commission may adopt such measures, including temporary or special pre-audit, as are necessary and appropriate to correct the deficiencies. It shall keep the general accounts of the Government and, for such period as may be provided by law, preserve the vouchers and other supporting papers pertaining thereto. (2) The Commission shall have exclusive authority, subject to the limitations in this Article, to define the scope of its audit and examination, establish the techniques and methods required therefor, and promulgate accounting and auditing rules and regulations, including those for the prevention and disallowance of irregular, unnecessary, excessive, extravagant, or unconscionable expenditures or uses of government funds and properties Section 3. No law shall be passed exempting any entity of the Government or its subsidiaries in any guise whatever, or any investment of public funds, from the jurisdiction of the Commission on Audit.

Section 4. The Commission shall submit to the President and the Congress, within the time fixed by law, an annual report covering the financial condition and operation of the Government, its subdivisions, agencies, and instrumentalities, including governmentowned or controlled corporations, and nongovernmental entities subject to its audit, and recommend measures necessary to improve their effectiveness and efficiency. It shall submit such other reports as may be required by law.

Organizational Roles and Responsibilities

The following organizations play central roles in budgeting, accounting and auditing arrangements. The COA audits the general accounts of the Government, promulgates accounting rules and regulations, and submits the annual financial report of the Government, its subdivisions, and agencies (including government owned or controlled corporations).

The Department of Finance (DOF) The DOF is responsible for (i) formulating, institutionalizing, and administering fiscal policies in coordination with other concerned subdivisions, agencies, and instrumentalities of the government; (ii) managing the financial resources of government; (iii) supervising the revenue operations of all LGUs; (iv) reviewing, approving and managing all public sector debt; and (v) rationalizing, privatizing and ensuring the public accountability of corporations and assets owned, controlled or acquired by the Government.187 The DOF oversees three operating bureaus: the Bureau of the Treasury (BTr), the Bureau of Internal Revenue (BIR), and the Bureau of Customs.

The Bureau of the Treasury (BTr) The BTr plays a pivotal role in the cash operations of the national government. It is responsible for (i) receiving and keeping national funds; (ii) managing and controlling disbursements of national funds; and (iii) maintaining accounts of financial transactions of all national government offices, agencies, and instruments.

Department of Budget and Management (DBM) The DBM is responsible for the design, reparation and approval of the accounting systems of government agencies. It is also responsible for coordinating and implementing the annual budget process. Furthermore, the Department manages the process of cash disbursement as well as monitoring compliance with appropriations.

Development and Budget Coordinating Council (DBCC) The DBCC comprises representatives from DBM, DOF, Bureau of Treasury, NEDA, and BSP. All agency budgetary requirements must pass through the Council. Its objectives are to (i) set budget parameters based on available resources; (ii) conduct budget hearings; and (iii) submit the resulting consolidated budget to the House of Representatives (particularly the Committee on Appropriations).

Accounting Information Systems

The national government accounting system is largely paper based. Financial reports from national agencies, including those with computerized systems, are manually processed and consolidated by COA. Existing computerized systems are of varying types.191 This variation is to be expected in such a diversified environment comprising a wide range of organizations with differing roles and objectives.

Government versus Commercial Accounting

Business accounting has often been used as a benchmark for evaluating government accounting. Two hundred years ago, Thomas Jefferson (quoted by Arthur Andersen, 1986) wished to see *the finance of the Union as clear and intelligible as a merchant's books, so that every member of Congress, and every man of any mind in the Union, should be able to comprehend them to investigate abuses, and consequently to control them'. Is it possible that government and business accounting are fundamentally alike in unimportant respects as public and private management are (Allison, 1980)? What are the important respects that set government accounting apart from its business counterpart?

In order to serve the three identified purposes, financial accounting and management accounting cannot be so neatly compartmentalized in the public sector, where management accounting refers to budgeting and control, rather than accounting solely in the service of managers. The budget is an expression of public policy and political preferences. It is an instrument of fiscal policy on revenue and spending to achieve macroeconomic objectives. It provides benchmarks for performance measured partly by the accounting system. Given their close relationship, it is often difficult to tell where budgeting ends and accounting begins. They reinforce each other in demonstrating and discharging fiscal accountability to the government's stakeholders, who are more numerous and diverse than the owners of a firm. Indeed, governments do not have owners.

524

The absence of ownership in government makes it problematic to apply the accounting equation (assets = liabilities + owners' equity) and its corollary (profit = revenuesexpenses) to the public sector. An exception may be local governments. These are municipal corporations chartered by the state to perform certain public services, which in many cases are private goods (for example water) or only quasipublic goods (for example elementary education). These entities have clear origins, and own identifiable assets and liabilities. Unfortunately, the assets and liabilities of the national government of a sovereign state are difficult to identify and harder still to measure in financial terms. With regard to assets, except in rare instances (such as the United States' purchase of Louisiana from France, or Alaska from Russia), few nations acquire new territories through buy-and-sell transactions. Most occupy their ancestral lands and some acquired their territories through military conquests or colonization. Historical costs, even if data are available, are not meaningful, yet market prices, even ifjustifiable. are hard to come by. The same problems arise in the case of natural resources and heritage assets. On the liability side, it is not easy to draw the line between a national government's contractual or legal obligations and its political

commitments and social responsibilities for the general welfare. In contrast to corporations' limited liabilities, governments in a democracy are prone to expand their responsibilities, resulting in larger budgets and frequent deficits (Buchanan and Wagner, 1977).

Accounting principles allow a business, whether private or state-owned, to recognize revenues only to the extent of goods or services provided. Governments uniquely provide public goods and finance them through taxation. Public goods are consumed collectively, and non-payers cannot be excluded— hence requiring tax financing. These characteristics sever the link between service delivery and revenue recognition, making it impossible to match revenues and expenses (Sunder, 1997). This accounting problem is also exacerbated by the involuntary nature of many transactions between government and people. The government's operating statement tracks resource flows, and only incidentally measures the government's service efforts and accomplishments. These unique characteristics of government are the primary source of the differences between government and commercial accounting. These differences, argues Sunder (1997, p. 198), 'do not constitute prima facie evidence that the former are defective and should be altered to conform to the latter'. More specifically, Nobes (1988, p. 198) challenged the assertion that 'Anglo-Saxon commercial accounting involving accrualsbased annual financial statements is necessary for accountability, control and decision-making relating to government'. From the research perspective, theories underlying government accounting standards are mostly normative, in contrast to the development of positive theory in (business) financial accounting. The latter (Watts, 1977; Watts and Zimmerman, 1978, 1990) draws its inspiration from the contract-cost theory of the firm originating from Coase (1937). A similar incipient conceptual revolution started tentatively with Zimmerman's (1977) paper linking government financial reporting to political incentives. It is time to resume the search for a positive theory of government accounting standards. One way would be to build on the work of Chester Barnard and Herbert Simon.

At about the same time Goase wrote his famous paper explaining the existence of the firm in terms of transaction costs, Barnard (1938) identified the functions of the executive as securing the co-operation of the stakeholders of an organization. Barnard's work is currently enjoying a revival, primarily through the efforts of Oliver Williamson (1990). Much earlier, Simon (1945) applied Barnard's insight to government in his hook Administrative Behavior. In Simon's view, an organization is in equilibrium if Barnard's executive succeeds in securing the contributions of stakeholders by offering them adequate inducements to stay in the organizational coalition. A business can be viewed in the same way (Gohen and Gyert, 1965). In both types of organization, the challenge for managers is to negotiate satisfactory terms of contracts to keep the coalition intact. In such a theory, owners are important as contributors of equity capital, but they are not the only group managers try to please. In other words, the owner-centred theory of the firm and the single-principal agency theory are a special case of the Barnard- Simon organization theory.

This theory can be used to identify potential users of government's financial information by postulating that they use the information to predict their inducements from government (Ghan, 1981). Recently, Sunder (1997) applied contract-cost theory to explain and justify the differences betw-een accounting for government and nonprofit organizations and business accounting. Much more research is needed before the multiple-stakeholder perspective can have an impact on standards. In the meantime, government accounting has shifted closer to the business (financial) accounting model.

Internal Auditing

The Internal Auditing Act 1962 (RA 3456) introduced internal auditing requirements to the national government. A 1965 amendment (RA 4177) extended the Act's coverage to government-owned and controlled corporations (GOCCs) and local government units (LGUs). In 1992, President Aquino directed that government internal-control systems be strengthened (AO 278) – the Association of Government Internal Audi- tors (AGIA), among others, was instructed to ensure that internal audit practices, methods, and procedures be improved through continuing education and be conducted in accordance with internal auditing standards.

192 The AGIA represents internal auditors in government and promotes their professional development. It had 1,177 members at January 1999.

Public Financial Management Reform Program

The objectives of the Government's public financial management reforms are to (i) allocate and manage expenditures via a Medium Term Expenditure Framework (MTEF); (ii) strengthen feedback mechanisms for budget formulation through enhanced budget and performance monitoring; (iii) improve the performance management environment by simplifying budgeting rules; (iv) introduce incentives for better performance management; and (v) increase management flexibility to ensure performance results.197 The reforms are based on a benchmarking study of the Philippine expenditure management system vis-à-vis its neighboring countries (Australia, Korea, Malaysia, New Zealand, Singapore, and Thailand) in terms of the three important expenditure outcomes: maintaining fiscal discipline, facilitating strategic prioritization at the oversight level, and enhancing the implementation efficiency of line agencies.198 The reform program comprises several activities as follows: 199 • Sectoral budget ceilings. Six-year sectoral budget ceilings were introduced for the Fiscal 2000 budget. These sectoral budgets were developed with the multi-sector Planning Committees of the National Economic and Development Authority (NEDA). These Committees include representatives from Congress, local government, academia, the private sector and nongovernment organizations. The process involved various government implementing agencies in a participative and proactive manner. Three-year budget baselines. The 6-year sectoral ceilings served as the basis for allocating resources to implementing agencies using a budget baseline approach. • Strengthening evaluation mechanisms. First, locally funded projects will be subjected to the same approval process that applies to those funded from foreign sources. Second, the performance measurement will be mainstreamed. A set of performance indicators will have to accompany all new policies or projects that are submitted to NEDA or DBM. The ultimate objective is to foster an evaluation culture.

• Improving government accounting and internal control. Adopting private sector accounting and reporting practices, such as full accrual accounting will enhance the usefulness of accounting information. It will also enable organizational outputs to be meaningfully costed.

526

•   Separating accounting and auditing functions. COA, the Philippines' supreme audit institution, undertakes accounting, internal control and auditing functions in government. These groupings are incongruous.

•   Improving procurement procedures. The DBM has launched the Electronic Procurement System to improve the efficiency and transparency of the government procurement process.200

Issue Synopsis: Government Budgeting and Accounting

Chapter VIII – Issues and Recommendations – identifies and describes constraints and proposes corrective actions. With minor departures, these include the following selected issues that have already been identified by the UNDP-sponsored studies:

•   The Commission on Audit is responsible for promulgating accounting and auditing rules. These responsibilities are defined in Article IX of the Constitution 1987. The coexistence of these responsibilities is inconsistent with the concept of auditor independence.

•   The absence of computerized accounting information systems, combined with complex accounting regulations (i) relegates the role of most government CPAs to that of highly qualified bookkeepers.

Little time is left for value-added activities, such as financial analysis; and (ii) means that financial reports are rarely prepared in time to be useful for decision-making purposes.

•   There is no consistent set of accounting standards for budgeting and reporting. Major reporting differences result.

•   Auditors spend the majority of their time on compliance auditing (checking transactions). Minimal time is spent on financial attest auditing as more effort is applied to value-for-money audits.

•   Comparatively attractive starting salaries attract high-quality personnel into government accounting. A flat earnings structure means that higher-level salaries are far from competitive. This creates retention problems and provides a supportive environment for graft and corruption.

Summary and Proposals

Over the past 25 years, there have been some notable institutional and conceptual innovations in government accounting, contributing to its greater visibility and influence. Its emphasis has shifted from bureaucratic control to accountability reporting to the public. In some countries, government accounting standards are no longer set by government officials, but by relatively independent boards. While acknowledging the importance of cash the lifeblood in government as in business contemporary accounting standards aim at tracking the long-term consequences of decisions and actions. Government officials are held accountable for their stewardship of both

financial and capital assets. Finally, it is not enough to keep the books accurately; the books have to be open to the public. When the public does not have the time or ability to inspect the accounts, governments have to make the task easier by preparing comprehensible as well as comprehensive financial statements.

Many challenges remain, especially at the global and international level. A major issue is the proper balance between international norms and domestic practices arising from national political ideology, economic system and culture. As a mechanism of governance, government accounting is subject to political forces that distribute power, and economic forces that determine the supply of and demand for resources. Therefore, unless accounting standards boards ally themselves with the institutions that can withhold something of value to a government a grant, a loan, an unqualified audit opinion, a favourable bond rating their pronouncements would remain

ineffectual. Unfortunately, at the international level, there are relatively few levers available to

527

a body such as the IFAC Public Sector Committee to enforce its standards. However, accountants could make the case that fiscal accountability is an international norm applicable to all governments regardless of their political and economic system. Once this transcendent value of fiscal accountability is embraced, it is a technical matter to work out the means of implementation. These include not only yearend financial statements the current focus of IPSASs—but also budgets, internal controls and external audits. 1 urge the IFAC Public

Sector Committee to rectify its neglect of the budget and to include 'actual versus budget' comparisons in financial statements. Furthermore, putting aside differences of opinions on accounting choices, the entire body of detailed standards should be framed by a set of broader principles aimed at promoting government fiscal accountability, such as:

•The objectives of government accounting are to safeguard the public treasury and pr()pert\, to accurately measure and communicate the government's fmancial condition so as to demonstrate financial accountability, and to facilitate decisionmaking. •Agovernment should prepare and publish its budgets, maintain complete financial records, provide full financial disclosure, and subject itself to independent audits.

•The form and content of financial reports should be guided by the rights and need to know of intended users.

•The accounting system should measure the cash and other financial consequences of past transactions and events, including, but not limited to, budget execution.

•The accounting system should be capable of keeping track of the levels and changes in assets, liabilities, revenues and expenditures or expenses, relative to budgeted amounts. These principles do not prescribe accounting choices. Rather, they provide a foundation for deliberating and setting government accounting standards.

Generally, accounting standards take on a greater social role as accountability requirements in countries that require higher standards of ethical behaviour. Government accounting standards in effect become government accountability standards. (Recently the U.S. General Accounting Office was renamed Government Accountability Office.). Government must answer for the resources or authority it receives from others in the society and economy. Government provides both public goods and private goods, in return for the authority to govern, as well as economic and financial resources, Government accountability requirements are expressed as the terms in the political contracts, social contracts, and economic contracts that government enters into with its stakeholders (see Exhibit 2). The asset-liability perspective of accrual accounting described in Exhibit 1 is compatible with this contract theory of government: the government's assets come from the stakeholders' voluntary and involuntary contributions, and its liabilities originate from providing incentives to the stakeholders. In conclusion, fundamental to the development of accrual accounting in developing countries is the ability to identify and measure the government's assets and liabilities. Corruption tends to result in the understatement of government's assets or the overstatement of government's liabilities. Unless financial integrity is assured, the credibility of government's financial information suffers. Thus both financial integrity assurance and accurate accrual accounting are accountants' professional contribution to developing countries.

References

Allen, R. and Tommasi, D. (2001), Managing Public Expenditure: A Reference Book for Transition Countries, OECD, Paris.

Bourmistrov, A. and Mellemvik, F. (2000) «Russian Local Government Accounting: New Norms and New Problems», in Caperchione E. and Mussari, R. eds., Comparative Issues in Local Government Accounting, Kluwer Academic Publishers, Boston, pp. 159- 174.

528

Bourmistrov, A. and Mellemvik, F. (2001), «Accounting and Democratic Governance: A Comparative Study of One Norwegian and One Russian County», in Bac, A. ed. International Comparative Issues in Government Accounting, Kluwer Academic Publishers, Dordrecht, The Netherlands, pp. 91-122.

Chan, J.L., Jones, R.H. and Lüder, K.G. (1996), «Modeling Government Innovations: An Assessment and Future Research Directions», Research in Governmental and Nonprofit Accounting, Vol. 9, pp. 1-19.

Chan, J.L. (2000), «A Sino-American Comparison of Budget and Accounting Coverage», in Caperchione, E. and Mussari, R., eds., Comparative Issues in Local Government Accounting, Kluwer Academic Publishers, Boston, pp. 11-34.

Chan, J.L., Cong, S.H. and Zhao, J.Y. (2001), «The Effects of Reform on China's Public budgeting and Accounting System», in Bac, A., ed. International Comparative Issues in Government Accounting, Kluwer Academic Publishers, Dordrecht, The Netherlands, pp. 297-314.

Chu, K-Y, and Hemming, R. (1991), «Public Expenditure Handbook: A Guide to Public Policy Issues in Developing Countries», International Monetary Fund, Washington, D.C. Coombs, Hugh M. and Mohamad Tayib, (2000), «Financial Reporting Practice: A Comparative Study of Local Authority Financial Reports Between the UK and 12 Malaysia», in Caperchione, E. and Mussari, M. eds., Comparative Issues in Local Government Accounting, Kluwer Academic Publishers, Boston,, pp. 53-68.

Deutsch, K.W. (1966), The Nerves of Government: Models of Political Communication and Control, The Free Press, New York.

Godfrey, A.D., Devlin, P.J. and Merrouche, C., (1996), «Governmental Accounting in Kenya, Tanzania and Uganda» in Chan, J.L., ed., Research in Governmental and Nonprofit Accounting, Vol. 9, JAI Press, Greenwich, Connecticut, pp. 193-208.

Godfrey, A.D., Merrouche, C. and Devlin, P.J. (1999), «A Comparative Analysis of the Evolution of Local Governmental Accounting in Algeria and Morocco,» in Copley, P.A. and Sanders, G.D., eds. Research in Governmental and Nonprofit Accounting, Vol. 10, JAI Press, Greenwich, Connecticut, pp. 201-234.

Grindle, Merilee S. (2000), «Ready or Not: The Developing World and Globalization,» in Nye, J.S. and Donahue, J.D., eds. Governance in a Globalizing World, Brookings Institution Press, ashington, D.C., pp. 178-207.

Hopwood, A. and Miller, P., eds. (1994), Accounting as a Social and Organizational Practice, Cambridge University Press, Cambridge.

International Federation of Accountants (IFAC) (1996), «Responding to an Increasing Demand for Accountability in the Public Sector,» IFAC Quarterly, October.

IFAC (2003), Handbook on International Public Sector Accounting Standards. IFAC, New York.

IFAC, International Public Sector Accounting Standards Board (2005), Exposure Draft 24, Financial Reporting Under the Cash Basis of Accounting – Disclosure Requirements for Recipients of External Assistance, IF AC, New York.

IFAC, International Public Sector Accounting Standards Board (2005), «Background and Update,» unpublished paper, March.

IFAC, Public Sector Committee (2000), Study 11, Government Financial Reporting: Accounting Issues and Practices. IFAC, New York, May.

Jaruga, A. (1988), «Governmental Accounting, Auditing and Financial Reporting in East European Countries,» in Chan, J.L. and Jones, R.H. eds., Governmental Accounting and Auditing: International Comparisons, Routledge, London, pp. 105-121. Keefer, P. and Khemani, S. (2004), «Democracy, Public Expenditure and the Poor,» World Bank Research Observer. World Bank, Washington, D.C.

529

Nowak, W.A. and Bakalarska, B. (2001), «Polish Public Sector Accounting in Transition: The Landscape after 1999 Step in the State Redefining,» in Bac, A. ed., International Comparative Issues in Government Accounting, Kluwer Academic Publishers, Dordrecht, The Netherlands, pp. 265-278.

Ouda, Hassan A.G. (2001), «Central Governmental Accounting of Egypt and the Netherlands: Similarities and Differences,» in Bac, A. ed., International Comparative Issues in Government Accounting, Kluwer Academic Publishers, Dordrecht, The Netherlands, pp. 71-90.

Rose-Ackerman, S. (1999), Corruption and Government: Causes, Consequences and Reform, Cambridge University Press, Cambridge.

Reuters (2003), «World Bank urges crackdown on government corruption», December 10.

Sachs, J.D. (2005), The End of Poverty: Economic Possibilities for Our Time, Penguin Books, New York.

Schiavo-Campo, S. and Tommasi, D. (1999), Managing Government Expenditure, Asian Development Bank, Manila.

Simon, H.A. (1954), Centralization vs. Decentralization in Organizing the Controller's Department, Controllership Foundation, New York.

Sutcliffe, P. (2003), «The Standards Programme of IFAC's Public Sector Committee,» Public Money and Management, January, pp. 11-12.

World Bank (1998), Public Expenditure Management Handbook, World Bank, Washington, D.C.

Iranian company valuation of intellectual capital: Evidence from Tehran Stock)Exchange (TSE

EFM CLASSIFICATION CODES 210 - Measuring and Managing Firm Value

Mostafa Emami

PhD Student, Department of Finance
©Michigan Technological University

Amrollah Amini (Ph.D)

Associate Professor
©Allame Tabatabaee University (ATU)

Alireza Emami

PhD Student, Department of Finance
©The Tehran University

*Presentor Address:
 888*W Campbell Rd Richardson TX 75080-3021*
 E-mail: memami@mtu.edu and Mostafa.Emami@modares.ac.ir
 Tel: +1(816) 237-0018 and +1(202) 670-0690 and +98(912)700 1816

Iranian company valuation of intellectual capital: Evidence from Tehran Stock Exchange (TSE)

Abstract: Konwledge, as a strategic advantage and a critical success factor (CSF), especially in knowledge societies, plays important roles in economics, business and managerial processes of modern and leading firms. Todays, it is well known that the higer the level of knowlege in a firm or in an industry, the higher the firm's or the industry's Intellectual Capital (IC) value. Since IC is a major part of firms total capital, most of the firms are very interested to measure their IC values. Two important questions in IC literature are 1)how a firm's IC value can be measured? 1)are there meaningful relationshipes amonge firms and industries' IC values with their share market prices? In this research, in order to answer the first question, we have proposed five simple calculation methods and calculated all Iranian firms' and industries' IC values based on each method. Also, to answer the second question, we have tested statistically our main research hypothesis that was a confirmation on existing meaningful relationships amonge firms and industries' IC values with their shares market prices in the Tehran Stock Exchange (TSE). Results of empirical study, at the confidence level %95, clearly confirm existing such a meaningful relationship in the TSE.

Key words: Knowledge, Intellectual Capita (IC), Tehran Stock Exchange (TSE).

1. INTRODUCTION

It is well known that the traditional accounting systems fail to adequately account for intellectual capital (IC) in a transparent manner. They usually try to consider intellectual property rights and ignore the increasing roles of intangible assets and knowledge and fail to account the real value of knowledge in their calculations.   There is an increasing need to correctly measure and capture the real value of intangible assets and knowledge in financial statements. To days and especially in konwledge societies, return on intellectual capital employed becomes more important than ROI. Also, the importance of financial capital in the determination of sustained profitability is strongly reduced. In other words, we belieive there is a positive correlation between the level of firms'

1

intangible assets and knowledge with their IC values. Because of increasing the relative importance of IC, as a major part of firms' total capital, most of the firms are interested to find good answers for two following questions:

1) How intellectual capital value can be defined, assessed and measured?

2) Statistically, is there a meaningful relationship between firms' IC values and their share market prices?

To answer the first question, we developed five simple financial quantitative calcualtion methods. Using each method and based on the 7 years data for interval 1997-2003 from the TSE, we have calculated the IC values for all Iranian firms were accepted in the TSE. On the other hands, to answer the second question, we have tested the main research hypothesis that was there is a meaningful relationship between firms' IC values and their share market prices.

The main aim of the present paper is to contribute towards the creation of IC measurement and valuation system. The financial method of intangible assets measurement presented in this paper aims to overcome some of the weaknesses of IC valuation, and contribute to the creation of complete financial statements, reflecting both companies' tangible and intangible assets.

Next section of the paper provides the literature. Section 3 is to explain the research methodology was appled in this research. Section 4 provides the statistical (regression) results. Finally, the paper ends with conclusions and final remarks in section 5.

2. THE LITERATURE

There is a huge number of papers on the concept and the elements of IC, its measurement and reporting methods, and its effects on the business excellence and performance superiority. For example, some researchers discussed on the meaurement and reporting of knowledge-based assets.[25] Some studied on the measurement of intangible assets in public sector using scaling techniques.[28] Also, Chen used a game theory to valuing IC and Kittsa cleared the relations between IC and intangible assets. [6,16] Hunt attempts to explain how to measure the knowledge and Andreou discusses on the impact of information technology and cultural differences on organizational behavior in the financial services industry.[1,10] Zhou introduces the concept of IC Web as a systematic linking of IC and knowledge management and Wexler studies the relations between IC and organizational memory.[31,32] Riahi-Belkaoui, according stakeholder views, studied the relationships between IC and firm performance of US multinational firms.[24] Bontis et al explain the IC Rate on Investment.[4] Das explains strategic alliances as a valuable way to manage IC.[7] Also Smith suggests a strategic point of view regarding to managing the intellectual properties.[9] Johnson believes IC can be leveraged through product and process management of human capital.[14,15] O'Donnell regards human interaction as the critical source of intangible value.[21] For further reading on the the measurement, reporting and management of IC see reference 23. In literature, most methods for valuing a firm's IC do not provide a complete set of IC measurements To overcome the weakness and contribute to creating a complete statement reflecting both companies' tangible and intangible assets, Rodov and Leliaert suggest financial method of intangible assets measurement (FIMIAN). [26]

Despite the increasing importance of intangible assets and IC, most accounting systems are still traditional and fail to adequately account for IC in a transparent manner. On the other hands, the importance of off-balance-sheet disclosure on intangibles in annual reports, specially in publicly quoted companies reports is strongly increased. This paper is aimed to help firms in valuing their real IC values.

3. RESEARCH METHODOLOGY

Our research is applied and descriptive. It is aimed to propose five simple and quantitative financial methods for valuing firm's IC. As a first step, using each proposed method, we have calculated IC values for all Iranian firms accepted in TES for interval 1997-2003. As the second step and in order to test main research hypothsis that was *there is a meaningful positive relationship between firms' IC values and their share market prices*, we have calculated the correlations between firms' IC values with their share market values. Since each proposed method provided a distinct set of IC values, we compared the methods by their correlation coefficients and determinnant coefficients values. It is clear that, the higher the correlation coefficient value, the higher the correlation of the proposed method to its share market value.

4. THE METHODS AND STATISTICAL RESULTS

4.1. THE METHODS

Five proposed methods for valuing firms' IC are as follows:

First Method : $IC_1 \square \dfrac{Rc \square RI}{WACC}$

Second Method : $IC_2 \square \square^\square{}_c \square^\square{}_I \square \square TA$

Third Method : $IC_3 \square \underline{\hspace{1.5cm}} \square \square \ \square \square \dfrac{\square}{-1} \ \boxminus \square \square \ WACC \square \square 1 \square IInft \square \square$

3

$$\text{Fourth Method}: IC4 = \square\square Tt \square 1 \square MV \square 1 \square t/\square InftBV \square t\square$$

$$\text{Fifth Method}: IC5 \square \square MV \square 1 \square t/ \square InfBV \square \square t\square$$

where,

IC: intelectual capital

Rc: firm's revenues

RI : average revenues in industry

WACC: weighted average cost of capital

$I_C\square$: firm's average revenues over *t* periods

$I_I\square$: industr's average revenues over *t* periods

$WACCT\square$: average of WACCs over T periods

$\square_C$: firm's average returns over T periods

$\square_C$: firm's average returns over T periods

$\square_I$: industry's average returns over T periods

TA: average total asset value over T periods

$\square$ $\square\square\square\square_c\square\square_I$ and $\square^\square I_{c\square}\square I_{I\square}$

I_{nft}: inflation rate in period *t*

$I_{nf\square}$: average inflation rate over T periods $_{ctA}\square \underline{R}_{ct}\square$: firm's

adjusted returns in period *t*

$R\square_1\square I_{nft}$

$_{ItA}\square \underline{R}_{It}\square$: firm's adjusted returns in period *t* $R\ \square_1\square I_{nft}$

$\square_{cA}$ and $\square_{IA}$: firm's and industry's adjusted average returns

BV_t and MV_t:firm's book and market value in period *t*

BV_t and MV_t:firm's average book and market value over t periods

Setting *WACC*=0.25 for all Iranian firms and using 7 years real data from the TSE, we have calculated the IC values and impleemnted regression analysis. The regression equations are as follows:

$$ShareMarketValue_t = \square_1 \square_1 \square_{1t}$$

$$ShareMarketValue_t = \square_2 \square_2 \square_{2t}$$

$$ShareMarketValue_t = \square_3 \square_3 \square_{3t}$$

$$ShareMarketValue_t = \square_4 \square_4 \square_{4t} \quad ShareMarketValue_t$$

$$= \square_5 \square_5 \square_{5t}$$

Tables 1 and 2 show the summary results of the regression analysis, and rank IC valuing methods. It is clear that a higher positive value of correlation determination is better. In other words, the higher the value of R, the higher the rank of the method. (see ANOVA in Ttables 3-13 in appendix)

Table 1: Summary of Results (regession between firms'IC values and shares market values)

Calculation Method	Multiple R	R Square	Adjusted R Square	Standard Error	Observations Numbers	ANOA Data in Appendix	Rank of Method
First Method	0.00625	3.91E-05	-0.00063	960802.3	1506	Table 3	5
Second Method	0.447881	0.200597	0.200134	741119.9	1729	Table 4	3
Third Method	0.115062	0.013239	0.012677	975284.7	1757	Table 5	4
Fourth Method	0.976012	0.952599	0.952573	213427.2	1763	Table 6	2
Fifth Method	0.976261	0.953086	0.95306	211873.8	1771	Table 7	1

Table 2: Summary of Results (regession between industries' IC values and their total shares market values)

Calculation Method	Multiple R	R Square	Adjusted R Square	Standard Error	Observations Numbers	ANOA Data in Appendix	Rank of Method
First Method	0.019007	0.000361	-0.00873	7886714	112	Table 8	5
Second Method	0.158109	0.024999	0.016135	6609426	112	Table 9	4
Third Method	0.348239	0.121271	0.113282	9012416	112	Table 10	3
Fourth Method	0.978947	0.958338	0.957959	1609632	112	Table 11	2
Fifth Method	0.979189	0.958812	0.958437	1600443	112	Table 12	1

5

5. CONCLUSIONS AND FINAL REMARKS

To days, despite the increasing importance of IC, most accounting systems fail to adequately account for IC in a transparent manner. The present paper was aimed to contribute towards the creation of IC measurement and valuation system and overcome some of the weaknesses of the IC valuation by answering two important questions; 1)how a firm's IC value can be measured?, and 2)is there a meaningful positive correlation between firms' IC and their share market prices? In this research, in order to answer the first question, five simple quantitative financial calculation methods were proposed. Also, based on each measuring method, the IC values, for all Iranian firms, were calculated. To answer the second question, we have statistically tested the correlation between the firms' IC values and their share market prices in the TSE. Results of the empirical study in the TSE, at the confidence level %95, clearly confirmed our main research hypothesis. Results of the empirical test clearly show that the IC values, were generated by the fourth and the fifth IC vlauing methods, were strongly correleted ($R \square 95\%$)to both the firms and the industries share market values. Considering the results, we can claim there is a strong and meaningful corelation between firms' IC values and their share market values.

REFERENCES

1- Andreou, A. N.; Boone, L. W. (2002) "The Impact of Information Technology and Cultural Differences on Organizational Behavior in the Financial Services Industry", *Journal of Intellectual Capital*, Vol. 3, No. 3, PP. 248-261.

2- Annell, E. (1989) Den Osynliga Balansra. Kningen Ledarskap. The Invisible Balance-sheet. Available at: www. Sveiby. Com. Au/Intang Ass/denosynl. Htm.

3- Barney, J. B. (1991) "Firm Resources and Sustainable Competitive Advantage", *Journal of Management*, Vol. 17, No. 1, PP. 99-120.

4- Bontis, N., Fitz-enz, J. (2002). Intellectual Capital ROI: A Causal Map of Human Capital Antecedents and Consequents", *Journal of Intellectual Capital*, Vol. 3, No. 3, PP. 223-247.

5- Brooking, A. (1997) "*Intellectual Capital*", International Thompson

6- Chen, S. (2003) "Valuing Intellectual Capital Using Game Theory", *Journal of Intellectual Capital*, Vol. 4, No. 2, PP. 191-201.

7- Das, S., Sen, P. K. & Sengupta, S. (2003) "Strategic Alliances: A Valuable Way to Manage Intellectual Capital", *Journal of Intellectual Capital,* Vol. 4, No. 1, PP. 10-19.

8- Edvinsson, L. and Malone, M. S. (1997) "*Intellectual Capital: Realising Your Company's True Value by Finding Its Hidden Brainpower*", Harper Business, London.

9- Hornery, S. (1999) "Speech Delivered at the International Symposium Measuring and Reporting Intellectual Captial: Experiences", Issues, and Prospects, OECD, Amsterdam, June.

10- Hunt, D. P. (2003) "The Concept of Knowledge and How to Measure It", Journal of Intellectual Capital, Vol. 4, No. 1, PP. 100-103.

11- Kaplan, R. and Norton, D. (1996) "Using the Balanced Scorecard as a Strategic Management System", Harvard Business Review.

12- Johnson, U., Martensson, M. & Skoog, M. (1999a) "Measuring and Managing Intangibles: Eleven Swedish Exploratory Case Strudies", Paper Presented at the International Symposium Measuting Reporting Intellectual Capital: Experiences, Issues, and Prospects, OECD, Amsterdam, June.

13- Johnson, U., Eklov, G., Holmgren, M. & Martensson, M. (1999b) "Human Resource Costing and Accounting Versus the Balanced Scorecard: A Literature Survey of Experience with the Concepts", Paper Presented at the International Symposium Measuring Reporting Intellectual Capital: Experiences, Issues, and Prospects, OECD, Amsterdam, June.

14- Johnson, W. H. A. (2002) "Leveraging Intellectual Capital through Product and Process Management of Human Capital", Journal of Intellectual Capital, Vol. 3, No. 4, PP. 415-429.

15- Johnson, W. H. A. 2003. Leveraging Intellectual Capital through Product and Process Management of Human Capital. Journal of Intellectual Capital, Vol. 4, No. 1, PP. 82-99.

16- Kittsa, B. Edvinsson L. & Beding, T. (2001) "Intellectual Capital: form Intangible Assets to Landscapes", Expert Systems with Applications, Vol. 20, PP. 35-50.

17- Leliaert, P. J., Candries, W. & Tilmans, R. (2003) "Identifying and Managing IC: A New Classification", Journal of Intellectual Capital, Vol. 4, No. 2, PP. 202-214.

18- Malcom, W. (2002) "International Encyclopedia of Business and Management", 2nd edn. New York: Thomson Business Press.

19- Mouritsen, J.; Larsen, H. T.; Bukh, P. N. D. (2001) "Intellectual Capital and Capable Firm: Narrating, Visualizing and Numbering for Managing Knowledge", Accounting Organizations and Society, Vol. 26, PP. 735-762.

20- Novicevic, M. M., Harvey, M., Pati, N., Kuffel. T. & Hench, T. (2002) "The Intangible/Intellectual Resource Curse Symptoms and Cures", Journal of Intellectual Capital, Vol. 3, No. 4, PP. 349-365.

21- O'Donnell, D., O'Regan, P., Coates, B., Kennedy T., Keary, B. & Berkery, G. (2003) "Human Interaction: The Critical Source of Intangible Value", Journal of Intellectual Capital, Vol. 4, No. 1, PP. 82-99.

22- Penrose, E. (1959) "The Theory of the Growth of the Firms", Basil Blackwell, Ox-Ford.

23- Petty, R. & Gurhrie, J. (2000) "Intellecture Capital Literatual Review: Measurement, Reporting and Management", Journal of Intellectual Capital, Vol. 1, No. 2, PP. 155-176.

24- Riahi-Belkaoui, A. (2003) "Intellectual Capital and Firm Performance of US Multinational Firms: A Study of the Resource- based and Stakeholder Views", Journal of Intellectual Capital, Vol. 4, No. 2, PP. 215-226.

25- Rodgers, W. (2003) "Meaurement and Reporting of Knowledge-based Assets", Journal of Intellectual Capital, Vol. 4, No. 2, PP. 181-190.

26- Rodov, I. & Leliaert, P. (2002), "FIMIAN: Financial Method of Intangible Assets Measurement", Journal of Intellectual Capital. Vol. 3, No. 3, PP. 323336.

27- Roos, J., Roos, G., Dragonetti, N. and Edvinsson, L. (1997) "Intellectual Capital: Navigating in the New Business Landscape", Macmillan Business, London.

28- Serrano Cinca, C., Mar Molinero, C. & Bossi Queiroz, A. (2003). The Measurement of Intangible Assets in Public Sector Using Scaling Techniques", Journal of Intellectual Capital, Vol. 4, No. 2, PP. 249-275.

29- Smith, M. & Hansen, F. (2002) "Managing Intellectual Property: A Strategic Point of View", Journal of Intellectual Capital, Vol. 3, No. 4, PP. 366-374.

30- Sveiby, K. E. (1997) "The New Organizational Wealth: Managing and Measuring Knowledge-Based Assets", Berrett-Koehler, New York, NY.

31- Wexler, M. N. (2002) "Organizational Memory and Intellectual Capital", Journal of Intellectual Capital, Vol. 3, No. 4, PP. 393-414.

32- Zhou, A. Z. & Fink, D. (2003) "The Intellectual Capital Web: A Systematic Linking of Intellectual Capital and Knowledge Management", Journal of Intellectual Capital, Vol. 4, No. 1, PP. 34-48.

Appendix

Table 3: AOVA (based on 7 years companies' data and first IC calculation method)

	df	SS	MS	F	Significance F			
Regression	1	5.42E+10	5.42E+10	0.058755	0.808508			
Residual	1504	1.39E+15	9.23E+11					
Total	1505	1.39E+15						
	Coefficients	Standard Error	t Stat	P-value	Lower 95%	Upper 95%	Lower 95.0%	Upper95.0%
Intercept	167242.9	25252.12	6.622925	4.89E-11	117709.7	216776	117709.7	216776
X Variable 1	0.011107	0.045823	0.242394	0.808508	-0.07878	0.10099	-0.07878	0.10099

Table 4: AOVA (based on 7 years companies' data and second IC calculation method)

	df	SS	MS	F	Significance F			
Regression	1	2.38E+14	2.38E+14	433.3625	4.67E-86			
Residual	1727	9.49E+14	5.49E+11					
Total	1728	1.19E+15						
	Coefficients	Standard Error	t Stat	P-value	Lower 95%	Upper 95%	Lower 95.0%	Upper95.0%
Intercept	240906.9	17827.98	13.51285	1.26E-39	205940.2	275873.6	205940.2	275873.6
X Variable 1	0.005891	0.000283	20.81736	4.67E-86	0.005336	0.006446	0.005336	0.006446

Table 5: AOVA (based on 7 years companies' data and third IC calculation method)

	df	SS	MS	F	Significance F			
Regression	1	2.24E+13	2.24E+13	23.54661	1.33E-06			

Residual	1755	1.67E+15	9.51E+11					
Total	1756	1.69E+15						
	Coefficients	Standard Error	t Stat	P-value	Lower 95%	Upper 95%	Lower95.0%	Upper95.0%
Intercept	254651.6	23286.46	10.93561	5.65E-27	208979.5	300323.7	208979.5	300323.7
X Variable 1	-0.05296	0.010915	-4.85248	1.33E-06	-0.07437	-0.03156	-0.07437	-0.03156

Table 6: AOVA (based on 7 years companies' data and fourth IC calculation method)

	df	SS	MS	F	Significance F			
Regression	1	1.61E+15	1.61E+15	35390.48	0			
Residual	1761	8.02E+13	4.56E+10					
Total	1762	1.69E+15						
	Coefficients	Standard Error	t Stat	P-value	Lower 95%	Upper 95%	Lower 95.0%	Upper95.0%
Intercept	54656.59	5196.669	10.51762	3.91E-25	44464.31	64848.88	44464.31	64848.88
X Variable 1	1.113967	0.005921	188.1236	0	1.102353	1.125581	1.102353	1.125581

Table 7: AOVA (based on 7 years companies' data and fifth IC calculation method)

	df	SS	MS	F	Significance F			
Regression	1	1.61E+15	1.61E+15	35938.69	0			
Residual	1769	7.94E+13	4.49E+10					
Total	1770	1.69E+15						
	Coefficients	Standard Error	t Stat	P-value	Lower 95%	Upper 95%	Lower 95.0%	Upper95.0%
Intercept	53979.82	5147.422	10.48677	5.29E-25	43884.15	64075.5	43884.15	64075.5
X Variable 1	1.286836	0.006788	189.575	0	1.273522	1.300149	1.273522	1.300149

Table 8: AOVA (based on 7 years industries' data and first IC calculation method)

	df	SS	MS	F	Significance F			
Regression	1	2.47E+12	2.47E+12	0.039754	0.84233			
Residual	110	6.84E+15	6.22E+13					
Total	111	6.84E+15						
	Coefficients	Standard Error	t Stat	P-value	Lower 95%	Upper 95%	Lower 95.0%	Upper95.0%
Intercept	4039326	758184.7	5.327628	5.34E-07	2536781	5541871	2536781	5541871
X Variable 1	0.347615	1.743441	0.199384	0.84233	-3.10748	3.802707	-3.10748	3.802707

Table 9: AOVA (based on 7 years industries' data and second IC calculation method)

	df	SS	MS	F	Significance F			
Regression	1	1.23E+14	1.23E+14	2.820346	0.095915			
Residual	110	4.81E+15	4.37E+13					
Total	111	4.93E+15						
	Coefficients	Standard Error	t Stat	P-value	Lower 95%	Upper 95%	Lower95.0%	Upper95.0%
Intercept	3518635	625949.8	5.621273	1.45E-07	2278148	4759121	2278148	4759121
X Variable 1	-0.00321	0.001913	-1.67939	0.095915	-0.007	0.000578	-0.007	0.000578

Table 11: AOVA (based on 7 years industries' data and third IC calculation method)

	df	SS	MS	F	Significance F			
Regression	1	1.23E+15	1.23E+15	15.18075	0.000168			
Residual	110	8.93E+15	8.12E+13					
Total	111	1.02E+16						
	Coefficients	Standard Error	t Stat	P-value	Lower 95%	Upper 95%	Lower95.0%	Upper95.0%
Intercept	4112923	889351.3	4.624633	1.03E-05	2350437	5875409	2350437	5875409
X Variable 1	-0.64607	0.165819	-3.89625	0.000168	-0.97469	-0.31746	-0.97469	-0.31746

Table 12: AOVA (based on 7 years industries' data and fourth IC calculation method)

	df	SS	MS	F	Significance F			
Regression	1	6.56E+15	6.56E+15	2530.288	9.44E-78			
Residual	110	2.85E+14	2.59E+12					
Total	111	6.84E+15						
	Coefficients	Standard Error	t Stat	P-value	Lower 95%	Upper 95%	Lower95.0%	Upper95.0%
Intercept	809362.3	165262	4.897449	3.36E-06	481851.6	1136873	481851.6	1136873
X Variable 1	1.131691	0.022498	50.30197	9.44E-78	1.087105	1.176277	1.087105	1.176277

Table 13: AOVA (based on 7 years industries' data and fifth IC calculation method)

	df	SS	MS	F	Significance F			
Regression	1	6.56E+15	6.56E+15	2560.674	5.03E-78			
Residual	110	2.82E+14	2.56E+12					
Total	111	6.84E+15						
	Coefficients	Standard Error	t Stat	P-value	Lower 95%	Upper 95%	Lower95.0%	Upper95.0%
Intercept	803639.2	164357.9	4.889567	3.47E-06	477920.2	1129358	477920.2	1129358
X Variable 1	1.306921	0.025827	50.6031	5.03E-78	1.255738	1.358104	1.255738	1.358104

18

Journal of Applied Sciences Research, 8(2): 983-991, 2012 ISSN 1819-544X
This is a refereed journal and all articles are professionally screened and reviewed

ORIGINAL ARTICLES

The Investigation Of The Relation Between Personnel's Emotional Intelligence And Professional Commitment (case study in National company of purging and Distribution of Oil Products in Iran (Shiraz))

¹Kamran Nazari, ²Mostafa Emami, ³Ali Reza Shakarbeigi

¹Department of Business Management, Payam Noor University, Kermanshah, Iran
²Young Researchers Club, Kermanshah Branch, Islamic Azad University, Kermanshah, Iran. ³Department of Law, Payam Noor University, Kermanshah, Iran

ABSTRACT

The main goal in this paper is to investigate the relation of emotional intelligence and career commitment of the personnel. The statistical society in this survey includes 300 employees of Iran (Shiraz) National Oil Products Infiltration and Distribution. Considering the sample volume by using Cockrun formula, 148 targets were selected which answered both questionaries, emotional intelligence standard by Mayer and Salvey and career commitment by and Mayer et al. in order to analyze the data, the software SPSS and also the average tests of some statistical society, Colmograph-Smironeph, Spearman adhesion coefficient and Freadman test were implemented. The results obtained from analyzing the information showed that in the studied society, there is some constant positive significant relation between self-controlling, sympathy, social skills and career commitment, and regarding the previous studies theories and backgrounds, these results were expected. But, unlike what we expected the analysis illustrated that self-controlling and social skills have negative significant relation with normative career commitment. The results, also, showed that in the considered statistical society, the emotional intelligence and career commitment were in a bad situation. Between the career commitment, the emotional career components and normative career commitment were in a bad situation and the constant career commitment, conversely, had a good situation.

Key words: emotional intelligence, career commitment, constant career commitment, normative career   commitment, emotional career commitment.

Introduction

In past decade, the issue presented in management literature has attracted the management researchers and scientists. The emotional intelligence is the issue in here. This issue that studies the personnel's feelings and emotions in working with others tries to explain the personnel's emotions place in their efficiency. A set of reports published from the investigation related to emotional intelligence issue, provided some promising results on personnel's emotional intelligence and their success. Some of these investigations show that the personnel with high emotional intelligent, has better functionality, organizational and career commitment, and are more satisfied of their own jobs than the others. These people have some characteristics such as self-controlling, selftraining, self-managing and controlling their emotions in workplace (Doostar, 1385).

The emotional intelligence includs the ability to pursuit and be incentive, to control the strokes, to control the emotion and to sympathy (Megarvey, 1997).

The emotional intelligent is known as the important resource of incitement, information, personal power, innovation, creativity and influence, that plays a vital role in improving the organization. Because, the emotional intelligent results in person's loyalty and organizational dependency, better compatibility with organization changes, technical improvements, human relations and making more logical decisions (Antonacopoulou & Gabriel, 2001).

J. Appl. Sci. Res., 8(2): 983-991, 2012

According to the subjects mentioned above and regarding the emotional intelligence importance, the main goal in this research is that is there any relation between emotional intelligent components and personnel's carrer commitment in Iran National (Shiraz) Oil Products Infiltration and Distribution Company, or not.

The emotional intelligence:

Corresponding Author: Kamran Nazari, Department of Business Management, Payam Noor University, Kermanshah, Iran
E-mail: Kamrann0156@yahoo.cm

The emotional intelligence is not a new concept, and Aristotle seems to be the first one who considered the importance of emotions in human relations. It is easy to get angry, everyone could get angry, but it is not easy to get angry on right person, at the correct time, for some sensible reason and in a correct way (Calman, 1382).

Here, the emotional intelligence means the academic studies and researches conducted on emotional intelligence and emotions, in twenty century. Based on the criterion presented with Thomas Cohen in his remarkable book, "scientific revolutions structure" about the paradigm, there could be seen some signs of maturation in emotional intelligence paradigm. The emotional intelligence has entered to psychology literature as a concept, which is rooted in Thorndike and Gardner works and is resulted from connecting intellectual and emotional minds, and the correlation between emotion and reason. The emotional intelligence is a new component in studies that many researchers are intended to use it in various fields. The emotional intelligence theory is some modern view about predicting the success factors in life, including work activities and efficient opposition against stressful factors as the mental disorders resource, because many characteristic significances such as sympathy, self-propensity, optimism, self-simulating, stress controlling, self-awareness and emotions managing, result in success in different fields of life. Emotional intelligence illustrates the social and personality emotional dimensions, which are often considered and appeared in daily activities (Saboori Moghadam, 1372).

Intelligence is one of the human's critical mechanisms that include the ability to be compatible with environment. Some part of intelligence is appeared in social and personal relations. Regarding to Thorndike, social intelligence includes ability to understand internal situations, incentives and self and others behavior and optimal functions according to the information. Gardner in his octoploid theory, considers the personal (inter and intera personal) intelligence and explains the person's ability to be aware of emotions, to distinguish between them and to use the data to give efficient answer against the environment, as one of the intelligent aspects (Plaamer & Donaldson, 2001). Obviously, since very early in the intelligence studies, cognitive aspects such as memory and problem solving have been emphasized. While, non-cognitive dimensions including emotional and functional abilities are not only acceptable but also necessary. Gradually, the insights on intelligence quotient have been replaced by studying other effective abilities in human functionality. For example, Thorndike (1920) explained the intelligent behavior including visual intelligence (fabricating skills and implementing the instruments), abstract intelligence (the ability to use the words, numbers and scientific principals) and social intelligence (recognizing the people and the ability to perform creative behaviors in human relations). Wechster, D (1943) offers that the intelligence non-cognitive aspects like emotional- sentimental, social and personal abilities to prospect self- abilities to be obtain success and compatibility in life, are important (Chiva & Alegre, 2008).

Basically, the emotional phenomenon, provide a particular resource for people about the environment and searching for them, and these data form the concepts, behaviors and feelings. It is supposed that people use various amounts of understanding, intellect and implementing these emotional data. The emotional intelligence theory provides a new insight about predicting the effective factors of success and also initial prevention from mental disorders, which is a supplementary to cognitive science and nervous science and the emotional intelligence abilities are so important for emotional self-controlling and subtle contraptions (King & Gardner, 2006).

Giving the general intelligence alone is not sufficient to reach success and the research show that in best situations the general intelligence is just 25% percent of success and the rest is depend on fortune, emotional and social intelligence (Golman, 1380).

Genetically, the emotional intelligence is not stable and is not formed just in childhood period, unlike the general intelligence which is slightly changed after adolescence. The emotional intelligence is more often learned and during the life it is formed based on the experiment. The research on determining the emotional intelligence level during the life show that the human is getting better and also is obtaining more skills to manage self-emotions (Golman, 1383).

The emotional intelligence frame, it's formal definition and the offers on how to measure it, were appeared in 1990, in two articles by Salovey, P & Mayer, J, for the first time. The initial definition was based on some two-part procedure, in which the first part includes total general data processing and the second part consists of personalizing the emotions, compatibly in order to improve the life progress. The emotional intelligence as some ability includes the capacity of understanding the instruments, recognizing, implementing and managing self and others emotions (Khaef Elahi & Doostar, 1382).

J. Appl. Sci. Res., 8(2): 983-991, 2012

Golman explains the emotional intelligence as the ability to keep the incentives and to resist against the problems, to control the anger and to postpone the success, to adjust the mental conditions and to prevent distress from disturbing the thoughts, to have sympathy with others and to be hopeful. According to Goldman, the emotional intelligence includes recognizing and controlling self-emotions, having sympathy with others and keeping satisfactory relations. In other words, the person with high emotional intelligence combines three emotional components (cognitive, physiological and behavioral components), successfully (Golman, 1380).

Since the critical components of emotional intelligence include the ability to understand the others emotions and to adjust self and others consistency, it is expected that the people with high emotional intelligence show better social skills and compatibility. Therefore, the social skills include the social life expeditors that help people to have efficient and reciprocal relations; moreover, the social skills are bilateral and the people with good social skills receive good behaviors and are liked with the others (Palmer & Donaldson, 2001).

Bar-on & Parker consider the emotional intelligence as a form of intelligence that is resulted from thoughts and emotions and they mean to reach the total structure of emotional, personal and social abilities that affect on ability to insist against requests and environmental stress (Chiva & Alegre, 2008).

In some research between 19 organizations in Arab states, it was illustrated that there is some negative significant relation between emotional intelligence and opposition. In this research, when the emotional intelligence was evaluated as the selected sample with supervisors, the adhesion coefficient was -0.52 and when emotional intelligence was evaluated by the personnel, the adhesion coefficient was -0.22, and it shows that the personnel and supervisors have different insights on the amount of emotional intelligence (Suliman & Shaikh, 2007; 208-220).

In some research conducted on big manufacturing organizations in England, the relation between emotional intelligence and leadership efficiency was investigated. In order to investigate the leadership efficiency, the supervisors' ideas were implemented. The selective sample included 38 supervisors and 1258 personnel. The Pierson adhesion coefficient between emotional intelligence and leadership efficiency was 39%, and it shows that there is some positive relation with 99% confidence between emotional intelligence and leadership efficiency. The emotional intelligence components in this research were: self- sentiment understanding, sentiments implementing, others feelings understanding and sentiments managing, and no significant relation was obtained between two first components with leadership efficiency and two other components (Stein & Sitarenio, 2009).

Koman & Wolff in some research between 81 teams in military organizations investigated the relation between emotional intelligence of group leaders and the amount of organizational intelligence in group level. In this research, also, the effect of group emotional intelligence on the group functionality was investigated. In fact, in this survey the group emotional intelligence is considered as interfering variable. The results of this research showed that the group emotional intelligence has completely positive relation with the leader emotional intelligence and also there is some positive relation between group emotional intelligence and functionality (Koman & Wolff, 2008).

In some study, Grant investigated the short-time and long-time training on the amount of emotional intelligence. The results in his study showed that the long-time training plan (in this study, 13 weeks) could improve the emotional intelligence, significantly (Grant, 2007).

Some research was conducted on 92 managers from general communications and 129 managers from Australia banks on the relation between emotional intelligence and financial function. The results illustrated that there is some significant positive relation between emotional intelligence and financial function of the banks (Heffernan & Droulers. M, 2008).

In some research on 8 ceramic companies in Spain, the results showed that the organizational learning capacity is as a regulator variable that could affect the relation between emotional intelligence and work satisfactory. The results illustrated that there is some positive relation between emotional intelligence and organization learning capacity. Also, the results of this research showed that there is no significant relation between emotional intelligence and work satisfactory, unless the organization learning capacity, affect the relation between these two variables, as a regulator factor (Chiva & Alegre, 2008).

In some research conducted on 156 professional personnel in New Zealand, it was illustrated that there is some positive relation between understanding the others feelings and social support (King & Gardner, 2006).

The adults showed better emotional intelligence skills than the others. Mayer, in his research, showed that the emotional intelligence improves with aging and experience from childhood to adulthood (Golman, 1383).

The research illustrate that people with lower emotional intelligence, facing with life stressful situations will have less conformity, and as a result they would get into trouble with depression, disappointment, and other negative consequences. Conversely, people with higher emotional intelligence, choose their life style in such a way that they face with less negative consequences and they also skilful in creating high quality relations. Totally, the emotional intelligence is related to the life events and helps the people to understand and predict the different daily aspects (Chiva & Alegre, 2008).

Siarochi et al pointed that the emotional intelligence regulates the relation between stress and psychological conformity. By psychological conformity, we mean the characteristics related to depression and disappointment and suicide tenets. In other research, they found that the people with skills in regulating the feelings are provided with higher social support, and this social support prevents them against depression and suicide tenets. Some people believe that today emotional intelligence plays a significant role in being succeeded in life and work. The studies show that bravery, sympathy, happiness and emotional self-awareness, as various factors of emotional intelligence, have the most effect on new success for employees, and also implementing the emotional intelligence test in selecting new employees shows that most newly employed persons would reach to significantly higher scores in bravery, sympathy, happiness and emotional self-awareness (Khaef Elahi and Doostdar, 1382). Investigating about 200 global organizations and companies indicates that one-third of differences is related to cognitive ability and technical skills and two-third of them is related to emotional potencies (Golman, 1998).

In some research conducted on 105 personnel from health care sector in U.S., it was concluded that sentimental intelligence has a critical role in investigating the relation between organizational commitment and ability to have sentimental conformity. This research showed that the personnel with high sentimental conformity ability, with a higher sentimental intelligence, will have more commitment. It means that, if it is proved that in some organization the emotional intelligence scores are in a high level, so it could be concluded that the personnel with higher sentimental intelligence will have more organizational commitment (Humphreys, Brunsen & Davis, 2005).

In some other research conducted on 200 officers in Niger police office, it was found that work experience, self-efficiency, emotional intelligence and incentive could affect on the amount of commitment (in order to analyze data in this research, we used the regression model and the Fischer statistics 5.856 was obtained: Aremu, 2005).

In some investigation on students graduated in gob course from 3 Malaysia, Poon found that for personnel with average to high sentimental intelligence, the work commitment will affect the work direction improvement. The results, also, showed some positive relation between work satisfactory and the amount of salary (Poon, 2004.

Career commitment:

The term carrer commitment is derived from psychology and has been improved from the current term organizational commitment (Hall *et al*, 2005). It has the study directions same as the organizational commitment (Herr, 2005). The definitions related to career commitment differ from the amount of work the person has to do in his work place to the important role of the work in life (Somech & Bogler, 2002).

The career commitment is considered as one of the most important determinant factors for the persons' work behaviors and it is the favorite issue for many managers and people in educational places (Kannan & Pillai, 2008).

The "career commitment theory" also presents that more the person invests on some issues, more hard is the commitment. Therefore, more encouraged the person to enter the work and more activities performed to provide such encouragement, 1988). The professional people, consider themselves as someone with full-time career which they should all their best for that and they feel limitless commitment on their career, because it is valuable for them (Favela & Fuzessery, 1974).

The career commitment is described as the insight of the person on his/ her career (Fjortof & W.I. Lee, 1994). The career commitment pointes to the dependency people have on their career. In fact, the career commitment includes believing the aims and the career values and having tendency to try considerably to reach the career and to get involved in it (Elias, 2006).

The career commitment is defined as the level of designating the functional standards to be performed (Jones, 2000). Wallas et al define the career commitment same as Allen and Mayer's for organizational commitment. They consider three normative, sentimental and continuum dimensions to the career commitment and define the career commitment as feeling personality with some career, needing to continue serving in some career and having a high sense of duty against it (Osinsky & Mueller, 2004).

In some study on accountants' career commitment, Arnya, Bullak and Arming, define the career commitment by replacing the word career for the term organizational in Porter's definition for organizational commitment.

1.   Believing the aims and their values and accepting them;

2.   Having tendency to do the best in performing the career; 3. Having tendency to continue and keep involvement in career.

So, the people with high commitment in their career do their best to perform their career and this would result in career success and fail internalizing as their own success or fail (Giffords, 2003).

Considering the career as some desired professional value is derived from initial activities conducted on career characteristics. Career commitment has mostly favored by Gouldner, who determined the difference between career commitment and organizational commitment for professional people in Borkeratic organizations (Tayler, 1988). And additionally, this interest toward the career commitment was formed after the researchers found that the career commitment in people has various positive effects (Hall *et al*, 2005).

Llee et al, address four reasons for the career commitment importance:

1.   Most of the time, in the life, is spent for the career.

2.   Because career commitment affects maintenance, keeping and remembering, therefore, it has considerable meanings to manage the human source.

3.   Because the career skills are resulted from experience, so, functionality could be related to the career commitment.

4.   Further studies on career commitment may show that how people combine different internal and external commitments (Elias, 2007).

J. Appl. Sci. Res., 8(2): 983-991, 2012

Career commitment is related to considerable aspects including functional improvement, replacement decrease and satisfactory increase in organizational and professional levels (Elias, 2006). The research show that personnel's high level commitment results in more incentive and satisfaction and therefore decreases the possibility to leave the organization (Huang, 2006).

The career commitment, probably, affects the functionality of personnel such as their observable theories, their opinions on work output and their involvement in professional groups. The career commitment is related to positive behaviors which are useful for the organization and consequently the people with higher career commitment would less get involved in inadvisable activities for organization (Greenfield, 2008).

A dutiful person is interested in keeping the involvement or presents a considerable endeavor, not because of getting advantage but for the reason that he/ she believes it is better to behave in such a way because it's true and because he/ she is expected to do so (Raju & Shrivastava, 1994).

Goals of research

This research by considering the importance of emotional intelligence and professional commitment of the workers pursues the following goals:

1. Survey the relation between emotional intelligence and professional commitments of the workers of Iran's national refinery and oil products Distribution Company (in Shiraz).

2. Presenting necessary solutions to improve emotional intelligence and increase professional commitment of the workers based on the findings of the research.

Method

As in this paper researcher tries to determine and survey emotional intelligence and its relation with professional commitment of the workers of Iran's national refinery and oil products distribution company (in Shiraz), so the paper follows the method of descriptive researches of quantifiable branch. Statistical population is 300 workers of Iran's national refinery and oil products distribution company (in Shiraz) and the research sample is 148 workers based on the following formula;

$$n = \frac{(300)(1/96)^2(0/5)(0/5)}{(0.5)^2(300-1) + (1/96)^2(0/5)(0/5)} = 148$$

Main information of this paper has been collected through two ways;

Library method: in this method books, theses, essays, information bases and internet sources were used to collect information about the history and literature of the matter.

Free method: In this method sage counseling and interview were used to design and analyze questionnaire. The main tool of this paper is the questionnaire which is one of the common tools of research and a direct way of getting research's data. Two kinds of questionnaire have been used to scale the variables. One of the questionnaires was Maier's and et al which was used for scaling the workers professional commitments and the other was emotional intelligence questionnaire of Maier and Slave which was used for scaling the components of emotional intelligence and descriptive and illative statistics have been used. Colmogrof-Smirnof tests of average of a statistical population, correlation factor of Spearman and Freedman test have been used.

Findings

In this research in order to test the research hypothesis, it must be determined whether the distribution of the collected data is normal or not. Being normal or not will be evaluated based on statistic test of Clomongr ofSnirnof, the results of this test are in following table;

Distribution of observations follow the normal distribution	H0:ρ=0
Distribution of observations don't follow the normal distribution	H1: $\rho\neq0$

Table 1: Colemogrof-Smirnof

variable	Sample amount	اماره ازمون	Sig amount	Test result
Emotional intelligence	148	0.993	0.278	Normal distribution
Professional commitment	148	0.991	0.280	Normal distribution

As we can see in table 1 the amount of اماره ازمون in level of 0.05 is less than the critical amount, so the zero hypothesis that means the data are normal is accepted and the corresponding hypothesis which means data are not distributed normally is rejected. Therefore as the data are normal in order to test these hypotheses Spearmen correlation test is used.

Based on the research's goals a main and fifteen particular hypotheses have been mentioned and tested which their results come as follow:

J. Appl. Sci. Res., 8(2): 983-991, 2012

main hypothesis

there is a positive and meaningful relation between emotional intelligence and professional commitments of the workers of Iran's national refinery and oil products distribution company (in Shiraz).

Particular hypotheses

Based on the main hypothesis fifteen particular hypotheses as follow came to the researcher's mind:

1. There is a positive and meaningful relation between self-control and emotional professional commitments of the workers of Iran's national refinery and oil products distribution company (in Shiraz).

2. There is a positive and meaningful relation between self-consciousness and emotional professional commitments of the workers of Iran's national refinery and oil products distribution company (in Shiraz).

3. There is a positive and meaningful relation between self- stimulation and emotional professional commitments of the workers of Iran's national refinery and oil products distribution company (in Shiraz).

4. There is a positive and meaningful relation between sympathy and emotional professional commitments of the workers of Iran's national refinery and oil products distribution company (in Shiraz).

5. There is a positive and meaningful relation between social skills and emotional professional commitments of the workers of Iran's national refinery and oil products Distribution Company (in Shiraz).

6. There is a positive and meaningful relation between self- control and continuous professional commitments of the workers of Iran's national refinery and oil products Distribution Company (in Shiraz).

7. There is a positive and meaningful relation between self-consciousness and continuous professional commitments of the workers of Iran's national refinery and oil products Distribution Company (in Shiraz).

8. There is a positive and meaningful relation between self-stimulation and continuous professional commitments of the workers of Iran's national refinery and oil products Distribution Company (in Shiraz).

9. There is a positive and meaningful relation between sympathy and continuous professional commitments of the workers of Iran's national refinery and oil products Distribution Company (in Shiraz).

10. There is a positive and meaningful relation between social skills and continuous professional commitments of the workers of Iran's national refinery and oil products Distribution Company (in Shiraz).

11. There is a positive and meaningful relation between self-control and regulated professional commitments of the workers of Iran's national refinery and oil products Distribution Company (in Shiraz).

12. There is a positive and meaningful relation between self-consciousness and regulated professional commitments of the workers of Iran's national refinery and oil products Distribution Company (in Shiraz).

13. There is a positive and meaningful relation between self- stimulation and regulated professional commitments of the workers of Iran's national refinery and oil products Distribution Company (in Shiraz).

14. There is a positive and meaningful relation between sympathy and regulated professional commitments of the workers of Iran's national refinery and oil products Distribution Company (in Shiraz).

15. There is a positive and meaningful relation between social skills and regulated professional commitments of the workers of Iran's national refinery and oil products Distribution Company (in Shiraz).

Conceptual model of the research

In this paper Meir and Solve's model has been used for emotional intelligence, and for professional commitment Meir's and et al model has been used which we can see in figure number 1.

Fig. 1: Conceptual model of the research

Dimensions of emotional intelligence	professional commitment
Self-regulation	Emotional professional commitment
self-consciousness	continuous professional commitment
self- stimulation	regulated professional commitment
sympathy	

J. Appl. Sci. Res., 8(2): 983-991, 2012

social skill

In order to survey the condition of emotional intelligence dimensions, the average test of statistical population has been used and its results are shown in the table 2.

Table 2: condition of emotional intelligence professional commitment's variables

variable	Variable's condition	average
emotional intelligence	undesirable	2.8659
professional commitment	undesirable	2.7569
self-control	undesirable	2.7799
self-consciousness	undesirable	2.8595
self- stimulation	mean	3.0714
sympathy	undesirable	2.8056
social skill	undesirable	2.5594
Emotional professional commitment	undesirable	2.0933
continuous professional commitment	undesirable	1.4683
regulated professional commitment	desirable	4.0488

In order to test the hypotheses Spearman correlation factor has been used. In table 3 we can see correlation and meaningfulness factors between emotional intelligence's and professional commitments' variables.

Table 3: Correlation and meaningfulness factors between emotional intelligence's and professional commitment's variables.

variables	Emotional commitment	professional	continuous professional commitment		regulated commitment	professional
	correlation factor	meaningfulnes s factors	correlation factor	meaningfulness factors	correlation factor	meaningfulness factors
self-control	0.433	0.000	0.301	0.009	-0.451	0.000
Selfconsciousness	0.190	0.105	0.190	0.105	0.057	0.635
self- stimulation	0.123	0.284	-0.074	0.518	-0.029	0.804
sympathy	0.384	0.003	0.298	0.011	-0.202	0.093
social skill	0.281	0.019	0.244	0.043	-0.303	0.013

The amount of correlation factor of emotional intelligence and professional commitment was 0.344 and because their meaningfulness factor was less than 0.05 and was 0.012 we come to this conclusion that there is a positive and meaningful relation between emotional intelligence and professional commitment, therefore the main hypothesis is accepted.

By considering table 3 we come to the following conclusions about particular hypotheses:

1.   There is no relation between self- consciousness and emotional professional commitment, continuous professional commitment and regulated professional commitment. As the meaningfulness factor is more than 0.05, therefore hypotheses 2, 7 and 12 are rejected.

J. Appl. Sci. Res., 8(2): 983-991, 2012

2.   As the meaningfulness factor is less than 0.05 and correlation is positive, there is a positive relation between self-control and emotional professional commitment. Therefore hypothesis 1 is accepted.

3.   As the meaningfulness factor is more than 0.05, there is no relation between self-control and regulated professional commitment. Therefore the hypothesis 11 is accepted.

4.   As the meaningfulness factor is less than 0.05 and correlation factor is negative, there is a negative relation between self-control and continuous professional commitment. Therefore hypothesis 6 is accepted

5.   As the meaningfulness factor is more than 0.05, there is no relation between self- stimulation and regulated professional commitment and continuous professional commitment. Therefore hypotheses 3,8 and13 are rejected.

6.   As the meaningfulness factor between sympathy and emotional professional commitment and continuous professional commitment is less than 0.05 and their correlation factors are positive. Therefore hypotheses 4 and 9 are accepted. However as the meaningfulness factor between sympathy and regulated professional commitment is more than 0.05, hypothesis 14 is rejected.

7.   As the meaningfulness factor between social skill and emotional professional commitment and continuous professional commitment is less than 0.05. Therefore hypotheses 5, 10 and 15 are accepted. However as the correlation factor between social skill and emotional professional commitment is positive, there is a positive relation between social skill and emotional professional commitment, but their correlation factors are negative, so there is a negative relation between social skill and regulated professional commitment.

Freedman test has been used to rank emotional intelligence's and professional commitment's variables. These variables are shown based on their importance in table 4.

Table 4: ranking of the intelligence's and professional commitment's variable.

Rank	emotional intelligence's variable	Average of score
1	stimulation	5.77
2	Self-consciousness	4088
3	self-control	4.42
4	sympathy	4.63
5	social skill	3.57
Rank	professional commitment's variable	Average of score
1	regulated professional commitment	2.88
2	emotional professional commitment	1.91
3	continuous professional commitment	1.20

Conclusion:

In nowadys world economic power and comfort of a country are functions of expert, commitment and capable human force. As a result of growing and developing organizations, one of the problems that they are faced is the reduction of professional commitments of their workers which has resulted in absence and delay of their workers, clash and contrast in work environments, growing lack of realism and reduction of energy for doing profitable activities. Different approaches have been offered to increase professional commitment in different sources; one of these approaches has prescribed the use of emotional intelligence's variables. Emotional intelligence is a matter which tries to explain and interpret the place of emotions and feelings in man's capabilities. Workers who have emotional intelligence are effective workers and eagerly accept organization goals and with high level of satisfaction try to gain the goals and they have the highest level of commitment and their approaches to control are a kind of self-control based on self-consciousness.

Emotional intelligence studies the role of individual emotions and feelings in their personal and social life, their works with others and it is an effort to explain and emplace individual emotions and feelings in their effectiveness. A set of researches and reports published by survey relevant to the matter of emotional or thrilling intelligence, have presented a hopeful conclusion about the relation between individual's emotional intelligences and their successes. Some of these researches claim that those workers who have a better function, work commitment and high level of job satisfaction, they have some features like; self- control, self- regulation, self- management and also are able to control their emotions , feelings and thrills in job environment (Xaefellahi and Dostar, 2006).

In this paper by considering the importance of emotional intelligence, the relation between emotional intelligence and professional commitments of workers of Iran's national refinery and oil products Distribution Company (in Shiraz) has been surveyed. Its findings show that in this statistical population there is a positive and meaningful relation between self-control, sympathy, social skill and emotional and continuous professional commitment. Based on relevant precedent theories and literature of the matter these findings were expected, however something that was unexpected was that; there was a negative meaningful relation between self-control, social skill and regulated professional commitment. These findings also showed that in the statistical population emotional intelligence and professional commitment had undesirable conditions. All components of emotional intelligence except for self-

J. Appl. Sci. Res., 8(2): 983-991, 2012

control which had a mean condition had undesirable conditions. But continuous professional commitment had a desirable condition. Based on the paper's goal and findings and the researcher's observations during the research, some advices and offers come as follow that will result in increasing the emotional intelligences of the workers and as its consequence increasing their professional commitment:

1. To increase sympathy workers must be sensitive to their own emotional signs and improve their effective eavesdrops.

2. By holding some training sessions we must inform the managers of the importance of nonmaterial requirements of the workers and also train them so that by relying on their cognition, knowledge and acquired skills will be capable to feel sympathy with the workers.

3. Social skills must be increased so that organizational structures will be more flexible and a premise will be prepared for increasing the horizontal relations and team work.

4. Managers and workers must try to use win-win strategy in their negotiations so that a desirable atmosphere will be made for negotiations in the organizations.

5. The organization must consider the workers emotional capabilities in choosing them and giving them promotions because based on this paper's findings worker's high level of emotional intelligence results in increasing their professional commitment and affecting the better function of the organization.

6. By considering this fact that the relation between emotional intelligence and job success and worker's professional commitment has been proved, the researcher's offer for human sources' managers and the organization industrial psychologists is to design some tests and mechanisms to evaluate applicants emotional intelligences before their entrance t o the organization.

References

Antonacopoulou, E.P., Y. Gabriel, 2001. Emotion, learning and organizational change: Towards an intergration of psycchanalytic and other perspectives" Journal of Organizational Change Management, 14(5): 435-451.

Aremu, A.O., 2005. "A confluence of credentialing,career experience,self-efficacy, Emotional intelligence & motivation on the career commitment of young police in Ibadan ,Nigeria" ,policing:international Journal of police strategies and management, 28(4): 609-618.

Carman, A., 2001. "staf burnout and patient satisfaction" Journal of occupational health psychology,7: 235-241.

Cherniss, C., 1992. "long term consequences of burn out : An exploratory study "journal of organizational behavior, 13: 2-11.

Chiva, R & J. Alegre, 2008." Emotional intelligence and job satisfaction: the role of organizational learning capability" ,personnel review, 37(6): 680-701.

Elias, R.Z., 2006. Theimpact of professional commitment and anticipatory socialization on accounting students ethical orientation; Journal of Business Ethics, pp: 83-90.

Freudenberger, H.J., 1974. "staff burn out"Jornal of social issues, 30: 15o-165.

Fullerton, G., 2003. When does commitment lead to loyalty?; Journal of Ghage Management, 14(4): 333-334.

Giffords, E.D., 2003. An examination of organizational and professional commitment among public; not profit and proprietary social service employees; Administration in Social Work, 27(3): 5-23.

Golman, Denial, 2001. "Emotional Intelligence" , Parsa, Nasrin, Tehran, Roshed Publication.

Golman, Denial, 2004. "Emotional Intelligence in Work" Ebrahimi, Bahman; Joyandeh, Mohsen,Tehran, Bahin Danesh Publication.

Grant, A.M., 2007. "Enhancing coaching skills and emotional intelligence through training" 39(5): 257-266.

Hall, M., D. Smith and K. Smith, 2005. Accountants commitment to their profession: multiple dimensions of professional commitment and opportunities for future research ; Behavioral Research in Accounting, 17: 89-109.

Heffernan, T., G. Oneill, T. Travaglion & M. Droulers, 2008. "relationshipe marketing" ,international Journal ofbank marketing, 26(3): 183-199.

Humphreys, J., B. Brunsen. & D. Davis, 2005. "Emotional structure and commitment:implications for health care management" ,Journal of health organization and management, 19(2): 120-129.

Jones, J., 2000. The impact of hospital mergers on organizational culture, organizational commitment, professional commitment , job satisfaction and intent to turnover on registeral nurses on medical, surgical hospital units; State University of New York.

Kanan, R. and S.M. pillai, 2008. An examination on the professional commitment of engineering college teacher; International Business Management, 2(6): 218-224.

Kerr, R., J. Garvin, N. Heaton. & E. Boyle, 2006. "emotional intelligence and leadership effectiveness" ,leadership & organizational development Journal, 27(4): 265-279.

King, M. & D. Gardner, 2006. "emotional intelligence and occupational stress among professional staff in NewZealand" ,international Journal of organizational analysis, 14(3): 186-203.

Koman, E.S. & S.B. Wolff, 2008."emotional intelligence competencies in the team and team leader ,Journal of management development, 27(1): 55-75.

J. Appl. Sci. Res., 8(2): 983-991, 2012

Maslach, C., & S.E. Jackson, 1993. "Manual of the Maslach Burn out Inventory"(2nded).Palo Alto: Consulting psychologist press Inc.

Mcgarvey, R., 1997. Final score:get more from employees by upping your EQ; Enterpreneur., 25(7): 78-81.

Osinsky, P. and C. Wmueller, 2004. Professional commitment of Russian provincial sp Paul .

Palmer, B, & C. Donaldson, 2001. "Emotional intelligence and life statisfaction"Retrieved from: http:///www.genos.com.au/pdg/EI-satisfaction.pdf.

Parry, J., 2006. The effect of workplace exposure on professionsl commitment : a longitudinal study of nursing professionals; Central Queensland University.ecialist; Journal of Work and Occupations, 31(2): 193-224.

Poon, J.M., 2004."Career commitment & career success : moderating rol of emotion perception",career development international., 9(4): 374-390.

Rraju, P.M and R.C. Shriavastava, 1994. Factors contributing to commitment to the teaching profession; International Journal of Educational Management, 8(5): 713.

Saborimoghadam, Hasan, 1993. "The Relation Between Control Focus and Individual's Work under Stress", M.A thesis of Clinical Psychology, Tahran Psychiatric Institute.

Stein, S.J., P. Papadogiannis, J.A. Yip. & G. Sitarenios, 2009. " Emotional Intelligence of leaders: aprofile top executives" , ,leadership & organizational development Journal., 30(1): 87-101.

Suliman, A.M. & F.N. Al-Shaikh, 2007. "Emotional intrlligence at work links to confilict and innovative", employee relations, 29(2): 208-220.

Ting, C. and S. Chun Hua, 2000. Understanding the professional Career commitment of medical laboratory professionals; The Journal of Health Sience, 2(4): 369-380.

Xaefallahi, Ahmadali; Dostar, Mohammad, 2003. "Emotional Intelligence's Dimensions", Chronicle Management and Development, 18: 52-62.

Developing fuzzy AHP approach to select appropriate TBM for excavation of Shiraz subway

Mostafa Emami (PHD)[1]
Associate Professor -Young Research Club, Islamic Azad University, Tehran, Iran
Amrolah Amini (PHD)
Associate Professor -Allameh Tabatabaei University, Tehran, Iran
Alireza Emami (PHD)
Associate Professor -University of Tehran, Tehran, Iran

Abstract

Today regarding to increasing of cities population and traffic, construction of subways is a solution. There are deferent methods for construction of subways. Extraction with full face machine (TBM) is a general method. This method has advantages and problems. Faster penetration rate than other methods is an important benefit of TBM. The high primal value of TBM is a problem. Therefore many economic & technical studies should be make before project start. If we result that we should use TBM the next step is TBM selection. According to variety of TBM types and effective parameters on excavation, the selection is difficult. For Shiraz subway, the FAHP method is used. There are 4 alternatives and 5 criteria. This types are selected by previous excavation experiments, zone position and tunneling aspects. After the calculations, weight of EPB shield machine maximized and this machine selected.

Keywords: Multi criteria decision making, Triangular fuzzy numbers , fuzzy AHP, TBM, Shiraz subway

[1] **Correspondent Address**:Mostafa Emami* (PHD)
Associate Professor -Young Research Club, Islamic Azad University, Tehran, Iran , Address: P O Box: ▮▮▮ Tehran –Iran
Tel:+ ( ) ▮▮▮ Cell:+▮▮▮ Fax:+▮▮▮ Contact:+▮▮▮
Email: MEMAMI@MTU.EDU MOSTAFA.EMAMI@MODARES.AC.IR

1-Introduction

The daily increase of population and expansion of cities in recent years necessitates fast and reliable transportation to prevent heavy traffic and time loss of citizens. Thus, the construction and expansion of the underground systems is in the long term programs of governments. This has led to the invention of different drilling methods and devices worldwide. Choosing the appropriate drilling method requires the familiarity with the way devices operate, the area of their operation, and the geological and geotechnic parameters and conditions of the project route. Maybe it is not possible to draw a clear cut line for the application of drilling devices because today most of them are designed and produced based on the geo technique properties of the project route and the companies daily introduce new machines that meet new needs based on technological developments. In this project the quality of choosing the appropriate drilling machine based on information available in different offices and the categorization of different producers is done, to which we point later. Choosing the drilling machine is very important because the wrong choice often leads to such problems as loss of life and property, changes in the plan and even the shutting down of the whole project.

There are different ways of choosing the right Tunnel Boring Machine (TBM), each of which has some advantages and disadvantages. Due to the existence of numerous parameters and their different effects, choosing the proper TBM is a time consuming process. To facilitate this selection, the multi-criteria decision making methods are suggested. The multi-criteria decision making methods consist of AHP, TOPSIS, ELECTRE, etc. For this study, the AHP method is utilized because the outcome of this method is close to the real outcome in previous similar works. Considering that in Iran numerous underground tunnels are under research for construction, the presentation of this article can persuade similar projects to employ AHP for choosing appropriate TBM. By choosing the appropriate TBM it is possible to considerably reduce the executive costs. For using this FAHP method, the information driven from research, experience, and the projects under construction were compared in pairs and the parameters were scored. Since the comparisons were based on the projects under construction and the outcome of research done by tunnel construction experts, the outcome can actually be the current judgment of experts. For the pair comparisons, the effusive and crude judgments must be avoided because it leads to wrong selection.

Multi-criteria selection method has been employed in different drilling projects. The following are some cases. Panou (2002) used the multi-criteria selection to choose one of the options (the tunnel way or surface). In his article, Nakamura (2006) used the multi-criteria selection for specifying the tunnel management system. Padma (2009) used the AHP for tunnel preservation system. Mikaeil and others (2009) used FAHP method to categorize the rate of TBM penetration in the hard rocks condition. Naghadehi and others (2009) presented an article titled "choosing the optimized subterraneous excavating method for Iran Jajarm's boxit mine using FAHP method"; however, no significant work has been done using the fuzzy multi-criteria selection method for choosing TBM, where the present article can be deemed a totally new work. The aim of this article is to choose the best TBM for Shiraz underground concerning the available options and standards via FAHP method. TBM photo is shown in fig.1.

2 -General geology of Shiraz

Shiraz plain, covering 225 square kilometers, is stretched from east to west. Shiraz city is built on the sedimentations of the third and the fourth geological ages. These sedimentations consist of clay stone, sandstone, conglomerate, tuf, tufit, zhips, and such alluvial sediments as clay, silt, sand, and gravel (GNU consulting company, 2007). The major part of Shiraz valley is covered with the young and none consolidated sedimentations most of which are in the form of sediments of glacial rivers with divergent profiles and grain size. New alluvial sediments along with lake sediments have covered the old place. Current sediments consist of silted and clay layers along with sand and grit. The more you go toward the west of the city, the more you see fines material. Geographical location of Shiraz city and shiraz palain are shown in fig.2 & fig.3.

2 -1-Technical specifications of the tunnel

The tunnel of the first line of the Shiraz underground is 8 kilometers long and two way(Fig.4). It starts from the Shiraz University square and starches to Laleh square, consisting of 9 stations ((GNU consulting company, 2007)). The maximum distance of the tunnel ceiling from the ground is 25 meters, where the minimum runs between 4 to 6 meters. The slope is 3 percents, the horizontal drilling diameter being 300 meters and the vertical drilling diameter being 2000 meters. The drilling diameter by the TBM is around 6.88 meters, where after segmenting and filling the back of segments it runs to the effective diameter of 6 meters.

2-2- specification of line 1 of Shiraz subway

This line having a 22/4 kilometers lingth from the Gole sorkh square and through Valie asr square reaches to Ehasan square.

The main depot is located at 1300 meters south east Gole sorkh square and depot no. 2 is adjacent to Ehsan square.

This line will be equipped by 20 underground and one surface stations. The first line will pass the land belonged to municipality along all its path.

In first 15 kilometers (Gole sorkh square to Zargari st.) the path will be constructed in terms of two separate tunnel with 7 meters approximate diameters and from zargari st and through Ghasrodasht,ghasrodasht sq, from golkhoon st. to chamran bridge, path will be developed as a shallow tunnel, from chamran bridge to mirza khuchak khan sq on the ground, adjacent to khoshk river and again as a shallow 10 meter wide tunnel from mirza kuchak khan sq to ehsan sq.

Main station and shootinggallery will be design and constructed with about 27 hectars area in order to stop about 120 wagons and cleaning operation and perfect accomplish of light and heavy reparation periodically. Station no.2 is consider merely for stopping about 18 wagon will be constructed at a 15 meters deep level in a 20000 m2 vast area(Alamut bridge and building company, 2005). Map of line 1 is shown in Fig.5.

2 -3- the result of geo technical experiments

Along the first line of Shiraz underground, i.e. from the front of the Shiraz University to the Laleh square, the boring operation was done in two initial and complementary phases. In the initial phase 12 bores and in the complementary phase 8 bores were drilled. The outcome of the geo technical experiments indicated the geological properties of the route (table 1). In the whole route no ground water was encountered, and regarding the grain size, most of the ingredients were grits. Regarding the shallowness, it is completely shallow, and its penetrability (S.P.T) differs from 8 to 50(Alamut bridge and building company, 2005).

The necessary cautions about the table:

1- Ground water is not encountered in any of the drilled bores, thus the respective column is left blank.

2- The dashed cells mean that no information is available about them in the reports of the geo technical

    experiments.

3 -Fuzzy Analytic Hierarchy Process

Analysis Hierarchical Process (AHP) is a multi-criteria decision making tool first proposed by Saati (1980). Since it was introduced, AHP have been one of the most useful multi-criteria decision making tools available to decision makers and researchers. Although AHP is sophisticated in recording knowledge, the conventional AHP is unable to veritably reflect the way human thinks (Kahraman, Cebeci & Ulukan, 2003). Although it uses a precise yardstick to compare the opinions of decision makers, the conventional AHP becomes confusing (Wang & Chen, 2007). AHP is criticized for using lopsided judgmental scales and its inability to properly consider the inherent uncertainty and carelessness of pair comparisons (Deng, 1999).

To overcome these deficiencies, FAHP is developed to resolve the expanded hierarchical issues. Decision makers found out that distanced judgment is more persuasive than rigid judgments. That's because the individual often cannot explicitly express his preferences regarding the fuzzy nature of comparison process (Kahraman et al, 2003). Since the relative importance specified by the AHP decision makers is oral, it is vague and imprecise. Decision makers often prefer to employ oral presentation rather than numerical value. Because due to the nature of pair comparisons they cannot explicitly express their opinions about priorities. In such conditions the best solution is to make decisions on the basis of multiple conditions and goals to achieve a relatively desirable level of achievement. These issues have caused the nature of decision making to be full of complexities and ambiguities in the most minor to most major cases. Consequently, most decisions are made in a fuzzy environment. Therefore, considering that the fuzzy logic method is proposed for decision making in uncertain and ambiguous situations, using this method can reduce ambiguities and increase the effectiveness of decisions made (Ertugrul & Karakasoglu, 2009).

3 -1-Triangular fuzzy numbers (TFNs)

Central to the fuzzy set theory is the notion of the fuzzy number. In applications it is often convenient to work with TFNs because of their computational simplicity(Giachetti & Young, 1997; Moon & Kang,2001), and they are useful in promoting representation and information processing in a fuzzy environment(Liang & Wang,1993). In addition,TFNs are the most utilized in FAHP studies(Chang,1996; Chiou & Tzeng,2001; Kou et al,2002; Zhu,1999).

ATFN A can be defined by a triplet (l, m, u) and the membership function $\mu_A(x)$ can bedefined by (Chiou & Tzeng,2001; Polat et al, 2007)

$$\mu_M(x) = \begin{cases} \dfrac{x-l}{m-l} & l \le x \le m \\ \dfrac{u-x}{u-m} & m \le x \le u \\ 0 & otehrwise \end{cases}$$

Where x is the mean value of A and l, m, u are real numbers. In this paper only the three relevant algebraic operations are illustrated. Define twoTFNs A and B by thetriplets A= $(l\ m\ u^1,\ ^{1\ 1},\ )$ and B= $(l\ m\ u^2,\ ^2,\ ^2)$. Then

addition: $A \oplus B$ $(l\ m\ u_1,\ _{1\ 1},\ )\oplus(l\ m\ u_2,\ _2,\ _2)$ $\square$ $\square(l_1\ l\ m_2,\ _1\square m\ u_2\ _1,\ \square u_2)$ multiplication: $A \otimes B$ $(l\ m\ u_1,\ _{1\ 1},\ )\otimes(l\ m\ u_2,\ _2,\ _2)$ $\square$ $\square(l_1\ l\ m_2,\ _1\square m\ u_2\ _1,\ \square u_2)$

$$(l\ m\ u_1,\ _{1\ 1},)^{-1} \square \ (1u\ ,1m\ ,1l\ ) \quad inverse:$$

where $\square$ represents approximately equal to. A TFN is shown in Fig.6

3-2- Literatsure review

Many methods and applications of FAHP are suggested by numerous researchers. Van Laarhoven and

Pedrcyz (1983) suggested the first principles of fuzzy logic employed in AHP. Buckley (1985) invented the trapezoidal fuzzy numbers to express decision makers' evaluation regarding each criterion. Chang (1996) introduced a new method of FAHP using triangular fuzzy numbers for pair comparisons. Traintaphyllou and Lin (1996) developed the methods of multi-indexed fuzzy decision making. These methods are based on AHP, the weighted sum model, the weighted product model and TOPSIS. Deng (1999) presented a fuzzy approach for the qualitative multi-criteria analysis in a simple and clear cut manner. Zhu, Jing, and Chang (1999) demonstrated the basic theory of triangular fuzzy numbers and improved the formula of the comparison of fuzzy numbers' size. Upon this, they introduced an actual example of oil discovery. Leung and Cao (2000) suggested a compatible fuzzy description while observing the tolerance deflection.

Chou and Liang (2001) proposed a multi-criteria fuzzy decision making model integrated with the theory of fuzzy collection, AHP, and anthrop for evaluating the performance of sailing companies. Bozdag, Kahraman, and Ruan (2003) presented four multi-purposed fuzzy decision making methods to come up with the best possible solution for the computerized integrated manufacturing system. One of these methods is FAHP, the others being Yager's weighted goals method, Blin's approach, and fuzzy synthetic evaluation. Chang, Cheng, and Wang (2003) put out a methodology of evaluating the performance of airports. They used the gray statistical model for choosing criteria and employed FAHP for specifying the weight of criteria. They finally utilized fuzzy integration and TOPSIS approach to rate the performance of airports. Hsieh, Lu, and Tzeng (2004) proposed a multi-criteria fuzzy approach for programming and choosing the options in general buildings of companies. FAHP method is for specifying the weight for assessing criteria among decision makers. Mikhailov and Tsvetinov (2004) employed the AHP new fuzzy regulation to assess services. The proposed fuzzy prioritizing method use paired comparisons in relation with the precise numerical value of comparisons and the initial prioritizing issue converts to non-linear programming.

Tang and Beynon (2005) used FAHP method to apply and expand static investment studies. They tried to align the owned machines with hired ones. Bashgil (2005) created an analytic tool to choose the best software for achieving the best customer satisfaction. Gu and Zhu (2006) devised the symmetrical fuzzy matrix as the area of goal indication. This matrix is created upon the fuzzy decision and FAHP method using the estimated fuzzy vector. Tuysuz and Kahranman (2006) invented an analytic tool to estimate the risk of projects suffering from insufficient and vague information. They used FAHP to assess the IT project risk of a Turkish company.

Ayag and Ozdemir (2006) proposed an intelligent approach based on FAHP to assess the tools' options. They first used FAHP under multiple indexes for weight and options and then performed the cost/benefit analysis using FAHP and provisions. Lee Chan and Kumar (2007) provided a model to create an organizational framework for a universal provider considering the risk factors. They used FAHP in selecting the universal provider. Chen and Chang (2008) invented an approach based on FAHP and Balanced Scorecard (BSC) the IT section of industry in Taiwan. Tang (2009) introduced an approach for the budget allocation of an aero space company using FAHP and Artificial Neurotic Network (ANN). Ertugrul and Karakasuglo (2009) employed a model by integrating BSC, FAHP, and TOPSIS the cement companies of Turkey. Torfi, Farahani, and Rezapour (2009) used a multi-criteria decision making approach by employing FAHP and FTOPSIS to assess the alternative options for preferred demands of users. Zheng, Ging, Shi, and Zhang (2010) developed FAHP model to assess the energy conservation in China's buildings. Also, Hsu, Lee, and Kreng (2010) mixed FAHP and fuzzy Delphi method to choose the technology for recycling lubricants.

3-3- FAHP methodology

In this study, we utilize Extent Analysis(EA) method, as originally proposed by Chang (1996). In this method,for each pair rows of pairwise comparisons matrix, the amount of Sk which is a triangular number, is calculated as follows (Ertugrul & Karakasoglu,2009):

$$S_k \square \square \ \square\square_{n \ ji} \quad \square_{n} \quad_{m} \quad _{ji}\square$$
$$m_g \square\square \qquad m_g \square$$ (١)
$$_{j\square 1} \qquad \square_{i\square \square 1\, j\, 1} \qquad \square$$

K represents the number of rows and i and j, respectively, indicate alternatives and indicators. In EA method after amounts of Sk calculation must their large degree compared with each other is calculated. A large degree on the M1 with M2 is indicated as (M1 ≥ M2) which is calculated as follows:

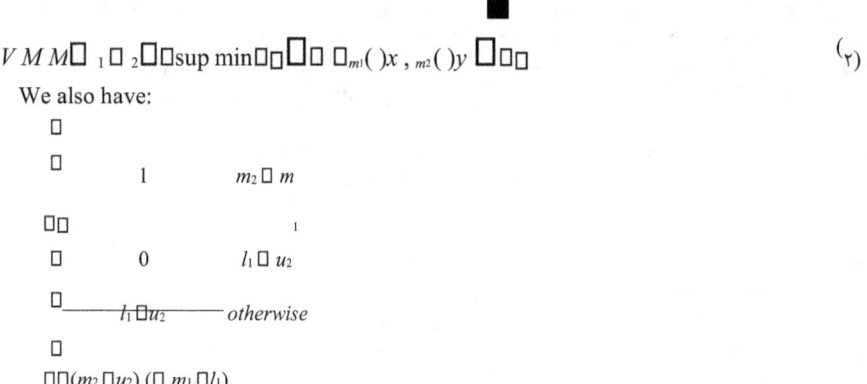

$$V\, M\, M\square_{1}\square_{2}\square\square \sup \min\square\square\square\square\ \square_{m_1}(\ )x\ ,_{m_2}(\ )y\ \square\square\square$$ (٢)

We also have:

$$\square$$
$$\square \qquad 1 \qquad\qquad m_2 \square m$$
$$\square\square \qquad\qquad\qquad\qquad _1$$
$$\square \qquad 0 \qquad\qquad l_1 \square u_2$$
$$\square \underline{\qquad l_1\square u_2 \qquad} otherwise$$
$$\square$$
$$\square\square(m_2\square u_2)\ (\square\ m_1\square l_1)$$

The large degree on the M with M1, M2, … , Mk is calculated as follows:

$$V\, M\, M\, M(\square_1, \quad _2,...,M_k)\ \square\, V\, M\, M\ and\ M\, M\ and\ M\, M\square(\square_1)\ (\square_2)\ ...(\square_k)\square\square\ \min V\, M$$

$$M(\square_i^{)}\ i\ \square 1,2,...,k$$ (٣)

Suppose that d(Ai) = min V(Si ≥Sk), k=1,2,3,…, n, k≠ i. Then the following weight vector is obtained.

$$A\ i_i(\ \square 1,2,...,n)$$ (۴)

that $A\ i^i(^{\square 1,2,...,n})$ are n elements. For normalization, the normalized weight vectors as follows which W is a non-fuzzy number:

$$W\ \square\ (\ (d\ A_1),d\ A(\ _2,..., (d\ A_n)))^T$$
(۵)

4 -Case Study

Choice of TBM suitable device for subway tunnel excavation in Shiraz is objective. In this decisionmaking problem, we have five criteria and four alternatives. Alternatives contain various devices, including EPB shield, combination shield, slurry shield and compressed air shield, that action of selection is based on experience from previous excavations, regional situation and different issues of tunneling.

Criteria include aggregation, permeability, safety, operational environment and investment. After identifying alternatives, criteria and objective of the problem, pairwise comparisons matrices of alternatives in terms of different criteria and pairwise comparisons matrix of criteria in terms of themselves are formed. Hierarchical structure of reaserch figure is shown in Fig.7. To form this matrices, nine point scale according to Table 1 has been used. Easier to indicate criteria and altenatives each with ID according to Table 2 has been introduced. You can see hierarchical structure of research in Figure 2. For this study FAHP method has been used. Chosen because the proximity of answers to real answer is in previous similar works. As previously mentioned, AHP method due to use AHP unequal judgment scales, disability in applying appropriate uncertainty and inherent careless in the process of pairewise comparison includes weaknesses (Kahraman et al, 2003). For this reason and to reduce uncertainties and to increase the effectiveness of the decisions, we use FAHP method for our work that in its kind and the appropriate device TBM selection is a new work.

In the intermediate mode of these modes, numbers of 2,4,6 and 8 belong to the desired alternative. In fuzzy mode, triangular fuzzy numbers are used for pair-wise comparisons that this action is done by using saati spectrum 1/9 to 9.

4 -1-Utilizing FAHP Method for selecting suitable device of TBM Shiraz Metro

Decision makers from different views may define different weight vectors. This usually not only makes vague evaluation but also provides several problems during the decision process (Chen, 2004). For this reason, we offer a group decision based on pairwise comparisons.

FAHP method has been selected to reduce uncertainty and ambiguity in decision making and to obtain subjective judgments of experts (Ertugrul & Karakasoglu, 2009). To fill the tables by experts, from 9-point spectrum of saati has been used. For this work, 1o experts in the field of tunneling was selected. To gather opinions of experts, special survey forms was provided and sent for them. Then ranking experts merged from

■

the following formula and comprehensive pairwise camparisons matrix was developed.

$$1_k$$

$$\square x_{ij} \square\square\square a\ b\ c_{ij}\ ,\ _{ij}\ ,\ _{ij}\ \square\ ,\ l_{ij}\ \square\ \min\square a_{jk}\square,m_{ij}\ \square\ \_k\ \square_{k\square1}b_{ijk}\ ,u_{ij}\ \square\ \max\square d_{ijk}\square$$

Pairwise comparison matrices of alternatives in relation with different criteria and pairwise comparison matrix of all of criteria in relation with one another are shown in Table 4 to 9. comparisons are shown as triangular fuzzy numbers.

Sk calculation for various alternatives in relation with criteria are summarized in tables 10 to 14. The table for calculating Sk for critria in relation with one another are also summarized in Table 15.

In the last stage of calculation, for each alternative, weighted average is calculated which is summarized in Table 16. Considering calculations done in tables 4 to 15 and forming table 16 under the FAHP method is obtained, slurry shield (A3) alternative as the best alternative for Shiraz Metro tunnel excavation is selected.

5 -Conclusions and recommendations

One of the most fundamental issues of mechanized Tvnlzny, especially Tvnlzny using TBM, is to select the type of machine which dig tunnel. There is methods for selecting which include AHP method as the most appropriate. But due to weakness mentioned before, we have proposed method FAHP, utilizing fuzzy set theory and triangular fuzzy numbers. Objective of this study is to determine the most appropriate TBM device for excavating tunnel of Shiraz metro. To solve this problem with regard to previous similar work and surveys of experts and consultants and experts about digging subway and tunneling area, 4 alternative and 5 criteria are considered. After processing, the most appropriate alternative (TBM with slurry shield) has been selected (by utilizing FAHP method). For future studies, Utilizing other methods of multi criteria decision making techniques such as fuzzy TOPSIS and ELECTERE III to solve similar problems and comparing results of the methods compared with existing method is proposed. Using artificial neural networks (ANN) and combining with FAHP method or comparison of these two approaches to solve similar problems can also be another suggestion that the results would be valuable. FAHP method can also be used in other areas related to tunneling and excavation and its branches.

References

Alamut bridge and building company,(2005) geo technical tests results report, subway project in Shiraz, Shiraz,

Baslığ il, H. (2005). The fuzzy analytic hierarchy process for software selection problems. Journal of Engineering and Natural Sciences, 3, 24–33.

Bozdağ , C. E., Kahraman, C., & Ruan, D. (2003). Fuzzy group decision making for selection among computer integrated manufacturing systems. Computer in Industry, 51, 13–29.

Buckley, J. J. (1985). Fuzzy hierarchical analysis. Fuzzy Sets and Systems,17, 233–247.

Chang, D. Y. (1996). Applications of the extent analysis method on fuzzy AHP. European Journal of Operational Research, 95, 649–655.

Chang, Y. H., Cheng, C. H., & Wang, T.C. (2003). Performance evaluation of international airports in the region of east Asia. In Proceedings of Eastern Asia Society for transportation studies (Vol. 4, pp. 213–230).

Chen, H. (2004). A research based on fuzzy AHP for multi-criteria supplier selection in supply chain. Master thesis, National Taiwan University of Science and Technology, Department of Industrial Management

Chou, T. Y., & Liang, G. S. (2001). Application of a fuzzy multi-criteria decision making model for shipping company performance evaluation.Maritime Policy & Management, 28(4), 375–392.

Deng, H. (1999). Multicriteria analysis with fuzzy pair-wise comparison. International Journal of Approximate Reasoning, 21, 215–231.

Ertuğ rul, I, & Karakasoğ lu, N. (2009). Performance evaluation of Turkish cement firms with fuzzy analytic hierarchy process and TOPSIS methods. Expert Systems with Applications, 36(1), 702–715.

GNU consulting company, reports of the metro line project in Shiraz, Shiraz, 1386

Gu, X., & Zhu, Q. (2006). Fuzzy multi-attribute decision making method based on eigenvector of fuzzy attribute evaluation space. Decision Support Systems, 41, 400–410.

Hsieh, T. Y., Lu, S. T., & Tzeng, G. H. (2004). Fuzzy MCDM approach for planning and design tenders selection in public office buildings. International Journal of Project Management, 22, 573–584.

Hsu,Y,L. Lee,C,W. Kreng,V,B.(2010). The application of Fuzzy Delphi Method and Fuzzy AHP in lubricant regenerative technology selection. Expert System with Applications,37,419-425

Kahraman, C., Cebeci, U., & Ulukan, Z. (2003). Multi-criteria supplier selection using fuzzy AHP. Logistics Information Management, 16(6), 382–394

Kahraman, C., Ruan, D., & Dog¨an, _I. (2003). Fuzzy group decision making for facility location selection. Information Sciences, 157, 135–153.

Lee, A. H. I., Chen, W. C., & Chang, C. J. (2008). A fuzzy AHP and BSC approach for evaluating performance of IT department in the manufacturing industry in Taiwan. Expert System with Applications,34, 96–107.

Leung, L. C., & Cao, D. (2000). On consistency and ranking of alternatives in fuzzy AHP. European Journal of Operational Research, 124, 102–113

Mikaeil, R., Naghadehi, M, Z., Sereshki, F.(2009). Multifactorial fuzzy approach to the penetrability classification of TBM in hard rock conditions. Tunnelling and Underground Space Technology, 24, 500-505

Mikhailov, L., & Tsvetinov, P. (2004). Evaluation of services using a fuzzy analytic hierarchy process. Applied Soft Computing,

5, 23–33.

Naghadehi, M,Z., Mikaeil, R., Ataei, M. (2009).The application of fuzzy analytic hierarchy process (FAHP) approach to selection of optimum underground mining method for Jajarm Bauxite Mine, Iran. Expert Systems With Applications, 36, 8218-8226

Nakamura, F. and Ohtsu, H. (2006) " Development of a tunnel management system for existing railroad tunnel", In Tunnelling and Underground Space Technology, 21: 312–313.

Padma, T. and Balasubramanie, P. (2009) " Knowledge based decision support system to assist work-related risk analysis in musculoskeletal disorder", In Knowledge-Based Systems, 22: 72-78.

Panou, K.D. and Sofianos, A.I. (2002) " fuzzy Multicriteria evaluation system for the assessment of tunnels visa-vis surface roads: theoretical aspects—part I" In Tunneling and Underground Space Technology, 17 : 195–207.

Tang, Y., & Beynon, M. J. (2005). Application and development of a fuzzy analytic hierarchy process within a capital investment study. Journal of Economics and Management, 1(2), 207–230.

Tang,Y,C.(2009). An approach to budget allocation for an aerospace company—Fuzzy analytic hierarchy process and artificial neural network. Expert System with Applications,72,3477-3489.

Torfi,F.,Farahani,R,Z & Rezapour,S.(2009). Fuzzy AHP to determine the relative weights of evaluation criteria and Fuzzy TOPSIS to rank the alternatives.Applied Soft Computing,Article in press

Triantaphyllou, E., & Lin, C. T. (1996). Development and evaluation of five fuzzy mutiattribute decision-making methods. International Journal of Approximate Reasoning, 14, 281–310.

Van Laarhoven, P. J. M., & Pedrcyz, W. (1983). A fuzzy extension of Saaty's priority theory. Fuzzy Sets and Systems, 11, 229–241

Wang, T. C., & Chen, Y. H. (2007). Applying consistent fuzzy preference relations to partnership selection. Omega, the International Journal of Management Science, 35, 384–388

Zheng,G.Jing,Y.Huang, H.Shi,G.Zhang,X.(2010). Developing a fuzzy analytic hierarchical process model for building energy conservation assessment. Renewable Energy,35,78-87.

Zhu, K., Jing, Y., & Chang, D. (1999). A discussion on extent analysis method and applications of fuzzy AHP. European Journal of Operational Research, 116, 450–456.

Fig.7

Goal

A
lternatives

๕rite
ei Criteria

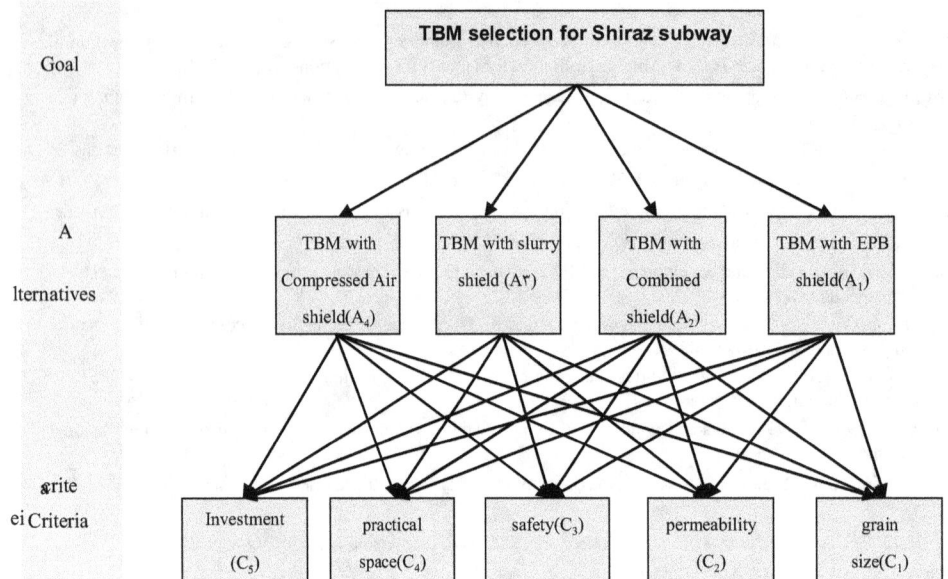

Empirical Investigation of Factors Moderating IT–Performance Relationship in Developed and Developing Countries

Mostafa Emami (PHD)[1]
Associate Professor -Young Research Club, Islamic Azad University, Tehran, Iran
Amrolah Amini (PHD)
Associate Professor -Allameh Tabatabaei University, Tehran, Iran
Alireza Emami (PHD)
Associate Professor -University of Tehran, Tehran, Iran

Abstract

This paper provides and tests a new conceptual model that offering an empirically based insight into the effects of IT-Performance moderators in developed and developing countries. Using data from 34 developed and 211 developing countries and applying Pearson Correlation Method and Structured Equation Model, we found that Economic, Business and Competition, Geographical, and Population factors with their interactions significantly moderate the relationship between IT diffusion and national level performance in both developed and developing countries. However, we found that National Health modertor variable significantly moderates the IT-performance relationship in developing but not in developed countrirs. Results of this research confirm fitness of the data with our proposed new model.

Key words: IT diffusion, national performance, developing countries, developed countries, structured equation model

1. Introduction

Most of researchers and development specialist believe that IT has a great impact on organizations performances and nations' developments. Although the amount of investment on IT has rapidly increased in recent years, however researchers are concern because of paradox in the results of IT. In other words, the application of IT to development goals has not always succeeded to date and there are many cases of partial or complete failure. [2][3] Accordingly, the main question of most researchers has now become how IT can be benefcal for development and what factors affect on IT diffusion with national performance. Although literature introduces a numerous factors affecting IT investment and usage and shows various differences in these factors between developed and developing countries, however, there are a few empirical researches to study their effects on IT-Performance relationship in a systematic way.

The purpose of this paper is to develop and test a new conceptual model that offering an empirically based insight into the effects of IT-Performance moderators in developed and developing countries. For this purpose, the remainder of the paper structured as follows. The following section summarizes the literature. Section 3 provides the new conceptual model and research hypotheses. Section 4 describes data and methodology. Section 5 provides the empirical results. Finally, the paper ends with conclusions and final remarks.

[1] [1] ***Correspondent Address**:Mostafa Emami* (PHD)

Associate Professor -Young Research Club, Islamic Azad University, Tehran, Iran , Address: P O Box: 1767778151 Tehran –Iran
Tel:+98(21)33440612Cell:+98(912)7001816Fax:+98(910)2294653Contact:+1(816)2370018+44(871)2185070+44(871)218-6050 Email: MEMAMI@MTU.EDU MOSTAFA.EMAMI@MODARES.AC.IR

2. The Literature

Brief review of the literature shows that there are numerous factors affecting IT usage and there are various differences in these factors between developed and developing countries. Tables 1 and 2 summarize factors moderating the relationship between IT and performance in general and in developed and developing countries.

Table 1: Most widely used variables in literature

Type of Variables	Factors	Measures
Independent Variable	Information Technology Diffusion (Investments)	☐ IT investment [7][13][21][35][36][40][43] ☐ IT use at country level [12][16][21][29][35] ☐ IT spending on hardware and software as percent of GDP [36] ☐ Computer hardware imports and production [12]
Dependent Variable	National Productivity Level	☐ Productivity growth at the macroeconomic level [12][13][21][24] Level of national wealth [35][40][43] ☐ Technical progress [11][35]
Common Used General Moderator Variables	Most widely-used, official-☐ source development data ☐ from the World Bank and ☐ other international agencies ☐	Total external debt to gross national income (Economic Indicator) GDP (current US$) (billions) (Economic Indicator) GNI per capita, Atlas method (current US$) (Economic Indicator) Life expectancy at birth, total (years) (Social Indicator) ☐ Population, total (millions) (Social Indicator) ☐ Population growth (annual %)(Social Indicator) ☐ Surface area (sq. km) (thousands) (Infrastructural &Natural Indicator)

Table 2: Factors affecting IT investment and diffusion

Factors	Factors
• Educational level [7][12][21][23][25][34][42] • Professional and Training level [23][7][21][25] • Perception of user toward IT [25] • Commitment level [26] • Enterprise readiness [27] • ICT readiness [27] • External Environment readiness [[27] • Human readiness [27] • Information readiness [27] • Completeness assets [12][13][21][29][35][40][43] • Telecommunications networks [12][21][29][40][43][35] • Skilled IT professionals [35][40][43] • Lack of resource for technology investments [34][35][40][42][43] • Structure of economy [7][12][21][29][35][36][40][43] • Openness to external influence [12][13][35][40][43] • Digital infrastructure [7][10][21] • Macro economy situation [10] • Ability to invest [10] • Knowledge citizens [10] • Competitiveness [10] • Access to skilled workforce [10]	• Cost of living and pricing [10] • Technology accumulation [35] • Lack of resources for technology investment [35] • Infrastructures [12][21][29][35] • Skilled human resource [12][21][29][35] • Property rights protection [12][36] • Lack of clean water, inadequate housing and freedom [34][42] • National culture and cross cultural differences [1][4][5][8][9][10][14][16][20][22][28][30][31][33][37][38][39][41] • Organizational culture [17][19] • Business Ethics [30] • Language and translation problems [8] • Culturally heterogeneous teams [6][15] • Culture of bureaucracy and institutional fragmentation [32] • Poverty [35] • Lack of infrastructure [35] • Inadequate education [35] • Incorrect assumptions and policy makings [35] • Legal similarity [38] • Political context [38][42]

As shown in Tables 1 and 2, there are huge number of factors moderating the relationship between IT diffusion and performance. In order to test their effects, we have categorized all factors into 5 general dimension; Economic Dimension, Business and Competition Dimension, Geographical and Infrastructural Dimension, Population, Gender and Literacy Dimension, and National Health Dimension. The main idea is that the relation between IT diffusion and national performance in developed and developing countries moderate by these five general factors (dimensions). We describe the conceptual model of this research in the next section.

3. The Model and Research Hypotheses

3.1 The Conceptual Model

In order to investigate the effects of moderator factors on the relationship between IT usage and country level performance, we developed the following general conceptual mode (Figure 1):

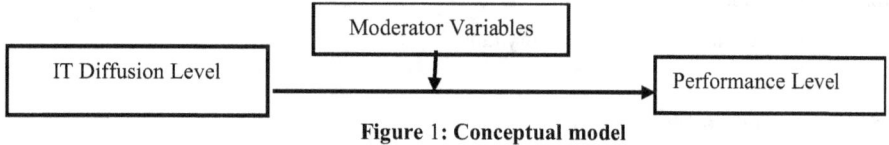

Figure 1: Conceptual model

Figure 2 shows the extended version of conceptual model.

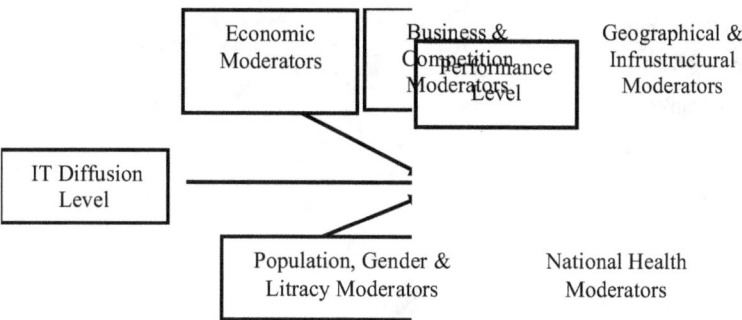

Figure 2: Extended version of the conceptual model

3.2 *The Operational Model and Variables*

In this section, we define independent, dependent and moderator variables and introduce the operational model of this research. The variables are as follows:

IT Diffusion Level (Independent Variables: X)

XTE1=Internet hosts country ranks

XTE2=Internet users country ranks

XTE3=Telephones-main lines in use country ranks

XTE4=Telephones-mobile cellular country ranks

XTE5=Television broadcast stations country ranks

Country level Performances (Dependent Variables:Y)

XEB4=Reserves of foreign exchange and gold country ranks

XEB1=Unemployment rate (%)country ranks

XEB6=Population below poverty line (%) country ranks

XEB13=Inflation rate(consumer prices)(%) country ranks

XEB18=GDP - per capita (PPP) country ranks

Economic Moderator Variables

XEB2=Stock of direct foreign investment - at home country ranks

XEB3=Stock of direct foreign investment - abroad country ranks

XEB7=Market value of publicly traded shares country ranks

4

XEB8=Labor force - by occupation–services (%) country ranks

XEB9=Labor force - by occupation–industry (%) country ranks

XEB11=Labor force country ranks

XEB12=Investment (gross fixed and % of GPD) country ranks

XEB15=Imports country ranks

XEB17=GDP - purchasing power parity country ranks

XEB20=GDP - composition by sector – services (%) country ranks

XEB23=Exports country ranks

XEB24=Economic aid - recipient country ranks

XEB25=Economic aid - donor country ranks

Business & Competition Moderators Variables

XDB2=Starting a business country ranks

XDB3=Dealing with licenses country ranks

XDB4=Employing workers country ranks

XDB5=Registering property country ranks

XDB6=Getting credit country ranks

XDB7=Protecting investors country ranks

XDB8=Paying taxes country ranks

XDB9=Trading across borders country ranks

XDB10=Enforcing contracts country ranks

XDB11=Closing a business country ranks

XDB12= Number of foreign companies listed in a country, country ranks

Geographical & Infrastructural Moderator Variables

XT1= Airports country ranks

XT2=Heliports country ranks

XT3=Merchant marine (ships) country ranks

XT4=Pipelines (km) country ranks

XT5=Railways (km) country ranks

XT6=Roadways (km) country ranks

XT7=Waterways (km) country ranks

XG1=Land Area - sq km country ranks

XG2=Total Area - sq km country ranks

National Health Moderators Variables

XP14=HIV/AIDS - people living with HIV/AIDS country ranks

XP17=Infant mortality rate – total (deaths/1,000 live births) country ranks

XP35=Total fertility rate (children born/woman) country ranks

XP11=Death Rate (deaths/1,000 population) country ranks

XP20=Life expectancy at birth – total (years) country ranks

Population, Gender & Literacy Moderators Variables

XP4=Age structure 15-64 years country ranks

XP10=Birth Rate (births/1,000 population) country ranks

XP26=Median age–total (years) country ranks

XP27=Net migration rate country ranks

XP28=Population country ranks

XP29=Population growth rate (%) country ranks

XP34=Sex ratio 15-64 years (male(s)/female) country ranks

XP23=Literacy–total (%) country ranks

This research examines following research hypotheses for developed and developing countries:

For developed countries:

H11a: (XTE1) correlates positively with (XEB4)

H12a: (XTE1) correlates negatively with (XEB1)

    H13a: (XTE1) correlates negatively with (XEB6)

    H14a: (XTE1) correlates negatively with (EXB13)

    H15a: (XTE1) correlates positively with (XEB18)

    H21a: (XTE2) correlates positively with (XEB4)

    H22a: (XTE2) correlates negatively with (XEB1)

    H23a: (XTE2) correlates negatively with (XEB6)

    H24a: (XTE2) correlates negatively with (EXB13)

    H25a: (XTE2) correlates positively with (XEB18)

    H31a: (XTE3) correlates positively with (XEB4)

    H32a: (XTE3) correlates negatively with (XEB1)

    H33a: (XTE3) correlates negatively with (XEB6)

    H34a: (XTE3) correlates negatively with (EXB13)

H35a: (XTE3) correlates positively with (XEB18)

H41a: (XTE4) correlates positively with (XEB4)

H42a: (XTE4) correlates negatively with (XEB1)

H43a: (XTE4) correlates negatively with (XEB6)

H44a: (XTE4) correlates negatively with (EXB13)

H45a: (XTE4) correlates positively with (XEB18)

H51a: (XTE5) correlates positively with (XEB4)

H52a: (XTE5) correlates negatively with (XEB1)

H53a: (XTE5) correlates negatively with (XEB6)

H54a: (XTE5) correlates negatively with (EXB13)

H55a: (XTE5) correlates positively with (XEB18)

H1am: Economic, Business and Competition, Geographical and Infrustructural, Population-GenderLiteracy, and National Health readiness factors moderate the relationships among (XTE1), (XTE2), (XTE3), (XTE4), and (XTE5) with (XEB4),(XEB1), (XEB6), (XEB13),and (XEB18) in developed courtiers.

For developing countries:

H11b: (XTE1) correlates positively with (XEB4)

H12b: (XTE1) correlates negatively with (XEB1)

H13b: (XTE1) correlates negatively with (XEB6)

H14b: (XTE1) correlates negatively with (EXB13)

H15b: (XTE1) correlates positively with (XEB18)

H21b: (XTE2) correlates positively with (XEB4)

H22b: (XTE2) correlates negatively with (XEB1)

H23b: (XTE2) correlates negatively with (XEB6)

H24b: (XTE2) correlates negatively with (EXB13)

H25b: (XTE2) correlates positively with (XEB18)

H31b: (XTE3) correlates positively with (XEB4)

H32b: (XTE3) correlates negatively with (XEB1)

H33b: (XTE3) correlates negatively with (XEB6)

H34b: (XTE3) correlates negatively with (EXB13)

H35b: (XTE3) correlates positively with (XEB18)

H41b: (XTE4) correlates positively with (XEB4)

H42b: (XTE4) correlates negatively with (XEB1)

H43b: (XTE4) correlates negatively with (XEB6)

H44b: (XTE4) correlates negatively with (EXB13)

H45b: (XTE4) correlates positively with (XEB18)

H51b: (XTE5) correlates positively with (XEB4)

H52b: (XTE5) correlates negatively with (XEB1)

H53b: (XTE5) correlates negatively with (XEB6)

H54b: (XTE5) correlates negatively with (EXB13)

H55b: (XTE5) correlates positively with (XEB18)

H1bm: Economic, Business and Competition, Geographica and Infrustructural, Population-GenderLiteracy, and National Health readiness factors signifcantly moderate the relationships among (XTE1),(XTE2), (XTE3), (XTE4), and (XTE5) with (XEB4),(XEB1), (XEB6), (XEB13),and (XEB18) in developing courtiers.

4. Data and Methodology

In this paper, we developed a conceptual model to investigate the effects of some key moderators on the relationship between the level of IT usage and national performance level in developed and developing countries. We used multiple measures to capture the independent, dependent and moderator variables.

In order to test the hypotheses, we divide the sample into developed and developing countries. Developed countries usually have economic systems based on continuous, self-sustaining economic growth in the tertiary and quaternary sectors and high standards of living. Countries not fitting this definition referred to as developing countries. Accordingly, in this research, developed countries are Andorra, Australia, Austria, Belgium, Canada, China, Denmark, Faroe Islands, Finland, France, Germany, Gibraltar, Greece, Hong Kong, Iceland, Ireland, Territories not administered by the Palestinian authority, Italy, Japan,
Luxembourg, Malta, Netherlands, New Zealand, Norway, Portugal, Singapore, Slovenia, Spain, South Korea, Sweden, Switzerland, Taiwan, United Kingdom, and United States of America (n1=34). Countries not including in this list referred to as developing countries (n2=211).

The main part of data is based on a well-structured international database for year 2008 [44]. This website strategizes historical information in the Library of Congress, World Fact Books and some other major international databases such as UNCTAD, World Bank database, International Monetary Funds (IMF) database, as well as some other international geography, economic, social and cultural related organizations. In order to calculate rank of each country in terms of number of foreign companies listed in a country, we used final World Exchange database for 2007 [45].

In order to analyze the data and compare the results in developed and developing counties, we applied Pearson Correlation Test (SPSS Software) and Structured Equation Model LISREL Software). Pearson Correlation Test and Partial Pearson Correlation Test show how each moderator variable significantly moderate each pair of IT-performance variables. Since there are 5 independent and 5 dependent variables in this research, we provided the effects of each moderator variable on 25 possible relations between independent and dependent variables. The results for developed and developing countries are provided in Tables 4 and 5 of the next section. Moreover, in order to analyze the data in a systematic way, we used Structured Equation Model (LISREL Software). Results of LISREL let to assess the fitness of the data with the proposed new conceptual model and explain the interactions between moderator variables and the roles of each moderator variables on IT-Performance relationship in developed and developing countries.

5. The Empirical Results

5.1 Results of Pearson and Partial Correlation Tests

The first and second parts of Table 3 show results of Pearson Correlation tests for developed countries and developing countries, respectively.

Results of Pearson Correlation tests for developed countries show that:

Hypotheses H11a and H12a supported, but H13a, H14a and H15a not supported.

Hypotheses H21a, H22a, and H23a supported, but H24a, H25a not supported.

Hypotheses H31a, H32a, and H33a, but H34a and H35a not supported.

Hypotheses H41a, H42a, and H43a supported, but H44a and H45a not supported. Hypotheses H51a

and H52a supported, but H53a, H54a and H55a not supported.

Hypothesis H1am supported.

Results of Pearson Correlation tests for developing countries show that:

Hypotheses H11b, H13b, H14b and H15b supported, but H12b not supported.

Hypotheses H21b, H22b, H23b, H24b and H25b supported.

8

Hypotheses H31b, H32b, H33b, H34b and H35b supported.

Hypotheses H41b, H42b, H43b, H44b and H45b supported.

Hypotheses H51b, H54b and H55b supported, but H52b and H53b not supported.

Hypothesis H1bm supported.

Table 3 : Results of Pearson Correlation tests for developed and developing countries

Developed Cointries	XEB4			XEB1			XEB6			XEB13			XEB18		
	Correlation	Sig	N	Correlation	Sig	N	Correlation	Sig	N	Correlation	Sig	N	Correlation	Sig	N
XTE1	0.778**	0.000	34	0.343*	0.024	34	0.218	0.108	34	-0.195	0.135	34	-0.106	0.275	34
XTE2	0.867**	0.000	34	0.406**	0.009	34	0.376*	0.014	34	-0.201	0.127	34	-0.184	0.149	34
XTE3	0.858**	0.000	34	0.456**	0.003	34	0.356*	0.017	34	-0.189	0.142	34	-0.204	0.124	34
XTE4	0.850**	0.000	34	0.469**	0.003	34	0.383*	0.013	34	-0.197	0.132	34	-0.226	0.099	34
XTE5	0.680**	0.000	34	0.358*	0.019	34	0.169	0.169	34	-0.101	0.285	34	-0.268	0.063	34
XEB4	1	---		0.215	0.111	34	0.240	0.086	34	-0.362*	0.018	34	-0.222	0.104	34
XEB1				1	---	34	0.454**	0.003	34	-0.073	0.340	34	-0.364*	0.017	34
XEB6							1	---	34	0.031	0.431	34	-0.203	0.125	34
XEB13										1	---	34	-0.220	0.105	34

Developing Countries	XEB4			XEB1			XEB6			XEB13			XEB18		
	Correlation	Sig	N	Correlation	Sig	N	Correlation	Sig	N	Correlation	Sig	N	Correlation	Sig	N
XTE1	0.624**	0.000		0.054	0.219		0.114*	0.050		0.260**	0.000	211	0.375**	0.000	211
XTE2	**			0.184**	0.004		0.318**	0.000		0.446**	0.000	211	0.230**	0.000	211
	** 0.847	** 0.000													
XTE3	0.849	0.000	211	0.216**	0.001		0.277**	0.000		0.475**	0.000	211	0.292**	0.000	211
XTE4	0.866	0.000	211	0.216**	0.001		0.368**	0.000		0.494**	0.000	211	0.171**	0.006	211
			211 211 211 211 211												
XTE5	0.720**	0.000			0.073			0.072		0.227**	0.000	211	0.222	0.001	211
XEB4				0.100 0.167**	0.007		0.101 0.148*	0.016		0.360**	0.000	211	0.299**	0.000	211
XEB1							0.244**	0.000		0.140*	0.021	211	0.065	0.173	211
XEB6										0.467**	0.000	211	-0.361**	0.000	211
XEB13			211			211			211			211	0.029	0.336	211

** Correlation is significant at the 0.01 level (1-tailed).

* Correlation is significant at the 0.05 level (1-tailed).

Tables 4 and 5 show the results of partial correlation for developed and developing countries, respectively.

Table 4: Results of partial correlation for developed countries

Table 5Corr: Results of partial correlation for developing countries

Hypotheses	Control	Independent	Dependent		Correlation	Significance (1-tailed)	n-2-m		Control	Independent	Dependent		Correlation	Significance (1-tailed)	df
Hypothesis H11a*	Control EM*	Independent XTE1	Dependent XEB4	Correlation 0.189		Significance 0.146	d31f	HypothesisH34a**	Control EM	Independent XTE3	XEB Dependent 13 -0.077	Correlation 0.336	Significance 31	-0.219	0.110(1-tailed) 31n-2-m	
H11b*	EM* GM BMXTE	XTE1	1XEB XEB4 4	0.091 0.55	0.096 0.000	208 31	H34b*	GM**EM*	XTEXTE33	XEB XEB13 13	-0.371 0.032	0.017	208			
	PM		XEB XEB4 4	0.491 0.498	0.000 0.002	208 31		PM**BM	XTEXTE33	XEB XEB13 13	-0.319 0.328	0.035	208			
	GM NM	XTE XTE1	1 XEB XEB4 4	0.391 0.787	0.000 0.000	208 31		NMGM	XTEXTE33	XEB XEB13 13	-0.189 0.185	0.146	208			
		XTE XTE1	1													
H12a*	PM EM*	XTE XTE1	1XEB XEB4 1	0.426 -0.214	0.000 0.116	208 31	H35a**	EMPM	XTEXTE33	XEB XEB18 13	0.006 0.245	0.486	208			
	NM BM	XTE XTE1	XEB XEB4 1	0.606 0.470	0.000 0.003	208 31		BM**NM	XTEXTE33	XEB XEB18 13	-0.580 0.371	0.000	208			
		XTE XTE1	1													
H12b**	EM**GM*	XTE XTE1	1XEB XEB1 1	-0.148 0.068	0.016 0.354	208 31	H35b*	GMEM*	XTEXTE33	XEB XEB18 18	0.001 0.075	0.498	208			
			XEB XEB1 1	-0.051 0.212	0.231 0.118	208 31										
	BM PM* GM NM*	XTE XTE1	1XEB XEB1 1	-0.034 0.224	0.312 0.105	208 31		PMBM	XTEXTE33	XEB XEB18 18	-0.212 0.308	0.118	208			
		XTE XTE1	1					NMGM	XTEXTE33	XEB XEB18 18	-0.150 0.460	0.202	208			
H13a**	PM EM**	XTE XTE1	1XEB XEB1 6	-0.095 -0.310	0.086 0.040	208 31	H41a*	EMPM*	XTEXTE43	XEB XEB4 18	0.369 -0.089	0.017	208			
	NM BM	XTE XTE1	XEB XEB1 6	0.018 0.174	0.396 0.166	208 31		BMNM	XTEXTE43	XEB XEB4 18	0.747 0.330	0.000	208			
		XTE XTE1	1													
H13b*	EM GM BM*PM	XTE XTE1	1XEB XEB6 6	-0.165 -0.017	0.008 0.463	208 31	H41b*	GMEM	XTEXTE44	XEB XEB4 4	0.715 0.313	0.000	208			
			XEB XEB6 6	-0.050 -0.075	0.234 0.340	208 31		PMBM	XTEXTE44	XEB XEB4 4	0.673 0.815	0.000	208			
		XTE XTE1	1XEB XEB6 6	-0.107 0.149	0.061 0.205	208 31		NMGM	XTEXTE44	XEB XEB4 4	0.882 0.651	0.000	208			
	GM*NM	XTE XTE1	1													
H14a**	PM* EM	XTE XTE1	1XEB XEB6 13	0.006 -0.082	0.465 0.324	208 31	H42a*	EM*PM	XTEXTE44	XEB XEB1 4	-0.029 0.785	0.436	208			
	NM*BM	XTE XTE1	XEB XEB6 13	-0.008 -0.242	0.457 0.088	208 31		BMNM	XTEXTE44	XEB XEB1 4	0.588 0.877	0.000	208			
		XTE XTE1	1													
H14b*	EM GM** BM*PM**	XTE XTE1	1 XEB XEB13 13	-0.125 -0.343	0.036 0.026	208 31	H42b*	GM*EM*	XTEXTE44	XEB XEB1 1	0.289 -0.007	0.051	208			
				0.072 -0.313	0.151 0.038	208 31		PMBM	XTEXTE44	XEB XEB1 1	0.445 0.131	0.005	208			
		XTE XTE1	1 XEB XEB13 13	0.001 -0.194	0.495 0.140	208 31		NMGM	XTEXTE44	XEB XEB1 1	0.344 0.162	0.025	208			
	GM*NM	XTE XTE1	1 XEB XEB13 13													
H15a**	PM* EM	XTE XTE1	1 XEB XEB13 18	0.001 0.172	0.494 0.170	208 31	H43a*	EM*PM*	XTEXTE44	XEB XEB6 1	-0.020 0.096	0.456	208			
	NM BM**			0.187 -0.497	0.003 0.002	208 31		BMNM	XTEXTE44	XEB XEB6 1	0.390 0.152	0.012	208			
		XTE XTE1	1 XEB XEB13 18													
H15b*	EM GM BM PM	XTE XTE1	1 XEB XEB18 18	0.258 0.147	0.000 0.207	208 31	H43b*	GM*EM	XTEXTE44	XEB XEB6 6	0.270 0.174	0.064	208			
				0.395 -0.034	0.000 0.425	208 31		PM*BM	XTEXTE44	XEB XEB6 6	0.227 0.244	0.102	208			
	GM NM	XTE XTE1	1 XEB XEB18 18	0.444 -0.051	0.000 0.389	208 31		NMGM	XTEXTE44	XEB XEB6 6	0.319 0.124	0.035	208			
		XTE XTE1	1 XEB XEB18 18													
H21a*	PM EM	XTE XTE1	2 XEB XEB18 4	0.137 0.495	0.024 0.002	208 31	H44a**	EMPM	XTEXTE44	XEB XEB13 6	-0.109 0.329	0.273	208			

10

Left block

Group	Comparison	XTE	n	XEB	est	est	p	p	N	df
	NM BM	XTE XTE1	2	XEB XEB18 4	0.394	0.767	0.000	0.000	208	31
H21b*	EM GM	XTE XTE2	2	XEB XEB4 4	0.244	0.768	0.000	0.000	208	31
	BM PM			XEB XEB4 4	0.787	0.717	0.000	0.000	208	31
	GM NM	XTE XTE2	2	XEB XEB4 4	0.624	0.894	0.000	0.000	208	31
		XTE XTE2	2							
H22a*	PM EM	XTE XTE2	2	XEB XEB4 1	0.752	-0.338	0.000	0.027	208	31
	NM BM			XEB XEB4 1	0.8	0.54343	0.000	0.001	208	31
		XTE XTE2	2							
H22b*	EM* GM*	XTE XTE2	2	XEB XEB1 1	-0.084	0.159	0.114	0.188	208	31
	BM*PM			XEB XEB1 1	0.091	0.337	0.095	0.027	208	31
		XTE XTE2	2	XEB XEB1 1	0.107	0.276	0.062	0.060	208	31
	GM*NM*	XTE XTE2	2							
H23a*	PM* EM*	XTE XTE2	2	XEB XEB1 6	0.052	-0.055	0.226	0.381	208	31
	NM BM			XEB XEB1 6	0.126	0.398	0.034	0.011	208	31
		XTE XTE2	2							
H23b*	EM* GM* BM	XTE XTE2	2	XEB XEB6 6	0.028	0.260	0.341	0.072	208	31
	PM*			XEB XE6B6	0.179	0.212	0.005	0.118	208	31
	GM*NM*	XTE XTE2	2	XEB XEB6 6	0.055	0.313	0.055	0.038	20	318
		XTE XTE2	2							
H24a**	PM EM	XTE XTE2	2	XEB XEB6 13	0.263	-0.126	0.000	0.243	208	31
	NM BM			XEB XEB6 13	0.117	-0.243	0.046	0.087	208	31
		XTE XTE2	2							
H24b*	EM* GM**	XTE XTE2	2	XEB XE13B13	-0.39	-0.425	0.288	0.007	208	31
	BM PM**			XEB XEB13 13	0.284	-0.349	0.000	0.023	208	31
	GM NM	XTE XTE2	2		0.130	-0.203	0.030	0.129	208	31
		XEB XEB13 13								
		XTE XTE2	2							
H25a**	PM EM	XTE XTE2	2	XEB XEB13 18	0.227	0.085	0.000	0.318	208	31
	NM BM**				0.312	-0.581	0.000	0.000	208	31
		XTE XTE2	2	XEB XEB13 18						
H25b*	EM* GM BM	XTE XTE2	2	XEB XEB18 18	-0.094	0.052	0.088	0.386	208	31
	PM				0.235	-0.179	0.000	0.160	208	31
	GM NM	XTE XTE2	2	XEB XEB18 18	0.366	-0.128	0.000	0.240	208	31
		XTE XTE2	2	XEB XEB18 18						
H31a*	PM EM	XTE XTE2	3	XEB XEB18 4	-0.126	0.445	0.034	0.005	208	31
	NM BM			XEB XEB18 4	0.273	0.754	0.000	0.000	208	31
		XTE XTE2	3							
H31b*	EM GM			XEB XEB4 4	0.216	0.561	0.001	0.000	208	31
	BM PM				0.790	0.693	0.000	0.000	208	31

Right block

Group	Comparison	XTE	XEB	est	est	p	N
	BMNM	XTEXTE44	XEB XEB13 6	-0.223	0.132	).106	208
H44b*	GM**EM*	XTEXTE44	XEB XEB13 13	-0.391	0.098	).012	208
	PM**BM	XTEXTE44	XEB XEB13 13	-0.324	0.349	).033	208
	NMGM	XTEXTE44	XEB XEB13 13	-0.200	0.198	).133	208
H45a**	EMPM	XTEXTE44	XEB XEB18 13	-0.102	0.300	).286	208
	BM**NM	XTEXTE44	XEB XEB18 13	-0.574	0.338	).000	208
H45b*	GMEM	XTEXTE44	XEB XEB18 18	-0.040	-0.300	).413	208
	PMBM	XTEXTE44	XEB XEB18 18	-0.248	0.161	).082	208
	NMGM	XTEXTE44	XEB XEB18 18	-0.171	0.302	).170	208
H51a*	EM*PM	XTEXTE54	XEB XEB4 18	0.276	-0.208	).060	208
	BMNM	XTEXTE54	XEB XEB4 18	0.593	0.221	).000	208
H51b*	GM*EM	XTEXTE55	XEB XEB4 4	0.265	0.307	).068	208
	PMBM	XTEXTE55	XEB XEB4 4	0.420	0.637	).007	208
	NMGM	XTEXTE55	XEB XEB4 4	0.755	0.474	).000	208
H52a*	EM*PM	XTEXTE55	XEB XEB1 4	0.036	0.601	).421	208
	BMNM	XTEXTE55	XEB XEB1 4	0.378	0.720	).015	208
H52b**	GM*EM	XTEXTE55	XEB XEB1 1	0.045	-0.092	).402	208
	PM*BM	XTEXTE55	XEB XEB1 1	0.245	0.016	).084	208
	NM*GM	XTEXTE55	XEB XEB1 1	0.114	0.005	).263	208
H53a**	EMPM	XTEXTE55	XEB XEB6 1	-0.157	-0.017	).192	208
	BMNM	XTEXTE55	XEB XEB6 1	0.125	0.084	).245	208
H53b**	GMEM**	XTEXTE55	XEB XEB6 6	-0.182	-0.201	).155	208
	PMBM	XTEXTE55	XEB XEB6 6	-0.047	-0.043	).397	208
	NMGM**	XTEXTE55	XEB XEB6 6	0.030	-0.183	).433	208
H54a**	EMPM	XTEXTE55	XEB XEB13 6	0.030	0.005	).435	208
	BMNM	XTEXTE55	XEB XEB13 6	-0.092	0.049	).306	208
H54b*	GMEM	XTEXTE55	XEB XEB13 13	-0.245	-0.200	).085	208

11

	GM NM	XTE XTE3	3XEB XEB4 4	0.632 0.882	0.000 0.000	208 31		PMBM*	XTEXTE55	XEB XEB13 13	-0.117 0.057		208
			XEB XEB4 4									).259	
		XTE XTE3 3						NMGM	XTEXTE55	XEB XEB13 13	-0.098 -0.114		208
		XTE XTE3 3										).294	
H32a*	PM EM*	XTE XTE3	3XEB XEB4 1	0.754 -0.123	0.000 0.247	208 31	H55a**	EMPM*	XTEXTE55	XEB XEB18 13	-0.175 -0.003		208
												).165	
	NM BM		XEB XEB4 1	0.841 0.595	0.000 0.000	208 31		BM**NM	XTEXTE55	XEB XEB18 13	-0.448 0.205		208
		XTE XTE3 3										).004	
H32b*	EM* GM* BMXTE XTE3		3XEB XEB1 1	-0.004 0.265	0.479 0.068	208 31	H55b*	GMEM*	XTEXTE55	XEB XEB18 18	-0.114 0.031		208
	PM		XEB XEB1 1	0.134 0.429	0.026 0.006	208 31						).264	
	GM NM	XTE XTE3 3	XEB XEB1 1	0.158 0.342	0.011 0.026	208 31		PMBM	XTEXTE55	XEB XEB18 18	-0.262 0.214		208
												).070	
		XTE XTE3 3						NMGM	XTEXTE55	XEB XEB18 18	-0.205 0.286		208
												).126	
H33a*	PM* EM*	XTE XTE3	3XEB XEB1 6	0.082 -0.138	0.117 0.222	208 31							
	NM BM		XEB XEB1 6	0.168 0.375	0.008 0.016	208 31							
		XTE XTE3 3											

** A variable that moderates the relation between independent anPM* XTE5 XEB18 d 208 dependent variables. By -0.031 0.329

controlling this variable, an insignificant relationship becomes significant.NM XTE5 XEB18208

0.229 0.000

| H33b* | EM* GM* | XTE XTE3 3 | | XEB XEB6 6 | -0.110 0.235 | 0.056 0.094 | 208 31 |

** A variable that moderates the relation between independent and dependent* A variablecontrolling this variable a significant relationship becomes insignificant. that moderates the relationship between independent and dependent variables. By variables. By controlling this variable, an insignificant relationship becomes significant.

BM PM* XTE XTE3 3 XEB XEB6 6 0.132 0.192 0.028 0.142 208 31 * A variable that moderates the relationship between independent and dependent variables. By controlling GM *NM XTE

XTE3 3 XEB XEB6 6 -0.12 0.303 0.429 0.043 208 31 this variable, a significant relationship becomes insignificant.

PM	XTE3	XEB6	0.208	0.001	208
NM*	XTE3	XEB6	0.097	0.081	208

5.2 Results of Structured Equation Models (LISREL)

5.2.1. Results of LISREL for developed countries

Figure [4] shows results of LISREL for developed countries. Let define the variables as follows: ITDIFFUS: IT Diffusion level
PERFORMA: National Performance level
ECONOMIC: Economic Moderator (EM)
BUSINESS: Business & Competition Moderator (BM)
GEOGRAPH: Geographical & Infrastructure Moderator (GM)
POPULATI: Population, Gender and Literacy Moderator (PM)
NATIONAL: National Health Moderator (NM)

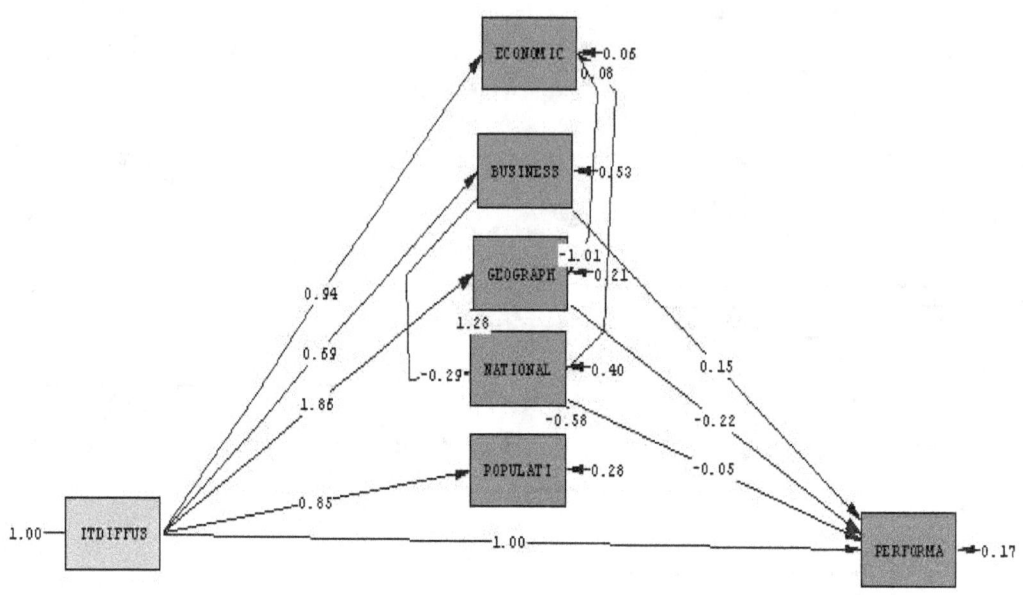

Chi-Square=13.41, df=8, P-value=0.09865, RMSEA=0.057

Figure 4: LISREL for developed countrie

As shown in Figure [4], the structure of the hypothetical model for interactions between IT diffusion, moderating factors and performance level in developed countries was supported for chi- square statistics ($\chi 2$=13.41 with 8 degree of freedom, p=0.09865). The Goodness of Fit Index (GFI) of the model was 0.98. The additional index values for the model were 1.00 for the Comparative Fit Index (CFI). These statistics suggest a good fit. The RMSEA was 0.057 (95% CIS 0.0; 0.094) with a p-value (for test of close fit RMSEA<0.05) of 0.36. These global goodness of fit statistics suggesting an acceptable fit of the data with the model. The path coefficient estimates were statistically significant with t-values from 2.86 to 43.42, indicating that the variables were linked to the model (a t-value of 1.96 or higher at the significance level of 0.05). Only t-value between National Health moderator (NATIONAL) and Performance level (PERFORMA) is less than 2, and therefore this relation is insignificant.

As shown in the above figure, IT diffusion affects on the moderator factors (ECONOMIC, BUSINESS, GEOGRAPH, POPULATI, and NATIONAL). The moderator factors in turn with their interactions affect on the Performance Level (PERFORMA). The Measurement Equations for the modelare as follows:

ECONOMIC = 0.18*NATIONAL + 0.57*ITDIFFUS, Errorvar.= 38.44, R^2 = 0.94 p-

values: (0.064)   (0.013)   (4.57)   t-values: 2.73   43.42

8.41

BUSINESS = 0.78*ITDIFFUS, Errorvar.= 1107.23, R^2 = 0.47

p-values: (0.057)   (108.31)   t-values: 13.65

10.22

GEOGRAPH = - 1.56*ECONOMIC + 1.73*ITDIFFUS, Errorvar.= 296.36, R^2 = 0.79 p -

values: (0.28)   (0.17)   (30.60)   t-values: -5.59   10.41   9.69

NATIONAL = -0.069*BUSINESS+ 0.37*GEOGRAPH - 0.65*POPULATI, Errorvar.= 47.69, R^2=

0.60

13

p-values:　(0.014)　　　(0.023)　　(0.080)　(4.70)　　　t-values:　-4.99

16.20　　　-8.06　　　10.15

POPULATI = 0.20*ITDIFFUS, Errorvar.= 26.72, R^2 = 0.72

p-values:　(0.0089)　　(2.61)　　t-values:　23.08

10.22

PERFORMA= 0.034*BUSINESS - 0.060*GEOGRAPH + 0.26*ITDIFFUS, Errorvar.= 18.98, R^2 = 0.83

p-values:　(0.0094)　(0.021)　　(0.017)　(1.86)　　t-values:　3.63

-2.86　　　14.93　　10.22

5.2.2. Results of LISREL for developing countries

Figure [5] shows results of LISREL for developking countries.

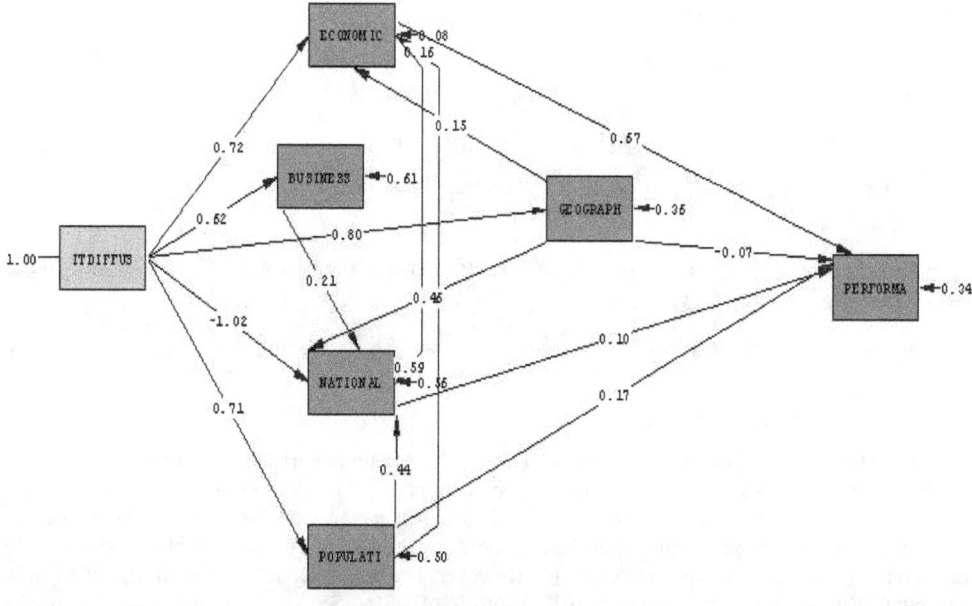

Chi-Square=4.35, df=6, P-value=0.62943, RMSEA=0.000

Figure 5: LISREL for developing countrie

As shown in Figure [5], the structure of the hypothetical model for interactions between IT diffusion, moderating factors and performance level in developing countries was supported for chi-square statistics ($\chi 2$=4.35 with 6 degree of freedom, p=0.62943). The Goodness of Fit Index (GFI) of the model was 0.99. The additional index values for the model were 1.00 for the Comparative Fit Index (CFI). These statistics suggest a good fit. The RMSEA was 0.00 (95% CIS 0.0; 0.075) with a p-value (for test of close fit RMSEA<0.05) of 0.84. These global goodness of fit statistics suggesting an acceptable fit of the data with the model. The path coefficient estimates were statistically significant with t-values from 2.08 to 19.26, indicating that the variables were linked to the model (a t-value of 1.96 or higher at the significance level of 0.05). Only t-value of the between Geographical & Infrastructure Readiness (GeographiReadi) and Performance level (Performance) is less than 2, and therefore this relation is insignificant.

14

As shown in Figure 5, IT diffusion affects on the moderator factors (ECONOMIC, BUSINESS, GEOGRAPH, POPULATI, and NATIONAL). The moderator factors in turn with their interactions affect on the Performance Level (PERFORMA). The Measurement Equations for the model is as follow:

$ECONOMIC = 0.12*GEOGRAPH + 0.23*POPULATI + 0.44*ITDIFFUS$, Errorvar.= 64.22, R^2 = 0.92

p-values: (0.027)   (0.041)   (0.023)   (6.28)   t-values: 4.65

5.72   19.26   10.22

$BUSINESS = 0.52*ITDIFFUS$, Errorvar.= 964.31, $R^2 = 0.39$ p-

values: (0.045)   (94.33)   t-values: 11.56

10.22

$GEOGRAPH = 0.58*ITDIFFUS$, Errorvar.= 427.00, $R^2 = 0.64$

p-values: (0.030)   (41.77)

t-values: 19.25   10.22

$NATIONAL = 0.72*ECONOMIC + 0.19*BUSINESS + 0.47*GEOGRAPH + 0.81*POPULATI - 0.76*ITDIFFUS$, Errorvar.= 695.39, $R^2 = 0.44$

p-values: (0.23) (0.059)   (0.093)   (0.15)   (0.13)   (68.03)   t-values: 3.17

3.21   5.11   5.55   -5.89   10.22

$POPULATI = 0.29*ITDIFFUS$, Errorvar.= 182.30, $R^2 = 0.50$

p-values: (0.020)   (17.83)   t-values: 14.56

10.22

$PERFORMA= 0.52*ECONOMIC + 0.065*NATIONAL + 0.19*POPULATI$, Errorvar.= 166.92, R^2 = 0.66 p-values: (0.067) (0.031) (0.076)   (16.33)   t-

values: 7.65   2.08   2.58   10.22

6. Conclusions and Final Remarks

This paper provides a new conceptual model and offering an empirically based insight into the effects of IT-Performance moderators in developed and developing countries. In order to test the model, we used data from 34 developed and 211 developing countries and applied both Pearson Correlation and Structured Equation Model. Pearson correlation and partial correlation results show how each of moderator variables moderates IT-performance relation in developed and developing countries. However, as a general conclusion from structured equation models, we found that four moderator variables ((ECONOMIC, BUSINESS, GEOGRAPH, and POPULATI) with their interactions significantly moderate the relationship between IT diffusion and national level performance in both developed and developing countries. Moreover, we found that NATIONAL modertor variable significantly moderates the IT-performance relationship in developing but not in developed countrirs. Results of this research confirm fitness of the data with our proposed new model and clearly explain the roles of each moderator variables on ITPerformance relationship in developed and developing countries.

References

Adam, M., and Myers, M. Have You Got Anything to Declare? Neo-colonialism, Information Systems, and the Imposition of Customs and Duties in a Third World Country, 2003, In Organizational Information Systems in the Context of Globalization, M. Korpela, R. Montealegre, and A. Poulymenakou (eds.), Kluwer Academic Publishers, Boston, 2003: 101-116.

Adkinson, W. F., Lenard, T. M., and Pickford, M. J. The Digital Economy Fact Book, 6th Ed., Washington D.C., The Progress and Freedom Foundation, 2004.

Avgerou, C., and Walsham, G. Information Technology in Context: Studies from the Perspective of Developing Countries, Ashgate Publishing, Aldershot, UK, 2000.

Avgerou, C. The Link Between ICT and Economic Growth in the Discourse of Development, in Organizational InformationSystems in the Context of Globalization, M. Korpela, R. Montealegre, and A. Poulymenakou (eds.), Kluwer Academic Publishers, Boston, 2003: 373-386.

Awasthi, V. N. Chow, C. W. and Wu, A. Cross-cultural Differences in the Behavioral Consequences of Imposing Performance Evaluation and Reward Systems: An Experimental Investigation, International Journal of Accounting, 36(3), 2001: 291-309.

Bada, A. O. Local Adaptation to Global Trends: A Study of an IT-Based Organizational Change Program in a Nigerian Bank," The Information Society, 18(2), 2002: 77-86.

Barrell, R. and Pain, N. Foreign Direct Investment, Technological Change and Economic Growth within Europe, Economic Journal, 107(445), 1997: 1770–1786.

Brett, J. M. Tinsiey, C. H. Janssens, M. Barsness Z. I. and Lytle A. L. New Approaches to the Study of Culture in Industrial/Organizational Psychology, In Eariey P.C., Erez M (Eds.), New Perspectives on Intemationai Industrial/Organizational Ssychology, San Francisco: New Lexington Press, 1997.

Brewster, C. Different Paradigms in Strategic HRM: Questions Raised by Comparative Research, in Wright, P. Dyer, L. Boudreau, J. and Milkovich, G. (eds) Research in Personnel and HRM. Supplement 4, Greenwich, CT: JAI Press, 1999.

Bui, T. X. Sankaran, S. and Sebastian I. M. A Framework for Measuring National Readiness, International Journal of Electronic Business, 1(1), 2003: 3-22.

Coe, D.T. Helpman, E. and Hoffmaister, A. W. North-south R & D Spillovers, The Economic Journal, 107(440), 1997: 134–149.

Caselli, F. and Coleman II, W. J. Cross-country Technology Diffusion: The Case of Computers, The American Economic Review, 91(2), 2001.

Dewan, S., and Kraemer, K.L. Information Technology and Productivity: Evidence from Country-level Data, Management Science 46, 4, 2000: 548–562.

Dowling, P. J. Welch, D. E. and Schuler, R. S. International Human Resource Management. Cincinnati, OH: South-Westem, 1999.

Dunkel, A. and Meierewert, S. Culture Standards and Their Impact on Teamwork–An Empirical Analysis of Austrian, German, Hungarian and Spanish Culture Differences, Journal for East European Management Studies, 2, 2004: 147-174.

Fang, X. and Rau, P-L. P. Culture Differences in Design of Portal Sites, Ergonomics, 46(1-3), 2003: 242-254.

Gerhart, B. and Fang, M. National Culture and Human Resource Management: Assumptions and Evidence, International Journal of Human Management, 16(6), 2005: 971-986.

Herscovitch, L. and Meyer, J. P. Commitment to Organizational Change: Extension of a Three Component Model, Journal of Applied Psychology, 87, 2002: 474–487.

Hofstede, G. Neuijen, B. Ohayv, D. D. and Sanders, G. Measuring Organizational Cultures: A Qualitative and Quantitative Study across Twenty Cases, Administrative Science Quarterly, 35(2), 1990: 286-316.

Hofstede, G. Cultural Consequences: Comparing Values, Behaviors, Institutions, and Organizations across Nations, Second Edition, Sage Publication Inc., Thousand Oaks, California, USA, 2001.

Kraemer, K. L. and Dedrick, J. Payoffs from Investment in Information Technology: Lessons from Asia-Pacific Region, World Development, 22, 1994: 1921–1931.

Liu, W., and Westrup, C. ICTs and Organizational Control across Cultures: The Case of a UK Multinational Operating in China, in Organizational Information Systems in the Context of Globalization, M. Korpela, R. Montealegre, and A. Poulymenakou (eds.), Kluwer Academic Publishers, Boston, 2003: 155-168.

16

Macome, E. On the Implementation of an Information System in the Mozambican Context: The EDM Case, in Organizational Information Systems in the Context of Globalization, M. Korpela, R. Montealegre, and A. Poulymenakou (eds.), Kluwer Academic Publishers, Boston, 2003: 169-184.

Madon, S. The Internet and Socio-Economic Development: Exploring the Interaction, Information Technology and People, 13(2), 2000: 85-101.

Mahmood Adam, M. A. and Swanberg, D. L. Factors Effecting Information Technology Usage: A Meta-Analysis of the Empirical Literature, Journal of Organizational Computing and Electronic Commerce, 11(2), 2001: 107-130.

Meyer, J. P. Srinivas, E. S. Lal, J. B. and Topolnytsky, L. Employee Commitment and Support for an Organizational Change: Test of the Three-component Model inTwo Cultures, Journal of Occupational and Organizational Psychology, 80, 2007: 185–211.

Mutula, S. M. and Brakel P. V. An evaluation of E-readiness Assessment Tools with Respect to Information Access: Towards an Integrated Information Rich Tool, International Journal of Information Management, 26(3), 2006: 212–223.

Pothukuchi, V. Damanpour, F. Choi, J. Chen, C. C. and Park, S. H. National and Organizational Culture Differences and International Joint Venture Performance, Journal of International Business Studies, 32(2), 2002: 243-265.

Robison, K. K. and Crenshaw, E. M. Post-industrial Transformations and Cyber-space: A Crossnational Analysis of Internet Development, Social Science Research, 31, 2002: 334–363.

Rossouw, G. J. Business Ethics in Developing Countries, Business Ethics Quarterely, 4(1), 1994: 4351.

Ryan, A. M. Chang, D. Ployhart, R. E. and Slade, L. A. Employee Attitude Surveys in a Multinational Organization: Considering Language and Culture in Assessing Measurement Equivalence, Personnel Psychology, 52, 1999: 37-58.

Saad, M. and Zawdie, G. From Technology Transfer to the Emergence of a Triple Helix Culture: The Experience of Algeria in Innovation and Technological Capability Development, Technology Analysis and Strategic Management, 17(1), 2005: 89–103.

Salter, S. B. and Sharp, D. J. Agency Effects and Escalation of Commitment Do Small National Culture Differences Matter? International Journal of Accounting, 36(1), 2001: 33-45.

Sen, A. Development as Freedom, Oxford University Press, Oxford, UK, 1999.

Shih, E. Kraemer, K. L. and Dedrick, J. IT Diffusion in Developing Countries, Communications of the ACM, 51(2), February 2008: 43-48.

Shih, E. Kraemer, K. L. and Dedrick, J. Research Note: Determinants of Country-level Investment in Information Technology, Management Science, 53(3), 2007: 521–528.

Shoib, G. M., and Nandhakumar, J. Cross-Cultural IS Adoption in Multinational Corporations: A Study of Rationality, in Organizational Information Systems in the Context of Globalization, M. Korpela, R. Montealegre, and A. Poulymenakou (eds.), Kluwer Academic Publishers, Boston, 2003:435-454.

Silva, L., and Figueroa, E. B. Institutional Intervention and the Expansion of ICTs in Latin America: The Case of Chile, Information Technology and People, 15(1), 2002: pp. 8-25.

Spony, G. The Development of a Work-value Model Assessing the Cumulative Impact of Individual and Cultural Differences on Managers' Work-value Systems: Empirical Evidence from French and British Managers, International Journal of Human Resource Management, 14(4), 2003: 658-679.

United Nations Development Program (UNDP) Human Development Report 2001: Making New Technologies Work for Human Development, Oxford University Press, New York, 2001.

Walsham, G. Cross-Cultural Software Production and Use: A Structurational Analysis, MIS Quarterly, (26:4), 2002: pp. 359-380.

Walsham, G. Robey, D. Sahay, S. Forwadr: Special issue on Information Systems in Developing Countries, MIS Quarterly, 31(2), 2007: 317-326.

17

World Bank Group, Information and Communication Technologies: A World Bank Group Strategy, Washington D.C., 2002.

Internet Sources:

http://www.theodora.com/wfb   http://www.world-exchange.org

Promoting Organizational Agility: An Applied Framework

Mostafa Emami (PHD)[1]

Associate Professor -Young Research Club, Islamic Azad University, Tehran, Iran

Amrolah Amini (PHD)

Associate Professor -Allameh Tabatabaei University, Tehran, Iran

Alireza Emami (PHD)

Associate Professor -University of Tehran, Tehran, Iran

Abstract

Purpose: prepare new methodology for agility in which organizations can respond to the business change drivers through new advanced technologies and procedures.

Design/ methodology/ approach: in this paper, we presented first main definitions and concepts of agility. Then, with literature review process on agility's models, main models of agility are determined to the further investigation. Following, some of the critiques on agility are discussed and analyzed and finally, the step-by-step and new methodology is presented as a comprehensive and holistic approach to agility evaluation and enhancement in any organization.

Finding: in this paper, holistic definition of agility, as well as step by-step method for agility evaluation and enhancement are discovered and explained.

Originality/value: because of environmental divers and need for achieving competitive advantage(s) through encountering challenges and opportunities, organizations need to be agile so that they can respond quickly (by attaining new and powerful capabilities) to changes in customers' demands and market conditions.

Implications and further investigation: the proposed conceptual methodology is applicable for any organization but it is based on literature review and therefore, need to be deployed and tested in real life organization in order to gain validity and functionality.

Keywords: change, agility, literature review, approaches, applied framework

1- Introduction

Uncertainty and change in the business environments had been a major topic in management research for a long time. Thompson (1967) stated that one of the most important functions for any organization is to manage uncertainties. Drucker (1968) described the concept of entrepreneurial task as the search for change, response to change, and exploitation of changes as opportunities. In existing era, many factors have pressures on organizations to get adaptability and flexibility about changes that occur in their business environment. As Hayen (1988) has pointed out, there is nothing new about change. However, today's change is taking place at a much faster speed than ever. The first set of conditions or factors that have pressures on today organizations are the series of socioeconomic, financial and political changes that occurred in the last quarter of the twentieth century. Further drivers for change are Changes in cost and efficiency; the adoption of agile manufacturing and industries' best practices; a

Correspondent Address:Mostafa Emami (PHD) [1] [1]

Associate Professor -Young Research Club, Islamic Azad University, Tehran, Iran , Address: P O Box: 1767778151 *Tehran –Iran*
Cell:+98(912)7001816Fax:+98(910)2294653Contact:+1(816)2370018+44(871)2185070+44(871)218-6050Tel:+98(21)33440612
Email: MEMAMI@MTU.EDU MOSTAFA.EMAMI@MODARES.AC.IR

need to manage supply chains more efficiently; a market shift from standardization to differentiated products; deregulation or new regulatory policies and/or government regulations; changing societal concerns, attitudes and lifestyles; and; changes in the degree of uncertainty. Therefore, to respond effectively to the above drivers, organizations need to be truly agile.

As it can be observed in following literature review, many agility models have been proposed for enhancement of responsiveness and flexibility, but noon of them (except Sharifi and Zhang, 1999) doesn't suggest practical methodology to agility evaluation and enhancement. On the other hand, many authors have proposed different concepts and components for agility and don't agree on its implementation or evaluation process. Meanwhile, their proposed frameworks are mainly based on manufacturing area and don't present holistic and comprehensive approach to agility evaluation and improvement in other organizational context (such as service and public sector organizations). As a new framework, our proposed

This paper is organized as following. At the first, definitions of agility and agile manufacturing are discussed so that the basic concepts and ideas of agility are explored and discussed. At section two, literature review on more cited and relatively practical models and approaches to design, implement and enhance agility's practices is presented. Following, critiques on agility concepts and frameworks are presented and then, we propose a practical methodology for agility implementation, which is based on above models. Finally, some recommendations for agility implementation and enhancement will be presented to the interested managers and practitioners.

2. Literature review
2.1. Definitions and Drivers of agility

At the beginning of the 21st Century, the world faces significant changes in almost all aspects, especially marketing competition, technological innovations and customer demands. Mass markets are continuing to fragment as customers become increasing demanding and their expectations rise. These developments have caused a major revision of business priorities and strategic visions (Sharifi and Zhang, 1999). Organizations have realized that agility is essential for their survival and competitiveness. Available literature on agility, scarce as it may be, has provided many conceptual overviews of its dimensions and has further conceptualized related elements. Also, a preliminary empirical assessment of management attention for agility is available to further indicate the relevance of the general agility concept as recognized by management (Naylor et al., 1999). Obviously, different facets of agility have been emphasized by various authors and this has lead to varied views reflected in the literature. According to Gunasekaran (1999), agility is the ability of surviving and prospering in a competitive environment of continuous and unpredictable change by reacting quickly and effectively to changing markets, driven by customerdefined products and services. Kidd (1994) defined agility as a rapid and proactive adaptation of enterprise elements to unexpected and unpredicted changes. The creators of "agile manufacturing" concept at the Iacocca Institute, of Lehigh University (USA) defined it as: A manufacturing system with capabilities (hard and soft technologies, human resources, educated management, information) to meet the rapidly changing needs of the marketplace (speed, flexibility, customers, competitors, suppliers, infrastructure, responsiveness). Main characteristics of agile manufacturing are delivering value to customers, being ready for changes in terms of market and technologies, and Prospering from the turbulent environment emerging (Helo, 2004). Also, Maskell suggests the most important aspects of agile manufacturing as customer prosperity, people and information, cooperation within and between firms, and fitting a company for change (Maskell, 2001). Likewise, Li Jin-Hai and et.al identify critical elements of real agile manufacturing as strategic processing, core competencies, multiple winners, integration, and information technology.

Yusuf et al. (1999) proposed that agility is the successful application of competitive bases such as speed, flexibility, innovation, and quality by the means of the integration of reconfigurable resources and best practices of knowledge-rich environment to provide customer-driven products and services in a fast changing environment. Despite the differences, all definitions of "agility" emphasize the speed and flexibility as the primary attributes of an agile organization (Gunasekaran, 1999; Sharifi and Zhang, 1999; Yusuf et al., 1999). An equally important attribute of agility is the effective response to change and uncertainty (Goldman et al., 1995; Kidd, 1994; Sharifi and Zhang, 2001). Some authors (Sharifi and Zhang, 1999) state that responding to change in proper ways and exploiting and taking advantages of changes are the main factors of agility. The next common component of published definitions of agility is a high quality and highly customized products (Gunasekaran, 1999; Kidd, 1994).

These definitions should be considered simultaneously in order to gain a better understanding of what constitute agility. In other words, although various definitions of agility are available in literature world, these definitions do not contrast with each other. Sarkis (2001) express that the concept of agility is in the process of being defined by both practitioners and researchers. Even a number of definitions for agility have been posited within the last few years, a common thread focuses on being able to function and compete within a state of dynamic and continuous (in table-1-, some of the best definitions of agility have been presented briefly).we define agility as organizational ability to sense, perceive, analyze and respond to the changes that occur in the turbulent environment based on competency, speed, cost, quality, responsiveness, team building, virtual structure, participation, knowledge and learning and at the same time, exploit from those changes.

Table-1- definitions of agility

Author(s)	Definition
Iacocca institute (1991)	A manufacturing system with extraordinary capabilities (Internal capabilities: hard and soft technologies, human resources, educated management, information) to meet the rapidly changing needs of the marketplace (speed, flexibility, customers, competitors, suppliers, infrastructure, responsiveness).
Sharifi and Zhange (1999, 2000)	Agility is a basic ability for any organization that is sensing, perceiving and anticipating changes in the business environment. Also, Ability to sense, respond to, and exploit anticipated or unexpected changes in the business environment is called agility.
Maskell (2001)	Agility is the ability to thrive and prosper in an environment of constant and unpredictable change.
Vernadat (1999)	Agility can be defined as the ability to closely align organization systems to changing business needs in order to achieve competitive performance.
Helo (2004)	Agility is a capability of responding to change in a dimension beyond flexibility.
Goldman *et al.* (1995)	Agility, for a company, is to be capable of operating profitably in a competitive environment of continually and unpredictably changing customer opportunities.
Hormozi (2001)	Agile organizations are flexible and quick to respond to fast moving market conditions.
Dove (1996)	Agility is the ability to manage and apply knowledge effectively so that an organization has the potential to thrive in a continuous changing and unpredicted business environment.
Kid (1994)	To operationalise agility, it can be defined as 'the synthesis of a number of enterprises that each have some core skills or competencies which they bring to a joint venturing operation thus enabling the cooperative enterprises to adapt and respond quickly to changing customer requirements.
Naylor and et.al (1995)	Agility means using market knowledge and a virtual corporation to exploit profitable opportunities in a volatile marketplace.
Power and Sohal (2001)	Agility means using market knowledge and a virtual corporation to exploit profitable opportunities in a volatile marketplace
Youssuf et.al (1999)	Agility is the successful exploration of competitive bases (speed, flexibility, innovation, proactivity, quality and productivity) through the integration of reconfigurable resources and best practices in a knowledge rich environment to provide customer driven products and services in a fast changing market environment.
Prince and Kay (2003)	Ability to respond to sudden changes and meet widely varied customer requirements in terms of price, specification, quantity, qualify and delivery is called agility.

Agility as a new paradigm for enhancing competitiveness has been widely researched since its inception in the early 1990s. The concept, in its various forms, is now recognized as a winning strategy for growth if not a basic one for survival in certain business environments. Agility implies not only the ability to respond to unanticipated change (responsibility) but also to act proactively with regard to change. You have frequently heard that if there is one constant thing, it is certainly change. Here, the most important question is what factors or drivers force organizations to get agility?

3

Many researches place primary importance on the external changes. Nagel and Dove (1991) identified some of the key drivers that shape the future competitive environment of the twenty first century as information availability, technology acceleration, globalized market and competition, wage and job skills shifts, resource limitation, and increasing customer expectation. Yusuf, Sarhadi and Gunasekaran (1999) determine drivers of agility as automation and price/cost consideration, widening customer choice and expectation, competing priorities, integration and proactivity, and achieving manufacturing requirements in synergy. Sharifi and Zhang (1999) also classify changes as due to market, competitive, customer requirements, technological, and social factors. Summarizing previous studies, Christopher (2001) identifies the general areas of business environment change as market volatility, intense competition, changes in customer requirements, accelerating technological change, and change in social factors. *In sum, it can be concluded from above that the main drivers of agility are increasingly competition, enhancing customer expectations, technology and innovation acceleration, globalization, social and cultural factors, market variability, information technology, special and loyal human resource scarcity or limitation, and so on (figure-1-).*

Figure-1-Factors influencing organizational environment

2.2. Agility models and approaches

Agile organization has been advocated as the 21st century's organization paradigm, and is seen as the winning strategy to become national and international leaders in an ever increasing competitive market of fast changing customer requirements (Youssuf et al., 1999). However, the ability to build agile organization and enhance it has not developed as rapidly as anticipated, because the development of technology to manage agile organization is still under way (Sharp et al., 1999). Thus, in embracing agile organization many important questions concerning agility need to be asked, such as what precisely is agility and how can it be measured? How will organizations know when they have it, as there are no simple metrics or indices available? How and to what degree does the organization's attributes affect companies' business performance? How to compare agility with competitiveness? If a company or organization wants to improve agility, how can it identify the principal obstacles to improvement? How to assist in achieving agility effectively? Answers to such questions are critical to the practitioners and to the theory of agile organization design. To assist managers in better achieving an agile organization, there have been numerous studies dedicated to design, implement, and improve the agility of an organization. In this section, we introduce some of the most cited and applied models of organizational agility so that the practical methodology of agility implementation process can be extracted and developed based upon them. It must be taken into account that election of following models is based on their conceptual and operational methodologies as well as their citations in relevant journals and books.

2.2.1. Goldman and et.al approach: researchers believe know Goldman, Nagel and Preiss (1995) as the first ones permeating the agility concept in the business world in order to respond successfully to the turbulent and changing environment. They described agility in the book "agile competitors and virtual organizations" (1995) as dynamic, context-specific, aggressively change-embracing and growth oriented. From this point of view, agility entails a continual readiness to change (sometimes radically) and there is no time when a company has completely fulfilled the goal of being agile. According to above definition, Agility is context-specific in that differences among markets limit the generalizability of detailed rules for becoming agile. Agile firms embrace change as they understand not only their current markets, product lines, competencies and customers, but also understand the potential for future customers and markets and the necessity of changing to meet those opportunities.

They identified four key dimensions of agile organization. The first dimension is enriching the customer. This entails a quick understanding of the unique requirements of each individual customer and rapidly providing it. The second dimension entails co-operation (intra-organizational, interorganizational co-operation such as supplier partnerships and perhaps emerging virtual relationships with competing organizations) in order to enhance competitiveness. The third dimension utilizes new organizational structure(s) to master change and uncertainty through techniques such as concurrent engineering and cross-functional teams. The fourth dimension leverages the impact of people, information and technology and recognizes the importance of employees as a company asset, placing greater emphasis on education, training and empowerment.

Figure-1-four principles of agility (Goldman et.al, 1995)

2.2.2. Ramesh and Devadasan model: Based on twenty agile manufacturing (AM) criteria, Ramesh and Devadasan (2007) concluded that agile manufacturing is function of flexible and lean manufacturing systems. They believe various definitions of agile manufacturing are not contrast with each other. But commonality among most of them is the enunciation that AM is the ability of manufacturing enterprise to quickly respond to the market requirements. Thus, AM calls for radical changes in the system, culture and management styles being currently followed in traditional manufacturing environment. They introduced twenty criteria on agile manufacturing as organizational structure, delegation of authority, manufacturing set ups, status of quality, status of productivity, employee's status, employee participation, nature of management, customer response adoption, product life cycle, product service life, design improvement, production methodology, manufacturing planning, cost management, automation type, information technology, integration, change in business and technical processes, time management, and outsourcing. Then, they designed the procedure to attain and enhance agility in organizations, which some the most important phases of their model are top management support and commitment, organizational structure study, studying the existing practices with reference to twenty agile criteria and estimating the deviations, identifying and implementing vital few activities, expand implementation based on the impact of preliminary efforts, and finally, analysis the result of implementation process.

2.2.3. Meredith and Francis model: Meredith and Francis (2000) have proposed the 16 dimensional reference model for implementing agile manufacturing, including components such as strategy, linkages, people, and processes (figure-2-). This reference model provides a tool with which to audit each company on its degree of agility and provides an integrated definition of the components of agility. The reference model is presented in the shape of a wheel to demonstrate that its components are interdependent. A wheel is weakened if any spoke is absent, broken or fragile. It is the same with agility. That is, if any of the 16 components is under-developed, then the firm's agile capability is weakened. In sum, the purpose of the wheel is to assist managers to audit the agile capability of their firms, identify agility blockages and develop a focused development plan.

The first quadrant focuses on strategic aspects of agility. Four policies/practices are specified: wide-deep scanning, strategic commitment, full deployment and agile scoreboard. The second quadrant focuses on organizational processes that support agility. Four policies/practices are specified: flexible assets and systems, fast new product acquisition, rapid problem-solving and rich information systems. The third quadrant focuses on outside linkages. Four policies/practices are specified: agility benchmarking, deep customer insight, aligned suppliers and performing partnerships. Finally, the fourth quadrant focuses on people and the management of the human resource of the firm. Four policies/practices are specified: adaptable structure; multi-skilled, flexible people; rapid, able decision-making; and continuous learning (Meredith and Francis, 2000).

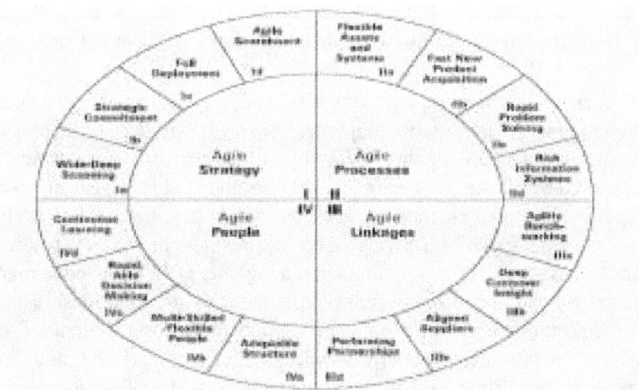

Figure-2- reference model of agility (Meredith and Francis, 2000)

2.2.3. Dove's model: Rick Dove (1994) is one of the first to discuss agility as the capability of a process to respond to the unanticipated change. Dove (1999) prefers to define agility succinctly as the ability to manage and apply knowledge as well as master to change proficiency. Though both knowledge management and change proficiency are still immature practices, he feel a sufficient foundation exists to guide an organizational engineering project to success. Figure-3- represents the key relationships and dynamics his investigations have revealed so far. In this model, infrastructure of agility are System Integrity Management, corporate change agents,

Reusable/Reconfigurable/Scalable (RRC) or (CAS) architecture principles, culture, learning science principles, IT, network and repository, KM change agents. As you see in following model, agility has two sides: change proficiency and knowledge management. At the left hand, processes, procedures and people of change proficiency are place on. Ant the right hand, competency and strategy of knowledge management are place in order to acquire, transfer, store and use of knowledge. According to Dove (1999) agility is achieved when change proficiency and knowledge management are balance.

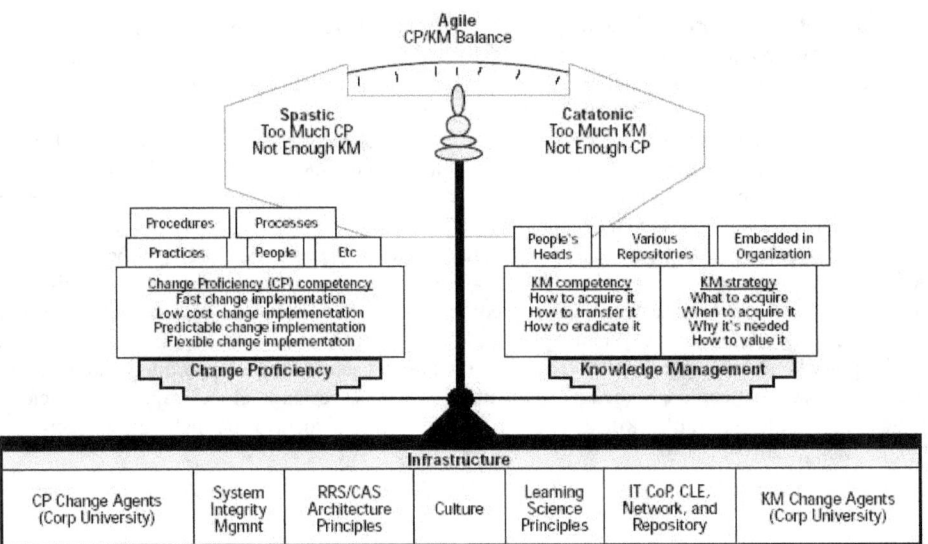

Figure-3- agility: knowledge management and change proficiency (Dove, 1999)

Dove and et.al (1996) define an agile enterprise as one that is broadly change-proficient; i.e., it exhibits competency at causing and dealing with change in the important competitive business practices of its business sector. According to them, there are three key concepts involved in this definition: change proficiency, critical business practices, and competency assessment. Sponsored by the Agility Forum, Rick Dove and et.al (1996) design a reference model structure that effectively captures and displays the essence of enterprise-wide competency at both proactive and reactive change(figure-4-). The reference model spans 24 interrelated critical business practices in 6 categories: strategic planning (3), business case justification (3), organizational relationship management (7), knowledge management (4), innovation management (4), and performance metrics (3)[1]. The seven organizational relationships focus on business units, employees, partners, suppliers, customers, information systems, and production systems. Each of the 24 practices is presented in a 3–5 page structure that provides: a generic definition, the framework and modules of a case-study practice that fits that definition, a set of generic proactive and reactive change issues, case-study responses for each issue, and finally, a change proficiency maturity synopsis that evaluates and displays the competency of the case example using the recently developed Change Proficiency Maturity Model (Dove and et.al, 1996). Figure-4- shows the change proficiency maturity profile for Remmele Engineering Corporation.

---

[1] - The numbers into ( ) represent amount of practices in each category. For example, "strategic planning" category has three practices as Strategic plan vision, Strategic plan dissemination, Strategic plan buy-In.

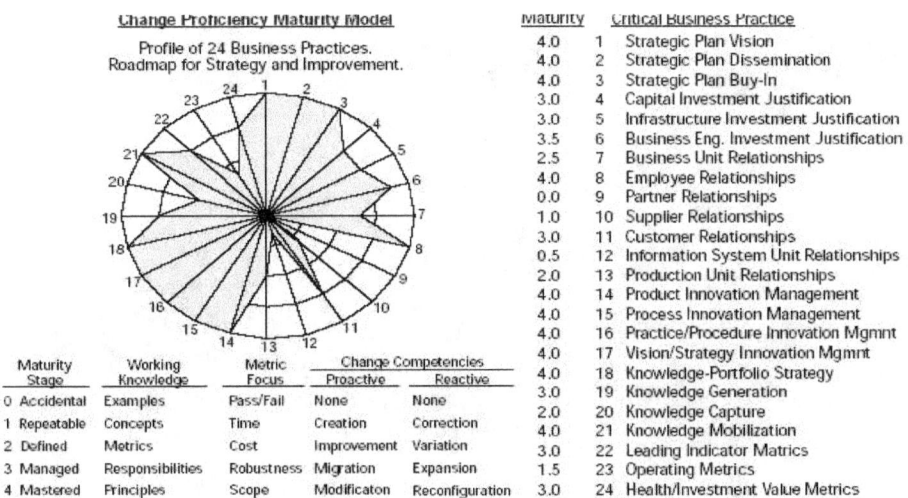

Change Proficiency Maturity Model	Maturity		Critical Business Practice

Profile of 24 Business Practices.
Roadmap for Strategy and Improvement.

Maturity	#	Critical Business Practice
4.0	1	Strategic Plan Vision
4.0	2	Strategic Plan Dissemination
4.0	3	Strategic Plan Buy-In
3.0	4	Capital Investment Justification
3.0	5	Infrastructure Investment Justification
3.5	6	Business Eng. Investment Justification
2.5	7	Business Unit Relationships
4.0	8	Employee Relationships
0.0	9	Partner Relationships
1.0	10	Supplier Relationships
3.0	11	Customer Relationships
0.5	12	Information System Unit Relationships
2.0	13	Production Unit Relationships
4.0	14	Product Innovation Management
4.0	15	Process Innovation Management
4.0	16	Practice/Procedure Innovation Mgmnt
4.0	17	Vision/Strategy Innovation Mgmnt
4.0	18	Knowledge-Portfolio Strategy
3.0	19	Knowledge Generation
2.0	20	Knowledge Capture
4.0	21	Knowledge Mobilization
3.0	22	Leading Indicator Matrics
1.5	23	Operating Metrics
3.0	24	Health/Investment Value Metrics

Maturity Stage	Working Knowledge	Metric Focus	Change Competencies	
			Proactive	Reactive
0 Accidental	Examples	Pass/Fail	None	None
1 Repeatable	Concepts	Time	Creation	Correction
2 Defined	Metrics	Cost	Improvement	Variation
3 Managed	Responsibilities	Robustness	Migration	Expansion
4 Mastered	Principles	Scope	Modificaton	Reconfiguration

Figure-4 - Change proficiency maturity profile for Remmele Engineering (Dove and et.al, 1996)

A five-stage maturity model framework was recently developed as a tool to assess existing corporate competency at change proficiency, as well as to prioritize and guide an Agility transformation or improvement strategy. The framework is based upon a progression through five stages of working knowledge and strategic focus for practices and procedures, with separate competency tracks for both proactive and reactive proficiencies. The framework is used to build a Change Proficiency Maturity Model for a specific business practice. They focus on change proficiency as a necessary and fundamental enabler for the agile enterprise. They also recognize that an agile enterprise can be as simple as a portfolio management company that constantly reshuffles the in-agile resources it controls, or as complex as a vertically integrated organization concerned about the Agility of each of its operating units, which in turn are concerned about the Agility of each of their key business processes. Complexity aside, all enterprises have frequent occasion to weather change, and each does so with its own degree of proficiency, or lack thereof. Some deal with each event as they come, some learn naturally from each event and get better at the next change, and some recognize competitive value in mastering the process of change.

Dove and et.al (1996) do not gauge a company's progress toward timeless mastery at change proficiency by accumulating points for practices like teaming, mass customization, virtual partnering, integrated product/process development, and other such very important concepts of the day. Instead, we look for more fundamental capabilities that allow a company to adopt and integrate whatever operating concepts are important today as well as those yet undefined that will become important tomorrow. Implementing today's competitive practices says nothing about the ability to implement tomorrow's.

2.2.5. Sharifi and Zhange methodology: In developing a model for achieving agility in manufacturing organizations, Zhang and Sharifi (2000) used three elements. Elements of their model are: (1)Agility drivers which are the changes/pressures from the business environment that necessitate a company to search for new ways of running its business in order to maintain its competitive advantage; (2) agility capabilities which are the essential capabilities that the company needs in order to positively respond to and take advantage of the changes; and (3) agility providers that are the means by which the so-called capabilities such as could be obtained (practices, methods, tools, techniques facilitating a capability for agility). As a result of surveying 1,000 companies, and conducting case studies in 12 of them, they concluded that practices related to people and organization issues were both more effective and important for manufacturers. They also found that the Internet, mass-customization and virtual organizations were only used by a small percentage of respondents, and usually only partially (Power and Sohal, 2001). Figure-5- presents conceptual model of agility implementation from point Sharifi and zhange view.

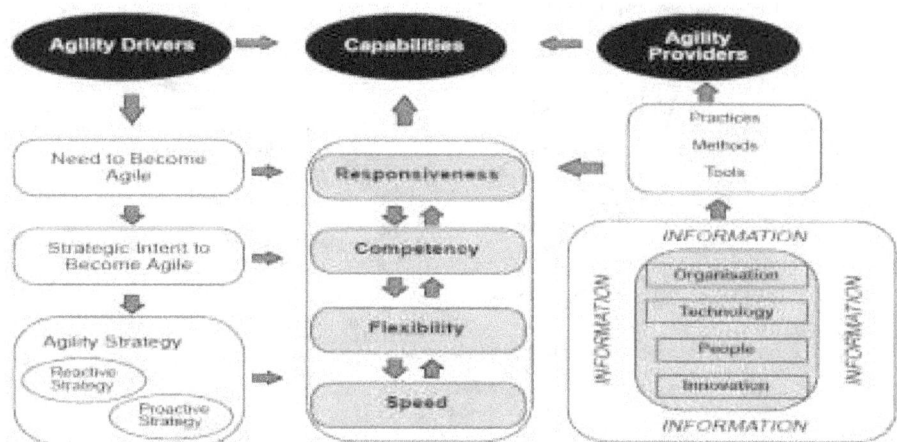

Figure-5-conceptual model of agility implementation (Sharifi and zhange, 2000)

As changes and pressures faced by companies may be different, the degree of agility required by individual companies will be different. This degree is defined as the ``agility need level'', which is a function of various factors such as turbulence of the business environment, the environment that the company competes in, and the characteristics of the company itself. Once the agility need level is determined for a company, the next step is to assess the current agility level of the company, i.e. how agile the company is now. The difference between the level of agility required and that the company already has may then be analyzed to provide a basis for further decision making. The next stage following the analysis of agility needs is to determine the required agility capabilities in order to become agile. This would require the detection, recognition and classification of changes faced by the company, as well as the analysis of the impact individual changes will bring to the company. The agility capabilities required may then be determined from the changes. The final stage in the methodology involves identifying agility providers that could bring about the required capabilities, implementing the identified providers, determining the level of agility achieved (through performance measurement), and formulating corrective measures to further improve the performance. A number of tools are being developed to assist manufacturing enterprises to carry out the above process, which have already been discussed. In sum, Sharifi and Zhange (2001) have proposed a methodology to examine the business environment of the company, determine the level of agility needed by the company, speculate on the strategic alternatives available for the company to pursue, determine the abilities of the company in response to unpredictable changes, determine the capabilities and priorities in implementing the capabilities required by the company to respond to changes (according to the specific circumstances surrounding it), identify the practices that could support the company's approach towards agility.

2.2.6. Youssuf, Sarhadi and Gunasekaran model: According to Youssuf and et.al (1999) agility is the successful exploration of competitive bases (speed, flexibility, innovation, reactivity, quality and profitability) through the integration of reconfigurable resources and best practices in a knowledge-rich environment to provide customerdriven products and services in a fast changing market environment. As we mentioned in definitions of agile manufacturing part, Youssuf and et.al (1999) have identified core concepts of agile manufacturing as core competence management, knowledge structure, virtual organization, and capability for reconfiguration(figure-6-). They propose three parallel steps to base competitive position in order to achieve agility: metrics, agility attributes and pathways or obstacles. Gunasekaran (1999) has proposed a conceptual model for the design of agile manufacturing systems based on the four key dimensions of strategies, technology, people and systems. He notes that most of the literature in this area focuses on strategies or techniques, but there is little or no focus on the integration issues. He also states that there is a lack of empirical studies testing hypotheses based on theory in this area.

Youssuf and et.al (1999) have stated that an agile organization must develop a strategic plan to launch new products in succession. Launching a single product hastily without a follow-up could be counter-productive. According to them, collectively literature reviews provide insights to what constitutes agile practices and attributes of an agile organization.

As mentioned above, attributes of agility are integration, competence, team building, technology, quality, change, partnership, market, education and welfare. Competitive bases, the pathways and obstacles to achieving these attributes are important issues for consideration if progress is to be achieved in moving towards agility. Also important is the metrics for the processes that are required for achieving agility.

2.2.7. Youssuf and Crocitto model: Youssuf and Crocitto (2003) have presented a human based model of organizational agility. They decided to expand on existing models of organizational agility by incorporating the role of people, advanced manufacturing technology, and organizational characteristics in organizational success; especially in the delivery of quality products and services. Their model emphasized on elements such as leadership, culture, information technology, organizational memberships, suppliers, customers, and reward system as fundamental aspects of agility. They suggest that above generic or human factors, along with advanced manufacturing and information technologies, can enhance flexibility and responsiveness of company gaining the agile manufacturing in the context. Then, if company reinforces capabilities such as quality, cost and speed, is can achieve agility in the turbulent environment (figure-7-).

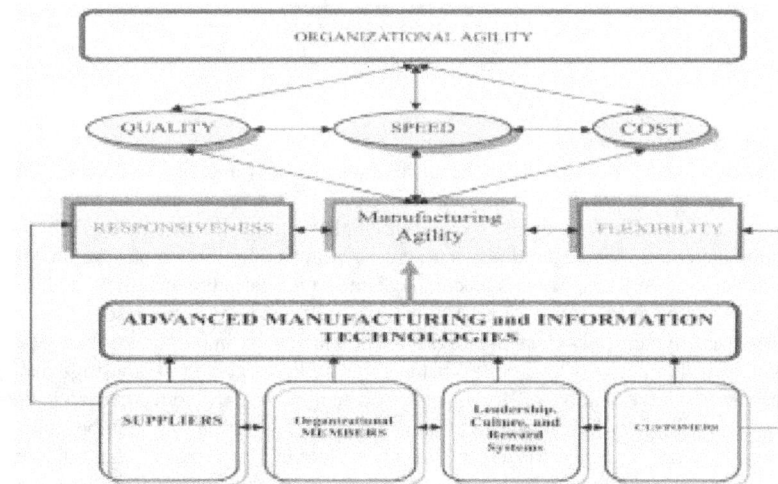

Figure-7-human side of organizational agility (Youssuf and Crocitto, 2003)

2.2.8. Chin-Torng Lin et.al model: According to Torng Lin and et.al (2005) the purpose of agile organization is to enrich/satisfy customers and employees. The main driving force behind agility is change. Even through change is nothing new; today's change is taking place at a much faster speed than ever before. Turbulence and uncertainty in the business environment have become the main causes of failure in the manufacturing industry. The number of changes and their type, specification or characteristic cannot be easily determined and are probably indefinite. So, they have developed a model containing four aspects to be truly agile. The first aspect is that customer requirement, competition criteria, market, technology, and social factors are changing competition in business environments (Agility drivers). In the second aspect, agile organization tries to Enrich and satisfy customers based on elements such as cost, time, function, and robustness. Agility capabilities included in the third aspect are flexibility, quickness, responsiveness, and competency. Finally, to be agile, organizations need to reinforce the agility enablers/pillars such as integration, competence, team building, technology, quality, change, partnership, market, education and welfare by leverage people and information technology (Foundation), master change and uncertainty (Control), and collaborative relationships (Strategy). However, these enablers have been presented earlier by Youssuf and et.al (1999). See figure-8-.

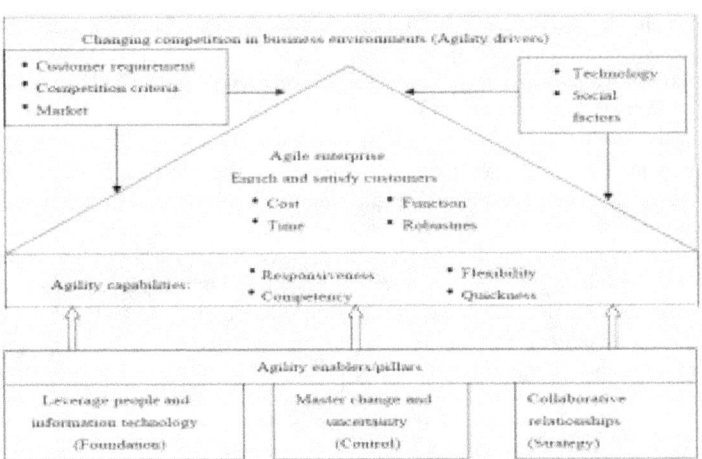

Figure-٨- conceptual model of agile enterprise (Torng Lin and et.al (٢٠٠٥)

3. Critiques on agility conceptualizations

Organizations have realized that agility is essential for their survival and competitiveness. As mentioned before, available literature on agility has provided conceptual overviews of dimensions and has further conceptualized related elements. Obviously, different facets of agility have been emphasized by various authors and this has lead to varied views reflected in the literature. Despite the differences, all definitions of agility emphasize the speed and flexibility as the primary attributes of an agile. Thus, There is no commonly accepted definition of agility, and there are a large number of opinions concerning the meaning of this term. The term of agility is used in the research on how organization can cope with unpredicted and dynamically changing environment. An equally important attribute of agility is the effective response to change and uncertainty as Dove (1996) believe that agility is equal to knowledge management and change proficiency. Also, there is large number of publications on agility that are concerned with the specific strategies, techniques, and manufacturing and/or management practices. There is also a vast number and variety of strategies, techniques, and manufacturing and/or management practices described as a part of the agile enterprise. Only a few studies address the conceptualization and development of an integrated view of the agile enterprise concept. Although, some agility frameworks make an attempt to present a more integrated and holistic model, it still presents a view mostly focused on production and the technological aspects of enterprise. Moreover, most agility related publications are focused on the theoretical descriptions of agility and agility frameworks, mainly in manufacturing context. Only few of those metrics and frameworks were investigated in empirical research (Sherehiy and et.al, 2007).

Two main approaches to understanding and defining agility have been distinguished among reviewed literature. The first approach is a very broad and imprecise concept that encompasses all definitions and description of various practices and technologies that have been implemented in industry during last two decades. For example, Yusuf et al. (1999) stated that agility is the synthesized use of the developed and well-know technologies and methods of manufacturing. This view is supported by Goldman et al. (1995), who describes AM as the assimilation of all flexible production technologies, together with experience gained from total quality management (TQM), ''JIT'' production, and lean production. Thus, according to this approach, agility is mutually compatible with lean manufacturing, CIM, TQM, materials requirement planning II (MRPII), JIT, and employee empowerment. Conversely, Gunasekaran (2002) also noted that AM is not lean, or flexible manufacturing, or CIM. To clarify the differences between the AM and current practices, Sanchez and Nagi (2001) stated that the lean manufacturing is a collection of operational techniques focused on productive use of resources, whereas agility is an overall strategy. Those authors contrast agile and flexible manufacturing in reference to the type of adaptation: flexible manufacturing is reactive adaptation, while agile is proactive. According to Tsourveloudis and Valavanis (2002), the flexibility is a capability of the whole factory to change from one task or production route to another, and agility is a strategic ability of the whole enterprise to adapt to unpredicted and sudden changes in the market.

The second approach to agility is much more narrow and focused. In this approach, the main emphasis is placed on the ability of rapid adaptation; however, it is not simply the speed of response. Agility is a rapid and proactive adaptation of enterprise elements to unexpected and unpredicted changes, and represents a new and radically different manufacturing business model. Enterprise elements are the goals, objectives, technology, and organization. It has been argued that since most of currently applied and well-known practices are not adjusted well to uncertainty and unpredictability of the dynamically changing business environment, those methods cannot be included into the concept of agility.

The development of an agile organization framework presents a serious challenge. First of all, the agility concepts are not yet clearly defined and conceptualized. Although the main and most important attributes of agility have been identified, those attributes are supposed to be applied to such complex structures as an enterprise. It has been proposed in the literature that, in reference to agility, the following components of the enterprise are most important: organization, people, and technology. Each of these elements is multidimensional and complex itself. Thus, numerous agility related concepts, practices and characteristics proposed in the literature can be summarized and classified in two main ways. First, it can be classified into groups according to the adherence or relevance to the main attributes of the agility. In the reviewed literature, a large diversity of agility attributes has been identified. Based on the review, the following main attributes for an agile enterprise can be distinguished: (1) flexibility and adaptability, (2) responsiveness, (3) speed, (4) integration and low complexity, (5) mobilization of core competences, (6) high quality and customized products, and (7) culture of change. It should be noted that among those attributes, the core and global characteristics of agility that can be applied to all aspects of enterprise include flexibility, responsiveness, quickness, culture of change, integration, and low complexity. These core characteristics should be reflected in most important aspects of enterprise: production/service, organization, and workforce. Flexibility is considered as the ability to pursue different business strategies and tactics, to quickly change from one strategy/task/job to another. The strategies should be of course different in some reasonable extent, which will not endanger the integrity and main mission of the enterprise. Responsiveness is an ability to identify changes and opportunities and respond reactively or proactively to them. The term "culture of change" is a description of environment supportive of experimentation, learning, and innovation and is focused on the continuous monitoring environment to identify changes. Culture of change is an environment where people on all organizational levels have positive and fearless attitude to changes, different opinions, new ideas, and technology. In order to respond to changes the management and workers at all levels have to continuously scan the business and work environment to identify changes and opportunities related to customers, suppliers, and competitors that may be exploited by the enterprise. The market and business environment have to be monitored in order to determine new technologies, practices and methods of production, management, and organization that can be used by the enterprise to successfully respond and adapt to the changes. The speed is ability to complete requirements of all other agile characteristics in shortest possible time. The ability to learn, carry out tasks and operations and make changes in shortest possible time. The integration and low complexity dimension is defined as close and simple relations between the individual system components, easy and effortless flow of the materials, information and communication between the system components, organizational structures, people, and technology. The described general attributes have to be translated into specific indices for each of the main enterprise structure: organization, workforce, technology, and operations.

The other classification of agile organization concepts and characteristics is based on their adherence to the enterprise structures. The global agility attributes can be established as goals for the high-level management and are applicable to whole enterprise. Starting from these general goals of agility, the more specific sub-goals and the means to achieve them could be derived. The more specific goals and ways to achieve them would depend on the specificity of the each particular enterprise. However, at the highest and global level of the enterprise can be established few domains that should be the main focus for enterprise while trying to achieve agility. These main domains are focus on customer satisfaction; cooperation, learning and knowledge management, and development of culture of change.

4. Organizational agility framework

As you saw in literature review section, Agility as the term is the ability of an organization to respond quickly and successfully to the changes and also exploit them. Hormozi (2001) acknowledges that successful implementation of agile manufacturing requires changes in five areas as government regulations, business cooperation, information technology, reengineering, and employee flexibility. Sharifi and Zhange (2000) state that any organization firstly should identify agility level need it based on agility drivers' identification. To determine the current level of agility the organization has, capabilities of organization to respond the changes occurring in the turbulent environment is assessed and determined what capabilities the organization lack. After determining agility level the organization needs and the level of agility it has, strategic intent to become agile is necessary and then strategy development and formulation is started. By determining current and desired level of agility, as well as strategic planning, the providers help the organization to enhance existing abilities and capabilities are specified and promoted. In this section we are going to develop a practical methodology for agility's practice implementation in any organization. Indeed, as you have seen and recognized in the above materials, researchers suggest three main phases to agility. Those are agility drivers, agility's capabilities, and agility enablers or providers. Researches have introduced many factors about drivers, capabilities, and enablers in the field. Here, we combine those elements to form new and complete model of organizational agility areas. Figure-9-shows this model.

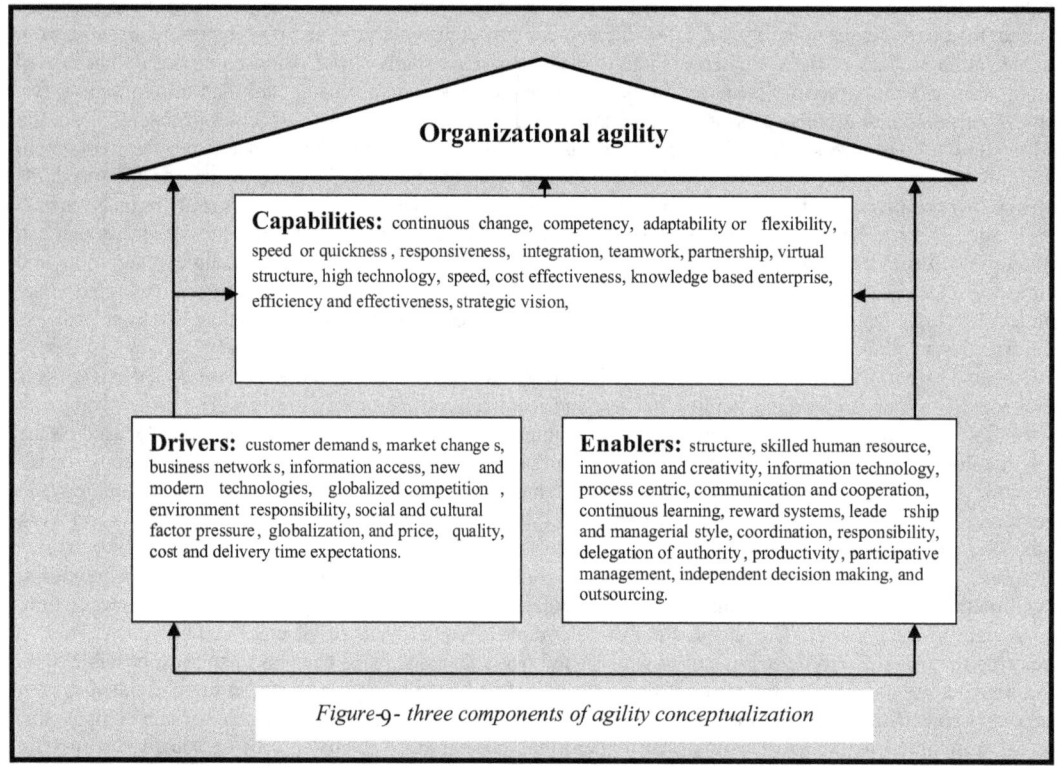

Organizational agility

Capabilities: continuous change, competency, adaptability or flexibility, speed or quickness, responsiveness, integration, teamwork, partnership, virtual structure, high technology, speed, cost effectiveness, knowledge based enterprise, efficiency and effectiveness, strategic vision,

Drivers: customer demand s, market change s, business network s, information access, new and modern technologies, globalized competition, environment responsibility, social and cultural factor pressure, globalization, and price, quality, cost and delivery time expectations.

Enablers: structure, skilled human resource, innovation and creativity, information technology, process centric, communication and cooperation, continuous learning, reward systems, leade rship and managerial style, coordination, responsibility, delegation of authority, productivity, participative management, independent decision making, and outsourcing.

Figure-9- three components of agility conceptualization

As you know, the aim of this paper is to prepare a conceptual model for agility evaluation and enhancement to respond rapidly to the changes in the environment. In other words, we are going to combine previous models and approaches to propose step-by-step methodology upon which organizations can improve their performance based on agility. In literature, previous models and methodologies don't prepare any step by step process for agility implementation (except somehow Sharifi and Zhange (1999) model). Although those models indicate three part of agility as drivers, capabilities, and enablers but don't agree on elements of these basic parts. Furthermore, steps such as strategy formulation, public and special environment consideration, performance measurement process, and developing action plans sometimes aren't clearly identified and stated. As you saw in agility approaches section, authors have stated many different definitions for agility concept and don't have agreement about defining it. We define agility as an organizational ability to respond to the business drivers using enablers in order to gain useful capabilities. In summary, main characteristics of this methodology than previous models are:

This model has step by step and systematic approach and guides organizations to implement easily and successfully.

Internal drivers of change is considered and determined in this model

Many factors, capabilities and providers have been identified in this model

Strategy formulation and action plans are highlighted in order to move away from current state to desired state.

After given period, it is needed to be measured performance (or level of agility that organization has gained) to re-analysis conditions and design improvement initiatives.

Some agility frameworks make an attempt to present a more integrated and holistic model, it still presents a view mostly focused on production and the technological aspects of enterprise, but, this model can be applied to any organization (whether profit, nonprofit, service, public and private).

Figure-10- presents the practical methodology of organizational agility measurement and enhancement. Based on below presented model, any organization needs to analyze the dynamic or static state of organizational environment (as a first stage). Through considering mission and vision statement, goals and objectives, policies and procedures, rules, market change, liquidity flow, strategies, structure, business processes, and so on, it can be carried out by managers and employees. This work is done for determining the factors that cause the internal and external environment is varied.

At second stage, it is important to be determined the drivers that press on organization to change or challenge the organizational life and survive. These are factors such as market environment's changes, level and intensity of competition, competitor characteristics; customer need, social and cultural factors, intra-organizational context, technology and innovation, globalization, environmental responsibility, and so on. Therefore, organizations need to determine quickly and successfully agility's drivers as they face with these factors and survive and life of them is being challenged. Results of this and previous stage can be placed into SWOT analysis model. In this place, organization should determine the level of agility they need to respond change or pressures. The level of agility needed for an organization is considered to be equivalent to the degree of turbulence of the business environment of the organization. The business environment is, as explained before, broken down into factors which are agility drivers, and for each a number of sub-factors are introduced which form the basis for designing the assessment questionnaire. The questions basically address the degree of turbulence of each sub-factor for the organization (Sharifi and Zhange, 2001).

Then, it can be identified and fostered capabilities to readiness for changes and to overcome them (third stage). The most important and comprehensive elements of agile capabilities are flexibility, speed, competency, and responsiveness. Sometimes, agile capabilities were identified such as speed, flexibility, cost, quality, innovation, and proactivity, teamwork, participation, knowledge and skills, virtual structure. In general, organizations should attempt to reinforce these factors so that they can respond to changes or pressures and exploit them to gain competitive advantage. This, in turn, forces the organization to search for ways and tools to obtain/enhance the required capabilities. Obviously, different organizations will experience different sets of changes as well as different levels of pressures resulting from each change. Consequently, different combinations of capabilities will have to be obtained for different organizations.

Fourth stage compromises generic enablers or providers as culture and values, leadership, organizational change, performance measurement, information technology, and customer service. As with capabilities, organization can improve mentioned factors so that their potential to survive and act as a leader in the competitive markets is enhanced. In sum, based on results of third and forth stages, organization can informed with the condition of organization from agility's perspective. In this place, existing level of organizational agility is determined.

With recognizing organization's states, top managers can formulate and develop the best strategies to improving conditions with many development approaches so that the level of organizational agility is enhanced or reinforced. After given period, managers carry out performance evaluation process to determine that the results expected are attained and to determine deviations from objectives and aims. By this, organizations again repeat this cycle (after given or specified period) to find deviations and gaps through environmental and gap analysis so that they respond to changes, uncertainties and turbulences and gain a sustainable competitive advantage.

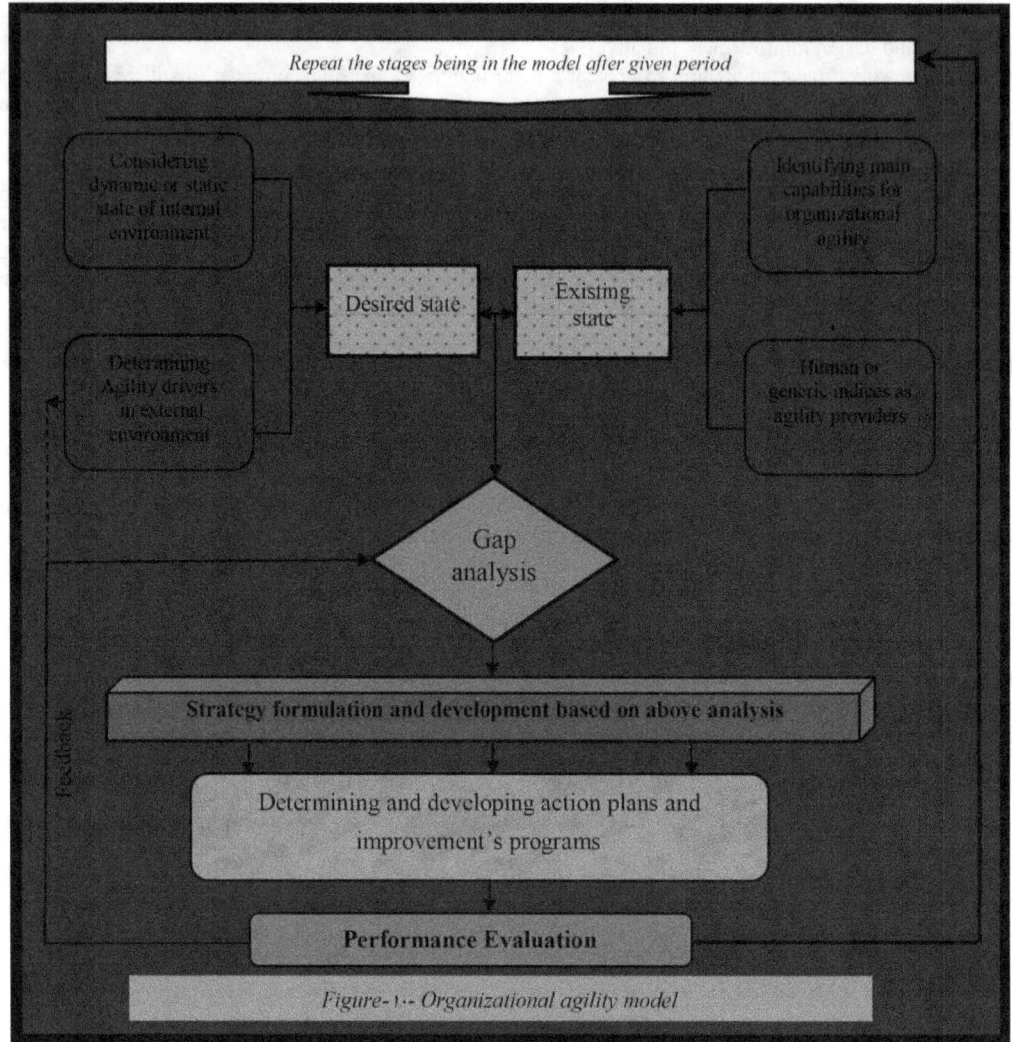

Figure-1-- Organizational agility model

By combining the results of previous stages, it can be implemented gap analysis to compare desired state with current state of organization. For improving conditions, many development approaches are designed so that the level of organizational agility is enhanced. After this, managers carry out performance measurement process to determine that the results expected are attained and to determine deviations from objectives and aims. By this, organizations again repeat this cycle (after given or specified period) to find deviations and gaps through environmental and gap analysis so that they respond to changes, uncertainties and turbulences and they can gain a sustainable competitive advantage.

5. Suggestions and Recommendations

Nowadays, many organizations are facing constantly and intensely increasing competition stimulated by technological innovations, changing market environments and changing customer demands. This critical situation has led to a major revision in business priorities, strategic vision, and in the viability of conventional and even relatively contemporary models (Sharifi and Zhang, 1999). In an increasingly competitive market, there is a need to develop and improve organizational flexibility and responsiveness. In the past decade, most companies adopted business process reengineering (BPR) and total quality management (TQM) and other improvement approaches in response to challenges and demands; however, these were not always successfully.

Although the methodology was developed based on a review of the literature pertaining to the subject, it was seen as necessary to validate its practical applicability. A comprehensive methodological approach to strategy building with regard to agility is needed among organizations and such a methodology could be developed in practice. The methodology proposed in this paper, though still to be fully developed and validated, constitutes an important effort in this regard and helps to bridge the gap between theory and practice in the agility's literature. For practitioners, the proposed methodology provides a basis for assessing their business situations and a guideline for recognizing missing capabilities and building up strategic policies in pursuit of agility as well competitive advantage.

6. Conclusion Today's organization must operate in a highly dynamic competitive environment subject to internally and externally induced change. While many of these changes could be considered continuous, there are some very disruptive changes that can dramatically impinge on the organization's ability to survive. Therefore, in this paper, we firstly introduced definitions of agility and agile manufacturing to understand the basic meaning of concept. Then, several and most important models and approaches to implement and retain agility in organization are presented. Based on above models and literature review, we propose a practical methodology for agility implement and improvement. As mentioned in this paper, any organization should consider internal and external environment to recognize changers that press on it. So, managers must improve and enhance capabilities and abilities of organization to respond and also exploit the change that occur in the environment. After this, gap analysis process can be act to determine current and best state of agility's level. If there is constrains to improve organizational responsiveness, corrective actions and programs are designed to improve the level of organizational agility. In sum, we believe proposed model can help managers to enhance responsiveness and competency of organizations to respond changes and also exploit them. However, we suggest researchers to examine the validity and effectiveness of proposed model.

References

At. Kearney Institute (2002). How Governments Can Improve Public Sector Performance, LSE public policy Group, London.

Brown, N; Bessant, J (2003).The Manufacturing Strategy-Capabilities Links in Mass Customization and Agile Manufacturing, International Journal of Operations and Production Management, 5(4), p.p 707-730.

Burgess, T (1994).Making the Leap to Agility, International Journal of Operations & Production Management, Vol. 14 No. 11.

Christopher, M; Towill, D (2001).An Integrated Model of the Design of Agile Supply Chains, Journal of Distribution & Logistic Management, V.31, N.4, p.p 235-246.

Crocitto, M; Youssuf, M (2003).Human Side of Organizational Agility, Industrial Management & Data System, 103/6, pp.388-397.

Dove, R ; Hartman, S and Benson, S (1996). An Agile Enterprise Reference Model, US Agility Forum, Bethlehem University.

Dove, R (1999). Knowledge Management, Responsibility, and the Agile Enterprise, Journal of Knowledge Management, 3 (1), pp.18-35.

Drucker, P (1968). Comeback of The Entrepreneur, Management Today, April, pp.23-30.

Hage, J., Aiken, M (1969). Routine technology, social structure and organizational goals. Administrative Science Quarterly, 14, p.p 366–376.

Fliedner, G and Vokurka, R (1997). Agility: Competitive Weapon of The 1990's and Beyond?, Production and Inventory Management Journal, Vol. 38 No. 3, pp. 19-24.

Giachetti, R; Martinez, L; Saenz, O; Chen, C (2003). Analysis of the Structural Measures of Flexibility and Agility Using a Measurement Theoretical Framework, Journal of Production Economics, 86 (1), 47-62.

Goldman, S.L., Nagel, R.N (1993). Management, technology and agility: the emergence of a new era in manufacturing. International Journal of Technology Management, 8 (1/2), 18–38.

Goldman, S; Nagel, R; Preiss, K (1995). Agile Competitors and Virtual Organizations, Kenneth: van No strand Reinhold.

Gunasekaran, A (1999). Agile Manufacturing: A Framework for Research and Development, International Journal of Production Economics, Vol. 62 No. 1-2, pp. 87-105.

Hayen, G (1988). Change, Challenge and Continuity: An Entrepreneurial Vision from an Electronics Multinational, International Journal of Technology Management, Vol. 3 No. 3.

Helo, P (2004). Managing Agility and Productivity in the Electronics Industry, Industrial Management and Data systems, v.104, n.7: 567-577.

Hormozi, A.M (2001). Agile Manufacturing: The Next Logical Step, Benchmarking: an International Journal, 8 (2): 132-143.

Iacocca Institute (1991). 21st Century Manufacturing Enterprise Strategy, V.1, Lehigh University, Bethelham, USA.

Jackson, M; Johansson, C (2003). An Agility Analysis from a Production System Perspective, Journal of Manufacturing Systems, vol.14, No .06: 482-488.

Kid, P.T (1994). A 21st Century Paradigm in Agile Manufacturing: Forging New Frontiers, AddisonWesley, Wokingham.

Levary, R (1992). Enhancing Competitive Advantage in Fast-Changing Manufacturing Environment, Ind England: 21-8.

Lin, Ching-Torng; Chiu, Hero and Chu, Po-Young (2004). Agility Index in The Supply Chain, International Journal Production Economics, 100(2):1-15.

Lin, Ching-Torng; Chiu, Hero and Chu, Po-Young (2005).Agility Evaluation Using Fuzzy Logic, International Journal of Production Economics, 101(2): pp.1-16.

Maskell, B (2001). The Age of Agile Manufacturing, Supply Chain Management: An International Journal; Vol.6, No 1: 5-11.

Meredith, S; Francis, D (2000). Journey Towards Agility: The Agile Wheel Explored The TQM Magazine, Vol.12, No. 2: 137-143.

Naylor, J.B; Naim, M.M and Berry, D (1999). Leagility: Integrating The Lean and Agile Manufacturing, International Journal of Production Economics, 62(1-2): 107-118.

Nagel, R., Dove, R. (1991), 21st century manufacturing enterprise strategy: an industry led view, Iacocca Institute, Lehigh University, Vol. 1.

Narasimhan, R; Swink, M and Soo Wook Kim (2006). Disentangling Leanness and Agility: An Empirical Investigation, Journal of Operations Management, No. 24(5): 440-457.

Power, D; Sohal, A (2005). Critical Success Factors in Agile Supply Chain Management, International Journal of Physical Distribution & Logistics Management, 31(4): 247-265.

Prince, J; Kay, J (2003). Combining Lean and Agile Characteristics, International Journal of Production Economics, 85(3): 305-318.

Ramesh, g; Devadasan, S (2007). Literature Review on the Agile Manufacturing Criteria, Journal of Manufacturing Technology Management, 18(2): 182-201.

Ren, J., Yusuf, Y.Y., Burns, N.D (2000). A prototype of measurement system for agile enterprise, International Conference on Quality, Reliability and Maintenance, Oxford, UK, pp. 247–252.

Ren, J., Yususf, Y.Y., Burns, N.D (2003). The effect of agile attributes on competitive priorities: a neural network approach. Integrated Manufacturing, 14 (6): 489–497.

Sanchez, L.M., Nagi, R (2001). A review of agile manufacturing systems, International Journal of Production Research, 39 (16): 3561–3600.

Sarkis, J (2001). Benchmarking for Agility, Benchmarking: An International Journal, 8, No. 2: 88107.

Government Accounting: An Assessment of Theory, Purposes and Standards

Mostafa Emami
M.Sc Eco.Fin , Department of Accounting, Tarbiat Modares University ,Iran,Tehran **Mehdi Parveizi**
Thecher of Islamic Azad University, Giylan gharb, Iran
Kamran Nazari
Department of Business Management, Payam Noor University, Kermanshah, Iran **Ehsan Rayegan**
Department of Accounting,Scool of Social Since , Razi University, Kermanshah, Iran

Abstract

Developments in governmental activities in recent years have raised concerns over whether the cash basis of accounting is sufficient for governmental accounting and reporting. Accrual accounting, previously thought to be only suitable in the private sector, has been seen to be an alternative for better reporting of government activities. Although there is a continuing debate over the use of cash versus accrual accounting, accrual accounting has been adopted in he governments of several countries including Australia, New Zealand and the United Kingdom. Government accounting and financial reporting aims to protect and manage public money and discharge accountability In order to achieve ambitious socioeconomic goals, developing countries require public sector institutional capacity for setting and implementing public policy, which in turn necessitates government accounting reform. The social value of government accounting reform therefore lies in its contribution to development goals, including poverty reduction. This rationale has led international and multilateral lenders and donors to endorse International Public Sector Accounting Standards (IPSAS) for adoption by developing countries. An emphasis on assuring financial integrity and a shift to accruals can make IPSAS more useful in government accounting reform in developing countries. All of these are heavily influenced by private sector practices, which favour the accrual basis and consolidated reporting. This article argues for a gradual symmetric approach to accruals and a combination of government-wide and fund reporting. The author also proposes some broad accounting principles to promote political and economic accountability .

Key words: Government Accounting, government, accounting reform, International Public Sector Accounting Standards (IPSAS.

Introduction

Miller (1995) p10 argues that a "healthy" accounting standard setting process needs representation from the entire spectrum of stakeholders to retain its integrity. He concludes that "a transparent due process allows outsiders to see the interactions and compromises among the key participants in the development of acceptable accounting rules". Prior Australian research has raised questions about the veracity of various aspects of the operation of the 'due process' for public sector standard setting. Ryan et.

521

Institute of Interdisciplinary Business Research

al. (1999) concluded that there were fundamental problems with the 'due process' as it operated in AAS29, which was released in 1993. There was a lack of input from account preparers and a close working relationship existed between the Treasuries and the standard setters. Carnegie and West (1997) conducted an analysis of the responses to ED 50 in relation to the recognition of infrastructure assets only. They contended that, for this particular issue, the standard setters placed more weight on a sample of 26 responses which were deemed to be "of particular interest" by the staff of the Australian Accounting Research Foundation (AARF) (p32). This led to their raising the concern that the PSASB may not have been responsive to its constituents. The Philippines realized fiscal surpluses between 1994 and 1997, prior to the Asian financial crisis.176 However, indicators have deteriorated significantly in the past 3 years. The Arroyo administration faces a worsening fiscal position. Unless the Government curbs expenses and improves revenue collection, the 2001 budget deficit could reach P200 billion ($4.2 billion).177 The weak fiscal position is creating tensions with multilateral development banks.178 Moreover, it restricts the Government's ability to address infrastructure issues and poverty reduction.

Furthermore, the Philippines experiences significant ongoing problems with corruption. With annual capital expenditure exceeding $3.5 billion, the procurement of goods and services, and implementation of infrastructure projects, by the Government present significant opportunities for graft.179 Government accounting and auditing arrangements were formulated in 1947. They have many strengths including the use of doubleentry bookkeeping, a mixed cash-accrual accounting base, a cadre of well-trained accountants, and potential access to a large external pool of trained accountants. Public management arrangements are characterized by institutional and regulatory rigidities. Efforts to modernize the public sector have gathered pace in recent years. Among other things, the Government intends to (i) develop a MediumTerm Expenditure Framework (MTEF); (ii) introduce output and outcome performance measures and targets; (iii) overhaul procurement practices; (iv) introduce 3-year baseline budgeting; (v) modernize auditing practices; (vi) introduce computerized financial management information systems; and (vii) prepare for the introduction of full accrual accounting.180he Constitution of the Philippines 1987 mandates the keeping of government accounts, the promulgation of accounting rules, the audit of financial reports, and the submission of reports covering the Government's financial operations and position.181 In particular, Article IX defines three constitutional commissions as being separate and independent bodies.

From Accountability to Accounting

The global rise of government accounting is fundamentally due to the greater demand for accountability in a democracy and market economy. Democratic governance and market transactions require and foster the norm of reciprocity the expectation of exchange of benefits of comparable value upon which accountability is based. Accounting information can be used to monitor and enforce the terms of economic, social and political contracts. When a government engages in market transactions whether buying or selling services, lending or borrowing money it is subject to economic accountability. When it levies taxes to finance public services, it incurs political accountability. The development of government accounting is related to the

522

Institute of Interdisciplinary Business Research

constitutional form of government that provides for separation of powers, and checks and balances among the legislative, executive, and judicial branches of government (Chan and Rubin, 1987). While all governments engage in some degree of planning and control, only democratic governments are mandated to open their books directly to auditors and indirectly to the public through financial reports. Fiscal transparency is therefore an attribute of limited government, for to give out information is to cede authority. Government officials rationally do not volunteer more information than is required or in their interest. It is therefore not surprising that, while some accounting is done on a voluntary basis, financial disclosure is often made only in response to demand. The regulatory structure for government financial disclosure mirrors the pattern of accountability in government and the political system. In an administrative hierarchy, the superior holds subordinates accountable and requires feedback information on their performance. A legislature monitors the conduct of the executive branch, for example, in executing the approved budget. Furthermore, a government has the incentive to disclose information in order to induce others to provide resources to it. These include potential buyers of government securities; vendors of goods and services on credit; and grantors of financial aid. In these voluntary exchanges, information is used to predict a government's ability to carry out the terms of contracts, .\fter the transactions are made, accounting information is used to monitor contractual performance. Governments are less inclined to disclose financial information to those without leverage over it, at least in the short-term, such as individual taxpayers. It is here that mandatory standards seek to increase the information access of those who are least able to demand it, or to enforce their right to know. The exercise of accountability requires institutions in both senses of the term: namely, organizations; and rules of the game (World Bank, 2002, p. 4). In government accounting, these refer to standard-setting bodies and the standards they promulgate. These institutions of government accounting in individual countries are extensively documented in the CIGAR literature and will not be covered in this article. It is, how ever, important to describe the general purposes of government accounting, in order to contrast it with

commercial accounting. The Commission on Audit shall have the power, authority, and duty to examine, audit, and settle all accounts pertaining to the revenue and receipts of, and expenditures or uses of funds and property, owned or held in trust by, or pertaining to, the Government, or

any of its subdivisions, agencies, or instrumentalities, including government- owned or controlled corporations with original charters, and on a post-audit basis: (a) constitutional bodies, commissions and offices that have been granted fiscal autonomy under this Constitution; (b) autonomous state colleges and universities; (c) other government owned or controlled corporations and their subsidiaries; and (d) such nongovernmental entities receiving subsidy or equity, directly or indirectly, from or through the Government, which are required by law or the granting institution to submit to such audit as a condition of subsidy or equity. However, where the internal control system of the audited agencies is inadequate, the Commission may adopt such measures, including temporary or special pre-audit, as are necessary and appropriate to correct the deficiencies. It shall keep the general accounts of the Government and, for such period as may be provided by law, preserve the vouchers and other supporting papers pertaining thereto. (2) The Commission shall have exclusive authority, subject to

523

the limitations in this Article, to define the scope of its audit and examination, establish the techniques and methods required therefor, and promulgate accounting and auditing rules and regulations, including those for the prevention and disallowance of irregular, unnecessary, excessive, extravagant, or unconscionable expenditures or uses of government funds and properties Section 3. No law shall be passed exempting any entity of the Government or its subsidiaries in any guise whatever, or any investment of public funds, from the jurisdiction of the Commission on Audit.

Section 4. The Commission shall submit to the President and the Congress, within the time fixed by law, an annual report covering the financial condition and operation of the Government, its subdivisions, agencies, and instrumentalities, including governmentowned or controlled corporations, and nongovernmental entities subject to its audit, and recommend measures necessary to improve their effectiveness and efficiency. It shall submit such other reports as may be required by law.

Organizational Roles and Responsibilities

The following organizations play central roles in budgeting, accounting and auditing arrangements. The COA audits the general accounts of the Government, promulgates accounting rules and regulations, and submits the annual financial report of the Government, its subdivisions, and agencies (including government owned or controlled corporations).

The Department of Finance (DOF) The DOF is responsible for (i) formulating, institutionalizing, and administering fiscal policies in coordination with other concerned subdivisions, agencies, and instrumentalities of the government; (ii) managing the financial resources of government; (iii) supervising the revenue operations of all LGUs; (iv) reviewing, approving and managing all public sector debt; and (v) rationalizing, privatizing and ensuring the public accountability of corporations and assets owned, controlled or acquired by the Government.187 The DOF oversees three operating bureaus: the Bureau of the Treasury (BTr), the Bureau of Internal Revenue (BIR), and the Bureau of Customs.

The Bureau of the Treasury (BTr) The BTr plays a pivotal role in the cash operations of the national government. It is responsible for (i) receiving and keeping national funds; (ii) managing and controlling disbursements of national funds; and (iii) maintaining accounts of financial transactions of all national government offices, agencies, and instruments.

Department of Budget and Management (DBM) The DBM is responsible for the design, reparation and approval of the accounting systems of government agencies. It is also responsible for coordinating and implementing the annual budget process. Furthermore, the Department manages the process of cash disbursement as well as monitoring compliance with appropriations.

Development and Budget Coordinating Council (DBCC) The DBCC comprises representatives from DBM, DOF, Bureau of Treasury, NEDA, and BSP. All agency budgetary requirements must pass through the Council. Its objectives are to (i) set budget parameters based on available resources; (ii) conduct budget hearings; and (iii) submit the resulting consolidated budget to the House of Representatives (particularly the Committee on Appropriations).

Accounting Information Systems

The national government accounting system is largely paper based. Financial reports from national agencies, including those with computerized systems, are manually processed and consolidated by COA. Existing computerized systems are of varying types.191 This variation is to be expected in such a diversified environment comprising a wide range of organizations with differing roles and objectives.

524

Government versus Commercial Accounting

Business accounting has often been used as a benchmark for evaluating government accounting. Two hundred years ago, Thomas Jefferson (quoted by Arthur Andersen, 1986) wished to see *the finance of the Union as clear and intelligible as a merchant's books, so that every member of Congress, and every man of any mind in the Union, should be able to comprehend them to investigate abuses, and consequently to control them'. Is it possible that government and business accounting are fundamentally alike in unimportant respects as public and private management are (Allison, 1980)? What are the important respects that set government accounting apart from its business counterpart?

In order to serve the three identified purposes, financial accounting and management accounting cannot be so neatly compartmentalized in the public sector, where management accounting refers to budgeting and control, rather than accounting solely in the service of managers. The budget is an expression of public policy and political preferences. It is an instrument of fiscal policy on revenue and spending to achieve macroeconomic objectives. It provides benchmarks for performance measured partly by the accounting system. Given their close relationship, it is often difficult to tell where budgeting ends and accounting begins. They reinforce each other in demonstrating and discharging fiscal accountability to the government's stakeholders, who are more numerous and diverse than the owners of a firm. Indeed, governments do not have owners.

The absence of ownership in government makes it problematic to apply the accounting equation (assets = liabilities + owners' equity) and its corollary (profit = revenuesexpenses) to the public sector. An exception may be local governments. These are municipal corporations chartered by the state to perform certain public services, which in many cases are private goods (for example water) or only quasipublic goods (for example elementary education). These entities have clear origins, and own identifiable assets and liabilities. Unfortunately, the assets and liabilities of the national government of a sovereign state are difficult to identify and harder still to measure in financial terms. With regard to assets, except in rare instances (such as the United States' purchase of Louisiana from France, or Alaska from Russia), few nations acquire new territories through buy-and-sell transactions. Most occupy their ancestral lands and some acquired their territories through military conquests or colonization. Historical costs, even if data are available, are not meaningful, yet market prices, even ifjustifiable. are hard to come by. The same problems arise in the case of natural resources and heritage assets. On the liability side, it is not easy to draw the line between a national government's contractual or legal obligations and its political

commitments and social responsibilities for the general welfare. In contrast to corporations' limited liabilities, governments in a democracy are prone to expand their responsibilities, resulting in larger budgets and frequent deficits (Buchanan and Wagner, 1977).

Accounting principles allow a business, whether private or state-owned, to recognize revenues only to the extent of goods or services provided. Governments uniquely provide public goods and finance them through taxation. Public goods are consumed collectively, and non-payers cannot be excluded— hence requiring tax financing. These characteristics sever the link between service delivery and revenue recognition, making it impossible to match revenues and expenses (Sunder, 1997). This accounting problem is also exacerbated by the involuntary nature of many transactions between government and people. The government's operating statement tracks resource flows, and only incidentally measures the government's service efforts and accomplishments. These unique characteristics of government are the primary source of the differences between government and commercial accounting. These differences, argues Sunder (1997, p. 198), 'do not constitute prima facie evidence that the former are defective and should be altered to conform to the latter'. More specifically, Nobes (1988, p. 198) challenged the assertion that 'Anglo-Saxon commercial accounting involving accrualsbased annual financial statements is necessary for accountability, control and

525

decision-making relating to government'. From the research perspective, theories underlying government accounting standards are mostly normative, in contrast to the development of positive theory in (business) financial accounting. The latter (Watts, 1977; Watts and Zimmerman, 1978, 1990) draws its inspiration from the contract-cost theory of the firm originating from Coase (1937). A similar incipient conceptual revolution started tentatively with Zimmerman's (1977) paper linking government financial reporting to political incentives. It is time to resume the search for a positive theory of government accounting standards. One way would be to build on the work of Chester Barnard and Herbert Simon.

At about the same time Goase wrote his famous paper explaining the existence of the firm in terms of transaction costs, Barnard (1938) identified the functions of the executive as securing the co-operation of the stakeholders of an organization. Barnard's work is currently enjoying a revival, primarily through the efforts of Oliver Williamson (1990). Much earlier, Simon (1945) applied Barnard's insight to government in his hook Administrative Behavior. In Simon's view, an organization is in equilibrium if Barnard's executive succeeds in securing the contributions of stakeholders by offering them adequate inducements to stay in the organizational coalition. A business can be viewed in the same way (Gohen and Gyert, 1965). In both types of organization, the challenge for managers is to negotiate satisfactory terms of contracts to keep the coalition intact. In such a theory, owners are important as contributors of equity capital, but they are not the only group managers try to please. In other words, the owner-centred theory of the firm and the single-principal agency theory are a special case of the Barnard- Simon organization theory.

This theory can be used to identify potential users of government's financial information by postulating that they use the information to predict their inducements from government (Ghan, 1981). Recently, Sunder (1997) applied contract-cost theory to explain and justify the differences betw-een accounting for government and nonprofit organizations and business accounting. Much more research is needed before the multiple-stakeholder perspective can have an impact on standards. In the meantime, government accounting has shifted closer to the business (financial) accounting model.

Internal Auditing

The Internal Auditing Act 1962 (RA 3456) introduced internal auditing requirements to the national government. A 1965 amendment (RA 4177) extended the Act's coverage to government-owned and controlled corporations (GOCCs) and local government units (LGUs). In 1992, President Aquino directed that government internal-control systems be strengthened (AO 278) – the Association of Government Internal Audi- tors (AGIA), among others, was instructed to ensure that internal audit practices, methods, and procedures be improved through continuing education and be conducted in accordance with internal auditing standards.

192 The AGIA represents internal auditors in government and promotes their professional development. It had 1,177 members at January 1999.

Public Financial Management Reform Program

The objectives of the Government's public financial management reforms are to (i) allocate and manage expenditures via a Medium Term Expenditure Framework (MTEF); (ii) strengthen feedback mechanisms for budget formulation through enhanced budget and performance monitoring; (iii) improve the performance management environment by simplifying budgeting rules; (iv) introduce incentives for better performance management; and (v) increase management flexibility to ensure performance results.197 The reforms are based on a benchmarking study of the Philippine expenditure management system vis-à-vis its neighboring countries (Australia, Korea, Malaysia, New Zealand,

Singapore, and Thailand) in terms of the three important expenditure outcomes: maintaining fiscal discipline, facilitating strategic prioritization at the oversight level, and enhancing the implementation efficiency of line agencies.198 The reform program comprises several activities as follows: 199 • Sectoral budget ceilings. Six-year sectoral budget ceilings were introduced for the Fiscal 2000 budget. These sectoral budgets were developed with the multi-sector Planning Committees of the National Economic and Development Authority (NEDA). These Committees include representatives from Congress, local government, academia, the private sector and nongovernment organizations. The process involved various government implementing agencies in a participative and proactive manner. Three-year budget baselines. The 6-year sectoral ceilings served as the basis for allocating resources to implementing agencies using a budget baseline approach. • Strengthening evaluation mechanisms. First, locally funded projects will be subjected to the same approval process that applies to those funded from foreign sources. Second, the performance measurement will be mainstreamed. A set of performance indicators will have to accompany all new policies or projects that are submitted to NEDA or DBM. The ultimate objective is to foster an evaluation culture.

• Improving government accounting and internal control. Adopting private sector accounting and reporting practices, such as full accrual accounting will enhance the usefulness of accounting information. It will also enable organizational outputs to be meaningfully costed.

• Separating accounting and auditing functions. COA, the Philippines' supreme audit institution, undertakes accounting, internal control and auditing functions in government. These groupings are incongruous.

• Improving procurement procedures. The DBM has launched the Electronic Procurement System to improve the efficiency and transparency of the government procurement process.200

Issue Synopsis: Government Budgeting and Accounting

Chapter VIII – Issues and Recommendations – identifies and describes constraints and proposes corrective actions. With minor departures, these include the following selected issues that have already been identified by the UNDP-sponsored studies:

• The Commission on Audit is responsible for promulgating accounting and auditing rules. These responsibilities are defined in Article IX of the Constitution 1987. The coexistence of these responsibilities is inconsistent with the concept of auditor independence.

• The absence of computerized accounting information systems, combined with complex accounting regulations (i) relegates the role of most government CPAs to that of highly qualified bookkeepers.

Little time is left for value-added activities, such as financial analysis; and (ii) means that financial reports are rarely prepared in time to be useful for decision-making purposes.

• There is no consistent set of accounting standards for budgeting and reporting. Major reporting differences result.

• Auditors spend the majority of their time on compliance auditing (checking transactions). Minimal time is spent on financial attest auditing as more effort is applied to value-for-money audits.

• Comparatively attractive starting salaries attract high-quality personnel into government accounting. A flat earnings structure means that higher-level salaries are far from competitive. This creates retention problems and provides a supportive environment for graft and corruption.

Summary and Proposals

Over the past 25 years, there have been some notable institutional and conceptual innovations in government accounting, contributing to its greater visibility and influence. Its emphasis has shifted from bureaucratic control to accountability reporting to the public. In some countries, government

527

accounting standards are no longer set by government officials, but by relatively independent boards. While acknowledging the importance of cash the lifeblood in government as in business contemporary accounting standards aim at tracking the long-term consequences of decisions and actions. Government officials are held accountable for their stewardship of both

financial and capital assets. Finally, it is not enough to keep the books accurately; the books have to be open to the public. When the public does not have the time or ability to inspect the accounts, governments have to make the task easier by preparing comprehensible as well as comprehensive financial statements.

Many challenges remain, especially at the global and international level. A major issue is the proper balance between international norms and domestic practices arising from national political ideology, economic system and culture. As a mechanism of governance, government accounting is subject to political forces that distribute power, and economic forces that determine the supply of and demand for resources. Therefore, unless accounting standards boards ally themselves with the institutions that can withhold something of value to a government a grant, a loan, an unqualified audit opinion, a favourable bond rating their pronouncements would remain

ineffectual. Unfortunately, at the international level, there are relatively few levers available to

a body such as the IFAC Public Sector Committee to enforce its standards. However, accountants could make the case that fiscal accountability is an international norm applicable to all governments regardless of their political and economic system. Once this transcendent value of fiscal accountability is embraced, it is a technical matter to work out the means of implementation. These include not only yearend financial statements the current focus of IPSASs—but also budgets, internal controls and external audits. 1 urge the IFAC Public

Sector Committee to rectify its neglect of the budget and to include 'actual versus budget' comparisons in financial statements. Furthermore, putting aside differences of opinions on accounting choices, the entire body of detailed standards should be framed by a set of broader principles aimed at promoting government fiscal accountability, such as:

•The objectives of government accounting are to safeguard the public treasury and pr()pert\, to accurately measure and communicate the government's fmancial condition so as to demonstrate financial accountability, and to facilitate decisionmaking. •Agovernment should prepare and publish its budgets, maintain complete financial records, provide full financial disclosure, and subject itself to independent audits.

•The form and content of financial reports should be guided by the rights and need to know of intended users.

•The accounting system should measure the cash and other financial consequences of past transactions and events, including, but not limited to, budget execution.

•The accounting system should be capable of keeping track of the levels and changes in assets, liabilities, revenues and expenditures or expenses, relative to budgeted amounts. These principles do not prescribe accounting choices. Rather, they provide a foundation for deliberating and setting government accounting standards.

Generally, accounting standards take on a greater social role as accountability requirements in countries that require higher standards of ethical behaviour. Government accounting standards in effect become government accountability standards. (Recently the U.S. General Accounting Office was renamed Government Accountability Office.). Government must answer for the resources or authority it receives from others in the society and economy. Government provides both public goods and private goods, in return for the authority to govern, as well as economic and financial resources, Government accountability requirements are expressed as the terms in the political contracts, social contracts, and economic contracts that government enters into with its stakeholders (see Exhibit 2).

528

The asset-liability perspective of accrual accounting described in Exhibit 1 is compatible with this contract theory of government: the government's assets come from the stakeholders' voluntary and involuntary contributions, and its liabilities originate from providing incentives to the stakeholders. In conclusion, fundamental to the development of accrual accounting in developing countries is the ability to identify and measure the government's assets and liabilities. Corruption tends to result in the understatement of government's assets or the overstatement of government's liabilities. Unless financial integrity is assured, the credibility of government's financial information suffers. Thus both financial integrity assurance and accurate accrual accounting are accountants' professional contribution to developing countries.

References

Allen, R. and Tommasi, D. (2001), Managing Public Expenditure: A Reference Book for Transition Countries, OECD, Paris.

Bourmistrov, A. and Mellemvik, F. (2000) «Russian Local Government Accounting: New Norms and New Problems», in Caperchione E. and Mussari, R. eds., Comparative Issues in Local Government Accounting, Kluwer Academic Publishers, Boston, pp. 159- 174.

Bourmistrov, A. and Mellemvik, F. (2001), «Accounting and Democratic Governance: A Comparative Study of One Norwegian and One Russian County», in Bac, A. ed. International Comparative Issues in Government Accounting, Kluwer Academic Publishers, Dordrecht, The Netherlands, pp. 91-122.

Chan, J.L., Jones, R.H. and Lüder, K.G. (1996), «Modeling Government Innovations: An Assessment and Future Research Directions», Research in Governmental and Nonprofit Accounting, Vol. 9, pp. 1-19.

Chan, J.L. (2000), «A Sino-American Comparison of Budget and Accounting Coverage», in Caperchione, E. and Mussari, R., eds., Comparative Issues in Local Government Accounting, Kluwer Academic Publishers, Boston, pp. 11-34.

Chan, J.L., Cong, S.H. and Zhao, J.Y. (2001), «The Effects of Reform on China's Public budgeting and Accounting System», in Bac, A., ed. International Comparative Issues in Government Accounting, Kluwer Academic Publishers, Dordrecht, The Netherlands, pp. 297-314.

Chu, K-Y, and Hemming, R. (1991), «Public Expenditure Handbook: A Guide to Public Policy Issues in Developing Countries», International Monetary Fund, Washington, D.C. Coombs, Hugh M. and Mohamad Tayib, (2000), «Financial Reporting Practice: A Comparative Study of Local Authority Financial Reports Between the UK and 12 Malaysia», in Caperchione, E. and Mussari, M. eds., Comparative Issues in Local Government Accounting, Kluwer Academic Publishers, Boston,, pp. 53-68.

Deutsch, K.W. (1966), The Nerves of Government: Models of Political Communication and Control, The Free Press, New York.

Godfrey, A.D., Devlin, P.J. and Merrouche, C., (1996), «Governmental Accounting in Kenya, Tanzania and Uganda» in Chan, J.L., ed., Research in Governmental and Nonprofit Accounting, Vol. 9, JAI Press, Greenwich, Connecticut, pp. 193-208.

Godfrey, A.D., Merrouche, C. and Devlin, P.J. (1999), «A Comparative Analysis of the Evolution of Local Governmental Accounting in Algeria and Morocco,» in Copley, P.A. and Sanders, G.D., eds. Research in Governmental and Nonprofit Accounting, Vol. 10, JAI Press, Greenwich, Connecticut, pp. 201-234.

Grindle, Merilee S. (2000), «Ready or Not: The Developing World and Globalization,» in Nye, J.S. and Donahue, J.D., eds. Governance in a Globalizing World, Brookings Institution Press, ashington, D.C., pp. 178-207.

Hopwood, A. and Miller, P., eds. (1994), Accounting as a Social and Organizational Practice, Cambridge University Press, Cambridge.

International Federation of Accountants (IFAC) (1996), «Responding to an Increasing Demand for Accountability in the Public Sector,» IFAC Quarterly, October.

IFAC (2003), Handbook on International Public Sector Accounting Standards. IFAC, New York.

IFAC, International Public Sector Accounting Standards Board (2005), Exposure Draft 24, Financial Reporting Under the Cash Basis of Accounting – Disclosure Requirements for Recipients of External Assistance, IF AC, New York.

IFAC, International Public Sector Accounting Standards Board (2005), «Background and Update,» unpublished paper, March.

IFAC, Public Sector Committee (2000), Study 11, Government Financial Reporting: Accounting Issues and Practices. IFAC, New York, May.

Jaruga, A. (1988), «Governmental Accounting, Auditing and Financial Reporting in East European Countries,» in Chan, J.L. and Jones, R.H. eds., Governmental Accounting and Auditing: International Comparisons, Routledge, London, pp. 105-121. Keefer, P. and Khemani, S. (2004), «Democracy, Public Expenditure and the Poor,» World Bank Research Observer. World Bank, Washington, D.C.

Nowak, W.A. and Bakalarska, B. (2001), «Polish Public Sector Accounting in Transition: The Landscape after 1999 Step in the State Redefining,» in Bac, A. ed., International Comparative Issues in Government Accounting, Kluwer Academic Publishers, Dordrecht, The Netherlands, pp. 265-278.

Ouda, Hassan A.G. (2001), «Central Governmental Accounting of Egypt and the Netherlands: Similarities and Differences,» in Bac, A. ed., International Comparative Issues in Government Accounting, Kluwer Academic Publishers, Dordrecht, The Netherlands, pp. 71-90.

Rose-Ackerman, S. (1999), Corruption and Government: Causes, Consequences and Reform, Cambridge University Press, Cambridge.

Reuters (2003), «World Bank urges crackdown on government corruption», December 10.

Sachs, J.D. (2005), The End of Poverty: Economic Possibilities for Our Time, Penguin Books, New York.

Schiavo-Campo, S. and Tommasi, D. (1999), Managing Government Expenditure, Asian Development Bank, Manila.

Simon, H.A. (1954), Centralization vs. Decentralization in Organizing the Controller's Department, Controllership Foundation, New York.

Sutcliffe, P. (2003), «The Standards Programme of IFAC's Public Sector Committee,» Public Money and Management, January, pp. 11-12.

World Bank (1998), Public Expenditure Management Handbook, World Bank, Washington, D.C.

530

FRAUD AND ADMINRATIVE CORRUPTION

Kamran Nazari

Department of Business Management, Payam Noor University, Kermanshah, Iran Mostafa Emami

Assistant Professor, Faculty of Economic and Managements Tarbiat Modares University, Tehran, Iran

Ali Reza Shakarbeigi

Department of Law, Payam Noor University, Kermanshah, Iran

Abstract

The Royal Government of Bhutan has been pursuing a very prudent, well thought out and balanced socio- economic development policy. Under the dynamic leadership of His Majesty the King, the country has achieved unprecedented economic growth in just over the last two decades. Blending socio economic growth with the real happiness of the people, His Majesty the King declared a vision and theme of Gross National Happiness, which not only provided a unique measurement yardstick but also gained wide recognition and acceptance. While developmental initiative brings about improvement in the living conditions of the people, Government has been very wary of many evils which are synonymous to the developmental activities. Fraud and corruption go hand in hand with the development process. Perhaps, it is only a question of degree and methodologies adopted in perpetrating corruption and fraud in different countries which may be in variance. His Majesty the King has always been very concerned on this issue and its likely effect in our small social set up. His Majesty has always aspired for a small, effective and clean government. Number of Royal kashas had been issued to step up due vigil over the public spending hoping for a clean and corruption free administrative set up.

To mark the Silver Jubilee Celebration of His majesty's enthronement, there is perhaps no other better alternatives than to express our solidarity on His Majesty's dynamism and reaffirm our commitment in establishing a corruption free society. The Royal Institute of Management has organized this seminar on Corruption and fraud and a much wider representation has been expected to deliberate on this issue. The Royal Audit Authority and the Division of Revenue and Customs have been advised to present a paper on the Extent and Magnitude of Corruption while papers on other themes will be covered by other agencies.

Key words: FRAUD, CORRUPTION, ROYAL AUDIT AUTHORITY, GOVERNMENTS

Introduction

Comparative academic studies have been focused on unethical behaviour, maladministration and mismanagement in public sector organizations. Governments all over the world and international organizations have designed strategies to fight corruption.

Corruption is a multi-faced phenomenon, linking multiple issues together such as abuse of entrusted power for private gains, low integrity, taking bribes, maladministration, fraud, and nepotism. The big question is how to prevent the increase of administrative corruption in a single country? But, how to get a grip on the control of corruption in a single-case comparison, and how to identify properly the most important implications of corruption? There are studies which

469

concentrate on explaining the effects of corruption (e.g. Mauro 1995; 1998; Rose-Ackerman 1999), elaborating upon the implications, forms, and types of corruption (e.g. Caiden 2001; Levin & Satarov 2000; Stohs & Brannick 1999), and analysing anti-corruption mechanisms and effective ways of minimizing harms and preventing corruption (e.g. Maor 2004; OECD 2000; Clark & Jos 2000; Johnston 1999; United Nations 2004; OECD 2003a). The proper diagnosis of the causes and logic behind corruption plays an important role in combating it (Quah 1999; Maor 2004; Schwartz 2003). Huberts, Lasthuizen and Peeters (2006: 290) make clear the fact that researchers will never be able to reveal all corruption to the public. They compare corruption to an iceberg, in which only the tip can be seen and only known facts can be taken into consideration.

Conventional histories of nineteenth and early twentieth century America portray its corrupt elements as similar, and at times equal, to those found in many of today's modern transition economies and developing regions. Nineteenth-century American urban governments vastly overpaid for basic services, such as street cleaning and construction, in exchange for kickbacks garnered by elected officials. Governments gave away public services for nominal official fees and healthy bribes.2 As late as the 1950s, reports Robert A. Caro (2002, pp. 403- 13), cash-filled envelopes floated in the hallowed halls of the U.S. Senate. Harry Truman made it into the Senate as an agent of the notoriously corrupt Pendergast machine (McCullough 1992).

Some of the greatest U.S. universities were funded by individuals infamous for their roles in extracting public resources through allegedly corrupt political influence— Leland Stanford and George D. Widener, whose surname adorns Harvard's largest library, come to mind. The presidential legacies of Ulysses Grant and Warren Harding were forever marred by the Crédit Mobilier and Teapot Dome scandals, respectively. The list could go on and on.

If the United States was once more corrupt than it is today, then America's history should offer lessons about how to reduce corruption. After all, the dominant political movement of the early twentieth century—Progressivism—was dedicated to the elimination of corruption. From 1901 to 1917, under Presidents T. Roosevelt, Taft, and Wilson, a national legislative an administrative agenda was justified in part by a perceived need to reduce corruption.

Municipalities and states throughout the twentieth century regularly elected reform slates that promised to exercise a strong hand to root out corruption. Crusading journalists and ambitious prosecutors have frequently taken aim at corruption. While scholars can debate the impact of these various forces, there is no doubt that U.S. history offers many examples of reform movements that claimed as a primary goal to reduce corruption, similar to the stated goals of reformers in developing countries today. In this volume we take stock of corruption and reform in American history. Because conceptual clarity is a pre-condition for measuring the level of and temporal change in corruption, the first three chapters—this introduction, the essay by John Wallis, and that by Rebecca Menes—each squarely confront what is meant by corruption.

Because corruption is generally illegal, or at least embarrassing, it tends to be hidden, and understandably, as the modern cross-national empirical literature has found, difficult to measure.

Time-series measurement is yet more difficult. Despite these problems there is great value in searching U.S. history for evidence on corruption and its time trend. Several of the chapters address the measurement of corruption over time. The Menes essay uses information on the number of corrupt mayors and municipal administrations. That by Stanley Engerman and Kenneth Sokoloff uses evidence on cost overruns for major governmental projects. This introductory essay uses data on the reporting of corruption by hundreds of newspapers for the 160 year period from 1815 to 1975. The contributions by Howard Bodenhorn and Wallis, Price Fishback and Shawn Kantor add evidence on the time path but focus on shorter time periods.

470

After the discussion of the meaning and measurement of corruption, two of the essays in this volume address the consequences of corruption or of weak legal regimes more generally.

Naomi Lamoreaux and Jean-Laurent Rosenthal discuss the rise of corporations during the late nineteenth century and how their emergence was accompanied by decreased protection of minority shareholder rights. David Cutler and Grant Miller examine the diffusion of plentiful water in America's cities during an era of legendary municipal corruption. Clearly corruption does not alone determine the extent of public good formation.

According to Lamoreaux and Rosenthal, the number of corporations in the late nineteenth century exploded, despite inadequate protection of minority shareholders, because returns to scale in production increased. Cutler and Miller argue, in a somewhat similar manner, that despite the corruption of municipal governments the increasing availability of municipal credit during the Gilded Age made large-scale water projects feasible. Of course, the increase in municipal credit availability must have had something to do with improvements in accountability, suggesting that some forms of corruption had been curtailed. Both essays suggest that despite substantial corruption in government and fraud in private dealings economic growth was curtailed far less in America than in today's developing economies.

The volume then turns to the causes and consequences of reform. Reform and regulation were often rationalized as tools to protect consumers and workers, but as three of the essays—by Fishback, Bodenhorn, and Marc Law and Gary Libecap—note the actual situation was often more complex. Fishback suggests the importance of a Stiglerian view of workplace safety regulation. Workplace safety regulations in the manufacturing and mining industries, he finds, were supported by unions and opposed by certain manufacturers. Because workplace safety laws in manufacturing disproportionately raised costs for small firms, the laws were championed by large firms. Because they were perceived as protecting workers, the laws were supported by unions.

Bodenhorn's essay emphasizes that reform can be the result of self-interested, competing politicians. He analyzes one of the first episodes of anti-corruption reform in U.S. history the fight against corruption in the chartering of New York State banks during the late 1830s.

Bodenhorn argues that reform emerged from the Whigs' desire to deprive their opponents Van Buren's Democratic Regency—of the rents of patronage. Deregulation was the weapon of choice against corruption since reducing chartering requirements limited the ability of government to manage their monopoly in a corrupt manner.

Though definition of fraud and corruption is not part of our paper, for proper understanding of the subject matter in the context of our presentation, fraud and corruption have been defined as follows;

Fraud : Fraud is usually characterized as an act of willful deceit, trickery, concealment or breach of confidence that are used to gain some unfair or dishonest advantage.

Corruption : Corruption is a much broader and multi - layered phenomenon. It is an unethical, illegal, dishonest act aimed at obtaining an unfair gain by one or more persons.

Definitions of corruption often found are:

Any form of unethical use of public authority for personal or private advantage ; the perversion of integrity by bribery or favor.

Action by a government functionary that is different from the standard, in order to favor someone in exchange for a reward. **Forms of corruption:**

It is intended to give an international dimension and perspective to this paper. As such, nature and forms of corruption presented in this paper depict a global scenario of corruption. It may not be necessary that some or all types of corruption discussed here may be prevalent in this country.

471

Many of us have wrong notions about our understanding as to what constitute corruption and fraud. Gift and presentations are generally not included under this category. Certainly, if gift and presentations of significant amounts are given with the intention of influencing present or future decisions in favour of the donors, it would be unethical to accept such calculated gestures. Similarly, acts of favouring close friends and relatives for employment related issues and contract works etc. in preference to others or carried out in a manner generally not permitted or not extended to others, would also constitute fraud and corruption. Many would still argue that such acts are gratuitous in nature and as such are not unethical. Perhaps, the question we should be asking is whether the recipients/ beneficiaries would or would not have got it in the normal course. '

In the professional circle, it has been generally understood that manifestations of corruption include, amongst others, the following:

 Bribery and extortion: commission, unreasonable gifts, Kickbacks etc.

 Fraud, embezzlement and theft: Forgery, manipulation of records, shortage of cash, pilferage of store etc.

 Misappropriation of resources :Irregular diversion of fund/properties/stores

 Undue favors in exchange for gains : Award of contracts to favored ones, Undue payments i.e. advances, escalation and not provided in the agreement etc

 Abuse of authority : Exercising discretionary powers for personal gains, Misuse of office equipment, Misuse of funds and human resources,

 Nepotism : Favoring near and dears

 Under/over assessments of taxes and duties with personal motives

 Tax evasion and smuggling

 Over/under invoicing with a view to financial benefit

 Unfair recruitment /promotion/placements/training

 Non compliance of rules and regulations with a view to gain

 Inaction by the rules enforcing authorities/regulatory bodies for violation Corruption is often kept in check by the media and the role of the press is directly confronted in the chapter by Matthew Gentzkow, Glaeser, and Goldin. In 1870, the press was partisan, histrionic, and prone to omit facts that went against acknowledged political biases. But by 1920, most newspapers eschewed party affiliations, used more moderate and civil language, and made at least a pretense of reporting the facts of the day without spin. The chapter argues that the rise of the independent press and the remarkable transformation in U.S. newspapers between 1870 and 1920 was fundamentally the result of the increasing financial returns to selling newspapers rather than placating politicians for patronage and other reasons. While the essay does not document the impact that the press may have had on corruption, it does discuss circumstantial evidence suggesting that the rise of the independent press was an important factor in movements to reform American political corruption.

Detection of Fraud and Corruption:

Most audits are conducted on a test basis using audit sampling and other techniques. To carry out 100% checking of all transactions would be an expensive proposition and meaningless as it would still not be possible to derive complete assurance and satisfaction on the existence and detection of fraud and corruption. Most corruption cases that are serious in nature often take place out side the records e.g. Bribery, commission, kickbacks, etc. It is also difficult to detect systematic frauds. Authorities normally succeed in detecting some of the fraud and corruption cases through in-depth investigations that would require;

472

Detailed scrutiny of accounts, records and operations

Unrestricted access to information

Unrestricted scope of examination

Investigations and interviews and obtaining written statements

Analysis and comparisons

Individuals wealth assessment and inquiring as to the sources

Gathering information from out side sources

Since both the Royal Audit Authority and the Division of Revenue and Custom primarily depend on the accounting records for their audit exercise, the cases of corruption noted do not give indication of extent and magnitude of corruption. Thus it would not be appropriate to draw conclusion from the observed cases. It is, however, evident that corruption in some form or other do exist in our society.

During the nineteenth century, the definition of corruption morphed into one specifically related to the bribery of public officials by private agents. Bribery was generally an illicit payment in exchange for some government controlled resource, such as a service or a public property or an exemption from government regulation. These forms of bribery, detailed in the chapter by Menes, form the lion's share of what is known about nineteenth century municipal corruption. City governments were corrupt in the purchase of inputs, such as street cleaning or construction services, and bribes were routinely given in exchange for overpayment for these inputs. City governments were corrupt in the distribution of publicly-owned property—land or access to a port— that was sold, not to the highest bidder for the good of the citizens, but to the most generous briber for the benefit of the few. Finally city governments were corrupt in the administration of rules, such as prohibitions on gambling and prostitution, and officials accepted bribes for leniency in the administration of such regulations.

In this volume we will use the word "corruption" to refer to what Wallis terms "venal corruption." We view corruption to have three central elements: (1) payments to public officials beyond their salaries; (2) an action associated with these payments that violates either explicit laws or implicit social norms; and (3) losses to the public either from that action or from a system that renders it necessary for actions to arise only from such payment. Two examples from the volume illustrate how these elements describe corruption.

Areas prone to Fraud and Corruption:

It is generally understood that certain areas are more prone to corruption than others.

The following areas are considered to be more prone to fraud and corruption:

Procurements

Construction works

Stores / equipment

Revenue receipts and cash collections / handling

Filing of tax returns i.e., incidence of under declaration of income, inflated expenditure etc.

Assessment of taxes and duties

Commission on Sales : Usually documentation is not adequate

The Determinants of Corruption

The economic approach to corruption (as in Rose-Ackerman 1975) starts with the costs and benefits facing potentially corrupt public officials. Since economics predicts that we should expect to see corruption when the benefits are high and costs are low, it is worth analyzing what factors should impact the benefits and costs of corrupt behavior by a government official. The benefits from being

473

corrupt are determined by the ability of a government official to increase someone's private wealth; the costs come from the expected penalties from being caught.

What determines the ability of a government official to increase someone's private wealth? The most obvious means is to pay the person out of the public purse. In extreme circumstances, the person can just be the official himself; embezzlement is one example of corrupt behavior. More usually, paying someone out of the public purse occurs in exchange for services of some form, either labor or subcontracting. If fees are close to the costs of contracting firms or the opportunity costs of workers, then the opportunities for corruption are limited. If fees are significantly above free market prices, then there is opportunity for corruption in the assignment of work. High public sector wages and discretion over hiring has traditionally created some of the best opportunities for corrupt earnings.

This simple analysis helps us to understand some of the most popular reforms attempted to arrest corruption. Civil service reform which would take patronage out of the hands of politicians and replace discretion with test-based rules would naturally serve limit the opportunity for corruption, especially when combined with a rigid pay scale for civil servants Rules concerning procurement fees have also tended to be a popular tool against corruption.

Competitive bids for public projects linked to the requirement that the government accept the low cost bid is one of the simplest means of limiting corruption in administration of government projects. The approach relies on the existence of a competitive supply of contractors.

The second means that public officials have to create private wealth is to transfer government property to private individuals for their own profit. The transfer of government land to traction companies was a popular form of corruption in the nineteenth century. Information about future government actions is a more subtle form of in-kind transfer. The returns to corruption in these cases depend on the size of the assets at the government's disposal and the discretion that individuals have in the distribution of these assets.

The third primary means that governments have to create private wealth is the manipulation of legal rulings or the enforcement of rules, such as regulations. Rules banning gambling and prostitution, for example, create the opportunity to extract bribes from potential providers. These bribes can be extracted by any and all members in the chain of enforcement.

As the amount of regulation increases, the opportunity to extract bribes also rises and leads reformers to fight against regulation and government monopoly (as in Bodenhorn's essay).

Conversely, the connection between the intrusiveness of regulation and the ability to extract bribes creates an incentive for politicians to push for further regulation. Even in a libertarian's dream world where government is restricted to enforcing disputes over property rights, there would still be considerable scope for corruption in the arbitration of these disputes. Every dispute over ownership creates the possibility for a corrupt ruling. After all, a corrupt judge can extract bribes even if when he rules in favor of the rightful owner. As the legal system has the ability to redistribute all of the wealth in society, the opportunities for corruption within the system are enormous. As corruption within the courts destroys the clear definition of property rights, this corruption has the potential to turn the libertarian dream into a Hobbesian nightmare. In practice, this ability may be limited by the ability of private litigants to rely on private arbitration and avoid a corrupt legal system.

Together these factors suggest that the benefits from corrupt practices for bribe-taking politicians or bribe-giving businessmen will rise with the size and discretion of the government and the amount of social and economic regulation. Benefits from corruption will also rise when the size of assets or damages involved in property rights disputes increases (Glaeser and Shleifer 2003). The late nineteenth century was a period of increasingly larger governments, more valuable public assets, more aggressive regulation, and bigger stakes litigation. The potential benefits from corruption rose along almost every conceivable dimension. The prediction is an absolute increase in the total amount of

474

corruption (measured in either bribes given or in social losses). But the increase in corruption might not translate into an increase relative to the size of government or the size of the economy.

The limits on corruption have customarily come from three sources: legal penalties, career or social costs, and internal psychic pain. Thus, the overall costs of corruption come from the size of the potential penalties and the probability that these costs are imposed which are in turn a function of information flows, social opprobrium, and the legal system.

The most obvious parameter influencing the cost of illegal corruption is thestated legal penalty for corrupt practices (the cost of corruption that violates social norms, but not laws, will not be connected to legal penalties). While this is certainly obvious, it is also important to remember that these penalties have changed significantly over time. For example, while Plunkitt's honest graft the use of insider information by politicians to enrich themselves was surely corruption, at least by our definition, it was fully legal during Plunkitt's time. Even the gifts of railway stock given to congressmen and others during the Crédit Mobilier scandal were perfectly legal at the time. In the 1790s, the number of laws regarding corruption was so modest that legal penalties against corruption were often negligible. Since that time, there has been a steady increase in the range of behaviors by public officials that are punishable by law and a steady increase in the attempt to craft laws, such as the RICO statute, that render illegal as yet unspecified forms of corrupt behavior.

Magnitude of Fraud and Corruption:

As already mentioned it is not possible to quantify the magnitude of corruption. Cases of fraud and corruption often reported, including those providing indication there of, includes:

I.   Bribery and Extortion
   Extending/availing undue favours
   Presentation of Gifts of large amounts

II. Fraud, Embezzlement and Irregular payments
   Forgery of documents
   Misuse of funds and properties
   Pilferage of stores
   Inclusion of dummy workers in Muster Rolls
   Double claims
   Intentional Irregular claims and payments
   Concealment of information

III. Procurement and construction works related corruption
   Direct procurements/ award of works from/ to some preferred suppliers/contractors
   Preferring a bidder without valid justification(s)
   Accepting a non responsive bid
   Non enforcing contractual terms
   Accepting defective, inferior and unspecified items
   Paying at higher rates than the agreed rates
   Incorporating terms and conditions prejudicial to the interest of procuring agencies
   Payment of unjustified escalation, freight, insurance claims etc.
   Extending undue favour to suppliers/ contractors i.e. unauthorized advances, non recovery of security money, non recovery of advances in time etc.
   Non processing and passing of bills in time without any reasons
   Indication of undue harassment to contractors for insignificant issues
   Disparities in enforcing contract terms

475

Payments made for works not executed/ materials not received

Procurements at exorbitant rates from private/ unauthorized sources

Payments made without any valid documents

Additional payments by showing excess measurements

Deliberately under estimating quantities of works and paying at higher rates for quantities beyond deviation limit

Non/short accountal of items procured

Procurement of excessive materials/supplies

Not inquiring into rates to be charged by the sub vendors and   paying at higher rates to the main vendors

Unjustified payment of compensation/recommending such payments

IV Misappropriation of public resources

Unauthorized diversion of funds

Payment/withdrawal of unauthorized /excessive advances

Retention of excessive cash in hand

Non/short accountal of revenue

Non/short deposit/remittances of revenue

Abnormal delays in accountal/deposit of revenue

Unauthorized issue of stores for private purposes

Non raising of bills for supplies/hiring charges to favour individuals

Non deduction of house rent from employees occupying Government accommodation

V   Abuse of Public Office and Nepotism

Use of facilities for personal purposes

Requiring public office to pay expenses of private nature

Awarding supply orders / contracts to relatives

Paying for self and relatives in preference to others

Granting discounts/write off to favoured ones

Using daily wages workers etc. for domestic purposes/personal works

Sanctioning loans without proper scrutiny and appraisal

VI Over/Under invoicing

Over invoicing sales to inflate sales to depict better results

Over invoicing to share the difference   Under invoicing

to share the difference **Division of the Surplus**

The division of the surplus from administrative corruption can be thought of as a cooperative game among the Payers and the Collector. The issue we face is that of dividing the potential gains from cooperation between the tax collector and a large number of taxpayers. We would like to have a rule that reflects the maximum tax liabilities of each payer and the fact that the tax collector is an essential party in the corruption process. It should be pointed out that this cannot be solved as a simple bargaining problem between a single taxpayer and the tax collector.

This is because there exists an aggregate revenue target, and therefore the current surplus available to be shared between the Collector and a Payer depends on the taxes that have already been collected elsewhere.

In this paper we use a simple solution to this problem – namely, the *Shapley value*. This solution concept defines the payoff to each person in a multiperson game as a function of their marginal

476

contributions to the total surplus (see Moulin, 1988, for an excellent overview). We could have defined a noncooperative game, as in Gul (1989). However, this would have greatly complicated the analysis without offering a more convincing approach. The outcome predicted by the Nash equilibrium of an extensive form game is very sensitive to the way we define the extensive form. Furthermore, the extensive form is never observed in practice, and therefore its choice is necessarily arbitrary. The Shapley value has the attractive feature of ignoring the details of the strategic game and defining the payoffs only in terms of observable actions. Therefore, it is much more amenable to being confronted with the data.

The Shapley value is the unique division of the total surplus that satisfies the following conditions:

• Individuals are treated symmetrically. That is, their identities are irrelevant; it is only the way they are able to affect payoffs that matters.

• The value is additive. That is, if two different situations or games are combined, the payoff to an individual is equal to the sum of his/her payoffs from each game.

It can also be shown that the Shapley value allocation to each individual is an amount equal to the expected marginal contribution of that individual in a randomly chosen coalition.

This potential marginal contribution can be interpreted in terms of each coalition member's relative power in the group. The power of the Collector in this particular surplus division game derives from his or her ability to effect a reduction in tax liabilities. The power of the Payers derives from their ability to pay their full tax liabilities and deprive the Collector of supplementary income in the form of bribes. **Recommendations**:

Existence of a proper system of check and balance reduces the risks of wrong doings and chances of indulging in fraud and corruption. Strong internal controls, proper rules and regulations, motivated employees, a rational taxation structure etc. tend to act as deterrent against perpetuating fraud and corruption. We are offering some suggestions and recommendations in controlling fraud and corruption for deliberations with the hope that more realistic recommendations will emerge from it.

Establishment of Adequate Regulatory Framework

Formulation of appropriate rules and regulations clearly stipulating punitive measures

Professional development programmers for accountants, auditors, taxofficials and administrators

Establishment of anti corruption Agency

Further strengthening legal System   Widening Tax Base

Power of Back Duty Investigations

Index linked Salaries of civil servants and others

Protection of salaries at least in monetary terms

Periodic transfers of employees

Rotation of duties

Appropriate representations on the Boards/ Committees avoiding conflicting decisions

Appropriate reward and incentive schemes- not necessarily directly linked to individual act of performance

Establishment of appropriate bodies to review reports on fraud and corruption

Rules and regulations to be developed with positive frame of mind. They should be perceived to be facilitating and not be seen as too prohibitive and restrictive.

A progressive and liberalized economic policy

Promoting self regulations of enterprises and greater accountability

Dissemination of information and creating awareness

Commissioning independent inquiries on large procurements and construction contracts by appropriate authorities

Establishment of independent quality control units to inspect quality of works, materials and equipment

Strengthening BCCI to look into grievances of business communities and offer business counseling / advise

A definitive and clear policy guidelines on privatization including post privatization commitments of corporations and role of government

Formulation of Unfair Trade Practices Act

Strengthening internal controls in the organizations

Introducing internal audits

Rules / laws with wider implication to be discussed and scrutinized at different levels before approval for their general acceptance and removing inconsistencies

Publicity and greater transparency

Adequate enforcement and monitoring by law enforcing bodies

Establishment of Consumer Protection and Advisory board

Announcements of adequate reward schemes to informers

Formulation of Essential commodities Act

Establishment of Bhutan Standards for manufactured and imported items

Development of Safety regulations

Strengthening Tax Administration and Audit System and other

Regulatory Bodies

Conclusions:

Corruption undermines the entire administrative system and functioning of the public offices. It adversely effects the integrity and morale of the employees of the public offices including those who are responsible to enforce laws, rules and regulations. It encourages those responsible to deliberately keep loopholes in the rules. Corruption may be prevalent at any level and any where thus effecting day to day activities and causing harassment and inconveniences to the general public. Detection of fraud and corruption alone is not sufficient. We must take preventive measures to control it. A proper study of causes of corruption and environment favouring it would help initiate effective remedial measures.

Individual cases of corruption can be rooted out by the application of organizational sanctions Systemic corruption cannot be handled so easily. There is no guarantee that if the most serious offenders are dismissed, or if everyone who is guilty is replaced, corruption will not persist. The old patterns will continue with new players. Moreover, in the wider society, systemic corruption impedes rather than aids change.

(a)   Systemic corruption perpetuates closed politics and restricts access, preventing the reflection of social change in political institutions.

(b)   Systemic corruption suppresses opposition contributing to increasing resentment.

Thus corruption, far from being an alternative to violence, is often accompanied by more violence.

(c)   Systemic corruption perpetuates and widens class, economic, and social divisions, contributing to societal strain and preventing cohesion.

478

(d)   Systemic corruption prevents policy change, particularly where this works against immediate market considerations. Individual or sectional interests are not the best guide to the public interest.

(e)   Systemic corruption blocks administrative reform, and makes deleterious administrative practices profitable, e.g., induced delays.

(f)   Systemic corruption diverts public resources and contributes to a situation of private affluence and public squalor, especially serious where affluence is confined to the few.

(g)   Systemic corruption contributes to societal anomie in shoring up or transmuting traditional values into inappropriate areas.

(h)   The effects of systemic corruption are not limited to a specific case: there is an accumulator effect upon public perceptions and expectations which subverts trust and cooperation far beyond the impact upon the individuals immediately concerned.

(i)   Systemic corruption is not confined to poor, developing, or modernizing countries, but found in all organizational societies."

Existence of adequate regulatory and legal framework as well as a clean and efficient civil service with high morale reduces the risk of rampant corruption in the society. A sound fiscal and monetary policy with due encouragement and incentives for investment will certainly act as deterrent against corruption. Corruption weakens the economy, efficiency and effectiveness of the government systems. Rampant corruption should not be allowed to occur at any cost.

References

CARTIER-BRESSON, J., "A Few Suggestions for a Comparative Analysis of Corruption in Western Europe", Revue Internationale de Politiques Comparées v. 4, n° 2, 2003.

CLARK, WILLIAM A. & JOS, PHILIP H. (2000). "Comparative Anti-Corruption Policy: The American, Soviet and Russian Cases", International Journal of Public Administration 23:1, 101– 148.

DOBEL, PATRICK J. (1999). Public Integrity. Baltimore and London: The Johns Hopkins University Press.

GALTUNG, FREDRIK (2006). Measuring the Immeasurable: Boundaries and Functions of (Macro) Corruption Indices. In Sampford, Charles & Shacklock, Arthur & Connors, Carmel & Galtung, Fredrik (eds). Measuring Corruption. Great Britain: Ashgate Publishing Limited: 101– 130.

HARISALO, RISTO & STENVALL, JARI (2001). Luottamus kansalaisyhteiskunnan peruskivenä: Kansalaisten luottamus ministeriöihin. [Trust as Cornerstone of Civic Society: Citizens trust to ministries]. Helsinki: Edita.

HOLMES, LESLIE (1993). The End of Communist Power. Anti-Corruption Campaign and Legitimation Crisis. New York: Oxford University Press.

HUBERTS, LEO & LASTHUIZEN, KARIN & PEETERS, CAREL (2006). Measuring Corruption: Exploring the Iceberg. In Sampford, Charles & Shacklock, Arthur & Connors, Carmel & Galtung, Fredrik (eds). Measuring Corruption. Great Britain: Ashgate Publishing Limited: 265– 293.

VAN HULTEN, MICHEL (2007). Ten years of Corruption (Perceptions) Indices. Methods – Results – What Next? An analysis.

JOHNSTON, MICHAEL (1999). A Brief History of anticorruption Mechanisms. In Schedler, Andreas & Diamond, Larry & Plattner, Marc F. (eds). The Self-Restraining State: Power and Accountability in New Democracies. Boulder:Lynne Rienner Publishers: 217–226.

KAUFMANN, DANIEL (2004). Corruption, Governance and Security: Challenges for the Rich

Countries and the World. In The Global Competitiveness Report 2004/2005. The World Bank: 83–102.

KONTTINEN, E. (1991). Perinteisesti moderniin: Professioiden yhteiskunnallinen synty Suomessa. [Traditionally to Modern: The Birth of Professions in Finland.] Tampere, Finland: Vastapaino.
KOSKINEN, PEKKA (2001). Johdatus rikosoikeuteen. [Introduction to Criminal Law.] Helsinki: University of Helsinki.

LANGSETH, PETTER (2006). Measuring Corruption. In Sampford, Charles & Shacklock, Arthur & Connors, Carmel & Galtung, Fredrik (eds). Measuring Corruption. Great Britain: Ashgate Publishing Limited: 7–44.

LEVIN, MARK & SATAROV, GEORGY (2000). Corruption and Institutions in
Russia, European Journal of Political Economy, vol. 16, no. 1: 113-132.

MAOR, MOSHE (2004). Feeling the Heat? Anticorruption Mechanisms in Comparative Perspective, Governance, vol. 17, no. 1: 1–28.

MAURO, P., "The Effects of Corruption on Growth, Investment and Government Expenditure", in Elliot, K. (ed.), Corruption and the Global Economy, pp. 83-108, 1997.

WEI, S-J., "How Taxing Ades, A. and R. Di Tella , "Rent, Competition and Corruption", Oxford University, mimeo,2005. is Corruption on International Investors?", NBER Working Paper, no. 6030, 2001.

WORLD BANK, Using Surveys for Public Sector Reform, Premnotes No. 23, Washington, 2005.

482

FRAUD AND ADMINRATIVE CORRUPTION

Kamran Nazari

Department of Business Management, Payam Noor University, Kermanshah, Iran Mostafa Emami

Assistant Professor, Faculty of Economic and Managements Tarbiat Modares University, Tehran, Iran

Ali Reza Shakarbeigi

Department of Law, Payam Noor University, Kermanshah, Iran

Abstract

The Royal Government of Bhutan has been pursuing a very prudent, well thought out and balanced socio- economic development policy. Under the dynamic leadership of His Majesty the King, the country has achieved unprecedented economic growth in just over the last two decades. Blending socio economic growth with the real happiness of the people, His Majesty the King declared a vision and theme of Gross National Happiness, which not only provided a unique measurement yardstick but also gained wide recognition and acceptance. While developmental initiative brings about improvement in the living conditions of the people, Government has been very wary of many evils which are synonymous to the developmental activities. Fraud and corruption go hand in hand with the development process. Perhaps, it is only a question of degree and methodologies adopted in perpetrating corruption and fraud in different countries which may be in variance. His Majesty the King has always been very concerned on this issue and its likely effect in our small social set up. His Majesty has always aspired for a small, effective and clean government. Number of Royal kashas had been issued to step up due vigil over the public spending hoping for a clean and corruption free administrative set up.

To mark the Silver Jubilee Celebration of His majesty's enthronement, there is perhaps no other better alternatives than to express our solidarity on His Majesty's dynamism and reaffirm our commitment in establishing a corruption free society. The Royal Institute of Management has organized this seminar on Corruption and fraud and a much wider representation has been expected to deliberate on this issue. The Royal Audit Authority and the Division of Revenue and Customs have been advised to present a paper on the Extent and Magnitude of Corruption while papers on other themes will be covered by other agencies.

Key words: FRAUD, CORRUPTION, ROYAL AUDIT AUTHORITY, GOVERNMENTS

Introduction

Comparative academic studies have been focused on unethical behaviour, maladministration and mismanagement in public sector organizations. Governments all over the world and international organizations have designed strategies to fight corruption.

Corruption is a multi-faced phenomenon, linking multiple issues together such as abuse of entrusted power for private gains, low integrity, taking bribes, maladministration, fraud, and nepotism. The big question is how to prevent the increase of administrative corruption in a single country? But, how to get a grip on the control of corruption in a single-case comparison, and how to identify properly the most important implications of corruption? There are studies which

469

concentrate on explaining the effects of corruption (e.g. Mauro 1995; 1998; Rose-Ackerman 1999), elaborating upon the implications, forms, and types of corruption (e.g. Caiden 2001; Levin & Satarov 2000; Stohs & Brannick 1999), and analysing anti-corruption mechanisms and effective ways of minimizing harms and preventing corruption (e.g. Maor 2004; OECD 2000; Clark & Jos 2000; Johnston 1999; United Nations 2004; OECD 2003a). The proper diagnosis of the causes and logic behind corruption plays an important role in combating it (Quah 1999; Maor 2004; Schwartz 2003). Huberts, Lasthuizen and Peeters (2006: 290) make clear the fact that researchers will never be able to reveal all corruption to the public. They compare corruption to an iceberg, in which only the tip can be seen and only known facts can be taken into consideration.

Conventional histories of nineteenth and early twentieth century America portray its corrupt elements as similar, and at times equal, to those found in many of today's modern transition economies and developing regions. Nineteenth-century American urban governments vastly overpaid for basic services, such as street cleaning and construction, in exchange for kickbacks garnered by elected officials. Governments gave away public services for nominal official fees and healthy bribes.2 As late as the 1950s, reports Robert A. Caro (2002, pp. 403- 13), cash-filled envelopes floated in the hallowed halls of the U.S. Senate. Harry Truman made it into the Senate as an agent of the notoriously corrupt Pendergast machine (McCullough 1992).

Some of the greatest U.S. universities were funded by individuals infamous for their roles in extracting public resources through allegedly corrupt political influence— Leland Stanford and George D. Widener, whose surname adorns Harvard's largest library, come to mind. The presidential legacies of Ulysses Grant and Warren Harding were forever marred by the Crédit Mobilier and Teapot Dome scandals, respectively. The list could go on and on.

If the United States was once more corrupt than it is today, then America's history should offer lessons about how to reduce corruption. After all, the dominant political movement of the early twentieth century—Progressivism—was dedicated to the elimination of corruption. From 1901 to 1917, under Presidents T. Roosevelt, Taft, and Wilson, a national legislative an administrative agenda was justified in part by a perceived need to reduce corruption.

Municipalities and states throughout the twentieth century regularly elected reform slates that promised to exercise a strong hand to root out corruption. Crusading journalists and ambitious prosecutors have frequently taken aim at corruption. While scholars can debate the impact of these various forces, there is no doubt that U.S. history offers many examples of reform movements that claimed as a primary goal to reduce corruption, similar to the stated goals of reformers in developing countries today. In this volume we take stock of corruption and reform in American history. Because conceptual clarity is a pre-condition for measuring the level of and temporal change in corruption, the first three chapters—this introduction, the essay by John Wallis, and that by Rebecca Menes—each squarely confront what is meant by corruption.

Because corruption is generally illegal, or at least embarrassing, it tends to be hidden, and understandably, as the modern cross-national empirical literature has found, difficult to measure.

Time-series measurement is yet more difficult. Despite these problems there is great value in searching U.S. history for evidence on corruption and its time trend. Several of the chapters address the measurement of corruption over time. The Menes essay uses information on the number of corrupt mayors and municipal administrations. That by Stanley Engerman and Kenneth Sokoloff uses evidence on cost overruns for major governmental projects. This introductory essay uses data on the reporting of corruption by hundreds of newspapers for the 160 year period from 1815 to 1975. The contributions by Howard Bodenhorn and Wallis, Price Fishback and Shawn Kantor add evidence on the time path but focus on shorter time periods.

After the discussion of the meaning and measurement of corruption, two of the essays in this volume address the consequences of corruption or of weak legal regimes more generally.

Naomi Lamoreaux and Jean-Laurent Rosenthal discuss the rise of corporations during the late nineteenth century and how their emergence was accompanied by decreased protection of minority shareholder rights. David Cutler and Grant Miller examine the diffusion of plentiful water in America's cities during an era of legendary municipal corruption. Clearly corruption does not alone determine the extent of public good formation.

According to Lamoreaux and Rosenthal, the number of corporations in the late nineteenth century exploded, despite inadequate protection of minority shareholders, because returns to scale in production increased. Cutler and Miller argue, in a somewhat similar manner, that despite the corruption of municipal governments the increasing availability of municipal credit during the Gilded Age made large-scale water projects feasible. Of course, the increase in municipal credit availability must have had something to do with improvements in accountability, suggesting that some forms of corruption had been curtailed. Both essays suggest that despite substantial corruption in government and fraud in private dealings economic growth was curtailed far less in America than in today's developing economies.

The volume then turns to the causes and consequences of reform. Reform and regulation were often rationalized as tools to protect consumers and workers, but as three of the essays—by Fishback, Bodenhorn, and Marc Law and Gary Libecap—note the actual situation was often more complex. Fishback suggests the importance of a Stiglerian view of workplace safety regulation. Workplace safety regulations in the manufacturing and mining industries, he finds, were supported by unions and opposed by certain manufacturers. Because workplace safety laws in manufacturing disproportionately raised costs for small firms, the laws were championed by large firms. Because they were perceived as protecting workers, the laws were supported by unions.

Bodenhorn's essay emphasizes that reform can be the result of self-interested, competing politicians. He analyzes one of the first episodes of anti-corruption reform in U.S. history the fight against corruption in the chartering of New York State banks during the late 1830s.

Bodenhorn argues that reform emerged from the Whigs' desire to deprive their opponents Van Buren's Democratic Regency—of the rents of patronage. Deregulation was the weapon of choice against corruption since reducing chartering requirements limited the ability of government to manage their monopoly in a corrupt manner.

Though definition of fraud and corruption is not part of our paper, for proper understanding of the subject matter in the context of our presentation, fraud and corruption have been defined as follows;

Fraud : Fraud is usually characterized as an act of willful deceit, trickery, concealment or breach of confidence that are used to gain some unfair or dishonest advantage.

Corruption : Corruption is a much broader and multi - layered phenomenon. It is an unethical, illegal, dishonest act aimed at obtaining an unfair gain by one or more persons.

Definitions of corruption often found are:

Any form of unethical use of public authority for personal or private advantage ; the perversion of integrity by bribery or favor.

Action by a government functionary that is different from the standard, in order to favor someone in exchange for a reward. **Forms of corruption:**

It is intended to give an international dimension and perspective to this paper. As such, nature and forms of corruption presented in this paper depict a global scenario of corruption. It may not be necessary that some or all types of corruption discussed here may be prevalent in this country.

Many of us have wrong notions about our understanding as to what constitute corruption and fraud. Gift and presentations are generally not included under this category. Certainly, if gift and presentations of significant amounts are given with the intention of influencing present or future decisions in favour of the donors, it would be unethical to accept such calculated gestures. Similarly, acts of favouring close friends and relatives for employment related issues and contract works etc. in preference to others or carried out in a manner generally not permitted or not extended to others, would also constitute fraud and corruption. Many would still argue that such acts are gratuitous in nature and as such are not unethical. Perhaps, the question we should be asking is whether the recipients/ beneficiaries would or would not have got it in the normal course.

In the professional circle, it has been generally understood that manifestations of corruption include, amongst others, the following:

Bribery and extortion: commission, unreasonable gifts, Kickbacks etc.

Fraud, embezzlement and theft: Forgery, manipulation of records, shortage of cash, pilferage of store etc.

Misappropriation of resources :Irregular diversion of fund/properties/stores

Undue favors in exchange for gains : Award of contracts to favored ones, Undue payments i.e. advances, escalation and not provided in the agreement etc

Abuse of authority : Exercising discretionary powers for personal gains, Misuse of office equipment, Misuse of funds and human resources,

Nepotism : Favoring near and dears

Under/over assessments of taxes and duties with personal motives

Tax evasion and smuggling

Over/under invoicing with a view to financial benefit

Unfair recruitment /promotion/placements/training

Non compliance of rules and regulations with a view to gain

Inaction by the rules enforcing authorities/regulatory bodies for violation Corruption is often kept in check by the media and the role of the press is directly confronted in the chapter by Matthew Gentzkow, Glaeser, and Goldin. In 1870, the press was partisan, histrionic, and prone to omit facts that went against acknowledged political biases. But by 1920, most newspapers eschewed party affiliations, used more moderate and civil language, and made at least a pretense of reporting the facts of the day without spin. The chapter argues that the rise of the independent press and the remarkable transformation in U.S. newspapers between 1870 and 1920 was fundamentally the result of the increasing financial returns to selling newspapers rather than placating politicians for patronage and other reasons. While the essay does not document the impact that the press may have had on corruption, it does discuss circumstantial evidence suggesting that the rise of the independent press was an important factor in movements to reform American political corruption.

Detection of Fraud and Corruption:
Most audits are conducted on a test basis using audit sampling and other techniques. To carry out 100% checking of all transactions would be an expensive proposition and meaningless as it would still not be possible to derive complete assurance and satisfaction on the existence and detection of fraud and corruption. Most corruption cases that are serious in nature often take place out side the records e.g. Bribery, commission, kickbacks, etc. It is also difficult to detect systematic frauds. Authorities normally succeed in detecting some of the fraud and corruption cases through in-depth investigations that would require;

Detailed scrutiny of accounts, records and operations

Unrestricted access to information

Unrestricted scope of examination

Investigations and interviews and obtaining written statements

Analysis and comparisons

Individuals wealth assessment and inquiring as to the sources

Gathering information from out side sources

Since both the Royal Audit Authority and the Division of Revenue and Custom primarily depend on the accounting records for their audit exercise, the cases of corruption noted do not give indication of extent and magnitude of corruption. Thus it would not be appropriate to draw conclusion from the observed cases. It is, however, evident that corruption in some form or other do exist in our society.

During the nineteenth century, the definition of corruption morphed into one specifically related to the bribery of public officials by private agents. Bribery was generally an illicit payment in exchange for some government controlled resource, such as a service or a public property or an exemption from government regulation. These forms of bribery, detailed in the chapter by Menes, form the lion's share of what is known about nineteenth century municipal corruption. City governments were corrupt in the purchase of inputs, such as street cleaning or construction services, and bribes were routinely given in exchange for overpayment for these inputs. City governments were corrupt in the distribution of publicly-owned property—land or access to a port— that was sold, not to the highest bidder for the good of the citizens, but to the most generous briber for the benefit of the few. Finally city governments were corrupt in the administration of rules, such as prohibitions on gambling and prostitution, and officials accepted bribes for leniency in the administration of such regulations.

In this volume we will use the word "corruption" to refer to what Wallis terms "venal corruption." We view corruption to have three central elements: (1) payments to public officials beyond their salaries; (2) an action associated with these payments that violates either explicit laws or implicit social norms; and (3) losses to the public either from that action or from a system that renders it necessary for actions to arise only from such payment. Two examples from the volume illustrate how these elements describe corruption.

Areas prone to Fraud and Corruption:

It is generally understood that certain areas are more prone to corruption than others.

The following areas are considered to be more prone to fraud and corruption:

Procurements

Construction works

Stores / equipment

Revenue receipts and cash collections / handling

Filing of tax returns i.e., incidence of under declaration of income, inflated expenditure etc.

Assessment of taxes and duties

Commission on Sales : Usually documentation is not adequate

The Determinants of Corruption

The economic approach to corruption (as in Rose-Ackerman 1975) starts with the costs and benefits facing potentially corrupt public officials. Since economics predicts that we should expect to see corruption when the benefits are high and costs are low, it is worth analyzing what factors should impact the benefits and costs of corrupt behavior by a government official. The benefits from being

473

corrupt are determined by the ability of a government official to increase someone's private wealth; the costs come from the expected penalties from being caught.

What determines the ability of a government official to increase someone's private wealth? The most obvious means is to pay the person out of the public purse. In extreme circumstances, the person can just be the official himself; embezzlement is one example of corrupt behavior. More usually, paying someone out of the public purse occurs in exchange for services of some form, either labor or subcontracting. If fees are close to the costs of contracting firms or the opportunity costs of workers, then the opportunities for corruption are limited. If fees are significantly above free market prices, then there is opportunity for corruption in the assignment of work. High public sector wages and discretion over hiring has traditionally created some of the best opportunities for corrupt earnings.

This simple analysis helps us to understand some of the most popular reforms attempted to arrest corruption. Civil service reform which would take patronage out of the hands of politicians and replace discretion with test-based rules would naturally serve limit the opportunity for corruption, especially when combined with a rigid pay scale for civil servants Rules concerning procurement fees have also tended to be a popular tool against corruption.

Competitive bids for public projects linked to the requirement that the government accept the low cost bid is one of the simplest means of limiting corruption in administration of government projects. The approach relies on the existence of a competitive supply of contractors.

The second means that public officials have to create private wealth is to transfer government property to private individuals for their own profit. The transfer of government land to traction companies was a popular form of corruption in the nineteenth century. Information about future government actions is a more subtle form of in-kind transfer. The returns to corruption in these cases depend on the size of the assets at the government's disposal and the discretion that individuals have in the distribution of these assets.

The third primary means that governments have to create private wealth is the manipulation of legal rulings or the enforcement of rules, such as regulations. Rules banning gambling and prostitution, for example, create the opportunity to extract bribes from potential providers. These bribes can be extracted by any and all members in the chain of enforcement.

As the amount of regulation increases, the opportunity to extract bribes also rises and leads reformers to fight against regulation and government monopoly (as in Bodenhorn's essay).

Conversely, the connection between the intrusiveness of regulation and the ability to extract bribes creates an incentive for politicians to push for further regulation. Even in a libertarian's dream world where government is restricted to enforcing disputes over property rights, there would still be considerable scope for corruption in the arbitration of these disputes. Every dispute over ownership creates the possibility for a corrupt ruling. After all, a corrupt judge can extract bribes even if when he rules in favor of the rightful owner. As the legal system has the ability to redistribute all of the wealth in society, the opportunities for corruption within the system are enormous. As corruption within the courts destroys the clear definition of property rights, this corruption has the potential to turn the libertarian dream into a Hobbesian nightmare. In practice, this ability may be limited by the ability of private litigants to rely on private arbitration and avoid a corrupt legal system.

Together these factors suggest that the benefits from corrupt practices for bribe-taking politicians or bribe-giving businessmen will rise with the size and discretion of the government and the amount of social and economic regulation. Benefits from corruption will also rise when the size of assets or damages involved in property rights disputes increases (Glaeser and Shleifer 2003). The late nineteenth century was a period of increasingly larger governments, more valuable public assets, more aggressive regulation, and bigger stakes litigation. The potential benefits from corruption rose along almost every conceivable dimension. The prediction is an absolute increase in the total amount of

474

corruption (measured in either bribes given or in social losses). But the increase in corruption might not translate into an increase relative to the size of government or the size of the economy.

The limits on corruption have customarily come from three sources: legal penalties, career or social costs, and internal psychic pain. Thus, the overall costs of corruption come from the size of the potential penalties and the probability that these costs are imposed which are in turn a function of information flows, social opprobrium, and the legal system.

The most obvious parameter influencing the cost of illegal corruption is thestated legal penalty for corrupt practices (the cost of corruption that violates social norms, but not laws, will not be connected to legal penalties). While this is certainly obvious, it is also important to remember that these penalties have changed significantly over time. For example, while Plunkitt's honest graft the use of insider information by politicians to enrich themselves was surely corruption, at least by our definition, it was fully legal during Plunkitt's time. Even the gifts of railway stock given to congressmen and others during the Crédit Mobilier scandal were perfectly legal at the time. In the 1790s, the number of laws regarding corruption was so modest that legal penalties against corruption were often negligible. Since that time, there has been a steady increase in the range of behaviors by public officials that are punishable by law and a steady increase in the attempt to craft laws, such as the RICO statute, that render illegal as yet unspecified forms of corrupt behavior.

Magnitude of Fraud and Corruption:

As already mentioned it is not possible to quantify the magnitude of corruption. Cases of fraud and corruption often reported, including those providing indication there of, includes:

I. Bribery and Extortion
  - Extending/availing undue favours
  - Presentation of Gifts of large amounts

II. Fraud, Embezzlement and Irregular payments
  - Forgery of documents
  - Misuse of funds and properties
  - Pilferage of stores
  - Inclusion of dummy workers in Muster Rolls
  - Double claims
    - Intentional Irregular claims and payments
    - Concealment of information

III. Procurement and construction works related corruption
  - Direct procurements/ award of works from/ to some preferred suppliers/contractors
  - Preferring a bidder without valid justification(s)
    - Accepting a non responsive bid
    - Non enforcing contractual terms
  - Accepting defective, inferior and unspecified items
    - Paying at higher rates than the agreed rates
    - Incorporating terms and conditions prejudicial to the interest of procuring agencies
    - Payment of unjustified escalation, freight, insurance claims etc.
    - Extending undue favour to suppliers/ contractors i.e. unauthorized advances, non recovery of security money, non recovery of advances in time etc.
    - Non processing and passing of bills in time without any reasons
    - Indication of undue harassment to contractors for insignificant issues
    - Disparities in enforcing contract terms

475

Payments made for works not executed/ materials not received

Procurements at exorbitant rates from private/ unauthorized sources

Payments made without any valid documents

Additional payments by showing excess measurements

Deliberately under estimating quantities of works and paying at higher rates for quantities beyond deviation limit

Non/short accountal of items procured

Procurement of excessive materials/supplies

Not inquiring into rates to be charged by the sub vendors and   paying at higher rates to the main vendors

Unjustified payment of compensation/recommending such payments

IV Misappropriation of public resources

Unauthorized diversion of funds

Payment/withdrawal of unauthorized /excessive advances

Retention of excessive cash in hand

Non/short accountal of revenue

Non/short deposit/remittances of revenue

Abnormal delays in accountal/deposit of revenue

Unauthorized issue of stores for private purposes

Non raising of bills for supplies/hiring charges to favour individuals

Non deduction of house rent from employees occupying Government accommodation

V   Abuse of Public Office and Nepotism

Use of facilities for personal purposes

Requiring public office to pay expenses of private nature

Awarding supply orders / contracts to relatives

Paying for self and relatives in preference to others

Granting discounts/write off to favoured ones

Using daily wages workers etc. for domestic purposes/personal works

Sanctioning loans without proper scrutiny and appraisal

VI Over/Under invoicing

Over invoicing sales to inflate sales to depict better results

Over invoicing to share the difference   Under invoicing

to share the difference **Division of the Surplus**

The division of the surplus from administrative corruption can be thought of as a cooperative game among the Payers and the Collector. The issue we face is that of dividing the potential gains from cooperation between the tax collector and a large number of taxpayers. We would like to have a rule that reflects the maximum tax liabilities of each payer and the fact that the tax collector is an essential party in the corruption process. It should be pointed out that this cannot be solved as a simple bargaining problem between a single taxpayer and the tax collector.

This is because there exists an aggregate revenue target, and therefore the current surplus available to be shared between the Collector and a Payer depends on the taxes that have already been collected elsewhere.

In this paper we use a simple solution to this problem – namely, the *Shapley value*. This solution concept defines the payoff to each person in a multiperson game as a function of their marginal

476

contributions to the total surplus (see Moulin, 1988, for an excellent overview). We could have defined a noncooperative game, as in Gul (1989). However, this would have greatly complicated the analysis without offering a more convincing approach. The outcome predicted by the Nash equilibrium of an extensive form game is very sensitive to the way we define the extensive form. Furthermore, the extensive form is never observed in practice, and therefore its choice is necessarily arbitrary. The Shapley value has the attractive feature of ignoring the details of the strategic game and defining the payoffs only in terms of observable actions. Therefore, it is much more amenable to being confronted with the data.

The Shapley value is the unique division of the total surplus that satisfies the following conditions:

•   Individuals are treated symmetrically. That is, their identities are irrelevant; it is only the way they are able to affect payoffs that matters.

•   The value is additive. That is, if two different situations or games are combined, the payoff to an individual is equal to the sum of his/her payoffs from each game.

It can also be shown that the Shapley value allocation to each individual is an amount equal to the expected marginal contribution of that individual in a randomly chosen coalition.

This potential marginal contribution can be interpreted in terms of each coalition member's relative power in the group. The power of the Collector in this particular surplus division game derives from his or her ability to effect a reduction in tax liabilities. The power of the Payers derives from their ability to pay their full tax liabilities and deprive the Collector of supplementary income in the form of bribes. **Recommendations**:

Existence of a proper system of check and balance reduces the risks of wrong doings and chances of indulging in fraud and corruption. Strong internal controls, proper rules and regulations, motivated employees, a rational taxation structure etc. tend to act as deterrent against perpetuating fraud and corruption. We are offering some suggestions and recommendations in controlling fraud and corruption for deliberations with the hope that more realistic recommendations will emerge from it.

Establishment of Adequate Regulatory Framework

Formulation of appropriate rules and regulations clearly stipulating punitive measures

Professional development programmers for accountants, auditors, taxofficials and administrators

Establishment of anti corruption Agency

Further strengthening legal System   Widening Tax Base

Power of Back Duty Investigations

Index linked Salaries of civil servants and others

Protection of salaries at least in monetary terms

Periodic transfers of employees

Rotation of duties

Appropriate representations on the Boards/ Committees avoiding conflicting decisions

Appropriate reward and incentive schemes- not necessarily directly linked to individual act of performance

Establishment of appropriate bodies to review reports on fraud and corruption

Rules and regulations to be developed with positive frame of mind. They should be perceived to be facilitating and not be seen as too prohibitive and restrictive.

A progressive and liberalized economic policy

Promoting self regulations of enterprises and greater accountability

Dissemination of information and creating awareness

477

Commissioning independent inquiries on large procurements and construction contracts by appropriate authorities

Establishment of independent quality control units to inspect quality of works, materials and equipment

Strengthening BCCI to look into grievances of business communities and offer business counseling / advise

A definitive and clear policy guidelines on privatization including post privatization commitments of corporations and role of government

Formulation of Unfair Trade Practices Act

Strengthening internal controls in the organizations

Introducing internal audits

Rules / laws with wider implication to be discussed and scrutinized at different levels before approval for their general acceptance and removing inconsistencies

Publicity and greater transparency

Adequate enforcement and monitoring by law enforcing bodies

Establishment of Consumer Protection and Advisory board

Announcements of adequate reward schemes to informers

Formulation of Essential commodities Act

Establishment of Bhutan Standards for manufactured and imported items

Development of Safety regulations

Strengthening Tax Administration and Audit System and other Regulatory Bodies

Conclusions:

Corruption undermines the entire administrative system and functioning of the public offices. It adversely effects the integrity and morale of the employees of the public offices including those who are responsible to enforce laws, rules and regulations. It encourages those responsible to deliberately keep loopholes in the rules. Corruption may be prevalent at any level and any where thus effecting day to day activities and causing harassment and inconveniences to the general public. Detection of fraud and corruption alone is not sufficient. We must take preventive measures to control it. A proper study of causes of corruption and environment favouring it would help initiate effective remedial measures.

Individual cases of corruption can be rooted out by the application of organizational sanctions Systemic corruption cannot be handled so easily. There is no guarantee that if the most serious offenders are dismissed, or if everyone who is guilty is replaced, corruption will not persist. The old patterns will continue with new players. Moreover, in the wider society, systemic corruption impedes rather than aids change.

(a)   Systemic corruption perpetuates closed politics and restricts access, preventing the reflection of social change in political institutions.

(b)   Systemic corruption suppresses opposition contributing to increasing resentment.

Thus corruption, far from being an alternative to violence, is often accompanied by more violence.

(c)   Systemic corruption perpetuates and widens class, economic, and social divisions, contributing to societal strain and preventing cohesion.

(d)   Systemic corruption prevents policy change, particularly where this works against immediate market considerations. Individual or sectional interests are not the best guide to the public interest.

(e)   Systemic corruption blocks administrative reform, and makes deleterious administrative practices profitable, e.g., induced delays.

(f)   Systemic corruption diverts public resources and contributes to a situation of private affluence and public squalor, especially serious where affluence is confined to the few.

(g)   Systemic corruption contributes to societal anomie in shoring up or transmuting traditional values into inappropriate areas.

(h)   The effects of systemic corruption are not limited to a specific case: there is an accumulator effect upon public perceptions and expectations which subverts trust and cooperation far beyond the impact upon the individuals immediately concerned.

(i)   Systemic corruption is not confined to poor, developing, or modernizing countries, but found in all organizational societies."

Existence of adequate regulatory and legal framework as well as a clean and efficient civil service with high morale reduces the risk of rampant corruption in the society. A sound fiscal and monetary policy with due encouragement and incentives for investment will certainly act as deterrent against corruption. Corruption weakens the economy, efficiency and effectiveness of the government systems. Rampant corruption should not be allowed to occur at any cost.

References

CARTIER-BRESSON, J., "A Few Suggestions for a Comparative Analysis of Corruption in Western Europe", Revue Internationale de Politiques Comparées v. 4, n° 2, 2003.

CLARK, WILLIAM A. & JOS, PHILIP H. (2000). "Comparative Anti-Corruption Policy: The American, Soviet and Russian Cases", International Journal of Public Administration 23:1, 101–148.

DOBEL, PATRICK J. (1999). Public Integrity. Baltimore and London: The Johns Hopkins University Press.

GALTUNG, FREDRIK (2006). Measuring the Immeasurable: Boundaries and Functions of (Macro) Corruption Indices. In Sampford, Charles & Shacklock, Arthur & Connors, Carmel & Galtung, Fredrik (eds). Measuring Corruption. Great Britain: Ashgate Publishing Limited: 101–130.

HARISALO, RISTO & STENVALL, JARI (2001). Luottamus kansalaisyhteiskunnan peruskivenä: Kansalaisten luottamus ministeriöihin. [Trust as Cornerstone of Civic Society: Citizens trust to ministries]. Helsinki: Edita.

HOLMES, LESLIE (1993). The End of Communist Power. Anti-Corruption Campaign and Legitimation Crisis. New York: Oxford University Press.

HUBERTS, LEO & LASTHUIZEN, KARIN & PEETERS, CAREL (2006). Measuring Corruption: Exploring the Iceberg. In Sampford, Charles & Shacklock, Arthur & Connors, Carmel & Galtung, Fredrik (eds). Measuring Corruption. Great Britain: Ashgate Publishing Limited: 265–293.

VAN HULTEN, MICHEL (2007). Ten years of Corruption (Perceptions) Indices. Methods – Results – What Next? An analysis.

JOHNSTON, MICHAEL (1999). A Brief History of anticorruption Mechanisms. In Schedler, Andreas & Diamond, Larry & Plattner, Marc F. (eds). The Self-Restraining State: Power and Accountability in New Democracies. Boulder:Lynne Rienner Publishers: 217–226.

KAUFMANN, DANIEL (2004). Corruption, Governance and Security: Challenges for the Rich

Countries and the World. In The Global Competitiveness Report 2004/2005. The World Bank: 83–102.

KONTTINEN, E. (1991). Perinteisesti moderniin: Professioiden yhteiskunnallinen synty Suomessa. [Traditionally to Modern: The Birth of Professions in Finland.] Tampere, Finland: Vastapaino.

KOSKINEN, PEKKA (2001). Johdatus rikosoikeuteen. [Introduction to Criminal Law.] Helsinki: University of Helsinki.

LANGSETH, PETTER (2006). Measuring Corruption. In Sampford, Charles & Shacklock, Arthur & Connors, Carmel & Galtung, Fredrik (eds). Measuring Corruption. Great Britain: Ashgate Publishing Limited: 7–44.

LEVIN, MARK & SATAROV, GEORGY (2000). Corruption and Institutions in Russia, European Journal of Political Economy, vol. 16, no. 1: 113-132.

MAOR, MOSHE (2004). Feeling the Heat? Anticorruption Mechanisms in Comparative Perspective, Governance, vol. 17, no. 1: 1–28.

MAURO, P., "The Effects of Corruption on Growth, Investment and Government Expenditure", in Elliot, K. (ed.), Corruption and the Global Economy, pp. 83-108, 1997.

WEI, S-J., "How Taxing Ades, A. and R. Di Tella , "Rent, Competition and Corruption", Oxford University, mimeo,2005. is Corruption on International Investors?", NBER Working Paper, no. 6030, 2001.

WORLD BANK, Using Surveys for Public Sector Reform, Premnotes No. 23, Washington, 2005.

481

Government Accounting: An Assessment of Theory, Purposes and Standards

Ehsan Rayegan
Department of Accounting,Scool of Social Since , Razi University, Kermanshah, Iran
Mehdi Parveizi
Thecher of Islamic Azad University, Giylan gharb, Iran
Kamran Nazari
Department of Business Management, Payam Noor University, Kermanshah, Iran
Mostafa Emami
M.Sc Eco.Fin , Department of Accounting, Tarbiat Modares University ,Iran,Tehran

Abstract

Developments in governmental activities in recent years have raised concerns over whether the cash basis of accounting is sufficient for governmental accounting and reporting. Accrual accounting, previously thought to be only suitable in the private sector, has been seen to be an alternative for better reporting of government activities. Although there is a continuing debate over the use of cash versus accrual accounting, accrual accounting has been adopted in he governments of several countries including Australia, New Zealand and the United Kingdom. Government accounting and financial reporting aims to protect and manage public money and discharge accountability In order to achieve ambitious socioeconomic goals, developing countries require public sector institutional capacity for setting and implementing public policy, which in turn necessitates government accounting reform. The social value of government accounting reform therefore lies in its contribution to development goals, including poverty reduction. This rationale has led international and multilateral lenders and donors to endorse International Public Sector Accounting Standards (IPSAS) for adoption by developing countries. An emphasis on assuring financial integrity and a shift to accruals can make IPSAS more useful in government accounting reform in developing countries. All of these are heavily influenced by private sector practices, which favour the accrual basis and consolidated reporting. This article argues for a gradual symmetric approach to accruals and a combination of government-wide and fund reporting. The author also proposes some broad accounting principles to promote political and economic accountability .

Key words: Government Accounting, government, accounting reform, International Public Sector Accounting Standards (IPSAS.

Introduction

Miller (1995) p10 argues that a "healthy" accounting standard setting process needs representation from the entire spectrum of stakeholders to retain its integrity. He concludes that "a transparent due process allows outsiders to see the interactions and compromises among the key participants in the development of acceptable accounting rules". Prior Australian research has raised questions about the veracity of various aspects of the operation of the 'due process' for public sector standard setting. Ryan et.

521

Institute of Interdisciplinary Business Research

al. (1999) concluded that there were fundamental problems with the 'due process' as it operated in AAS29, which was released in 1993. There was a lack of input from account preparers and a close working relationship existed between the Treasuries and the standard setters. Carnegie and West (1997) conducted an analysis of the responses to ED 50 in relation to the recognition of infrastructure assets only. They contended that, for this particular issue, the standard setters placed more weight on a sample of 26 responses which were deemed to be "of particular interest" by the staff of the Australian Accounting Research Foundation (AARF) (p32). This led to their raising the concern that the PSASB may not have been responsive to its constituents. The Philippines realized fiscal surpluses between 1994 and 1997, prior to the Asian financial crisis.176 However, indicators have deteriorated significantly in the past 3 years. The Arroyo administration faces a worsening fiscal position. Unless the Government curbs expenses and improves revenue collection, the 2001 budget deficit could reach P200 billion ($4.2 billion).177 The weak fiscal position is creating tensions with multilateral development banks.178 Moreover, it restricts the Government's ability to address infrastructure issues and poverty reduction.

Furthermore, the Philippines experiences significant ongoing problems with corruption. With annual capital expenditure exceeding $3.5 billion, the procurement of goods and services, and implementation of infrastructure projects, by the Government present significant opportunities for graft.179 Government accounting and auditing arrangements were formulated in 1947. They have many strengths including the use of doubleentry bookkeeping, a mixed cash-accrual accounting base, a cadre of well-trained accountants, and potential access to a large external pool of trained accountants. Public management arrangements are characterized by institutional and regulatory rigidities. Efforts to modernize the public sector have gathered pace in recent years. Among other things, the Government intends to (i) develop a MediumTerm Expenditure Framework (MTEF); (ii) introduce output and outcome performance measures and targets; (iii) overhaul procurement practices; (iv) introduce 3-year baseline budgeting; (v) modernize auditing practices; (vi) introduce computerized financial management information systems; and (vii) prepare for the introduction of full accrual accounting.180he Constitution of the Philippines 1987 mandates the keeping of government accounts, the promulgation of accounting rules, the audit of financial reports, and the submission of reports covering the Government's financial operations and position.181 In particular, Article IX defines three constitutional commissions as being separate and independent bodies.

From Accountability to Accounting

The global rise of government accounting is fundamentally due to the greater demand for accountability in a democracy and market economy. Democratic governance and market transactions require and foster the norm of reciprocity the expectation of exchange of benefits of comparable value upon which accountability is based. Accounting information can be used to monitor and enforce the terms of economic, social and political contracts. When a government engages in market transactions whether buying or selling services, lending or borrowing money it is subject to economic accountability. When it levies taxes to finance public services, it incurs political accountability. The development of government accounting is related to the

522

Institute of Interdisciplinary Business Research

constitutional form of government that provides for separation of powers, and checks and balances among the legislative, executive, and judicial branches of government (Chan and Rubin, 1987). While all governments engage in some degree of planning and control, only democratic governments are mandated to open their books directly to auditors and indirectly to the public through financial reports. Fiscal transparency is therefore an attribute of limited government, for to give out information is to cede authority. Government officials rationally do not volunteer more information than is required or in their interest. It is therefore not surprising that, while some accounting is done on a voluntary basis, financial disclosure is often made only in response to demand. The regulatory structure for government financial disclosure mirrors the pattern of accountability in government and the political system. In an administrative hierarchy, the superior holds subordinates accountable and requires feedback information on their performance. A legislature monitors the conduct of the executive branch, for example, in executing the approved budget. Furthermore, a government has the incentive to disclose information in order to induce others to provide resources to it. These include potential buyers of government securities; vendors of goods and services on credit; and grantors of financial aid. In these voluntary exchanges, information is used to predict a government's ability to carry out the terms of contracts, .\fter the transactions are made, accounting information is used to monitor contractual performance. Governments are less inclined to disclose financial information to those without leverage over it, at least in the short-term, such as individual taxpayers. It is here that mandatory standards seek to increase the information access of those who are least able to demand it, or to enforce their right to know. The exercise of accountability requires institutions in both senses of the term: namely, organizations; and rules of the game (World Bank, 2002, p. 4). In government accounting, these refer to standard-setting bodies and the standards they promulgate. These institutions of government accounting in individual countries are extensively documented in the CIGAR literature and will not be covered in this article. It is, how ever, important to describe the general purposes of government accounting, in order to contrast it with

commercial accounting. The Commission on Audit shall have the power, authority, and duty to examine, audit, and settle all accounts pertaining to the revenue and receipts of, and expenditures or uses of funds and property, owned or held in trust by, or pertaining to, the Government, or

any of its subdivisions, agencies, or instrumentalities, including government- owned or controlled corporations with original charters, and on a post-audit basis: (a) constitutional bodies, commissions and offices that have been granted fiscal autonomy under this Constitution; (b) autonomous state colleges and universities; (c) other government owned or controlled corporations and their subsidiaries; and (d) such nongovernmental entities receiving subsidy or equity, directly or indirectly, from or through the Government, which are required by law or the granting institution to submit to such audit as a condition of subsidy or equity. However, where the internal control system of the audited agencies is inadequate, the Commission may adopt such measures, including temporary or special pre-audit, as are necessary and appropriate to correct the deficiencies. It shall keep the general accounts of the Government and, for such period as may be provided by law, preserve the vouchers and other supporting papers pertaining thereto. (2) The Commission shall have exclusive authority, subject to

523

the limitations in this Article, to define the scope of its audit and examination, establish the techniques and methods required therefor, and promulgate accounting and auditing rules and regulations, including those for the prevention and disallowance of irregular, unnecessary, excessive, extravagant, or unconscionable expenditures or uses of government funds and properties Section 3. No law shall be passed exempting any entity of the Government or its subsidiaries in any guise whatever, or any investment of public funds, from the jurisdiction of the Commission on Audit.

Section 4. The Commission shall submit to the President and the Congress, within the time fixed by law, an annual report covering the financial condition and operation of the Government, its subdivisions, agencies, and instrumentalities, including governmentowned or controlled corporations, and nongovernmental entities subject to its audit, and recommend measures necessary to improve their effectiveness and efficiency. It shall submit such other reports as may be required by law.

Organizational Roles and Responsibilities

The following organizations play central roles in budgeting, accounting and auditing arrangements. The COA audits the general accounts of the Government, promulgates accounting rules and regulations, and submits the annual financial report of the Government, its subdivisions, and agencies (including government owned or controlled corporations).

The Department of Finance (DOF) The DOF is responsible for (i) formulating, institutionalizing, and administering fiscal policies in coordination with other concerned subdivisions, agencies, and instrumentalities of the government; (ii) managing the financial resources of government; (iii) supervising the revenue operations of all LGUs; (iv) reviewing, approving and managing all public sector debt; and (v) rationalizing, privatizing and ensuring the public accountability of corporations and assets owned, controlled or acquired by the Government.187 The DOF oversees three operating bureaus: the Bureau of the Treasury (BTr), the Bureau of Internal Revenue (BIR), and the Bureau of Customs.

The Bureau of the Treasury (BTr) The BTr plays a pivotal role in the cash operations of the national government. It is responsible for (i) receiving and keeping national funds; (ii) managing and controlling disbursements of national funds; and (iii) maintaining accounts of financial transactions of all national government offices, agencies, and instruments.

Department of Budget and Management (DBM) The DBM is responsible for the design, reparation and approval of the accounting systems of government agencies. It is also responsible for coordinating and implementing the annual budget process. Furthermore, the Department manages the process of cash disbursement as well as monitoring compliance with appropriations.

Development and Budget Coordinating Council (DBCC) The DBCC comprises representatives from DBM, DOF, Bureau of Treasury, NEDA, and BSP. All agency budgetary requirements must pass through the Council. Its objectives are to (i) set budget parameters based on available resources; (ii) conduct budget hearings; and (iii) submit the resulting consolidated budget to the House of Representatives (particularly the Committee on Appropriations).

Accounting Information Systems

The national government accounting system is largely paper based. Financial reports from national agencies, including those with computerized systems, are manually processed and consolidated by COA. Existing computerized systems are of varying types.191 This variation is to be expected in such a diversified environment comprising a wide range of organizations with differing roles and objectives.

524

Government versus Commercial Accounting

Business accounting has often been used as a benchmark for evaluating government accounting. Two hundred years ago, Thomas Jefferson (quoted by Arthur Andersen, 1986) wished to see *the finance of the Union as clear and intelligible as a merchant's books, so that every member of Congress, and every man of any mind in the Union, should be able to comprehend them to investigate abuses, and consequently to control them'. Is it possible that government and business accounting are fundamentally alike in unimportant respects as public and private management are (Allison, 1980)? What are the important respects that set government accounting apart from its business counterpart?

In order to serve the three identified purposes, financial accounting and management accounting cannot be so neatly compartmentalized in the public sector, where management accounting refers to budgeting and control, rather than accounting solely in the service of managers. The budget is an expression of public policy and political preferences. It is an instrument of fiscal policy on revenue and spending to achieve macroeconomic objectives. It provides benchmarks for performance measured partly by the accounting system. Given their close relationship, it is often difficult to tell where budgeting ends and accounting begins. They reinforce each other in demonstrating and discharging fiscal accountability to the government's stakeholders, who are more numerous and diverse than the owners of a firm. Indeed, governments do not have owners.

The absence of ownership in government makes it problematic to apply the accounting equation (assets = liabilities + owners' equity) and its corollary (profit = revenuesexpenses) to the public sector. An exception may be local governments. These are municipal corporations chartered by the state to perform certain public services, which in many cases are private goods (for example water) or only quasipublic goods (for example elementary education). These entities have clear origins, and own identifiable assets and liabilities. Unfortunately, the assets and liabilities of the national government of a sovereign state are difficult to identify and harder still to measure in financial terms. With regard to assets, except in rare instances (such as the United States' purchase of Louisiana from France, or Alaska from Russia), few nations acquire new territories through buy-and-sell transactions. Most occupy their ancestral lands and some acquired their territories through military conquests or colonization. Historical costs, even if data are available, are not meaningful, yet market prices, even ifjustifiable. are hard to come by. The same problems arise in the case of natural resources and heritage assets. On the liability side, it is not easy to draw the line between a national government's contractual or legal obligations and its political

commitments and social responsibilities for the general welfare. In contrast to corporations' limited liabilities, governments in a democracy are prone to expand their responsibilities, resulting in larger budgets and frequent deficits (Buchanan and Wagner, 1977).

Accounting principles allow a business, whether private or state-owned, to recognize revenues only to the extent of goods or services provided. Governments uniquely provide public goods and finance them through taxation. Public goods are consumed collectively, and non-payers cannot be excluded— hence requiring tax financing. These characteristics sever the link between service delivery and revenue recognition, making it impossible to match revenues and expenses (Sunder, 1997). This accounting problem is also exacerbated by the involuntary nature of many transactions between government and people. The government's operating statement tracks resource flows, and only incidentally measures the government's service efforts and accomplishments. These unique characteristics of government are the primary source of the differences between government and commercial accounting. These differences, argues Sunder (1997, p. 198), 'do not constitute prima facie evidence that the former are defective and should be altered to conform to the latter'. More specifically, Nobes (1988, p. 198) challenged the assertion that 'Anglo-Saxon commercial accounting involving accrualsbased annual financial statements is necessary for accountability, control and

525

decision-making relating to government'. From the research perspective, theories underlying government accounting standards are mostly normative, in contrast to the development of positive theory in (business) financial accounting. The latter (Watts, 1977; Watts and Zimmerman, 1978, 1990) draws its inspiration from the contract-cost theory of the firm originating from Coase (1937). A similar incipient conceptual revolution started tentatively with Zimmerman's (1977) paper linking government financial reporting to political incentives. It is time to resume the search for a positive theory of government accounting standards. One way would be to build on the work of Chester Barnard and Herbert Simon.

At about the same time Goase wrote his famous paper explaining the existence of the firm in terms of transaction costs, Barnard (1938) identified the functions of the executive as securing the co-operation of the stakeholders of an organization. Barnard's work is currently enjoying a revival, primarily through the efforts of Oliver Williamson (1990). Much earlier, Simon (1945) applied Barnard's insight to government in his hook Administrative Behavior. In Simon's view, an organization is in equilibrium if Barnard's executive succeeds in securing the contributions of stakeholders by offering them adequate inducements to stay in the organizational coalition. A business can be viewed in the same way (Gohen and Gyert, 1965). In both types of organization, the challenge for managers is to negotiate satisfactory terms of contracts to keep the coalition intact. In such a theory, owners are important as contributors of equity capital, but they are not the only group managers try to please. In other words, the owner-centred theory of the firm and the single-principal agency theory are a special case of the Barnard- Simon organization theory.

This theory can be used to identify potential users of government's financial information by postulating that they use the information to predict their inducements from government (Ghan, 1981). Recently, Sunder (1997) applied contract-cost theory to explain and justify the differences betw-een accounting for government and nonprofit organizations and business accounting. Much more research is needed before the multiple-stakeholder perspective can have an impact on standards. In the meantime, government accounting has shifted closer to the business (financial) accounting model.

Internal Auditing

The Internal Auditing Act 1962 (RA 3456) introduced internal auditing requirements to the national government. A 1965 amendment (RA 4177) extended the Act's coverage to government-owned and controlled corporations (GOCCs) and local government units (LGUs). In 1992, President Aquino directed that government internal-control systems be strengthened (AO 278) – the Association of Government Internal Audi- tors (AGIA), among others, was instructed to ensure that internal audit practices, methods, and procedures be improved through continuing education and be conducted in accordance with internal auditing standards.

192 The AGIA represents internal auditors in government and promotes their professional development. It had 1,177 members at January 1999.

Public Financial Management Reform Program

The objectives of the Government's public financial management reforms are to (i) allocate and manage expenditures via a Medium Term Expenditure Framework (MTEF); (ii) strengthen feedback mechanisms for budget formulation through enhanced budget and performance monitoring; (iii) improve the performance management environment by simplifying budgeting rules; (iv) introduce incentives for better performance management; and (v) increase management flexibility to ensure performance results.197 The reforms are based on a benchmarking study of the Philippine expenditure management system vis-à-vis its neighboring countries (Australia, Korea, Malaysia, New Zealand,

526

Singapore, and Thailand) in terms of the three important expenditure outcomes: maintaining fiscal discipline, facilitating strategic prioritization at the oversight level, and enhancing the implementation efficiency of line agencies.198 The reform program comprises several activities as follows: 199 • Sectoral budget ceilings. Six-year sectoral budget ceilings were introduced for the Fiscal 2000 budget. These sectoral budgets were developed with the multi-sector Planning Committees of the National Economic and Development Authority (NEDA). These Committees include representatives from Congress, local government, academia, the private sector and nongovernment organizations. The process involved various government implementing agencies in a participative and proactive manner. Three-year budget baselines. The 6-year sectoral ceilings served as the basis for allocating resources to implementing agencies using a budget baseline approach. • Strengthening evaluation mechanisms. First, locally funded projects will be subjected to the same approval process that applies to those funded from foreign sources. Second, the performance measurement will be mainstreamed. A set of performance indicators will have to accompany all new policies or projects that are submitted to NEDA or DBM. The ultimate objective is to foster an evaluation culture.

• Improving government accounting and internal control. Adopting private sector accounting and reporting practices, such as full accrual accounting will enhance the usefulness of accounting information. It will also enable organizational outputs to be meaningfully costed.

• Separating accounting and auditing functions. COA, the Philippines' supreme audit institution, undertakes accounting, internal control and auditing functions in government. These groupings are incongruous.

• Improving procurement procedures. The DBM has launched the Electronic Procurement System to improve the efficiency and transparency of the government procurement process.200

Issue Synopsis: Government Budgeting and Accounting

Chapter VIII – Issues and Recommendations – identifies and describes constraints and proposes corrective actions. With minor departures, these include the following selected issues that have already been identified by the UNDP-sponsored studies:

• The Commission on Audit is responsible for promulgating accounting and auditing rules. These responsibilities are defined in Article IX of the Constitution 1987. The coexistence of these responsibilities is inconsistent with the concept of auditor independence.

• The absence of computerized accounting information systems, combined with complex accounting regulations (i) relegates the role of most government CPAs to that of highly qualified bookkeepers.

Little time is left for value-added activities, such as financial analysis; and (ii) means that financial reports are rarely prepared in time to be useful for decision-making purposes.

• There is no consistent set of accounting standards for budgeting and reporting. Major reporting differences result.

• Auditors spend the majority of their time on compliance auditing (checking transactions). Minimal time is spent on financial attest auditing as more effort is applied to value-for-money audits.

• Comparatively attractive starting salaries attract high-quality personnel into government accounting. A flat earnings structure means that higher-level salaries are far from competitive. This creates retention problems and provides a supportive environment for graft and corruption.

Summary and Proposals

Over the past 25 years, there have been some notable institutional and conceptual innovations in government accounting, contributing to its greater visibility and influence. Its emphasis has shifted from bureaucratic control to accountability reporting to the public. In some countries, government

527

accounting standards are no longer set by government officials, but by relatively independent boards. While acknowledging the importance of cash the lifeblood in government as in business contemporary accounting standards aim at tracking the long-term consequences of decisions and actions. Government officials are held accountable for their stewardship of both

financial and capital assets. Finally, it is not enough to keep the books accurately; the books have to be open to the public. When the public does not have the time or ability to inspect the accounts, governments have to make the task easier by preparing comprehensible as well as comprehensive financial statements.

Many challenges remain, especially at the global and international level. A major issue is the proper balance between international norms and domestic practices arising from national political ideology, economic system and culture. As a mechanism of governance, government accounting is subject to political forces that distribute power, and economic forces that determine the supply of and demand for resources. Therefore, unless accounting standards boards ally themselves with the institutions that can withhold something of value to a government a grant, a loan, an unqualified audit opinion, a favourable bond rating their pronouncements would remain

ineffectual. Unfortunately, at the international level, there are relatively few levers available to

a body such as the IFAC Public Sector Committee to enforce its standards. However, accountants could make the case that fiscal accountability is an international norm applicable to all governments regardless of their political and economic system. Once this transcendent value of fiscal accountability is embraced, it is a technical matter to work out the means of implementation. These include not only yearend financial statements the current focus of IPSASs—but also budgets, internal controls and external audits. 1 urge the IFAC Public

Sector Committee to rectify its neglect of the budget and to include 'actual versus budget' comparisons in financial statements. Furthermore, putting aside differences of opinions on accounting choices, the entire body of detailed standards should be framed by a set of broader principles aimed at promoting government fiscal accountability, such as:

•The objectives of government accounting are to safeguard the public treasury and pr()pert\, to accurately measure and communicate the government's fmancial condition so as to demonstrate financial accountability, and to facilitate decisionmaking. •Agovernment should prepare and publish its budgets, maintain complete financial records, provide full financial disclosure, and subject itself to independent audits.

•The form and content of financial reports should be guided by the rights and need to know of intended users.

•The accounting system should measure the cash and other financial consequences of past transactions and events, including, but not limited to, budget execution.

•The accounting system should be capable of keeping track of the levels and changes in assets, liabilities, revenues and expenditures or expenses, relative to budgeted amounts. These principles do not prescribe accounting choices. Rather, they provide a foundation for deliberating and setting government accounting standards.

Generally, accounting standards take on a greater social role as accountability requirements in countries that require higher standards of ethical behaviour. Government accounting standards in effect become government accountability standards. (Recently the U.S. General Accounting Office was renamed Government Accountability Office.). Government must answer for the resources or authority it receives from others in the society and economy. Government provides both public goods and private goods, in return for the authority to govern, as well as economic and financial resources, Government accountability requirements are expressed as the terms in the political contracts, social contracts, and economic contracts that government enters into with its stakeholders (see Exhibit 2).

528

The asset-liability perspective of accrual accounting described in Exhibit 1 is compatible with this contract theory of government: the government's assets come from the stakeholders' voluntary and involuntary contributions, and its liabilities originate from providing incentives to the stakeholders. In conclusion, fundamental to the development of accrual accounting in developing countries is the ability to identify and measure the government's assets and liabilities. Corruption tends to result in the understatement of government's assets or the overstatement of government's liabilities. Unless financial integrity is assured, the credibility of government's financial information suffers. Thus both financial integrity assurance and accurate accrual accounting are accountants' professional contribution to developing countries.

References

Allen, R. and Tommasi, D. (2001), Managing Public Expenditure: A Reference Book for Transition Countries, OECD, Paris.

Bourmistrov, A. and Mellemvik, F. (2000) «Russian Local Government Accounting: New Norms and New Problems», in Caperchione E. and Mussari, R. eds., Comparative Issues in Local Government Accounting, Kluwer Academic Publishers, Boston, pp. 159- 174.

Bourmistrov, A. and Mellemvik, F. (2001), «Accounting and Democratic Governance: A Comparative Study of One Norwegian and One Russian County», in Bac, A. ed. International Comparative Issues in Government Accounting, Kluwer Academic Publishers, Dordrecht, The Netherlands, pp. 91-122.

Chan, J.L., Jones, R.H. and Lüder, K.G. (1996), «Modeling Government Innovations: An Assessment and Future Research Directions», Research in Governmental and Nonprofit Accounting, Vol. 9, pp. 1-19.

Chan, J.L. (2000), «A Sino-American Comparison of Budget and Accounting Coverage», in Caperchione, E. and Mussari, R., eds., Comparative Issues in Local Government Accounting, Kluwer Academic Publishers, Boston, pp. 11-34.

Chan, J.L., Cong, S.H. and Zhao, J.Y. (2001), «The Effects of Reform on China's Public budgeting and Accounting System», in Bac, A., ed. International Comparative Issues in Government Accounting, Kluwer Academic Publishers, Dordrecht, The Netherlands, pp. 297-314.

Chu, K-Y, and Hemming, R. (1991), «Public Expenditure Handbook: A Guide to Public Policy Issues in Developing Countries», International Monetary Fund, Washington, D.C. Coombs, Hugh M. and Mohamad Tayib, (2000), «Financial Reporting Practice: A Comparative Study of Local Authority Financial Reports Between the UK and 12 Malaysia», in Caperchione, E. and Mussari, M. eds., Comparative Issues in Local Government Accounting, Kluwer Academic Publishers, Boston,, pp. 53-68.

Deutsch, K.W. (1966), The Nerves of Government: Models of Political Communication and Control, The Free Press, New York.

Godfrey, A.D., Devlin, P.J. and Merrouche, C., (1996), «Governmental Accounting in Kenya, Tanzania and Uganda» in Chan, J.L., ed., Research in Governmental and Nonprofit Accounting, Vol. 9, JAI Press, Greenwich, Connecticut, pp. 193-208.

Godfrey, A.D., Merrouche, C. and Devlin, P.J. (1999), «A Comparative Analysis of the Evolution of Local Governmental Accounting in Algeria and Morocco,» in Copley, P.A. and Sanders, G.D., eds. Research in Governmental and Nonprofit Accounting, Vol. 10, JAI Press, Greenwich, Connecticut, pp. 201-234.

Grindle, Merilee S. (2000), «Ready or Not: The Developing World and Globalization,» in Nye, J.S. and Donahue, J.D., eds. Governance in a Globalizing World, Brookings Institution Press, ashington, D.C., pp. 178-207.

529

Hopwood, A. and Miller, P., eds. (1994), Accounting as a Social and Organizational Practice, Cambridge University Press, Cambridge.

International Federation of Accountants (IFAC) (1996), «Responding to an Increasing Demand for Accountability in the Public Sector,» IFAC Quarterly, October.

IFAC (2003), Handbook on International Public Sector Accounting Standards. IFAC, New York.

IFAC, International Public Sector Accounting Standards Board (2005), Exposure Draft 24, Financial Reporting Under the Cash Basis of Accounting – Disclosure Requirements for Recipients of External Assistance, IF AC, New York.

IFAC, International Public Sector Accounting Standards Board (2005), «Background and Update,» unpublished paper, March.

IFAC, Public Sector Committee (2000), Study 11, Government Financial Reporting: Accounting Issues and Practices. IFAC, New York, May.

Jaruga, A. (1988), «Governmental Accounting, Auditing and Financial Reporting in East European Countries,» in Chan, J.L. and Jones, R.H. eds., Governmental Accounting and Auditing: International Comparisons, Routledge, London, pp. 105-121. Keefer, P. and Khemani, S. (2004), «Democracy, Public Expenditure and the Poor,» World Bank Research Observer. World Bank, Washington, D.C.

Nowak, W.A. and Bakalarska, B. (2001), «Polish Public Sector Accounting in Transition: The Landscape after 1999 Step in the State Redefining,» in Bac, A. ed., International Comparative Issues in Government Accounting, Kluwer Academic Publishers, Dordrecht, The Netherlands, pp. 265-278.

Ouda, Hassan A.G. (2001), «Central Governmental Accounting of Egypt and the Netherlands: Similarities and Differences,» in Bac, A. ed., International Comparative Issues in Government Accounting, Kluwer Academic Publishers, Dordrecht, The Netherlands, pp. 71-90.

Rose-Ackerman, S. (1999), Corruption and Government: Causes, Consequences and Reform, Cambridge University Press, Cambridge.

Reuters (2003), «World Bank urges crackdown on government corruption», December 10.

Sachs, J.D. (2005), The End of Poverty: Economic Possibilities for Our Time, Penguin Books, New York.

Schiavo-Campo, S. and Tommasi, D. (1999), Managing Government Expenditure, Asian Development Bank, Manila.

Simon, H.A. (1954), Centralization vs. Decentralization in Organizing the Controller's Department, Controllership Foundation, New York.

Sutcliffe, P. (2003), «The Standards Programme of IFAC's Public Sector Committee,» Public Money and Management, January, pp. 11-12.

World Bank (1998), Public Expenditure Management Handbook, World Bank, Washington, D.C.

Government Accounting: An Assessment of Theory, Purposes and Standards

Ehsan Rayegan

Department of Accounting,Scool of Social Since , Razi University, Kermanshah, Iran

Mehdi Parveizi

Thecher of Islamic Azad University, Giylan gharb, Iran

Kamran Nazari

Department of Business Management, Payam Noor University, Kermanshah, Iran

Mostafa Emami

M.Sc Eco.Fin , Department of Accounting, Tarbiat Modares University ,Iran,Tehran

Abstract

Developments in governmental activities in recent years have raised concerns over whether the cash basis of accounting is sufficient for governmental accounting and reporting. Accrual accounting, previously thought to be only suitable in the private sector, has been seen to be an alternative for better reporting of government activities. Although there is a continuing debate over the use of cash versus accrual accounting, accrual accounting has been adopted in he governments of several countries including Australia, New Zealand and the United Kingdom. Government accounting and financial reporting aims to protect and manage public money and discharge accountability In order to achieve ambitious socioeconomic goals, developing countries require public sector institutional capacity for setting and implementing public policy, which in turn necessitates government accounting reform. The social value of government accounting reform therefore lies in its contribution to development goals, including poverty reduction. This rationale has led international and multilateral lenders and donors to endorse International Public Sector Accounting Standards (IPSAS) for adoption by developing countries. An emphasis on assuring financial integrity and a shift to accruals can make IPSAS more useful in government accounting reform in developing countries. All of these are heavily influenced by private sector practices, which favour the accrual basis and consolidated reporting. This article argues for a gradual symmetric approach to accruals and a combination of government-wide and fund reporting. The author also proposes some broad accounting principles to promote political and economic accountability .

Key words: Government Accounting, government, accounting reform, International Public Sector Accounting Standards (IPSAS.

Introduction

Miller (1995) p10 argues that a "healthy" accounting standard setting process needs representation from the entire spectrum of stakeholders to retain its integrity. He concludes that "a transparent due process allows outsiders to see the interactions and compromises among the key participants in the development of acceptable

521

accounting rules". Prior Australian research has raised questions about the veracity of various aspects of the operation of the 'due process' for public sector standard setting. Ryan et.

*Tel:989127001816-18162370018 Email: Mostafa.Emami@Modares.ac.ir
Institute of Interdisciplinary Business Research

al. (1999) concluded that there were fundamental problems with the 'due process' as it operated in AAS29, which was released in 1993. There was a lack of input from account preparers and a close working relationship existed between the Treasuries and the standard setters. Carnegie and West (1997) conducted an analysis of the responses to ED 50 in relation to the recognition of infrastructure assets only. They contended that, for this particular issue, the standard setters placed more weight on a sample of 26 responses which were deemed to be "of particular interest" by the staff of the Australian Accounting Research Foundation (AARF) (p32). This led to their raising the concern that the PSASB may not have been responsive to its constituents. The Philippines realized fiscal surpluses between 1994 and 1997, prior to the Asian financial crisis.176 However, indicators have deteriorated significantly in the past 3 years. The Arroyo administration faces a worsening fiscal position. Unless the Government curbs expenses and improves revenue collection, the 2001 budget deficit could reach P200 billion ($4.2 billion).177 The weak fiscal position is creating tensions with multilateral development banks.178 Moreover, it restricts the Government's ability to address infrastructure issues and poverty reduction.

Furthermore, the Philippines experiences significant ongoing problems with corruption. With annual capital expenditure exceeding $3.5 billion, the procurement of goods and services, and implementation of infrastructure projects, by the Government present significant opportunities for graft.179 Government accounting and auditing arrangements were formulated in 1947. They have many strengths including the use of doubleentry bookkeeping, a mixed cash-accrual accounting base, a cadre of well-trained accountants, and potential access to a large external pool of trained accountants. Public management arrangements are characterized by institutional and regulatory rigidities. Efforts to modernize the public sector have gathered pace in recent years. Among other things, the Government intends to (i) develop a MediumTerm Expenditure Framework (MTEF); (ii) introduce output and outcome performance measures and targets; (iii) overhaul procurement practices; (iv) introduce 3-year baseline budgeting; (v) modernize auditing practices; (vi) introduce computerized financial management information systems; and (vii) prepare for the introduction of full accrual accounting.180he Constitution of the Philippines 1987 mandates the keeping of government accounts, the promulgation of accounting rules, the audit of financial reports, and the submission of reports covering the Government's financial operations and position.181 In particular, Article IX defines three constitutional commissions as being separate and independent bodies.

From Accountability to Accounting

The global rise of government accounting is fundamentally due to the greater demand for accountability in a democracy and market economy. Democratic governance and market transactions require and foster the norm of reciprocity the expectation of exchange of benefits of comparable value upon which accountability is based. Accounting information can be used to monitor and enforce the

522

terms of economic, social and political contracts. When a government engages in market transactions whether buying or selling services, lending or borrowing money it is subject to economic accountability. When it levies taxes to finance public services, it incurs political accountability. The development of government accounting is related to the

Institute of Interdisciplinary Business Research

constitutional form of government that provides for separation of powers, and checks and balances among the legislative, executive, and judicial branches of government (Chan and Rubin, 1987). While all governments engage in some degree of planning and control, only democratic governments are mandated to open their books directly to auditors and indirectly to the public through financial reports. Fiscal transparency is therefore an attribute of limited government, for to give out information is to cede authority. Government officials rationally do not volunteer more information than is required or in their interest. It is therefore not surprising that, while some accounting is done on a voluntary basis, financial disclosure is often made only in response to demand. The regulatory structure for government financial disclosure mirrors the pattern of accountability in government and the political system. In an administrative hierarchy, the superior holds subordinates accountable and requires feedback information on their performance. A legislature monitors the conduct of the executive branch, for example, in executing the approved budget. Furthermore, a government has the incentive to disclose information in order to induce others to provide resources to it. These include potential buyers of government securities; vendors of goods and services on credit; and grantors of financial aid. In these voluntary exchanges, information is used to predict a government's ability to carry out the terms of contracts, .\fter the transactions are made, accounting information is used to monitor contractual performance. Governments are less inclined to disclose financial information to those without leverage over it, at least in the short-term, such as individual taxpayers. It is here that mandatory standards seek to increase the information access of those who are least able to demand it, or to enforce their right to know. The exercise of accountability requires institutions in both senses of the term: namely, organizations; and rules of the game (World Bank, 2002, p. 4). In government accounting, these refer to standard-setting bodies and the standards they promulgate. These institutions of government accounting in individual countries are extensively documented in the CIGAR literature and will not be covered in this article. It is, how ever, important to describe the general purposes of government accounting, in order to contrast it with

commercial accounting. The Commission on Audit shall have the power, authority, and duty to examine, audit, and settle all accounts pertaining to the revenue and receipts of, and expenditures or uses of funds and property, owned or held in trust by, or pertaining to, the Government, or

any of its subdivisions, agencies, or instrumentalities, including government- owned or controlled corporations with original charters, and on a post-audit basis: (a) constitutional bodies, commissions and offices that have been granted fiscal autonomy under this Constitution; (b) autonomous state colleges and universities; (c) other government owned or controlled corporations and their subsidiaries; and (d) such nongovernmental entities receiving subsidy or equity, directly or indirectly, from or through the Government, which are required by law or the granting institution to submit to such audit as a condition of subsidy or equity. However, where the internal control system of the audited agencies is inadequate, the Commission may adopt such measures, including temporary or special pre-audit, as are necessary and appropriate to correct the deficiencies. It shall keep the general

523

accounts of the Government and, for such period as may be provided by law, preserve the vouchers and other supporting papers pertaining thereto. (2) The Commission shall have exclusive authority, subject to

the limitations in this Article, to define the scope of its audit and examination, establish the techniques and methods required therefor, and promulgate accounting and auditing rules and regulations, including those for the prevention and disallowance of irregular, unnecessary, excessive, extravagant, or unconscionable expenditures or uses of government funds and properties Section 3. No law shall be passed exempting any entity of the Government or its subsidiaries in any guise whatever, or any investment of public funds, from the jurisdiction of the Commission on Audit.

Section 4. The Commission shall submit to the President and the Congress, within the time fixed by law, an annual report covering the financial condition and operation of the Government, its subdivisions, agencies, and instrumentalities, including governmentowned or controlled corporations, and nongovernmental entities subject to its audit, and recommend measures necessary to improve their effectiveness and efficiency. It shall submit such other reports as may be required by law.

Organizational Roles and Responsibilities

The following organizations play central roles in budgeting, accounting and auditing arrangements. The COA audits the general accounts of the Government, promulgates accounting rules and regulations, and submits the annual financial report of the Government, its subdivisions, and agencies (including government owned or controlled corporations).

The Department of Finance (DOF) The DOF is responsible for (i) formulating, institutionalizing, and administering fiscal policies in coordination with other concerned subdivisions, agencies, and instrumentalities of the government; (ii) managing the financial resources of government; (iii) supervising the revenue operations of all LGUs; (iv) reviewing, approving and managing all public sector debt; and (v) rationalizing, privatizing and ensuring the public accountability of corporations and assets owned, controlled or acquired by the Government.187 The DOF oversees three operating bureaus: the Bureau of the Treasury (BTr), the Bureau of Internal Revenue (BIR), and the Bureau of Customs.

The Bureau of the Treasury (BTr) The BTr plays a pivotal role in the cash operations of the national government. It is responsible for (i) receiving and keeping national funds; (ii) managing and controlling disbursements of national funds; and (iii) maintaining accounts of financial transactions of all national government offices, agencies, and instruments.

Department of Budget and Management (DBM) The DBM is responsible for the design, reparation and approval of the accounting systems of government agencies. It is also responsible for coordinating and implementing the annual budget process. Furthermore, the Department manages the process of cash disbursement as well as monitoring compliance with appropriations.

Development and Budget Coordinating Council (DBCC) The DBCC comprises representatives from DBM, DOF, Bureau of Treasury, NEDA, and BSP. All agency budgetary requirements must pass through the Council. Its objectives are to (i) set budget parameters based on available resources; (ii) conduct budget hearings; and (iii) submit the resulting consolidated budget to the House of Representatives (particularly the Committee on Appropriations).

Accounting Information Systems

The national government accounting system is largely paper based. Financial reports from national agencies, including those with computerized systems, are manually processed and consolidated by COA. Existing computerized systems are of varying types.191 This variation is to be expected in such a diversified environment comprising a wide range of organizations with differing roles and objectives.

525

Government versus Commercial Accounting

Business accounting has often been used as a benchmark for evaluating government accounting. Two hundred years ago, Thomas Jefferson (quoted by Arthur Andersen, 1986) wished to see *the finance of the Union as clear and intelligible as a merchant's books, so that every member of Congress, and every man of any mind in the Union, should be able to comprehend them to investigate abuses, and consequently to control them'. Is it possible that government and business accounting are fundamentally alike in unimportant respects as public and private management are (Allison, 1980)? What are the important respects that set government accounting apart from its business counterpart?

In order to serve the three identified purposes, financial accounting and management accounting cannot be so neatly compartmentalized in the public sector, where management accounting refers to budgeting and control, rather than accounting solely in the service of managers. The budget is an expression of public policy and political preferences. It is an instrument of fiscal policy on revenue and spending to achieve macroeconomic objectives. It provides benchmarks for performance measured partly by the accounting system. Given their close relationship, it is often difficult to tell where budgeting ends and accounting begins. They reinforce each other in demonstrating and discharging fiscal accountability to the government's stakeholders, who are more numerous and diverse than the owners of a firm. Indeed, governments do not have owners.

The absence of ownership in government makes it problematic to apply the accounting equation (assets = liabilities + owners' equity) and its corollary (profit = revenuesexpenses) to the public sector. An exception may be local governments. These are municipal corporations chartered by the state to perform certain public services, which in many cases are private goods (for example water) or only quasipublic goods (for example elementary education). These entities have clear origins, and own identifiable assets and liabilities. Unfortunately, the assets and liabilities of the national government of a sovereign state are difficult to identify and harder still to measure in financial terms. With regard to assets, except in rare instances (such as the United States' purchase of Louisiana from France, or Alaska from Russia), few nations acquire new territories through buy-and-sell transactions. Most occupy their ancestral lands and some acquired their territories through military conquests or colonization. Historical costs, even if data are available, are not meaningful, yet market prices, even ifjustifiable. are hard to come by. The same problems arise in the case of natural resources and heritage assets. On the liability side, it is not easy to draw the line between a national government's contractual or legal obligations and its political

commitments and social responsibilities for the general welfare. In contrast to corporations' limited liabilities, governments in a democracy are prone to expand their responsibilities, resulting in larger budgets and frequent deficits (Buchanan and Wagner, 1977).

Accounting principles allow a business, whether private or state-owned, to recognize revenues only to the extent of goods or services provided. Governments uniquely provide public goods and finance them through taxation. Public goods are consumed collectively, and non-payers cannot be excluded—hence requiring tax financing. These characteristics sever the link between service delivery and revenue recognition, making it impossible to match revenues and expenses (Sunder, 1997). This accounting problem is also exacerbated by the involuntary nature of many transactions between government and people. The government's operating statement tracks resource flows, and only incidentally measures the government's service efforts and accomplishments. These unique characteristics of government are the primary source of the differences between government and commercial accounting. These differences, argues Sunder (1997, p. 198), 'do not constitute prima facie evidence that the former are defective and should be altered to conform to the latter'. More specifically, Nobes (1988, p. 198) challenged the assertion that 'Anglo-Saxon commercial accounting involving accrualsbased annual financial statements is necessary for accountability, control and

526

decision-making relating to government'. From the research perspective, theories underlying government accounting standards are mostly normative, in contrast to the development of positive theory in (business) financial accounting. The latter (Watts, 1977; Watts and Zimmerman, 1978, 1990) draws its inspiration from the contract-cost theory of the firm originating from Coase (1937). A similar incipient conceptual revolution started tentatively with Zimmerman's (1977) paper linking government financial reporting to political incentives. It is time to resume the search for a positive theory of government accounting standards. One way would be to build on the work of Chester Barnard and Herbert Simon.

At about the same time Goase wrote his famous paper explaining the existence of the firm in terms of transaction costs, Barnard (1938) identified the functions of the executive as securing the co-operation of the stakeholders of an organization. Barnard's work is currently enjoying a revival, primarily through the efforts of Oliver Williamson (1990). Much earlier, Simon (1945) applied Barnard's insight to government in his hook Administrative Behavior. In Simon's view, an organization is in equilibrium if Barnard's executive succeeds in securing the contributions of stakeholders by offering them adequate inducements to stay in the organizational coalition. A business can be viewed in the same way (Gohen and Gyert, 1965). In both types of organization, the challenge for managers is to negotiate satisfactory terms of contracts to keep the coalition intact. In such a theory, owners are important as contributors of equity capital, but they are not the only group managers try to please. In other words, the owner-centred theory of the firm and the single-principal agency theory are a special case of the Barnard- Simon organization theory.

This theory can be used to identify potential users of government's financial information by postulating that they use the information to predict their inducements from government (Ghan, 1981). Recently, Sunder (1997) applied contract-cost theory to explain and justify the differences betw-een accounting for government and nonprofit organizations and business accounting. Much more research is needed before the multiple-stakeholder perspective can have an impact on standards. In the meantime, government accounting has shifted closer to the business (financial) accounting model.

Internal Auditing

The Internal Auditing Act 1962 (RA 3456) introduced internal auditing requirements to the national government. A 1965 amendment (RA 4177) extended the Act's coverage to government-owned and controlled corporations (GOCCs) and local government units (LGUs). In 1992, President Aquino directed that government internal-control systems be strengthened (AO 278) – the Association of Government Internal Audi- tors (AGIA), among others, was instructed to ensure that internal audit practices, methods, and procedures be improved through continuing education and be conducted in accordance with internal auditing standards.

192 The AGIA represents internal auditors in government and promotes their professional development. It had 1,177 members at January 1999.

Public Financial Management Reform Program

The objectives of the Government's public financial management reforms are to (i) allocate and manage expenditures via a Medium Term Expenditure Framework (MTEF); (ii) strengthen feedback mechanisms for budget formulation through enhanced budget and performance monitoring; (iii) improve the performance management environment by simplifying budgeting rules; (iv) introduce incentives for better performance management; and (v) increase management flexibility to ensure performance results.197 The reforms are based on a benchmarking study of the Philippine expenditure management system vis-à-vis its neighboring countries (Australia, Korea, Malaysia, New Zealand,

527

Singapore, and Thailand) in terms of the three important expenditure outcomes: maintaining fiscal discipline, facilitating strategic prioritization at the oversight level, and enhancing the implementation efficiency of line agencies.198 The reform program comprises several activities as follows: 199 • Sectoral budget ceilings. Six-year sectoral budget ceilings were introduced for the Fiscal 2000 budget. These sectoral budgets were developed with the multi-sector Planning Committees of the National Economic and Development Authority (NEDA). These Committees include representatives from Congress, local government, academia, the private sector and nongovernment organizations. The process involved various government implementing agencies in a participative and proactive manner. Three-year budget baselines. The 6-year sectoral ceilings served as the basis for allocating resources to implementing agencies using a budget baseline approach. • Strengthening evaluation mechanisms. First, locally funded projects will be subjected to the same approval process that applies to those funded from foreign sources. Second, the performance measurement will be mainstreamed. A set of performance indicators will have to accompany all new policies or projects that are submitted to NEDA or DBM. The ultimate objective is to foster an evaluation culture.

•   Improving government accounting and internal control. Adopting private sector accounting and reporting practices, such as full accrual accounting will enhance the usefulness of accounting information. It will also enable organizational outputs to be meaningfully costed.

•   Separating accounting and auditing functions. COA, the Philippines' supreme audit institution, undertakes accounting, internal control and auditing functions in government. These groupings are incongruous.

•   Improving procurement procedures. The DBM has launched the Electronic Procurement System to improve the efficiency and transparency of the government procurement process.200

Issue Synopsis: Government Budgeting and Accounting

Chapter VIII – Issues and Recommendations – identifies and describes constraints and proposes corrective actions. With minor departures, these include the following selected issues that have already been identified by the UNDP-sponsored studies:

•   The Commission on Audit is responsible for promulgating accounting and auditing rules. These responsibilities are defined in Article IX of the Constitution 1987. The coexistence of these responsibilities is inconsistent with the concept of auditor independence.

•   The absence of computerized accounting information systems, combined with complex accounting regulations (i) relegates the role of most government CPAs to that of highly qualified bookkeepers.
Little time is left for value-added activities, such as financial analysis; and (ii) means that financial reports are rarely prepared in time to be useful for decision-making purposes.

•   There is no consistent set of accounting standards for budgeting and reporting. Major reporting differences result.

•   Auditors spend the majority of their time on compliance auditing (checking transactions). Minimal time is spent on financial attest auditing as more effort is applied to value-for-money audits.

•   Comparatively attractive starting salaries attract high-quality personnel into government accounting. A flat earnings structure means that higher-level salaries are far from competitive. This creates retention problems and provides a supportive environment for graft and corruption.

Summary and Proposals

Over the past 25 years, there have been some notable institutional and conceptual innovations in government accounting, contributing to its greater visibility and influence. Its emphasis has shifted from bureaucratic control to accountability reporting to the public. In some countries, government

528

accounting standards are no longer set by government officials, but by relatively independent boards. While acknowledging the importance of cash the lifeblood in government as in business contemporary accounting standards aim at tracking the long-term consequences of decisions and actions. Government officials are held accountable for their stewardship of both

financial and capital assets. Finally, it is not enough to keep the books accurately; the books have to be open to the public. When the public does not have the time or ability to inspect the accounts, governments have to make the task easier by preparing comprehensible as well as comprehensive financial statements.

Many challenges remain, especially at the global and international level. A major issue is the proper balance between international norms and domestic practices arising from national political ideology, economic system and culture. As a mechanism of governance, government accounting is subject to political forces that distribute power, and economic forces that determine the supply of and demand for resources. Therefore, unless accounting standards boards ally themselves with the institutions that can withhold something of value to a government a grant, a loan, an unqualified audit opinion, a favourable bond rating their pronouncements would remain

ineffectual. Unfortunately, at the international level, there are relatively few levers available to a body such as the IFAC Public Sector Committee to enforce its standards. However, accountants could make the case that fiscal accountability is an international norm applicable to all governments regardless of their political and economic system. Once this transcendent value of fiscal accountability is embraced, it is a technical matter to work out the means of implementation. These include not only yearend financial statements the current focus of IPSASs—but also budgets, internal controls and external audits. 1 urge the IFAC Public

Sector Committee to rectify its neglect of the budget and to include 'actual versus budget' comparisons in financial statements. Furthermore, putting aside differences of opinions on accounting choices, the entire body of detailed standards should be framed by a set of broader principles aimed at promoting government fiscal accountability, such as:

•The objectives of government accounting are to safeguard the public treasury and pr()pert\, to accurately measure and communicate the government's fmancial condition so as to demonstrate financial accountability, and to facilitate decisionmaking. •Agovernment should prepare and publish its budgets, maintain complete financial records, provide full financial disclosure, and subject itself to independent audits.

•The form and content of financial reports should be guided by the rights and need to know of intended users.

•The accounting system should measure the cash and other financial consequences of past transactions and events, including, but not limited to, budget execution.

•The accounting system should be capable of keeping track of the levels and changes in assets, liabilities, revenues and expenditures or expenses, relative to budgeted amounts. These principles do not prescribe accounting choices. Rather, they provide a foundation for deliberating and setting government accounting standards.

Generally, accounting standards take on a greater social role as accountability requirements in countries that require higher standards of ethical behaviour. Government accounting standards in effect become government accountability standards. (Recently the U.S. General Accounting Office was renamed Government Accountability Office.). Government must answer for the resources or authority it receives from others in the society and economy. Government provides both public goods and private goods, in return for the authority to govern, as well as economic and financial resources, Government accountability requirements are expressed as the terms in the political contracts, social contracts, and economic contracts that government enters into with its stakeholders (see Exhibit 2).

529

The asset-liability perspective of accrual accounting described in Exhibit 1 is compatible with this contract theory of government: the government's assets come from the stakeholders' voluntary and involuntary contributions, and its liabilities originate from providing incentives to the stakeholders. In conclusion, fundamental to the development of accrual accounting in developing countries is the ability to identify and measure the government's assets and liabilities. Corruption tends to result in the understatement of government's assets or the overstatement of government's liabilities. Unless financial integrity is assured, the credibility of government's financial information suffers. Thus both financial integrity assurance and accurate accrual accounting are accountants' professional contribution to developing countries.

References

Allen, R. and Tommasi, D. (2001), Managing Public Expenditure: A Reference Book for Transition Countries, OECD, Paris.

Bourmistrov, A. and Mellemvik, F. (2000) «Russian Local Government Accounting: New Norms and New Problems», in Caperchione E. and Mussari, R. eds., Comparative Issues in Local Government Accounting, Kluwer Academic Publishers, Boston, pp. 159- 174.

Bourmistrov, A. and Mellemvik, F. (2001), «Accounting and Democratic Governance: A Comparative Study of One Norwegian and One Russian County», in Bac, A. ed. International Comparative Issues in Government Accounting, Kluwer Academic Publishers, Dordrecht, The Netherlands, pp. 91-122.

Chan, J.L., Jones, R.H. and Lüder, K.G. (1996), «Modeling Government Innovations: An Assessment and Future Research Directions», Research in Governmental and Nonprofit Accounting, Vol. 9, pp. 1-19.

Chan, J.L. (2000), «A Sino-American Comparison of Budget and Accounting Coverage», in Caperchione, E. and Mussari, R., eds., Comparative Issues in Local Government Accounting, Kluwer Academic Publishers, Boston, pp. 11-34.

Chan, J.L., Cong, S.H. and Zhao, J.Y. (2001), «The Effects of Reform on China's Public budgeting and Accounting System», in Bac, A., ed. International Comparative Issues in Government Accounting, Kluwer Academic Publishers, Dordrecht, The Netherlands, pp. 297-314.

Chu, K-Y, and Hemming, R. (1991), «Public Expenditure Handbook: A Guide to Public Policy Issues in Developing Countries», International Monetary Fund, Washington, D.C. Coombs, Hugh M. and Mohamad Tayib, (2000), «Financial Reporting Practice: A Comparative Study of Local Authority Financial Reports Between the UK and 12 Malaysia», in Caperchione, E. and Mussari, M. eds., Comparative Issues in Local Government Accounting, Kluwer Academic Publishers, Boston,, pp. 53-68.

Deutsch, K.W. (1966), The Nerves of Government: Models of Political Communication and Control, The Free Press, New York.

Godfrey, A.D., Devlin, P.J. and Merrouche, C., (1996), «Governmental Accounting in Kenya, Tanzania and Uganda» in Chan, J.L., ed., Research in Governmental and Nonprofit Accounting, Vol. 9, JAI Press, Greenwich, Connecticut, pp. 193-208.

Godfrey, A.D., Merrouche, C. and Devlin, P.J. (1999), «A Comparative Analysis of the Evolution of Local Governmental Accounting in Algeria and Morocco,» in Copley, P.A. and Sanders, G.D., eds. Research in Governmental and Nonprofit Accounting, Vol. 10, JAI Press, Greenwich, Connecticut, pp. 201-234.

Grindle, Merilee S. (2000), «Ready or Not: The Developing World and Globalization,» in Nye, J.S. and Donahue, J.D., eds. Governance in a Globalizing World, Brookings Institution Press, ashington, D.C., pp. 178-207.

Hopwood, A. and Miller, P., eds. (1994), Accounting as a Social and Organizational Practice, Cambridge University Press, Cambridge.

International Federation of Accountants (IFAC) (1996), «Responding to an Increasing Demand for Accountability in the Public Sector,» IFAC Quarterly, October.

IFAC (2003), Handbook on International Public Sector Accounting Standards. IFAC, New York.

IFAC, International Public Sector Accounting Standards Board (2005), Exposure Draft 24, Financial Reporting Under the Cash Basis of Accounting – Disclosure Requirements for Recipients of External Assistance, IF AC, New York.

IFAC, International Public Sector Accounting Standards Board (2005), «Background and Update,» unpublished paper, March.

IFAC, Public Sector Committee (2000), Study 11, Government Financial Reporting: Accounting Issues and Practices. IFAC, New York, May.

Jaruga, A. (1988), «Governmental Accounting, Auditing and Financial Reporting in East European Countries,» in Chan, J.L. and Jones, R.H. eds., Governmental Accounting and Auditing: International Comparisons, Routledge, London, pp. 105-121. Keefer, P. and Khemani, S. (2004), «Democracy, Public Expenditure and the Poor,» World Bank Research Observer. World Bank, Washington, D.C.

Nowak, W.A. and Bakalarska, B. (2001), «Polish Public Sector Accounting in Transition: The Landscape after 1999 Step in the State Redefining,» in Bac, A. ed., International Comparative Issues in Government Accounting, Kluwer Academic Publishers, Dordrecht, The Netherlands, pp. 265-278.

Ouda, Hassan A.G. (2001), «Central Governmental Accounting of Egypt and the Netherlands: Similarities and Differences,» in Bac, A. ed., International Comparative Issues in Government Accounting, Kluwer Academic Publishers, Dordrecht, The Netherlands, pp. 71-90.

Rose-Ackerman, S. (1999), Corruption and Government: Causes, Consequences and Reform, Cambridge University Press, Cambridge.

Reuters (2003), «World Bank urges crackdown on government corruption», December 10.

Sachs, J.D. (2005), The End of Poverty: Economic Possibilities for Our Time, Penguin Books, New York.

Schiavo-Campo, S. and Tommasi, D. (1999), Managing Government Expenditure, Asian Development Bank, Manila.

Simon, H.A. (1954), Centralization vs. Decentralization in Organizing the Controller's Department, Controllership Foundation, New York.

Sutcliffe, P. (2003), «The Standards Programme of IFAC's Public Sector Committee,» Public Money and Management, January, pp. 11-12.

World Bank (1998), Public Expenditure Management Handbook, World Bank, Washington, D.C.

ENTREPRENEURSHIP, RELIGION, AND BUSINESS ETHICS

Mostafa Emami
Department Of Accounting , Tarbiat Modares University ,Iran.
Mostafa.Emami@Modares.a c.ir

Kamran Nazari
Department of Business Management, Payam Noor University, Kermanshah, Iran
kamranno57@yahoo.com

ABSTRACT

Interest in entrepreneurship has heightened in recent years, especially in business schools. Much of this interest is driven by student demand for courses in entrepreneurship, either because of genuine interest in the subject, or because students see entrepreneurship education as a useful hedge given uncertain corporate careers This paper reports a study of the importance of religious faith to entrepreneurs and the relationship of that faith to their ethical judgments. The importance of religious faith to entrepreneurs was similar to the importance of religious faith to other business respondents. Literature offers numerous definitions of ethics.Crane and Matten (2004, p.8) define business ethics as "the study of business situations, activities, and ecisions where issues of right and wrong are dressed". Based on Jones's definition of ethical decisions (Jones, 1991, cited in Chau and Siu, 2000) ,Entrepreneurs who identified religious interests as being of high importance, and also entrepreneurs who were highly orthodox in their faith, expressed more sensitive ethical judgments on at least five of sixteen ethical issues than did entrepreneurs who indicated that religious interests were of low or no importance.

Keywords: *Entrepreneurship, Religion, Business, Ethics, Society*

INTRODUCTION

In recent years, the reputation of business has been seriously damaged by a range of financial scandals. Virtually all countries have had their Enron (Elliot and Schroth, 2002), Parmalat, Ahold, Vivendi, Lernout and Hauspie or MCI-Worldcom. We have seen cases with false accounts, manipulation of information, questionable initial public offerings, corruption of public agents, personal enrichment of top managers (Buelens, 2002, p. 15; Byrne et al., 2002). Many of these cases have led to bankruptcy, personnel being dismissed and financial losses for the individual investors. A common feature is unethical behavior by high-level managers and entrepreneurs, and also by professionals – accountants, lawyers, bankers – following conflicts of interests (Hamilton, 2002).

The ethical content of business behavior has for some time been a matter of public concern. Coupled with the growth of interest in entrepreneurship, the ethics of entrepreneurial behavior becomes subject to the same type of scrutiny. Also, religious commitment has traditionally been thought to be related to the level of morality in personal and public life. In this paper, we examine the ethical attitudes of a group of entrepreneurs, looking specifically for significant differences between those entrepreneurs who describe themselves as more religious and those who consider themselves less religious in their personal lives. We also consider the possible effect of religious orthodoxy on the ethical attitudes of entrepreneurs.

During the past several decades, the significant and growing scholarly interest in entrepreneurs and new venture creation has resulted in the shaping of entrepreneurship as a rigorous academic field of study, including the creation of several dedicated scholarly journals, modification of business school curricula, and rise of entrepreneurship-specific research conferences. In a similar manner, the field of business ethics – including the study of both the ethical behavior and societal impact of profit-seeking firms – has during the last twenty years also achieved recognition and legitimacy as a rigorous and important field of study. Yet the intersection of entrepreneurship and ethics, though receiving more recent research attention, remains relatively embryonic.

ENTREPRENEURSHIP

Interest in entrepreneurship as a phenomenon rests in the perceived contributions entrepreneurs make to public policy goals such as economic growth, increased productivity, job creation, technological innovation, deregulation and privatisation, and structural adjustments or realignments (Gibb 1996; Shane 1996). Although the effects of entrepreneurship are rarely contested, a common observation about the

J. Basic. Appl. Sci. Res., 2(1)685-689, 2012

ISSN 2090-4304
Journal of Basic and Applied

© 2012, TextRoad Publication

Scientific Research *www.textroad.com*

Application of Fuzzy TOPSIS Technique for Strategic Management Decision

Mostafa Emami [a*]**, Kamran Nazari** [b]**, Haniyeh**

Fardmanesh [c] [a]

Department Of Accounting , Tarbiat Modares University ,Iran. [b]

Payam-noor University, Iran

[c] Department of Management, University of Tehran, Tehran, Iran

ABSTRACT

MCDM (Multi Criteria Decision Making) Fuzzy TOPSIS such as is concerned with structuring and solving decision and planning problems involving multiple criteria. The purpose is to support decision makers facing such problems. Typically, there does not exist a unique optimal solution for such problems and it is necessary to use decision maker's preferences to differentiate between solutions. This paper discusses the use of MCDA for supporting strategic management. By considering the technical issues associated with the content of strategic decisions, and also the social aspects that characterize the processes within which they are created. This paper presents a fuzzy TOPSIS technique for strategy selection problem. By using TOPSIS technique we support strategy selection decisions. **KEY WORDS:** Multi-Criteria, Strategic management, Fuzzy, scenario planning.

1. INTRODUCTION

Multiple-criteria decision-making or multiple-criteria decision analysis is a sub-discipline of operations research that explicitly considers multiple criteria in decision-making environments. Whether in our daily lives or in professional settings, there are typically multiple conflicting criteria that need to be evaluated in making decisions. Cost or price is usually one of the main criteria. Some measure of quality is typically another criterion that is in conflict with the cost. Strategic management is a field that deals with the major intended and emergent initiatives taken by general managers on behalf of owners, involving utilization of resources, to enhance the performance of firms in their external environments. It entails specifying the organization's mission, vision and objectives, developing policies and plans, often in terms of projects and programs, which are designed to achieve these objectives, and then allocating resources to implement the policies and plans, projects and programs (Nag, Hambrick, and Chen, 2007). Most papers use multi-attribute value analysis, such as Phillips (1986) and Goodwin and Wright (2001). On a more theoretical level, Belton and Stewart (2002) discussed the potential use of MCDA and scenario planning. Stewart (Stewart, 1997; Stewart, 2005) presented several technical issues about this integration and provided a thoughtful discussion on how it could be made. Montibeller et al. (2006) suggested a framework for conducting a multi-attribute value analysis under multiple scenarios, in the same way as Belton and Stewart (2002), but with an emphasis on the robustness of strategies.

The popular view of strategic decisions is that they typically involve a high degree of uncertainty, high stakes, major resource implications, and long-term consequences (Johnson, Scholes and Whittington, 2005). This view is associated with the traditional conceptualization of strategic decisions as the product of intentional attempts at rational choice, and context-setters for subsequent strategic action (Schwenk, 1995).

Notwithstanding the above criticisms, we believe like others (Laroche, 1995) that the view and quest of intentional decision making is an undeniable aspect of organizational life. In our experience, managers act in accordance to the belief that strategic decisions must be intentional acts and the result of a well-designed rational process. Indeed that is the main reason that they look for our help as decision analysts. There is, therefore, a clear role for Decision Analysis in these contexts, to support strategic decision making.

2. MATERIALS AND METHODS

2.1. Nature of decision in strategic management

The research data corroborate this view, demonstrating that firms with high performance in profitability, growth, and marketplace reputation have superior (that is, fast, high-quality, and widely supported) strategic decision-making processes. These processes support the emergence of effective strategy. Firms that were more modest performers had strategic decision-making processes that were slower and more political. Their strategies were more predictable and less effective. Executives in these firms often recognized that their strategic decision making was flawed, but they did not know how to fix it.

Will Mulcaster argues that while much research and creative thought has been devoted to generating alternative strategies, too little work has been done on what influences the quality of strategic decision making

---

*Corresponding Author: Mostafa Emami, Tarbiat Modares University,Tehran, Iran P.O BO:1767778151 . Tel:989127001816-18162370018E- mail: Mostafa.Emami@Modares.ac.ir

and the effectiveness with which strategies are implemented. For instance, in retrospect it can be seen that the financial crisis of 2008–9 could have been avoided if the banks had paid more attention to the risks associated with their investments, but how should banks change the way they make decisions to improve the quality of their decisions in the future? Mulcaster's Managing Forces framework addresses this issue by identifying forces that should be incorporated into the processes of decision making and strategic implementation. The forces are: Time; Opposing forces; Politics; Perception; Holistic effects; Adding value; Incentives; Learning capabilities; Opportunity cost; Risk; Style—which can be remembered by using the mnemonic 'TOPHAILORS'.

2.2. Using of MCDM for decision making process

Since the 1980s scenario planning has been suggested as an alternative way of considering uncertainty in strategic decisions, instead of traditional forecasting. The main idea is to construct a small set of possible future scenarios that describe how the main uncertainties surrounding the problem would behave (e.g., interest rates, prices of commodities, demographic trends). Each scenario presents a coherent story that may happen in the future and is used to explore how different strategies would perform under such circumstances (Schoemaker, 1993, Van der Heijden, 2004, Schoemaker, 1995). Once scenarios are ready and strategies are devised, a table can be built, which describes qualitatively the outcomes of each strategy under each scenario.

Scenario planning has been widely employed in practice and seems to be a tool which managers are comfortable to work with (Schoemaker, 1993, Van der Heijden, 2004). Scenario planning has proved to be a powerful tool to increase awareness about future uncertainties and enhance creativity in thinking about possible strategies. However, the literature on scenario planning is limited in discussing how to identify/design highquality strategies from a scenario analysis. Even more, the scenario planning literature does not acknowledge the need to evaluate these strategies against multiple organisational objectives, despite ample evidence of multiple objectives in strategic decision making (Eisenhardt, K.M and Zbaracki, 2005). The fact that strategic decisions involve invariably multiple strategic objectives, suggests the adoption of MCDA as the evaluation tool for strategic choices.

The popularity and advantages of scenario planning, combined with the power of evaluation of MCDA, provides a potent set of decision-support tools for strategic decisions (Montibeller and Belton, 2006). Indeed, since the 1980s there are suggestions of considering the use of MCDA with scenario planning.

Let a set of n strategic options be: $= \{ , , ... , \}$. There are m criteria: , ,... each k-th criterion measures the achievement of one strategic objective of the organization. There is a set of n scenarios

, , ... , . A model is built for each s-th scenario, which provides the overall evaluation of the i-th alternative under the scenario:

$$= \quad (\quad)$$

686

Where w is the weight of the k-th criterion under the s-th scenario and v is the value of the i-th alternative on the k-th criterion. Notice that this model allows different weights for distinct scenarios, in order to reflect different future priorities.

One important change that an organization may experience, when using MCDA for strategic with its strategic objectives and also in better scoping the strategic choices it is considering (Barcus and Montibeller, 2008).

Since evaluation of strategy is a thinking human based evaluation, in this paper, we use a fuzzy approach in MCDM model. One of the most important models in MCDM methods is TOPSIS. In this research, a TOPSISbased model is used to obtain appropriateness of given strategy in from of fuzzy logic for each scenario.

In this model, desirability of a strategy in fuzzy from is given such that in different profiles, the right and left distance of any fuzzy number from ideal value (best) and non ideal value (worst) are measured. This is the standard measuring of desirability of a strategy. Following steps are designed to obtain desirability of strategy, using TOPSIS method:

1. Multiplying the fuzzy numbers weight of criteria (w_i) by value of criteria for each strategy (r_{ij}) according to table 2:

$$N_{ij} \square R_{ij} \square W_i$$

Where N_{ij} is a triangular fuzzy number like this:

$$N_{ij} \square (\square_{ij}, r_{ij}, \square_{ij}) \square (\square_i, y_i, \square_i) \square$$

$$(\square_{ij}.y_i \square r_{ij}.\square_i, r_{ij}.y_i, \square_{ij}.y_i \square r_{ij}.\square_i)$$

2. Choosing the profile of $\square_0$.

3. Calculating following real numbers for each project and then producing matrix of $L_\square$ and $R_\square$:

$$x_{ij\square} \square \min\{x_{ij} \square R\square_{Nij}(x_{ij}) \square \square_0\}$$

$$x_{ij\square} \square \max\{x_{ij} \square R\square_{Nij}(x_{ij}) \square \square_0\}$$

J. Basic. Appl. Sci. Res., 2(1)685-689, 2012

The resulted matrix from $x_{ij}{}^\square$ is called $L_\square$ (meeting point of profile $\square_0$ with left side equation of fuzzy number).

The resulted matrix from $x_{ij}{}^\square$ is called $R_\square$ (meeting point of profile $\square_0$ whit right side equation of fuzzy number).

Ideal solution and non ideal one for matrixes of $L_\square$ and $R_\square$ due to n strategy (j=1,2,........n), m criterion (i=1,2,..........m), is defined as follows: Ideal solution for $L_\square$:

$$A_{L^\square_\square} \square \{(\max_j x_{ij}{}^\square) \big| j \square 1,2,...,n\} \square$$

$$\{x_{1\square\square}, x_{2\square\square}, x_{1\square\square},...,x_{n\square\square}\} \text{ Non ideal}$$

solution for $L_\square$:

$$A_{L^\square_\square} \square \{(\min_j x_{ij}{}^\square) \big| j \square 1,2,...,n\} \square$$

$\{x_{1\square\square}, x_{2\square\square}, x_{1\square\square},...,x_{n\square\square}\}$ Ideal solution

for $R_{\square}$:

$$A_R{}^{\square}{}_{\square} \square \{(\max_j x_{ij}{}^{\square})\big| j \,\square\, 1, 2,...,n\} \,\square$$

$\{x_{1\square\square}, x_{2\square\square}, x_{1\square\square},...,x_{n\square\square}\}$ Non ideal

solution for $R_{\square}$:

$$A_R{}^{\square}{}_{\square} \square \{(\min_j x_{ij}{}^{\square})\big| j \,\square\, 1,2,...,n\} \,\square$$

$\{x_{1\square\square}, x_{2\square\square}, x_{1\square\square},...,x_{n\square\square}\}$

4. Calculation the distance of the strategies of each matrix from it ideal or non ideal solution is done using following equations:

The distance of strategy (j) of $L_{\square}$ from ideal solution

$$dL_{\square j} \,\square\square\square \square_{\square\; i\square1} (x_{ij\square} \,\square\, x_{i\square\square})_2 \square\square \,,\, j \,\square\, 1,2,...,n$$

The distance of strategy (j) of $L_{\square}$ from non ideal solution:

$$dL_j \,\square\square \square_{\square\; i\square1}{}^{\square\; m} (x_{ij} \,\square\, x_i) {}_2{}^{\square} \,\square \,,\, j \,\square\, 1,2,...,n$$

The distance of strategy (j) of $R_{\square}$ from ideal solution:

$$dR_{\square j} \,\square\; \square\square \square_{\square\; i\square1}{}^{m} (x_{ij\square} \,\square\, x_{i\square\square})_2 \square\square \,,\, j \,\square\, 1,2,...,n$$

The distance of strategy (j) of $R_{\square}$ from non ideal solution:

$$dR_{\square j} \,\square\square\square \square_{\square\; i\square1}{}^{m} (x_{ij\square} \,\square\, x_{i\square\square})_2 \square\square \,,\, j \,\square\, 1,2,...,n$$

5. Calculation of strategy (j) relative closeness to ideal solution of $L_{\square}$ and $R_{\square}$ by using following equations:

$$C * L_j \square \frac{dL_{\square j}}{dL_j \,\square\, dL_j} \square \,\square \quad j \,\square\, 1,2,...,n$$

$$C * R_j \square \frac{dR_{\square j}}{dR_j \,\square\, dR_j} \square \qquad \square \quad j \,\square\, 1,2,...,n$$

6. Fuzzy desirability U_j in $\square_0$ profile is defined as follows:

$$U_j \square \{(C * L_j, \square_0), (C * R_j, \square_0)\} , \text{ if}$$

$$C * L_j \square C * R_j$$

$$U_j \square \{(C * R_j, \square_0), (C * L_j, \square_0)\} , \text{ if}$$

688

$$C * L_j \square C * R_j$$

In other words, right and left side value of fuzzy desirability U_j is obtained using $C*L_j$ and $C*R_j$.

In TOPSIS model, the priority depends on relative closeness of each choice to ideal solution. That is why the sixth step equation is used.

Since in our proposed method, left and right distances of any fuzzy number from ideal and non ideal solutions are used to measure desirability strategies, and then the above equations are used as left and right sides of ideal fuzzy solution.

By creating various profiles and repeating the step (2-6), desirability fuzzy solution for all strategies is produced.

3. RESULTS AND DISCUSSION

Most of the MCDA applications reported in the literature assess single-point outcomes, which try to represent the performance of an option if it were implemented. Particularly in strategic decision-making, however, considering long-term consequences is relevant and, many times, crucial. One relatively simple way of considering long-term consequences in these cases is by applying time discounting, as in net present value (NPV) analysis. This can be used for assessing the strategy's performance under each criterion, for example the NPV for profit (French, Bedford, and Atherton, 2005; Barcus and Montibeller, 2008). A key challenge of NPV analysis is always to define a suitable discount rate. In private companies this may be relatively straightforward, as it is linked with the cost of capital. However, the same cannot be said about public decisions, where the level of discounting is debatable – a large rate can make costs in the long-term future negligible and favor shorttermism (Santos, Belton and Howick, 2002).

Another avenue is the use of system dynamics models to simulate multiple long-term responses of a system, given some policy as input. These responses can then be employed to assess the policy's performances in a MCDA model.

4. Conclusion

Since MCDA has been less employed than it is expected for supporting strategic decision making in strategic management. This seems somehow contradictory, as dealing with multiple and conflicting strategic objectives is a crucial issue for making strategic decisions. For addressing this problem, this paper presented a new approach for using of MCDA in strategic management. In particular, we advocated the use of scenario planning to consider uncertainties, associated with an appraisal of robustness of strategic options against different scenarios. Therefore, the evaluation and selection of strategy for strategy management is customarily done using, technical and financial information. In this article, Authors proposed a new methodology to provide a simple approach to assess alternative strategy and help decision maker to select the best one. By using TOPSIS technique we support strategy selection decisions. Also this article applied improved TOPSIS to make comparison more intuitionitic and reduce or eliminate assessment.

REFERENCES

Belton, V. and Stewart, T., 2002. Multiple Criteria Decision Analysis: An Integrated Approach. Kluwer: Dordrecht.

Barcus, A. and Montibeller, G. 2008. Supporting the Allocation of Software Development Work in Distributed Teams with Multi-criteria Decision Analysis. OMEGA, 36: 464-475.

French, S., Bedford, T. and Atherton, E. 2005 Supporting ALAEP decision maing lby cost benefit analysis and multi-attribute utility theory. Journal of Risk Research, 8(3): 207-223.

Goodwin, P. and Wright, G., 2001. Enhancing Strategy Evaluation in Scenario Planning: A Role for Decision Analysis, Journal of Management Studies, 38:1-16.

Laroche, H. 1995. From Decision to Action in Organizations: a social representation perspective. Organization Science, 6: 62-75.

Mintzberg, H. 1987. 5 Ps for Strategy, California Management Review, 30(1): 11-24.

Mintzberg, H., & Waters, J. A. 1990. Does Decision get in the way? Organization Studies, 11:1-6.

Montibeller, G., Belton, V. 2006. Causal Maps and the Evaluation of Decision Options – A review. Journal of the Operational Research Society, 57(7): 779-771.

Montibeller, G., Belton, V., 2006. Causal Maps and the Evaluation of Decision Options – A review. Journal of the Operational Research Society, 57(7): 779-771

Nag, R.; Hambrick, D. C. and Chen, M.-J, 2007. What is strategic management, really? Inductive derivation of a consensus definition of the field. Strategic Management Journal. 28(9):935–95.

Johnson, G., Scholes, K., and Whittington, R. 2005. Exploring Corporate Strategy: text and cases (7th ed). London: Prentice Hall.

Phillips, L. D., 1986. Decision Analysis and its Application in the Industry. In: Mitra, G. (ed.) Computer Assisted Decision Making, 189-197.

Pennings (Ed.), Organizational Strategy and Change. Jossey Bass, San Francisco.

Starbuck, W. H. 1985. Acting First and Thinking Later: theory versus reality in strategic change. In J. M.

Santos S., V., Belton, and S., Howick, 2002. Adding Value to Performance Measurement by Using System Dynamics and Multicriteria Analysis. Int. J. of Operations and Production Management, 22(11): 12461272.

Schwenk, C. R. 1995. Strategic Decision Making. Journal of Management Studies, 21(3): 471-493.

Schoemaker, P.J.H. 1993. Multiple Scenario Development: Its conceptual and behavioral foundation, Strategic *Management Journal,* 14(3): 193 - 213

Schoemaker, P.J.H. 1995. Scenario Planning: A tool for strategic thinking. *Sloan Management Review*, 36(2): 25-40.

Stewart, T.J., 1997. Scenario analysis and multicriteria decision making. In: Climaco, J. (Ed.) Multicriteria Analysis, Springer, Berlin, pp. 519-528.

Stewart, T.J. 2005. Dealing with uncertainties in MCDA. In: Figueira, J., Greco, S. and Ehrgott, M. (Eds.) Multiple Criteria Decision Analysis – State of the Art Surveys, Springer, New York, pp. 445-470.

Van der Heijden, K. 2004. Scenarios: The Art of Strategic Conversation (2nd ed.). Wiley, Chichester.

Eisenhardt, K.M and Zbaracki, 2005, M.J. Strategic Decision Making. Strategic Management Journal, Vol. 13(S2): 17-37.

field of entrepreneurship research is that it lacks consensus about its object of study (Cornelius et al. 2006; Schildt et al. 2006). Bull and Willard lamented that "the term has been used for more than two centuries, but we continue to extend, reinterpret, and revise the definition" (1993: 185). It is worth exploring the conceptual legacy of entrepreneurship as an object of study, both to identify the essence of the construct and to provide perspective for contemporary understandings and possible future extensions.

For 250 years, attempts to define and explain entrepreneurship as a phenomenon have been widely based on functional arguments. Differing interpretations of entrepreneurship can be distinguished based on how two related questions are answered: (1) what unique function does the entrepreneur play in the economy, and (2) what unique characteristics of individuals enable them to perform this function?

A medieval French term originally referring simply to 'people who get things done,' the meaning of the term 'entrepreneur' evolved by the early 18th century to refer to business contractors. Richard Cantillon, a practicing businessman of dubious means turned reflective penman of economic treatises, is credited with first imbuing the term with a new and more significant meaning. In 1755 Cantillon used the term to identify those individuals in the economic system who accept risk to make a financial profit rather than depend on a regular salary for income. These 'entrepreneurs' were thereafter demarcated as distinct from the masses, being postulated as the driving force behind the seemingly perpetual motion of the economy's circular flow of money and goods (Pressman 1999). Thus was the first formal conception of the 'risk-taking entrepreneur' as the catalyst of economic production.

Since Cantillon, attributing the catalytic power of entrepreneurship to the entrepreneur's willingness to take on risk has been a persistent theme among entrepreneurship scholars (see Hébert and Link 1988). Although, as the concept of risk-taking was debated and refined by successive scholars, over time differences of opinion emerged (cf. Brockhaus 1980; Koh 1996; Miner 1997). In the early 20th century, Knight made the distinction between uncertainty that is measurable, which he termed 'risk,' and uncertainty that is not measurable, which he termed 'true uncertainty' (1921: 20). Risk, he contended, could simply be insured. It is therefore in the area of meeting the challenge of uncertainty that a space for the entrepreneur is made in the economic system. To Knight, the entrepreneur is a specialist in uncertainty bearing – someone uniquely capable and willing to take responsibility for controlling productive resources in an uncertain environment (1921: 244-55).

Subsequent interpretations of the concept can be viewed with reference to a general equilibrium model of the economy (Chiles et al. 2007). On one side are the ideas of Schumpeter, considered by many to be the grandfather of contemporary entrepreneurship theory, who positioned entrepreneurs as the causal agents responsible for creating disequilibrium in the economy (Schumpeter 1934; 1943).

Schumpeter vehemently opposed the idea of the entrepreneur as a risk taker. Instead, he conceptualised entrepreneurship as the act of carrying out new combinations of productive resources. Schumpeter insisted that "'everyone is an entrepreneur only when he actually 'carries out new combinations'" (1934: 78). Thus, he viewed the act of innovation as the defining characteristic of an entrepreneur, although he takes pains to make clear that an entrepreneur is not the same as a technological inventor. Schumpeter saw his definition as a permutation consistent with the classic definition of Jean-Baptiste Say, that "the entrepreneur's function is to combine the productive factors, to bring them together" (Schumpeter 1934: 76). Schumpeter's ideas spawned one of the most influential and lasting concepts in the study of entrepreneurship – that of the 'innovative entrepreneur' (e.g. Baumol 1993; Drucker 1985).

In direct contrast, Kirzner positioned entrepreneurs as the causal agents that move an economy back toward equilibrium. He argued that the defining act is that of 'opportunity discovery', and the unique characteristic of entrepreneurs is their attentiveness to opportunity. In this way, valuable opportunities arising from economic disequilibrium are recognised, and through the pursuit of these opportunities for profit, economic equilibrium is gradually restored (Kirzner 1973; 1997a; 1997b). Based on Kirzner's ideas, the concept of entrepreneurship as essentially the "processes of discovery, evaluation, and exploitation of opportunities" (Shane and Venkataraman 2000: 218) sits among risk-bearing and innovation as one of the most widely accepted definitions of the field.

ENTREPRENEURSHIP AND ETHICS

Max Weber's work, The Protestant Ethic and the Spirit of Capitalism has been an influential part of the sociology literature for just over 100 years where it remains both a powerful and controversial thesis (Swatos and Kaelber, 2005; Howard, 2005). While Weber is considered by most to be a sociologist, his prolific works in economics, specifically addressing questions related to the impact of religious values and culture on the advent and evolution of economic systems, places him at the confluence of the economics and sociology; a field that Weber described as "social economics" (Swedberg, 1999).

Entrepreneurs have long been recognized as being "a breed apart," in that some of their attitudes and motivations are thought to differ from those of the population at large. Successful entrepreneurs have a high propensity to make decisions on their own, to be action-oriented, to assume risk, and to persevere in the face of uncertainty and adversity. In a word, they tend to exhibit a high degree of individualism.

In an earlier study, the authors found that entrepreneurs differ from non-entrepreneurs in some of their attitudes toward ethical issues (3 pp.64-72). On certain issues, particularly those requiring individual courage, entrepreneurs exhibited a more stringent standard of ethical propriety. On other issues, particularly those which involved individual profiting at the expense of others, entrepreneurs adopted a less ethical stance than nonentrepreneurs. Furthermore, the study found that entrepreneurs were more likely to perceive moderate or extreme pressure to engage in unethical behavior.

Although the emergence of academic research connecting entrepreneurship and ethics is fairly recent, increased interest in the topic has produced a good deal of initial scholarship. In addition, there are certain foundational works in management that have direct bearing on the connection between ethics and entrepreneurship. Normative, descriptive, and prescriptive research (c.f. Dees & Starr, 1992) are all represented in this body of work. A synthetic understanding of the variety of theoretical and empirical work in this area offers fascinating insights into the way in which ethics and entrepreneurship are related, and the questions raised by thinking about this interconnectedness. In surveying the literature, the existing research connecting ethics and entrepreneurship tends to fall into one of three primary areas of inquiry: entrepreneurial ethics, social venturing, and entrepreneurship and society Much of the existing literature linking ethics and entrepreneurship is focused on entrepreneurial ethics at the micro level. Emphasis is on the entrepreneur, with an interest in ethical dilemmas that may be especially relevant to the new venture setting, although some work also looks at the organizational dynamics of new ventures, and the impact on ethical behavior at the firm level. This stream of research asks at least six key questions.

How do entrepreneurs differ from non-entrepreneurs with respect to ethics? One line of inquiry questions whether or not systematic trait differences between entrepreneurs and non-entrepreneurs carry over into corresponding systematic differences in ethical perception and action. While some research calls into question the existence of stable, systematic differences between entrepreneurs and non-entrepreneurs on dimensions such as risk tolerance (Xu & Ruef, 2004), Buchholz and Rosenthal (2005) argue that the qualities required for successful entrepreneurship – imagination, creativity, novelty, sensibility – are systematically and theoretically crucial to ethical decision-making, suggesting that ethics and entrepreneurship are closely aligned. Similarly, others (Dunham, McVea, & Freeman, 2008) argue that entrepreneurial success requires moral imagination, in addition to an effective handling of the strategic dimensions of starting a new venture. Some research indicates that entrepreneurs may indeed generally place a greater emphasis on ethical behavior (Bucar & Hisrich, 2001) and exhibit higher levels of moral reasoning (Teal & Carroll, 1999). Other research shows fairness – or procedural justice – to be an important element in managing the relationship between entrepreneurs and key investors, leading to a set of desirable outcomes for the entrepreneur (Sapienza & Korsgaard, 1996). Such a focus on ethics and fairness on the part of the entrepreneur may bring its own risks, however; others (Goel & Karri, 2006; Karri & Goel, 2008; Sarasvathy & Dew, 2008) have debated whether or not entrepreneurs tend to 'over-trust,' making them more vulnerable to others' opportunism.

On the other hand, other research finds that entrepreneurs possess a strong 'action bias' that may prevent them from adequately considering ethical issues (Bhide, 1996). Longenecker, McKinney, and Moore (1988; 1989a) suggest that entrepreneurs are more focused than large firm managers on personal financial gain, even if it comes at others' expense or violates norms of fairness. Although this effect has fluctuated over time (Longenecker et al., 2006), some scholars, like Kets de Vries (1985), caution about "specific negative factors that could permeate the personality of entrepreneurs and dominate their behavior" (Kuratko, 2007:5; see also Osborne, 1991). This 'dark side' of entrepreneurship - - specifically, the propensity of entrepreneurs to act as rule-breakers that push institutional boundaries - - is a theme explored empirically by Zhang and Arvey (this issue), who examine the longitudinal connection between adolescent nonconformity and entrepreneurial status in adulthood. The relationship between rule-breaking and entrepreneurship is also analyzed normatively by Brenkert (this issue), who explores the ethical tension represented by entrepreneurial rule-breaking.

This tension has been highlighted in the context of entrepreneurial activity in large organizations as well, where it can be difficult to tell the difference between corporate entrepreneurs and 'rogue' middle managers (Kuratko & Goldsby, 2004). At the organizational level of analysis itself, ethics and corporate entrepreneurship has also been explored by describing 'institutional entrepreneurship' that pursues social causes (Maguire, Hardy, & Lawrence, 2004). How do stakeholders influence corporate entrepreneurship (Kuratko, Hornsby, & Goldsby, 2007)? And when a firm's innovative behavior runs counter to established societal norms, is this an example of organizational misconduct, or "positive ethical deviance" (Hartman, Wilson, & Arnold, 2005:343; see also Warren, 2003)?

Small business owners tend to prioritize the interests of customers ahead of employees or stockholders (Vitell, Dickerson, & Festervand, 2000); they have also been shown to have differential approaches to community involvement, and these differing initiatives have heterogeneous effects on organizational performance (Besser & Miller, 2004). Furthermore, the "profit-maximization-for-shareholder-gain" objective commonly ascribed to large firms seems "inappropriate for the small business" (Spence, 2004:118), and smaller ventures tend to have a correspondingly supportive view of their competitors (Spence, Coles, & Harris, 2001). Future research in this area, therefore, could focus on the development of a 'stakeholder theory of entrepreneurship', specifically addressing the theoretical and practical challenges faced by entrepreneurs in balancing the claims of the stakeholders that are specific to – and commonplace in – new ventures. How do entrepreneurial stakeholders and their dynamic interactions qualitatively differ in character from the traditionally considered largecorporation stakeholders? How would a stakeholder theory of entrepreneurship account for the wide range of entrepreneurial stakeholder scenarios, from venture-backed IPO companies to small family firms?

We also strongly agree with the arguments made by Mintzberg et al. (2002, p. 67) that corporations have become too focused on the creation of short-term shareholder wealth and too greedy at the expense of the longterm interest of the corporation and its shareholders:

> "Greed has been raised to some sort of higher calling; corporations have been urged to ignore broader social responsibilities in favor of narrow shareholder value; chief executives have been regarded as if they alone create economic performance ... A syndrome of selfishness has taken hold of our corporations and our societies, as well as our minds" (Mintzberg et al., 2002, p. 67).

Greed, insatiable consumption, and self-serving behavior have become not only acceptable in society, but may be seen as a desirable trait in some segments of our society. Unrestricted greed is not what we or Cooke (1997) advocate. What Cooke (1997) clearly notes is that "greed", or the quest to obtain superior returns, is the motivating force for publicly held firms to innovate and engage in risky entrepreneurial initiatives. Publicly held corporations have a fiduciary duty to act on the behalf of their owners. To do otherwise is not moral. For example, Miles and White (1998), in an analysis of the social irresponsibility of Sirgy and Lee's (1996) quality of life approach to marketing (QOL), note that when firms adopt a QOL orientation, the firms' customers tend to pay a price premium, employees tend to earn less, investors tend to earn lower risk adjusted returns, fewer jobs tend to be created, and social welfare is often diminished. In general, publicly held corporations should not invest in projects without a probability of earning for their principals a market based, risk adjusted rate of return (even if an investment has great social benefits). In addition, one must be very careful when the corporation leaves its original purpose of generating 98 Morgan P. Miles et al.wealth and embarks on doing social "good". Freedman offers the following example: Take the corporate executive who says 'I have responsibilities over and above that of making a profit'. If he feels that he has such responsibilities, he is going to spend money in a way that is not in the interest of the shareholders. Where does he get that money?...What right does the executive have to spend his stockholders money? To spend his employees' money? Or his customers' money. Who gave him the right to decide how their money should be spent? If 'socially responsive' business executives would stop and think, they would recognize that in effect they are acting irresponsibly. Let me give you an example that has often impressed me. During the 1930's, German businessmen used some corporate money to support Hitler and the Nazis. Was this a proper exercise of social responsibility? (Friedman quoted in McClaughry, 1972, p. 5) In the case that is offered by Friedman, it is clear that not all stakeholders would agree that using corporate funds to support the Nazi movement was a social "good". This illustrates the major problem in advocating any corporate initiative as being socially responsible. The "virtue" of any corporate initiative is, like beauty, in the eye of the beholder and is based on social and cultural values. Individuals, not corporations, should be allowed to use the proceeds of their investments to support those initiatives as they see fit and not be forced to support social initiatives (such as the Nazi party) with which that they do not agree.

THE RISE OF UNETHICAL PRACTICES IN BUSINESS

We have observed that non-ethical behaviour occurs at all levels in business. Most cases, fortunately, do not have the magnitude of the scandals seen in the press, but they exist in a range of forms. Somewhat unfair attitudes are multiplying rapidly in business, especially when times are difficult.Adanger is that people do not even realise their behaviour is inappropriate. The fading away of norms has perfidious effects. Some managers even believe that certain 'dirty tricks' are good management practices: delaying payment to suppliers to improve the cash flow is seen as efficient, even if a different

Australian Journal of Business and Management Research   Vol.1 No.11 [59-69] | February-2012

agreement was made. Just-in-time management has led, in some cases, to the extreme situation that, in order to win the contract, a supplier will promise to deliver on time, knowing in advance that he cannot deliver, and that he will have to find an excuse or hope the customer's behaviour will justify the delay. An honest entrepreneur who admits that he cannot meet the extreme requests will have no chance of the contract and excludes himself from the competition. Another danger is the snowballing effect: if a supplier is not paid on time, he in turn is unable to pay his own suppliers. In some extreme cases, the only defence measure is to refuse to deliver, again a rather unethical practice, and in some cases approaching blackmail. Thus, unethical behaviour encourages and breeds other unethical practices in business.

This may lead to the simplistic conclusion that business is bad; and business cannot be ethical. Such a judgement is too easy, especially when coming from the protected position of the academic or ethicist. Business is not bad, it is just difficult – and, in difficult times, the first goal of a business is to survive. This is valid for a company, and also for an individual, and thus for the individual within a company: the manager or the entrepreneur.It is therefore worthwhile to analyse the reasons behind non-ethical behaviour in business.

There are different sets of reasons for the rise of unethical behaviour in business: some are the consequence of the general evolution of society, others are basically due to the evolution of the business environment and to its internal organisation. The evolution of society in recent decades has been characterised by the increasing individualism of people. The Anglo-Saxon dominant business model has increased the importance of money in society and the glorification of material consumption (Capra, 2003, p. 230). In our modern society, the media have acquired a disproportional importance.

The role models offered by television have not always constituted good examples, on the contrary: Media reality shows and political talk shows often favour superficiality and show, rather than thoroughness and honesty. The globalisation of the economy has had harmful side effects. It has led to larger structures, with more centralisation, and a greater concentration of power.

The race to increase productivity leads to depersonalization as the distance between head office and the anonymous workers increases. It is easier for a CEO of a multinational to close a factory and to lay off thousands of workers far away from the head offices in Paris or Detroit, than for the boss of a small family company to lay off people he knows personally from having worked with them for several years.The dominance of financial considerations is another evolution in business and society. The system is now focused on the shorttermism of the stock market. This favours immediate results.

Financial communication is gaining in importance. Business leaders have learnt to use the system, and in the financial media we can see a prevalence of show over content. Shareholder value is the ultimate value of the business: harsh decisions are taken with the excuse of shareholder value, hiding behind the anonymity of the individual investor. Another consequence of the dominance of the Anglo-American business model is the 'juridisation' of business. Every important deal is signed and laid down in a contract. Here again, a perfidious side effect is that many business people use the letter of the contract rather than the spirit of the contract. Worse, the contract is often invoked over something that is not explicitly stated in the contract, rather than trying to solve the problem. To avoid being sued, managers are very prudent when perpetrating unethical acts: they make sure that nothing is written down and that their responsibility cannot be proved. Paradoxically, the inefficiency of the law, the slow pace of justice, is another reason for the recent increase in unethical practices. Some claims are legally defendable, others are not because they are based on good faith, on promises without written agreement. However, even with the law on your side, it is very difficult, costly and time-consuming to win a court case. Even then, it will not restore the harm done to the company, especially the opportunity costs of a lost contract at a given time. It cannot restore the lasting harm done to people who have lost their jobs because of a missed order.

Some entrepreneurs deliberately abuse the imperfections of the juridical system to perpetrate unethical actions. They know that the cost of a lawsuit is disproportionate to the loss of a deal, especially with international transactions. They will sometimes use this to negotiate a discount under pressure. In such situations, litigations are long and costly: moreover, they take time, and absorb a lot of management's energy which should be directed to the development of the business.

On the other hand, many instances of unethical behaviour are not illegal: ethics goes beyond the law. Other cases are difficult to prove, and the imperfections in the justice system are a real handicap in encouraging business ethics. Some of the reasons for non-ethical behaviour are features of the internal organisation: the rewards and evaluation systems of business and of managers are not always in line with the long-term vision. Further, there is considerable difficulty in translating the strategy set at the top into practical implementation at the lower levels. Contradictions are not easily handled by more junior managers. Entrepreneurs operate in a dynamic environment with many uncertainties such as changes in competition, changes in technology, supply and demand fluctuations, labour issues, legal and public environmental regulations (Hannafey, 2003). Modern business is subject to pressures from all stakeholders on top of time pressures, scarce resources, social and financial pressures, and stiff competition. Shareholders want better value and a better stock price; managers look for their bonuses, and the personnel strive for higher wages and better working conditions; customers expect a higher quality at a lower price; suppliers seek to raise their prices; banks look for interest and guarantees; the government anticipates collecting taxes and imposes constraints on business. All these stakeholders exert some pressure on the entrepreneur, who thus has to juggle with all kinds of constraints and contradictory expectations such that ''Entrepreneurs experience powerful competitive market pressures so keenly that these forces may alter their perspectives on ethics'' (Hannafey, 2003; referring to Chau and Siu, 2000).

ENTREPRENEURSHIP AND SOCIETY

The third broad area of scholarly inquiry involving ethics and entrepreneurship takes a much more macro view of entrepreneurship, exploring the role of new ventures on the relationship between business and society. There is an exhaustively large body of research on questions involving the connections between entrepreneurship, economic development, and social welfare, primarily in the economics literature. We will not attempt to comprehensively review all of that work here; rather, we will attempt to give an overview that touches on several persistent questions. Employing both philosophical and empirical approaches, this body of literature explores at least six such questions.

From the standpoint of economic theory, what role does entrepreneurship play in social welfare? There is a tremendous clash in economic theory as to the social and moral role and impact of entrepreneurship. Although scholars have convincingly argued that Smithian capitalism contains a strong entrepreneurial and ethical focus (Newbert, 2003; Werhane, 1991, 2000), the mainstream neoclassical view is that entrepreneurship is either an allocation mechanism or an aberration. As an alternative, Schumpeter ([1934]1983) suggests that entrepreneurship is the driving market force for 'creative destruction', revolutionizing the existing economic structure by destroying the old equilibrium and creating a new one, via innovation - - a perspective inherently concerned with "disequilibria, decision making, uncertainty", and therefore focused on "how the economic and its variables change endogenously in a historical and political context" (Thanawala, 1994:360). Etzioni (1987) argues that such entrepreneurial creative destruction dramatically affects the evolution of ethical and societal elements, placing the entrepreneur in a central position with respect to society's ethical demands.

An explicit focus on moral perspectives or approaches to ethics could potentially enrich our current economic theories of entrepreneurship (c.f. Minniti & Levesque, 2008). For instance, Sarasvathy (2002) provocatively suggests that the traditional economic frameworks employed to discuss entrepreneurship are limited in their usefulness, and therefore should be discarded in favor of a new, more imaginative economic framework that better incorporates the ethical demands of entrepreneurship within society. What would this new paradigm look like?

Alternatively, how would the incorporation of a more explicit treatment of ethical issues inform or modify our existing economic theories of entrepreneurship?

What is the role of entrepreneurship in macroeconomic development? Empirically, entrepreneurship is viewed as a primary mode of economic development; indeed most job creation occurs in small, entrepreneurial firms (Acs & Audretsch, 1992; Birch, 1987; van Praag & Versloot, 2007). Going further, Kirchhoff (1991) suggests that entrepreneurship may be the wellspring of most economic growth. Researchers continue to examine entrepreneurship's role in the growth and development of economic markets, and although there is general consensus that entrepreneurial activity is of critical importance, there is disagreement about the specific relationship between venturing and economic development. Much of the research builds upon the assumption that economic growth is driven by entrepreneurial innovation; while the dominant view centers around product innovation as an economic driver (e.g., Romer, 1986), other scholars argue for the importance of process innovation (Corriveau, 1994). Other work (e.g., Acs et al., 2009; Audretsch, Bonte, & Keilbach, 2008) suggests that entrepreneurship produces knowledge spillovers arising from agglomeration, which in turn drive economic growth. Some researchers eschew this association between innovation and economic growth, proposing instead that imitative entrepreneurship is a much more powerful economic driver than the less-common innovative activities (Baumol, 1986, 1993; Schmitz, 1989). Powell (1990) concurs, suggesting that the need for imitative entrepreneurship is especially acute in emerging economies, where it has also been shown to have the most impact on economic growth (Minniti & Levesque, in press). Baumol (1990) also suggests that the mode of entrepreneurship pursued by entrepreneurs depends heavily on the quality and extent of supporting societal institutions already in place, a theory confirmed by other scholars (e.g., Sobel, 2008). Yet differential institutional environments – whether in developed or transition economies – have very different effects on entrepreneurial activity (Aidis, Estrin, & Mickiewicz, 2008; Dore, 2006; Galbraith, 2006; Henrekson, 2005; Minniti, 2008; Phan, Venkataraman, & Velamuri, 2008).

Within this scholarly discussion about economic impact, there is a particular interest in the societal influence of entrepreneurial activity on the emerging economies and societies of developing, transition, or third-world countries (Brown, 2002; Bruton, Ahlstrom, & Obloj, 2008; Harper, 1991; Jarillo, 1989; McMillan & Woodruff, 2002) as well as the benefits to the developing-world entrepreneurs themselves (Nussbaum, 2000). Yet these environments can be particularly challenging to entrepreneurs because of corruption, which represents the breakdown of institutional ethics. As such, Anokhin and Schulze (this issue) empirically explore the relationship between corruption and entrepreneurial innovation, which has implications for the relationship between entrepreneurship and economic development. All of this work highlights a number of related questions for future research: From the standpoint of macroeconomic development, which modes of entrepreneurship are most desirable, and under what conditions? How do entrepreneurs in a corrupt environment deal with risks of expropriation? How does the relationship between corruption and entrepreneurship factor into macroeconomic growth? What are the policy implications?

What other societal roles does entrepreneurship play? As part of the debate about entrepreneurship and economic development, some scholars argue that the link between venturing and macroeconomic growth is tenuous at best, and that the true benefit to societal welfare arising from entrepreneurship is the diversification of the socioeconomic portfolio. For example, Shapero (1985) argues that the true benefit to the quality of life in a society stems from the diversification of economic entities which respond to the environment in different ways – using the Irish potato famine as a disastrous counterexample of the perils of an undiversified socioeconomic portfolio.

At the very least, a number of other social metrics may be interrelated with macroeconomic development, but their impact can be specifically considered, irrespective of their influence on economic outcomes. For instance, it is suggested that entrepreneurs can play an overarching and prominent role in building a 'good society' (Brenkert, 2002); indeed the primacy of entrepreneurship within a societal framework is in many ways a pivotal indicator of socioeconomic views on self-determination, freedom, wealth disparity, and distributive justice (Nielsen, 2002). Small and medium-sized enterprises, which are oftentimes entrepreneurial firms, have ubiquitous societal influence on norms of civic engagement and the building of social capital (Spence & Schmidpeter, 2003). Entrepreneurial activity is connected with political policies that advance socioeconomic freedom (Bjornskov & Foss, 2008; Sen, 1999). As a direct link between individual citizens and economic entities, entrepreneurs and their new ventures have an immediate and particular salience to stakeholder evaluations and judgments about business citizenship (Wood & Lodgson, 2002).

As previously discussed, institutions play an important role in fostering or discouraging entrepreneurship. But what happens when there are 'voids' in place of functioning institutions? Mair and Marti (this issue), show that in such situations, new ventures – in addition to creating economic benefits to entrepreneurs themselves – also play a key role in institution building. Entrepreneurs may create new networks of stakeholders, ultimately creating markets where they did not exist before (Sarasvathy & Dew, 2005). On the other hand, alreadyestablished entrepreneurial networks, in the absence of robust institutions and markets, can actually serve as a barrier to entry to new ventures, dampening additional entrepreneurial activity and creating substantial transaction costs for newcomers trying to establish new ventures (Aidis et al., 2008). More research is required to better understand how entrepreneurs deal with institutional voids. Under what conditions does entrepreneurship in developing economies engender a virtuous cycle, instead of devolving into collusion and corruption? As with other lines of research connecting entrepreneurship and society, what are the implications for policy?

How do entrepreneurs enact social change? Much of the research connecting entrepreneurship and society suggests that the entrepreneur can stimulate positive political change by discarding obsolete or anachronistic social patterns and helping to enact new ones – but what do we know about this process? For one thing, Van de Ven, Sapienza and Villanueva (2007) suggest that entrepreneurs are aware of their own role in advancing societal interests; indeed they argue that the portrayal of entrepreneurs as self-interested, rugged individualists is "incomplete", and hence "explanations of entrepreneurial behavior will be more theoretically complete and empirically accurate if they address both self- and collective interests simultaneously than when they are based only on either self-interests or collective interests." As previously discussed, Mair and Marti (this issue) show in rich detail of how one particular entrepreneurial actor navigates a resource- and institution-constrained environment and ultimately does 'institutional work' in that environment - ultimately having an impact on the shaping of nascent institutions. Entrepreneurs that advance social change are often part of larger social movements (Vasi, 2009), and they engage in certain activities such as framing their objectives to appeal to diverse stakeholders and using nonmarket and political means (Maguire et al., 2004) in order to achieve those objectives. Ultimately, Peter Drucker suggested that social entrepreneurs can "change the performance capacity of society" (Gendron, 1996), but compelling questions remain; for instance, what strategic techniques are most effective at connecting entrepreneurial actions with larger social changes? Research could also further unpack the entrepreneurial processes by which institutions are created, modified, or replaced – which might start to build a "theory of entrepreneurial ethics-in-practice" (Dees & Starr, 1992:103).

In what ways can entrepreneurship be socially unproductive? While entrepreneurship is described as an inherently containing a moral imperative (Anderson & Smith, 2007; Carr, 2003), or at the least, being consonant with ethical conduct (Surie & Ashley, 2008), other work points out that entrepreneurship can actually be societally detrimental. For example, Baumol (1990) points out that opportunistic entrepreneurial rent seeking can encourage corruption and its consequences; Davidson and Ekelund (1994) propose that such outcomes are better characterized as an evolutionary process that indicates the presence of pareto optimality mechanisms, and therefore represent timing problems. Nevertheless the uncomfortable fact remains that entrepreneurial innovation can result in "losses and hardships for some members of society" because entrepreneurship is "destructive of some stakeholders' wellbeing even as it creates new wellbeing among other stakeholders" (Dew & Sarasvathy, 2007:267). It is also possible that certain new enterprises might profit at the expense of societal or public goods; that is, the venture could appropriate private gains while imposing societal costs – these ventures are what Davidsson and Wicklund (2001:90) refer to as "robber enterprises". From a policy standpoint, does this suggest that entrepreneurship should be governed by certain societal constraints? How should we ethically account for stakeholders who are disadvantaged by entrepreneurship? Under what circumstances are such outcomes morally problematic? How would different moral frameworks address this problem?

What are the ethics of opportunity exploitation? The 'Austrian school' of economics places a fundamental emphasis on the entrepreneur, but in contrast to the Schumpeterian view, scholars in this tradition suggest that venturing opportunities are instead created by extant market disequilibria (Kirzner, 1997). The role of the entrepreneur in this view, therefore, is to discover and capitalize on such opportunities (Shane & Venkataraman, 2000). This raises some interesting questions regarding the ethics of opportunity exploitation. While exploitation is often viewed as a desirable, morally-neutral description of either entrepreneurial initiative (e.g., Choi & Shepherd, 2004) or organizational learning (March, 1991), an important yet unexplored area of research is the ethical considerations of entrepreneurial opportunity exploitation (Hannafey, 2003). Future research might examine such questions as: What are the moral implications of entrepreneurial creative destruction? Under what circumstances is opportunity exploitation indefensible? How might entrepreneurs distinguish between ethically sound value creation and opportunistic exploitation? What patterns emerge in the cultural or institutional factors that influence entrepreneurial exploitation? What are entrepreneurs' special or particular societal obligations, as distinct from managers in mature firms? Additional research along these lines is needed to advance our understanding of entrepreneurial opportunity exploitation.

RELIGION AND ECONOMIC BEHAVIOR

Religion has long been identified as an important determinant of economic behavior. In the early part of the twentieth century, Max Weber's The Protestant Ethic and the Spirit of Capitalism, (6) and R. H. Tawney's Religion and the Rise of Capitalism (5) elaborated at some length on this relationship. Both of these scholars perceived Protestantism as providing a favorable climate for the entrepreneurial activity essential for economic progress. A more recent exploration of the relationship between religion and economic activity, this time in the context of a less developed country, can be found in Amy L. Sherman's The Soul of Development: Biblical Christianity and Economic Transformation in Guatemala. In this book, Sherman documents a positive effect of religious orthodoxy upon both the attitudes and actions favorable for economic progress.

The specific relationship between religion and ethical attitudes has not been subject to a great deal of empirical research, and the research which has been conducted has not yielded unequivocal results. A recent paper by Barnett, Bass and Brown found that strongly religious persons expressed a stronger belief in universal moral principles than others do, and from this finding they inferred that religious belief would have a positive impact on ethical attitudes (1, pp 1161-1174). George Wuthnow found a consistently positive effect of religion, as measured both by the stated importance of religion in respondents' lives and by their participation in religious communities, upon ethical attitudes (7, pp. 79-115). However, while the effect was consistently positive, Wuthnow considered it to be relatively modest. In contrast to the aforementioned studies, Clark and Dawson found that the more religious exhibited a more tolerant attitude toward ethically questionable situations than did the less religious (2, pp. 359-372).

SUMMARY AND CONCLUSIONS

In conclusion, we are quite pleased that our paper has resulted in additional work on this important topic and hope that subsequent research and theory are offered for public debate. Recent history has indicated that market economies tend to produce more goods and services and generate a much higher level of public welfare than command economies. Ray's

(2004) position suggests that we return to a more authoritarian, command economy, and that would stifle the discovery and creation of life saving/ life sustaining innovations for all, greatly reducing social welfare over the long term. This examination of religious faith and entrepreneurial ethics is limited by a number of considerations. First, the data pertain to ethical attitudes, not ethical behavior. We examine what entrepreneurs say about particular issues not what they would do when facing such situations— notoriously difficult information to discover.

Also, this investigation considers a relatively small group of entrepreneurs. Some, in fact, may question the use of the term "entrepreneur," since we cannot distinguish founders or high-tech entrepreneurs from other selfemployed individuals.

Consideration of the effect of religious orthodoxy on ethical judgments was limited to orthodox entrepreneurs of the Christian faith. This was necessary because of the small numbers of respondents in other religions. It would be appropriate to examine this question as it pertains to other groups. The questions asked, moreover, did not probe deeply into the nature of respondents' religious beliefs. In spite of such limitations, however, the study does provide some evidence of a relationship of between religious faith and entrepreneurial ethical attitudes.

The religious faith factor appears to affect judgments on some ethical issues far more than others. Further analysis may provide a key to the nature of issues most likely to be affected. The degree of orthodoxy affected ethical judgments, but the effect was quite similar to the effect of attaching high importance to religious interests. Since the former (the highly orthodox) was a subset of the latter (high importance), there may have been considerable overlap between the two groups.

At most, therefore, the factor of orthodoxy slightly sharpened the differences observed earlier in the responses of those for whom religious interests had high importance. In both cases, however, the religious element did result in judgments of greater ethical sensitivity.

REFERENCES

1. Ackoff, R. L. 1987. Business Ethics and the Entrepreneur. Journal of Business Venturing, 2: 185-91.
2. Aidis, R., Estrin, S., & Mickiewicz, T. 2008. Institutions and Entrepreneurship Development in Russia: A Comparative Perspective. Journal of Business Venturing, 23(6): 656-672.
3. Anokhin, S., & Schulze, W. S. 2009. Entrepreneurship, Innovation, and Corruption. Journal of Business Venturing, in press(in press): tbd.
4. Audretsch, D. B., Bonte, W., & Keilbach, M. 2008. Entrepreneurship Capital and Its Impact on Knowledge Diffusion and Economic Performance. Journal of Business Venturing, 23(6): 687-698.
5. Barlow, H. D. 1993. From Fiddle Factors to Networks of Collusion: Charting the Waters of Small Business Crime. Crime, Law, and Social Change, 20: 319-337.
6. Baron, D. P. 2007. Corporate Social Responsibility and Social Entrepreneurship. Journal of Economics and Management Strategy, 16(3): 683-717.
7. Clark, James W. and Dawson, Lyndon E. "Personal Religiousness and Ethical Judgements: An Empirical Analysis,"Journal of Business Ethics, (15, 1996), 359-372.
8. Longenecker, Justin G., McKinney, Joseph A. and Moore, Carlos W. "Egoism and Independence: Entrepreneurial Ethics," Organizational Dynamics, (Winter, 1988), 64-72.
9. Maguire, S., Hardy, C., & Lawrence, T. B. 2004. Institutional Entrepreneurship in Emerging Fields: HIV/AIDS Treatment Advocacy in Canada. Academy of Management Journal, 47(5): 657-679.
10. Mair, J., & Marti, I. 2006. Social Entrepreneurship Research: A Source of Explanation, Prediction, and Delight. Journal of World Business, 41(1): 36-44.
11. March, J. G. 1991. Exploration and Exploitation in Organizational Learning. Organization Science, 2: 71-87.
12. Martin, K., & Freeman, R. E. 2004. The Separation of Technology and Ethics in Business Ethics. Journal of Business Ethics, 53(4): 353-364.
13. McVea, J. F. 2009. A Field Study of Entrepreneurial Decision-Making and Moral Imagination. Journal of Business Venturing, in press(in press): tbd.
14. Minniti, M. 2008. The Role of Government Policy on Entrepreneurial Activity: Productive, Unproductive, or Destructive? Entrepreneurship Theory and Practice, 32(5): 779-790.
15. Monllor, J., & Attaran, S. 2008. Opportunity Recognition of Social Entrepreneurs: An Application of the Creativity Model. International Journal of Entrepreneurship and Small Business, 6(1): 54-67.
16. Morris, M. H., Schindehutte, M., Walton, J., & Allen, J. 2002. The Ethical Context of Entrepreneurship: Proposing and Testing a Developmental Framework. Journal of Business Ethics, 40: 331-361.
17. Newbert, S. L. 2003. Realizing the Spirit and Impact of Adam Smith's Captialism through Entrepreneurship. Journal of Business Ethics, 46: 251-261.

18. Nicholls, A. 2006. Social Entrepreneurship: New Models of Sustainable Social Change. New York: Oxford University Press.

19. Norman, W., & MacDonald, C. 2004. Getting to the Bottom of 'Triple Bottom Line'. Business Ethics Quarterly, 14(2): 243-262.

20. Nussbaum, M. C. 2000. Women and Human Development: The Capabilities Approach. New York: Cambridge University Press.

21. Osborne, R. L. 1991. The Dark Side of the Entrepreneur. Long Range Planning, 24(3): 26-31.

22. Payne, D., & Joyner, B. 2006. Successful U.S. Entrepreneurs: Identifying Ethical Decision-Making and Social Responsibility Behaviors. Journal of Business Ethics, 65(3): 203-217.

23. Perrini, F. 2006a. The New Social Entrepreneurship: What Awaits Social Entrepreneurship Ventures? Cheltenham, U.K.: Edward Elgar.

24. Phan, P. H., Venkataraman, S., & Velamuri, S. R. 2008. Entrepreneurship in Emerging Reagions around the World: Theory, Evidence and Implications. Cheltenham, U.K.: Edward Elgar.

25. Reynolds, S. 2006. Moral Awareness and Ethical Predispositions: Investigating the Role of Individual Differences in the Recognition of Moral Issues. Journal of Applied Psychology, 91(1): 233-243.

26. Robinson, J., Mair, J., & Hockerts, K. 2009. International Perspectives on Social Entrepreneurship. London: Palgrave Macmillan.

27. Romer, P. M. 1986. Increasing Returns and Long-Run Growth. Journal of Political Economy, 94(5): 1002-1037.

28. Sapienza, H. J., & Korsgaard, A. 1996. Procedural Justice in Entrepreneur-Investor Relations. Academy of Management Journal, 39(3): 544-574.

29. Sarasvathy, S. 2004b. The Questions We Ask and the Questions We Care About: Reformulating Some Problems in Entrepreneurship Research. Journal of Business Venturing, 19(5): 707-717.

30. Schminke, M., Ambrose, M. L., & Neubaum, D. O. 2005. The Effect of Leader Moral Development on Ethical Climate and Employee Attitudes. Organizational Behavior and Human Decision Processes, 97(2): 135-151.

31. Schumpeter, J. A. [1934]1983. The Theory of Economic Development. New Brunswick, New Jersey: Transaction Publishers.

32. Seelos, C., & Mair, J. 2007. Profitable Business Models and Market Creation in the Context of Deep Poverty: A Strategic View. Academy of Management Perspectives, 21(4): 49-63.

33. Shapero, A. 1985. Why Entrepreneurship? A Worldwide Perspective. Journal of Small Business Management, 23: 1-5.

34. Sobel, R. S. 2008. Testing Baumol: Institutional Quality and the Productivity of Entrepreneurship. Journal of Business Venturing, 23(6): 641-655.

35. Solymossy, E., & Masters, J. K. 2002. Ethics through an Entrepreneurial Lens: Theory and Observation. Journal of Business Ethics, 38: 227-241.

36. Starr, J. A., & MacMillan, I. C. 1990. Resource Cooptation Via Social Contracting: Resource Acquisition Strategies for New Ventures. Strategic Management Journal, 11: 79-92.

37. Tenbrunsel, A. E., Smith-Crowe, K., & Umphress, E. E. 2003. Building Houses on Rocks: The Role of Ethical Infrastructure in Organizations. Social Justice Research, 16(3): 285-307.

38. 5. Tawney, R. H., Religion and the Rise of Capitalism (New York: Harcourt, Brace and World, Inc., 1926).

39. Venkataraman, S. 2002. Stakeholder Value Equilibration and the Entrepreneurial Process. The Ruffin Series, 3: 45-58.

40. Vitell, S. J., Dickerson, E. B., & Festervand, T. A. 2000. Ethical Problems, Conflicts and Beliefs of Small Business Professionals. Journal of Business Ethics, 28(1): 15-24.

41. Waddock, S. A., & Post, J. E. 1991. Social Entrepreneurs and Catalytic Change. Public Administration Review, 51(5): 393-401.

42. Warren, D. E. 2003. Constructive and Destrictuve Deviance in Organizations. Academy of Management Review, 28(4): 622-632.

43. Wempe, J. 2005. Ethical Entrepreneurship and Fair Trade. Journal of Business Ethics, 60(3): 211-220.

44. Wood, D. J., & Lodgson, J. M. 2002. Business Citizenship: From Individuals to Organizations. The Ruffin Series, 3: 59-94.

45. 6. Weber, Max. The Protestant Ethic and the Spirit of Capitalism, trans. T. Parsons (London: Unwin Paperbacks, 1984)

46. 7. Wuthnow, George. God and Mammon in America. (The Free Press, 1994), 79-115

47. Zahra, S., Gedajlovic, E., Neubaum, D. O., & Shulman, J. M. 2009. A Typology of Social Entrepreneurs: Motives, Search Processes and Ethical Challenges. Journal of Business Venturing, in press(in press): tbd.

Journal of Applied Sciences Research, 8(3): 1594-1607, 2012 ISSN 1819-544X
This is a refereed journal and all articles are professionally screened and reviewed

ORIGINAL ARTICLES

Emotional Intelligence: Understanding, Applying, and Measuring

[1]Kamran Nazari, [2]Mostafa Emami

[1]Department of Business Management, Payam Noor University, Kermanshah, Iran
[2]Young Researchers Club, South Tehran Branch, Islamic Azad University, Tehran, Iran.

ABSTRACT

Interest in emotional intelligence has bloomed over the last few years. That it has become a standard concept in general and applied psychology, as well as in applied business settings, is indubitable. Emotional Intelligence - EQ - is a relatively recent behavioural model, rising to prominence with Daniel Goleman's 1995 Book called 'Emotional Intelligence'. The early Emotional Intelligence theory was originally developed during the 1970s and 80s by the work and writings of psychologists Howard Gardner (Harvard), Peter Salovey (Yale) and John 'Jack' Mayer (New Hampshire). Emotional Intelligence is increasingly relevant to organizational development and developing people, because the EQ principles provide a new way to understand and assess people's behaviours, management styles, attitudes, interpersonal skills, and potential. Emotional Intelligence is an important consideration in human resources planning, job profiling, recruitment interviewing and selection, management development, customer relations and customer service, and more. Emotional Intelligence links strongly with concepts of love and spirituality: bringing compassion and humanity to work, and also to 'Multiple Intelligence' theory which illustrates and measures the range of capabilities people possess, and the fact that everybody has a value. The EQ concept argues that IQ, or conventional intelligence, is too narrow; that there are wider areas of Emotional Intelligence that dictate and enable how successful we are. Success requires more than IQ (Intelligence Quotient), which has tended to be the traditional measure of intelligence, ignoring esential behavioural and character elements. We've all met people who are academically brilliant and yet are socially and inter-personally inept. And we know that despite possessing a high IQ rating, success does not automatically follow.

Key words: emotion, Emotional Intelligence, intellectual quotient.

Introuction

Since the publication of the best selling book Emotional Intelligence by Daniel Goleman (1995), the topic of emotional intelligence has witnessed unparalleled interest. Programs seeking to increase emotional intelligence have been implemented in numerous settings, and courses on developing one's emotional intelligence have been introduced in universities and even in elementary schools throughout the United States. But what exactly is emotional intelligence? As is the case with all constructs (i.e. intelligence or personality), several schools of thought exist which aim to most accurately describe and measure the notion of emotional intelligence. At the most general level, emotional intelligence (E.I.) refers to the ability to recognize and regulate emotions in ourselves and others (Goleman, 2001). Peter Salovey and John Mayer, who originally used the term "emotional intelligence" in published writing, initially defined emotional intelligence as:

A form of intelligence that involves the ability to monitor one's own and others' feelings and emotions, to discriminate among them and to use this information to guide one's thinking and actions (Salovey & Mayer, 1990).

Later, these authors revised their definition of emotional intelligence, the current characterization now being the most widely accepted. Emotional intelligence is thus defined as:

The ability to perceive emotion, integrate emotion to facilitate thought, understand emotions, and to regulate emotions to promote personal growth (Mayer & Salovey, 1997).

J. Appl. Sci. Res., 8(3): 1594-1607, 2012

Another prominent researcher of the emotional intelligence construct is Reuven Bar-On, the originator of the term "emotion quotient". Possessing a slightly different outlook, he defines emotional intelligence as being concerned with understanding oneself and others, relating to people, and adapting to and coping with the immediate surroundings to be more successful in dealing with environmental demands (Bar-On, 1997). Regardless of the discrepancies betweendefinitions of emotional intelligence, it is clear that what is being referred to is distinct from standard intelligence, or I.Q.

Corresponding Author: Kamran Nazari,Department of Business Management, Payam Noor University, Kermanshah, Iran
E-mail: Kamrann0156@yahoo.com

Intelligence quotients (I.Q.'s) were developed and used during the initial part of the 20 century as measures of intelligence. French psychologist Alfred Binet pioneered the modern intelligence testing movement in developing a measure of mental age in children, a chronological age that typically corresponds to a given level of performance (Myers, 1998). More modern studies linked a person's I.Q. with their potential for success in general (Weschler, 1958) as well as with elements such as leadership success (Lord, DeVader, & Alliger, 1986). However, the validity of the general academic measure of I.Q. was soon challenged on the grounds that it did not consider situational factors such as environment or cultural setting when predicting achievement (Riggio, Murphy, & Pirozzolo, 2002). Theorists began to hypothesize that perhaps cognitive intelligence as measured by I.Q. tests did not encompass intelligence in its entirety, but that perhaps several types of intelligences could coincide within one person.

An influential psychologist in the areas of learning, education, and intelligence, E.L. Thorndike proposed that humans possess several types of intelligence, one form being called social intelligence, or the ability to understand and manage men and women, boys and girls, and to act wisely in human relations (Thorndike, 1920). Even David Wechsler, the originator of the Wechsler Adult Intelligence Scale (WAIS) intelligence tests, referred to both non-intellective and intellective elements of intelligence. The non-intellective elements, which included affective, personal, and social factors, he later hypothesized were essential for predicting one's ability to succeed in life (Wechsler, 1940). Later in the century, Howard Gardner again raised the notion of multiple intelligences. A Harvard-educated developmental psychologist, Gardner proposed a theory of multiple intelligences which dictated that individuals possess aptitudes in several areas, including verbal, mathematical, musical, spatial, movement oriented, environmental, intrapersonal (the examination and knowledge of one's own feelings) and interpersonal (the ability to read the moods, intentions, and desires of others) spheres (Myers, 1998). These intelligences were thought by Gardner to be as important as the type of intelligence typically measured by I.Q. tests (Gardner, 1983).

The History of EQ:

Charles Darwin was the first to recognize the value of emotions. He noted that the emotional system energizes behavior needed to stay alive. Emotions cannot be stopped, they happen instinctually and immediately in response to situations and people. In the 1920s E.I. Thorndike identified "social intelligence" as the ability to act wisely in human relations. In 1988, Reuven Bar-On coined the term emotional intelligence in his doctoral dissertation. In 1990, John Mayer and Peter Salovey did groundbreaking research on emotional intelligence, pointing to the importance of knowing yourself as well as understanding others. In 1995, Daniel Goleman introduced the important of EQ in the workplace, noting that IQ is a less powerful predictor of outstanding leadership than EQ. The highest estimate of how much difference IQ (intellectual quotient) accounts for in how well people perform in their careers is no higher than 10% and perhaps as low as 4% (Sternberg, 1997). IQ is considered a threshold competence, a minimum capability that all must have. Once you're in a group of similar IQs, IQ will no longer distinguish you in the group.

EQ (emotional intelligence) data suggests that older groups score significantly higher than younger groups in most EQ scales. Respondents in their late 40s obtained the highest mean scores. On the North American sample, females appear to have stronger interpersonal skills than males, but males have higher intrapersonal capacity, are better at managing emotions, and are more adaptable. Women are more aware of emotions, demonstrate more empathy towards others, and are more socially responsible. Men have better self-regard, are more self-reliant, cope better with stress, and are more optimistic than women in the studies conducted. No significant differences in emotional intelligence were found between various ethnic groups in North America. Higher-level employees are more likely to have inflated views of their emotional intelligence and less congruence with the perceptions of others than lower-level employees. Data shows that when there is no easy right or wrong answer to a problem or decision, people usually decide one direction or another based on emotions.

There is a moderate yet significant relationship between EQ and physical health and significant differences in psychological health and a moderate, yet statistically significant relationship between EQ and performance at school. However, EQ is not something we have been taught to improve since childhood. So, it makes sense that most people have an average EQ score.

1596

J. Appl. Sci. Res., 8(3): 1594-1607, 2012

Who's stressing about IQ?:

You cite the meta-analysis of Judge *et al.* (2004) to support the notion that general intelligence predicts leadership effectiveness only when leaders are in low stress situations. Judge *et al.* only synthesized studies using dichotomized data (high and low stress situations). Unless the data came from an experimental setting, stress should be scored as a continuous variable and the following regression should be estimated: Yleader perf.=a+βIQ+βstress+βIQ   stress. There are established meta-analytic techniques to synthesize interaction effects of this nature (Kanetkar, Evans, Everell, Irving, & Millman, 1995). Fiedler & Link (1994) actually looked at the IQstress interaction (in 13 samples)—alas, this datawas not included in Judge *et al.* In most of the models Fiedler and Link tested, both IQ and stress had positive slopes and the interaction was positive too . This result suggests exactly the opposite to what you said (and dispels another myth in the making). The relation of IQ to leader performance is stronger in high stress than in low stress situations. Referring specifically to leader performance in situations with interpersonal stress, Fiedler (1995) noted: "Our studies do not support the hypothesis… that intelligence tests are not useful in predicting leadership performance in complex or intellectually demanding tasks. On the contrary…intelligence tests seem to predict performance somewhat better in intellectually demanding and complex tasks, than in simple or routine ones" .

Neurological Substrates of EI:

The EI theory of performance posits that each of the four domains of EI derives from distinct neurological mechanisms that distinguish each domain from the others and all four from purely cognitive domains of ability. In turn, at a higher level of articulation, the EI competencies nest within these four EI domains. This distinction between EI-based competencies and purely cognitive abilities like IQ can now be drawn more clearly than before owing to recent findings in neuroscience. Research in the newly emerging field of affective neuroscience (Davidson, Jackson, & Kalin, 2000) offers a fine-grained view of the neural substrates of the EI-based range of behavior and allows us to see a bridge between brain function and the behaviors described in the EI model of performance.

From the perspective of affective neuroscience, the defining boundary in brain activity between emotional intelligence and cognitive intelligence is the distinction between capacities that are purely (or largely) neocortical and those that integrate neocortical and limbic circuitry. Intellectual abilities like verbal fluency, spatial logic, and abstract reasoning—in other words, the components of IQ—are based primarily in specific areas of the neocortex. When these neocortical areas are damaged, the corresponding intellectual ability suffers. In contrast, emotional intelligence encompasses the behavioral manifestations of underlying neurological circuitry that primarily links the limbic areas for emotion, centering on the amygdala and its extended networks throughout the brain, to areas in the prefrontal cortex, the brain's executive center.

Key components of this circuitry include the dorsolateral, ventromedial, and orbitofrontal sectors of the prefrontal cortex (with important functional differences between left and right sides in each sector) and the amygdala and hippocampus (Davidson, Jackson, & Kalin, 2000). This circuitry is essential for the development of skills in each of the four main domains of emotional intelligence. Lesions in these areas produce deficits in the hallmark abilities of EI—Self-Awareness, Self-Management (including Motivation), Social Awareness skills such as Empathy, and Relationship Management, just as lesions in discrete areas of the neocortex selectively impair aspects of purely cognitive abilities such as verbal fluency or spatial reasoning (Damasio, 1994, 1999).

The first component of emotional intelligence is Emotional Self-Awareness, knowing what one feels. John Mayer (see, for example, Mayer & Stevens, 1994) uses the term meta-mood, the affective analogue of metacognition, for key aspects of Emotional Self-Awareness. The neural substrates of Emotional Self-Awareness have yet to be determined with precision. But Antonio Damasio (1994), on the basis of neuropsychological studies of patients with brain lesions, proposes that the ability to sense, articulate, and reflect on one's emotional states hinges on the neural circuits that run between the prefrontal and verbal cortex, the amygdala, and the viscera. Patients with lesions that disconnect the amygdala from the prefrontal cortex, he finds, are at a loss to give words to feelings, a hallmark of the disorder alexithymia. In some ways, alexithymia and Emotional SelfAwareness may be mirror concepts, one reflecting a deficiency in the workings of these neural substrates, the other efficiency (Taylor, Parker, & Bagby, 1999). The second component of EI, Emotional Self-Management, is the ability to regulate distressing affects like anxiety and anger and to inhibit emotional impulsivity. PET (positron-emission tomography) measurements of glucose metabolism reveal that individual differences in metabolic activity in the amygdala are associated with levels of distress or dysphoria—the more activity, the greater the negative affect (Davidson, Jackson, & Kalin, 2000). In contrast, metabolic activity in the left medial prefrontal cortex is inversely related to levels of activity in the amygdala—an array of inhibitory neurons in the prefrontal area, animal studies have shown, regulate activation of the amygdala. In humans, the greater the activity level in the left medial prefrontal cortex, the more positive the person's emotional state. Thus a major locus of the ability to regulate negative affect appears to be the circuit between the amygdala and the left prefrontal cortex.

This circuitry also appears instrumental in the motivational aspect of Emotional Self-Management; it may sustain the residual affect that propels us to achieve our goals. David McClelland (1975) has defined motivation as "an affectively toned associative network arranged in a hierarchy of strength and importance in the individual," which determines what goals we seek (p. 81). Davidson proposes that the left medial prefrontal cortex is the site of "affective working memory." Damage to this region is associated with a

1597

J. Appl. Sci. Res., 8(3): 1594-1607, 2012

loss of the ability to sustain goal-directed behavior; loss of the capacity to anticipate affective outcomes from accomplishing goals diminishes the ability to guide behavior adaptively (Davidson, Jackson, & Kalin, 2000). In other words, Davidson proposes that the prefrontal cortex allows us to hold in mind or remind ourselves of the positive feelings that will come when we attain our goals and at the same time allows us to inhibit the negative feelings that would discourage us from continuing to strive toward those goals.

Social Awareness, the third EI component, which encompasses the competency of Empathy, also involves the amygdala. Studies of patients with discrete lesions to the amygdala show impairment of their ability to read nonverbal cues for negative emotions, particularly anger and fear, and to judge the trustworthiness of other people (Davidson, Jackson, & Kalin, 2000). Animal studies suggest a key role in recognizing emotions for circuitry running from the amygdala to the visual cortex; Brothers (1989), reviewing both neurological findings and comparative studies with primates, cites data showing that certain neurons in the visual cortex respond only to specific emotional cues, such as a threat. These emotion-recognition cortical neurons have strong connections to the amygdala.

Finally, Relationship Management, or Social Skill, the fourth EI component, poses a more complex picture. In a fundamental sense, the effectiveness of our relationship skills hinges on our ability to attune ourselves to or influence the emotions of another person. That ability in turn builds on other domains of EI, particularly SelfManagement and Social Awareness. If we cannot control our emotional outbursts or impulses and lack Empathy, there is less chance we will be effective in our relationships. Indeed, in an analysis of data on workplace effectiveness, Richard Boyatzis, Ruth Jacobs, and I have found that Emotional Self-Awareness is a prerequisite for effective Self-Management, which in turn predicts greater Social Skill. A secondary pathway runs from Self-Awareness to Social Awareness (particularly Empathy) to Social Skill. Managing relationships well, then, depends on a foundation of Self-Management and Empathy, each of which in turn requires SelfAwareness. This evidence that Empathy and Self-Management are foundations for social effectiveness finds support at the neurological level. Patients with lesions in the prefrontal-amygdala circuits that undergird both Self-Management and Empathy show marked deficits in relationship skills, even though their cognitive abilities remain intact (Damasio, 1994). When Damasio administered an EI measure to one such patient, he found that though the patient had an IQ of 140, he showed marked deficits in self-awareness and empathy (Bar-On, 2000b). Primate studies find parallel effects. Monkeys in the wild who had this prefrontal-amygdala circuitry severed were able to perform food gathering and similar tasks to maintain themselves but lacked all sense of how to respond to other monkeys in the band, even running away from those who made friendly gestures (Brothers, 1989).

The Business Case for EI Competencies:

The data documenting the importance for outstanding performance of each of the twenty emotional intelligence competencies have been building for more than two decades. I have reviewed the data for each competence (Goleman, 1998b), as have Cherniss and Adler (2000). Moreover the data continue to build, both informally, as organizations worldwide do internal studies to identify the competencies that distinguish outstanding from average performers, and formally, as academic researchers continue to focus studies on one or another of these capabilities. David McClelland (1975) was perhaps the first to propose the concept of competence as a basis for identifying what differentiates outstanding from average performers at work. McClelland (1998) reviewed data from more than thirty different organizations and for executive positions in many professions, from banking and managing to mining geology, sales, and health care. He showed that a wide range of EI competencies (and a narrow range of cognitive ones) distinguished top performers from average ones. Those that distinguished most powerfully were Achievement Drive, Developing Others, Adaptability, Influence, Self-Confidence, and Leadership. The one cognitive competence that distinguished as strongly was Analytic Thinking. Although each competence contributes on its own to workplace effectiveness, I believe it is less useful to consider them one by one than it is to examine them in their clusters, where one can also assess the synergies of strengths in several competencies that enable outstanding performance, as McClelland (1998) has shown. For that reason, I review here only selected examples of data linking the EI competencies to workplace performance. Readers who seek a fuller review should consult Goleman (1998b) or the classic work of Boyatzis (1982) and Spencer and Spencer (1993).

The Self-Awareness Cluster: Understanding Feelings and Accurate Self-Assessment:

The first of the three Self-Awareness competencies, Emotional Self-Awareness, reflects the importance of recognizing one's own feelings and how they affect one's performance. At a financial services company emotional self-awareness proved crucial in financial planners' job performance (Goleman, 1998b). The interaction between a financial planner and a client is delicate, dealing not only with hard questions about money but also, when life insurance comes up, the even more discomforting issue of mortality; the planners' Self-Awareness apparently helped them handle their own emotional reactions better.

At another level, Self-Awareness is key to realizing one's own strengths and weaknesses. Among several hundred managers from twelve different organizations, Accurate Self-Assessment was the hallmark of superior performance (Boyatzis, 1982). Individuals with the Accurate Self-Assessment competence are aware of their abilities and limitations, seek out feedback and learn from their mistakes, and know where they need to improve and when to work with others who have complementary strengths. Accurate Self-Assessment was the competence found in virtually every "star performer" in a study of several hundred knowledge

J. Appl. Sci. Res., 8(3): 1594-1607, 2012

workers— computer scientists, auditors and the like—at companies such as AT&T and 3M (Kelley, 1998). On 360-degree competence assessments, average performers typically overestimate their strengths, whereas star performers rarely do; if anything, the stars tended to underestimate their abilities, an indicator of high internal standards (Goleman, 1998). The positive impact of the Self-Confidence competence on performance has been shown in a variety of studies. Among supervisors, managers, and executives, a high degree of Self-Confidence distinguishes the best from the average performers (Boyatzis, 1982). Among 112 entry-level accountants, those with the highest sense of Self-Efficacy, a form of Self-Confidence, were rated by their supervisors ten months later as having superior job performance. The level of Self-Confidence was in fact a stronger predictor of performance than the level of skill or previous training (Saks, 1995). In a sixty-year study of more than one thousand high-IQ men and women tracked from early childhood to retirement, those who possessed SelfConfidence during their early years were most successful in their careers (Holahan & Sears, 1995).

The Self-Management Cluster: Managing Internal States, Impulses, and Resources:

The Self-Management cluster of EI abilities encompasses six competencies. Heading the list is the Emotional Self-Control competence, which manifests largely as the absence of distress and disruptive feelings. Signs of this competence include being unfazed in stressful situations or dealing with a hostile person without lashing out in return. Among small business owners and employees, those with a stronger sense of control over not only themselves but the events in their lives are less likely to become angry or depressed when faced with job stress or to quit (Rahim & Psenicka, 1996). Among counselors and psychotherapists, superior performers tend to respond calmly to angry attacks by a patient, as do outstanding flight attendants dealing with disgruntled passengers (Boyatzis & Burrus, 1995; Spencer & Spencer, 1993). And among managers and executives, top performers are able to balance their drive and ambition with Emotional Self-Control, harnessing their personal needs in the service of the organization's goals (Boyatzis, 1982). Those store managers who are best able to manage their own stress and stay unaffected have the most profitable stores, by such measures as sales per square foot, in a national retail chain (Lusch & Serkenci, 1990).

The Trustworthiness competence translates into letting others know one's values and principles, intentions and feelings, and acting in ways that are consistent with them. Trustworthy individuals are forthright about their own mistakes and confront others about their lapses. A deficit in this ability operates as a career derailer (Goleman, 1998).

The signs of the Conscientiousness competence include being careful, self-disciplined, and scrupulous in attending to responsibilities. Conscientiousness distinguishes the model organizational citizens, the people who keep things running as they should. In studies of job performance, outstanding effectiveness in virtually all jobs—from the bottom to the top of the corporate ladder—depends on Conscientiousness (Barrick & Mount, 1991). Among sales representatives for a large U.S. appliance manufacturer, those who were most conscientious had the largest volume of sales (Barrick, Mount, & Straus, 1993).

If there is any single competence our present times call for, it is Adaptability. Superior performers in management ranks exhibit this competence (Spencer & Spencer, 1993). They are open to new information and can let go of old assumptions and so adapt how they operate. Emotional resilience allows an individual to remain comfortable with the anxiety that often accompanies uncertainty and to think "out of the box," displaying on-the-job creativity and applying new ideas to achieve results. Conversely, people who are uncomfortable with risk and change become naysayers who can undermine innovative ideas or be slow to respond to a shift in the marketplace. Businesses with less formal and more ambiguous, autonomous, and flexible roles for employees open flows of information, and multidisciplinary team-oriented structures experience greater innovation (Amabile, 1988).

David McClelland's landmark work The Achieving Society (1961) established Achievement Orientation as the competence that drives the success of entrepreneurs. In its most general sense, this competence, which I call Achievement Drive, refers to an optimistic striving to continually improve performance. Studies that compare star performers in executive ranks to average ones find that stars display classic achievement-oriented behaviors—they take more calculated risks, they support enterprising innovations and set challenging goals for their employees, and so forth. Spencer and Spencer (1993) found that the need to achieve is the competence that most strongly sets apart superior and average executives. Optimism is a key ingredient of achievement because it can determine one's reaction to unfavorable events or circumstances; those with high achievement are proactive and persistent, have an optimistic attitude toward setbacks, and operate from hope of success. Studies have shown that optimism can contribute significantly to sales gains, among other accomplishments (Schulman, 1995). Those with the Initiative competence act before being forced to do so by external events. This often means taking anticipatory action to avoid problems before they happen or taking advantage of opportunities before they are visible to anyone else. Individuals who lack Initiative are reactive rather than proactive, lacking the farsightedness that can make the critical difference between a wise decision and a poor one. Initiative is key to outstanding performance in industries that rely on sales, such as real estate, and to the development of personal relationships with clients, as is critical in such businesses as financial services or consulting (Crant, 1995; Rosier, 1996).

The Social Awareness Cluster: Reading People and Groups Accurately:

J. Appl. Sci. Res., 8(3): 1594-1607, 2012

The Social Awareness cluster manifests in three competencies. The Empathy competence gives people an astute awareness of others' emotions, concerns, and needs. The empathic individual can read emotional currents, picking up on nonverbal cues such as tone of voice or facial expression. Empathy requires Self-Awareness; our understanding of others' feelings and concerns flows from awareness of our own feelings. This sensitivity to others is critical for superior job performance whenever the focus is on interactions with people. For instance, physicians who are better at recognizing emotions in patients are more successful than their less sensitive colleagues at treating them (Friedman & DiMatteo, 1982). The ability to read others' needs well comes naturally to the best managers of product development teams (Spencer & Spencer, 1993). And skill in Empathy correlates with effective sales, as was found in a study among large and small retailers (Pilling & Eroglu, 1994). In an increasingly diverse workforce, the Empathy competence allows us to read people accurately and avoid resorting to the stereotyping that can lead to performance deficits by creating anxiety in the stereotyped individuals (Steele, 1997). Social Awareness also plays a key role in the Service competence, the ability to identify a client's or customer's often unstated needs and concerns and then match them to products or services; this empathic strategy distinguishes star sales performers from average ones (Spencer & Spencer, 1993). It also means taking a long-term perspective, sometimes trading off immediate gains in order to preserve customer relationships. A study of an office supply and equipment vendor indicated that the most successful members of the sales team were able to combine taking the customer's viewpoint and showing appropriate assertiveness in order to steer the customer toward a choice that satisfied both the customer's and the vendor's needs (McBane, 1995).

Organizational Awareness, the ability to read the currents of emotions and political realities in groups, is a competence vital to the behind-the-scenes networking and coalition building that allows individuals to wield influence, no matter what their professional role. Insight into group social hierarchies requires Social Awareness on an organizational level, not just an interpersonal one. Outstanding performers in most organizations share this ability; among managers and executive generally, this emotional competence distinguishes star performers. Their ability to read situations objectively, without the distorting lens of their own biases and assumptions, allows them to respond effectively (Boyatzis, 1982).

Competence Comes in Multiples:

Although there is theoretical significance in showing that each competence in itself has a significant impact on performance, it is also in a sense an artificial exercise. In life—and particularly on the job—people exhibit these competencies in groupings, often across clusters, that allow competencies to support one another. Emotional competencies seem to operate most powerfully in synergistic groupings, with the evidence suggesting that mastery of a "critical mass" of competencies is necessary for superior performance (Boyatzis, Goleman, & Rhee, 2000). Along with competency clusters comes the notion of a tipping point—the point at which strength in a competence makes a significant impact on performance. Each competence can be viewed along a continuum of mastery; at a certain point along each continuum there is a major leap in performance impact. In McClelland's analysis (1998) of the competencies that distinguish star performers from average ones, he found a tipping point effect when people exhibited excellence in six or more competencies. McClelland argues that a critical mass of competencies above the tipping point distinguishes top from average performers. The typical pattern is that stars are above the tipping point on at least six EI competencies and demonstrate strengths in at least one competency from each of the four clusters. This effect has been replicated in Boyatzis's research (1999b), which demonstrated that meeting or surpassing the tipping point in at least three of the four EI clusters was necessary for success among high-level leaders in a large financial services organization. Boyatzis found that both a high degree of proficiency in several aptitudes in the same cluster and a spread of strengths across clusters are found among those who exhibit superior organizational performance. Using information about the profit produced by partners at a large financial services company, Boyatzis (1999a) was able to analyze the financial impact of having a critical mass of strengths above the tipping point in different EI clusters. At this company, strengths in the Self-Awareness cluster added 78 percent more incremental profit; in the Self-Management cluster, 390 percent more profit, and the Relationship Management cluster, 110 percent more. The extremely large effect from strengths in the Self-Management competencies suggests the importance of managing one's emotions—using abilities such as self-discipline, integrity, and staying motivated toward goals—for individual effectiveness. Organizations and individuals interface in ways that require a multitude of EI abilities, each most effective when used in conjunction with others. Emotional Self-Control, for instance, supports the Empathy and the Influence competencies. Finding a comfortable fit between an individual and an organization is easier when important aspects of organizational culture (rapid growth, for example) link to a grouping of competencies rather than a single competency. Other researchers have reported that competencies operate together in an integrated fashion, forming a meaningful pattern of abilities that facilitates successful performance in a given role or job (Nygren & Ukeritis, 1993). Spencer and Spencer (1993) have identified distinctive groupings of competencies that tend to typify high-performing individuals in specific fields, including health care and social services, technical and engineering, sales, client management, and leadership at the executive level.

EI Leadership, Climate, and Organizational Performance:

J. Appl. Sci. Res., 8(3): 1594-1607, 2012

I have indicated how EI can affect an individual's success in an organization. But how does it affect organizational success overall? The evidence suggests that emotionally intelligent leadership is key to creating a working climate that nurtures employees and encourages them to give their best. That enthusiasm, in turn, pays off in improved business performance. This trickle-down effect emerged, for example, in a study of CEOs in U.S. insurance companies. Given comparable size, companies whose CEOs exhibited more EI competencies showed better financial results as measured by both profit and growth (Williams, 1994).

A similar relationship between EI strengths in a leader and business results was found by McClelland (1998) in studying the division heads of a global food and beverage company. The divisions of the leaders with a critical mass of strengths in EI competencies outperformed yearly revenue targets by a margin of 15 to 20 percent. The divisions of the leaders weak in EI competencies underperformed by about the same margin (Goleman, 1998).The relationship between EI strengths in a leader and performance of the unit led appears to be mediated by the climate the leader creates. In the study of insurance CEOs, for example, there was a significant relationship between the EI abilities of the leader and the organizational climate (Williams, 1994). Climate reflects people's sense of their ability to do their jobs well. Climate indicators include the degree of clarity in communication; the degree of employees' flexibility in doing their jobs, ability to innovate, and ownership of and responsibility for their work; and the level of the performance standards set (Litwin & Stringer, 1968; Tagiuri & Litwin, 1968). In the insurance industry study, the climate created by CEOs among their direct reports predicted the business performance of the entire organization, and in three-quarters of the cases climate alone could be used to correctly sort companies by profits and growth. Leadership style seems to drive organizational performance across a wide span of industries and sectors and appears to be a crucial link in the chain from leader to climate to business success. A study of the heads of forty-two schools in the United Kingdom suggests that leadership style drove up students' academic achievement by directly affecting school climate. When the school head was flexible in leadership style and demonstrated a variety of EI abilities, teachers attitudes were more positive and students' grades higher; when the leader relied on fewer EI competencies, teachers tended to be demoralized and students underperformed academically (Hay/McBer, 2000). Effective school leaders not only created a working climate conducive to achievement but were more attuned to teachers' perceptions of such aspects of climate and organizational health as clarity of vision and level of teamwork. The benefits of an understanding and empathic school leader were reflected in the teacher-student relationship as well. In a related follow-up analysis, Lees and Barnard (1999) studied the climates of individual classrooms, concluding that teachers who are more aware of how students feel in the classroom are better able to design a learning environment that suits students and better able to guide them toward success. Teachers who have a leader who has created a positive school climate will be better equipped to do the same in their own classrooms. Indeed, several dimensions of school climate identified in the earlier study correspond to dimensions of classroom climate. For instance, clarity of vision in a school's purpose parallels clarity of purpose in class lessons; challenging yet realistic performance standards for teachers translate into like standards for students. A similar effect of EI-based leadership on climate and performance was demonstrated in a study of outstanding leaders in health care (Catholic Health Association, 1994). For this study, 1,200 members of health care organizations were asked to nominate outstanding leaders based on criteria such as organizational performance and anticipation of future trends. The members were then asked to evaluate the effectiveness of the nominees in fifteen key situations that leaders face—among them organizational change, diversity, and institutional integrity. The study revealed that the more effective leaders in the health care industry were also more adept at integrating key EI competencies such as Organizational Awareness and relationship skills like persuasion and influence.The link between EI strengths in a leader and the organization's climate is important for EI theory. A Hay/McBer analysis of data on 3,781 executives, correlated with climate surveys filled out by those who worked for them, suggests that 50 to 70 percent of employees' perception of working climate is linked to the EI characteristics of the leader (Goleman, 2000b). Research drawing on that same database sheds light on the role of EI competencies in leadership effectiveness, identifying how six distinct styles of EI-based leadership affect climate. Four styles—the visionary (sometimes called the "authoritative"), the affiliative, the democratic, and the coaching—generally drive climate in a positive direction. Two styles—the coercive and the pacesetting— tend to drive climate downward, particularly when leaders overuse them (though each of these two can have positive impact if applied in appropriate situations Visionary leaders are empathic, self-confident, and often act as agents of change. Affiliative leaders, too, are empathic, with strengths in building relationships and managing conflict. The democratic leader encourages collaboration and teamwork and communicates effectively— particularly as an excellent listener. And the coaching leader is emotionally self-aware, empathic, and skilled at identifying and building on the potential of others. The coercive leader relies on the power of his position, ordering people to execute his wishes, and is typically handicapped by a lack of empathy. The pacesetting leader both sets high standards and exemplifies them, exhibiting initiative and a very high drive to achieve—but to a fault, too often micromanaging or criticizing those who fail to meet her own high standards rather than helping them to improve. The most effective leaders integrate four or more of the six styles regularly, switching to the one most appropriate in a given leadership situation. For instance, the study of school leaders found that in those schools where the heads displayed four or more leadership styles, students had superior academic performance relative to students in comparison schools. In schools where the heads displayed just one or two styles, academic performance was poorest. Often the styles here were the pacesetting or coercive ones, which tend to undermine teacher morale and enthusiasm (Hay/McBer, 2000). Among life insurance company CEOs, the very best in terms of corporate growth and profit were those who drew upon a wide range of leadership styles (Williams, 1994). They were adept at all four of the styles that have a positive impact on climate—visionary, democratic, affiliative, and coaching—matching them with the appropriate circumstances. They rarely exhibited the coercive or pacesetting styles.Granted, the factors influencing organizational performance are diverse and complex. But

J. Appl. Sci. Res., 8(3): 1594-1607, 2012

the EI theory of performance at the collective level predicts positive links between EI leadership, organizational climate, and subsequent performance. Hay/McBer data indicate not only that EI-based leadership may be the most important driver of climate but also that climate in turn may account for 20 to 30 percent of organizational performance (Goleman, 2000b). If these data are borne out, the implications are greatly supportive of employing EI as a criterion for selection, promotion, and development: such an application becomes a competitive strategy.

Gender Differences in Emotional Intelligence:

Competing evidence exists surrounding whether or not males and females differ significantly in eneral levels of emotional intelligence. Daniel Goleman (1998) asserts that no gender differences in E.I. exist, admitting that while men and women may have different profiles of strengths and weaknesses in different areas of emotional intelligence, their overall levels of E.I. are equivalent. However, studies by Mayer and Geher (1996), Mayer, Caruso, and Salovey (1999), and more recently Mandell and Pherwani (2003) have found that women are more likely to score higher on measures of emotional intelligence than men, both in professional and personal settings. The discrepancy may be due to measurement choice. Brackett and Mayer (2003) found that females scored higher than males on E.I. when measured by a performance measure (the Mayer-Salovey-Caruso Emotional Intelligence Test). However, when using self-report measures such as the Bar-On Emotion Quotient Inventory (EQ-i) and the Self-Report Emotional Intelligence Test (SREIT), they found no evidence for gender differences. Perhaps gender differences exist in emotional intelligence only when one defines E.I. in a purely cognitive manner rather than through a mixed perspective. It could also be the case that gender differences do exist but measurement artifacts such as over-estimation of ability on the part of males are more likely to occur with self-report measures. More research is required to determine whether or not gender differences do exist in emotional intelligence.

Implications for the Future: EI and Higher Education:

Given the value of the personal and organizational effectiveness of EI-based capabilities, there is a clear need to integrate that valuation into our organizations' functions. Organizations need to hire for emotional intelligence along with whatever other technical skills or business expertise they are seeking. When it comes to promotions and succession planning, EI should be a major criterion, particularly to the extent that a position requires leadership. When those with high potential are being selected and groomed, EI should be central. And in training and development, EI should again be a major focus.

However, because EI competencies entail emotional capacities in addition to purely cognitive abilities, modes of learning that work well for academic subjects or technical skills are not necessarily well suited for helping people improve an emotional competence (Goleman, 1998b). For this reason the Consortium for Research on Emotional Intelligence in Organizations has summarized empirical findings on the mode of learning best for emotional competencies and formulated guidelines for their effective development. The consortium has posted a technical report on its Web site (www.eiconsortium.org) and has fostered a book for HR professionals on how to make training in EI skills most effective (Cherniss & Adler, 2000). Given our new understanding of the crucial role emotional competence plays in individual, group, and organizational success, the implication for education is clear: We should be helping young people master these competencies as essential life skills. There are already numerous school-based programs in the basics of EI, programs that deliver social and emotional learning (SEL). The Collaborative for Social and Emotional Learning has vetted the best models, and acts as a clearinghouse for these programs through its Web site (www.casel.org).

But as of this writing, when it comes to preparing young people in the essential emotional intelligence skills that matter most for their success in the workplace, for piloting their careers, and for leadership, we face a serious gap. The SEL programs cover the early school years but not higher education. Only a scattered handful of pioneering SEL courses exist at the college or professional level. And yet the data showing the crucial role EI skills play in career success make a compelling case for reenvisioning higher education in order to give these capabilities their place in a well-rounded curriculum.

Given that employers themselves are looking for EI capacities in those they hire, colleges and professional schools that offered appropriate SEL training would benefit both their graduates and the organizations they work for. The most forward-thinking educators will, I hope, recognize the importance of emotional intelligence in higher education, not just for the students, not just for the students' employers, but for the vitality of an economy as a whole. As Erasmus, the great humanist writer, tells us, "The best hope of a nation lies in the proper education of its youth."

Measures of Mayer and Salovey's Model:

Mayer and Salovey began testing the validity of their four-branch model of emotional intelligence with the Multibranch Emotional Intelligence Scale (MEIS). Composed of 12 subscale measures of emotional intelligence, evaluations with the Multibranch Emotional Intelligence Scale indicate that emotional intelligence is a distinct intelligence with 3 separate sub factors: emotional perception, emotional understanding, and emotional management. The Multibranch Emotional Intelligence Scale found only limited

1602

J. Appl. Sci. Res., 8(3): 1594-1607, 2012

evidence for the branch of emotional intelligence related to integrating emotions. Additionally, examination of the Multibranch Emotional Intelligence Scale found evidence for **discriminant validity** in that emotional intelligence was independent of general intelligence and self-reported empathy, indicating its ability to measure unique qualities of an individual not encompassed by earlier tests. There were, however, certain limitations to the Multibranch Emotional Intelligence Scale. Not only was it a lengthy test (402 items) but it also failed to provide satisfactory evidence for the integration branch of the Four Branch Model (Mayer, Salovey, & Caruso, 2002). For these and other reasons, Mayer and Salovey decided to design a new ability measure of emotional intelligence.

The current measure of Mayer and Salovey's model of emotional intelligence, the Mayer-Salovey-Caruso Emotional Intelligence Test (MSCEIT) was normed on a sample of 5,000 men and women. The MSCEIT is designed for individuals 17 years of age or older and aims to measure the four abilities outlined in Salovey and Mayer's model of emotional intelligence. Each ability (perception, facilitation of thought, understanding, and regulation) is measured using specific tasks. Perception of emotion is measured by rating the extent and type of emotion expressed on different types of pictures. Facilitation of thought is measured by asking people to draw parallels between emotions and physical sensations (e.g., light, colour, temperature) as well as emotions and thoughts. Understanding is measured by asking the subject to explain how emotions can blend from other emotions (e.g., how emotions can change from one to another such as anger to rage). Regulation (or management) of emotions is measured by having people choose effective self and other management techniques (Brackett & Mayer, 2003). With less than a third of the items of the original Multibranch Emotional Intelligence Scale, the Mayer-Salovey-Caruso Emotional Intelligence Test is comprised of 141 items. The scale yields six scores: an overall emotional intelligence score (expressed as an emotional intelligence quotient, or EIQ), two area scores (Experiential Emotional Intelligence, or EEIQ and Strategic Emotional Intelligence, or SEIQ) and four branch scores corresponding to the four branches of emotional intelligence. Each score is expressed in terms of a standard intelligence with a mean score of 100 (average score obtained in the general population) and a standard deviation of 15. Additionally, the manual provides qualitative ratings that correspond to each numeric score. For example, an individual who receives an overall EIQ of 69 or less would be rated 'considerable development' whereas someone scoring 130 or more would be rated 'significant strength' (Mayer, Salovey, & Caruso, 2002).

The Impact of EI on Organizational Effectiveness:

Look deeply at almost any factor that influences organizational effectiveness, and you will find that emotional intelligence plays a role. For instance, as this volume is being completed, the United States continues an unprecedented period of economic prosperity and growth. The downside of this fortunate circumstance for many organizations is that it has become increasingly more difficult to retain goodemployees, particularly those with the skills that are important in the high-tech economy. So what aspects of an organization are most important for keeping good employees? A Gallup Organization study of two million employees at seven hundred companies found that how long an employee stays at a company and how productive she is there is determined by her relationship with her immediate supervisor (Zipkin, 2000). Another study quantified this effect further. Spherion, a staffing and consulting firm in Fort Lauderdale, Florida, and Lou Harris Associates, found that only 11 percent of the employees who rated their bosses as excellent said that they were likely to look for a different job in the next year.

However, 40 percent of those who rated their bosses as poor said they were likely to leave. In other words, people with good bosses are four times less likely to leave than are those with poor bosses (Zipkin, 2000). What is it about bosses that influences their relationship with employees? What skills do bosses need to prevent employees from leaving? The most effective bosses are those who have the ability to sense how their employees feel about their work situation and to intervene effectively when those employees begin to feel discouraged

or dissatisfied. Effective bosses are also able to manage their own emotions, with the result that employees trust them and feel good about working with them. In short, bosses whose employees stay are bosses who manage with emotional intelligence.

When I ask employees and their bosses to identify the greatest challenges their organizations face, they mention these concerns:
• People need to cope with massive, rapid change.
• People need to be more creative in order to drive innovation.
• People need to manage huge amounts of information.
• The organization needs to increase customer loyalty.
• People need to be more motivated and committed.
• People need to work together better.
• The organization needs to make better use of the special talents available in a diverse workforce.
• The organization needs to identify potential leaders in its ranks and prepare them to move up.
• The organization needs to identify and recruit top talent.
• The organization needs to make good decisions about new markets, products, and strategic alliances.
• The organization needs to prepare people for overseas assignments.

These are the intense needs that face all organizations today, both public sector and private. And in virtually every case, emotional intelligence must play an important role in satisfying the need. For instance, coping with massive change involves, among other

1603

J. Appl. Sci. Res., 8(3): 1594-1607, 2012

things, the ability to perceive and understand the emotional impact of change on ourselves and others. To be effective in helping their organizations manage change, leaders first need to be aware of and to manage their own feelings of anxiety and uncertainty (Bunker, 1997). Then they need to be aware of the emotional reactions of other organizational members and act to help people cope with those reactions. At the same time in this process of coping effectively with massive change, other members of the organization need to be actively involved in monitoring and managing their emotional reactions and those of others.

Let us consider one other challenge, one that might seem less emotional than many of the others in the list. How might emotional intelligence play a role in helping organizational leaders make good decisions about new products, markets, and strategic alliances? Making such decisions involves much more than emotional intelligence. Good data must be assembled, and these data must be analyzed using the most sophisticated tools available. However, in the end, data almost never produce a clear-cut answer. Many important variables can be quantified but not all.

Analytical tools can organize most of the information needed for a clear and coherent picture, but almost always there is also some ambiguity and guesswork involved. There comes a point when organizational leaders must rely on their intuition or gut feeling. Such feelings will sometimes point in the right direction and sometimes in the wrong direction. The leaders who are most likely to have feelings that point in the right direction are the ones who have a good sense of why they are reacting as they are. They have learned to discriminate between feelings that are irrelevant and misleading and feelings that are on target. In other words, emotional intelligence enables leaders to tune into the gut feelings that are most accurate and helpful in making difficult decisions.

Emotional intelligence influences organizational effectiveness in a number of areas:
• Employee recruitment and retention;
• Development of talent;
• Teamwork;
• Employee commitment, morale, and health;
• Innovation;
• Productivity;
• Efficiency;
• Sales;
• Revenues;
• Quality of service;
• Customer loyalty;
• Client or student outcomes.

The influence of EI begins with the retention and recruitment of talent. For instance, as Claudio FernándezAráoz points out in Chapter Eight, the extent to which candidates' emotional intelligence is considered in making top executive hiring decisions has a significant impact on the ultimate success or failure of those executives. The emotional intelligence of the persons doing the hiring is also crucial for good hiring decisions.

Emotional intelligence also affects the development of talent. For instance, Kathy Kram and I (Chapter Eleven) show how relationships at work can contribute to the development of talent. However, not all relationships are equally effective in doing so. The emotional intelligence of the mentor, boss, or peer will influence the potential of a relationship with that person for helping organizational members develop and use the talent that is crucial for organizational effectiveness. (See Chapter Ten for further discussion of emotional intelligence and the development of talent.)

Sources of EI in Organizations:

If individual and group emotional intelligence contribute to organizational effectiveness, what in the organization contributes to individual and group emotional intelligence? Such a question is especially important for anyone who wishes to harness the power of emotional intelligence for organizational improvement. Emotional intelligence, as Goleman (1995a) pointed out in his first book on the topic, emerges primarily through relationships. At the same time, emotional intelligence affects the quality of relationships. Kram note that both formally arranged relationships and naturally occurring relationships in organizations contribute to emotional intelligence. Relationships can help people become more emotionally intelligent even when they are not set up for that purpose. The model suggests that ultimately any attempts to improve emotional intelligence in organizations will depend on relationships. Even formal training interventions or human resource policies will affect emotional intelligence through their effect on relationships among individuals and groups in the organization.

Conclusion:

1604

J. Appl. Sci. Res., 8(3): 1594-1607, 2012

Several studies have found that emotional intelligence can have a significant impact on various elements of everyday living. Palmer, Donaldson, and Stough (2002) found that higher emotional intelligence was a predictor of life satisfaction. Additionally, Pellitteri (2002) reported that people higher in emotional intelligence were also more likely to use an adaptive defense style and thus exhibited healthier psychological adaptation. Performance measures of emotional intelligence have illustrated that higher levels of E.I. are associated with an increased likelihood of attending to health and appearance, positive interactions with friends and family, and owning objects that are reminders of their loved ones (Brackett, Mayer, & Warner, in press). Mayer, Caruso, and Salovey (1999) found that higher emotional intelligence correlated significantly with higher parental warmth and attachment style, while others found that those scoring high in E.I. also reported increased positive interpersonal relationships among children, adolescents, and adults (Rice, 1999; Rubin, 1999). emotional intelligence can be beneficial in many areas of life. However, the application of its usefulness has been most frequently documented in the professional workplace. Cherniss (2000) outlines four main reasons why the workplace would be a logical setting for evaluating and improving emotional intelligence competencies:

1. Emotional intelligence competencies are critical for success in most jobs.
2. Many adults enter the workforce without the competencies necessary to succeed or excel at their job.
3. Employers already have the established means and motivation for providing emotional intelligence training.
4. Most adults spend the majority of their waking hours at work.

A strong interest in the professional applications of emotional intelligence is apparent in the way organizations have embraced E.I. ideas. The American Society for Training and Development, or example, has published a volume describing guidelines for helping people in organizations ultivate emotional intelligence competencies which distinguish outstanding performers from average ones (Cherniss and Adler, 2000).

As previously noted, considerable research in the emotional intelligence field has focused on leadership, a fundamental workplace quality. Even before research in the area of E.I. had begun, the Ohio State Leadership Studies reported that leaders who were able to establish mutual trust, respect, and certain warmth and rapport with members of their group were more effective (Fleishman and Harris, 1962). This result is not surprising given that many researchers have argued that effective leadership fundamentally depends upon the leader's ability to solve the complex social problems which can arise in organizations (Mumford, Zaccaro, Harding, Jacobs, & Fleishman, 2000).

The cost-effectiveness of emotional intelligence in the workplace has been an area of interest. Several studies have reported the economic value of hiring staff based on emotional intelligence. In a report to Congress, the Government Accounting Office (1998) outlined the amount saved when the United States Air Force used Bar On's Emotional Quotient Inventory (EQ-I) to select program recruiters. By selecting those individuals who scored highest in emotional intelligence as recruiters, they increased their ability to select successful recruiters by threefold and saved $3 million annually. A similar study by Boyatzis (1999) found that when partners in a multinational consulting firm were assessed on E.I. competencies, partners who scored above the median on nine or more competencies delivered $1.2 million more profit than did other partners.

Cherniss and Goleman (1998) estimated that by not following training guidelines established to increase emotional intelligence in the workplace, industry in the United States is losing between $5.6 and $16.8 billion a year. They found that the impact of training employees in emotional and social competencies with programs which followed their guidelines was higher than for other programs, and by not implementing these programs companies were receiving less of an impact and consequently losing money.

Three main models of emotional intelligence exist. The first model by Peter Salovey and John Mayer perceives E.I. as a form of pure intelligence, that is, emotional intelligence is a cognitive ability. A second model by Reuven Bar-On regards E.I. as a mixed intelligence, consisting of cognitive ability and personality aspects. This model emphasizes how cognitive and personality factors influence general well-being. The third model, introduced by Daniel Goleman, also perceives E.I. as a mixed intelligence involving cognitive ability and personality aspects. However, unlike the model proposed by Reuven Bar-On, Goleman's model focuses on how cognitive and personality factors determine workplace success.

• Salovey and Mayer's model of E.I. is measured using the Mayer-Salovey-Caruso Emotional Intelligence Test (MSCEIT), a performance measure which requires the participant to complete tasks associated with emotional intelligence. Both Bar-On and Goleman's models utilize self-report measures of emotional intelligence. Bar-On's model is measured using the Emotion Quotient Inventory (EQ-i) and Goleman's model is measured using the Emotional Competency Inventory (ECI), the Emotional Intelligence Appraisal (EIA), and the Work Profile Questionnaire – Emotional Intelligence Version (WPQei).

• Research has found that significant relationships exist between all three models of E.I.. In addition, emotional intelligence has been consistently compared to three other constructs: personality, alexithymia (difficulty in feeling and distinguishing emotions), and leadership. Many traits contained in the Big Five Personality Factor Model are similar to those described by Bar-On and Goleman in their models of emotional intelligence. Alexithymia has been found to be inversely related to emotional intelligence. Studies in leadership have found transformational leadership (leadership which inspires, motivates, and develops others while generating awareness of organizational goals) leads to increased employee effectiveness and satisfaction. Studies have also found that transformational leadership is significantly related to higher E.I.

- Studies in gender differences are inconclusive. Although some research has found that women are more emotionally intelligent than men, other studies have found no significant differences between genders. More research is required in this regard.
- Emotional intelligence has been found to be a predictor of life satisfaction, healthy psychological adaptation, positive interactions with peers and family, and higher parental warmth. Lower emotional intelligence has also been found to be associated with violent behaviour, illegal use of drugs and alcohol, and participation in delinquent behaviour.
- Emotional intelligence has been extensively researched in workplace settings. It has been related to increased success among those who share similar positions (e.g., senior managers). Additionally, hiring individuals with higher levels of emotional intelligence as well as training existing staff to be more emotionally intelligent has been associated with financial gains in the private sector. Training in emotional intelligence in the workplace can occur at all levels, and several evaluated programs have found success in developing more emotionally intelligent workforces.

References

Antonakis, J., 2003. Why "emotional intelligence" does not predict leadership effectiveness. The International Journal of Organizational Analysis, 11: 355-361.

Ashkanasy, N.M., & C.S. Daus, 2005. Rumors of the death of emotional intelligence in organizational behavior are vastly exaggerated. Journal of Organizational Behavior, 26: 441-452.

Bechara, A., & H. Damasio, 2005. The somatic marker hypothesis: A neural theory of economic decision. Games and Economic Behavior, 52: 336-372.

Dasborough, M.T., & N.M. Ashkanasy, 2002. Emotion and attribution of intentionality in leader–member relationships. The Leadership Quarterly, 13: 615-634.

Dasborough, M.T., & N.M. Ashkanasy, 2003. Is emotional intelligence training for leaders justified? Australian Journal of Psychology, 55(supplement), pp120-121.

Daus, C.S., & N.M. Ashkanasy, 2003. Will the real emotional intelligence please stand up? The Industrial and Organizational Psychologist, 41: 69-72.

Daus, C.S., & N.M. Ashkanasy, 2005. The case for an ability-based model of emotional intelligence in organizational behavior. Journal of Organizational Behavior, 26: 453-466.

Davidson, J.E., & C.L. Downing, 2000. Contemporary models of intelligence (pp. 34–52). In R. J. Sternberg (Ed.), Handbook of intelligence. New York: Cambridge University Press.

Duncan, J., H. Emslie & P. Williams, 1996. Intelligence and the frontal lobe: The organization of goal-directed behavior. Cognitive Psychology, 30: 257-303.

Edwards, J.R., 1995. Alternatives to difference scores as dependent variables in the study of congruence in organizational research. Organizational Behavior and Human Decision Processes, 64: 307-324.

Fiedler, F.E., & T.G. Link, 1994. Leader intelligence, interpersonal stress, and task performance. In R. J. Sternberg & R. K. Wagner (Eds.), Mind in context: Interactional perspectives on human intelligence., pp: 152-167. Cambridge: University of Cambridge.

Fiedler, F.E., 1995. Cognitive resources and leadership performance-A rejoinder. Applied Psychology-An International Review, 44: 50-56.

Fonlupt, P., 2003. Perception and judgment of physical causality involve different brain structures. Cognitive Brain Research, 17: 248-254.

Frangou, S., X. Chitins, & S.C.R. Williams, 2004. Mapping IQ and gray matter density in healthy young people. NeuroImage, 23: 800-805.

Gardner, H., 1983. Frames of mind. New York: Basic Books.

George, J.M., 2000. Emotions and leadership: The role of emotional intelligence. Human Relations, 53: 10271055.

Gignac, G.E., 2005. Evaluating the MSCEIT V2.0 via CFA: Comment on Mayer et al. (2003). Emotion, 5: 233235.

Gilovich, T., K. Savitsky, & V.H. Medvec, 1998. The illusion of transparency: Biased assessments of others' ability to read one's emotional states. Journal of Personality and Social Psychology, 75: 332-346.

Goleman, D., R. Boyatzis, & A. McKee, 2002. Primal leadership. Boston: HBS Press.

Hinson, J.M., T.L. Jameson & P. Whitney, 2002. Somatic markers, working memory, and decision making. Cognitive, Affective, & Behavioral Neuroscience, 2: 341-353.

Houdé, O., L. Zago, F. Crivello, S. Moutier, A. Pineau, B. Mazoyer & N. Tzourio-Mazoyer, 2001. Access to deductive logic depends on a right ventromedial prefrontal area devoted to emotion and feeling: Evidence from a training program. NeuroImage, 14: 1486-1492.

House, R.J., & R.N. Aditya, 1997. The social scientific study of leadership: Quo vadis? Journal of Management, 23: 409-473.

Joint Committee on Standards (JCS) 1999. Standards for educational and psychological testing. Washington DC: American Educational Research Association.

1606

J. Appl. Sci. Res., 8(3): 1594-1607, 2012

Jordan, P.J., & A.C. Troth, 2004. Managing emotions during team problem solving: Emotional intelligence and conflict resolution. Human Performance, 17: 195-218.

Judge, T.A., J.E. Bono, R. Ilies & M.W. Gerhardt, 2002. Personality and leadership: A qualitative and quantitative review. Journal of Applied Psychology, 87: 765-780.

Kanetkar, V., M.G. Evans, S.A. Everell, D. Irving, & Z. Millman, 1995. The effect of scale changes on metaanalysis of multiplicative and main effects models. Educational and Psychological Measurement, 55: 206224.

LeDoux, J.E., 1995. In search of an emotional system in the brain: Leaping from fear to emotion and consciousness. In M. S. Gazzaniga (Ed.), The Cognitive Neurosciences (pp. 1049–1061). Cambridge, MA: MIT Press.

Locke, E.A., 2005. Why emotional intelligence is an invalid concept. Journal of Organizational Behavior, 26: 425-431.

Lopes, P.N., P. Salovey, S. Cote & M. Beers, 2005. Emotion regulation ability and the quality of social interaction. Emotion, 5: 113-118.

Matthews, G., M. Zeidner, & R.D. Roberts, 2002. Emotional intelligence: science and myth. Cambridge, MA: MIT Press.

Mayer, J.D., R.D. Roberts & S.G. Barsade, 2008. Human abilities: Emotional intelligence. Annual Review of Psychology, 59: 507-536.

Mayer, J.D., & P. Salovey, 1997. What is emotional intelligence? In P. Salovey & D. J. Sluyter (Eds.), Emotional development and emotional intelligence: Educational implications (pp. 3–31). New York: Basic Books.

Mischel, W., 1968. Personality and assessment. New York: Wiley.

Naqvi, N., B. Shiv & A. Bechara, 2006. The role of emotion in decision making: A cognitive neuroscience perspective. Current Directions in Psychological Science, 15: 260-264.

Narr, K.L., R.P. Woods, P.M. Thompson, P. Szeszko, D. Robinson, T. Dimtcheva, *et al.*, 2007. Relationship between IQ and regional cortical gray matter thickness in healthy adults. Cerebral Cortex, 17: 2163-2171.

Offerman, L.R., J.R. Bailey, N.L. Vasilopoulos, C. Seal, & M. Sass, 2004. The relative contribution of emotional competence and cognitive ability to individual and team performance. Human Performance, 17: 219-243.

Oberauer, K., R. Shulze, O. Wilhelm, & H.-M. Süss, 2005. Working memory and intelligence—Their correlation and their relation: Comment on Ackerman, Beier, and Boyle (2005). Psychological Bulletin, 131: 61-65.

Obonsawin, M.C., J.R. Crawford, J. Page, P. Chalmers, R. Cochrane, & G. Low, 2002. Performance on tests of frontal lobe function reflect general intellectual ability. Neuropsychologia, 40: 970-977.

Popper, K.R., 1963. Conjectures and refutations: The growth of scientific knowledge. New York: Harper Torchbooks.

Prati, L.M., C. Douglas, G.R. Ferris, A.P. Ammeter & M.R. Buckley, 2003. Emotional intelligence, leadership effectiveness, and team outcomes. International Journal of Organizational Analysis, 11: 21-40.

Roberts, R.D., R. Schulze, K. O'Brien, C. MacCann, J. Reid, & A. Maul, 2006. Exploring the validity of the Mayer–Salovey–Caruso emotional intelligence test (MSCEIT) with established emotions measures. Emotion, 6: 663-669.

Rubin, R.S., D.C. Munz, & W.H. Bommer, 2005. Leading from within: The effects of emotion recognition and personality on transformational leadership behavior. Academy of Management Journal, 48: 845-858.

Salas, E., J.E. Driskell, & S. Hughs, 1996. The study of human stress and performance. In J. E. Driskell & E. Salas (Eds.), Stress and human performance (pp. 1–46). Manwah, NJ: Lawrence Erlbaum Associates.